# The Puzzles of Power

# The Puzzles of Power
## An Introduction to Political Science

Second Edition
Edited by Michael Howlett and David Laycock

Toronto  Oxford  New York
Oxford University Press
1998

Oxford University Press
70 Wynford Drive, Don Mills, Ontario M3C 1J9
http://www.oupcan.com

*Oxford   New York*
*Athens   Auckland   Bangkok   Bogotá   Buenos Aires   Calcutta*
*Cape Town   Chennai   Dar es Salaam   Delhi   Florence   Hong Kong   Istanbul*
*Karachi   Kuala Lumpur   Madrid   Melbourne   Mexico City   Mumbai*
*Nairobi   Paris   São Paulo   Singapore   Taipei   Tokyo   Toronto   Warsaw*

and associated companies in
*Berlin   Ibadan*

*Oxford* is a trade mark of Oxford University Press

**Canadian Cataloguing in Publication Data**

Main entry under title

The puzzles of power : an introduction to political science

2nd ed.
Includes bibliographical references
ISBN 0–19–541377–6

1. Political science.   2. Canada—Politics and government.
I. Howlett, Michael, 1955–   .   II. Laycock, David H. (David Howard), 1954–   .

JA66.P89 1998        320        C98–931496–0

Cover Design:  Sonya Thursby/Opus House

Text Design:  Brett Miller

# Contents

# Preface

This edition of *The Puzzles of Power* is intended to aid political science students in their introduction to the discipline. Each section deals with a specific subfield identified by the Canadian political science community and is designed to provide students with an overview of current and past approaches to key analytical questions and concepts in the subfield. Each section includes an introductory essay about the subfield, a set of study questions intended to aid tutorial and classroom discussion, and two or three selected readings from important books and journals to illustrate key points and arguments with which students of the subfield must grapple. The introductory essays and the readings seek to connect the experiences of Canadian students to the contemporary puzzles of power.

Our colleagues at Simon Fraser University tackled revisions of and additions to their introductions with enthusiasm and care. Their comments, along with those of various students and instructors who worked with the first edition, have helped improve this edition in numerous ways. In particular we would like to thank Darin Barney, Andrew Heard, and Doug Ross for their considered, and frank, assessment of the strengths and weaknesses of the first edition. We would also like to thank Euan White, Ric Kitowski, and Phyllis Wilson, at Oxford University Press, and Richard Tallman, all of whom handled the development and editorial work with speed and their customary, reassuring, professionalism.

Accurate portrayal of our colleagues' approaches to research methods and subjects has been one of our major concerns in putting this volume together. Not all approaches and subjects, of course, could receive the attention some might prefer. However, we are confident that the essays and readings in this edition will assist students' efforts to puzzle through politics.

# Part I

# Puzzling Through Politics

## Introduction

Michael Howlett and David Laycock

To both introductory students and experienced teachers, political science is a formidable discipline. Its breadth of subject matter is comparable to that of geography or sociology, but political science is also more methodologically varied than most other disciplines. In this book we attempt to provide students with an introduction to the diversity within political science.

To get a preliminary sense of what the methodological diversity of political science entails, it is helpful to think of political scientists employing a wide range of techniques for puzzling through power. Broadly speaking, the methods used by political scientists differ in two important regards: in the extent to which they feel political puzzles can be resolved through the application of methods common to the natural sciences, and in terms of units within which they define the political.

The first dimension involves different philosophical assumptions made by political scientists about the nature of political inquiry and the nature of politics. Many political scientists believe that reliable and readily quantifiable information can be gathered on political actors and institutions and on the various social and economic factors that affect political activity. On the basis of these empirical inquiries, they argue that political theories can be constructed that accurately explain and occasionally even predict conditions and phenomena found in everyday political life. Other political scientists question our ability to attach revealing numerical values to politically significant matters such as security, stability, power, alienation, and legitimacy. Whether and how a political analyst conceives of the political universe, and how each selects, measures, and weighs relevant data, depends on how each interprets the basic characteristics of the political puzzle.

The second dimension is equally problematic. Defining the nature of the political is not a simple matter. For a variety of historical reasons, students of politics have focused on various aspects of political life in their studies. While political institutions such as governments, executives, legislatures, and legal systems have garnered attention, so have elements of political behaviour such as the social, cultural, and ethnolinguistic characteristics of populations and their interrelationships with political institutions. In addition, political scientists have focused on specific political institutions, such as systems of public administration or systems of states, as in the case of international relations, or on subunits of state, as in the study of provincial politics and local governments. Others have concentrated almost exclusively on the theoretical and philosophical issues involved in the study of politics. This diversity within political science has led to the creation of diverse areas of study, which may or may not share a commonly accepted philosophy and methodology.[1]

Thus to understand the concerns of contemporary political science it is necessary to recognize political scientists' substantially differing overall approaches to the study of the discipline, and to acknowledge the discipline's division into numerous subfields of study. The readings in this section address the first issue. The remainder of this introduction and the balance of the text address the second.

It is important to remember that the study of political puzzles has an ancient history. It has always concerned how people use power relating to each other, often forming complex institutions of government to structure their pursuit of common and conflicting goals and objectives. For ancient Greeks the purpose of government was to enable individuals in communities to achieve 'the good life'. Politics was studied to promote human flourishing. Although we seldom state this goal explicitly in our contributions to professional journals, this remains an important aim of contemporary political science.

Political studies have been concerned not only with the successes of governments in promoting human ends, but also with reasons for their failure to do so. While political scientists have analysed the institutional basis for co-operative endeavours in community life, they have also considered varied manifestations of intra- and inter-community conflict, in war, insurrection, revolution, and rebellion. Problems endemic to governments and other authoritative social institutions, such as corruption, discrimination, and injustice, have also commanded our attention.

Like all human sciences, political science has been profoundly influenced by other fields of inquiry. In its ancient Greek beginnings, the study of politics was seen as a part of the larger enterprise of philosophy. To achieve the good life, one had to begin by systematically understanding the relationships between human nature and the rest of nature. After this, one attempted to understand relationships between moral standards for rule-governed behaviour in political communities and how these could be used to classify and evaluate the various uses of state power to organize and control conflict over scarce resources. The study of politics was the exclusive province of philosophers until at least the middle of the eighteenth century. For many philosophers, politics was a significant concern, but subsidiary to ruminations on ethics, metaphysics, or the nature of divine inspiration.

By the eighteenth century, politics was increasingly studied under the rubric of political economy, which sought to understand the interaction between economic and political institutions, dynamics, and behaviour. Political economists were broadly educated and often undertook their investigations under the wing of philosophy, as Adam Smith's appointment in the department of moral philosophy at the University of Edinburgh indicated. As sociology became a distinct discipline during the nineteenth century, the study of politics was increasingly affected by sociologists' concern with the behaviour of social groups and classes.

Over the last 50 years, many political scientists have sought to acquire scientific status for their research by adopting the quantitative techniques and behavioural assumptions of psychologists and economists. As of 1998, much published work in political science journals uses analytical and statistical techniques that only economists would have employed two decades ago. Political science methods and objects of investigation have thus evolved, since Plato, in symbiotic relationships with the other human and social sciences.

One of the most striking examples of this symbiosis is in the realm of 'rational choice' (or, as economists usually call it, 'public choice') theory. In this case, however, economic assumptions about human nature and economic models of market behaviour have replaced more traditional political assumptions and models of social choice. Rational choice theory takes from post-seventeenth-century economic theory of market activity the idea that all publicly significant human behaviour is an expression of self-interested 'utility maximization', in the sense that all individuals pursue goals that reflect their perceived self-interest. Whether in the voting booth, complex government bureaucracies, political party competition, or decisions about participation in the activities of organized interests, it is argued, individuals focus on their perceived interests. Rational choice theory contends that we do this to such an extent that assuming this is central to human behaviour is the key to modelling and theorizing not just individual behaviours but also institutional behaviour and all other elements of political life. This approach to human behaviour and its political extensions have been broadly criticized by political and other social scientists, but rational choice theory none the less has enjoyed increasing popularity among professional political scientists over the past 20 years.[2]

Symbioses with other disciplines in the modern era have, for political studies, often resulted from its expansion beyond traditional concerns with government structures and processes. Political scientists are in many cases changing their definitions of politics to accommodate their desire to study the exercise of power outside of the primarily male-populated institutions of government, parties, and interest groups. Feminist political scientists, for example, are now systematically investigating the political significance of power relations in the family and the workplace, thus analytically implementing the feminist slogan, 'the personal is political.'

Many political scientists have accepted the contention, by no means novel with feminism, that the locations and techniques of political power reach well beyond the phenomena of electoral competition, lobbying activities, and bureaucratic administration studied in traditional political science. Political scientists interested in developing novel approaches to the logic and consequences of the many faces of power readily examine subject matter or adopt analytical techniques of neighbouring disciplines. The development of women's studies over the past 25 years, for example, has drawn our attention to the fact that until recently, few political scientists displayed sensitivity to the way their use of gendered pronouns implicitly marginalized women as political thinkers, political actors, and political analysts. As Carole Pateman points out in the section below on political philosophy, linguistic practices are politically powerful, and students of politics need to appreciate their significance for relations between women and men.

As many of our subfield introductions and selections illustrate, how one defines the domain of 'the political' has a decisive impact on how one studies political life. Contemporary political scientists focus not only on states and their activities—and, of course, on relations between states—but also on social-group and organizational dynamics, and on these groups' interactions with various policy-making processes, institutions, and agencies of modern states. Attempts by interest groups and social movements to alter policies adopted and implemented by governments are ubiquitous features of contemporary political life.

Students of political phenomena today can choose a variety of subfields, such as political behaviour, comparative politics, political economy, and public policy. They can also specialize in subfields dealing with the more traditional concerns of political philosophy, international relations, and the study of national and subnational governments.

Each of these subfields has its own wide range of concerns and perspectives on political life, and often its own specific methodologies for investigating those concerns and issues. As a discipline, political science has an overall orientation towards producing hypotheses and valid generalizations about political phenomena through careful theorization and testing.[3] But no *paradigm*—or unified methodology of research, analysis, and theory testing—establishes absolutely authoritative instruments and assumptions of inquiry across the spectrum of political studies. Each subfield addresses empirical and conceptual concerns in its own fashion.

Political theory and political philosophy tend to emphasize the use, interpretation, and clarification of historically situated normative ideas and concepts to account for patterns of human interaction in institutional settings. In other words, what counts as most important in political analysis is a matter of prior choices and orientations to basic moral values. By contrast, political sociologists often rely extensively on quantitative and statistical methods when investigating political behaviour. Also reasonably distinctive are the search for cross-culturally sensitive methods of comparing different nations' political experiences of comparative politics, and the institutional analysis of public administration or public policy. Some subfields combine elements of these and other methods. The study of national and subnational governments offers many examples of such methodological hybridization.

To become a political scientist, then, one must be prepared to produce and apply generalizations regarding different dimensions of political life. A command of several methodologies and approaches to the study of political phenomena is necessary. One must be both a generalist and a specialist to make headway in understanding the puzzles of politics.

❧

The two selections in this first section address the fundamental methodological debate in political science concerning the appropriateness of a purely 'scientific' approach to the subject.

Alan Zuckerman argues in our first selection that it may be possible to occupy some middle ground in this debate, undertaking a systematic analysis of politics without ignoring the difficulties surrounding the use of the scientific method. As Zuckerman notes, it is up to students to weigh carefully the strengths and weaknesses in both the arguments for and applications of different methods in political studies before attempting their own investigations.

Alan Isaak's chapter from a text on the methodology of political science argues that political science is a science in much the same fashion that chemistry is, and claims that arguments trying to deprive political science of its scientific status either misconstrue the nature of science or undermine the acquisition of most meaningful forms of knowledge about politics. There is a long tradition of philosophical rejections of this position, many of which deny that value neutrality is possible or desirable in political explanation. To these critics of political science as science, the puzzles of politics cannot be resolved if analysts fail to note that human beings with real value preferences are both the subjects and objects of inquiry.[4]

## Notes

1. It is this second dimension that Gabriel Almond has tried to capture using the metaphor of political scientists conducting their work like separate groups of diners at a banquet, conversing only at their table while choosing from a variety of menu items, that is, methodologies and approaches to issues in the discipline. See Gabriel A. Almond 'Separate Tables: Schools and Sects in Political Science', *PS: Political Science and Politics* 21, 4 (1988): 828.
2. For discussions of rational choice theory, see Dennis Mueller, *Public Choice II* (Cambridge: Cambridge University Press, 1989); John Elster, ed., *Rational Choice* (New York: New York University Press, 1986); Kristen R. Munroe, ed., *The Economic Approach to Politics: A Critical Assessment of the Theory of Rational Action* (New York: Harper Collins, 1991); Donald Green and Ian Shapiro, *Pathologies of Rational Choice Theory: A Critique of Applications in Political Science* (New Haven: Yale University Press, 1994).
3. See the selections by Zuckerman and Isaak in this section.
4. For a good example of this argument, see Charles Taylor, 'Neutrality in Political Science', in Peter Laslett and W.G. Runciman, eds, *Philosophy, Politics and Society*, 3rd series (Oxford: Basil Blackwell, 1969).

## Study Questions for the Readings

1. What does Zuckerman see as the fundamental assumptions behind the effort to study politics and political life in a systematic, 'scientific' fashion? Are these reasonable assumptions?
2. Define each of the following terms and describe their interrelationships: theory, hypothesis, concepts, variables.
3. How can a theory in political science be tested? In your answer be sure to deal with the issues of measurement and the operationalization of key concepts.
4. How does Isaak define 'science'? Are there other plausible definitions?
5. What does Isaak consider the strongest arguments for seeing political science as a science?
6. If political science is *not* a science, is it still worth doing? Why?

# The Point of Departure

Alan S. Zuckerman

When we do political science, we set out to discover uniformities in the political world. We assume that the swirl of political events—wars, elections, coups, riots, incidences of corruption, and other political phenomena—can be understood in rather simple and precise ways. We develop concepts, hypotheses, and theories in order to describe and explain politics. Using the assumptions and methods of one or more of the research schools of political science, we are guided in our search by the rules of logic and the proper use of evidence. Political science, like any science, uses analytic techniques to posit and explore regularities in the world around us.

On first encounter, many students may find it strange that political science draws attention to both the general and the abstract. Some students come to the study of politics with a deep interest in current events. They expect to learn the particulars of politics: the relevant names, dates, and events; who said what to whom, and what did he or she mean by that? When they consider how we know what we know, they may believe analysis follows the principle that the closer one is to the phenomena, the more one knows. Other students seek to improve, perhaps even transform, the communities in which they live. Still others may pursue both of these goals. And all students may be puzzled by the effort to detect uniformities and offer hypotheses that apply to diverse cases of politics and by the methodological concerns that accompany this effort.

As a generalizing science, political science is not bound to the study of current events or to issues of political relevance. When we analyse something in the news, we do so with an eye to the more abstract theoretical issues at stake. We want to explain, for example, the collapse of the Communist regimes in Eastern Europe not only to know more about what we witnessed but also to address general questions, such as the formation of political movements and revolution in authoritarian regimes, revolution in industrial societies, and the conditions under which revolution occurs without violence. In political science, interest in the particular draws attention to general issues.

Neither citizenship training nor preparation for the revolution directs the study of politics. In the university, there is virtue in simply trying to know how the world works. At the same time, you have every right to care deeply about what you study. There is no rule that political scientists may have no preferences about the issues of war and peace or prosperity and poverty, just as there is no expectation that cancer researchers will be impartial about what they study. However, you must be objective, in the sense of being willing to test your ideas and accept the results of fair tests, even if they negate your preferences.

Political science offers theories that enable us to analyse political phenomena. Consider the goal of developing an explanation of revolution that can account for the transformation of power that occurred in Eastern Europe and Russia at the end of the 1980s, the Russian Revolution of 1917, and the revolutions in France, Cuba, and Germany, as well. To solve this puzzle, it is first necessary to decide what the concept 'revolution' signifies. Are all of these events examples of the same concept? How would you define revolution so that we

From Alan S. Zuckerman, *Doing Political Science: An Introduction to Political Analysis* (Boulder, Co.: Westview Press, 1991). Reprinted by permission of the author.

could decide which of these cases is a true revolution and which is not? You will ask the 'what' questions: 'What is a revolution?' or 'What would indicate the presence of a revolution?' After all, no one actually sees a revolution as such, and we need to develop operations by which we can establish the defining characteristics of this phenomenon. Having defined revolution, you must then explain its presence by answering the 'why' questions. These questions may come in simple or complicated form: 'Why do revolutions occur?' or 'What factors are present whenever a revolution occurs?' or 'In what ways do the phenomena that designate the presence of the explanatory concepts vary so as to influence the phenomena that indicate the presence or absence of a revolution?' As you analyse, you decide what is important and what may be ignored. You move beyond the swirl of events and crises to search for underlying themes, and you offer concepts, hypotheses, and theories. As you do political science, you struggle to develop systematic and testable knowledge about politics.

There are several schools of research in political science, and alternative assumptions—about which questions to ask, concepts to use, hypotheses to test—and diverse views about the theories most likely to lead to powerful explanations characterize the discipline. Some political scientists focus attention on the behaviour of individuals; others reason as if there were only groups. There is also disagreement over the relative importance of detailed descriptions of particular cases and over the power of abstract logic in analyses. No single approach to research represents all of orthodox political science.

## What We Assume in Order to Do Political Science

All analyses entail assumptions about how the world should be studied. These suppositions lead us to ask particular kinds of questions, to use specific methods, and to propose certain kinds of answers. Clearly, you cannot seek to know the world without taking some principles as givens.

To do political science, you must accept the tenet that all knowledge is public. This apparently innocuous assumption implies several critical points.

1. There are no hidden truths, no hidden sources of truth, and no purveyors of truth who can never be wrong. 'All must submit to the same base-line of evidence. Quite literally, this means that nothing is sacred.'[1] Because everyone can be mistaken, your effort to understand the world of politics should include an evaluation of the claims that are presented to you as knowledge. You have the right and, indeed, the obligation to assess whatever your teachers seek to teach you and whatever you read in articles and books. (Incidentally, you should judge the merits of this point, as well.) One of the most important goals of this book is to help make you a more critical reader and consumer of knowledge. When you do political science, you learn, evaluate, and, where appropriate, challenge claims to knowledge about politics.

2. Whoever analyses politics must provide support that will convince other persons. Emotional attachments, personal hunches, and intuitive understandings do not adequately justify knowledge claims. The point is not that personal intuitions are wrong but that they are not necessarily relevant. To substantiate a claim that you have analysed a political problem—interpreted the rate of voting in elections, accounted for the level of homelessness, or explained the outbreak of a war or revolution—you must present the credentials that warrant the analysis. Ultimately, you need to convince the reader or listener to accept your answer, but you should first persuade yourself of the merits of your analysis on rational grounds.

3. You should assess knowledge by standards that are beyond anyone's control. Logical coherence and adequate evidence are the most widely accepted criteria by which we judge claims to

knowledge. Logical coherence entails precise definitions of key concepts, as well as careful and justified derivations of deductions (that is, the conclusions that are implied by initial principles) and inductions (the generalizations that are implied by empirical evidence). You also need to assess whether the evidence assembled is adequate to the task at hand. As you read this book you will encounter numerous examples that elaborate the principles of logical coherence and adequate evidence.

4. To do political science, you must assume that the political world is an orderly place. As Ernest Gellner instructs us, 'Assume the regularity of nature, the systematic nature of the world, not because it is demonstrable, but because anything which eludes such a principle also eludes real knowledge: *if* cumulative and communicable knowledge is to be possible at all, then the principle of orderliness must apply to it.'[2] It is not possible to see, much less understand, something that is completely unlike anything else. And because you can only know something that displays recurrent patterns, you must begin with the assumption that there *are* regularities in our world.

5. Gellner describes another critical characteristic of the patterns that exist in the world: 'The orderliness of the world is also assumed to be systematic: not only are there regularities to be discovered, but these form a system, such that if we are successful with our inquiries, the more specific regularities turn out in the end to be corollaries of more general ones.'[3] This assumption urges you to extend your ideas, to push your ability to analyse the world to its limits. You need not assume that you will tie all the corollaries together, but you should be willing to expand your quest.

6. At the same time, you should not assume that order is self-evident. Do not suppose that all you must do to understand politics is read the newspaper or watch the news on television. Rather, you must analyse actively, proposing and testing ideas about the nature of the world's order. Only the active use of our intellects allows us to

posit uniformities and bring logic and evidence to bear on our propositions and hypotheses.

7. Empirical sciences—like political science —recognize the centrality of our minds in the effort to know the world but insist that there is a reality outside our effort to know it. 'In order to learn about the physical world through perception, we must be able to extract the relevant information from the items we perceive; and our available theories . . . permit us to do that.'[4]

But even though theories enable us to observe the world, we are not caught in an infinite regress in which our thoughts determine what we observe. 'Testing would be circular if what we observed were wholly determined by the theories under test, but observation always involves an interaction with an independent physical world that plays a crucial role in determining what we can observe in a given set of circumstances. Thus, even the most theory-laden observations can surprise us.'[5]

Scientists assume a granular world, to borrow an image from Ernest Gellner[6]—that is, a world in which discrete phenomena exist in and of themselves, whether or not we posit their existence. They strive to bring our concepts and hypotheses in line with the discrete items, without necessarily ever seeing the granular matter.

8. The assumption of the granular nature of the world allows us to use the facts of the world (which really are not more than widely accepted descriptions) to test our explanations: 'The very act of looking at data as *data*, as evidence for or against theories or interpretations which are inherently conjectural, *rather than as examples of theories as seen as inherently part of the very nature of things*, completely transforms the situation. It signals that everything is conjectural.'[7] This assumption also precludes the view that the world out there is beyond our ken, a jungle of elements that we cannot explore.

9. You have the right, if not the obligation, to offer your own explanation of politics, as well. Remember that when we do political science, we offer concepts, hypotheses, and theories in order

to discover the uniformities present in the world of politics. Hence, you should advance your own analyses, even as you learn, assess, and challenge those of others. And reason and evidence should guide your efforts.

Although you have enormous power over claims to knowledge, you are also tightly constrained by the rules of analysis. Gellner maintains that the effort to study the world as it exists— empirical analysis—requires that an individual be freed from the chains of intellectual orthodoxies. But this freedom is not unbridled license, which would entail that all claims to knowledge are equally personal and equally plausible. Rather, the rules of logic and evidence serve as checks to make sure that you adhere to standards that are beyond your control:

> Knowledge is and can only be about *my* experience, my *data*. . . . But it all depends on how you read this. Is knowledge about *my* data, or about my *data*? The reason why empiricism clings so to experience is not because it is mine . . . but because it is *outside my control*, because it is *given* to me and there is little or nothing that I can do about it.
>
> The point . . . is not that this or that self becomes the judge, but that there *is* a judge at all, some judge, for everything becomes subject to judgement, to conjecture. The self is introduced not in order to introduce private caprice, but for the opposite reason, to curb it: a *judge* is required to reduce all other participants to the status of mere witnesses, allowed to present evidence, which is then assessed.[8]

By applying the rules of logic and evidence, not your unchecked hunches and personal experience, you can accept or reject the analyses offered by others and give others reasons to accept your interpretations. You thus use public standards to guide your decisions regarding claims to knowledge and to control your own explanations of politics.

There are several important implications in this discussion. First, because there is always a gap between the creations of our minds and the world itself, each of us is likely to analyse the world in a somewhat different way. Second, differences in how we interpret the world derive from and help to refine the various research schools of political science and the clashing theoretical systems and approaches that characterize all fields of knowledge. Third, we do not rejoice in these disagreements; instead, we strive to minimize their importance by following rules of analysis that enable us to demonstrate the meaning of our claims and the concepts and hypotheses of our analyses. Finally, although each of us analyses the world somewhat differently, every perspective is not necessarily as good as all the others. Indeed, the standard of public knowledge, the rules of analysis, and the specific requirements of logic and evidence help us to decide among the alternative visions. There can be no analysis without rules of analysis, and there can be no analysis without the evaluation of analysis.

## The Language of Political Science: Theories, Hypotheses, Concepts, and Variables

Explanations—claims about how the world works—lie at the heart of political analysis. They answer the question, 'Why did a phenomenon occur when it did or in the way it did?' with a response that is part of a general argument. W.H. Newton-Smith and Harold Brown tell us that 'science begins when, having noted correlations, we seek an explanation of why they obtain.'[9] We seek to discover 'explanatory truths' in science, and 'explanatory power comes from theories.'[10] 'A complete explanation is one that provides a set of premises that is acceptable in our current theoretical framework, and that is sufficient for deducing a description of the item to be explained.'[11] We explain by demonstrating that the political phenomenon, event, or set of events that we are analysing represents an instance of a general process.

Explanations answer 'why' questions. 'Why did the French Revolution occur?' seeks an explanation of a particular event. 'Why do revolutions occur in industrial democracies?' focuses the analysis on a type of society or political system. 'Why do revolutions occur?' points to the most general level, seeking to specify the conditions under which any and all revolutions occur. Although political scientists ask all these questions, the goal of providing abstract and general knowledge leads us to prefer questions about types of regimes and even about all regimes rather than questions about revolutions in particular countries. After all, when we explain why all revolutions or certain types of revolutions occur, we account for particular events as well, but the reverse is not true. When we explain, we claim that the world is organized in such a way that the phenomenon under question has to occur or is particularly likely to occur.

In political science and other empirical sciences, we explain by offering hypotheses. These statements specify the relationship among the phenomena being explained, the dependent variables, and the explanatory (or independent) variables. Each hypothesis requires a more general 'covering hypothesis', which allows us to specify and justify the particular hypothesis as an instance of this more general claim. Hypotheses are situated within categories of related explanations or theories. They also require tests that assess the empirical adequacy of the hypothesis. And, as always, we use the standards of empirical knowledge—logic and evidence—to direct our efforts to know the world.

Hypotheses come in various forms, specifying that the explanatory variable influences, affects, predicts, rises with, is inversely related to, is a necessary condition for, is a sufficient condition for, is both a necessary and sufficient condition for, accounts for the variation in, or is tied in some other way to the dependent variable. In the next

chapters, you will examine a hypothesis that attempts to account for variations in the level of voting in national elections—the dependent variable—by relating it to variations in the level of education—the explanatory variable. This hypothesis suggests that the higher the level of education is, the higher the level of turnout will be. You will also consider a hypothesis that accounts for turnout by relating it to specific characteristics of the political system, contending that the more the electoral rules facilitate voting and the greater the level of electoral competitions among the political parties is, the higher the level of turnout will be. Hypotheses detail the precise relationship among the explanatory variables and that which is to be explained.

You must be able to test your hypotheses with empirical evidence. Barrington Moore Jr emphasizes the centrality of this simple but absolutely critical statement: 'The effort requires constructing the argument in such a way that disproof is possible through resort to evidence.'[12] Harold Brown tells us that 'the ability to recognize that a particular set of items has the requisite properties . . . constitutes the critical step in theory construction.'[13] Similarly, W.H. Newton-Smith notes, 'In the long run . . . the ultimate test of the superiority of one theory over another is observational success.'[14] Referring back to the previous example, you must be able to observe whether turnout rises as a direct function of education. Hence, hypotheses must include precisely defined and measured variables. It follows, as well, that you must be able to specify the meaning of the linking verbs, such as 'influences', 'predicts', 'varies with', or any of the other words you might use to relate a set of explanatory and dependent variables. If you cannot test the hypothesis directly or derive testable implications, you do not have a hypothesis. And if you do not have a hypothesis, you do not have an explanation.

Political scientists work with *nominal* definitions, which indicate how the concept is to be used. In other words, we specify that *for our purposes* something is this and not that. Such definitions do not provide the true or essential characteristics of the political phenomena in question—this could only be done if the concept were a perfect representation of the component of the world that we claim it represents. Because we cannot be sure of this claim and because we have reason to think that we can never provide a concept with this kind of power, we strive to offer concepts that come closer and closer to that reality, to the 'grains' of our granular world. But we do not claim that they are abstract equivalents, or a representation in words, of the world as it exists. We work by the rule that precisely defined concepts allow us to think clearly.

It is useful to distinguish between *abstract* and *operational* definitions. Abstract definitions correlate terms and sets of characteristics without connecting either to observable phenomena. If we define turnout in an election as participation in the voting process, we have a reasonable abstract definition. But if we want to make the concept of turnout empirically useful, we need to provide an operational definition. We need to provide a technique, method, or measure—an operation—that will connect the abstract concept with what is observable and verifiable. We must devise an operation, such as determining the percentage of adults with the right to vote who go to the polls. This figure can be calculated, verified, and compared over time.

Notice that we do not see turnout as such, just as we never directly see an election, a revolution, a government, a war, or any other of the abstractions we deal with in political science. (We only see people voting, fighting, holding meetings, and so forth.) But because we want to make the study of political science objectively verifiable, we use operational definitions to connect unobservable abstractions to publicly observable phenomena. In this way, we specify the variables in our hypotheses.

To assess the utility of an operational definition, you should examine the validity and reliability of the measures or indicators you use. When you can show that the indicators adequately detail the presence of the concept's defining characteristics, you have reason to use the hypotheses that contain these variables.

Validity examines whether the indicators come sufficiently close to the concept's abstract definition. For example, let us assume that the abstract definition of education is the process of learning about the world and the operational definition is the number of years of formal schooling. (Notice that it is relatively easy to observe the characteristics of the operational definition but not those of the abstract definition.) You weigh the validity of this operationalization when you ask whether there are other ways of learning about the world and whether the omission of learning that takes place at home or on the streets—to name two such alternatives—invalidates the operational definition. Questions of validity might also be used to ascertain whether the concept of party identification, defined abstractly as a psychological attachment to a political party, is properly measured by the answer to the question, 'Generally speaking, do you think of yourself as a Republican or Democrat or ———?' Similarly, those who deny that scores on the Scholastic Aptitude Tests really measure intelligence are raising questions about the adequacy of this particular operational definition. Note that in order to assess a concept's validity, you must know its abstract definition. Questions of validity examine the gap between the abstract and operational definitions of a concept.

To assess the reliability of a set of measures, you must first determine if the information in the operationalization is dependable. You must ask whether the techniques used to measure the components of the concept produce consistent and accurate results. As an example, imagine the problems that could result from defining political corruption as an affirmative response to the question, 'Have you ever taken a bribe?' After all, it is unlikely that a corrupt person would answer in the affirmative. We also assess reliability when we decide if we should accept the answers people give in surveys asking whether or not they voted in the most recent election. We must consider the possibility that a significant number will say they have voted, even when they have not, in hopes of appearing to be good citizens. But just because you can raise questions about a measure's dependability does not mean that the operationalization is useless. You need to draw reasonable conclusions, knowing that there are no perfect operationalizations.

As long as you keep in mind that our measures are efforts to make our concepts and hypotheses useful—not exact equivalents of the abstract definitions—you will make the most of your ability to analyse politics without violating the distinction between what is in our minds and what is real. Remember this rule: *Measurements must be made, and all measures have problems.*

Hypotheses in political science specify the relationship among the explanatory variables and that which is being explained; variables that specify the motives of the actors or that establish causal relationships are not necessarily included. Some students are puzzled by this point because it violates their implicit understanding of the meaning of explanation. Consider the justifications for hypotheses that do not refer to motives or causes. First, it is not always possible to attribute motives to actors, to test for the presence of those motives, or to make the link between the presence of the motive and the action. Furthermore, the stated motives—which are all we ever get from surveys, interviews, or discussions—are sometimes really justifications that follow and rationalize actions. In addition, a causal explanation is not the only form of explanation. Cause implies constant conjunction, temporal precedence, and nonspuriousness. This means that the explanatory variable precedes in time and is always associated with the presence of the dependent variable and that the dependent variable is brought about by *that* explanatory variable and no

other. However, a successful explanation in political analysis does not have to meet such stringent conditions.

Given the need to test our hypotheses and the assumption that the world is an orderly place, we should keep our hypotheses as simple as possible. There is no reason to search for what are sometimes called 'full' explanations if that implies including all possible explanatory factors. Politics is not so complicated that it excludes parsimonious analyses. Indeed, the guiding rule leads us in the opposite direction: search for the simplest explanation, the one with the fewest number of explanatory variables. We use this preference for simple hypotheses to choose among competing explanations when all are equally able to solve the problem at hand. Here, as in many aspects of your life, strive to keep it simple.

Hypotheses are strengthened when they are tied to strong theories. A theory is a set of propositions that are deductively connected to each other in ways that explain the phenomena in question. Newton-Smith defines a 'successful' theory as 'one whose success includes not only observational success but theoretical success. Theoretical success is a matter both of the generation of novel predictions which themselves are theoretical and of the explanation of accepted theories.'[15] The more a particular hypothesis is logically implied by and leads to other hypotheses, the more reason we have to use it and accept its explanation of the phenomena being studied. And the greater the theoretical scope of a hypothesis, the more reason we have to think that it is part of an interrelated set of ideas that helps us understand a larger portion of the political world. This does not contradict the standard of parsimony, which should be applied to each hypothesis but not the set of related hypotheses. Indeed, we strive to place our simple hypotheses in a complex and wide-ranging web of ideas.

Philosophers of science often use the metaphor of a net to describe the relationship among the hypotheses of a theory. Karl Popper, for example, compares theories to 'nets in which to capture the world', suggesting an image of tightly woven intellectual systems. 'The finer is the mesh', he says, the more of the world that we capture with our ideas and the more we can claim to know about the world.[16] In other words, by linking more and more hypotheses and propositions together, we improve our understanding and explanation of the world around us. David Hull prefers the image of 'patchwork nets'[17] as a more realistic description of the weave of intellectual systems. Theories vary in the extent to which their sets of propositions and hypotheses are tightly and precisely linked to each other.

Let's look at some illustrations of hypotheses and theories. (a) The statement, 'The stronger a voter's identification is with a political party, the more likely he or she is to vote for that party' is a hypothesis in which party identification—a psychological state—is used to explain vote choice—a political act. (b) The statement, 'When parents share the same party identification, their children have a very strong identification with that party' is a hypothesis in which the party identifications of the parents explain the strength of the voter's party identification. (c) The statement, 'The stronger a person's attachment to a social group is, the more likely the person is to act in accordance with the expectations of that group' is yet another hypothesis, which may be used to explain the first and second hypotheses. It covers them with a more general claim, and in so doing, it explains and provides the justification for each.

Together, the three hypotheses compose a theory of the relationship between psychological attachments to social groups and vote choice. Given statement (c) and the proposition that identification with one's parents' loyalties is an example of such a psychological attachment, it follows that where parents have the same party loyalties, their children will also have those political identifications. Given statement (c) and the proposition that identification with a political party is an example of a psychological attachment, it follows

that persons who identify with a political party will vote for that party.

Another theory explains the pattern of working-class politics under capitalism. Hypothesis (a) holds that the greater the level of economic organization is among the working class, the greater the level of electoral support for socialist parties is among that class. Hypothesis (b) holds that the greater the proportion of the working class who labour in large factories is, the greater the economic organization of that class is. Hypothesis (c) holds that the greater the level of capitalism is, the greater the level of revolutionary activity among the working class is. Here, too, we have a general hypothesis that specifies the relationships among a set of variables, while covering other hypotheses.

To explain or analyse, we must propose specific hypotheses, place them into theories by linking them to more general hypotheses, and test the hypotheses. By examining the logical power of the derivations, testing the hypotheses with relevant empirical evidence, and examining rival explanations, we determine if our hypotheses can explain the political phenomena in question. As more tests are passed—tests of logical coherence, of validity and reliability of measures, or of observations about the strength and nature of the relationships proposed—our reasons to accept the explanations are strengthened.

These standards for the acceptance of claims to knowledge are the criteria used by the community of scholars that studies politics. Hence, when we demonstrate that an explanation of the rate of turnout conforms to data from national or state elections, we are testing and supporting the knowledge claim. When we demonstrate that the explanatory hypothesis is properly deduced from a more general law, we are showing that our analysis accords with the rules of logic. Other members of the community of scholars who share these criteria for the acceptance of knowledge claims can then assess and decide whether to agree with our analysis.

Two related conclusions follow: First, those outside the circle of scholars need accept neither the explanation nor the criteria by which it is assessed. Second, all knowledge is relative to the methods that produce and evaluate it.

There is no claim that political scientists produce absolute truth about politics. All that is claimed is that successful analyses meet the criteria of knowledge established by those who study politics. Lest you be dismayed by the limited nature of the claim, I should point out that it applies, as well, to other sciences. All knowledge that fits under the heading of science is relative to the theories and fields of study from which it comes. Consider Harold Brown's admonition: 'We have excellent grounds for taking the well-tested claims of current science to be true, while remembering that these results remain tentative and subject to reconsideration, and that the best established scientific knowledge of our day may yet have to be revised.'[18] The standards of a discipline can come under attack and can change, but they do so only when they are challenged by those who have mastered these very standards. The goal of this book is to help *you* master them, as well.

Some scholars offer a stronger defence of these standards. Gellner insists that they, more than any other form of reasoning, provide the means to increase our knowledge of the world. He argues that they are the standards of 'science—of that transcultural, cumulative and qualitatively superior form of knowledge which has so totally transformed the modern world'.[19] He and others contend that we must accept the principle of public knowledge and use the rules of logic and evidence to test claims about the world; if we ignore these standards, our ability to understand and explain political phenomena is diminished.

## The Cacophonous Sound of Political Science

Political science appears to contain a fundamental paradox. Political scientists share a language of analysis—which emphasizes concepts, variables, indicators, hypotheses, and theories—and a vision of the discipline that focuses on the explanation of political phenomena. However, they display deep conflicts over appropriate assumptions, foci, and methods of analysis, and they offer hypotheses and theories that directly contradict one another. They frequently describe the same phenomenon but offer very different analyses of it. They may even observe the world in different ways. And the research schools of political science voice much agreement on the methods and goals of analysis but much disagreement on the results of analysis.

In a field like political science where there are multiple and competing theories, there are also multiple and competing analyses. This is true because each theory contains concepts, variables, and hypotheses that necessarily depict politics in a particular way. Consider the two examples of theories that I presented earlier. In the first theory, the decision to vote for a particular party is explained as the result of a psychological attachment to that party. In the second theory, vote choice is explained as the result of the voter's position in a particular social class. Such multiple theories characterize the analysis of electoral choice and almost all other political phenomena. The diversity of political science derives, as well, from the multiple and competing schools for research that encompass the various theories. . . .

Within the research schools of political science (and all sciences), there is intellectual order. For those who speak the same language of theory and method, the conversations are complex and fascinating, yielding powerful analyses. But you must resist the temptation to merge the approaches. They are offered as alternatives to one another, and you need to understand them as different and sometimes contradictory ways to analyse politics. As you do political science, you will gradually decide which you prefer.

Some of the challenges of political science stem from the diversity of the discipline itself.

Political science has no theoretical orthodoxy. There is no approach that you must select and no theory that you need accept as true. You may even choose to use some methods of analysis while ignoring others. Some see this as a virtue because there is little that must be accepted uncritically as truth and because there are no defenders of a holy writ. Others see this as a problem because there is little evidence of an accumulation of accepted knowledge claims about politics. As a result, it may seem as if each analysis treats its problem as if it were the only analysis. Whatever your preferences in this regard, you must understand and evaluate each of the competing theories and assess the relative merits of the competitors. And when you submit your own hypotheses, you must be ready to justify your analyses in the face of powerful criticisms within the discipline.

## Notes

1.  Ernest Gellner, *Relativism and the Social Sciences* (Cambridge: Cambridge University Press, 1985), 88–9.
2.  Ibid., 89. Emphasis in original.
3.  Ibid.
4.  Harold I. Brown, *Observation and Objectivity* (New York: Oxford University Press, 1987), vi.
5.  Ibid.
6   Gellner, *Relativism and the Social Sciences*, 89.
7.  Ibid., 22. Emphasis in original.
8.  Ibid., 20–1. Emphasis in original. See also W.H. Newton-Smith, *The Rationality of Science* (Boston: Routledge & Kegan Paul, 1981); Brown, *Observation and Objectivity*.
9.  Newton-Smith, *The Rationality of Science*, 211.
10. Ibid., 223.
11. Brown, *Observation and Objectivity*.
12. Barrington Moore Jr, *Injustice: The Social Bases of Obedience and Revolt* (White Plains, NY: M.E. Sharp, 1978), 381.
13. Brown, *Observation and Objectivity*, 28.
14. Newton-Smith, *The Rationality of Science*, 224.
15. Ibid.
16. Karl Popper, *Conjectures and Refutations: The Growth of Scientific Knowledge* (New York: Harper Torchbooks, 1965), cited in Dickinson McGaw and George Watson, *Political and Social Inquiry* (New York: Wiley, 1976).
17. David L. Hull, *Science as a Process: An Evolutionary Account of the Social and Conceptual Development of Science* (Chicago: University of Chicago Press, 1988), 493.
18. Brown, *Observation and Objectivity*, 220.
19. Gellner, *Relativism and the Social Sciences*, 53. Newton-Smith, *The Rationality of Science*, and Brown, *Observation and Objectivity*, make similar claims.

# Is Political Science a Science?

Alan C. Isaak

Arguments made by those who are sceptical of or in opposition to [the applicability of scientific methods to the study of politics][1] . . . may not demonstrate that it is impossible to study politics scientifically, [but] they suggest that the road to empirical knowledge is a rough one; there are obstacles that every political scientist must be aware of. It is with this in mind that we begin our analysis of the anti-science arguments.

## Arguments Against the Possibility of a Science of Politics

Science or scientific method is characterized by a number of assumptions and principles. . . . First, scientists assume some form of determinism or 'law of universal causation'. Again, this means that the political scientist who accepts scientific method plunges into his work assuming that nothing in politics just happens. The second major characteristic of science is its empirical basis. This implies a number of features, including an observational foundation, intersubjectivity, and the value-free nature of science. The objectives of science are summarized in the third characteristic, its systematic nature. They are to formulate and verify empirical generalizations, develop systematic theory, and finally explain and predict. The arguments against the possibility of a science of politics invariably attempt to demonstrate that political science does not and/or cannot have one or more of these characteristics. This strategy

From *Scope and Methods of Political Science: An Introduction to the Methodology of Political Inquiry*, Third Edition (Pacific Grove, Calif.: Brooks/Cole Publishing Company, 1984). Reprinted by permission of Harcourt Brace & Company.

correctly assumes that if political science must have these characteristics to be legitimately labelled 'scientific', then such a demonstration, if successful, would illustrate the quicksand upon which the scientific study of politics rests. At that point, the behaviourally or scientifically oriented political scientist would be well advised to put the brakes on, admit the futility of his activities, and return to more traditional ways of doing things.

### The Complexity of Political Phenomena

One argument against the possibility of a science of politics claims that no regularities can be discovered because political phenomena are too complex. Because of a variety of usages, the meaning of 'complex' is not clear. However, the basic point seems to be that in politics there are too many variables and possible relationships between them to find any order. In contradistinction, physicists and chemists are able to discover relationships and construct theories because the phenomena that interest them are less complex. This directly attacks the third characteristic of science. If political phenomena are so complex that they cannot be organized into generalizations—that is, if relationships are not discoverable—then there can be no science of politics; that is, there can be no scientific explanations and predictions of political phenomena. Let us turn to the writings of the well-known contemporary political scientist Hans Morgenthau for a statement of this position. After noting the complexity of social phenomena and difficulty involved in isolating causal factors, he concludes: 'The social sciences can, at best, do what is their regular task; that is, present a series of hypothetical possibilities, each of which may occur under certain conditions—

and which of them will actually occur is any-body's guess.'[2]

A reply to this argument should first point out that the degree of complexity of political phe-nomena is an empirical, not a logical, question. That is, it is debatable whether the social sciences are more complex than the natural sciences, and the debate can only be resolved by systematically examining each science. But it is not even neces-sary for our purposes to resolve the controversy, since there are no logical grounds for this criticism of scientific political science. From the fact that it is difficult to sort out political factors and measure relationships (research-oriented political scientists need not be reminded of this), one cannot logical-ly conclude that the discovery of generalizations is impossible. Note that the critic is not denying that relationships exist, only that the political scientist can discover them.

This is the logical-methodological answer. But, in addition, several empirical points can be offered to strengthen our case. Philosopher of science Adolf Grunbaum has wondered what someone living before Galileo and holding to the complexity thesis would have thought about the possibility of a science of motion. This observa-tion is perhaps especially relevant in today's rapid-ly changing world, in which the word *impossible* is used with greater and greater discretion. (Thirty years ago, what would the betting odds be on the landing of men on the moon?) The point is that it is foolish to state on empirical grounds (even assuming that the evidence is sound) that some-thing is logically impossible. In Grunbaum's words, 'This argument rests its case on what is not known, and therefore, like all such arguments, it has no case.'[3] Furthermore, we can refer the scep-tic to the relationships that have been discovered in the fields of psychology, sociology, economics, and even political science; the discovery of a sin-gle law logically refutes the impossibility argu-ment, and, on a positive note, the social sciences are more highly developed than many of their critics care to admit or seem to realize. The neater

and apparently less complex nature of the natural sciences is probably more the result of the labora-tory conditions under which most physicists and chemists work, conditions that allow them to con-trol the factors they study, than it is on any inher-ent lack of explanatory factors.

This argument boils down to the mistaken translation of a practical problem into a logically insurmountable barrier. As we have already implied, every political scientist knows how diffi-cult it is to find order in the world of politics—but this does not prevent him from attempting to dis-cover generalizations. Sometimes, he even suc-ceeds. Contrary to the image of science held by many laymen, scientists, whether natural or social, realize that no complete description or explana-tion of any empirical phenomenon is possible. Something is always left out. Thus, to chastise political science for something that is true even of physics is perhaps unfair. If political scientists are sobered by the practical wisdom implied by the complexity argument, if their rose-coloured glass-es are shattered, then it has been useful—Utopian optimism is out of place in science. But if the reac-tion is to give up the scientific enterprise, then political science has been dealt a destructive blow.

## Human Indeterminacy

So much for the complexity thesis. Another argu-ment against the possibility of a science of politics is based upon the so-called indeterminacy of human behaviour. Russell Kirk, one of the most vigorous opponents of the scientific study of pol-itics, has put it this way: 'Human beings are the least controllable, verifiable, law-obeying and pre-dictable of subjects.'[4] Up to a point, this is a ver-sion of the complexity argument—one of the reasons for the complexity of political phenomena is the unpredictable behaviour of political actors. The reply is the same. But there is an additional feature that makes the argument a new and prob-ably more uncompromising one. This feature is a belief in freedom of the will. Because humans are free to choose their course of action at any given point in the political process, their actions cannot be classified, and so generalizations describing their behaviour cannot be formulated. This argument is more uncompromising than the previous one, because the claim is not that it is extremely difficult to isolate causal factors, but that there are no causal factors in the first place.

As many philosophers have shown, this is a bogus argument. The ability to formulate laws of human behaviour and freedom of the will are not incompatible. Those who opt for freedom of the will are usually saying that people are able to act without external restraints. 'But would they also claim that what they do is not determined even by the sort of people they are, considered as a whole, individuals possessing a certain disposition, a certain character, certain motives, and so on?'[5] In other words, a free choice need not be uncaused. It is, rather, largely the result of the particular characteristics of the chooser. These characteristics, in turn, are subject to description; that is, inclusion in general laws that relate them to other factors. John Hospers neatly summarizes this whole reply when he points out that, 'Freedom . . . is the opposite of compulsion, not of causality.'[6] The distinction is important, for it allows us to accept scientific determinism while retaining a notion of legal and social responsibility. We are subject to punishment if we 'freely' rob a bank; that is, if we are not forced by someone else to do so. It also allows us to exempt some, children for instance, from the laws of responsibility, for in their state of immaturity they are not always aware of the implications of actions. Martin Landau has suggested that the doctrine of free will has such great staying power because it has become a basic moral principle. 'It has been sustained and sanctioned to such an extent that in some quarters it is a sin to hold otherwise.'[7]

Some critics would now reject the defence just presented with a statement of indeterminism—'Not every fact has a cause.' Unfortunately for social scientists, most of the uncaused ones are found in the social, economic, and political realms. This position strikes directly at the first assumption of our model of science. Now let us recall that determinism should not be considered an empirical statement about the universe; there is no point in trying to disprove it, for the failure to discover determining conditions does not prove that there are none. That is why it is not empirical—it fails to meet the testability and verifiability criteria. Instead, the thesis of determinism should be 'construed as a regulative principle that formulates in a comprehensive way one of the major objectives of positive science, namely, the discovery of the determinants for the occurrence of events'.[8] In other words, without some sort of assumption that events have causes, the whole attempt to describe and explain the world of politics might as well be given up. This suggestion is no doubt appealing to some. But why end science at this point? And I say 'end' because progress has been made in the social sciences, including political science. For one engaged in the enterprise of understanding political phenomena, the assumption of determinism seems unavoidable. Why, when starting out to gain knowledge, should one want to limit himself before he begins? Perhaps political science will never produce the kind of knowledge that characterizes physics and chemistry, but it is worth the try and something is better than nothing. We can't tell what we can't do until we try to do it.

The Reaction Problem

It is often argued that even if people are not completely indeterminate, they have another characteristic that makes it impossible to systematically analyse and predict their political behaviour. Much research in political science is based on the reactions of those being studied. What readily comes to mind is the survey research technique in which human subjects are questioned to elicit responses that will describe their opinions, attitudes, or general states of mind. This kind of research depends upon the reactions of the subjects. It appears to be an effective way to find out certain things about people. But some critics of scientific political science point out that since the subjects are aware of the fact that they are being studied, their responses cannot be taken as valid indicators of their opinions. How many attempt to please the interviewer with their answers? How many try to offend? How many try to see through the questions to figure out what the interviewer is after? The point in each case is that the political scientist cannot be sure that he is obtaining accurate measures of the factors he is studying. As long as people know they are being studied, there is a good chance that they will adjust their behaviour.

The problem of human reaction is not limited to survey research. There are research methods that place the political scientist in real-world political situations so that he can observe political behaviour up close. Typical studies of this sort have been conducted in government bureaucracies, labour unions, and political conventions. For decades, anthropologists have known about and employed this technique and have given it a name: *participant observation*. Many readers have become familiar with this technique through the books of anthropologists like Margaret Mead and Ruth Benedict, who spent considerable time living in other cultures as participating members. The objective of participant observation is not only to observe behaviour first-hand but to get a feel for the culture by actually being part of it. The problem is that in being aware of their role as objects of research, those being studied may change their behaviour.[9]

Thus, the issue of human reaction boils down to the introduction of another factor, the researcher, into the research situation. That the reaction of subjects is a real problem was clearly demonstrated in a study of worker motivation carried out in the Hawthorne, Illinois, Western Electric plant during the late 1920s. Asked to discover ways to increase worker productivity, the team of psychologists discovered accidentally that not only did an increase in lighting increase

productivity, but a decrease in lighting had the same effect. The conclusion was that the workers were not responding to the level of lighting or other changes in working conditions so much as to the fact that they were being studied, that someone was paying attention to them. Thus was born the 'Hawthorne Effect'.[10] In the light of claims that this is a problem peculiar to the study of human behaviour, it is instructive to note comments made by the great animal psychologist, Pavlov. In discussing the actions of researchers, Pavlov once wrote, 'His slightest movements—blinking of the eyelids or movement of the eyes, posture, respiration, and so on—all acted as stimuli which, falling upon the dog, were sufficient to vitiate the experiments by making exact interpretations of the results extremely difficult.'[12]

What we have here is a practical research problem, not an insurmountable methodological barrier. When the subjects of research are aware that they are being observed, they sometimes behave out of character. However, within certain limits, the extent to which this is occurring can be determined. When conducting survey research, the same attitudes can be measured by using several slightly different questions scattered throughout the questionnaire. Each can be used as a cross-check against the others. The lesson is that one should always attempt to find several sources of data to test a hypothesis. The greater the correspondence among the different types of evidence, the more confidence the political scientist can place in his conclusions.

The same basic rule applies to participant observation. No matter how extensive, such observations are at best suggestive—not conclusive. In conjunction with other methods, they can prove useful. There are many types of research that do not depend upon human reaction. The examination of documents and other historical records falls into this category. This type of research, which constitutes a significant portion of all political research, is not subject to the kinds of problems we have been considering.

## The Influence of Values

Another argument against the possibility of a science of politics questions its presumed value-free nature. Here is the main difference between the natural and social sciences; practitioners of the former do not have to deal with values—protons and molecules are neither good nor bad—but social scientists do, because people are moral beings and thus social scientists are irretrievably immersed in value questions. This is especially true of political science, for several reasons. First, political science is a policy science. Politics is mainly concerned with goals and the means to achieve them—policies. Politics involves policies and policies involve values.

A second reason is the importance of value concepts—attitudes, opinions, and ideologies—to political science. No political scientist denies that values hold a significant place in his discipline. Much of politics involves the value commitments of political actors, and so political scientists must study values. The first claim of the anti-scientist is, however, that because political scientists study values, they must be influenced by them. It would seem that no lengthy argument is required to demonstrate the weakness of this claim. There is a logical difference between having one's own values and studying attitudes and opinions. The latter can be treated in the same manner as any other political phenomena. They are just as susceptible to scientific treatment (for instance the tremendous progress that has been made in the analysis of opinions and attitudes). To admit this, the political scientist does not have to deny that he has values—this is patently foolish.

Looking at the other value aspect of political science, its link to policy-making, to say that we are interested in policies is not to claim that we are formulating basic values or goals for a society. The political scientist may do this, but not legitimately as a political scientist. While playing his professional role, he can only give instrumental value judgements, answers to means—not ends of

questions. This is what a policy science is all about. Given the objective of preventing urban riots, the political scientist's task is to demonstrate how the goal can be achieved. This becomes an empirical question—the normative aspect (urban riots should be prevented) is no longer the concern (as an ultimate value) of the political scientist (although it may deeply concern the [person]).

However, the anti-scientist might accept this analysis and then point out that because the political scientist is also a value-holding person, he cannot prevent his own values from influencing his professional research. Thus, every study and approach in political science is value-influenced. This is the heart of the matter. To quote Russell Kirk again, 'Although the complete behaviorist may deny the existence of "value-judgments" and normative understandings, nevertheless he does not escape, in his researches, the influence of his own value-judgments.'[12]

What we are faced with here is a half-truth. That values influence research is undeniably true; but this influence is not inevitable.[13] Furthermore, there are ways to tell when values are distorting supposedly objective work. After all, when someone like Kirk argues that values exert an influence he must believe that there is a way to uncover this influence. Otherwise, how else could he make the claim? Every social scientist knows how difficult it is to prevent his values from intruding. But he does not have to throw up his hands; scientific method enables us to sort out what is *fact* and what is *value*. If the principle of intersubjectivity is followed by observant and critical scientists, then few biased propositions in political science will indefinitely exist.

A common rebuttal is that even if one admits the possibility of purging the content of political research of its value-biasedness, the fact remains that the political scientist must make other kinds of value judgements that inevitably affect his objectivity. First of all, when he decides to use scientific method, he is making a value judgement—he could just as well choose not to use it. There are several replies to this confusing position. One will be discussed in a moment because it is significant in its own right. We need say here only that one does not select a way of studying politics the way he does a new automobile—either one is as good as another or it is all a matter of personal taste and cost. Scientific method is a label applied to a set of assumptions and principles that those studying the world have formulated, developed, and accepted as the best foundation for their work. Scientists do not arbitrarily impose science upon a society. Thus, while a political scientist might 'choose' the scientific approach, it is really not the same kind of choice as, 'Democracy is the best form of government.'

A second kind of value judgement that occurs before the research is done has to do with the selection of research topics. No one denies that political scientists choose to study the causes of urban riots, for instance, because the problem interests them or because they think that the black ghetto is dysfunctional or evil. But the results of their work need not be biased by their values. Once they plunge into their research, the original value choice is methodologically irrelevant. The claim that ghetto living conditions lead to urban riots can be tested intersubjectively. Until it is, it should be considered a hypothesis—a guess, educated or otherwise, about a relationship between two factors. It is difficult to understand why the selection of a research topic *has* to bias the results of research. Political scientists might, because of their value commitments, ignore certain factors or data so that their conclusions and values agree. But here again we see the significance of scientific method; this kind of biased research will not survive the criticism of colleagues. This argument really ties in with the one we just considered, which emphasizes political science's interest in policy questions. Whether beginning with a society's, government's, or individual political scientist's attempt to solve a particular social or political problem, there is no doubt that much political science research begins with a normative

commitment. This refers both to the President, who wants to decrease the incidence of urban disturbances because they threaten the existing political system,[14] and to the political scientist, who studies racism because he believes it is morally wrong.

We can conclude from this sampling of arguments that there are no valid arguments demonstrating the impossibility of a science of politics, and that many of them are useful if they make manifest to the political scientist some of the difficulties of his discipline. For instance, while the complexity of political phenomena is no *logical* barrier, it creates serious problems. The same can be said of values and free will. In criticizing arguments against the possibility of a science of politics, we are not taking a complacent attitude toward the many problems facing political science. There is no full-blown science of politics just around the corner. As we have already said, Utopian optimism is out of place in any science. The crucial point is that a science of politics is possible, and any attempt to end the pursuit of political knowledge at this point is premature and unreasonable.

## Ethics and Scientific Political Research

There are a number of commentators who while accepting the possibility of studying politics scientifically, nevertheless argue for ethical reasons against its advisability. . . . [M]ost political scientists would reject the notion that it is possible to formulate a set of ultimate ethical principles. However, each profession establishes modes of acceptable conduct for its members, either overtly through formal guidelines or unintentionally as a result of typical patterns of behaviour.[15] The main point is that these standards are logically independent of those used to evaluate scientific rigour. In other words, it is perfectly possible that a particular technique considered methodologically sound will not measure up ethically. Is it proper for a political scientist studying decision-making in the White House to find and cultivate an inside informer? Is it ethical for a political scientist to infiltrate a radical political organization, participate as a regular member, and unbeknownst to its members keep a systematic record of their activities?[16] What about a student of public attitudes who deceives his subjects to elicit completely open responses from them?

While apparently scientifically appropriate, each case raises the question: Should the subjects of political research always be made aware that they are being studied? We have already dealt with the problem of human reaction. If the subjects of research are unaware of their status as subjects, perhaps the methodological problem is solved. But are the human rights of the subjects violated in the process?

Lest someone think that our examples are hypothetical, it should be pointed out that similar real-world cases are not unusual. One of the most famous and far-reaching cases in its political implications involved the placement of tape recorders in a jury room, without the knowledge of the jurors, as part of a large-scale study of the American jury system.[17] The researchers and consulting lawyers wanted to test a number of hypotheses about how jurors behave and what factors affect their decisions. They concluded that interviewing the jurors would lead to the aforementioned reaction problem. Thus, a method for obtaining data which does not involve this limitation was developed and approved by a federal district court judge; it included the use of tape recorders. After a year of data collection without incident, reports of the project began to filter into the public domain, and there was a great hue and cry against it. Congressional hearings and investigations were held during which it was charged that the study was actually another example of the Communist strategy of infiltration and subversion. The result of all this was an act of Congress making it a federal crime to record federal jury deliberations.

Whether political scientists like it or not, political research is often evaluated not only methodologically but also ethically and politically. Scientifically legitimate research may be impossible if it violates cultural norms of the society. While there is, as one might expect, a great deal of controversy over what is and what is not acceptable, there seem to be several criteria that all accept. The most obvious and important universal principle is that research should be neither physically nor psychologically harmful to human subjects. Government agencies and universities have established guidelines that those engaged in research are expected to follow. Even though this area is the least controversial, there is still no universally accepted set of boundaries that indicate how far a researcher can go in obtaining data necessary for research.

There are ethical concerns that involve stages of the research process other than the collection of data. These deal with such questions as, 'Who is sponsoring the research?' and 'What, if any, are the social and political objectives of the sponsor?' For the political scientist, the first question gets at the special relationship between government and political science, a relationship that takes on real significance since so much political research is funded by government agencies. Can political scientists be scientific when their research is being supported by political decision-makers who might be affected by the findings of the research or who might wish to use the research for political purposes?

The most famous case in point is Project Camelot, a massive endeavour initiated in 1964 by the United States Department of Defence to discover the causes of social and political turmoil in developing nations.[18] On the surface, it appeared to be a legitimate, perhaps even highly significant research project and many social scientists joined the team. However, after several months of preliminary work, many of them reached the conclusion that the ultimate purpose of the project was to provide the Department of Defence with the basic information needed to develop successful counterinsurgency strategies in such hot spots as Chile. In short, the feeling grew that the scientific community was being used by the government. This resulted in great opposition from the community and an attempt by the State Department, then engaged in a power struggle with the Department of Defence, to abort the whole project. With the affair proving more and more embarrassing, President Johnson ended Project Camelot only seven months after its inception. Most involved probably uttered a sigh of relief, but not before a new type of criticism was made. Ironically, the same social scientific community, which several months before had questioned the motives of the government in developing the research, now condemned Washington for summarily ending it. The charge was censorship. The termination had occurred not because the research was methodologically unsound or ethically questionable, but because it was embarrassing the United States in the international political arena. Let us quote a leading critic of Project Camelot, the sociologist Irving L. Horowitz.

> In conclusion, two important points must be clearly kept in mind and clearly apart. First, Project Camelot was intellectually, and from my own perspective, ideologically unsound. However, and more significantly, Camelot was not cancelled because of its faulty intellectual approaches. Instead, its cancellation came as an act of government censorship, and an expression of contempt for social science so prevalent among those who need it most. Thus it was political expedience, rather than its lack of scientific merit, that led to the demise of Camelot because it threatened to rock State Department relations with Latin America.[19]

Project Camelot demonstrates that ethical and political problems often come together. The political scientist is faced not only with the great ethical questions common to all social sciences, but a whole host of political problems resulting from the special subject matter of political science as well. Political science and government interface, that is, they have many points of contact. In light of this relationship, what should be the role of the political scientist? Should it be only to study politics or to use one's special knowledge to work for or against political change? It now becomes obvious that we are back to the basic point raised by the post-behaviouralists. It is not merely an academic point, for not only do political scientists receive research support from government, but they also serve as advisers to decision-makers and they become decision-makers themselves.

## Alternative Routes to Political Knowledge

Not all political scientists who reject the viability of *scientific* political knowledge reject the possibility of political knowledge. Some claim that scientific method provides one route to knowledge, but there are other routes, such as metaphysics, theology, and intuition. The scientist is usually characterized as a sort of scholarly bigot, applying the seal of approval only to facts ground out of his own rigid set of rules, which he labels *scientific* method. This, however, is an unfair criticism and it fails to understand what science is all about.

The scientist does not deny that theological, metaphysical, or intuitive knowledge exists. He only claims that none of these is knowledge *about the world*. There is no way to verify a theological or intuitive explanation of an empirical event. Thus, the scientist does not have to be arrogant about the knowledge he produces or might produce. All he has to say is, 'If man can ever know the world, it must be through the application of scientific method.' He might then argue that science is not a conspiracy to impose a particular approach or methodology on the study of politics (or anything else). Scientific method develops as scientists do scientific work. It is the basic set of principles that have been formulated and refined to describe and explain the world of observation and experience. The logic or foundation of this activity is the concern of philosophers of science (including us). But neither the scientist nor the philosopher of science arbitrarily creates this foundation. Given the objectives of accurately describing and soundly explaining the world (of politics, for instance), certain principles seem to follow—they are necessary to do the job. It is interesting to note that even he who advocates a non-empirical approach, such as theology, to analyse the world, usually begins making observations about the world and using them as evidence. At this point, whether he realizes it or not, he is using the same methods as the scientist. The point is that science is not imposed upon society by scientists. Rather, it is a more sophisticated version of the methods we all use to cope with the world in our day-to-day lives.

But why bother with the difficult and often frustrating enterprise of science if it is really nothing more than common sense with luxuries added? Is the scientist perpetrating a fraud, going through the motions and accepting credit that he doesn't deserve? Another kind of attack on a science of politics questions the superiority of scientific over commonsensical knowledge and claims that pursuing scientific method is a waste of time. How many of us have heard someone comment after reading a report of political research, 'We knew this already'? Philosopher of science Ernest Nagel has given us a number of answers to this significant charge.[20] We will here only summarize and reinterpret them so as to make them relevant to students of politics. We will examine several reasons why scientific knowledge is superior to commonsensical knowledge and why, therefore, an attempt to create a science of politics is a worthwhile undertaking.

An initial shortcoming of common sense is its tendency to accept presumed facts without questions, as a matter of faith. Propositions such as, 'All politicians are corrupt', become part of the folk wisdom of American politics and are either never explained or explained improperly. If we accept a fact simply because it is obvious, reasonable, or self-evident, we may never be aware of the underlying conditions that account for it. The same can be said of the superficial explanations that often pass as scientific. For instance, several commonsensical propositions, which are accepted by many as sound historical explanations, claim that economic depressions are caused by Republican administrations and a Democratic administration will always be followed by war. First, their truth can be questioned. But assuming that there is a correlation between political parties and economics of war, accepting such a commonsensical fact as an explanation of a historical or societal trend might be incorrect. The point is, commonsensically, we will never know—scientifically, we might find out. Perhaps the correlation is spurious, to speak statistically. It might be purely coincidental that the election of a Democratic President usually precedes a war; or the relationships may be deeper and more complex. Scientific method, with its stress on empiricism, intersubjectivity, and systematic generalizations, can probably be employed to sort out some of the more basic factors that common sense does not perceive. Once again it must be emphasized that scientific method is not a philosopher's stone, capable of providing ready answers to every question. Nor is common sense being rejected out of hand. In our day-to-day lives, there is usually no other basis for decisions. We are, instead, taking a more modest position which claims that the application of scientific method to problems of political analysis uncovers many of the mistakes and inconsistencies of common-sense knowledge and therefore leads to a more reliable brand of knowledge than its more primitive ancestor.

These shortcomings of commonsensical knowledge lead to several practical problems for those attempting to use it for purposes of explanation and prediction. First, although commonsensical knowledge may be true to a point, because it isn't explained its limits are seldom realized. A user of scientific method, on the other hand, knows approximately how far he can go in applying the knowledge he discovers, because in sorting out explanatory factors, he has become aware of its limits. Suppose we explain the relatively low rate of voting turnout in the United States on the basis of a widespread apathy, which is interpreted as an expression of basic satisfaction with the political system. This makes sense, so we accept it as commonsensically true. But suppose that as a matter of fact it is applicable only to certain segments of the population, the White middle class for instance. Other segments—Blacks, the poor, and the isolated—don't vote because they feel alienated from society. Their behaviour has nothing to do with satisfaction; on the contrary, much dissatisfaction goes along with alienation. The scientific study of voting behaviour would be more likely to discover these facts than common sense. Therefore, the scientist would be less likely to overapply his explanation. He would know the basic difference between middle-class and lower-class nonvoting, a difference that the advocate of common sense would be more likely to miss. The relevance of this analysis for practical policy-making is clear.

Another serious problem that common-sense knowledge must face is its currency in accounting for political change. If explanatory factors are unknown, then if conditions change, especially the less obvious ones (which really means the more important ones), a realization of inadequacy possibly leading to disillusionment might be the result for an advocate of common-sense knowledge. But if a sound scientific explanation has been given, and if we are aware of the implications of changing conditions, we will have a much better chance of anticipating the change. For instance, taking another oversimplified hypothetical case, let us assume that it is a commonsensical truth that urban disturbances occur primarily because of an increasing disrespect for law and order. However, if the primary conditions for such disturbances are urban living

conditions (the ghetto, unemployment, and so forth), then if such conditions become worse, the common-sense explanation is not able to explain and predict the increase in riots and demonstrations and thus point out what steps ought to be taken to prevent them. Once again, common sense, in most cases, is not so much wrong as incomplete and superficial.

But isn't common sense sometimes correct— is a common reply? Correct, perhaps; substantiated, no. This is the gist of these last few pages. Knowledge is not knowledge until it has been substantiated, using the procedures that have been labelled *scientific method*. While we might say, 'I knew that all the time', we didn't know it— we sensed it, we intuited, we believed it.

On the other hand, common sense is useful as a source of hypotheses—relationships to be tested. No productive scientist can ignore the world of his own psychic experiences; it might not be a totally reliable world, but because he is human, it is his starting point. Several pages ago we referred to the acceptance of widespread political corruption in America as commonsensical folk wisdom. While not necessarily proof that such wisdom is generally true, the experiences of Watergate should provide an imaginative political scientist with some potentially fruitful leads. It is often said that a poet experiences and sees the same things as the average man except that he sees them differently. The same could be said of the scientist. The great scientist is great not because he knows more about scientific method; all competent ones have that knowledge. He is great because of imagination, insight, and the ability to draw implications from what he observes. But every imaginative insight must be subjected to the test of intersubjectivity. It is at this point that scientific method becomes relevant. This is what distinguishes the insights of the scientist from those of the poet.

In conclusion, let us make several points. First, while science begins with common-sense *observation*, scientific knowledge is not equivalent to commonsensical knowledge. Second, while the accumulated wisdom of common sense is sometimes duplicated by scientific procedures, it does not follow that science is a waste of time. Nothing is obvious until it has been empirically and systematically substantiated. This is not to deny that at times political science devotes its resources

to the more easily studied at the expense of the perhaps more significant and harder to find phenomena. But, finally, let us note that political science discovers things that are unknown by and even in violation of common sense.

## Notes

1. For a bitter refutation of the scientific study of politics, see Herbert J. Storing, ed., *Essays on the Scientific Study of Politics* (New York: Holt, Rinehart & Winston, 1962).

2. Hans J. Morgenthau, *Scientific Man versus Power Politics* (Chicago: University of Chicago Press, 1946), 130.

3. Adolf Grunbaum, 'Causality and the Science of Human Behavior', in Herbert Feigl and May Brodbeck, eds, *Readings in the Philosophy of Science* (New York: Appleton-Century-Crofts, 1953), 770.

4. Russell Kirk, 'Is Social Science Scientific?', in Nelson W. Polsby, Robert A. Dentler, and Paul A. Smith, eds, *Politics and Social Life* (Boston: Houghton Mifflin, 1963), 63.

5. Quentin Gibson, *The Logic of Social Enquiry* (London: Routledge & Kegan Paul, 1960), 22.

6. John Hospers, *An Introduction to Philosophical Analysis* (Englewood Cliffs, NJ: Prentice-Hall, 1954), 271.

7. Martin Landau, *Political Theory and Political Science* (New York: Macmillan, 1972), 27.

8. Ernest Nagel, *The Structure of Science* (New York: Harcourt Brace Jovanovich, 1961), 605.

9. Participant observation should not be confused with the memoirs of decision-makers who have left office. Such writings are legion, and while an important source of data for historians and political scientists, they must be placed in the category of personal recollections rather than systematic research.

10. F.J. Roethlisberger and W.J. Dickson, *Management and the Worker* (Cambridge, Mass.: Harvard University Press, 1939).

11. Ivan Petrovich Pavlov, *Essential Works of Pavlov*, ed. Michael Kaplan (New York: Bantam Books, 1966), 108–9.

12. Kirk, 'Is Social Science Scientific?', 63.

13. For a discussion of ways of sorting out one's values, see William E. Connolly, 'Theoretical Self-Conscious', in William E. Connolly and Glen Gordon, eds, *Social Structure and Political Theory* (Lexington, Mass.: D.C. Heath, 1974), 40–66.

14. Two studies resulting from such motivations are *The Report of the National Advisory Commission on Civil Disorders* (New York: E.P. Dutton & Co., 1968); and *The Walker Report to the National Commission on the Causes and Prevention of Violence* (New York: New American Library, 1968).

15. See the discussion of codes for political scientists in 'Ethical Problems of Academic Political Scientists', *PS: Political Science and Politics* (Summer 1968): 3–28. For a thorough discussion of a number of ethical issues pertaining to political science, see Amy Gutmann and Dennis Thompson, eds, *Ethics and Politics* (Chicago: Nelson-Hall, 1984).

16. For the use of such a technique, see Scott McNall, 'The Career of the Radical Rightist', in Scott McNall, ed., *The Sociological Perspective* (Boston: Little, Brown, 1974), 392–406.

17. Ted Vaughn, 'Governmental Intervention in Social Research: Political and Ethical Dimensions in the Wichita Jury Recordings', in Gideon Sjoberg, *Ethics, Politics and Social Research* (Cambridge, Mass.: Schenkman, 1967), 50–77.

18. The best description of the whole affair is Irving Louis Horowitz, 'The Life and Death of Project Camelot', in Norman K. Denzin, ed., *The Values of Social Science* (Chicago: Transaction Books, 1970), 159–84.

19. Ibid., 183.

20. Nagel, *The Structure of Science*, ch. 1. Also see Karl W. Deutsch, 'The Limits of Common Sense', in Polsby, Dentler, and Smith, *Politics and Social Life*, 51–8.

# Part II

# Political Philosophy

## Introduction

David Laycock and Darin Barney

By the time they reach university, many students are very cynical about politicians and political life. Many see politics as typically rife with corruption or as inherently incapable of 'delivering the goods' for the average person. Why should we take politics seriously? Is it, or can it be, anything but a one-sided game involving the pursuit of naked self-interest by the clever or privileged? How might those who are not so cynical construct a positive rationale for political life that none the less takes the cynic's challenge seriously?

Political philosophy is that part of political science that attempts to offer satisfactory answers to these basic questions. It has been doing so ever since they were first posed strikingly by one of Plato's major characters in *The Republic*, over two thousand years ago.[1] From political philosophy we get many basic concepts in political science, such as justice, equality, and freedom, as well as thoughtful suggestions as to how these can be understood to shed light on contemporary political problems. Since Aristotle, political philosophy has provided some of the most challenging and insightful models for blending political explanations with other types of explanations to yield understanding of political phenomena. Finally, political philosophy has always offered prescriptions for social and political reform and visions of wholesale political reconstruction. Unlike much contemporary social science, political philosophy employs and explicitly defends particular models of human nature in its explanations and proposals for reform of the political community.

The term 'political theory' is often used interchangeably with that of 'political philosophy'. Here we use 'political philosophy' to denote normative efforts to account for and transform politics. This is not meant to provoke debate, but merely to avoid confusion for readers beginning to study politics systematically. As the introduction and selections in Part I suggest, such systematic study employs many different methods and approaches, and applies them to widely varied political phenomena. Studies of comparative politics, international relations, public administration, and public policy all employ—in fact, require—clear theories to organize, classify, and assess the relative significance of empirical data that can aid in explanations of selected features of political life. Political philosophy is a specific but fundamental type of political theory that synthesizes: (1) analysis of political phenomena and human nature; (2) evaluation of existing political institutions; and (3) philosophically defended prescriptions for political life.[2]

## Politics and Ethics: Classical Greeks to Modernity

Serious reflection on the nature and purposes of political association has been going on in Western cultures for close to 2,500 years. At its origins in classical Greek thought, systematic discussion of political phenomena was inextricably linked to philosophy, particularly ethics and metaphysics, and to rudimentary efforts to establish a scientific account of both human and non-human nature. Thus in Plato's *Republic* we find Socrates making arguments about justice and the good society based on then current understandings of human nature and of the character and accessibility of knowledge.

Aristotle insisted, however, that political science was more than a branch of ethics or metaphysics. He argued that the study of politics was the 'architectonic' science. By this he meant that an understanding of political association was necessary to provide an overall design for human investigation of the world and pursuit of 'the good life'. This was a significant departure from most pre-Platonic thinking about politics, which tended to consider political activity and power as largely uncontrollable by human reason.

Aristotle's human-centric view of political institutions and all other forms of interaction with the physical world set the agenda for centuries of political thought. After Aristotle's extraordinary achievements in natural science, philosophy, and political science, those who thought seriously about politics were more inclined to see political life as a largely human rather than divine creation. How power, community resources, social and economic benefits, honour, and freedom are distributed became not only matters of practical conflict but also subjects of conceptual, methodological, and moral debate. Justice, for example, became something towards which humans could strive in social relations, not just a divine dispensation.

Since Aristotle's time, and especially since the rebirth of classical thought in the European Renaissance, much of the general Greek orientation towards the study of politics has remained. However, the content of much political theorizing has changed dramatically in the writings of influential political theorists. For example, it was virtually self-evident to Aristotle that neither slaves nor women were capable of even moderately rational contributions to public life. Over the past 300 years, however, liberal and socialist thinkers have gradually made compelling cases for conferring citizenship on both women and other marginalized groups. They have done so on the grounds that all humans deserve equal respect, translated in the political sphere into equal political rights.

Such a broad historical comparison vividly demonstrates the connection between assumptions about human nature and proposals for political participation. Answers to the question of 'who should rule' are basic to any political philosophy and political order. However, we need not look at 2,000-year comparisons to underscore this point. Many contemporary religious fundamentalists, for example, continue to believe that women should work only as mothers and homemakers because it is against their nature to rub shoulders with men in the sordid world of politics and business. Most modern feminists, of course, insist there is nothing innately masculine about directing public life or innately feminine about accepting patriarchal rule in households, business enterprises, or political associations. The often intense and rhetorically exaggerated encounters between fundamentalists and feminists testify to the highly political and philosophically complex relationships between claims about human nature and patterns of participation in political life.

This contemporary debate also reminds us that the common denominator of many key political debates is power. Power is to political relationships what money is to economic relationships: the currency of competition and exchange and a necessary tool for the pursuit of important human purposes. In sixteenth-century Florence, Niccolo Machiavelli contended that statecraft and the hard-headed study of political power should replace a concern with justice at the centre of political analysis. In *The Prince* (1532), Machiavelli rejected the Aristotelian idea, accepted with minor modification by medieval Catholic thinkers, that effective political actors could or even should consistently operate on the basis of ethical or moral principles. Politics, Machiavelli insisted, is beyond the enveloping reach of conventional justice and related ethical concerns. He contended that the essence of politics is less likely to be discovered in ethical speculation than in consideration of *raison d'état*, or self-interested pursuit of territory and power by states and their leaders.

This theme was taken up in a systematic and uncompromisingly logical fashion by the English philosopher Thomas Hobbes in *Leviathan* (1651). Hobbes contended that justice is impossible in the absence of a government, because no person has a good reason to support consistently any interests other than his/her own. He claimed that humans are dangerous competitors for glory, riches, and power, and that in 'the state of nature', competition for power degenerates into a mutually destructive 'war of each against all'. The political conclusion he drew was that only a state with absolute power—a 'leviathan'—can prevent such a brutal competition. As self-interested maximizers of their long-run interest, rational citizens see that they must adopt a prudential political obligation to obey the laws of the Sovereign and keep the peace.

## Modern Political Thought

Hobbes presented a fundamental political philosophical challenge to classical notions of human nature, the character of political obligation, and the nature of justice and political power. In the eighteenth and nineteenth centuries, liberals, conservatives and eventually socialists followed Hobbes in debating principles for the philosophically and morally defensible distribution of power and its rewards. Answers to the question of the relationship between power and justice have remained central to all philosophical defences of existing and proposed political orders.

The liberal tradition since Hobbes has provided a variety of answers to this basic question relating power to justice. All liberal theory, starting notably with John Locke's *Second Treatise of Government* (1690), has rejected the idea that either justice or human well-being can be secured when a state holds absolute power. Locke introduced the idea that individuals have natural rights to 'life, liberty, and estate', recognition and protection of which provide the basis for legitimate state power. To Locke the reason for establishing the state was essentially the same as that for limiting its powers: to establish an institution that facilitates individual pursuit of property.

Since Locke's time, liberals have argued over how individual rights can be reconciled with state power. That a large sphere of personal liberty was crucial to all that we value in 'progressive' societies was the primary contention of John Stuart Mill. In his 1859 classic, *On Liberty*, Mill sought to make the case for extensive human liberty for both men and women—whose inclusion in this case was itself a radical move in the nineteenth century. Using both 'utilitarian' and rights-based arguments, Mill contended that overall social utility, or the greatest good for the greatest number in society, would be advanced if individuals' actions were unconstrained up to the point that they clearly produced harm to others. Mill was confident that the development of individual human capacities through such free, autonomous behaviour ultimately benefited fellow citizens and enabled meaningful democratic decision-making. But his concern that intolerant majorities might limit the freedom of minorities led Mill to argue that liberty had an intrinsic value for individuals that should supersede arguments for state and social interference with individual lives based on perceived or actual benefits to majorities.

Liberals since Mill's time have argued over the merits of utilitarian and rights-based foundations for setting various boundaries to state intervention in 'civil society'. Most of us feel ourselves pulled in both directions on many issues. Should we have an absolute right to decide how we use a car, to which we claim exclusive ownership, in our efforts to go to work quickly and securely? Or do the needs of the community to reduce pollution, develop efficient public transportation, and perhaps even redesign accommodation patterns and neighbourhood structures place justifiable limits on our chosen modes of transportation? How do we relate to and build a community, making trade-offs between our individual and collective needs and interests? How can we determine whether there are collective community interests, to which we owe some obligation, or simply individuals' interests, the simultaneous pursuit of which will indirectly maximize social good? These kinds of questions bring the issues of power, justice, liberty, and equality to a focus in the quintessential modern political problem of democratic government.

Locke's case for limited government based on citizen rights and the consent of the governed did much to prepare the ground for later discussions of democratic government. But Locke's purpose was to make a strong case against arbitrary government rather than to rationalize a system of widespread public control over government. Jean-Jacques Rousseau's *Discourse on the Origins of Inequality* (1757) and *Social Contract* (1762) situated the perennial questions regarding individual-community relations in the context of a demanding model of popular sovereignty or democratic control over basic decisions made by the state. Rousseau's insistence that neither liberty nor community could be achieved without high levels of economic, social, and political equality among men[3] helped set the agenda for many future debates over the expectations and institutions of democratic society and government.

In his early writings, for example, Karl Marx accepted Rousseau's suggestion that human freedom was only an abstract possibility prior to the achievement of broadly based social equality.[4] In his later work, especially *Capital*,[5] Marx set this moral commitment in the context of a theory of history and critique of capitalism. This theory and critique featured conflicting relations between owners and non-owners of property as the major dynamic driving economic, social, and political activity. For Marx, this theory of 'historical materialism' implied that only the supersession of capitalism could enable the creation of a truly democratic political community.

Socialist political theory represented a major departure from liberal political studies, by insisting that economic power and social structure were highly political matters, and that the political implications of these economic and social variables deserved the attention of political philosophers as much as the foundations of individual autonomy and state sovereignty. Marxist perspectives in the social sciences have been enormously influential in shaping research agendas and debates in universities around the world, especially since the Russian Revolution of 1917. Interpreting Marx's theoretical and polemical writings, later Marxists repoliticized the analysis of power by linking it to issues of alienation, exploitation and inter-class distributive justice.[6] Such Marxist analysis has challenged political philosophy to avoid the complacency to which its academic practitioners are susceptible.[7]

The twentieth century has seen many theoretical and practical debates over the meaning and practice of liberty and equality in democratic politics. Central to this debate are the questions of whether and how equality promotes or undermines liberty, and with which aspects of human experience equality should be concerned.[8] Equality has been understood in three broad senses: equality of legal right, equality of opportunity, and equality of condition. In the first sense, one now finds something close to consensus. Institutionalization of formal legal equality has been disappointing, since its introduction has often had far less impact on social distributions of power and resources than its advocates anticipated. Nevertheless, few public figures or political theorists now argue that historically deprived groups—such as women, Native peoples, immigrants, and workers[9]—are undeserving of legal citizenship rights.

Over the last century debates have been much more heated over the meaning and desirability of the second notion of equality, equality of opportunity. Since the late nineteenth century, liberals have argued that a combination of public education, broadly defined civil liberties, and basic social services would ensure that anyone who really wished to could succeed in the social, economic, political, or cultural spheres of their choice. This was possible, liberals contended, because political power was dispersed, had a plurality of sources, and did not spring exclusively from economic power. Liberals argued that the separation of economic and political power in liberal democratic capitalist societies ensured that energetic and resourceful individuals had something close to an equal opportunity to excel in their chosen endeavours.

For some, this scenario has never seemed realistic or descriptive of the situations many people face in Western societies. Many theorists have insisted that structural bases of power (economic, social, and political) 'nest' or accumulate in conjunction with one another, effectively preventing some social groups from fully participating in society. This is true whether, like classical socialists, one sees capitalism as the basis of all other inequality, or whether one sees patriarchy as its primary source, as do many modern feminists. Accordingly, to tackle these perceived foundations of political, social, and economic power, both socialists and feminists reject the liberal account of equality of opportunity and argue that society must be reconfigured to produce something much closer to equality of condition. This third notion of equality envisions a serious effort to redistribute opportunities among citizens along radically egalitarian lines, by moving to more equal distributions of resources than contemporary liberal capitalist societies have been willing to consider. None of the advocates of this third view of equality, however, have proposed exactly equal distributions of goods and services.

## Contemporary Political Philosophy and the Questioning of Modernity

By the middle of the twentieth century, debates about the proper scope and reach of the state were supplemented by fundamental questions about the integrity of the modern project itself. World War II had mobilized the formidable resources of the state as never before, and culminated in a pair of atrocities—the Holocaust and the dropping of atomic bombs on the civilian population of Japan. The horrific gravity of these state actions compelled many political theorists to reappraise the core suppositions underlying modern political life. The Enlightenment had promised an endless trajectory of progress towards freedom along a path illuminated by the cool light of reason. Faced with the discoveries at Auschwitz and the images of Hiroshima, political philosophers were forced to ask: Is this the cost of freedom? Is this the outcome of Enlightenment rationality? Have we reached the terminus of progress?

Political philosophers in the latter half of the twentieth century have worked out a number of responses to these questions. Some conservative thinkers, such as Leo Strauss and the Canadian George Grant, have recommended seeking counsel in the wisdom of ancient philosophy.[10] Modern political thinkers, they argued, had replaced the ancient love of goodness with a love of unbridled liberty, and had encouraged people to see themselves as the makers of their world rather than as beings limited by the transcendent mysteries of the universe. This hubris inevitably produced disappointment, moral confusion, and spiritually empty lives. These thinkers joined the German philosopher Martin Heidegger in calling for a return to meditative thinking as a way out of the morass in which the modern world had landed itself.[11]

The critical theorists of the Frankfurt School argued that the aspirations of the Enlightenment were still valid and should be used as standards against which the practices of modern political life could be judged. Beginning in the 1940s, thinkers such as Max Horkheimer and Theodore Adorno argued that capitalism had succeeded in draining the twin pillars of the Enlightenment—reason and freedom—of their real meaning.[12] These terms had been turned upside down to legitimize the domination inherent in the class inequality of capitalism. Mass culture industries threatened to create what Herbert Marcuse called a 'one-dimensional society',[13] in which individuality could be reduced to a matter of which running-shoe logo a person wears on her t-shirt and freedom of consumer choice. For the critical theorists, the task was not to abandon the modern ideals of reason and liberty but to rescue them from the distorting influence of capitalism.

These and related ideas fuelled counter-culture and protest movements throughout the industrialized world in the postwar period. But protest movement victories against the institutions of modern capitalism and liberal states were fleeting. As a result, many thinkers began to question attempts to rescue the Enlightenment project of progress, reason, and freedom. They argued that modernity had exhausted itself and sought the development of new, post-modern social and political agendas.

Post-modern political thought is not *anti*-modern; it is, more accurately, *hyper*-modern. Thomas Hobbes articulated two key arguments of modern political thought by asserting that truth and falsehood were simply names given to phenomena by human beings, not natural attributes, and that the central concern of politics was power, not justice. The nineteenth-century German philosopher Friedrich Nietzsche vividly described the eventual impact of these positions: Western society had arrived at a place that was 'beyond good and evil', where truth and morality were completely historical and contingent upon the human will to power.[14] Rather than reacting with despair to this apparent collapse of a fixed moral universe—or, as Nietzsche would put it, the death of God—post-modern thinkers have sought to illuminate the political and social implications of the new era.

The best-known example of such theorizing involves the French philosopher Michel Foucault. Foucault argues that human society and experience are structured by discourses that define the true, real, normal, and good in opposition to the false, unreal, abnormal, and bad. He denies that any of these discourses are grounded in anything necessary or natural. Instead, they reflect the operations of power in human relationships.[15] Human nature itself is constructed by discourse and subject to the disciplines of power.

For Foucault, politics concerns how the discourses and relationships reflecting particular configurations of power come to be institutionalized, regularized, and enmeshed across society at many levels. Thus, not only the state, but also things like madness, the human body, disciplinary systems (including schools, hospitals, and prisons), sexuality, and the construction of the 'self' became questions of political significance.[16] Foucault proposed that thoughtful people concerned with politics should develop genealogies, or 'histories of the present', to detail these discursive constructions.

Subsequent post-modernists have surmised that, if truth is established by power through discourse, then the focus of political analysis should be language rather than ideas. Jean-François Lyotard defined post-modernism as an 'incredulity towards meta-narratives'.[17] What he meant was that political relationships and arrangements are largely the outcome of language games played out within parameters set by the so-called grand narratives of history—Progress, Liberation, and the advance of Reason—which are just stories that legitimate a narrow range of acceptable behaviours. According to Lyotard, post-modernists should be suspicious of these stories and trust instead the little narratives—the small stories of everyday people—that exist despite, beyond, or beneath the broad sweep of grand narratives.

Jacques Derrida took political philosophy even further down the linguistic road by asserting that, like everything else, political life is a 'text' and should be interpreted as such.[18] His French contemporary, Jean Baudrillard, sees social and political life as a complex of symbolic codes that are decreasingly grounded in anything immediate or 'real'. In this view, something like democracy is no longer attached to external objective standards or measures. Instead, it is simply a slick copy of a copy whose original was lost long ago. This society of copies of copies without real original referents—of 'simulacra', as Baudrillard calls them—constitutes a world of 'hyperreality', in which Disneyland becomes more 'real' than any actual neighbourhood.[19]

Post-modernism has pressed many political philosophers and students of politics to theorize more expansively and inclusively. With its emphasis on language and texts, post-modernism reminds us that power in our society operates in many ways not directly framed by established political institutions. Post-modern theory also directs attention to political practices and identities at the margins of the mainstream. This may account for post-modernism's attraction for analysts of the politics of customarily marginalized citizens, including women, ethnic minorities, and gays and lesbians. If nothing else, post-modernists have helped direct the attention of more traditional political theorists to important questions of pluralism and difference in the heterogeneous polities of the late twentieth century.

Post-modernism can be seen as a threat to the more philosophical aspects of political philosophy. Philosophy has traditionally been defined by the belief that essential truths exist and can be found out through contemplation. *Political* philosophy believes that human communities can and should be modelled on these truths. The post-modern assertion that 'the truth is made rather than found' purports to pull the rug out from under conventional political philosophy.[20] If the post-modernists are correct, then most political philosophy is a great hoax, enlisting dubious appeals to nature in order to legitimize subjective political preferences.

Ironically, this puts political philosophy back where it began, in Plato's *Republic*. There, Thrasymachus took the proto-post-modern position that 'justice is the advantage of the stronger.' Though he tried, Socrates could not bring Thrasymachus to see justice as something more enduring than whatever the prevailing order said it was. Nevertheless, Socrates went on expounding the virtues of true justice to those who would listen.

Similarly, political philosophy continues to address the vexing political issues of the day despite post-modern obstinance, and often attempts to answer the difficult questions posed by post-modernists. For instance, the critical theorist Jurgen Habermas respects the linguistic emphasis of post-modern theory, but remains optimistic regarding the unfinished business of the Enlightenment. For Habermas, the route to real liberty and equality is through discursive democracy, an ethics of political practice involving truly rational and undistorted communication that reaches consensus about shared ends.[21]

The work of Jurgen Habermas is just one example of why reports of the death of political philosophy should be considered exaggerations. As the twentieth century draws to a close, we see deep economic restructuring, the political integration of diverse communities throughout the world, the rise of new social movements, and massive technological and environmental challenges. All of these have political implications that demand the kind of serious thinking political philosophers have historically undertaken.

Since the fall of Eastern bloc communism, much political philosophy has addressed questions about how liberal polities can justly accommodate the plurality of human aspirations, needs, and practices. Accordingly, issues surrounding the complex politics of identity, community, cultural rights, and citizenship animate current debates in political philosophy. Steeped as they are in the complicated politics of multiculturalism, nationalism, regionalism, and bilingualism, Canadian thinkers such as Charles Taylor and Will Kymlicka have made crucial contributions to these debates.[22] Taylor's insights into the 'politics of recognition' and Kymlicka's theory of 'multicultural citizenship' typify the enduring worthiness of the enterprise of political philosophy as it moves into its third millennium.

The first selection reprinted here makes the case for democratizing the domains of political theory and practice in Western societies. Carole Pateman argues that this can be done by understanding women's experience as subjects and objects of political power in home, family, school, and cultural, social, and working environments. This argument, in effect, contends that the 'modern project' of making good on the promises of liberty, equality, and justice will not be completed so long as women are not equal beneficiaries. Carole Pateman has been at the forefront of feminist theorizing since this article was published and has been instrumental in promoting a research agenda that reflects the practical challenge presented by the women's movement to politics as usual in most Western countries.[23]

The second selection is taken from a series of lectures given on CBC radio by McGill University political philosopher Charles Taylor. In this opening chapter to *The Malaise of Modernity*, he sketches a modern landscape where most citizens lack the security and clear purpose for their lives once provided by religious or other social beliefs that connected individuals to communities. While his view of the character of modern life owes a good deal to Nietzsche, Taylor's conclusions regarding how to address modernity's 'malaise' differ substantially from those of post-modernists. Taylor has written much on these and related themes,[24] and is regarded as one of the English-speaking world's pre-eminent political philosophers.

In the final selection, taken from his influential book *Multicultural Citizenship: A Liberal Theory of Minority Rights*, political philosopher Will Kymlicka addresses what he sees as 'the greatest challenge facing democracies today' in increasingly heterogenous societies. Kymlicka has been in the forefront of contemporary liberal theorists' approaches to the politically explosive issue of minority rights. In the excerpts here, Kymlicka outlines the history of liberal approaches to the question of minority rights and argues that state protection of minority 'societal cultures' is consistent with liberal conceptions of freedom and equality. For Kymlicka, an approach to this issue must be both 'morally defensible and politically viable', and must also explain why such protection is basic to peaceful democratic politics in modern, culturally diverse polities. Through his contributions to making multiculturalism a focus of revealing analysis by political philosophers, Kymlicka demonstrates the continuing relevance of political philosophy to students of politics.

## Notes

1. These questions are posed by Thrasymachus in Book I of *The Republic*, Plato's classic treatise on the relationship between justice and the political order, written around 380 BC.

2. Political theory and political philosophy are often treated as interchangeable terms, with the assumption that they have an important role in the discipline of political science. That it should play an important role may be obvious, but *what* role it should play is not obvious or uncontentious. See, for example, the discussions in John G. Gunnell, 'Political theory and political science', in David Miller, ed., *The Encyclopedia of Political Thought* (Oxford: Basil Blackwell, 1987), 386–90; David Held, 'Editor's Introduction', in Held, ed., *Political Theory Today* (Stanford, Calif.: Stanford University Press, 1991), 1–21; William Galston, 'Political Theory in the 1980s: Perplexity Amidst Diversity', in Ada Finifter, ed., *Political Science: The State of the Discipline II* (Washington: American Political Science Association, 1993), 27–53.

3. Despite his standing as a critic of existing autocratic regimes and advocate of democracy, Rousseau was not an advocate of gender equality. See his *Emile*, as well as Carole Pateman's article in this section.

4. See especially his *Economic and Philosophic Manuscripts of 1844* and *The German Ideology*, large excerpts from which are reprinted in, among others, Robert Tucker, ed., *The Marx-Engels Reader*, 2nd edn (New York: W.W. Norton, 1980).

5. The complete work has been translated into English by many writers; for excerpts from Capital and other related works, see Tucker, ed., *The Marx-Engels Reader*.

6. For introductions to some of these approaches, see Tom Bottomore, ed., *Modern Interpretations of Marx* (Oxford: Blackwell Publisher, 1981); Terrell Carver, ed., *The Cambridge Companion to Marx* (New York: Cambridge University Press, 1991).

7. For an acknowledgment of this by a prominent member of the political science establishment, see Charles Lindblom, 'Another State of Mind', Presidential Address, American Political Science Association, in *American Political Science Review* 76, 1 (Mar. 1982): 9–21.

8. For stimulating recent discussions of this issue, see Steven Lukes, 'Equality and Liberty: Must they Conflict?', in Held, ed., *Political Theory Today*, 48–66; Robert A. Dahl, *A Preface to Economic Democracy* (Berkeley: University of California Press, 1985), chs 1, 2. The classic nineteenth-century delineation of this conflict, Alexis de Tocqueville's *Democracy in America*, has been immensely influential since its publication in 1835.

9. Property ownership requirements for the right to vote were only slowly lifted through the latter half of the nineteenth century and early part of the twentieth century in most Western democracies. For an overview, see J.M. Barbalet, *Citizenship* (Minneapolis: University of Minnesota Press, 1988), chs 2–4.

10. See Leo Strauss, *The City and Man* (Chicago: Rand McNally, 1964); George Grant, *Philosophy in the Mass Age* (Toronto: Copp Clark, 1959).

11. Martin Heidegger, *Discourse on Thinking*, trans. John M. Anderson and Hans Freund (New York: Harper & Row, 1966).

12. Max Horkheimer and Theodore Adorno, *Dialectic of Enlightenment* (New York: Herder & Herder, 1972). For a good history of the Frankfurt School, see Martin Jay, *The Dialectical Imagination: A History of the Frankfurt School and the Institute for Social Research* (Boston: Little, Brown, 1973).

13. Herbert Marcuse, *One Dimensional Man* (Boston: Beacon Press, 1964).

14. Friedrich Nietzsche, *Beyond Good and Evil*, trans. Walter Kaufmann (New York: Vintage, 1989); Nietzsche, *The Genealogy of Morals*, trans. Francis Golfinng (Garden City, NY: Doubleday, 1956).

15. For a good survey of Foucault's work, see Paul Rabinow, ed., *The Foucault Reader* (New York: Pantheon, 1984).

16. In particular, see Michel Foucault, *Discipline and Punish: The Birth of the Prison*, trans. Alan Sheridan (New York: Pantheon, 1975); Foucault, *The History of Sexuality: An Introduction*, trans. Robert Hurley (New York: Pantheon, 1976).

17. Jean-François Lyotard, *The Post-Modern Condition* (Minneapolis: University of Minnesota Press, 1985).

18. Jacques Derrida, *Of Grammatology*, trans. Gayatri Spivak (Baltimore: Johns Hopkins University Press, 1976).

19. For an anthology of Baudrillard's writing, see *Selected Writings*, ed. Mark Poster (Stanford, Calif.: Stanford University, 1988).

20. Richard Rorty, *Philosophy and the Mirror of Nature* (Princeton, NJ: Princeton University Press, 1979); Rorty, *Contingency, Irony and Solidarity* (Cambridge: Cambridge University Press, 1989).

21. Jurgen Habermas, *The Theory of Communicative Action*, trans. Thomas McCarthy (Boston: Beacon Press, 1984).

22. Charles Taylor, *Sources of the Self* (Cambridge, Mass.: Harvard University Press, 1989); Taylor, *Multiculturalism and 'The Politics of Recognition'* (Princeton, NJ: Princeton University Press, 1992); Will Kymlicka, *Liberalism, Community and Culture* (Oxford: Clarendon Press, 1989); Kymlicka, *Multicultural Citizenship: A Liberal Theory of Minority Rights* (Oxford: Clarendon Press, 1995).

23. Pateman's more recent work includes *The Sexual Contract* (Stanford, Calif.: Stanford University Press, 1988); *The Disorder of Women: Democracy, Feminism and Political Theory* (Cambridge: Polity Press, 1989); and Carole Pateman and Elizabeth Gross, eds, *Feminist Challenges: Social and Political Theory* (Boston: Northeastern University Press, 1987). For two good examples of this new wave of feminist theorizing about democratic politics that builds effectively on the authors' political engagement, see Iris Marion Young, *Justice and the Politics of Difference* (Princeton, NJ: Princeton University Press, 1990); Anne Phillips, *Engendering Democracy* (London: Polity Press, 1991).

24. See Taylor's *Sources of the Self* and *Multiculturalism and 'The Politics of Recognition'*, written by Taylor as an engaged and troubled Canadian citizen.

## Study Questions for the Readings

1. Why does Pateman think that democratic theory ignored the question of gender and power for so long? Which questions were central to democratic theory, if this was not?
2. Why does Pateman believe a modern democratic theory must take the feminist case seriously? Is she right about this?
3. What does a feminist critique of conventional politics mean by saying that 'the personal is political'?
4. What are the three malaises of modernity identified by Taylor?
5. What are the roots of these three malaises?
6. What dangers do these malaises pose to us as Canadians? Which, in your view, is the most worrisome?
7. What does Kymlicka see as 'the greatest challenge facing democracies today'? Why?
8. What are 'group-specific rights', as contrasted with 'individual rights'? Why does Kymlicka believe that the former are a necessary complement to the latter in multicultural liberal societies?
9. What does it mean to say that an individual's freedom requires access to a 'societal culture'? Do you agree?
10. How does Kymlicka's version of liberal equality require a liberal state to provide benefits and opportunities to members of both national majorities and national minorities?

# Feminism and Democracy

## Carole Pateman

A feminist might dispose briskly of the subject of this essay. For feminists, democracy has never existed; women have never been and still are not admitted as full and equal members and citizens in any country known as a 'democracy'. A telling image that recurs throughout the history of feminism is of liberal society as a series of male clubs—usually, as Virginia Woolf points out in *Three Guineas*, distinguished by their own costumes and uniforms—that embrace parliament, the courts, political parties, the military and police, universities, workplaces, trade unions, public (private) schools, exclusive clubs and popular leisure clubs, from all of which women are excluded or to which they are mere auxiliaries. Feminists will find confirmation of their view in academic discussions of democracy which usually take it for granted that feminism or the structure of the relationship between the sexes are irrelevant matters. The present volume at least acknowledges that feminism might have something significant to say to democratic theorists or citizens, albeit in a token paper by a token woman writer. In the scope of a short essay it is hardly possible to demolish the assumption of two thousand years that there is no incompatibility between 'democracy' and the subjection of women or their exclusion from full and equal participation in political life. Instead, I shall indicate why feminism provides democracy—whether in its existing liberal guise or in the form of a possible future participatory or self-managing

democracy—with its most important challenge and most comprehensive critique.

The objection that will be brought against the feminists is that after a century or more of legal reforms and the introduction of universal suffrage women are now the civil and political equals of men, so that feminism today has little or nothing to contribute to democratic theory and practice. This objection ignores much that is crucial to an understanding of the real character of liberal democratic societies. It ignores the existence of widespread and deeply held convictions, and of social practices that give them expression, that contradict the (more or less) formally equal civic status of women. The objection is based on the liberal argument that social inequalities are irrelevant to political equality. Thus, it has to ignore the problems that have arisen from the attempt to universalize liberal principles by extending them to women while at the same time maintaining the division between private and political life which is central to liberal democracy, and is also a division between women and men. If liberal theorists of democracy are content to avoid these questions, their radical critics, along with advocates of participatory democracy, might have expected to confront them enthusiastically. However, although they have paid a good deal of attention to the class structure of liberal democracies and the way in which class inequality undercuts formal political equality, they have rarely examined the significance of sexual inequality and the patriarchal order of the liberal state for a democratic transformation of liberalism. Writers on democracy, whether defenders or critics of the status quo, invariably fail to consider, for example, whether their discussions of freedom or consent have any relevance to

From Graeme Duncan, ed., *Democratic Theory and Practice* (Cambridge: Cambridge University Press, 1983), 204–17. © 1983 Cambridge University Press. Reprinted with the permission of Cambridge University Press.

women. They implicitly argue as if 'individuals' and 'citizens' are men.

It is frequently overlooked how recently democratic or universal suffrage was established. Political scientists have remained remarkably silent about the struggle for womanhood suffrage (in England there was a continuous organized campaign for 48 years from 1866 to 1914) and the political meaning and consequences of enfranchisement. Women's position as voters also appears to cause some difficulty for writers on democracy. Little comment is excited, for example, by Schumpeter's explicit statement, in his extremely influential revisionist text, that the exclusion of women from the franchise does not invalidate a polity's claim to be a 'democracy'. In Barber's fascinating account of direct democracy in a Swiss canton, womanhood suffrage (gained only in 1971) is treated very equivocally. Barber emphasizes that women's enfranchisement was 'just and equitable'—but the cost was 'participation and community'. Assemblies grew unwieldy and participation diminished, atomistic individualism gained official recognition, and the ideal of the citizen-soldier could no longer be justified.[1] The reader is left wondering whether women should not have sacrificed their just demand for the sake of men's citizenship. Again, in Verba, Nie, and Kim's recent cross-national study of political participation it is noted, in a discussion of the change in Holland from compulsory to voluntary voting, that 'voting rights were universal.' The footnote, on the same page, says that in both electoral systems there was 'a one man one vote system'.[2] Did women vote? Unrecognized historical ironies abound in discussions of democracy. Feminists are frequently told today that we must not be offended by masculine language because 'man' really means 'human being', although when, in 1867 in support of the first women's suffrage bill in Britain, it was argued that 'man' (referring to the householder) was a generic term that included women, the argument was firmly rejected. Another recent example of the way in which

women can be written out of democratic political life can be found in Margolis's *Viable Democracy*. He begins by presenting a history of 'Citizen Brown', who is a man and who, we learn, in 1920 obtained 'his latest major triumph, the enfranchisement of women'.[3] Thus the history of women's democratic struggles disappears and democratic voting appears as the sole creation—or gift—of men.

Such examples might be amusing if they were not symptomatic of the past and present social standing of women. Feminism, liberalism, and democracy (that is, a political order in which citizenship is universal, the right of each adult individual member of the community) share a common origin. Feminism, a general critique of social relationships of sexual domination and subordination and a vision of a sexually egalitarian future, like liberalism and democracy, emerges only when individualism, or the idea that individuals are by nature free and equal to each other, has developed as a universal theory of social organization. However, from the time, 300 years ago, when the individualist social contract theorists launched the first critical attack on patriarchalism the prevailing approach to the position of women can be exemplified by the words of Fichte, who asks, 'Has woman the same rights in the state which man has? This question may appear ridiculous to many. For if the only ground of all legal rights is reason and freedom, how can a distinction exist between two sexes which possess both the same reason and the same freedom?' He replies to this question as follows:

> Nevertheless, it seems that, so long as men have lived, this has been differently held, and the female sex seems not to have been placed on a par with the male sex in the exercise of its rights. *Such a universal sentiment must have a ground, to discover which was never a more urgent problem than in our days.*[4]

The anti-feminists and anti-democrats have never found this 'urgent problem' difficult to solve.

Differential rights and status have been and are defended by appeal to the 'natural' differences between the sexes, from which it is held to follow that women are subordinate to their fathers or husbands and that their proper place is in domestic life. The argument from nature stretches back into mythology and ancient times (and today often comes dressed up in the scientific garb of sociobiology) and its longevity appears to confirm that it informs us of an eternal and essential part of the human condition. But, far from being timeless, the argument has specific formulations in different historical epochs and, in the context of the development of liberal-capitalist society, it appears in a form which obscures the patriarchal structure of liberalism beneath the ideology of individual freedom and equality.

It is usually assumed that the social contract theorists, and Locke in particular, provided the definite counter to the patriarchal thesis that paternal and political power are one and the same, grounded in the natural subjection of sons to fathers. Locke certainly drew a sharp distinction between natural or familial ties and the conventional relations of political life, but although he argued that sons, when adult, were as free as their fathers and equal to them, and hence could only justifiably be governed with their own consent, it is usually 'forgotten' that he excluded women (wives) from this argument. His criticism of the patriarchalists depends upon the assumption of natural individual freedom and equality, but only men count as 'individuals'. Women are held to be born to subjection. Locke takes it for granted that a woman will, through her marriage contract, always agree to place herself in subordination to her husband. He agrees with the patriarchalists that wifely subjection has 'a Foundation in Nature' and argues that in the family the husband's will, as that of the 'abler and the stronger', must always prevail over 'that of his wife in all things of their common Concernment'.[5] The contradiction between the premise of individual freedom and equality, with its corollary of the conventional basis of authority, and the assumption that women (wives) are naturally subject has since gone unnoticed. Similarly, there has been no acknowledgement of the problem that if women are naturally subordinate, or born into subjection, then talk of their consent or agreement to this status is redundant. Yet this contradiction and paradox lie at the heart of democratic theory and practice. The continuing silence about the status of wives is testament to the strength of the union of a transformed patriarchalism with liberalism. For the first time in history, liberal individualism promised women an equal social standing with men as naturally free individuals, but at the same time socio-economic developments ensured that the subordination of wives to husbands continued to be seen as natural, and so outside the domain of democratic theorists or the political struggle to democratize liberalism.

The conviction that a married woman's proper place is in the conjugal home as a servant to her husband and mother to her children is now so widespread and well established that this arrangement appears as a natural feature of human existence rather than historically and culturally specific. The history of the development of the capitalist organization of production is also the history of the development of a particular form of the sexual division of labour (although this is not the history to be found in most books). At the time when the social contract theorists attacked the patriarchal thesis of a natural hierarchy of inequality and subordination, wives were not their husbands' equals, but nor were they their economic dependants. Wives, as associates and partners in economic production, had an independent status. As production moved out of the household, women were forced out of the trades they controlled and wives became dependent on their husbands for subsistence or competed for individual wages in certain areas of production.[6] Many working-class wives and mothers have had to continue to try to find paid employment to ensure the survival of their families, but by the mid-nineteenth century the ideal, the natural and respectable, mode of life had come to be seen as that of the middle-class, breadwinning paterfamilias and his totally dependent wife. By then the subjection of wives was complete; with no independent legal or civil standing they had been reduced to the status of property, as the nineteenth-century feminists emphasized in their comparisons of wives to the slaves of the West Indies and American South. Today, women have won an independent civil status and the vote; they are, apparently, 'individuals' as well as citizens—and thus require no special attention in discussions of democracy. However, one of the most important consequences of the institutionalization of liberal individualism and the establishment of universal suffrage has been to highlight the practical contradiction between the formal political equality of liberal democracy and the social subordination of women, including their subjection as wives within the patriarchal structure of the institution of marriage.

It is indicative of the attitude of democratic theorists (and political activists) towards feminism that John Stuart Mill's criticism of the argument from (women's) nature, and the lessons to be learned from it, are so little known. The present revival of the organized feminist movement has begun to rescue *The Subjection of Women* from the obscurity into which Mill's commentators have pushed it, although it provides a logical extension of the arguments of his academically acceptable *On Liberty*. *The Subjection* is important for its substantive argument, but also because the ultimately contradictory position that Mill takes in the essay illustrates just how radical feminist criticism is, and how the attempt to universalize liberal principles to both sexes pushes beyond the confines of liberal democratic theory and practice.

In *The Subjection* Mill argues that the relation between women and men, or, more specifically, between wives and husbands, forms an unjustified exception to the liberal principles of individual rights, freedom, and choice, to the principles of equality of opportunity and the allocation of occupational positions by merit that, he believes, now govern other social and political institutions. In the modern world, consent has supplanted force and the principle of achievement has replaced that of ascription—except where women are concerned. Mill writes that the conjugal relation is an example of 'the primitive state of slavery lasting on. . . . It has not lost the taint of its brutal origin.'[7] More generally, the social subordination of women is 'a single relic of an old world of thought and practice, exploded in everything else.'[8] Mill opens *The Subjection* with some pertinent comments on the difficulty feminists face in presenting an intellectually convincing case. Domination by men is rooted in long-standing customs, and the idea that male supremacy is the proper order of things derives from deep feelings and sentiments rather than rationally tested beliefs (and, it might be added, men have a lot to lose by being convinced). Thus feminists must not expect their opponents to 'give up practical principles in which they have been born and bred and which are the basis of much of the existing order of the world, at the first argumentative attack which they are not capable of logically resisting.'[9] Mill is very conscious of the importance of the appeal to nature. He notes that it provides no criterion to differentiate the subordination of women from other forms of domination because all rulers have attempted to claim a grounding in nature for their position. He also argues that nothing at all can be said about the respective natures of women and men because we have only seen the sexes in an unequal relationship. Any differences in their moral and other capacities will become known when men and women can interact as independent and equal rational beings.

However, despite Mill's vigorous attack on the appeal to custom and nature he ultimately falls back on the very argument that he has carefully criticized. His failure consistently to apply his principles to domestic life has been noted by recent feminist critics, but it is less often pointed out that his inconsistency undermines his defence of womanhood suffrage and equal democratic citizenship. The central argument of *The Subjection* is that husbands must be stripped of their legally sanctioned despotic powers over their wives. Most of the legal reforms of the marriage law that Mill advocated have now been enacted (with the significant exception of marital rape, to which I shall return), and the implications of his unwillingness to extend his criticism to the sexual division of labour within the home are now fully revealed. Mill argues that because of their upbringing, lack of education, and legal and social pressures, women do not have a free choice whether or not to marry: 'wife' is the only occupation open to them. But although he also argues that women must have equal opportunity with men to obtain a proper education that will enable them to support themselves, he assumes that, if marriage were reformed, most women would *not* choose independence.

Mill states that it is generally understood that when a woman marries she has chosen her career, like a man when he chooses a profession. When a woman becomes a wife, 'she makes choice of the management of a household, and the bringing up of a family, as the first call on her exertions, . . . she renounces . . . all [occupations] not consistent with the requirement of this.'[10] Mill is reverting here to ascriptive arguments and the belief in women's natural place and occupation. He is falling back on the ancient tradition of patriarchal political theory that, as Susan Okin has shown in *Women in Western Political Thought*,[11] asserts that whereas men are, or can be, many things, women are placed on earth to fulfil one function only: to bear and rear children. Mill neatly evades the question of how, if women's task is prescribed by their sex, they can be said to have a real choice of occupation, or why equal opportunity is relevant to women if marriage itself is a 'career'. Mill compares an egalitarian marriage to a business partnership in which the partners are free to negotiate their own terms of association, but he relies on some very weak arguments, which run counter to

liberal principles, to support his view that equality will not disturb the conventional domestic division of labour. He suggests that the 'natural arrangement' would be for wife and husband each to be 'absolute in the executive branch of their own department . . . any change of system and principle requiring the consent of both.'[12] He also suggests that the division of labour between the spouses could be agreed in the marriage contract—but he assumes that wives will be willing to accept the 'natural' arrangement. Mill notes that duties are already divided 'by consent . . . and general custom'[13] [and] modified in individual cases; but it is exactly 'general custom', as the bulwark of male domination, that he is arguing against in the body of the essay. He forgets this when he suggests that the husband will generally have the greater voice in decisions as he is usually older. Mill adds that this is only until the time of life when age is irrelevant; but when do husbands admit that this has arrived?[14] He also forgets his own arguments when he suggests that more weight will be given to the views of the partner who brings the means of support, disingenuously adding 'whichever this is' when he has already assumed that wives will 'choose' to be dependent by agreeing to marry.

Anti-feminist movements and propagandists in the 1980s also claim that the domestic division of labour supported by Mill is the only natural one. They would not be disturbed by the implications of this arrangement for the citizenship of women but advocates of democracy should be. Mill championed womanhood suffrage for the same reasons that he supported votes for men; because it was necessary for self-protection or the protection of individual interests and because political participation would enlarge the capacities of individual women. The obvious problem with his argument is that women as wives will largely be confined to the small circle of the family and its daily routines and so will find it difficult to use their vote effectively as a protective measure. Women will not be able to learn what their interests are without experience outside domestic life. This point is even more crucial for Mill's arguments about political development and education through participation. He writes in general terms of the elevation of the individual 'as a moral, spiritual, and social being'[15] that occurs under free government, but this is a large claim to make for the periodic casting of a vote (although the moral transformation of political life through enfranchisement was a central theme of the womanhood suffrage movement). Nor did Mill himself entirely believe that this 'elevation' would result from the suffrage alone. He writes that 'citizenship', and here I take him to be referring to universal suffrage, 'fills only a small place in modern life, and does not come near the daily habits or inmost sentiments.'[16] He goes on to argue that the family, 'justly constituted', would be the 'real school of the virtues of freedom'. However, this is as implausible as the claim about the consequences of liberal democratic voting. A patriarchal family with the despotic husband at its head is no basis for democratic citizenship; but nor, *on its own*, is an egalitarian family. Mill argues in his social and political writings that only participation in a wide variety of institutions, especially the workplace, can provide the political education necessary for active, democratic citizenship. Yet how can wives and mothers, who have 'chosen' domestic life, have the opportunity to develop their capacities or learn what it means to be a democratic citizen? Women will therefore exemplify the selfish, private beings, lacking a sense of justice or public spirit, that result when an individual is confined to the narrow sphere of everyday family life.[17] Mill's failure to question the apparently natural division of labour within the home means that his arguments for democratic citizenship apply only to men.

It might be objected that it is unreasonable and anachronistic to ask of Mill, writing in the 1860s, that he criticize the accepted division of labour between husband and wife when only very exceptional feminists in the nineteenth century were willing to question the doctrine of the separate spheres of the sexes. But if that objection is granted,[18] it does not excuse the same critical failure by contemporary democratic theorists and empirical investigators. Until the feminist movement began, very recently, to have an impact on academic studies, not only has the relation between the structure of the institution of marriage and the formal equality of citizenship been ignored, but women citizens have often been excluded from empirical investigations of political behaviour and attitudes or merely referred to briefly in patriarchal not scientific terms.[19] A reading of *The Subjection* should long ago have placed these matters in the forefront of discussions of democracy. Perhaps the appearance of empirical findings showing, for example, that even women active in local politics are inhibited from running for office because of their responsibility for child care and a belief that office-holding is not a proper activity for women,[20] will be taken more seriously than the feminist writings of even eminent philosophers.

The problems surrounding women's citizenship in the liberal democracies may have been sadly neglected, but the failure of democratic theorists to confront the woman and wife question runs much deeper still. Democratic citizenship, even if interpreted in the minimal sense of universal suffrage in the context of liberal civil rights, presupposes the solid foundation of a practical, universal recognition that all members of the polity are social equals and independent 'individuals', having all the capacities implied by this status. The most serious failure of contemporary democratic theory and its language of freedom, equality, consent, and of the individual, is that women are so easily and inconspicuously excluded from references to the 'individual'. Thus the question never arises whether the exclusion reflects social and political realities. One reason why there is no consciousness of the need to ask this question is that democratic theorists conventionally see their subject-matters encompassing the political or public sphere, which for radical theorists includes the economy and the workplace. The sphere of personal and domestic life—the sphere that is the 'natural' realm of women—is excluded from scrutiny. Despite the central role that consent plays in this argument democratic theorists pay no attention to the structure of sexual relations between men and women and, more specifically, to the practice of rape and the interpretation of consent and non-consent which define it as a criminal offence. The facts about rape are central to the social realities which are reflected in and partly constituted by our use of the term 'individual'.

Among Mill's criticisms of the despotic powers of nineteenth-century husbands is a harsh reminder that a husband had the legal right to rape his wife. Over a century later a husband still has that right in most legal jurisdictions. Locke excludes women from the status of 'free and equal individual' by his agreement with the patriarchal claim that wives were subject to their husbands by nature; the content of the marriage contract confirms that, today, this assumption still lies at the heart of the institution of marriage. The presumed consent of a woman, in a free marriage contract, to her subordinate status gives a voluntarist gloss to an essentially ascribed status of 'wife'. If the assumption of natural subjection did not still hold, liberal democratic theorists would long ago have begun to ask why it is that an ostensibly free and equal individual should always agree to enter into a contract which subordinates her to another such individual. They would long ago have begun to question the character of an institution in which the initial agreement of a wife deprives her of the right to retract her consent to provide sexual services to her husband, and which gives him the legal right to force her to submit. If contemporary democratic theorists are to distance themselves from the patriarchal assumptions of their predecessors they must begin to ask whether a person can be, at one and the same time, a free democratic citizen and a wife who gives up a vital aspect of her freedom and individuality, the freedom to refuse consent and say 'no' to the violation of the integrity of her person.

A woman's right of refusal of consent is also a matter of more general importance. Outside of marriage rape is a serious criminal offence, yet the evidence indicates that the majority of offenders are not prosecuted. Women have exemplified the beings whom political theorists have regarded as lacking the capacities to attain the status of individual and citizen or to participate in the practice of consent, but women have, simultaneously, been perceived as beings who, in their personal lives, always consent, and whose explicit refusal of consent can be disregarded and reinterpreted as agreement. This contradictory perception of women is a major reason why it is so difficult for a woman who has been raped to secure the conviction of her attacker(s). Public opinion, the police, and the courts are willing to identify enforced submission with consent, and the reason why this identification is possible is that it is widely believed that if a woman says 'no' her words have no meaning, since she 'really' means 'yes'. It is widely regarded as perfectly reasonable for a man to reinterpret explicit rejection of his advances as consent.[21] Thus women find their speech is persistently and systematically invalidated. Such invalidation would be incomprehensible if the two sexes actually shared the same status as 'individuals'. No person with a secure, recognized standing as an 'individual' could be seen as someone who consistently said the opposite of what they meant and who, therefore, could justifiably have their words reinterpreted by others. On the other hand, invalidation and reinterpretation are readily comprehensible parts of a relationship in which one person is seen as a natural subordinate and thus has an exceedingly ambiguous place in social practices (held to be) grounded in convention, in free argument and consent.

Political theorists who take seriously the question of the conceptual foundations and social conditions of democracy can no longer avoid the feminist critique of marriage and personal life. The critique raises some awkward and often embarrassing questions, but questions that have to be faced if 'democracy' is to be more than a men's club writ large and the patriarchal structure of the liberal democratic state is to be challenged. The assumptions and practices which govern the everyday, personal lives of women and men, including their sexual lives, can no longer be treated as matters remote from political life and the concerns of democratic theorists. Women's status as 'individuals' pervades the whole of their social life, personal and political. The structure of everyday life, including marriage, is constituted by beliefs and practices which presuppose that women are naturally subject to men—yet writers on democracy continue to assert that women and men can and will freely interact as equals in their capacity as enfranchised democratic citizens.

The preceding argument and criticism are relevant to discussions of both liberal democracy and participatory democracy, but particularly to the latter. Liberal theorists continue to claim that the structure of social relations and social inequality is irrelevant to political equality and democratic citizenship, so they are no more likely to be impressed by feminists than by any other radical critics. Advocates of participatory democracy have been reluctant to take feminist arguments into account even though these arguments are, seen in one light, an extension of the participatory democratic claim that 'democracy' extends beyond the state to the organization of society. The resistance to feminism is particularly ironical because the contemporary feminist movement has, under a variety of labels, attempted to put participatory democratic organization into practice.[22] The movement is decentralized, anti-hierarchical, and tries to ensure that its members collectively educate themselves and gain independence through consciousness-raising, participatory decision-making, and rotation of tasks and offices.

Feminists deny the liberal claim that private and public life can be understood in isolation from each other. One reason for the neglect of J.S. Mill's feminist essay is that his extension of liberal

principles to the institution of marriage breaches the central liberal separation, established by Locke, between paternal and political rule; or between the impersonal, conventional public sphere and the family, the sphere of natural affection and natural relations. Proponents of participatory democracy have, of course, been willing to challenge commonplace conceptions of the public and the private in their discussions of the workplace, but this challenge ignores the insights of feminism. It is rarely appreciated that the feminists and participatory democrats see the division between public and private very differently. From the feminist perspective participatory democratic arguments remain within the patriarchal-liberal separation of civil society and state: domestic life has an exceedingly ambiguous relation to this separation, which is a division within public life itself. In contrast, feminists see domestic life, the 'natural' sphere of women, as private, and thus as divided from a public realm encompassing both economic and political life, the 'natural' arenas of men.[23]

By failing to take into account the feminist conception of 'private' life, by ignoring the family, participatory democratic arguments for the democratization of economic life have neglected a crucial dimension of democratic social transformation (and I include my *Participation and Democratic Theory* here). It is difficult to find any appreciation of the significance of the integral relation between the domestic division of labour and economic life, or the sexual division of labour in the workplace, let alone any mention of the implications of the deeper matters touched on in this essay, in writings on industrial democracy. It is the feminists, not the advocates of workplace democracy, who have investigated the very different position of women workers, especially married women workers, from that of male employees. Writers on democracy have yet to digest the now large body of feminist research on women and paid employment or to acknowledge that unless it is brought into the centre of reflection, debate, and political action, women will remain as peripheral in a future participatory 'democracy' as they are at present in liberal democracies.

I have drawn attention to the problem posed by the assumption that women's natural place is a private one, as wife and mother in the home, for arguments about the educative and developmental consequences of political participation. It might be argued that this problem is much less pressing today than in Mill's time because many married women have now entered the public world of paid employment and so they, if not housewives, already have their horizons widened and will gain a political education if enterprises are democratized. In Australia, for example, in 1977 women formed 35 per cent of the labour force and 63 per cent of these women were married.[24] The reality behind the statistics, however, is that women's status as workers is as uncertain and ambiguous as our status as citizens and both reflect the more fundamental problem of our status as 'individuals'. The conventional but implicit assumption is that 'work' is undertaken in a workplace, not within the 'private' home, and that a 'worker' is male—someone who has his need for a clean place of relaxation, clean clothes, food, and care of his children provided for him by his wife. When a wife enters paid employment it is significant for her position as 'worker' that no one asks who performs these services for her. In fact, married women workers do two shifts, one in the office or factory, the other at home. A large question arises here why members of enterprises who are already burdened with two jobs should be eager to take on the new responsibilities, as well as exercise the opportunities, that democratization would bring.

The relative importance of the two components of the wife's double day, and so the evaluation of women's status as workers, is reflected, as Eisenstein notes, in the popular use of 'the term "working mother" which simultaneously asserts women's first responsibility to motherhood and her secondary status as worker.'[25] Again, the question has to be asked how workers of secondary status could, without some very large changes being made, take their place as equal participants in a democratized workplace. The magnitude of the changes required can be indicated by brief reference to three features of women's (paid) work-life. The sexual harassment of women workers is still a largely unacknowledged practice but it reveals the extent to which the problem of sexual relations, consent, and women's status as 'individuals' is also a problem of the economic sphere.[26] Secondly, women still have to win the struggle against discrimination by employers and unions before they can participate as equals. Finally, it has to be recognized that the workplace is structured by a sexual division of labour which poses still further complex problems for equality and participation. Women are segregated into certain occupational categories ('women's work') and they are concentrated in non-supervisory and low-skilled and low-status jobs. It is precisely workers in such jobs that empirical research has shown to be the least likely to participate.

The example of the workplace, together with the other examples discussed in this essay, should be sufficient to show the fundamental importance to democratic theory and practice of the contemporary feminist insistence that personal and political life are integrally connected. Neither the equal opportunity of liberalism nor the active, participatory democratic citizenship of all the people can be achieved without radical changes in personal and domestic life. The struggles of the organized feminist movement of the last 150 years have achieved a great deal. An exceptional woman can now become prime minister—but that particular achievement leaves untouched the structure of social life of unexceptional women, of women as a social category. They remain in an uncertain position as individuals, workers, and citizens, and popular opinion echoes Rousseau's pronouncement that 'nature herself has decreed that women . . . should be at the mercy of man's judgement.'[27] The creation of a free and egalitarian sexual and personal life is the most difficult to achieve of all the changes necessary to build a truly democratic society precisely because it is not something remote from everyday life that can be applauded in abstract slogans while life, and the subjection of women, goes on as usual. Democratic ideals and politics have to be put into practice in the kitchen, the nursery, and the bedroom; they come home, as J.S. Mill wrote, 'to the person and hearth of every male head of a family, and of everyone who looks forward to being so.'[28] It is a natural biological fact of human existence that only women can bear children, but that fact gives no warrant whatsoever for the separation of social life into two sexually defined spheres of private (female) existence and (male) public activity. This separation is ultimately grounded in the mistaken extension of the argument from natural necessity to child-rearing. There is nothing in nature that prevents fathers from sharing equally in bringing up their children, although there is a great deal in the organization of social and economic life that works against it. Women cannot win an equal place in democratic productive life and citizenship if they are deemed destined for one ascribed task, but nor can fathers take an equal share in reproductive activities without a transformation in our conception of 'work' and of the structure of economic life.

The battle joined 300 years ago when the social contract theorists pitted conventionalist arguments against the patriarchalists' appeal to nature is far from concluded, and a proper, democratic understanding of the relation of nature and convention is still lacking. The successful conclusion of this long battle demands some radical reconceptualization to provide a comprehensive theory of a properly democratic practice. Recent feminist theoretical work offers new perspectives and insights into the problem of democratic theory and practice, including the question of individualism and participatory democracy, and an appropriate conception of 'political' life.[29] It has been hard to imagine what a democratic form of social life might look like for much of the past century. Male-dominated political parties, sects, and their theoreticians have attempted to bury the old 'Utopian' political movements which are part of the history of the struggle for democracy and women's emancipation, and which argued for prefigurative forms of political organization and activity. The lesson to be learnt from the past is that a 'democratic' theory and practice that is not at the same time feminist merely serves to maintain a fundamental form of domination and so makes a mockery of the ideals and values that democracy is held to embody.

## Notes

1. B.R. Barber, *The Death of Communal Liberty* (Princeton: Princeton University Press, 1974), 273. The comment on citizen-soldiers is very revealing. There is no reason why women should not be armed citizens and help defend the *patrie* (as guerrilla fighters and armies have shown). However, one of the major arguments of the anti-suffragists in Britain and the USA was that the enfranchisement of women would fatally weaken the state because women by nature were incapable of bearing arms. I have commented on these issues in C. Pateman, 'Women, Nature and the Suffrage', *Ethics* 90, 4 (1980): 564–75. Some other aspects of the patriarchal argument from nature are discussed below.

2. S. Verba, N. Nie, and J.-O. Kim, *Participation and Political Equality* (Cambridge: Cambridge University Press, 1978), 8.

3. M. Margolis, *Viable Democracy* (Harmondsworth: Penguin, 1979), 9.

4. J.G. Fichte, *The Science of Rights*, trans. A.E. Kroeger (London: Trubner, 1889), Appendix, s. 3.1 439 (my emphasis).

5. J. Locke, *Two Treatises of Government*, 2nd edn, ed. P. Laslett (Cambridge: Cambridge University Press, 1967), I, ss. 47, 48; II, s. 82.

6. For amplification of these necessarily brief comments, see T. Brennan and C. Pateman, '"Mere Auxiliaries to the Commonwealth": Women and the Origins of Liberalism', *Political Studies* 27

(1979): 183–200; R. Hamilton, *The Liberation of Women: A Study of Patriarchy and Capitalism* (London: Allen and Unwin, 1978); H. Hartmann, 'Capitalism, Patriarchy and Job Segregation by Sex', *Signs* 1, 3, pt. 2 (1976): 137–70; A. Oakley, *Housewife* (Harmondsworth: Penguin, 1976), chs 2 and 3.

7. J.S. Mill, *The Subjection of Women*, in J.S. Mill and H. Taylor, *Essays on Sex Equality*, ed. A. Rossi (Chicago: Chicago University Press, 1970), 130.
8. Ibid., 146.
9. Ibid., 128.
10. Ibid., 179.
11. Susan Okin, *Women in Western Political Thought* (Princeton: Princeton University Press, 1979).
12. Mill, *The Subjection of Women*, 169.
13. Ibid., 170.
14. It is worth noting that Mill implicitly distinguishes between the actions and beliefs of individual husbands and the power given to 'husbands' over 'wives' within the structure of the institution of marriage. He notes that marriage is not designed for the benevolent few to whom the defenders of marital slavery point, but for every man, even those who use their power physically to ill-treat their wives. This important distinction is still frequently overlooked today when critics of feminism offer examples of individual 'good' husbands personally known to them.
15. Mill, *The Subjection of Women*, 237.
16. Ibid., 174.
17. Mill, and many other feminists, see the lack of a sense of justice (a consequence of confinement to domestic life) as the major defect in women's characters. The assertion that the defect is natural to women is central to the belief—ignored by writers on democracy—that women are inherently subversive of political order and a threat to the state; on this question, see C. Pateman, '"The Disorder of Women": Women, Love and the Sense of Justice', *Ethics* 91, 1 (1980): 20–34.
18. It need not be granted. *The Subjection* owes a good deal to William Thompson's (much neglected) *Appeal of One Half the Human Race, Women, Against the Pretensions of the Other Half, Men, to Retain them in Political, and Hence in Civil and Domestic, Slavery* (New York: Source Book Press, 1970), originally published in 1825. Thompson was very willing to

question these matters in his vision of a co-operative-socialist and sexually egalitarian future.
19. For an early critique, see, for example, M. Goot and E. Reid, 'Women and Voting Studies: Mindless Matrons or Sexist Scientism', *Sage Professional Papers in Contemporary Sociology* 1 (1975); more recently, for example, J. Evans, 'Attitudes to Women in American Political Science', *Government and Opposition* 15, 1 (1980): 101–14.
20. M.M. Lee, 'Why Few Women Hold Public Office: Democracy and Sexual Roles', *Political Science Quarterly* 91 (1976): 297–314.
21. A detailed discussion of the paradoxical manner in which political theorists have treated women's consent, and references to the empirical evidence on which these comments are based, can be found in C. Pateman, 'Women and Consent', *Political Theory* 8, 2 (1980): 149–68. In some legal jurisdictions, for example the states of New South Wales, South Australia, and Victoria in Australia, rape within marriage is now a criminal offence. Legal reform is extremely welcome, but the wider social problem remains: one of the saddest conclusions I reached during my research was that rather than rape being 'a unique act that stands in complete opposition to the consensual relations that ordinarily obtain between the sexes . . . rape is revealed as the extreme expression of, or an extension of, the accepted and 'natural' relation between men and women' (161).
22. On the other hand, the experience of women in the 'participatory democratic' New Left was a major impetus to the revival of the feminist movement. The New Left provided an arena for political action, the development of skills, and was ideologically egalitarian—but it remained male supremacist in its organization and, especially, its personal relations: see S. Evans, *Personal Politics* (New York: Knopf, 1979).
23. For some comments on the ambiguous place of the family, see my '"The Disorder of Women"'; on the wider question of public and private, see C. Pateman, 'Feminist Critiques of the Public-Private Dichotomy', in S. Benn and G. Gaus, eds, *Conceptions of the Public and Private in Social Life* (London: Croom Helm, forthcoming).
24. A steady increase in the employment of married women has been one of the most striking features

of the post-war development of capitalism. However, it is worth re-emphasizing that (working-class) wives have always been in the paid workforce. In Britain in 1851 about a quarter of married women were employed (Oakley, *Housewife*, 44). Moreover, domestic service, until the late 1930s, was a major occupation for (usually single) women. One reason that Mill is able to overlook the fundamental importance of wives' (private) childbearing duties for their public status is that middle-class mothers had other women to look after their children; similarly, upper- and middle-class suffragettes could go to prison secure in the knowledge that domestic servants were caring for their homes and children. On this point, see J.

Liddington and J.Norris, *One Hand Tied Behind Us: The Rise of the Women's Suffrage Movement* (London: Virago, 1978).

25. Z.R. Eisenstein, *The Radical Future of Liberal Feminism* (New York: Longman, 1980), 207–8.
26. On sexual harassment, see, for example, C.A. Mackinnon, *Sexual Harassment of Working Women* (New Haven: Yale University Press, 1979).
27. J.-J. Rousseau, *Emile*, trans. B. Foxley (London: Dent, 1911), 328.
28. Mill, *The Subjection of Women*, 136.
29. See, for example, the discussion by R.P. Petchesky, 'Reproductive Freedom: Beyond "A Woman's Right to Choose"', *Signs* 5, 4 (1980): 661–85.

# Three Malaises

## Charles Taylor

I want to write here about some of the malaises of modernity. I mean by this features of our contemporary culture and society that people experience as a loss or a decline, even as our civilization 'develops'. Sometimes people feel that some important decline has occurred during the last years or decades—since the Second World War, or the 1950s, for instance. And sometimes the loss is felt over a much longer historical period: the whole modern era from the seventeenth century is frequently seen as the time frame of decline. Yet although the time scale can vary greatly, there is certain convergence on the themes of decline. They are often variations around a few central melodies. I want to pick out two such central themes here, and then throw in a third that largely derives from these two. These three by no means exhaust the topic, but they do get at a great deal of what troubles and perplexes us about modern society.

The worries I will be talking about are very familiar. No one needs to be reminded of them; they are discussed, bemoaned, challenged, and argued against all the time in all sorts of media. That sounds like a reason not to talk about them further. But I believe that this great familiarity hides bewilderment, that we don't really understand these changes that worry us, that the usual run of debate about them in fact misrepresents them—and thus makes us misconceive what we can do about them. The changes defining modernity are both well known and very perplexing, and that is why it's worth talking still more about them.

The first source of worry is individualism. Of course, individualism also names what many people consider the finest achievement of modern civilization. We live in a world where people have a right to choose for themselves their own pattern of life, to decide in conscience what convictions to espouse, to determine the shape of their lives in a whole host of ways that their ancestors couldn't control. And these rights are generally defended by our legal systems. In principle, people are no longer sacrificed to the demands of supposedly sacred orders that transcend them.

Very few people want to go back on this achievement. Indeed, many think that it is still incomplete, that economic arrangements, or patterns of family life, or traditional notions of hierarchy still restrict too much our freedom to be ourselves. But many of us are also ambivalent. Modern freedom was won by our breaking loose from older moral horizons. People used to see themselves as part of a larger order. In some cases, this was a cosmic order, a 'great chain of Being', in which humans figured in their proper place along with angels, heavenly bodies, and our fellow earthly creatures. This hierarchical order in the universe was reflected in the hierarchies of human society. People were often locked into a given place, a role and station that was properly theirs and from which it was almost unthinkable to deviate. Modern freedom came about through the discrediting of such orders.

But at the same time as they restricted us, these orders gave meaning to the world and the activities of social life. The things that surround us were not just potential raw materials or instruments for our projects, but they had the significance given them by their place in the chain of being. The eagle was not just another bird, but the king of a whole domain of animal life. By the same token, the rituals and norms of society had more

From Charles Taylor, *The Malaise of Modernity* (Toronto: House of Anansi, 1991), 1–12. Reprinted with permission of Stoddart Publishing Co. Limited.

than merely instrumental significance. The discrediting of these orders has been called the 'disenchantment' of the world. With it, things lost some of their magic.

A vigorous debate has been going on for a couple of centuries as to whether this was an unambiguously good thing. But this is not what I want to focus on here. I want to look rather at what some have seen to be the consequences for human life and meaning.

The worry has been repeatedly expressed that the individual lost something important along with the larger social and cosmic horizons of action. Some have written of this as the loss of a heroic dimension to life. People no longer have a sense of higher purpose, of something worth dying for. Alexis de Tocqueville sometimes talked like this in the last century, referring to the 'petits et vulgaires plaisirs' that people tend to seek in the democratic age.[1] In another articulation, we suffer from a lack of passion. Kierkegaard saw 'the present age' in these terms. And Nietzsche's 'last men' are at the final nadir of this decline; they have no aspiration left in life but to a 'pitiable comfort'.[2]

This loss of purpose was linked to a narrowing. People lost the broader vision because they focused on their individual lives. Democratic equality, says Tocqueville, draws the individual towards himself, 'et menace de le renfermer enfin tout entier dans la solitude de son propre cœur.'[3] In other words, the dark side of individualism is a centring on the self, which both flattens and narrows our lives, makes them poorer in meaning, and less concerned with others or society.

This worry has recently surfaced again in concern at the fruits of a 'permissive society', the doings of the 'me generation', or the prevalence of 'narcissism', to take just three of the best-known contemporary formulations. The sense that lives have been flattened and narrowed, and that this is connected to an abnormal and regrettable self-absorption, has returned in forms specific to contemporary culture. This defines the first theme I want to deal with.

The disenchantment of the world is connected to another massively important phenomenon of the modern age, which also greatly troubles many people. We might call this the primacy of instrumental reason. By 'instrumental reason' I mean the kind of rationality we draw on when we calculate the most economical application of means to a given end. Maximum efficiency, the best cost-output ratio, is its measure of success.

No doubt sweeping away the old orders has immensely widened the scope of instrumental reason. Once society no longer has a sacred structure, once social arrangements and modes of action are no longer grounded in the order of things or the will of God, they are in a sense up for grabs. They can be redesigned with their consequences for the happiness and well-being of individuals as our goal. The yardstick that henceforth applies is that of instrumental reason. Similarly, once the creatures that surround us lose the significance that accrued to their place in the chain of being, they are open to being treated as raw materials or instruments for our projects.

In one way this change has been liberating. But there is also a widespread unease that instrumental reason not only has enlarged its scope but also threatens to take over our lives. The fear is that things that ought to be determined by other criteria will be decided in terms of efficiency or 'cost-benefit' analysis, that the independent ends that ought to be guiding our lives will be eclipsed by the demand to maximize output. There are lots of things one can point to that give substance to this worry: for instance, the ways the demands of economic growth are used to justify very unequal distributions of wealth and income, or the way these same demands make us insensitive to the needs of the environment, even to the point of potential disaster. Or else, we can think of the way much of our social planning, in crucial areas like risk assessment, is dominated by forms of cost-benefit analysis that involve grotesque calculations, putting dollar assessments on human lives.[4]

The primacy of instrumental reason is also evident in the prestige and aura that surround technology, and makes us believe that we should seek technological solutions even when something very different is called for. We see this often enough in the realm of politics, as Bellah and his colleagues forcefully argue in their new book.[5] But it also invades other domains, such as medicine. Patricia Benner has argued in a number of important works that the technological approach in medicine has often sidelined the kind of care that involves treating the patient as a whole person with a life story, and not as the locus of a technical problem. Society and the medical establishment frequently undervalue the contribution of nurses, who more often than not provide this humanly sensitive caring, as against that of specialists with high-tech knowledge.[6]

The dominant place of technology is also thought to have contributed to the narrowing and flattening of our lives that I have just been discussing in connection with the first theme. People have spoken of a loss of resonance, depth, or richness in our human surroundings. Almost 150 years ago, Marx, in the *Communist Manifesto*, remarked that one of the results of capitalist development was that 'all that is solid melts in air.' The claim is that the solid, lasting, often expressive objects that served us in the past are being set aside for the quick, shoddy, replaceable commodities with which we now surround ourselves. Albert Borgman speaks of the 'device paradigm', whereby we withdraw more and more from 'manifold engagement' with our environment and instead request and get products designed to deliver some circumscribed benefit. He contrasts what is involved in heating our homes, with the contemporary central heating furnace, with what this same function entailed in pioneer times, when the whole family had to be involved in cutting and stacking the wood and feeding the stove or fireplace.[7] Hannah Arendt focused on the more and more ephemeral quality of modern objects of use and argued that 'the reality and reliability of the human world rest primarily on the fact that we are surrounded by things more permanent than the activity by which they are produced.'[8] This permanence comes under threat in a world of modern commodities.

This sense of threat is increased by the knowledge that this primacy is not just a matter of a perhaps unconscious orientation, which we are prodded and tempted into by the modern age. As such it would be hard enough to combat, but at least it might yield to persuasion. But it is also clear that powerful mechanisms of social life press us in this direction. A manager in spite of her own orientation may be forced by the conditions of the market to adopt a maximizing strategy she feels is destructive. A bureaucrat, in spite of his personal insight, may be forced by the rules under which he operates to make a decision he knows to be against humanity and good sense.

Marx and Weber and other great theorists have explored these impersonal mechanisms, which Weber has designated by the evocative term of 'the iron cage'. And some people have wanted to draw from these analyses the conclusion that we are utterly helpless in the face of such forces, or at least helpless unless we totally dismantle the institutional structures under which we have been operating for the last centuries—that is, the market and the state. This aspiration seems so unrealizable today that it amounts to declaring us helpless.

I want to return to this below, but I believe that these strong theories of fatality are abstract and wrong. Our degrees of freedom are not zero. There is a point to deliberating what ought to be our ends, and whether instrumental reason ought to have a lesser role in our lives than it does. But the truth in these analyses is that it is not just a matter of changing the outlook of individuals, it is not just a battle of 'hearts and minds', important as this is. Change in this domain will have to be institutional as well, even though it cannot be as sweeping and total as the great theorists of revolution proposed.

This brings us to the political level, and to the feared consequences for political life of individualism and instrumental reason. One I have already introduced. It is that the institutions and structures of industrial-technological society severely restrict our choices, that they force societies as well as individuals to give a weight to instrumental reason that in serious moral deliberation we would never do, and which may even be highly destructive. A case in point is our great difficulties in tackling even vital threats to our lives from environmental disasters, like the thinning ozone layer. The society structured around instrumental reason can be seen as imposing a great loss of freedom, on both individuals and the group—because it is not just our social decisions that are shaped by these forces. An individual lifestyle is also hard to sustain against the grain. For instance, the whole design of some modern cities makes it hard to function without a car, particularly where public transport has been eroded in favour of the private automobile.

But there is another kind of loss of freedom, which has also been widely discussed, most memorably by Alexis de Tocqueville. A society in which people end up as the kind of individuals who are 'enclosed in their own hearts' is one where few will want to participate actively in self-government. They will prefer to stay at home and enjoy the satisfactions of private life, as long as the government of the day produces the means to these satisfactions and distributes them widely.

This opens the danger of a new, specifically modern form of despotism, which Tocqueville calls 'soft' despotism. It will not be a tyranny of terror and oppression as in the old days. The government will be mild and paternalistic. It may even keep democratic forms, with periodic elections. But in fact, everything will be run by an 'immense tutelary power',[9] over which people will have little control. The only defence against this, Tocqueville thinks, is a vigorous political culture in which participation is valued, at several levels of government and in voluntary associations as well. But the atomism of the self-absorbed individual militates against this. Once participation declines, once the lateral associations that were its vehicles wither away, the individual citizen is left alone in the face of the vast bureaucratic state and feels, correctly, powerless. This demotivates the citizen even further, and the vicious cycle of soft despotism is joined.

Perhaps something like this alienation from the public sphere and consequent loss of political control is happening in our highly centralized and bureaucratic political world. Many contemporary thinkers have seen Tocqueville's work as prophetic.[10] If this is so, what we are in danger of losing is political control over our destiny, something we could exercise in common as citizens. This is what Tocqueville called 'political liberty'. What is threatened here is our dignity as citizens. The impersonal mechanisms mentioned above may reduce our degrees of freedom as a society, but the loss of political liberty would mean that even the choices left would no longer be made by ourselves as citizens, but by irresponsible tutelary power.

These, then, are the first three malaises about modernity that I want to deal with in this book. The first fear is about what we might call a loss of meaning, the fading of moral horizons. The second concerns the eclipse of ends, in face of rampant instrumental reason. And the third is about a loss of freedom.

Of course, these are not uncontroversial. I have spoken about worries that are widespread and mentioned influential authors, but nothing here is agreed. Even those who share some form of these worries dispute vigorously how they should be formulated. And there are lots of people who want to dismiss them out of hand. Those who are deeply into what the critics call the 'culture of narcissism' think of the objectors as hankering for an earlier, more oppressive age. Adepts of modern technological reason think the critics of the primacy of the instrumental are reactionary and obscurantist, scheming to deny the world the benefits of science. And there are proponents of mere negative freedom who believe that the value of political liberty is overblown, and that a society in which scientific management combines with maximum independence for each individual is what we ought to aim at. Modernity has its boosters as well as its knockers.

Nothing is agreed here, and the debate continues. But in the course of this debate, the essential nature of the developments, which are here being decried, there being praised, is often misunderstood. And as a result, the real nature of the moral choices to be made is obscured. In particular, I will claim that the right path to take is neither that recommended by straight boosters nor that favoured by outright knockers. Nor will a

simple trade-off between the advantages and costs of, say, individualism, technology, and bureaucratic management provide the answer. The nature of modern culture is more subtle and complex than this. I want to claim that both boosters and knockers are right, but in a way that can't be done justice to by a simple trade-off between advantages and costs. There is in fact both much that is admirable and much that is debased and frightening in all the developments I have been describing, but to understand the relation between the two is to see that the issue is not how much of a price in bad consequences you have to pay for the positive fruits, but rather how to steer these developments towards their greater promise and avoid the slide into the debased forms.

## Notes

1.  Alexis de Tocqueville, *De la Démocratie en Amérique*, vol. 2 (Paris: Garnier-Flammarion, 1981), 385.
2.  'Erbämliches Behagen'; *Also Sprach Zarathustra*, Zarathustra's Preface, sect. 3.
3.  Tocqueville, *De la Démocratie*, 127.
4.  For the absurdities of these calculations, see R. Bellah et al., *The Good Society* (Berkeley: University of California Press, 1991), 114–19.
5.  Ibid., ch. 4.
6.  See especially Patricia Benner and Judith Wrubel, *The Primacy of Caring: Stress and Coping in Health and Illness* (Menlo Park, Calif.: Addison-Wesley, 1989).
7.  Albert Borgman, *Technology and the Character of Contemporary Life* (Chicago: University of Chicago Press, 1984), 41–2. Borgman even seems to echo Nietzsche's picture of the 'last men' when he argues that the original liberating promise of technology can degenerate into 'the procurement of frivolous comfort' (p. 39).
8.  Hannah Arendt, *The Human Condition* (Garden City, NY: Doubleday, Anchor Edition, 1959), 83.
9.  Tocqueville, *De la Démocratie*, 385.
10. See, for instance, R. Bellah et al., *Habits of the Heart* (Berkeley: University of California Press, 1985).

# Multicultural Citizenship

## Will Kymlicka

Most countries today are culturally diverse. According to recent estimates, the world's 184 independent states contain over 600 living language groups, and 5,000 ethnic groups. In very few countries can the citizens be said to share the same language, or belong to the same ethnonational group.[1]

This diversity gives rise to a series of important and potentially divisive questions. Minorities and majorities increasingly clash over such issues as language rights, regional autonomy, political representation, education curriculum, land claims, immigration and naturalization policy, even national symbols, such as the choice of national anthem or public holidays. Finding morally defensible and politically viable answers to these issues is the greatest challenge facing democracies today. In Eastern Europe and the Third World, attempts to create liberal democratic institutions are being undermined by violent nationalist conflicts. In the West, volatile disputes over the rights of immigrants, indigenous peoples, and other cultural minorities are throwing into question many of the assumptions which have governed political life for decades. Since the end of the Cold War, ethnocultural conflicts have become the most common source of political violence in the world, and they show no sign of abating.[2]

. . . There are no simple answers or magic formulas to resolve all these questions. Some conflicts are intractable, even when the disputants are motivated by a sense of fairness and tolerance, which all too often is lacking. Moreover, every dispute has its own unique history and circumstances that need to be taken into account in devising a fair and workable solution. My aim is to step back and present a more general view of the landscape—to identify some key concepts and principles that need to be taken into account, and so clarify the basic building blocks for a liberal approach to minority rights.

The Western political tradition has been surprisingly silent on these issues. Most organized political communities throughout recorded history have been multiethnic, a testament to the ubiquity of both conquest and long-distance trade in human affairs. Yet most Western political theorists have operated with an idealized model of the polis in which fellow citizens share a common descent, language, and culture. Even when the theorists themselves lived in polyglot empires that governed numerous ethnic and linguistic groups, they have often written as if the culturally homogeneous city-states of Ancient Greece provided the essential or standard model of a political community.[3]

To achieve this ideal of a homogeneous polity, governments throughout history have pursued a variety of policies regarding cultural minorities. Some minorities were physically eliminated, either by mass expulsion (what we now call 'ethnic cleansing') or by genocide. Other minorities were coercively assimilated, forced to adopt the language, religion, and customs of the majority. In yet other cases, minorities were treated as resident aliens, subjected to physical segregation and economic discrimination, and denied political rights.

Various efforts have been made historically to protect cultural minorities, and to regulate the potential conflicts between majority and minority cultures. Early in this century, bilateral treaties regulated the treatment of fellow nationals in

From *Multicultural Citizenship: A Liberal Theory of Minority Rights* (Oxford: Oxford University Press, 1995), 1–6, 76–84, 108–15.

other countries. For example, Germany agreed to accord certain rights and privileges to ethnic Poles residing within its borders, so long as Poland provided reciprocal rights to ethnic Germans in Poland. This treaty system was extended, and given a more multilateral basis, under the League of Nations.

However, these treaties were inadequate. For one thing, a minority was only ensured protection from discrimination and oppression if there was a 'kin state' nearby which took an interest in it. Moreover, the treaties were destabilizing, because where such kin states did exist, they often used treaty provisions as grounds for invading or intervening in weaker countries. Thus Nazi Germany justified its invasion of Poland and Czechoslovakia on the grounds that these countries were violating the treaty rights of ethnic Germans on their soil.

After World War II, it was clear that a different approach to minority rights was needed. Many liberals hoped that the new emphasis on 'human rights' would resolve minority conflicts. Rather than protecting vulnerable groups directly, through special rights for the members of designated groups, cultural minorities would be protected indirectly, by guaranteeing basic civil and political rights to all individuals regardless of group membership. Basic human rights such as freedom of speech, association, and conscience, while attributed to individuals, are typically exercised in community with others, and so provided protection for group life. Where these individual rights are firmly protected, liberals assumed, no further rights needed to be attributed to the members of specific ethnic or national minorities:

> the general tendency of the postwar movements for the promotion of human rights has been to subsume the problem of national minorities under the broader problem of ensuring basic individual rights to all human beings, without reference to membership in ethnic groups. The leading assumption has been that members of national minorities do not need, are not entitled to, or cannot be granted rights of a special character. The doctrine of human rights has been put forward as a substitute for the concept of minority rights, with the strong implication that minorities whose members enjoy individual equality of treatment cannot legitimately demand facilities for the maintenance of their ethnic particularism. (Claude, 1955: 211)

Guided by this philosophy, the United Nations deleted all references to the rights of ethnic and national minorities in its Universal Declaration of Human Rights.

The shift from group-specific minority rights to universal human rights was embraced by many liberals, partly because it seemed a natural extension of the way religious minorities were protected. In the sixteenth century, European states were being torn apart by conflict between Catholics and Protestants over which religion should rule the land. These conflicts were finally resolved, not by granting special rights to particular religious minorities, but by separating church and state, and entrenching each's individual freedom of religion. Religious minorities are protected indirectly, by guaranteeing individual freedom of worship, so that people can freely associate with other co-religionists, without fear of state discrimination or disapproval.

Many postwar liberals have thought that religious tolerance based on the separation of church and state provides a model for dealing with ethnocultural differences as well. On this view, ethnic identity, like religion, is something which people should be free to express in their private life, but which is not the concern of the state. The state does not oppose the freedom of people to express their particular cultural attachments, but nor does it nurture such expression—rather, to adapt Nathan Glazer's phrase, it responds with 'benign neglect' (Glazer, 1975: 25; 1983: 124). The members of ethnic and national groups are protected against discrimination and prejudice, and they are

free to try to maintain whatever part of their ethnic heritage or identity they wish, consistent with
the rights of others. But their efforts are purely
private, and it is not the place of public agencies
to attach legal identities or disabilities to cultural
membership or ethnic identity. This separation of
state and ethnicity precludes any legal or governmental recognition of ethnic groups, or any use of
ethnic criteria in the distribution of rights,
resources, and duties.[4]

Many liberals, particularly on the left, have
made an exception in the case of affirmative
action for disadvantaged racial groups. But in a
sense this is the exception that proves the rule.
Affirmative action is generally defended as a temporary measure which is needed to move more
rapidly towards a 'colour-blind' society. It is
intended to remedy years of discrimination, and
thereby move us closer to the sort of society that
would have existed had we observed the separation of state and ethnicity from the beginning.
Thus the UN Convention on Racial Discrimination
endorses affirmative action programs only where
they have this temporary and remedial character.
Far from abandoning the ideal of the separation of
state and ethnicity, affirmative action is one
method of trying to achieve that ideal.

Some liberals, particularly on the right, think
it is counter-productive to pursue a 'colour-blind'
society through policies that 'count by race'.
Affirmative action, they argue, exacerbates the
very problem it was intended to solve, by making
people more conscious of group differences, and
more resentful of other groups. This dispute
among liberals over the need for remedial affirmative action programs is a familiar one in many liberal democracies.[5]

But what most postwar liberals on both the
right and left continue to reject is the idea of permanent differentiation in the rights or status of the
members of certain groups. In particular, they
reject the claim that group-specific rights are
needed to accommodate enduring cultural differences, rather than remedy historical discrimina-

tion. As we will see in subsequent chapters, postwar liberals around the world have repeatedly
opposed the idea that specific ethnic or national
groups should be given a permanent political
identity or constitutional status.[6]

However, it has become increasingly clear
that minority rights cannot be subsumed under
the category of human rights. Traditional human
rights standards are simply unable to resolve some
of the most important and controversial questions
relating to cultural minorities: which languages
should be recognized in the parliaments, bureaucracies, and courts? Should each ethnic or national group have publicly funded education in its
mother tongue? Should internal boundaries (legislative districts, provinces, states) be drawn so
that cultural minorities form a majority within a
local region? Should governmental powers be
devolved from the central level to more local or
regional levels controlled by particular minorities,
particularly on culturally sensitive issues of immigration, communication, and education? Should
political offices be distributed in accordance with
a principle of national or ethnic proportionality?
Should the traditional homelands of indigenous
peoples be reserved for their benefit, and so protected from encroachment by settlers and resource
developers? What are the responsibilities of
minorities to integrate? What degree of cultural
integration can be required of immigrants and
refugees before they acquire citizenship?

The problem is not that traditional human
rights doctrines give us the wrong answer to these
questions. It is rather that they often give no
answer at all. The right to free speech does not tell
us what an appropriate language policy is; the
right to vote does not tell us how political boundaries should be drawn, or how powers should be
distributed between levels of government; the
right to mobility does not tell us what an appropriate immigration and naturalization policy is.
These questions have been left to the usual
process of majoritarian decision-making within
each state. The result, I will argue, has been to

render cultural minorities vulnerable to significant injustice at the hands of the majority, and to exacerbate ethnocultural conflict.

To resolve these questions fairly, we need to supplement traditional human rights principles with a theory of minority rights. The necessity for such a theory has become painfully clear in Eastern Europe and the former Soviet Union. Disputes over local autonomy, the drawing of boundaries, language rights, and naturalization policy have engulfed much of the region in violent conflict. There is little hope that stable peace will be restored, or that basic human rights will be respected, until these minority rights issues are resolved.

It is not surprising, therefore, that minority rights have returned to prominence in international relations. For example, the Conference on Security and Co-operation in Europe (CSCE) adopted a declaration on the Rights of National Minorities in 1991, and established a High Commissioner on National Minorities in 1993. The United Nations has been debating both a Declaration on the Rights of Persons Belonging to National or Ethnic, Religious and Linguistic Minorities (1993), and a Draft Universal Declaration on Indigenous Rights (1988). The Council of Europe adopted a declaration on minority language rights in 1992 (the European Charter for Regional or Minority Languages). Other examples could be given.[7]

However, these declarations remain controversial. Some were adopted hastily, to help prevent the escalation of conflict in Eastern Europe. As a result, they are quite vague, and often seem motivated more by the need to appease belligerent minorities than by any clear sense of what justice requires. Both the underlying justification for these rights, and their limits, remain unclear.

I believe it is legitimate, and indeed unavoidable, to supplement traditional human rights with minority rights. A comprehensive theory of justice in a multicultural state will include both universal rights, assigned to individuals regardless of group membership, and certain group-differentiated rights or 'special status' for minority cultures.

Recognizing minority rights has obvious dangers. The language of minority rights has been used and abused not only by the Nazis, but also by apologists for racial segregation and apartheid. It has also been used by intolerant and belligerent nationalists and fundamentalists throughout the world to justify the domination of people outside their group, and the suppression of dissenters within the group. A liberal theory of minority rights, therefore, must explain how minority rights are limited by principles of individual liberty, democracy, and social justice. . . .

## Defining Cultures

. . . [T]he term 'culture' has been used to cover all manner of groups, from teenage gangs to global civilizations. The sort of culture that I will focus on, however, is a *societal* culture—that is, a culture which provides its members with meaningful ways of life across the full range of human activities, including social, educational, religious, recreational, and economic life, encompassing both public and private spheres. These cultures tend to be territorially concentrated, and based on a shared language.[8]

I have called these 'societal cultures' to emphasize that they involve not just shared memories or values, but also common institutions and practices. Ronald Dworkin has said that the members of a culture have 'a shared vocabulary of tradition and convention' (Dworkin, 1985: 231). But that gives us an abstract or ethereal picture of cultures. In the case of societal culture, this shared vocabulary is the everyday vocabulary of social life, embodied in practices covering most areas of human activity. And in the modern world, for a culture to be embodied in social life means that it must be institutionally embodied—in schools, media, economy, government, etc.

Such 'societal cultures' did not always exist, and their creation is intimately linked with the process of modernization (Gellner, 1983). Modernization involves the diffusion throughout a society of a common culture, including a standardized language, embodied in common economic, political, and educational institutions. This occurs for a variety of reasons. It is a functional requirement of a modern economy, with its need for a mobile, educated, and literate workforce. Second, it reflects the need for a high level of solidarity within modern democratic states. The sort of solidarity essential for a welfare state requires that citizens have a strong sense of common identity and common membership, so that they will make sacrifices for each other, and this common identity is assumed to require (or at least be facilitated by) a common language and history. Third, the diffusion of a common culture seems required by the modern commitment to equality of opportunity. The provision of standardized public education throughout a society, for example, has been seen as essential to ensure equality of opportunity for people from different classes, races, and regions of the society.

Most contemporary liberals write as if this process of building a common culture extends through the entire country, so that there is just one such culture in each country. For example, Dworkin suggests that the United States contains a single 'cultural structure' based on a 'shared language' (Dworkin, 1985: 232–3; 1989: 488).

The claim that all Americans share a common culture based on the English language is clearly false. Yet there is a kernel of truth in it. The United States has integrated an extraordinary number of people from very different backgrounds into a common culture. The vast majority of Americans do in fact participate in the same societal culture, based on the English language. At other times and places, differences in ethnicity, race, region, class, gender, and religion were often assumed to preclude the possibility of a common culture. But in the United States and other modern societies, the common culture is capacious, integrating a rich array of groups.

If there is not a single culture in the United States, there is a dominant culture that incorporates most Americans, and those who fall outside it belong to a relatively small number of minority cultures. To understand the impressive integrative power of this common culture, but also its limits, it is worth examining how immigrants and national minorities relate to the dominant American culture.

When immigrants come to the United States, they bring their language and historical narratives with them. But they have left behind the set of institutionalized practices, conducted in their mother tongue, which actually provided culturally significant ways of life to people in their original homeland. They bring with them a 'shared vocabulary of tradition and convention', but they have uprooted themselves from the social practices which this vocabulary originally referred to and made sense of.

Some immigrants might hope to re-create these practices in their entirety in their new country. But that is effectively impossible without significant government support, which is rarely if ever provided. On the contrary, . . . immigration policy in the United States is intended to integrate immigrants within the existing English-speaking culture. Immigrants come as individuals or families, rather than entire communities, and settle throughout the country, rather than forming 'homelands'. They are expected to learn the English language and American history, and to speak English in public life—e.g., at school, work, and when interacting with governments and other public agencies. . . .

Immigrants are no longer expected to assimilate entirely to the norms and customs of the dominant culture, and indeed are encouraged to maintain some aspects of their ethnic particularity. But this commitment to 'multiculturalism' or 'polyethnicity' is a shift in *how* immigrants integrate into the dominant culture, not whether they integrate. The rejection of 'Anglo-conformity' primarily has involved affirming the right of immigrants to maintain their ethnic heritage in the private sphere—at home, and in voluntary associations. To a lesser extent, it also involved reforming the public institutions of the dominant culture so as to provide some recognition or accommodation of their heritage. But it has not involved the establishment of distinct and institutionally complete societal cultures alongside the Anglophone society. (By 'institutionally complete', I mean containing a full range of social, educational, economic, and political institutions, encompassing both public and private life.)

Under these conditions, the immigrants' mother tongue is often spoken at home, and passed on to the children, but by the third generation English has become the mother tongue, and the original language is increasingly lost. This process is speeded up, of course, by the fact that public schooling is only provided in English. In fact, it is very difficult for languages to survive in modern industrialized societies unless they are used in public life. Given the spread of standardized education, the high demands for literacy in work, and widespread interaction with government agencies, any language which is not a public language becomes so marginalized that it is likely to survive only amongst a small élite, or in a ritualized form, not as a living and developing language underlying a flourishing culture.[9]

So while there are many aspects of their heritage that immigrants will maintain and cherish, this will take the form not of re-creating a separate societal culture, but rather of contributing new options and perspectives to the larger Anglophone culture, making it richer and more diverse. For the third generation, if not sooner, learning the original mother tongue is not unlike learning a foreign language. Learning the old language may be rewarding as a hobby or business skill, but for the children of immigrants, it is the Anglophone culture which defines their options, not the culture from which their parents uprooted themselves.[10]

The situation of national minorities in the United States—i.e., groups whose homeland has been incorporated through conquest, colonization, or federation—is very different. At the time of their incorporation, each group constituted an ongoing societal culture, separate from the Anglophone culture. They did not have to re-create their culture in a new land, since their language and historical narratives were already embodied in a full set of social practices and institutions, encompassing all aspects of social life. These practices and institutions defined the range of socially meaningful options for their members.

These groups have fought to retain their existence as distinct societal cultures, although not all have been accorded the language and self-government rights necessary to do so. Indeed, some groups have faced enormous pressure to assimilate. In the case of many Indian tribes, for example, there have been prohibitions on the use of their mother tongue, and attempts to break open their lands for settlement so that they have become minorities in their historical homelands. Yet they have persisted, and their status as self-governing 'domestic dependent nations' is now more firmly recognized. The determination they have shown in maintaining their existence as distinct cultures, despite these enormous economic and political pressures, shows the value they attach to retaining their cultural membership.

So the typical situation of immigrant groups and national minorities is very different. Of course, I have over-simplified the contrast. The extent to which immigrant groups have been allowed or encouraged to integrate varies considerably, as does the extent to which national minorities have been able to maintain a separate culture. . . .

But, as a general rule, both in the United States and in other Western democracies, dominant cultures have had far less success accommodating national groups than ethnic groups. In multination states, national minorities have resisted integration into the common culture, and instead sought to protect their separate existence by consolidating their own societal cultures.

American Indian tribes and Puerto Ricans, like the Aboriginal peoples and Québécois in Canada, are not just subgroups within a common culture, but genuinely distinct societal cultures.

In short, for a culture to survive and develop in the modern world, given the pressures towards the creation of a single common culture in each country, it must be a societal culture.[11] Given the enormous significance of social institutions in our lives, and in determining our options, any culture which is not a societal culture will be reduced to ever-decreasing marginalization. The capacity and motivation to form and maintain such a distinct culture is characteristic of 'nations' or 'peoples' (i.e., culturally distinct, geographically concentrated, and institutionally complete societies). Societal cultures, then, tend to be national cultures.

This connection is confirmed from another direction, by studies of nationalism. Most analysts of nationalism have concluded that the defining feature of nations is that they are 'pervasive cultures', 'encompassing cultures', or 'organizational cultures' (e.g., A. Smith, 1986: 2; Margalit and Raz, 1990: 444; Tamir, 1993; Poole, 1993). In short, just as societal cultures are almost invariably national cultures, so nations are almost invariably societal cultures.

## Liberalism and Individual Freedom

I believe that societal cultures are important to people's freedom, and that liberals should therefore take an interest in the viability of societal cultures. To show this, however, I need briefly to consider the nature of freedom, as it is conceived within the liberal tradition.[12]

The defining feature of liberalism is that it ascribes certain fundamental freedoms to each individual. In particular, it grants people a very wide freedom of choice in terms of how they lead their lives. It allows people to choose a conception of the good life, and then allows them to reconsider that decision, and adopt a new and hopefully better plan of life.

Why should people be free to choose their own plan of life? After all, we know that some people will make imprudent decisions, wasting their time on hopeless or trivial pursuits. Why then should the government not intervene to protect us from making mistakes, and to compel us to lead the truly good life? There are a variety of reasons why this is not a good idea: governments may not be trustworthy; some individuals have idiosyncratic needs which are difficult for even a well-intentioned government to take into account; supporting controversial conceptions of the good may lead to civil strife. Moreover, paternalistic restrictions on liberty often simply do not work—lives do not go better by being led from the outside, in accordance with values the person does not endorse. Dworkin calls this the 'endorsement constraint', and argues that 'no component contributes to the value of a life without endorsement . . . it is implausible to think that someone can lead a better life against the grain of his profound ethical convictions than at peace with them' (Dworkin, 1989: 486).[13]

However, the fact that we can get it wrong is important, because (paradoxically) it provides another argument for liberty. Since we can be wrong about the worth or value of what we are currently doing, and since no one wants to lead a life based on false beliefs about its worth, it is of fundamental importance that we be able rationally to assess our conceptions of the good in the light of new information or experiences, and to revise them if they are not worthy of our continued allegiance.[14]

This assumption that our beliefs about the good life are fallible and revisable is widely endorsed in the liberal tradition—from John Stuart Mill to the most prominent contemporary American liberals, such as John Rawls and Ronald Dworkin. (Because of their prominence, I will rely heavily on the works of Rawls and Dworkin in the rest of this chapter.) As Rawls puts it, individuals 'do not view themselves as inevitably tied to the pursuit of the particular conception of the good and its final ends which they espouse at any given time'. Instead, they are 'capable of revising and changing this conception'. They can 'stand back' from their current ends to 'survey and assess' their worthiness (Rawls, 1980: 544; cf. Mill, 1982: 122; Dworkin, 1983).

So we have two preconditions for leading a good life. The first is that we lead our life from the inside, in accordance with our beliefs about what gives value to life. Individuals must therefore have the resources and liberties needed to lead their lives in accordance with their beliefs about value, without fear of discrimination or punishment. Hence the traditional liberal concern with individual privacy, and opposition to 'the enforcement of morals'. The second precondition is that we be free to question those beliefs, to examine them in light of whatever information, examples, and arguments our culture can provide. Individuals must therefore have the conditions necessary to acquire an awareness of different views about the good life, and an ability to examine those views intelligently. Hence the equally traditional liberal concern for education, and freedom of expression and association. These liberties enable us to judge what is valuable, and to learn about other ways of life.

It is important to stress that a liberal society is concerned with both of these preconditions, the second as much as the first. It is all too easy to reduce individual liberty to the freedom to pursue one's conception of the good. But in fact much of what is distinctive to a liberal state concerns the forming and revising of people's conceptions of the good, rather than the pursuit of those conceptions once chosen.

Consider the case of religion. A liberal society not only allows individuals the freedom to pursue their existing faith, but it also allows them to seek new adherents for their faith (proselytization is allowed), or to question the doctrine of their church (heresy is allowed), or to renounce their faith entirely and convert to another faith or to atheism (apostasy is allowed). It is quite conceivable to have the freedom to pursue one's current

faith without having any of these latter freedoms. There are many examples of this within the Islamic world. Islam has a long tradition of tolerating other monotheistic religions, so that Christians and Jews can worship in peace. But proselytization, heresy, and apostasy are generally prohibited. This was true, for example, of the 'millet system' of the Ottoman Empire . . . . Indeed, some Islamic states have said the freedom of conscience guaranteed in the Universal Declaration of Human Rights should not include the freedom to change religion (Lerner, 1991: 79–80). Similarly, the clause in the Egyptian constitution guaranteeing freedom of conscience has been interpreted so as to exclude freedom of apostasy (Peters and de Vries, 1976: 23). In such a system, freedom of conscience means there is no forced conversion, but nor is there voluntary conversion. A liberal society, by contrast, not only allows people to pursue their current way of life, but also gives them access to information about other ways of life (through freedom of expression), and indeed requires children to learn about other ways of life (through mandatory education), and makes it possible for people to engage in radical revision of their ends (including apostasy) without legal penalty. These aspects of a liberal society only make sense on the assumption that revising one's ends is possible, and sometimes desirable, because one's current ends are not always worthy of allegiance. A liberal society does not compel such questioning and revision, but it does make it a genuine possibility.

## Societal Cultures as Context of Choice

I have just outlined what I take to be the predominant liberal conception of individual freedom. But how does this relate to membership in societal cultures? Put simply, freedom involves making choices amongst various options, and our societal culture not only provides these options, but also makes them meaningful to us.

People make choices about the social practices around them, based on their beliefs about the value of these practices (beliefs which, I have noted, may be wrong). And to have a belief about the value of a practice is, in the first instance, a matter of understanding the meanings attached to it by our culture.

I noted earlier that societal cultures involve 'a shared vocabulary of tradition and convention' which underlies a full range of social practices and institutions (Dworkin, 1985: 231). To understand the meaning of a social practice, therefore, requires understanding this 'shared vocabulary'— that is, understanding the language and history which constitute that vocabulary. Whether or not a course of action has any significance for us depends on whether, and how, our language renders vivid to us the point of that activity. And the way in which language renders vivid these activities is shaped by our history, our 'traditions and conventions'. Understanding these cultural narratives is a precondition of making intelligent judgements about how to lead our lives. In this sense, our culture not only provides options, it also 'provides the spectacles through which we identify experiences as valuable' (Dworkin, 1985: 228).[15]

What follows from this? According to Dworkin, we must protect our societal culture from 'structural debasement or decay' (1985: 230).[16] The survival of a culture is not guaranteed, and, where it is threatened with debasement or decay, we must act to protect it. Cultures are valuable, not in and of themselves, but because it is only through having access to a societal culture that people have access to a range of meaningful options. Dworkin concludes his discussion by saying, 'We inherited a cultural structure, and we have some duty, out of simple justice, to leave that structure at least as rich as we found it' (1985: 232–3).

In this passage and elsewhere, Dworkin talks about 'cultural structures'. This is a potentially misleading term, since it suggests an overly formal and rigid picture of what (as I discuss below) is a very diffuse and open-ended phenomenon.

Cultures do not have fixed centres or precise boundaries. But his main point is, I think, sound enough. The availability of meaningful options depends on access to a societal culture, and on understanding the history and language of that culture—its 'shared vocabulary of tradition and convention' (Dworkin, 1985: 228, 231).[17]

This argument about the connection between individual choice and culture provides the first step towards a distinctively liberal defence of certain group-differentiated rights. For meaningful individual choice to be possible, individuals need not only access to information, the capacity to reflectively evaluate it, and freedom of expression and association. They also need access to a societal culture. Group-differentiated measures that secure and promote this access may, therefore, have a legitimate role to play in a liberal theory of justice.[18]

Of course, many details remain to be filled in, and many objections need to be answered. In particular, this connection between individual choice and societal cultures raises three obvious questions: (1) is individual choice tied to membership in one's own culture, or is it sufficient for people to have access to some other culture? (2) if (as I will argue) people have a deep bond to their own culture, should immigrant groups be given the rights and resources necessary to re-create their own societal cultures? and (3) what if a culture is organized so as to preclude individual choice—for example, if it assigns people a specific role or way of life, and prohibits any questioning or revising of that role? I will start answering these questions in the rest of the chapter, although a full answer will only emerge in later chapters. . . .

## The Equality Argument

Many defenders of group-specific rights for ethnic and national minorities insist that they are needed to ensure that all citizens are treated with genuine equality. On this view, 'the accommodation of differences is the essence of true equality',[19] and group-specific rights are needed to accommodate our differences. I think this argument is correct, within certain limits.

Proponents of 'benign neglect' will respond that individual rights already allow for the accommodation of differences, and that true equality requires equal rights for each individual regardless of race or ethnicity.[20] . . . this assumption that liberal equality precludes group-specific rights is relatively recent, and arose in part as an (over-) generalization of the racial desegregation movement in the United States. It has some superficial plausibility. In many cases, claims for group-specific rights are simply an attempt by one group to dominate and oppress another.

But some minority rights eliminate, rather than create, inequalities. Some groups are unfairly disadvantaged in the cultural marketplace, and political recognition and support rectify this disadvantage. I will start with the case of national minorities. The viability of their societal cultures may be undermined by economic and political decisions made by the majority. They could be outbid or outvoted on resources and policies that are crucial to the survival of their societal culture. The members of majority cultures do not face this problem. Given the importance of cultural membership, this is a significant inequality which, if not addressed, becomes a serious injustice.

Group-differentiated rights—such as territorial autonomy, veto powers, guaranteed representation in central institutions, land claims, and language rights—can help rectify this disadvantage, by alleviating the vulnerability of minority cultures to majority decisions. These external protections ensure that members of the minority have the same opportunity to live and work in their own culture as members of the majority.

. . . [T]hese rights may impose restrictions on the members of the larger society, by making it more costly for them to move into the territory of the minority (e.g., longer residency requirements, fewer government services in their language), or by giving minority members priority in the use of certain land and resources (e.g., indigenous hunting and fishing rights). But the sacrifice required of non-members by the existence of these rights is far less than the sacrifice members would face in the absence of such rights.

Where these rights are recognized, members of the majority who choose to enter the minority's homeland may have to forgo certain benefits they are accustomed to. This is a burden. But without such rights, the members of many minority cultures face the loss of their culture, a loss which we cannot reasonably ask people to accept.

Any plausible theory of justice should recognize the fairness of these external protections for national minorities. They are clearly justified, I believe, within a liberal egalitarian theory, such as Rawls's and Dworkin's, which emphasizes the importance of rectifying unchosen inequalities. Indeed inequalities in cultural membership are just the sort which Rawls says we should be concerned about, since their effects are 'profound and pervasive and present from birth' (Rawls, 1971: 96; cf. Dworkin, 1981).[21]

This equality-based argument will only endorse special rights for national minorities if there actually is a disadvantage with respect to cultural membership, and if the rights actually serve to rectify the disadvantage. Hence the legitimate scope of these rights will vary with the circumstances. In North America, indigenous groups are more vulnerable to majority decisions than the Québécois or Puerto Ricans, and so their external protections will be more extensive. For example, restrictions on the sale of land which are necessary in the context of indigenous peoples are not necessary, and hence not justified, in the case of Quebec or Puerto Rico.[22]

At some point, demands for increased powers or resources will not be necessary to ensure the same opportunity to live and work in one's culture. Instead, they will simply be attempts to gain benefits denied to others, to have more resources to pursue one's way of life than others have. This was clearly the case with apartheid, where whites constituting under 20 per cent of the population controlled 87 per cent of the land mass of the country, and monopolized all the important levers of state power.

One could imagine a point where the amount of land reserved for indigenous peoples would not be necessary to provide reasonable external protections, but rather would simply provide unequal opportunities to them. Justice would then require that the holdings of indigenous peoples be subject to the same redistributive taxation as the wealth of other advantaged groups, so as to assist the less well off in society. In the real world, of course, most indigenous peoples are struggling to maintain the bare minimum of land needed to sustain the viability of their communities. But it is possible that their land holdings could exceed what justice allows.[23]

The legitimacy of certain measures may also depend on their timing. For example, many people have suggested that a new South African constitution should grant a veto power over certain important decisions to some or all of the major national groups. This sort of veto power is a familiar feature of various 'consociational democracies' in Europe, and . . . under certain circumstances it can promote justice. But it would probably be unjust to give privileged groups a veto power before there has been a dramatic redistribution of wealth and opportunities (Adam, 1979: 295). A veto power can promote justice if it helps protect a minority from unjust policies that favour the majority; but it is an obstacle to justice if it allows a privileged group the leverage to maintain its unjust advantages.

So the ideal of 'benign neglect' is not in fact benign. It ignores the fact that the members of a national minority face a disadvantage which the members of the majority do not face. In any event, the idea that the government could be neutral with respect to ethnic and national groups is patently false. . . . one of the most important determinants of whether a culture survives is whether its language is the language of government—i.e.,

the language of public schooling, courts, legislatures, welfare agencies, health services, etc. When the government decides the language of public schooling, it is providing what is probably the most important form of support needed by societal cultures, since it guarantees the passing on of the language and its associated traditions and conventions to the next generation. Refusing to provide public schooling in a minority language, by contrast, is almost inevitably condemning that language to ever-increasing marginalization.

The government therefore cannot avoid deciding which societal cultures will be supported. And if it supports the majority culture, by using the majority's language in schools and public agencies, it cannot refuse official recognition to minority languages on the ground that this violates 'the separation of state and ethnicity'. This shows that the analogy between religion and culture is mistaken. As I noted earlier, many liberals say that just as the state should not recognize, endorse, or support any particular church, so it should not recognize, endorse, or support any particular cultural group or identity. . . . But the analogy does not work. It is quite possible for a state not to have an established church. But the state cannot help but give at least partial establishment to a culture when it decides which language is to be used in public schooling, or in the provision of state services. The state can (and should) replace religious oaths in courts with secular oaths, but it cannot replace the use of English in courts with no language.

This is a significant embarrassment for the 'benign neglect' view, and it is remarkable how rarely language rights are discussed in contemporary liberal theory.[24] As Brian Weinstein put it, political theorists have had a lot to say about 'the language of politics'—that is, the symbols, metaphors, and rhetorical devices of political discourse—but have had virtually nothing to say about 'the politics of language'—that is, the decisions about which languages to use in political, legal, and educational forums (Weinstein, 1983:

7–13). Yet language rights are a fundamental cause of political conflict, even violence, throughout the world, including Canada, Belgium, Spain, Sri Lanka, the Baltics, Bulgaria, Turkey, and many other countries (Horowitz, 1985: 219–24).

One could argue that decisions about the language of schooling and public services should be determined, not by officially recognizing the existence of various groups, but simply by allowing each political subunit to make its own language policy on a democratic basis. If a national minority forms a majority in the relevant unit, they can decide to have their mother tongue adopted as an official language in that unit. But this is because they are a local majority, not because the state has officially recognized them as a 'nation'.

This is sometimes said to be the American approach to language rights, since there is no constitutional definition of language rights in the United States. But in fact the American government has historically tried to make sure that such 'local' decisions are always made by political units that have an Anglophone majority. . . . decisions about state borders, or about when to admit territories as states, have been explicitly made with the aim of ensuring that there will be an Anglophone majority. States in the American Southwest and Hawaii were only offered statehood when the national minorities residing in those areas were outnumbered by settlers and immigrants. And some people oppose offering statehood to Puerto Rico precisely on the grounds that it will never have an Anglophone majority (Rubinstein, 1991; Glazer, 1983: 280).

This illustrates a more general point. Leaving decisions about language to political subunits just pushes back the problem. What are the relevant political units—what level of government should make these decisions? Should each neighbourhood be able to decide on the language of public schooling and public services in that neighbourhood? Or should this decision be left to larger units, such as cities or provinces? And how do we decide on the boundaries of these subunits? If we draw municipal or provincial boundaries in one way, then a national minority will not form even a local majority. But if we draw the boundaries another way, then the national minority will form a local majority. In a multination state, decisions on boundaries and the division of powers are inevitably decisions about which national group will have the ability to use which state powers to sustain its culture.[25]

For example, . . . the Inuit in Canada wish to divide the Northwest Territories in two, so that they will form the majority in the eastern half. This is seen as essential to the implementation of their right of self-government. Some liberals object that this proposal violates the separation of state and ethnicity by distributing public benefits and state powers so as to make it easier for a specific group to preserve its culture. But all decisions regarding boundaries and the distribution of powers in multination states have this effect. We can draw boundaries and distribute legislative powers so that a national minority has an increased ability within a particular region to protect its societal culture, or we can draw boundaries and distribute legislative powers so that the majority nation controls decisions regarding language, education, immigration, etc. on a country-wide basis.

The whole idea of 'benign neglect' is incoherent, and reflects a shallow understanding of the relationship between states and nations. In the areas of official languages, political boundaries, and the division of powers, there is no way to avoid supporting this or that societal culture, or deciding which groups will form a majority in political units that control culture-affecting decisions regarding language, education, and immigration.

So the real question is, what is a fair way to recognize languages, draw boundaries, and distribute powers? And the answer, I think, is that we should aim at ensuring that all national groups have the opportunity to maintain themselves as a distinct culture, if they so choose. This ensures that the good of cultural membership is equally protected for the members of all national groups. In a democratic society, the majority nation will always have its language and societal culture supported, and will have the legislative power to protect its interests in culture-affecting decisions. The question is whether fairness requires that the same benefits and opportunities should be given to national minorities. The answer, I think, is clearly yes.

Hence group-differentiated self-government rights compensate for unequal circumstances which put the members of minority cultures at a systemic disadvantage in the cultural marketplace, regardless of their personal choices in life. This is one of many areas in which true equality requires not identical treatment, but rather differential treatment in order to accommodate differential needs.[26]

This does not mean that we should entirely reject the idea of the cultural marketplace. Once the societal cultures of national groups are protected, through language rights and territorial autonomy, then the cultural marketplace does have an important role to play in determining the character of the culture. Decisions about which particular aspects of one's culture are worth maintaining and developing should be left to the choices of individual members. For the state to intervene at this point to support particular options or customs within the culture, while penalizing or discouraging others, would run the risk of unfairly subsidizing some people's choices (Kymlicka, 1989b). But that is not the aim or effect of many rights for national minorities, which are instead concerned with external protections . . . .

Let me now turn to polyethnic rights for ethnic groups. I believe there is an equality-based argument for these rights as well, which also invokes the impossibility of separating state from ethnicity, but in a different way. I argued [earlier] that the context of choice for immigrants, unlike national minorities, primarily involves equal access to the mainstream culture(s). Having uprooted themselves from their old culture, they are expected to become members of the national societies which already exist in their new country. Hence promoting the good of cultural membership for immigrants is primarily a matter of enabling integration, by providing language training and fighting patterns of discrimination and prejudice. Generally speaking, this is more a matter of rigorously enforcing the common rights of citizenship than providing group-differentiated rights. In so far as common rights of citizenship in fact create equal access to mainstream culture, then equality with respect to cultural membership is achieved.

But even here equality does justify some group-specific rights. Consider the case of public holidays. Some people object to legislation that exempts Jews and Muslims from Sunday closing legislation on the ground that this violates the separation of state and ethnicity. But almost any decision on public holidays will do so. In the major immigration countries, public holidays currently reflect the needs of Christians. Hence government offices are closed on Sunday, and on the major religious holidays (Easter, Christmas). This need not be seen as a deliberate decision to promote Christianity and discriminate against other faiths (although this was undoubtedly part of the original motivation). Decisions about government holidays were made when there was far less religious diversity, and people just took it for granted that the government work-week should accommodate Christian beliefs about days of rest and religious celebration.

But these decisions can be a significant disadvantage to the members of other religious faiths. And having established a work-week that favours Christians, one can hardly object to exemptions for Muslims or Jews on the ground that they violate the separation of state and ethnicity. These groups are simply asking that their religious needs be taken into consideration in the same way that the needs of Christians have always been taken into account. Public holidays are another significant embarrassment for the 'benign neglect' view, and it is interesting to note how rarely they are discussed in contemporary liberal theory.

Similar issues arise regarding government uniforms. Some people object to the idea that Sikhs or Orthodox Jews should be exempted from requirements regarding headgear in the police or military. But here again it is important to recognize how the existing rules about government uniforms have been adopted to suit Christians. For example, existing dress-codes do not prohibit the wearing of wedding rings, which are an important religious symbol for many Christians (and Jews). And it is virtually inconceivable that designers of government dress-codes would have ever considered designing a uniform that prevented people from wearing wedding rings, unless this was strictly necessary for the job. Again, this should not be seen as a deliberate attempt to promote Christianity. It simply would have been taken for granted that uniforms should not unnecessarily conflict with Christian religious beliefs. Having adopted dress-codes that meet Christian needs, one can hardly object to exemptions for Sikhs and Orthodox Jews on the ground that they violate 'benign neglect'.

One can multiply the examples. For example, many state symbols such as flags, anthems, and mottoes reflect a particular ethnic or religious background ('In God We Trust'). The demand by ethnic groups for some symbolic affirmation of the value of polyethnicity (e.g., in government declarations and documents) is simply a demand that their identity be given the same recognition as the original Anglo-Saxon settlers.

It may be possible to avoid some of these issues by redesigning public holidays, uniforms, and state symbols. It is relatively easy to replace religious oaths with secular ones, and so we should. It would be more difficult, but perhaps not impossible, to replace existing public holidays and work-weeks with more 'neutral' schedules for schools and government offices.[27]

But there is no way to have a complete 'separation of state and ethnicity'. In various ways, the ideal of 'benign neglect' is a myth. Government decisions on languages, internal boundaries, public holidays, and state symbols unavoidably involve recognizing, accommodating, and supporting the needs and identities of particular ethnic and national groups. Nor is there any reason to regret this fact. There is no reason to regret the existence of official languages and public holidays, and no one gains by creating unnecessary conflicts between government regulations and religious beliefs. The only question is how to ensure that these unavoidable forms of support for particular ethnic and national groups are provided fairly—that is, how to ensure that they do not privilege some groups and disadvantage others. In so far as existing policies support the language, culture, and identity of dominant nations and ethnic groups, there is an argument of equality for ensuring that some attempts are made to provide similar support for minority groups, through self-government and polyethnic rights.

## References

Adam, Heribert. 1979. 'The Failure of Political Liberalism', in H. Adam and H. Giliomee, eds, *Ethnic Power Mobilized: Can South Africa Change?* New Haven: Yale University Press: 258–85.

Ajzenstat, Janet. 1984. 'Liberalism and Assimilation: Lord Durham Revisited', in S. Brooks, ed., *Political Thought in Canada: Contemporary Perspectives.* Toronto: Irwin: 239–57.

_____. 1988. *The Political Thought of Lord Durham.* Montreal and Kingston: McGill-Queen's University Press.

Asch, Michael. 1984. *Home and Native Land: Aboriginal Rights and the Canadian Constitution.* Toronto: Methuen.

Barsh, Russel, and J. Henderson. 1980. *The Road: Indian Tribes and Political Liberty.* Berkeley: University of California Press.

_____. 1982. 'Aboriginal Rights, Treaty Rights and Human Rights: Indian Tribes and Constitutional Renewal', *Journal of Canadian Studies* 17: 55–81.

Bloed, Arie. 1994. 'The CSCE and the Protection of National Minorities', *CSCE ODHIR Bulletin* 1, 3: 1–4.

Brilmayer, Lea. 1992. 'Groups, Histories, and International Law', *Cornell International Law Journal* 25, 3: 555–63.

Brotz, H. 1980. 'Multiculturalism in Canada: A Muddle', *Canadian Public Policy* 6, 1: 41–6.

Buchanan, Allen. 1975. 'Revisability and Rational Choice', *Canadian Journal of Philosophy* 5: 395–408.

Caney, Simon. 1991. 'Consequentialist Defenses of Liberal Neutrality', *Philosophical Quarterly* 41, 165: 457–77.

Capotorti, F. 1979. *Study on the Rights of Persons Belonging to Ethnic, Religious and Linguistic Minorities*. UN Doc. E/CN.4/Sub.2/384 Rev. 1. New York: United Nations.

Castles, Stephen, and Mark Miller. 1993. *The Age of Migration: International Population Movements in the Modern Age*. Basingstoke: Macmillan.

Clarke, F. 1934. *Quebec and South Africa: A Study in Cultural Adjustment*. London: Oxford University Press.

Claude, Inis. 1955. *National Minorities: An International Problem*. Cambridge, Mass.: Harvard University Press.

Clinton, Robert. 1990. 'The Rights of Indigenous Peoples as Collective Group Rights', *Arizona Law Review* 32, 4: 739–47.

Copp, David. 1992. 'The Concept of a Society', *Dialogue* 31, 2: 183–212.

Crowe, Keith. 1974. *A History of the Original Peoples of Northern Canada*. Montreal and Kingston: McGill-Queen's University Press.

Deganaar, J. 1987. 'Nationalism, Liberalism, and Pluralism', in J. Butler, ed., *Democratic Liberalism in South Africa: Its History and Prospect*. Middletown, Conn.: Wesleyan University Press: 236–398.

Dworkin, Ronald. 1981. 'What is Equality? Part II: Equality of Resources', *Philosophy and Public Affairs* 10, 4: 283–345.

_____. 1983. 'In Defense of Equality', *Social Philosophy and Policy* 1, 1: 24–40.

_____. 1985. *A Matter of Principle*. London: Harvard University Press.

_____. 1989. 'Liberal Community', *California Law Review* 77, 3: 479–504.

_____. 1990. 'Foundations of Liberal Equality', in Grethe Petersen, ed., *The Tanner Lectures on Human Values, 11*. Salt Lake City: University of Utah Press: 1–119.

Edwards, John. 1985. *Language, Society and Identity*. Oxford: Basil Blackwell.

Gellner, Ernest. 1983. *Nations and Nationalism*. Oxford: Basil Blackwell.

Glazer, Nathan. 1975. *Affirmative Discrimination: Ethnic Inequality and Public Policy*. New York: Basic Books.

_____. 1978. 'Individual Rights against Group Rights', in A. Tay and E. Kamenka, eds, *Human Rights*. London: Edward Arnold: 87–103.

_____. 1983. *Ethnic Dilemmas: 1964–1982*. Cambridge, Mass.: Harvard University Press.

Gordon, Milton. 1975. 'Toward a General Theory of Racial and Ethnic Group Relations', in N. Glazer and D. Moynihan, eds, *Ethnicity, Theory and Experience*. Cambridge, Mass.: Harvard University Press.

_____. 1978. *Human Nature, Class, and Ethnicity*. New York: Oxford University Press.

_____. 1981. 'Models of Pluralism: The New American Dilemma', *Annals of the Academy of Political and Social Science* 454: 178–88.

Government of Canada. 1991. *Shared Values: The Canadian Identity*. Ottawa: Supply and Services.

Gurr, Ted. 1993. *Minorities at Risk: A Global View of Ethnopolitical Conflict*. Washington: Institute of Peace Press.

Hannum, Hurst. 1990. *Autonomy, Sovereignty, and Self-Determination: The Adjudication of Conflicting Rights*. Philadelphia: University of Pennsylvania Press.

_____, ed. 1993. *Basic Documents on Autonomy and Minority Rights*. Boston: Martinus Nijhoff.

Hindess, Barry. 1993. 'Multiculturalism and Citizenship', in Chandran Kukathas, ed., *Multicultural Citizens: The Philosophy and Politics of Identity*. St Leonards: Centre for Independent Studies: 33–45.

Horowitz, D.L. 1985. *Ethnic Groups in Conflict*. Berkeley: University of California Press.

Hurka, Thomas. 1994. 'Indirect Perfectionism: Kymlicka on Liberal Neutrality', *Journal of Political Philosophy* (forthcoming).

Johnson, Gerald. 1973. *Our English Heritage*. Westport, Conn.: Greenwood Press.

Knopff, Rainer. 1979. 'Language and Culture in the Canadian Debate: The Battle of the White Papers', *Canadian Review of Studies in Nationalism* 6, 1: 66–82.

_____. 1982. 'Liberal Democracy and the Challenge of Nationalism in Canadian Politics', *Canadian Review of Studies in Nationalism* 9, 1: 23–39.

Kukathas, Chandran. 1991. *The Fraternal Conceit: Individualist versus Collectivist Ideas of Community.* St Leonards: Centre for Independent Studies.

_____. 1992. 'Are There any Cultural Rights?', *Political Theory* 20, 1: 105–39.

Kymlicka, Will. 1989a. *Liberalism, Community, and Culture.* Oxford: Oxford University Press.

_____. 1989b. 'Liberal Individualism and Liberal Neutrality', *Ethics* 99, 4: 883–905.

_____. 1991. 'Liberalism and the Politicization of Ethnicity', *Canadian Journal of Law and Jurisprudence* 4, 2: 239–56.

_____. 1995a. 'Dworkin on Freedom and Culture', in Justine Burley, ed., *Reading Dworkin.* Oxford: Basil Blackwell (forthcoming).

_____. 1995b. 'Concepts of Community and Social Justice', in Fen Hampson and Judith Reppy, eds, *Global Environmental Change and Social Justice* (forthcoming).

Laczko, Leslie. 1994. 'Canada's Pluralism in Comparative Perspective', *Ethnic and Racial Studies* 17, 1: 20–41.

Laforest, Guy. 1991. 'Libéralisme et nationalisme au Canada à l'heure de l'accord du Lac Meech', *Carrefour* 13, 2: 68–90.

Lerner, Natan. 1991. *Group Rights and Discrimination in International Law.* Dordrecht: Martinus Nijhoff.

Lyons, David. 1981. 'The New Indian Claims and Original Rights to Land', in J. Paul, ed., *Reading Nozick: Essays on Anarchy, State and Utopia.* Totowa, NJ: Rowman & Littlefield.

McDonald, Michael. 1992. 'Liberalism, Community, and Culture', *University of Toronto Law Journal* 42: 113–31.

McNeill, William. 1986. *Polyethnicity and National Unity in World History.* Toronto: University of Toronto Press.

McRae, Kenneth. 1979. 'The Plural Society and the Western Political Tradition', *Canadian Journal of Political Science* 12, 4: 675–88.

Maré, Gerhard. 1992. *Brothers Born of Warrior Blood: Politics and Ethnicity in South Africa.* Johannesburg: Raven Press.

Margalit, Avishai, and Joseph Raz. 1990. 'National Self-Determination', *Journal of Philosophy* 87, 9: 439–61.

Mason, Andrew. 1990. 'Autonomy, Liberalism and State Neutrality', *Philosophical Quarterly* 40, 160: 433–52.

Mill, J.S. 1982. *On Liberty*, ed., G. Himmelfarb. Hardmondsworth: Penguin.

Moore, Margaret. 1993. *Foundations of Liberalism.* Oxford: Oxford University Press.

Morton, F.L. 1985. 'Group Rights versus Individual Rights in the Charter: The Special Cases of Natives and the Québécois', in N. Nevitte and A. Kornberg, eds, *Minorities and the Canadian State.* Oakville, Ont.: Mosaic Press: 71–85.

Mulgan, Richard. 1989. *Maori, Pākehā and Democracy.* Auckland: Oxford University Press.

Nettheim, Garth. 1988. '"Peoples" and "Populations": Indigenous Peoples and the Rights of Peoples', in James Crawford, ed., *The Rights of Peoples.* Oxford: Oxford University Press: 107–26.

Nielsson, Gunnar. 1985. 'States and "Nation-Groups": A Global Taxonomy', in Edward Tiryakian and Ronald Rogowski, eds, *New Nationalisms of the Developed West.* Boston: Allen & Unwin: 27–56.

Penz, Peter. 1992. 'Development Refugees and Distributive Justice: Indigenous Peoples, Land and the Developmentalist State', *Public Affairs Quarterly* 6, 1: 105–31.

_____. 1993. 'Colonization of Tribal Lands in Bangladesh and Indonesia: State Rationales, Rights to Land, and Environmental Justice', in Michael Howard, ed., *Asia's Environmental Crisis.* Boulder, Colo.: Westview Press: 37–72.

Peters, R., and G. de Vries. 1976. 'Apostasy in Islam', *Die Welt des Islams* 17: 1–25.

Poole, Ross. 1993. 'Nationalism and the Nation State in Late Modernity', *European Studies Journal* 10, 1: 161–74.

Porter, John. 1975. 'Ethnic Pluralism in Canadian Perspective', in N. Glazer and D. Moynihan, eds, *Ethnicity, Theory and Experience.* Cambridge, Mass.: Harvard University Press: 267–304.

Rawls, John. 1971. *A Theory of Justice.* London: Oxford University Press.

_____. 1975. 'Fairness to Goodness', *Philosophical Review* 84: 536–54.

_____. 1980. 'Kantian Constructivism in Moral Theory', *Journal of Philosophy* 77, 9: 515–72.

_____. 1988. 'The Priority of Right and Ideas of the Good', *Philosophy and Public Affairs* 17, 251–76.

Rorty, Richard. 1991. *Objectivity, Relativism, and Truth: Philosophical Papers I*. Cambridge: Cambridge University Press.

Rosenfeld, Michel. 1991. *Affirmative Action and Justice: A Philosophical and Constitutional Inquiry*. New Haven: Yale University Press.

Rubinstein, Alvin. 1993. 'Is Statehood for Puerto Rico in the National Interest?', *In Depth: A Journal for Values and Public Policy* (Spring): 87–99.

Russell, John. 1993. 'Nationalistic Minorities and Liberal Traditions', in Philip Bryden et al., eds, *Protecting Rights and Liberties: Essays on the Charter and Canada's Political, Legal and Intellectual Life*. Toronto: University of Toronto Press: 205–41.

Schwartz, Brian. 1986. *First Principles, Second Thoughts: Aboriginal Peoples, Constitutional Reform and Canadian Statecraft*. Montreal: Institute for Research on Public Policy.

Sharp, Andrew. 1990. *Justice and the Maori: Maori Claims in New Zealand Political Argument in the 1980s*. Auckland: Oxford University Press.

Sigler, Jay. 1983. *Minority Rights: A Comparative Analysis*. Westport, Conn.: Greenwood Press.

Skutnabb-Kangas, Tove. 1988. 'Multilingualism and the Education of Minority Children', in T. Skutnabb-Kangas and J. Cummings, eds, *Minority Education: From Shame to Struggle*. Clevedon: Multilingual Matters: 9–44.

Smith, Anthony. 1986. *The Ethnic Origins of Nations*. Oxford: Basil Blackwell.

_____. 1993. 'A Europe of Nations—or the Nation of Europe?', *Journal of Peace Research* 30, 2: 129–35.

Sowell, Thomas. 1990. *Preferential Policies: An International Perspective*. New York: Morrow.

Steinberg, Stephen. 1981. *The Ethnic Myth: Race, Ethnicity, and Class in America*. New York: Atheneum.

Svensson, Frances. 1979. 'Liberal Democracy and Group Rights: The Legacy of Individualism and its Impact on American Indian Tribes', *Political Studies* 27, 3: 421–39.

Tamir, Yael. 1993. *Liberal Nationalism*. Princeton, NJ: Princeton University Press.

Taylor, Charles. 1985. *Philosophy and the Human Sciences: Philosophical Papers* 2. Cambridge: Cambridge University Press.

_____. 1991. 'Shared and Divergent Values', in Ronald Watts and D. Brown, eds, *Options for a New Canada*. Toronto: University of Toronto Press: 53–76.

Thornberry, Patrick. 1991. *International Law and the Rights of Minorities*. Oxford: Oxford University Press.

Todorov, Tzvetan. 1993. *On Human Diversity: Nationalism, Racism and Exoticism in French Thought*. Cambridge, Mass.: Harvard University Press.

Tully, James. 1994. 'Aboriginal Property and Western Theory: Recovering a Middle Ground', *Social Philosophy and Policy* 11, 2: 153–80.

van den Berghe, Pierre. 1981a. *The Ethnic Phenomenon*. New York: Elsevier.

_____. 1981b. 'Protection of Ethnic Minorities: A Critical Appraisal', in R. Wirsing, ed., *Protection of Ethnic Minorities: Comparative Perspectives*. New York: Pergamon: 343–55.

Van Dyke, Vernon. 1977. 'The Individual, the State, and Ethnic Communities in Political Theory', *World Politics* 29, 3: 343–69.

_____. 1982. 'Collective Entities and Moral Rights: Problems in Liberal-Democratic Thought', *Journal of Politics* 44: 21–40.

Waldron, Jeremy. 1989. 'Autonomy and Perfectionism in Raz's *Morality of Freedom*', *Southern California Law Review* 62, 3–4: 1097–152.

_____. 1992. 'Superseding Historic Injustice', *Ethics* 103, 1: 4–28.

Walzer, Michael. 1982. 'Pluralism in Political Perspective', in M. Walzer, ed., *The Politics of Ethnicity*. Cambridge, Mass.: Harvard University Press: 1–28.

Weaver, Sally. 1985. 'Federal Difficulties with Aboriginal Rights in Canada', in M. Boldt and J. Long, eds, *The Quest for Justice: Aboriginal Peoples and Aboriginal Rights*. Toronto: University of Toronto Press: 139–47.

Weinstein, Brian. 1983. *The Civic Tongue: Political Consequences of Language Choices*. New York: Longman.

# Notes

1. For these estimates (and their imprecision), see Laczko, 1994; Gurr, 1993; Nielsson, 1985. Iceland and the Koreas are commonly cited as two examples of countries which are more or less culturally homogeneous.

2. For surveys of minority rights claims worldwide, see Sigler, 1983; Gurr, 1993; Van Dyke, 1977; Capotorti, 1979; Hannum, 1990.

3. On the assumption of cultural homogeneity in Western political thought, see McRae, 1979; Van Dyke, 1977; Walzer, 1982: 1–3; McNeill, 1986: 23. On the reality of cultural heterogeneity throughout history, and its causes, see McNeill, 1986. On the ever-increasing scale of this diversity, see Castles and Miller, 1993: 8.

4. For liberal endorsements of this position, see Glazer, 1975: 220; 1978: 98; 1983: 124; Gordon, 1975: 105; Porter, 1975: 295; van den Berghe, 1981b: 347; Ajzenstat, 1984: 251–2; Rorty, 1991: 209; Kukathas, 1991: 22; Edwards, 1985; Brotz, 1980: 44.

5. For this debate, see Rosenfeld, 1991; Sowell, 1990.

6. For a variety of examples, see Barsh and Henderson, 1980: 241–8; 1982: 69–70; Clinton, 1990; Gordon, 1975, 1978, 1981; Glazer, 1975: 220; Van Dyke, 1982: 28–30; Svensson, 1979: 430–3; Adam, 1979; Deganaar, 1987; Knopff, 1982: 29–39; Laforest, 1991; Ajzenstat, 1988: ch. 8; Morton, 1985: 73–83; Schwartz, 1986: ch. 1; Brotz, 1980: 44–5; Asch, 1984: 75–88, 100–4; Weaver, 1985: 141–2. For more references and discussion, see Kymlicka, 1989a: ch. 7; 1991.

7. For a summary of these developments, see Lerner, 1991; Thornberry, 1991; Bloed, 1994; Hannum, 1993.

8. For an interesting exploration of the idea of a 'society' and its requirements for a certain level of institutional completeness and intergenerational continuity, see Copp, 1992.

9. For example, American studies indicate 'an almost complete breakdown in the transmission of non-English languages between the second and third generations' (Steinberg, 1981: 45). One reason why languages which do not achieve the status of a public language are unlikely to survive is that people lack the opportunity or incentive to use and develop them in cognitively stimulating ways (Skutnabb-Kangas, 1988).

10. As Clarke notes, language is sometimes a 'technical accomplishment', and sometimes the 'main support for a distinct cultural identity' (Clarke, 1934: 20). Over time, the immigrant language shifts from the latter to the former. As the immigrants slowly lose their mother tongue, so at the same time, and as a consequence, the dominant language is (in a different sense) taken away from its original ethnic speakers. That is, as immigrants become members of the larger Anglophone culture, the descendants of the original Anglo-Saxon settlers cease to have any exclusive or privileged say over the development and use of the English language. This helps explain why North American English has diverged from English in Britain, where Anglo-Saxons continue to be the overwhelming majority of the speakers of the language (Johnson, 1973: 117).

11. In earlier times, cultures did not have to form societal culture to survive, since there were fewer society-wide institutions shaping people's options. (The language of public schools was not an issue when there were no public schools.) Indeed, the very idea of a 'societal culture' is a modern one. In medieval times, the idea that the various economic classes or castes would share a common culture was unheard of. Thus Todorov is historically correct when he says that 'Culture is not necessarily national (it is even only exceptionally so). It is first of all the property of a region, or of an even smaller geographical entity; it may also belong to a given layer of a population, excluding other groups from the same country; finally, it may also include a group of countries' (Todorov, 1993: 387). However, as Todorov himself notes, there is a powerful tendency in the modern world for culture to become national in scope.

12. The following argument is presented in much more detail in Kymlicka, 1989a: chs 2–4; 1990: ch. 6.

13. Liberals often make an exception where individuals are particularly vulnerable to weakness of will (e.g., paternalistic legislation against addictive

drugs). The connection between rational revisability, the endorsement constraint, and the liberal
prohibition on state paternalism is quite complicated. For Rawls's discussion of perfectionism, see
Rawls, 1988: 260, 265. For Dworkin's account, see
1989: 486–7; 1990. For general discussions, see
Kymlicka, 1989b; Waldron, 1989; Moore, 1993:
ch. 6; Caney, 1991; Mason, 1990; McDonald,
1992: 116–21; Hurka, 1994.

14. Allen Buchanan calls this the 'rational revisability'
model of individual choice (Buchanan, 1975). The
claim that we have a basic interest in being able
rationally to assess and revise our current ends is
often phrased in terms of the value of 'autonomy'.
This label may be misleading, since there are
many other conceptions of autonomy. For example, on one account of autonomy, the exercise of
choice is intrinsically valuable, because it reflects
our rational nature (this view is ascribed to Kant).
Another account of autonomy argues that non-
conformist individuality is intrinsically valuable
(this view is often ascribed to Mill). I am making
the more modest claim that choice enables us to
assess and learn what is good in life. It presupposes that we have an essential interest in identifying and revising those of our current beliefs
about value which are mistaken. When I use the
term autonomy, therefore, it is in this (relatively
modest) sense of 'rational revisability'. I discuss
these different conceptions of autonomy in
Kymlicka, 1989a: ch. 4; 1990: ch. 6.

15. I discuss this in greater length in Kymlicka 1989a:
ch. 8; 1995a. Of course, the models we learn
about in our culture are often closely related to the
models in other cultures. For example, models
derived from the Bible will be part of the structure
of many cultures with a Christian influence. And
there are international bodies, like the Catholic
Church, which actively seek to ensure this com-
monality amongst models in different cultures. So
in saying that we learn about conceptions of the
good life through our culture, I do not mean to
imply that the goods are therefore culture-specific,
although some are.

16. In explaining his notion of the decay of a cultural
structure, Dworkin says that 'We are all beneficiaries or victims of what is done to the language we
share. A language can diminish; some are richer

and better than others' (1985: 229). This is misleading if he means that some languages are inherently richer than others. All human languages have
an equal capacity for evolution and adaptation to
meet the needs of their speakers (Edwards, 1985:
19; Skutnabb-Kangas, 1988: 12). However, the
range of options available in one's language can
clearly decay.

17. I should note that Dworkin made his brief
comments about 'cultural structures' in the context
of an argument regarding public funding of the
arts, and they were not intended to provide a
comprehensive description or theory about the
nature of cultures. However, since he is one of the
few liberal theorists to address explicitly the question of the relationship between freedom and culture, I have tried to draw out the implications of
his view. See also his claim that people 'need a
common culture and particularly a common language even to have personalities, and culture and
language are social phenomena. We can only have
the thoughts, and ambitions, and convictions that
are possible within the vocabulary that language
and culture provide, so we are all, in a patent and
deep way, the creatures of the community as a
whole' (Dworkin, 1989: 488; cf. Dworkin, 1985:
228, and the discussion in Kymlicka, 1995a).

18. In Rawls's terminology, we can say that access to
such a culture is a 'primary good'—i.e., a good
which people need, regardless of their particular
chosen way of life, since it provides the context
within which they make those particular choices. I
explore how this argument relates to Rawls's
account of 'primary goods' in more depth in
Kymlicka, 1989a: ch. 7. For related arguments
about the dependence of freedom on culture, see
Taylor, 1985; Tamir, 1993: chs 1–2; Margalit and
Raz, 1990.

19. This phrase is from the judgement of the Canadian
Supreme Court in explaining its interpretation of
the equality guarantees under the Canadian
Charter of Rights. *Andrews v. Law Society of British
Columbia* 1 SCR 143; 56 DLC (4th) 1. See also
Government of Canada, 1991: 10.

20. For examples of this view, see Knopff, 1979;
Morton, 1985; Kukathas, 1992; Hindess, 1993;
Maré, 1992: 107–10; Rawls, 1975: 88, 93; and the
references cited in note 4.

21. I explored this relationship between national rights and liberal egalitarian justice in Kymlicka, 1989a: ch. 9. For what it is worth, I continue to endorse the argument in that chapter, but I should have been clearer about its scope. I would now describe the argument in that chapter as an equality-based defence of certain external protections for national minorities. I did not use those terms at the time, in part because I did not have a very clear conception of the variety of rights, groups, and moral justifications that are involved in the debate.

22. I am here disagreeing with Tamir, who argues that the larger a national minority is, the more rights it should have (1993: 75). In my view, if a national group is large enough, it may have little need for group-differentiated rights, since it can ensure its survival and development through the usual operation of the economic marketplace and democratic decision-making. (This might be true, for example, if a binational state contained two nations of roughly equal size and wealth.)

23. On the role of indigenous land claims in a liberal egalitarian framework, see Kymlicka, 1995b; Penz, 1992, 1993; Russell, 1993; Tully, 1994. It is important to note that the equality argument for land claims is not based on notions of compensatory justice. The compensatory argument says that because indigenous peoples were the legal owners of their traditional lands, and because their lands were taken away illegally, they should be compensated for this historical wrong. Since the debate over land claims is often couched in the language of compensatory justice, I should say a word about this. I take it as given that indigenous peoples have suffered terrible wrongs in being dispossessed of their lands, and that they should be compensated for this in some way. Moreover, I believe that indigenous peoples continue to have certain property rights under the common law (in former British colonies), wherever these have not been explicitly extinguished by legislation. (That is to say, the *terra nullius* doctrine is wrong in terms both of morality and the common law.) But it is a mistake, I think, to put too much weight on historical property rights. For one thing, these claims do not, by themselves, explain why indigenous peoples have rights of self-government. Many groups have been wrongfully dispossessed of property and other economic opportunities, including women, blacks, and Japanese immigrants in the United States and Canada during World War II. Each of these groups may be entitled to certain forms of compensatory justice, but this does not by itself explain or justify granting powers of self-government (rather than compensatory programs to promote integration and equal opportunity within the mainstream). Suffering historical injustice is neither necessary nor sufficient for claiming self-government rights. . . .

Moreover, the idea of compensating for historical wrongs, taken to its logical conclusion, implies that all the land which was wrongly taken from indigenous peoples in the Americas or Australia or New Zealand should be returned to them. This would create massive unfairness, given that the original European settlers and later immigrants have now produced hundreds of millions of descendants, and this land is the only home they know. Changing circumstances often make it impossible and undesirable to compensate for certain historical wrongs. As Jeremy Waldron puts it, certain historical wrongs are 'superseded' (Waldron, 1992b). Also, the land held by some indigenous groups at the time of contact was itself the result of the conquest or coercion of other indigenous groups (Mulgan, 1989: 30–1; Crowe, 1974: 65–81). The compensatory argument would presumably require rectifying these pre-contact injustices as well. (For other difficulties with compensatory claims, see Brilmayer, 1992.)

The equality argument does not try to turn back the historical clock, nor to restore groups to the situation they would have been in [in] the absence of any historical injustice. (These compensatory aims actually fit more comfortably with Nozick's libertarian theory of entitlement than with a liberal egalitarian theory of distributive justice—see Lyons, 1981.) The aim of the equality argument is to provide the sort of land base needed to sustain the viability of self-governing minority communities, and hence to prevent unfair disadvantages with respect to cultural membership now and in the future. In short, the equality argument situates land claims within a theory of distributive justice, rather than compensatory justice.

Waldron assumes that indigenous land claims are all based on claims for compensatory justice (Waldron, 1992). In fact, however, most indigenous groups focus, not on reclaiming all of what they had before European settlement, but on what they need now to sustain themselves as distinct societies (see the declaration of the World Council of Indigenous Peoples, quoted in Nettheim, 1988: 115; Sharp, 1990: 150–3). Historical factors are, of course, relevant in other ways. The 'historical agreement' argument I discuss below is very much history-based.

24. The only attempt I know of to reconcile official languages with 'benign neglect' is by Rainer Knopff. He argues that language has two functions: it can function as the vehicle for the transmission of a particular culture, but it can also function as 'a culturally neutral, or utilitarian, means of communication which allows those of different cultures to participate in the same political community' (Knopff, 1979: 67). By placing the emphasis on the utilitarian function, governments 'can enact official languages without at the same time legislating official cultures . . . in enacting "official languages", one does not necessarily imply that the cultures which these languages transmit and represent thereby become "official cultures"' (Knopff, 1979: 67). Culture, Knopff argues, 'remains a purely private affair' in Canada, for while English and French have official backing as the 'utilitarian' languages, all languages compete on equal terms for 'cultural' allegiance. It is the 'task of the individual members of a culture to show the excellence of their product on the cultural marketplace, as it were. If they succeed, the language of that culture will become attractive to others . . . if [a] culture, and hence, language cannot show itself to be worthy of choice in the light of standards of the good, then it deserves to disappear' (Knopff, 1979: 70). This view of language as a 'culturally neutral medium' has been thoroughly discredited in the literature. In any event, it is simply not true that teaching in the English language in public schools is totally divorced from the teaching of the history and customs of the Anglophone society.

25. Some commentators say that governments should draw boundaries and distribute powers so as to protect the viability of national minorities, but that they should not state in law that they are doing this. This enables the state to continue claiming that it treats all ethnic and national differences with 'benign neglect'. For example, van den Berghe argues that deliberately designing or revising federal units to protect minority cultures is consistent with 'benign neglect', so long as it does not involve the explicit legal recognition of groups. He thinks it is one thing to define the powers and boundaries of a political subunit so as to ensure the protection of a minority culture (what he calls 'indirect consociationalism'), but quite another for the constitution or statute law to cite the existence of that minority as the reason for those arrangements (what he calls 'group rights') (van den Berghe, 1981a: 348). But surely this is hypocritical. If the agreed purpose of indirect consociationalism is to protect minority cultures, then anyone who values honesty and transparency in government (as liberals claim to do) should want that justification to be clear to everyone. Van den Berghe's solution violates the 'publicity condition' which Rawls imposes on liberal theories of justice (Rawls, 1971: 133). None the less, this attitude seems to be widely shared. While most Canadians accept that the powers and boundaries of Quebec were fixed to accommodate the needs of the Francophone minority in Canada, many objected to the government's proposal to state in the constitution that Quebec formed a 'distinct society' as the homeland of the French Canadian nation, because they saw this as violating the principle that the constitution should not recognize particular ethnic or national groups. Quebecers, however, are no longer willing to have their special status hidden away. They view it is as a matter of basic respect that their separate identity be recognized and affirmed at the level of constitutional principle (Taylor, 1991: 64).

26. This is similar to the debate over affirmative action for women or people with disabilities. Like self-government rights, affirmative action programs asymmetrically distribute rights or opportunities on the basis of group membership. Proponents argue that they are required for genuine equality. Critics respond that the economic marketplace (like the cultural marketplace) already respects equality, by treating job applicants without regard for their

group membership. However, an equality-based argument for group-specific affirmative action can be made if the actual operation of the economic marketplace works to the disadvantage of certain groups. As with self-government rights, the equality argument for affirmative action seeks to show how the structure of common individual rights is intended to treat all people equally, but in fact works to the disadvantage of the members of a particular collectivity. Many group-specific claims can be seen in this way—that is, as compensating for the disadvantages and vulnerabilities of certain groups within the structure of common individual rights.

Of course, as I discussed earlier, affirmative action for women or people with disabilities differs in many ways from self-government rights for national minorities, since they are compensating for very different kinds of injustices. The former is intended to help disadvantaged groups integrate into society, by breaking down unjust barriers to full integration. The latter is intended to help cultural communities maintain their distinctiveness, by protecting against external decisions. This means that the former are (in theory) temporary, whereas the latter are permanent, barring dramatic shifts in population.

27. Imagine that schools and government offices (and presumably private businesses as well) were open seven days a week all year round, including Christmas and Easter, and that each student and employee was allowed to choose two days off per week, two weeks' vacation per year, plus, say, five additional holidays per year. This would maximize each individual's ability to adapt their schedule to their religious beliefs. But I do not know whether this is realistic or even desirable, given the extent to which social life is built around common weekends and holidays. As an atheist, I have no commitment to resting on the sabbath or celebrating religious holidays. But I do like the fact that most of my friends and family, regardless of their religion, language, and ethnicity, do not work on the weekends or on certain public holidays. Maintaining friendships and other voluntary associations would be much more difficult if society (including schools and other government institutions) were not organized in this way. Perhaps a better solution would be to have one major holiday from each of the largest religious groups in the country. We could have one Christian holiday (say, Christmas), but replace Easter and Thanksgiving with a Muslim and Jewish holiday. This would maintain the value of common holidays, and would also encourage people of each faith to learn something about the beliefs of other faiths.

# Part III

# Political Behaviour

## Introduction

Lynda Erickson

Within the discipline of political science, the term 'political behaviour' has an ambiguous status. This is because it connotes both a particular area of research, described as human behaviour in the political realm, and an approach or way of studying political phenomena, usually labelled behaviouralism.[1] As a subject area, political behaviour tends to focus on the study of individuals, not institutions or structures, and includes topics such as political attitudes, public opinion, and voting behaviour. It explores such questions as: do Canadians support self-determination for Aboriginal peoples?[2] What reasons persuade Quebecers to endorse separatism?[3] Is public opinion influenced by polling results?[4] And what decides elections?[5] Behaviouralism refers more generically to the use of scientific methods and perspectives and is associated with a major debate that developed within the discipline about the nature of political science and what constitutes knowledge about politics. Since method and approach are central issues in the study of political behaviour, a brief account of behaviouralism and the 'behavioural debate' is a good way to begin our introduction to this area of the discipline.

After World War II, a number of political scientists in the United States became dissatisfied with the traditional methods that dominated research and writing in their discipline. At that time two kinds of analysis tended to occupy scholars in political science. One was philosophical. It featured historical treatments of classical theorists or involved discussions of philosophical issues, such as the nature of democracy, what is justice, and what constitutes the most desirable form of governing. The other kind of analysis was descriptive and focused on collecting information about political structures and processes and elaborating on how they worked. According to those who were dissatisfied with traditional political science, philosophical approaches did not, in themselves, produce a sufficient understanding of political phenomena. And descriptive approaches were not rigorous enough. There were few special methods for collecting and analysing information, and analysis often intermingled researchers' preferences for how politics should proceed and how institutions should work with their descriptions of how political processes and structures did function.[6]

These critics of traditional scholarship believed that the discipline needed to be more systematic in its approach to data collection and that it needed to adopt a new kind of theoretical approach, one that was empirical, not normative, and that helped to explain and possibly predict political phenomena. They argued that the methods and perspectives of science should be adopted to generate theories and gather evidence about the political world. Since these critics of traditional scholarship viewed political behaviour as a form of social behaviour, they urged political scientists to use the knowledge and concepts of other social sciences as a source of ideas for their research on political phenomena. Some of these scientifically oriented scholars began to refer to their work as 'behavioural science' and subsequently the term 'behaviouralism' became identified with the kind of political science they advocated.[7]

While there were some differences among behaviouralists in what they considered were the central features of the behavioural approach, the basic elements of a scientific study of politics, as they described it, can be characterized as follows. Firstly, scientific research is empirical. That is, it is based on evidence from actual events, circumstances, or behaviour and conclusions are drawn about how things are, not how they ought to be. Secondly, this empirical work must be rigorous and systematic. Researchers must, therefore, be as precise and consistent as possible in collecting evidence, paying close attention to issues of measurement and, where possible, quantifying their data. Thirdly, scientific work is intersubjective. That is, researchers' evidence and scientific claims can be and are checked by others in their field. Finally, the objective of research is to produce theories and explanations about the empirical world. Using logic and evidence, scientists develop and test generalizations about why and/or how things occur in order to explain and predict the variety of phenomena they study.[8]

The behaviouralist view that politics should be studied scientifically drew a number of criticisms.[9] Some stemmed from scepticism about the theoretical objectives of behaviouralists. It was argued that the kind of generalizations that characterize explanations in the natural sciences cannot be made in political science because people and their politics are simply too diverse and the reasons for their activities are too varied. Certainly, attempting to find universal laws that would apply to all instances of a phenomenon was fruitless, it was argued, as was the search for overarching theories that would explain politics and political life across time and space.

Many behaviouralists were willing to concede that it was unlikely universal 'laws' of politics would be produced. Most generalizations in political science would take the form of 'tendencies'. In other words, explanations would be of the sort that said: when conditions 'x' are present a particular event 'y' is *likely* to occur. In addition, attempts to produce overarching theories were largely abandoned by behaviouralists in later years. But for many critics, even the quest for 'weaker' generalizations covering more limited circumstances was considered inappropriate and unproductive. While not accepting the argument that generalizations are inherently impossible, most contemporary research in political behaviour is sensitive to the changing circumstances of political life and the changes in people's understandings of their situations that limit the scope of generalizations.

Another set of criticisms of behaviouralism was directed to its focus on rigorous, systematic empirical work. Political life, it was argued, is generally too complex to be categorized by scientific study. Measuring, especially quantifying, political phenomena simplifies them too much and distorts their features—or, those aspects of political life that are quantifiable are, for the most part, trivial.

Even initially, these arguments about rigour and measurement were less convincing in some areas of politics than others. Electoral research, for example, lends itself naturally to the use of numbers and the analysis of public opinion, and mass politics has produced a substantial literature based on survey research and quantitative work. But political research that entails systematic empirical analysis and quantitative data now reaches beyond these areas and is practised extensively, including within fields as diverse as public administration, comparative politics, and international relations. Much of this work has contributed to our understanding of government and politics. So the issue of whether such work oversimplifies political phenomena, or is concerned with merely the trivial, must now be answered on a case-by-case basis. A blanket rejection of this kind of research is no longer justifiable.

Questions of measurement remain an issue in other respects for those engaged in the study of political behaviour. It seems obvious to say that how we measure something affects the results we get in our research, but in the study of political behaviour the implications of this are particularly important. For example, in survey research, small changes in question wording can alter results substantially. A study of the 1988 Canadian general election found that survey respondents who were asked their opinion on the free trade agreement that had been negotiated between Canada and the United States prior to that election responded differently depending on the wording of the question posed to them. Half the respondents were asked whether they supported the free trade agreement reached by 'the Mulroney government'. The other half were asked whether they supported the free trade agreement reached by 'Canada'. Among those respondents who were asked about the 'Mulroney' agreement, the proportion saying they supported it was as much as 10 per cent lower than was the percentage in favour of the 'Canadian' agreement.[10]

In the debate about behaviouralism and the scientific study of politics, some of the most strongly worded criticisms came because of concern about the possible elimination of values from political science and the study of politics. Early behaviouralists tended to make a clear distinction between what they called facts and values, and were inclined to argue that scientists' claims about the political world were based on facts. Scientific work is empirical and personal values were not to intrude.

Many critics took issue with an approach they said excluded discussion of moral issues or debate about contemporary policy concerns from the arena of political science. They pointed out that a central aspect of the discipline has been its concern with fundamental issues that involve questions of right and wrong and judgements about the nature of the good society. Rejection of this kind of analysis would impoverish the discipline. In addition, they argued, participation in contemporary policy controversies that involves value judgements about issues of public concern is an important contribution political scientists can make to their societies.

While behaviouralists did advocate that more scientific study be undertaken in political science, this did not mean they wanted to eliminate other approaches in the discipline. Duncan MacRae described a sentiment shared by many behaviouralists when he argued, 'we must not lose sight of the nonscientific aspects of knowledge, which are also part of our discipline. . . . Our concern with normative political theory keeps before us the goals we are seeking and the ways in which regimes may contribute to them.'[11] The problem seems to be that we use the term 'political science' to refer to the discipline as a whole, both those parts of it that would claim to be scientific and those that do not.

Another set of criticisms of the behaviouralist position on values concerned the view that political research could be value free. Critics argued that the values and personal perspectives of political scientists affect their work in a number of often subtle ways, including influencing what researchers choose to study, how they interpret their data, and even what data they will consider relevant for explaining particular phenomena.

These arguments are now convincing to many contemporary practitioners of behavioural research. They recognize that, in the course of scientific study, evidence must be interpreted by researchers, and there often are credible alternative interpretations and hence different explanations for the same phenomena. Factors outside of the research data themselves influence the conclusions drawn from evidence. In other words, the distinction between facts and values is not a straightforward one.

The role of values and presuppositions in empirical research has since been widely debated among scholars who study the nature of science, and the issue is widely acknowledged to be more complex than the early behaviouralists assumed it was. What researchers consider to be a relevant and well-verified claim (i.e., a 'fact') in the context of their research may be influenced by their presuppositions about what elements are important in explaining the phenomena they are studying and their criteria for verification. These features of scientific inquiry are not limited to political science, or even the social sciences, but they are especially noticed there.

This does not mean that judgements in the social sciences are made just on grounds of personal preference and that 'anything goes' when it comes to scientific explanations. Nor does it absolve researchers of the need to provide evidence for their claims. Good arguments must be given in support of explanations and conclusions and empirical evidence must be presented to substantiate a position. These arguments and evidence are then judged by other scholars in the field.[12]

## The Study of Political Behaviour in Canada

The behavioural movement, in its earliest years, was primarily a product of American political science. As in many other countries, the study of political behaviour using rigorous empirical methods came later in Canada. National election surveys, which were an important cornerstone of the early behavioural movement, were first conducted in the 1940s in the United States, whereas the first national election survey in Canada was not conducted until 1965. And at the national meetings of the professional political science association in Canada, where, for the purposes of organizing the presentation of papers, there are separate sections for the different subject areas of the discipline, a section for something like political behaviour was not established until 1971. That section was first called 'political sociology'.

Although late in coming to Canada, national election surveys have been conducted by political scientists for every general election since 1965 (with the exception of the 1972 vote), and they now play a critically important role in the study of political behaviour in Canada. These surveys employ random sampling techniques similar to those used in the commercial polling reported in newspapers and other media. But the national election surveys have used much longer questionnaires and much larger samples than those used in most commercial polls. The longer questionnaires allow researchers to collect data on a wider range of opinion and behaviour and to learn more about the social and demographic characteristics of the respondents. In addition to helping us to study voting in national elections, these surveys are also used to examine other kinds of political behaviour, such as engaging in political discussions and attending to the political media, as well as to study the nature and correlates of a range of political preferences and attitudes. After the original research teams complete their initial work on the surveys, the data become available for other researchers to use.

One set of national election surveys, undertaken immediately following the 1974, 1979, and 1980 national elections, included a panel study in which a number of the respondents interviewed in the 1974 study were reinterviewed in 1979 and again in 1980.[13] The panel data were then used to track change and stability in people's attitudes and behaviour over a number of years.[14] The 1988 national election study was the first to use computer-assisted telephone interviewing (CATI) technology to collect its data, and this technology has seen continued use in subsequent national eclection surveys. CATI technology has made it easier for the national election research teams to track Canadians' opinions over the length of the election campaigns by using rolling cross-section samples (a cross-section of Canadians is interviewed each day of the campaign) and to interview each survey respondent twice: once during the campaign and once after polling day. As a result, estimating the impact of election campaigns became a more reliable endeavour.[15] The rolling cross-sample technique has also allowed researchers to trace the apparent effects of specific campaign events, such as the leaders' debates or campaign blunders, on voting preferences.

While voting studies at the local, provincial, and national levels remain an important focus of research in this field, work on other aspects of Canadians' political attitudes and behaviours has flourished, as have studies of the attitudes and behaviour of special groups within the Canadian population. For example, one major study of Canadians' attitudes and judgements about democratically related rights and freedoms included a survey of political élites (MPs and MLAs), legal élites, and administrative élites as well as citizens.[16] Surveys of delegates at party conventions have been routine in the study of party leadership selection.[17] And these have recently been augmented by surveys of party members who participated in the televoting used to choose some provincial party leaders.[18]

The objective of all of these behavioural investigations, whether focused on the general public, subgroups within the public, or certain élites, is, firstly, to describe what people think and how they behave politically, and, secondly, to explain why they think and behave as they do. In this respect, then, theories, understood as explanations for which empirical support must be received, remain as central to behavioural inquiry as they were at the outset of the behavioural revolution. Debates rage as to which theories are likely to provide more effective or powerful explanations and what kind of evidence is most reliable, but neither the importance of theory nor the relevance of evidence to behavioural inquiry is questioned.

❧

In the readings below, the first article, by David Northrup, illustrates the importance of methodological concerns in the study of political attitudes. Northrup finds it is not simply the kinds of questions researchers ask of their respondents that affect the answers given to interviewers. The gender of the interviewer also appears to have some impact. The other selection, by Sniderman et al., uses some of the data from the study of Canadian opinion on rights and freedoms described above. This article also illustrates the use of comparative data, in this case from the United States as well as Canada, and shows how findings from research in political behaviour can contribute to debates about democracy. Such debates are typically considered to be within the domain of traditional political philosophy (or what is called normative theory), because that is where value questions about the 'proper ordering' of the state are explicitly addressed. When, as they so often do, these debates involve empirical assumptions about how people behave politically, systematic empirical research that addresses such assumptions can usefully be brought to bear on the normative debate.

## Notes

1. D. Kavanagh, *Political Science and Political Behaviour* (London: George Allen & Unwin, 1983).
2. Paul M. Sniderman, Joseph F. Fletcher, Peter H. Russell, and Philip E. Tetlock, *The Clash of Rights: Liberty, Equality and Legitimacy in Pluralist Democracy* (New Haven: Yale University Press, 1996).
3. André Blais and Richard Nadeau, 'To be or not to be a sovereignist: Quebeckers' perennial dilemma', *Canadian Public Policy* 18 (1992): 89–103.
4. R. Johnston, A. Blais, H.E. Brady, and J. Crête, *Letting the People Decide: Dynamics of a Canadian Election* (Montreal and Kingston: McGill-Queen's University Press, 1992).
5. H. Clarke, L. LeDuc, J. Jensen, and J. Pammett, *Absent Mandate: Canadian Electoral Politics in an Era of Restructuring*, 3rd edn (Toronto: Gage, 1996).
6. David Easton, 'Political Science in the United States, Past and Present', in David Easton and Corinne S. Schelling, eds, *Divided Knowledge: Across Disciplines, Across Cultures* (Newbury Park, Calif.: Sage Publications, 1991), 37–58.
7. A. Somit and J. Tanenhaus, *The Development of American Political Science: From Burgess to Behavioralism* (New York: Irvington Publishers, 1982).
8. For a book of readings that illustrates the kind of research undertaken by political scientists identified as working within the behavioural mode at this time in the United States, see H. Eulau, S. Eldersveld, and M. Janowitz, eds, *Political Behavior: A Reader in Theory and Research* (Glencoe, Ill.: Free Press, 1956).

9. See, for example, B. Crick, *The American Science of Politics* (London: Routledge & Kegan Paul, 1959); H.J. Storing, ed., *Essays on the Scientific Study of Politics* (New York: Holt, Rinehart and Winston, 1962); C. McCoy and J. Playford, eds, *Apolitical Politics* (New York: Thomas Y. Crowell, 1967); S. Wolin, 'Political Theory as a Vocation', *American Political Science Review* 63 (1969): 1062–82.

10. Johnston et al., *Letting the People Decide.* The effect of question wording was greatest early in the campaign in that election. Later in the campaign, after the electorate had been exposed to a vigorous public debate and widespread propaganda about the agreement in the context of the election campaign, the effect of the question wording declined.

11. D. MacRae, 'The Science of Politics and Its Limits', in H. Weisberg, ed., *Political Science: The Science of Politics* (New York: Agathon Press, 1983), 24–48.

12. For discussion of some of these issues about facts and values and political science, see M.E. Hawkesworth, 'The Science of Politics and the Politics of Science', in Hawkesworth and M. Kogan, eds, *Encyclopedia of Government and Politics* (London: Routledge, 1992).

13. Clarke et al., *Absent Mandate.*

14. A number of subsequent surveys have also used interlocking panels to study political change. See ibid., Appendix.

15. Johnston et al., *Letting the People Decide.*

16. Sniderman et al., *Clash of Rights.*

17. George Perlin, ed., *Party Democracy in Canada: The Politics of National Party Conventions* (Scarborough. Ont.: Prentice-Hall, 1988); R.K. Carty, L.J. Erickson, and D.E. Blake, eds, *Leaders and Parties in Canadian Politics: The Experience of the Provinces* (Toronto: HBJ Holt, 1992); Keith Archer and Alan Whitehorn, *Political Activists: The NDP in Convention* (Toronto: Oxford University Press, 1997).

18. D.K. Stewart, 'The Changing Leadership Electorate: An Examination of Participants in the 1992 Alberta Conservative Leadership Election', *Canadian Journal of Political Science* 30 (1997): 107–28.

## Study Questions for the Readings

1. Given that gender of the interviewer appears to have some impact on how (some) people answer survey questions, does that mean that these people 'misreport' their attitudes?

2. If people's reported attitudes vary with the context of the survey and the way in which questions are asked, what implications does this have for survey research? Are survey data reliable empirical evidence?

3. What examples have you seen of polling results that you think may have been affected by the way the survey questions were worded? Could they have been asked in a way that would have reduced the question effect?

4. Do you think any of the results in the Charter Survey may have been 'contaminated' by the way the questions were worded? If so, what alternative question(s) would you propose?

5. The survey upon which 'The Fallacy of Democratic Élitism' is based was undertaken in 1987. Do you think that pluralism among political élites in Canada has increased or decreased since that time? Why or why not?

6. What democratic rights are the subject of this study? Are there other democratic rights that they have not investigated? If so, would these rights conflict with the rights that are the subject of this study?

# Gender, Gender, Gender:
## The Effect of the Interviewer's Gender on Respondent's Answers to Affirmative Action Items

David A. Northrup

## Introduction

Hyman and his colleagues, in their exhaustive review of what has become known as interviewer effect, demonstrated that variations in interviewer behaviour, characteristics (age, class, race, gender, etc.), and the interaction between interviewer and respondent can affect sample survey estimates.[1] However, according to Bradburn there is little support, 'popular notions notwithstanding', for concluding that interviewer characteristics 'with the exception of training and experience [have a] consistent effect' on survey results. Bradburn suggests that improved training and the use of professional interviewers have ensured that interviewer effects are minimized. The exception, Bradburn notes, are those characteristics of the interviewer that are 'visible' to the respondent.[2]

The two interviewer characteristics most visible in a face-to-face survey, and easiest for the respondent to determine in a telephone survey, are the race and gender of the interviewer.[3] The impact of race on survey results is well documented.[4] While most researchers report that White respondents defer to Black interviewers on questions of racial tolerance, others find evidence of deference by both White and Black respondents to interviewers of the opposite race. This effect may be seen as a particular type of social

Revised and abridged from Institute for Social Research, York University, Working Papers Series, with the permission of the author, who would like to thank Mirka Ondrack, Christine Klucha, John Pollard, and Anne Oram, colleagues at the Institute for Social Research, and Robert MacDermid, Political Science at York, for assistance with this paper.

desirability, or what Schuman and Converse have called the 'desire not to offend a polite stranger'.[5] Race-of-interviewer effects have also been found in surveys of adolescents.[6] Ethnicity of interviewer effects have been confirmed for ethnically sensitive questions in a survey of Cubans, Chicanos, Native Americans, and Chinese,[7] but these effects are not evident for non-ethnically sensitive questions.[8]

The impact of the interviewer's gender on response has received much less scrutiny by survey researchers, and the results of this work are much less consistent than those on race-of-interviewer effects. Hyman reports on a survey where the results 'reveal consistencies which are suggestive' of what he terms the 'respondent reaction to the interview situation'.[9] (Perhaps a more cumbersome, but certainly more accurate description than the commonly used term 'gender-of-interviewer effect'.) Johnson and DeLamater report that both men and women were more positive about being interviewed by women rather than by men and that women also reported more willingness to be honest when interviewed by women.[10] However, after reviewing 144 items about sexual behaviour, they conclude that 'interviewer gender is not associated with substantial differences in reported sexual behaviour among youth.' Schofield finds more honest reporting by both men and women when the age of the interviewer is close to the age of the respondent and when their gender is the same.[11] But Reiss, in his study on premarital sex, found reporting was not influenced by the interviewer's gender.[12]

More recently, Fowler and Mangione have found, by reinterviewing respondents in a face-to-face survey, that both men and women rated female interviewers higher on friendliness, professionalism, and overall performance than they rated male interviewers.[13] Fowler and Mangione 'wonder' about the instant 'kind of relationship' established by female interviewers. They caution, however, against drawing firm conclusions about gender-of-interviewer effects until more data are available and suggest that these types of differences may be ameliorated in telephone interviews.

The increasing social and political importance of gender has resulted in an increase in the number of surveys exploring affirmative action and items measuring gender-related issues. As a result, it is critical that we systematically explore the extent to which the gender of the interviewer affects respondents' behaviour in surveys. An initial attempt to measure the impact of gender on response is explored in this paper. More specifically, variations in support for what can broadly be labelled as 'affirmative action items' are considered.

A recently completed Canada-wide survey measuring AIDS awareness, understanding, and attitudes, as well as two other recent national surveys, used affirmative action items to help measure political ideology and attitudes. Data from these three surveys will be reviewed in this paper.

## The Studies

The AIDS survey (AIDS in Canada: Knowledge, Behaviour, and Attitudes of Adults) was completed in 1988 with 2,330 Canadians.[14] The Attitudes Towards Civil Liberties and the Canadian Charter of Rights and Freedoms (Charter of Rights Study) was completed with 2,084 Canadians in 1987.[15] The Royal Commission on Electoral Reform and Party Financing, the most recent survey considered in this paper, was completed in 1990 with 2,950 Canadians.[16]

All interviewing (completed in English and French) was conducted from the centralized facilities of the Institute for Social Research (ISR) in Toronto. For each survey the households (as well as the respondent when there were two or more

adults in the household) were randomly selected. The response rate for each survey, calculated as completions over estimated number of eligible households, was between 64 and 67 per cent. In order to correct for oversampling of the smaller Canadian provinces as well as the overrepresentation of one-person households in each survey, a weighted data set is used in the analysis presented in this paper.

Different questions were used in the three surveys. Two specifically addressed support for government action (AIDS survey: 'Do you support programs which favour the hiring and promoting of women to make up for their lack of opportunities in the past?' Charter of Rights survey: 'A certain proportion of the top jobs in government should go to women' [agree or disagree]). The electoral reform survey measured support for having more women in the pre-eminent legislative body in Canada: 'As you may know there are many more men than women in the House of Commons. In your view, how serious a problem is this?' (four-point seriousness scale).

## Results

### The AIDS Survey

Many of the questions in the AIDS survey dealt with sensitive issues such as sexual practices, number of sexual partners, and whether the respondent knew anyone with AIDS or anyone who was a homosexual. As a result, it is important to determine if the gender of the interviewer affected respondents' answers. Did men, for example, need to 'brag about their sexual prowess' when interviewed by a woman? Did willingness to indicate acquaintance with a homosexual or someone who had AIDS vary according to the interviewer's gender?

For male respondents, there is a consistency in the pattern of responses to the 'AIDS' items (the first four items of Table 1). When interviewed by men as opposed to women, men are less likely to report they 'know someone who is a homosexual' (41 per cent to 44 per cent), and to 'personally know someone who has AIDS' (8 per cent compared to 11 per cent). They are also less likely to agree that an 'infected person should be required by law to name their sexual partners' (80 per cent compared to 84 per cent) and more likely to state they have had more than one partner over the last year (44 per cent compared to 47 per cent) when interviewed by women. Although none of these differences are statistically significant, the pattern suggests that male responses to male interviewers

are in the direction of what could be called a 'more traditional value system'.

The last three items presented in the table were part of a battery of items used to determine political attitudes and ideology. These questions were included in the survey to determine the extent to which attitudes about AIDS correlated with attitudes on a number of other more common sociopolitical issues. The first two items evidence a 'gender effect'. Men, whether interviewed by a man or a woman, are less likely than women to agree that 'efforts to prevent the sale of

## Table 1: AIDS Survey: Response to Items by the Gender of the Interviewer (percentage distribution)

| Question and Response | Gender of Interviewer/Respondent | | | |
| --- | --- | --- | --- | --- |
| | Man/ Man | Woman/ Man | Man/ Woman | Woman/ Woman |
| Per cent who 'personally knew someone with AIDS' | 8 | 11 | 11 | 12 |
| Per cent who 'know anyone who is a homosexual' | 41 | 44 | 40 | 46 |
| 'A doctor carries out a blood test and finds a person has been infected with the AIDS virus. Do you think the infected person should be required by law to name his or her sexual partners?' Per cent saying 'yes' | 80[a] | 84 | 87 | 87[b] |
| Per cent of respondents 'who had more than 1 partner in the last 5 years' and fear of AIDS 'stopped them from having sex' [at least once] | 44 | 47 | 48 | 46 |
| Proportion saying 'efforts to prevent the sale of pornography' should be increased | 75 | 73 | 81 | 83 |
| Per cent responding 'yes' to: 'should censors have the right to ban or require cuts to films?' | 47[a] | 44[a] | 65[b] | 61[b] |
| 'Do you approve of programs which favour the hiring and promotion of women to make up for their lack of opportunities in the past?' Per cent responding 'yes approve' | 59[a] | 68[b] | 70[b] | 73[b] |
| Minimum number of cases (except third item, which has approximately one-third the number of cases) | 325 | 790 | 320 | 860 |

Groups indicated [a] are significantly different from groups indicated [b] at the .05 level (anova).

pornography should be increased' (75 and 73 per cent for men interviewed by men and women while the corresponding figures for women are 81 and 83 per cent respectively). Men are also less supportive of allowing 'censors the right to ban or cut films' than are women (between 44 and 47 per cent of men compared to 61 to 65 per cent of women, a significant difference at the 0.5 level).

The pattern for the last item in the table is quite different and reminiscent of the response pattern for the four 'AIDS' items reviewed above. Men, when interviewed by male interviewers, are less likely (59 per cent) to be supportive of 'pro-grams for hiring and promoting women to make up for their lack of opportunities in the past' than are men interviewed by women (68 per cent). This proportion of men supporting affirmative action programs, when they were interviewed by women, is close to the proportion of women supporting these programs whether interviewed by men (70 per cent) or women (73 per cent). The man/man group is significantly different from the other three groups (.05). This difference is what has been traditionally described as 'gender-of-interviewer effect'.

There is no evidence to suggest the gender of the interviewer affects women's response.

## Table 2: Charter of Rights Study: Response to Items by the Gender of the Interviewer and Respondent (percentage distribution)

| Question and Response | Gender of Interviewer/Respondent | | | |
| | Man/ Man | Woman/ Man | Man/ Woman | Woman/ Woman |
|---|---|---|---|---|
| Proportion saying 'it should be against the law to write or speak in such a way as to promote hatred' | 72 | 70 | 70 | 74 |
| Proportion saying a 'certain proportion of the top jobs in government should go to French Canadians' | 35 | 32 | 26 | 32 |
| Proportion saying 'films showing sexually explicit acts should be allowed' | 63[a] | 58[a] | 36[b] | 35[b] |
| Proportion saying 'the Charter of Rights is a good thing for Canada' | 80 | 79 | 73 | 75 |
| Proportion saying 'large companies should have quotas about the number of women they hire' | 23[b] | 25[b] | 34 | 39[a] |
| Proportion saying 'it is very important to guarantee equality between men and women' | 65 | 73 | 70 | 72 |
| Proportion saying 'a certain proportion of the top jobs in government should go to women' | 37[a] | 58[b] | 48[ac] | 58[ad] |
| Minimum number of cases (except second and last items have approximately half the number of cases) | 275 | 640 | 260 | 640 |

Groups indicated [a] are significantly different from groups indicated [b] at the .05 level (anova).
Groups indicated [c] are significantly different from groups indicated [d] at the .05 level (anova).

## The Charter of Rights Study

The items included in the Charter of Rights table can be divided into three groups. For the first pair of items, 'it should be against the law to speak in such a way as to promote hatred', and 'a proportion of the top government jobs should go to French Canadians', there is no systematic variation in response according to either the gender of the respondent or the gender of the interviewer (Table 2). This is the most common response pattern in the data set.

A gender effect, however, is present in the third, fourth, and fifth items. The item concerned with banning or allowing 'films that show sexually explicit acts' is similar to the AIDS survey item about censorship (censors' right to ban or require cuts to films). The results are also similar. Again men give the more 'permissive' response. Men, when interviewed by men (63 per cent), are more likely (but not at a level of statistical significance) to say 'films that show sexually explicit acts' should be allowed, than when they are interviewed by women (58 per cent). The proportion of women saying these films should be allowed is significantly less than the proportion of men and is independent of the gender of the interviewer (36 and 35 per cent).

Also, men (23 and 25 per cent) are less likely than women (34 to 39 per cent) to agree that 'large companies should have quotas about the number of women they hire.' These differences in response between men and women are statistically significant. Although the differences are less striking and not statistically significant, men (79 and 80 per cent) more often than women demonstrate support for the Canadian Charter of Rights by saying it 'is a good thing' (73 and 75 per cent).

The final two items evidence a gender-of-interviewer effect. As was the case in the AIDS Survey, we find that men when interviewed by other men express more conservative positions than when they are interviewed by women. Thus we find 65 per cent of men say 'it is very impor-

tant to guarantee equality between men and women' when interviewed by a man, whereas 8 per cent more, or 73 per cent of men, express belief in guaranteeing equality between the sexes when interviewed by a woman. Male response, when the interviewer was a woman, is about the same as female response, which does not vary by interviewer gender (70 and 72 per cent). The same pattern holds for the final item in the table, 'proportion of the top government jobs should be set aside for women.' Again men interviewed by men are least supportive of this type of affirmative action (37 per cent). Men interviewed by women (58 per cent) and women interviewed by either men (48 per cent) or women (58 per cent) are more supportive (the difference between the man/man group and the other three groups is significant at the .05 level).

The different level and pattern of support for the two affirmative action items deserves comment. Support for 'quotas in large companies' is lower than support for 'setting aside a certain proportion of the top jobs in government' for each of the four interviewer-respondent combinations. Part of this difference may be a consequence of the wording in each item. 'Quotas' may sound harsher and more demanding than a 'certain proportion'. This difference in tone is somewhat analogous to the 'forbid' and 'not allow' experiments reported by Schuman and Presser.[17] The argument is that even though the terms have the same affective meaning, to 'forbid' has a harsher connotation than to 'not allow'. It is also possible that some respondents may support affirmative action in government, but not in large companies, as they may feel a claim for affirmative action by their government is more reasonable than a claim for affirmative action by 'regulating' a 'private-sector' organization.

In any case, neither of these two arguments provides a suitable answer as to why the gender-of-interviewer effect was present only in the government item. A possible hypothesis may be that the harsher tone as expressed in quotas for large companies, and the differences between private- and public-sector support for affirmative action, may mitigate the male respondent's need to give the socially acceptable response.

Unlike the case in the AIDS survey, there is a hint of gender-of-interviewer effect for women respondents in the Charter of Rights study. In both the affirmative action items, women are more supportive of affirmative action when interviewed by other women than when they are interviewed by men. Five per cent more women support quotas when interviewed by women than when interviewed by men. The difference rises to 10 per cent (and is significant) in the second affirmative action item. Women may feel more comfortable expressing their support for affirmative action to other women than to men. Alternative explanations include a desire not to offend men (underreporting) or a need to support other women (overreporting).

The Electoral Reform Survey

As is the case in the first two surveys, there are items in the electoral reform survey that do not evidence either a gender-of-respondent or a gender-of-interviewer effect (Table 3). The first item, asking if corporations should be allowed 'to advertise and promote their position during their election campaigns', is not affected by the gender of the respondent—45 and 46 per cent of men vote to allow corporations to advertise their position, while 43 and 48 per cent of women do so. Although this pattern, where neither gender of respondent nor gender of interviewer impacted on response was most common, gender and gender-of-interviewer effects are present in the electoral reform survey.

Men interviewed by either sex (67 per cent for both scenarios) are more in favour of 'reimbursing some of the money spent by parties and candidates during an election' than are women when interviewed by men (60 per cent) or other women (61 per cent). Likewise, men (28 and

27 per cent) are more likely than women (23 and 22 per cent) to indicate that elections work better in Canada than in the United States.

There is strong evidence for gender-of-interviewer effects in the electoral reform survey. When interviewed by women, men are 10 per cent more likely to say having 'many more men than women in the House of Commons' is a 'very serious' or 'serious problem' than when they are interviewed by men (significant at the .05 level). The proportion of men who, when interviewed by women, think government would be 'much better' or 'better' if there were 'as many women as men in the House' is, at 44 per cent, 14 per cent higher than the number of men who think this is the case when they complete the interview with male interviewers. Finally, although the difference is very small and not significant, we also find that men, when interviewed by men (26 per cent), are more likely to say 'everyone would be better off if women stayed at home and raised their children' than when they are interviewed by women (23 per cent).

The pattern of response for women, while lacking the statistical significance of the pattern for men, is also suggestive of a gender-of-interviewer effect. In the item asking how serious a problem underrepresentation of women is in the House of Commons, women, when interviewed by men, are 4 per cent less likely to identify this as a serious problem than when they are interviewed by other women. The difference between response according to the gender of the interviewer is larger (9 per cent) on the item asking if having more women would improve the quality of government (33 per cent of women think it would improve government when interviewed by men and 42 per cent when interviewed by other women).

In all three studies, for the affirmative action items, some men give different answers to female interviewers than to male interviewers. Differences range from 10 per cent on the question about women in the House of Commons to 21 per cent on the question of setting aside a proportion

## Table 3: Electoral Reform Survey: Response to Items by the Gender of the Interviewer and Respondent (percentage distribution)

| Question and Response | Gender of Interviewer/Respondent | | | |
| --- | --- | --- | --- | --- |
| | Man/ Man | Woman/ Man | Man/ Woman | Woman/ Woman |
| Per cent responding 'be allowed' to: 'Should corporations be allowed to advertise and promote their positions during election campaigns?' | 46 | 45 | 43 | 48 |
| Per cent responding 'government should reimburse some of the  money spent by parties and candidates during an election' | 67 | 67 | 60 | 61 |
| Per cent responding 'Elections work better in Canada than in the US' | 28 | 27 | 23 | 22 |
| Per cent responding 'very serious' or 'serious' problem to: 'As you may know, there are many more men than women in the House of Commons. In your view how serious a problem is this?' | 20[a] | 30[b] | 36[b] | 40[b] |
| Per cent saying 'If there were as many women as men in the House, government would be either much better or better' | 30[a] | 44[b] | 33[a] | 42[b] |
| Per cent 'basically agreeing' to  item: 'Everyone would be better off if women stayed at home and raised children' | 26 | 23 | 27 | 26 |
| Minimum number of cases (except first two items which have approximately half the  number of cases) | 520 | 750 | 440 | 715 |

Groups indicated [a] are significantly different from groups indicated [b] at the .05 level (anova).

of top jobs in government for women. Men are more supportive of traditional roles and attitudes. When asked about affirmative action issues in each of the three surveys, the difference in men's response according to the gender of the interviewer is statistically significant. There is again limited evidence that women adjust their responses according to the gender of the interviewer. And, as was the case for men, these differences, based upon the gender of the interviewer, are largest for the affirmative action type items.

## Discussion

Although gender-of-interviewer effects are either not present or have limited impact on items central to each study, we have found consistent evidence for gender-of-interviewer effects for affirmative action type questions. For male respondents, the gender of the interviewer is a powerful determinant of response for these types of questions. In all three surveys men gave more supportive answers to female interviewers than they did to male interviewers. It is difficult to be certain why this should be so; however, social desirability may help explain differing male response. Sudman and Bradburn argue that respondents face a dilemma in the interview situation.[18] By participating in the interview they are demonstrating a 'motivation to be a good respondent and provide the information that is asked for'. At the same time they want to answer in a way 'that reflects well on themselves'. In earlier work, the authors demonstrated that seemingly innocuous questions such as ownership of a library card or whether the respondent was registered to vote are subject to overreporting by 11 to 21 per cent.[19] The questions on affirmative action are likely to be at least as sensitive as questions about owning a library card. Reporting support for 'women's issues' may, for some men, be seen as the correct, or socially desirable, response. When men are interviewed by other men, the private 'one-on-one' situation may, for some men, create a 'conspiratorial' situation where they feel they really can say what they think. Conversely, perhaps some men are adjusting their response to suit what they believe other men (the interviewers) want to hear.[20]

The findings for gender of interviewer are similar to those for race-of-interviewer effects. In both cases, effects are found only for items that address issues relating to the interviewer characteristic of race or gender. Also, in both types of effects, those with a 'prominent' position in society give socially desirable answers to the more socially disadvantaged (men deferring to women and Whites to Blacks). Although Hatchett and Schuman and others question the asymmetry of the race-of-interviewer effect and show that Whites as well as Blacks are influenced by the interviewer's race, the evidence presented here, like some of the reviews of race-of-interviewer effect, follow the pattern of the more socially advantaged deferring to the more socially disadvantaged.[21]

The extent to which the combined impact of race and gender of interviewer modifies or mag-nifies differences in reporting by respondents on topics with a gender and race component (for example, support for a Black woman candidate in an election) is an interesting question. How would answers from White men vary when the interviewer was a Black woman rather than a White man?

The implications of gender-of-interviewer effects for analysis of survey data are quite straightforward. The implications for the collection of survey data are less clear. Survey organizations must routinely add the gender of the interviewer to their data sets. This information needs to be used by researchers when analysing data, especially data that may be sensitive to the gender of the interviewer. For example, research on the 'gender gap' in politics, attitudes towards abortion, affirmative action, and so forth needs to look at gender-of-interviewer effects. Otherwise, because most survey firms employ mainly women as interviewers, we may constantly be incorrectly reporting male attitudes about gender-based issues.[22] Identification of gender-of-interviewer effects tells us as much about our respondents' values as knowing how the relative proportion of men and women answer a particular question.

The other difficult question to answer is whether or not survey organizations should attempt to match the gender of the interviewer to the respondent. Electing to do so indicates that the organization assumes responses to questions that may be sensitive to the gender of the respondent are more valid when obtained from an interviewer of the same sex. This assumption may or may not be true. Certainly the variation in response by the gender of the interviewer may help in understanding attitudes and determining values. Because most interviewers are female, perhaps a more reasonable strategy would be for survey firms to increase the proportion of male interviewers so that the impact of the gender of the interviewer on survey data can be a standard part of data analysis.

Recently, researchers have reminded us that the survey interview is as much an interaction between the respondent and interviewer as it is the completion of a standardized measurement

tool.[23] Clearly, one of the critical background factors that influences that interaction between the respondent and the interviewer is their gender.

## Notes

1. Herbert H. Hyman, J. Feldman, and C. Stember, *Interviewing in Social Research* (Chicago: University of Chicago Press, 1954).
2. Norman M. Bradburn, 'Response Effects', in Peter H. Rossi, James D. Wright, and Andy B. Anderson, eds, *The Handbook of Survey Research* (Orlando: Academic Press, 1983).
3. Patrick Cotter, Jeffery Cohen, and Philip B. Coulter, 'Race-of-Interviewer Effects in Telephone Interviews', *Public Opinion Quarterly* 46 (1981): 278–84, demonstrated that race-of-interviewer effects are found in telephone surveys. Other research has found ethnicity-of-interviewer effects in telephone surveys: see Steven D. Reese, Wayne A. Danielson, Pamela J. Shoemaker, Tsan-Kuo Chang, and Huei-Ling Hsu, 'Ethnicity of Interviewer Effects Among Mexican Americans and Anglos', *Public Opinion Quarterly* 50 (1981): 563–72.
4. Howard Schuman and Jean M. Converse, 'The Effect of Black and White Interviewers on Black Response', *Public Opinion Quarterly* 35 (1971): 44–8. Shirley Hatchett and Howard Schuman, 'White Respondents and Race of Interviewer Effects', *Public Opinion Quarterly* 39 (1975–6); 523–8; Cotter, Cohen, and Coulter, 'Race-of-Interviewer Effects in Telephone Interviews'; Barbara A. Anderson, Brian D. Silver, and Paul R. Abramson, 'The Effects of Race of the Interviewer on Measures of Electoral Participation by Blacks in SRC National Election Studies', *Pubic Opinion Quarterly* 52 (1988): 53–83; Steven E. Finkel, Thomas M. Guterbock, and Marian J. Borg, 'Race of Interviewer Effects in a Pre-election Poll', *Public Opinion Quarterly* 55 (1991): 313–30.
5. Schuman and Converse, 'Effect of Black and White Interviewers on Black Response'.
6. Bruce A. Campbell, 'Race of Interviewer Effects Among Southern Adolescents', *Public Opinion Quarterly* 45 (1981): 231–44.
7. Reese et al., 'Ethnicity of Interviewer Effects Among Mexican Americans and Anglos'.
8. Michael F. Weeks and R. Paul Moore, 'Ethnicity and Interviewer Effects on Ethnic Respondents', *Public Opinion Quarterly* 45 (1981): 244–9.
9. Hyman, Feldman, and Stember, *Interviewing in Social Research*.
10. Weldon T. Johnson and John D. DeLamater, 'Response Effects in Sex Surveys', *Public Opinion Quarterly* 40 (1976): 165–81.
11. M. Schofield, *The Sexual Behaviour of Young People* (London: Longman, 1965).
12. I.L. Reiss, *The Social Context of Premarital Sexual Permissiveness* (New York: Rinehart and Winston, 1967).
13. Floyd J. Fowler Jr and Thomas W. Mangione, *Standardizing Survey Interviewing: Minimizing Interviewer-Related Error* (Newbury Park, Calif.: Sage, 1990).
14. The survey was funded by the Federal Centre for AIDS, Health and Welfare Canada. Michael Ornstein, York University, was the principal investigator.
15. The survey was funded by the Social Sciences and Humanities Research Council of Canada. Paul M. Sniderman, Stanford University, was the principal investigator. Co-investigators were Peter H. Russell, University of Toronto, Philip E. Tetlock, University of California at Berkeley, and Joseph F. Fletcher, University of Toronto.
16. The survey was funded by the Royal Commission on Electoral Reform and Party Financing. André Blais, Université de Montréal, and Elizabeth Gidengil, McGill University, were the principal investigators.
17. Howard Schuman and Stanley Presser, *Questions and Answers in Attitude Surveys: Experiments on Question Form, Wording, and Content* (New York: Academic Press, 1981).
18. Seymour Sudman and Norman M. Bradburn, *Asking Questions: A Practical Guide to Questionnaire Design* (San Francisco: Jossey-Bass, 1982).

19. Norman M. Bradburn, Seymour Sudman, and associates, *Improving Interview Method and Questionnaire Design* (San Francisco: Jossey-Bass, 1979).

20. By using logistic regression techniques, we can determine the relative importance of gender of interviewer in predicting response to affirmative action items and determine if any of the variation in response according to the gender of the interviewer identified in the cross-tabulations is accounted for by other factors. Briefly summarized, the results of the logit regression show that, after the gender of the respondent, the gender of the interviewer was the most powerful predictor of attitudes towards affirmative action. Indeed, the interviewer's gender was either as powerful as, or a more powerful predictor of response than, age, education, income, and marital status, variables more traditionally used to explain attitudes and values. Finally, in the logit models, the hints in the cross tabular data that suggest women's response may also be affected by the gender of the interviewer are not substantiated. A complete discussion of the logistic regression can be found in an earlier version of the paper in the Institute for Social Research's publication series.

21. Hatchett and Schuman, 'White Respondents and Race of Interviewer Effects'.

22. Fowler and Mangione, *Standardizing Survey Interviewing*.

23. Lucy Suchman and Brigitte Jordan, 'Validity and the Collaborative Construction of Meaning in Face to Face Surveys', in Judith M. Tanur, ed., *Questions About Questions: Inquiries into the Cognitive Bases of Surveys* (New York: Russell Sage, 1992), 241–67.

# The Fallacy of Democratic Élitism:
## Élite Competition and Commitment to Civil Liberties

Paul M. Sniderman, Joseph F. Fletcher, Peter H. Russell, Philip E. Tetlock, Brian J. Gaines

It is now widely accepted that political élites are more committed to civil liberties than the public at large; indeed, so much more so that it is commonly supposed that élites serve as a bulwark against mass intolerance.[1] But notwithstanding the seeming surfeit of evidence, we think that the thesis of democratic élitism deserves a sober, second thought.

Our argument is this. The engine of modern democratic politics is competition between élites, characteristically organized around the electoral system. This electoral competition, as Schumpeter famously observed, defines the democratic method itself, which is 'that institutional arrangement for arriving at political decisions in which individuals acquire the power to decide by means of a competitive struggle for the people's vote.'[2]

The competitive struggle for the people's vote is waged on a number of fronts, among them issues of civil liberties and civil rights. In part, political parties divide on issues of civil liberties out of political advantage, in part out of political conviction. Either way, the effect is to encourage divergence among élites competing for popular support in their orientation to civil liberties. As against previous research, then, which has emphasized the contrast between the mass public and élites taken as a whole, we want to suggest that élite-mass differences tend to be eclipsed, both in size and in political significance, by differences in commitment to basic rights that divide political élites themselves.

From *British Journal of Political Science* 21 (1991): 349–70. Reprinted with the permission of Cambridge University Press.

## The Thesis of Democratic Élitism

Previous research has stressed the extent to which the politically aware and influential support civil liberties more than ordinary citizens. In turn, this has invited the conclusion—paradoxical at first sight—that it is political élites who serve as custodians of democratic values: a conclusion drawn by researchers since Stouffer's seminal study. As McClosky and Brill observe:[3]

> While the level of mass public support for civil liberties may be disappointing to many civil libertarians, they may take comfort from the fact, as Stouffer did, that the community leaders, who are more tolerant than the general public, are likely to exercise a disproportionate influence on public policy.[4]

The classic argument on élites, masses, and democratic values hinges on two claims. The first—we shall call this 'the consensus claim'—asserts that the active political minority tend to be overwhelmingly in agreement with key democratic values, while the general public tends to be sharply divided on them—except as abstract pieties. No one of course takes the position that the consensus among élites is perfect: on the contrary, there is a clear-eyed appreciation of the unevenness of their support for basic rights. Nevertheless, in contrasting élite and mass samples—whether drawn by Stouffer, or by McClosky and his colleagues, or by Nunn and his colleagues or by Sullivan and his[5]—élites have invariably been found to be more committed to civil liberties than the mass public.

The conclusion to draw from the survey evidence contrasting élite and mass commitment to civil liberties has seemed obvious: élites, previous research suggests, are a better bet than the ordinary citizen—not necessarily a sure bet, mind you, merely a better one—to stand by democratic values under pressure. As McClosky has written: 'The evidence suggests that it is the articulate classes rather than the public who serve as *the major repositories of the public conscience and as carriers of the Creed. Responsibility for keeping the system going, hence, falls most heavily on them.*'[6]

To declare that the politically aware and influential are 'the major repositories of the public conscience' and the 'carriers of the [democratic] Creed' is to make a strong claim. But why are the politically active and aware more committed to civil liberties than the public? Not because they constitute a 'natural' élite. On the contrary, the claim is that the politically active acquire their commitment to democratic values largely through political activity itself. This claim we shall call 'the participation claim'.

First sketched by Key and Dahl in 1961, the participation claim has been most systematically expounded over 20 years later, by McClosky and Brill in 1983.[7] They argue that the more politically active and involved tend, as a consequence of their very involvement in politics, to be more likely: (1) to be *exposed* to the norms of civil liberties that constitute the society's creed; (2) to *comprehend* these civil libertarian norms; and (3) to be more strongly motivated to *accept* them.[8] Consistent with this claim, they present innumerable contrasts of élite and mass samples, showing that the former tend to be regularly and strikingly more in favour than the latter of freedoms of speech and press, of symbolic speech, of assembly and religion, of privacy and of lifestyle.[9]

The consensus claim and the participation claim fit naturally together. The more politically active and aware have an advantage over the ordinary citizen in understanding the subtleties and complexities of issues of civil liberties by virtue of the company they keep. They interact more with those who care about democratic principles and

hence are more exposed to civil libertarian norms;[10] they are under more pressure to ensure that their opinions on specific issues are consistent with their attitudes on larger principles and hence are more likely to favour democratic values in controversial cases; and they are more motivated to accept the established principles of democratic politics, if not to win acceptance and get ahead, then to avoid being branded a deviant and rejected as a dissenter.[11]

We dub the coupling of the consensus and the participation claims the thesis of democratic élitism. This coinage fits past practice.[12] It also conforms with fair usage, and on two different counts: firstly, the consensus claim clearly strikes an élitist note given its stress on the power of political involvement to promote tolerance and commitment to democratic values in a liberal society.[13] For the record it is worth emphasizing that in invoking the concept of élites, we do not have in mind a sharply demarcated ruling class or power élite; on the contrary, we mean only to refer to those who are particularly active in public affairs and hence uncommonly informed about political issues and influential in decisions about them. Our definition and those employed in previous studies comparing élites with the general public thus coincide—a point of agreement worth emphasis since it means that our substantive differences with the classic findings are not a function of definitional differences.

As for the notion of democratic values, we have in mind, at the core, an array of basic rights—for example, the right to hold unpopular opinions, to voice one's political preferences, to join others and to urge others to join in a public cause, and so on. For some purposes it is useful to draw a line between democratic values, on the one hand, and liberal values on the other. But for us the crucial consideration is comparability with previous research. Hence we are committed to ensuring that our usage of the notion of democratic values parallels previous usage, both conceptually and operationally, a parallelism necessary so that the different conclusions we draw cannot be dismissed as due to the different measurement procedures we use.

For our part, we believe the thesis of democratic élitism suffers a number of flaws. The most serious of these flaws is neglect of the institutions of democratic politics—most notably, the electoral system. People learn as a consequence of political involvement, but what they learn depends very much on the company they keep. To take an empirically extreme but therefore conceptually vivid example, the person who immerses himself in the John Birtch Society may well be transformed by the experience, but the effect of this experience is unlikely to be a special devotion to civil liberties and civil rights. Political socialization at the élite level involves exposure not simply to the values of the larger culture but also to the norms of particular political groups; and insofar as these political groups themselves divide over issues of civil liberties, the differences in support for civil liberties among élites can matter more than the differences between élites and the public at large.

## The Data

We shall base our primary analysis upon a study of attitudes towards civil liberties that we conducted in the wake of the establishment of the [Canadian] Charter of Rights and Freedoms . . . . Having set out our case using the Canadian data, we shall demonstrate that an even stronger version of our argument is supported by studies which were conducted in the United States and form the largest part of the empirical basis for the theory of democratic élitism.

The Charter data were collected, in 1987, by the Institute of Social Research at York University, as part of the Charter of Rights project.[14] A representative sample of the Canadian public was drawn using a modified random digit dialling technique (RDD), with an additional random selection within each household.[15] The overall response rate was 63.5 per cent, yielding a sample size of

2,084. In addition, we obtained a special élite sample, made up of members of Parliament, both federal and provincial. MPS, MPPS, and MLAS were interviewed from the Progressive Conservative, Liberal, New Democratic, and Social Credit parties and from the Parti Québécois. The selection within each party was random, with the proportions across parties fixed to give a larger share of the sample to the two parties, the Conservative and Liberal parties, with the largest share of parliamentary seats.

Each respondent was interviewed over the telephone, respondents from both samples being asked the same questions, some incidental variations aside. At the end of the telephone interview, respondents were asked to complete a self-administered questionnaire. To those from whom an address was obtained (approximately 83 per cent), a mail questionnaire was sent, along with the means to return it. Seventy-five per cent of the mass sample and 63 per cent of the political élite sample returned completed questionnaires. Full details of data collection procedures are set out in the technical documentation of the Charter project, available from the Institute for Social Research.[16]

## Findings

### The Politics of Liberty

Our starting point is élite and mass attitudes towards the value of liberty, expressed in support for quintessential rights such as freedom of expression and assembly. The Charter study accordingly asked whether members of extreme political groups should be allowed to hold a public rally. The results, displayed in Table 1, snugly fit the thesis of democratic élitism: political élites overwhelmingly support freedom of assembly. Differently put, even the least sympathetic élites, the Conservative and Liberal élites, are markedly more sympathetic than the public at large.

But of course, following the research of Sullivan, Piereson, and Marcus, this type of result is open to objection: élites may appear more tolerant because the groups (or acts) that studies of tolerance conventionally investigate are more threatening to the ordinary citizen than to élites.[17] Since political élites have repeated, and often cordial, interactions with people subscribing to a broad range of points of view, they may find some groups less threatening than the average citizen does, in which case élite support for the rights of such groups may reflect not higher levels of tolerance, but rather lower levels of aversion towards the group to be tolerated.

To ensure élite-mass comparability, the 'content-controlled' method was employed.[18] The method requires respondents to select from a list of groups the one they like the least, with each respondent then being asked whether *this* particular group should, or should not, be allowed to hold a public rally. The majority of political élites back freedom of association, even in the case of the group they most dislike. In contrast, the public fails this test of civil liberties, with two-thirds of them denying that the group they like the least should be allowed to hold a rally.

Consider, next, freedom of expression. We asked: 'Should groups like the Nazis and Ku Klux Klan be allowed to appear on public television to state their views?' Respondents were supplied with two alternative responses: 'No, because it would be offensive to certain racial or religious groups', or 'Yes, because it should be allowed no matter who is offended.'[19]

Two findings stand out in Table 1. Firstly, consistent with the thesis of democratic élitism, there is a marked difference between the responses of the mass public and of political élites as a whole. However, secondly and more provocatively, there is a striking variation among political élites in their commitment to civil liberties; indeed, so much so that the range of commitment across political parties overlaps that of the public at large. Thus, comparable majorities of Liberals, the separatist Parti Québécois (PQ), and the public at large believe that the Nazis and the Ku Klux

Klan should not be allowed public air time to express their point of view.

The differences among élites in reaction to issues of civil liberties have an element of contingency. Which party is most, and which least, in favour of civil liberties is partly bound up with the political coloration of specific controversies. On the specific question of free speech for extreme right-wing groups, for example, the Conservatives and the social democratic NDP are jointly the most favourable towards freedom of expression. But consider an issue of freedom of expression featuring an element of traditional morality: 'Should films showing sexually explicit acts be allowed or should they be banned?'

Sex films are some distance from classic cases of political expression, and some would take the position that such films do not raise genuine issues of civil liberties. But that is just our point: the boundaries of civil liberties are inherently contestable, and the terms of the debate are set in part by the electoral interests and ideological commitments of political actors. Table 1 illustrates these political dynamics. Once again there is marked variation among élites in their support for civil liberties, but now the Conservatives and the Social Credit Party are the least approving of freedom of expression—not surprisingly, considering the emphasis both attach to the preservation of traditional moral values. At the other extreme are the NDP and PQ, an overwhelming majority of whom are opposed to banning films.

Patently, on this issue of censorship there is no élite consensus. On the one side, there is nothing to choose on this issue between the views of the public and those of the governing Conservative Party; on the other, there is everything to choose between the positions of political élites across parties.

The Politics of Order

Issues of civil liberties require people to choose between competing values—for example, between

## Table 1: The Politics of Liberty: A Comparison of Mass and Élite Attitudes

Do you think members of extreme political groups should be allowed to hold public rallies in our cities, or should not be allowed to do so?

| | Mass (%) | Élite (%) | Élite Sample by Party | | | | |
| | | | PC (%) | Lib (%) | NDP (%) | PQ (%) | SC (%) |
|---|---|---|---|---|---|---|---|
| Should | 61 | 87 | 82 | 79 | 97 | 93 | 90 |
| Should not | 39 | 13 | 18 | 21 | 3 | 7 | 10 |
| Total | 100 | 100 | 100 | 100 | 100 | 100 | 100 |
| N | (1,947) | (512) | (122) | (144) | (106) | (106) | (33) |

The group you most dislike [content-controlled] should be allowed to hold public rallies in our cities. Do you strongly agree, agree, disagree, or strongly disagree?

| | Mass (%) | Élite (%) | Élite Sample by Party | | | | |
| | | | PC (%) | Lib (%) | NDP (%) | PQ (%) | SC (%) |
|---|---|---|---|---|---|---|---|
| Strongly agree | 6 | 13 | 13 | 13 | 13 | 9 | 23 |
| Agree | 26 | 52 | 53 | 47 | 65 | 44 | 54 |
| Uncertain | 2 | 2 | 1 | 2 | 4 | 1 | 6 |
| Disagree | 22 | 17 | 16 | 19 | 9 | 25 | 9 |
| Strongly disagree | 43 | 16 | 17 | 20 | 8 | 21 | 8 |
| Total | 100 | 100 | 100 | 100 | 100 | 100 | 100 |
| N | (1,889) | (466) | (111) | (126) | (104) | (96) | (30) |

Should groups like the Nazis and Ku Klux Klan be allowed to appear on public television to state their views?

| | Mass (%) | Élite (%) | Élite Sample by Party | | | | |
| | | | PC (%) | Lib (%) | NDP (%) | PQ (%) | SC (%) |
|---|---|---|---|---|---|---|---|
| Yes* | 20 | 38 | 47 | 31 | 52 | 22 | 32 |
| Uncertain** | 22 | 22 | 20 | 14 | 23 | 26 | 36 |
| No*** | 58 | 40 | 33 | 55 | 25 | 52 | 32 |
| Total | 100 | 100 | 100 | 100 | 100 | 100 | 100 |
| N | (1,219) | (305) | (69) | (75) | (77) | (62) | (21) |

Do you think that films that show sexually explicit acts should be allowed, or should they be banned?

| | Mass (%) | Élite (%) | Élite Sample by Party | | | | |
| | | | PC (%) | Lib (%) | NDP (%) | PQ (%) | SC (%) |
|---|---|---|---|---|---|---|---|
| Allowed | 48 | 68 | 47 | 65 | 86 | 84 | 49 |
| Banned | 52 | 32 | 53 | 35 | 14 | 16 | 51 |
| Total | 100 | 100 | 100 | 100 | 100 | 100 | 100 |
| N | (2,039) | (496) | (117) | (141) | (106) | (101) | (31) |

Note: Entries are vertical percentages, rounded to the nearest whole number. PC = Progressive Conservative,
Lib = Liberal, NDP = New Democratic Party, PQ = Parti Québécois, SC = Social Credit.

   * 'Yes, should be allowed no matter who is offended.'

  ** 'Neither' or 'Undecided'.

*** 'No, because they would offend certain racial or religious groups.'

freedom and order. There are unavoidable trade-offs between the rights of citizens to urge their political views and the responsibility of authorities to ensure public order and safety. Accordingly, we asked: 'Should a town or city be able to limit public demonstrations that city officials think might turn violent against persons and property?'

A genuine conflict is posed here: when should freedom of assembly trump public safety? Support for civil liberties meets its toughest challenge from competing values in hard cases.[20] It does not matter what people think of the Bill of Rights so far as a Boy Scout march in Peoria is concerned: it does matter so far as a Nazi march in Skokie is concerned. Moreover, the nub of the issue here is not whether a demonstration should be limited if there is a clear evidence of a high risk of violence, but—and this is rather different—whether it should be restricted if 'city officials think' it might turn violent, surely a difference of which political élites should be cognizant if they are to play the role assigned to them by the thesis of democratic élitism.

It is sobering, therefore, to inspect the reactions of citizens and political élites, set out in Table 2. Eight out of ten of the public favour limits on public demonstrations if public officials believe that there is a risk of violence. But, and this is the crucial point, Liberal élites, Conservative élites, and Parti Québécois élites are just as likely to take the same position and Social Credit élites even more so. The New Democrats offer a marked contrast, not only to the public at large, but to other political élites: they are between two and three times as likely to disapprove of local officials exercising a regulative authority over public demonstrations. All the same, even in the NDP élite, the modal position is to approve of such authority.

Let us next consider when freedom of speech and morality come into conflict. We asked which of two positions came closer to our respondents' own view: 'The government has no right to decide what should or should not be published' or 'To

protect its moral values, a society sometimes has to forbid certain things from being published.'[21]

We do not want to imply that one of these positions is the 'objectively' correct position from the point of view of democratic theory. Our concern instead is whether political élites require a different level of proof than ordinary citizens before siding with community standards over individual rights. What, after all, can it mean to say that élites are more committed to civil liberties if they are not, at a minimum, more wary of assigning power to government when the exercise of that power can encroach on citizens' rights? But, as Table 2 demonstrates, political élites (again with the exception of the NDP) are if anything more likely than the public to support the principle of government censorship in order to protect 'society's moral values'.

Consider another example of value conflict inherent in issues of civil liberties. There is inevitably room for debate over whether it is the function of law to protect the values of the community or to ensure individual autonomy. So we asked whether 'Our laws should aim to: enforce the community's standards of right and wrong', or 'Protect a citizen's right to live by any moral standard he chooses.'[22]

Élite reactions, as Table 2 shows, cover a wide range. At one extreme, 62 per cent of Conservatives believe that the aim of the law should be to enforce community standards of right and wrong, while at the other, only 19 per cent of the Parti Québécois élite agree, with Liberal and New Democrat élites neatly spaced between. Indeed, the differences between the party élites are so substantial that it does not make sense to talk of a distinctively élite point of view on the tension between community standards and individual rights. Moreover, and this is the second part of our claim, the choice presupposed by the thesis of democratic élitism is a misleading choice. If you ask what difference it makes whether decisions pertaining to civil liberties are made by élites or ordinary citizens, the answer

## Table 2: The Politics of Order: A Comparison of Mass and Élite Attitudes

Should a town or city be able to limit public demonstrations that city officials think might turn violent against persons and property?

| | | | | Élite Sample by Party | | | |
|---|---|---|---|---|---|---|---|
| | Mass (%) | Élite (%) | PC (%) | Lib (%) | NDP (%) | PQ (%) | SC (%) |
| No | 13 | 21 | 16 | 18 | 37 | 16 | 4 |
| Uncertain | 8 | 7 | 7 | 3 | 16 | 4 | 4 |
| Yes | 79 | 72 | 77 | 79 | 47 | 80 | 92 |
| Total | 100 | 100 | 100 | 100 | 100 | 100 | 100 |
| N | (1,230) | (306) | (69) | (78) | (76) | (62) | (21) |

Which of these comes closer to your own view?
(1) The government has no right to decide what should or should not be published.
(2) To protect its moral values, a society sometimes has to forbid certain things from being published.

| | | | | Élite Sample by Party | | | |
|---|---|---|---|---|---|---|---|
| | Mass (%) | Élite (%) | PC (%) | Lib (%) | NDP (%) | PQ (%) | SC (%) |
| (1) No right | 21 | 19 | 19 | 20 | 24 | 10 | 26 |
| Uncertain | 13 | 11 | 8 | 8 | 18 | 12 | 6 |
| (2) Forbid | 66 | 70 | 73 | 73 | 58 | 79 | 68 |
| Total | 100 | 100 | 100 | 100 | 100 | 100 | 100 |
| N | (1,225) | (309) | (68) | (77) | (79) | (65) | (21) |

Our laws should aim to:   (1) Enforce the community's standards of right and wrong.
(2) Protect a citizen's right to live by any moral standard he chooses.

| | | | | Élite Sample by Party | | | |
|---|---|---|---|---|---|---|---|
| | Mass (%) | Élite (%) | PC (%) | Lib (%) | NDP (%) | PQ (%) | SC (%) |
| (2) Protect | 25 | 34 | 19 | 36 | 27 | 64 | 13 |
| Uncertain | 18 | 24 | 19 | 19 | 41 | 17 | 13 |
| (1) Enforce | 57 | 42 | 62 | 46 | 32 | 19 | 73 |
| Total | 100 | 100 | 100 | 100 | 100 | 100 | 100 |
| N | (1,220) | (311) | (69) | (78) | (79) | (65) | (21) |

Do you think the search of a young man seen near a house where the police know that drugs are sold is a reasonable search, or does it violate the young man's rights?

| | | | | Élite Sample by Party | | | |
|---|---|---|---|---|---|---|---|
| | Mass (%) | Élite (%) | PC (%) | Lib (%) | NDP (%) | PQ (%) | SC (%) |
| Violation | 41 | 43 | 23 | 45 | 60 | 50 | 25 |
| Reasonable | 59 | 57 | 77 | 55 | 40 | 50 | 75 |
| Total | 100 | 100 | 100 | 100 | 100 | 100 | 100 |
| N | (2,049) | (507) | (123) | (142) | (108) | (102) | (33) |

Note: Entries are vertical percentages, rounded to the nearest whole number. PC = Progressive Conservative, Lib = Liberal, NDP = New Democratic Party, PQ = Parti Québécois, SC = Social Credit. 'Uncertain' includes both the response 'Undecided' and the response 'Neither'.

depends on *which* élites are in power; and, as it happens, looking at the reaction of the party that currently controls the federal government, it makes no difference whatever.

Consider, finally, a paradigmatic example of when the values of order and liberty come into conflict in contemporary society—namely, the issue of crime. We asked respondents: 'To consider an instance where the police see a young man they do not recognize walking very near a house where they know drugs are being sold. They search him and find he is carrying drugs.' Then we asked whether this search is reasonable or a violation of the young man's rights.

As Table 2 demonstrates, there is again a very sharp divergence in the reactions of political élites. Conservatives overwhelmingly say that the search is legitimate; the NDP characteristically reject the search as a violation of the young man's rights; while both Liberals and the PQ split right down the middle. And again, the crucial consideration for the politics of civil liberties is not whether decisions get made by élites or mass publics but rather *which* élites are charged with responsibility for them. Insofar as what counts is a readiness to place a heavier weight on considerations of freedom *per se* as against competing values—the traditional test by which the superiority of the élites is asserted— the case of civil liberties would be better served if a randomly selected citizen made a decision on this issue as opposed to an elected member of the political party currently governing Canada.

### The Politics of Responsibility and Threat: Wiretapping and Emergency Powers

Issues of civil liberties can be complex, not only because they entail weighing competing values, but also because they require weighing competing conjectures about future states of the world. Thus, sometimes the difficulty is not whether a freedom should be curtailed so that the state can deal responsibly with a crime that has been committed, but rather whether some restrictions are in

order because there is a risk that a crime is about to be committed.

Considerations that call for qualification of civil liberties on the ground of what is about to happen we shall call threats. Threats are inherently difficult to balance against civil liberties because there is inherent uncertainty about what might happen. Do élites, in balancing the rights of citizens against threats to the larger community, systematically give greater weight than the public does to forestalling harm and hence lesser weight to protecting civil liberties?

Our first test focuses on wiretapping, perhaps the most evocative symbol of the intrusive powers of government. No doubt there are abuses in most democracies of the government's powers of surveillance, particularly on the grounds of protecting national security but also in the interest of fighting crime. In Canada, however, these abuses have received special notoriety, with a royal commission established specifically to hold public hearings and to investigate illegal surveillance and related abuses, including illegal break-ins, the unauthorized opening of mail, and improper access to tax data.[23] Given both the notoriety and recent incidence of wiretapping abuses, our sample of political élites must have been familiar— indeed, some on a firsthand basis—with the potential for harm of the government's police and security powers.[24]

With wiretapping, much depends on circumstance and justification. Hence, respondents were asked whether they approved of wiretapping, not in the abstract, but rather in a particular circumstance. An array of specific situations and justifications were explored. Respondents were asked whether Canada's security service should be permitted to tap the telephones of people who: (1) hold ideas that may lead to the overthrow of our democratic system; (2) are agents of a foreign government; (3) are suspected of terrorism; and (4) are suspected of being spies.[25] To avoid order effects, these wiretapping situations were randomly varied.[26]

Of the array of justification for wiretapping, the crucial one for our purposes is surveillance on the grounds that people hold 'dangerous' ideas. Specifically, both élite and mass samples were asked if wiretapping is justified in the case of people who hold ideas that may lead to the overthrow of the democratic system. A person who weighs threats heavily has good reason, from his point of view, to approve of surveillance. But notice that by design the 'threat' here is conjectural. Nothing was said about an actual act to overthrow the government; merely that the person held 'certain ideas that may lead to the overthrow of our democratic system'.

The results are striking on two counts, neither consistent with the thesis of democratic élitism. Firstly, as Table 3 demonstrates, there is a profound difference between the reactions of the élites who are accustomed to making up the federal government and those whose traditional role has been in opposition. A majority of Liberals, and a still larger majority of Conservatives, endorse the wiretapping of people whose thoughts—not their acts—may be revolutionary, whereas an overwhelming majority of the NDP and Parti Québécois élites are opposed to such surveillance. Secondly, the public is less, not more, approving of wiretapping in the crucial case of belief: specifically, 63 per cent of ordinary citizens oppose the wiretapping of someone whose ideas are politically threatening, compared with 40 per cent of the Conservative élite and 47 per cent of the Liberal élite.

So far as the thesis of democratic élitism is concerned, the crucial comparison is between the public at large and particular groups of élites who actually control, or are likely to control, the government. The answer, Table 3 suggests, is that those who are accustomed to political responsibility, far from requiring a higher standard of proof before limiting individual rights than the public at large, are content with a lower standard. So, reviewing the potential justifications for the tapping of telephones, we see that the ordinary citizen is less, not more, likely to approve of wiretapping than Conservatives and Liberal élites are. It is accordingly difficult to argue that the politically active—simply by virtue of being active in politics—are sensitive to the abuses of power, certainly so far as issues of surveillance and encroachments on civil liberties are concerned.

We want to put the thesis of democratic élitism to a still more severe test by exploring issues raised in the aftermath of the imposition of the War Measures Act in 1970. Following the kidnapping of a British trade commissioner and a Quebec minister, the Prime Minister of Canada, Pierre Trudeau, suspended certain civil liberties and civil rights, initially across the whole of Canada, subsequently in Quebec only, taking as his authority the War Measures Act. Pursuant to regulations passed under the Act, police were authorized to search and hold suspects for questioning without normal legal protections.

Such unfettered power is now more difficult to exercise, thanks to a lengthy debate about the War Measures Act and its replacement by a new Act that imposes new restrictions on the actions taken by the government. It might be supposed, therefore, that Canadians, or at any rate Canadian political élites, have pondered the lessons of the 'October Crisis' of 1970. Whatever their immediate reactions in the heat of the Quebec Crisis— and these were overwhelmingly in favour of imposition of the War Measures Act, as reflected not merely in their expressed attitudes but also in the near-unanimous parliamentary vote (with only NDP MPs dissenting)—it would not seem unreasonable that the seriousness of this threat to people's most basic rights and freedoms would loom larger on sober, second thought. Accordingly, we asked: 'If the cabinet says there is a national emergency, and a majority in Parliament agrees, is it all right to suspend the usual civil rights?'

Both mass and élite reactions are recorded in Table 3. The first thing to notice is the extent to which people had formed opinions about this issue. The ordinary citizen plainly had some

## Table 3: The Politics of Responsibility: A Comparison of Mass and Élite Attitudes

Do you think the security service should be able to wiretap the telephones of people who hold ideas that may lead to the overthrow of our democratic system?

|  | Mass (%) | Élite (%) | Élite Sample by Party | | | | |
|---|---|---|---|---|---|---|---|
|  |  |  | PC (%) | Lib (%) | NDP (%) | PQ (%) | SC (%) |
| No | 63 | 59 | 40 | 47 | 81 | 75 | 27 |
| Yes | 37 | 41 | 60 | 53 | 19 | 25 | 73 |
| Total | 100 | 100 | 100 | 100 | 100 | 100 | 100 |
| N | (517) | (137) | (28) | (41) | (37) | (25) | (6) |

Do you think the security service should be able to wiretap the telephones of people who are agents of a foreign government?

|  | Mass (%) | Élite (%) | Élite Sample by Party | | | | |
|---|---|---|---|---|---|---|---|
|  |  |  | PC (%) | Lib (%) | NDP (%) | PQ (%) | SC (%) |
| No | 51 | 44 | 31 | 41 | 48 | 62 | 40 |
| Yes | 49 | 56 | 69 | 59 | 52 | 38 | 60 |
| Total | 100 | 100 | 100 | 100 | 100 | 100 | 100 |
| N | (512) | (104) | (27) | (28) | (20) | (20) | (10) |

Do you think the security service should be able to wiretap the telephones of people who are suspected of terrorism?

|  | Mass (%) | Élite (%) | Élite Sample by Party | | | | |
|---|---|---|---|---|---|---|---|
|  |  |  | PC (%) | Lib (%) | NDP (%) | PQ (%) | SC (%) |
| No | 33 | 26 | 9 | 13 | 43 | 52 | 0 |
| Yes | 67 | 74 | 91 | 87 | 57 | 48 | 100 |
| Total | 100 | 100 | 100 | 100 | 100 | 100 | 100 |
| N | (533) | (133) | (31) | (40) | (29) | (26) | (7) |

Do you think the security service should be able to wiretap the telephones of people who are suspected of being spies?

|  | Mass (%) | Élite (%) | Élite Sample by Party | | | | |
|---|---|---|---|---|---|---|---|
|  |  |  | PC (%) | Lib (%) | NDP (%) | PQ (%) | SC (%) |
| No | 42 | 33 | 22 | 19 | 54 | 52 | 8 |
| Yes | 58 | 67 | 78 | 81 | 46 | 48 | 92 |
| Total | 100 | 100 | 100 | 100 | 100 | 100 | 100 |
| N | (473) | (140) | (39) | (34) | (23) | (34) | (10) |

## Table 3: (continued)

If the cabinet says there is a national emergency, and a majority in Parliament agrees, is it all right to suspend the usual civil rights?

| | Mass (%) | Élite (%) | Élite Sample by Party PC (%) | Lib (%) | NDP (%) | PQ (%) | SC (%) |
|---|---|---|---|---|---|---|---|
| No | 26 | 29 | 14 | 15 | 53 | 37 | 11 |
| Uncertain | 22 | 11 | 6 | 7 | 18 | 18 | 0 |
| Yes | 52 | 60 | 80 | 78 | 29 | 45 | 89 |
| Total | 100 | 100 | 100 | 100 | 100 | 100 | 100 |
| N | (1,225) | (308) | (69) | (77) | (78) | (63) | (21) |

Note: Entries are vertical percentages, rounded to the nearest whole number. PC = Progressive Conservative, Lib = Liberal, NDP = New Democratic Party, PQ = Parti Québécois, SC = Social Credit. 'Uncertain' includes both the response 'Undecided' and the response 'Neither'.

difficulty figuring out what position to take, with one in five undecided. In contrast, political élites were markedly more likely to know where they stood. More exactly, political élites who were likely to face making a decision about national emergency—that is, Liberals and Conservatives—were more likely to know where they stood on the issue, with members of the NDP and PQ, the minority parties, more similar to the public at large. Still more important, and quite contrary to the thesis of democratic élitism, members of the two major federal parties gave overwhelming support to parliamentary suspension of civil liberties 'if the cabinet says there is a national emergency'. Indeed, they were far more likely to approve of such a suspension than the average citizen was: eight out of every ten Conservatives and Liberals believed that Parliament should be able to suspend civil liberties at the cabinet's pleasure—hardly a sign that political élites have learned wariness about the enormous risks inherent in the suspension of civil rights. Indeed, only among the NDP did a majority of élites oppose the parliamentary suspension of civil rights.[27] Finally, it is striking that a plurality of the Parti Québécois—and, indeed, a clear majority of those with an opinion on the issue—favoured the principle of parliamentary suspension, suggesting that even those who have been victims of

this power can support it, if they themselves might one day exercise power.

Taking all these findings into account, there is less than compelling evidence that political élites, merely by virtue of being political élites, are distinctively reliable guardians of civil liberties. There is a marked divergence within élites by party; indeed so much that what counts is not whether élites or ordinary citizens, but rather which élites, make civil liberties policy.

### Schumpeter's Argument

Democratic politics, Schumpeter insisted, hinges on organized competition between blocs of élites. The public plays its role, not by directly acting on its own views but only indirectly, by choosing between competing groups of élites.[28] We have shown that, in Canada, the groups of political élites that compete for popular support differ significantly in their attitudes towards civil liberties. However, it is essential to consider how generalizable our findings are: do they apply to Canadian political élites distinctively, or—as Schumpeter's argument would suggest—to democratic politics more broadly?

There are two quite distinct sampling issues. The first concerns politics. The pattern we have uncovered may be peculiar to the politics of Canada. The second, and less obvious, sampling issue concerns the issues themselves. Élites, as McClosky and his co-workers appreciate, are not always in agreement: they reach consensus on issues where the norms have been settled ('clear' norms) and exhibit cleavage where it remains legitimate to differ ('contested' norms).[29] Our findings, it may therefore be argued, simply illustrate the difference between élite reactions to clear norms on the one hand and to contested norms on the other.

We address both issues by demonstrating that McClosky's own published results support an even stronger version of our argument. Ideally, it would be desirable to carry out a comparison between Democratic and Republican élites that was strictly analogous to our comparison of Canadian party élites. However, since McClosky's data are not available for analysis, it is necessary to translate our argument into a comparison not of partisan but of ideological élites. Fortunately, McClosky's own work established the close correspondence between ideological and partisan élites in politics, with the Republican Party being distinctively the party of conservatism and the Democratic Party the party of liberalism—a finding reconfirmed by subsequent research.[30]

Drawing on McClosky's published results,[31] Table 4 compares the attitudes of liberal and conservative élites and of liberal and conservative citizens across a large and diverse array of civil liberties issues, including: what may be shown on television; whether government has the right to forbid publications in order to protect moral values; whether communities may censor teachers' curricula; whether a person who is arrested has the right to remain silent; whether the police have a right to search a car stopped for a traffic violation; whether it is permissible to violate people's rights in order to stop crime; whether the police may arrest a protestor for calling them a dirty name; whether local officials may deny a religious cult the use of a public park for a meeting; whether demonstrators may be allowed to

hold a mass protest march; whether homosexuals may be arrested or fined if a majority passes a law to do so; whether a majority, voting in a referendum, may legally ban the public expression of certain opinions; and, finally, whether refusing to hire a professor because of his political beliefs is justified.

The results are strikingly consistent. Firstly, whatever the issue, and the diversity of issues should be emphasized, conservative élites are no more approving of civil liberties than ordinary conservative citizens are. In short, although conservative élites are far more politically active, aware, and sophisticated than are ordinary conservative citizens, McClosky's own data show that they are in no degree more sympathetic to civil liberties.

Secondly, and this deserves special emphasis, conservative élites are markedly *less* approving of civil liberties than are ordinary *liberal* citizens. This result is consistent across issue, but we want to give at least one specific example to drive home the point. Consider the question of whether demonstrators should be allowed to hold a mass protest march for an unpopular cause: 35 per cent of élites who are strong conservatives oppose the right to assemble in this circumstance, compared with only 9 per cent of ordinary citizens who are strong liberals, or indeed 14 per cent of ordinary citizens who are moderate liberals.

It is worth remarking that the differences between élites and mass who are liberal tend to be non-existent or trivial; but our argument is not that there are no differences whatever between élites taken as a whole and the public taken as a whole. Indeed, so far as Table 4 is a reliable guide, one reason there will tend to be some differences—even if being active in politics has no effect whatever on one's view of civil liberties—is because the world of politics tends to be habituated by proportionately more liberals than are found in society at large.

McClosky and Brill present these data to demonstrate the close connection, in the United

## Table 4: The American Comparison: Mass and Élite Attitudes Compared

| | Percentage of Community Leaders Agreeing | | | | Percentage of Mass Public Agreeing | | | |
|---|---|---|---|---|---|---|---|---|
| | Strong Liberal | Moderate Liberal | Moderate Conserv. | Strong Conserv. | Strong Liberal | Moderate Liberal | Moderate Conserv. | Strong Conserv. |
| **PART A** | (N = 262) | (N = 111) | (N = 87) | (N = 135) | (N = 257) | (N = 255) | (N = 257) | (N = 257) |
| The government has no right to decide what should be published. | 56 | 47 | 38 | 32 | 38 | 24 | 26 | 23 |
| The government has a right to forbid what should be published. | 32 | 41 | 54 | 59 | 48 | 55 | 59 | 66 |
| Once an arrested person says he/she wishes to remain silent, authorities . . . . . . should stop questioning. | 69 | 58 | 52 | 40 | 67 | 52 | 51 | 42 |
| . . . should persist questioning. | 15 | 20 | 24 | 40 | 12 | 18 | 20 | 32 |
| When a community pays its teacher's salary, it . . . . . . does not buy . . . . | 51 | 35 | 26 | 19 | 45 | 25 | 30 | 18 |
| . . . has . . . . a right to censor her/him. | 31 | 47 | 60 | 71 | 35 | 49 | 52 | 75 |
| Television programs that show people actually making love . . . . . . should be permitted. | 43 | 30 | 23 | 16 | 45 | 35 | 28 | 24 |
| . . . should not be allowed. | 41 | 51 | 70 | 72 | 41 | 50 | 62 | 68 |
| Should police be able to search cars stopped for traffic violations? No | 43 | 24 | 25 | 13 | 42 | 32 | 28 | 25 |
| Yes | 46 | 66 | 67 | 79 | 46 | 54 | 60 | 69 |
| In dealing with muggings and other street crimes, which is more important? To protect suspect rights | 27 | 7 | 2 | 4 | 16 | 9 | 7 | 4 |
| To stop crime | 40 | 60 | 69 | 79 | 54 | 63 | 72 | 80 |

# Table 4: (continued)

| | Percentage of Community Leaders Agreeing | | | | | Percentage of Mass Public Agreeing | | | | |
|---|---|---|---|---|---|---|---|---|---|---|
| | Strong Liberal | Moderate Liberal | Middle Road | Moderate Conserv. | Strong Conserv. | Strong Liberal | Moderate Liberal | Middle Road | Moderate Conserv. | Strong Conserv. |
| **PART B** | (N = 99) | (N = 272) | (N = 338) | (N = 375) | (N = 54) | (N = 82) | (N = 270) | (N = 562) | (N = 646) | (N = 80) |
| What would you do if the police arrested a protestor for calling them a dirty name? — Take action | 60 | 31 | 19 | 11 | 6 | 45 | 25 | 9 | 9 | 6 |
| Nothing | 7 | 21 | 37 | 54 | 69 | 12 | 23 | 41 | 49 | 58 |
| What would you do if local officials denied an unpopular cult public park access? — Take action | 43 | 28 | 22 | 13 | 17 | 24 | 19 | 8 | 7 | 10 |
| Nothing | 11 | 20 | 29 | 44 | 44 | 21 | 30 | 38 | 45 | 43 |
| **PART C** | (N = 91) | (N = 271) | (N = 334) | (N = 374) | (N = 52) | (N = 35) | (N = 190) | (N = 305) | (N = 394) | (N = 58) |
| Should demonstrators be allowed to hold a protest march for some unpopular cause? — Yes | 93 | 86 | 74 | 56 | 44 | 85 | 77 | 56 | 47 | 50 |
| No | 2 | 7 | 12 | 29 | 35 | 9 | 14 | 24 | 32 | 36 |
| If the majority makes homosexuality a crime, should homosexuals be fined or arrested? — No | 89 | 77 | 54 | 37 | 33 | 94 | 74 | 62 | 40 | 38 |
| Yes | 3 | 8 | 21 | 37 | 39 | 0 | 10 | 18 | 33 | 34 |
| If the majority votes to ban public expression of certain opinions, should this be law? — No | 90 | 82 | 69 | 53 | 50 | 88 | 74 | 60 | 55 | 64 |
| Yes | 3 | 9 | 13 | 24 | 21 | 6 | 13 | 19 | 24 | 16 |
| **PART D** | (N = 89) | (N = 271) | (N = 336) | (N = 372) | (N = 52) | (N = 34) | (N = 183) | (N = 286) | (N = 368) | (N = 50) |
| Refusing to hire a professor because of her/his unusual political beliefs . . . . . . is unjustifiable. | 49 | 31 | 16 | 7 | 6 | 53 | 30 | 18 | 10 | 4 |
| . . . may be necessary. | 26 | 50 | 69 | 85 | 85 | 21 | 46 | 67 | 81 | 90 |

Sources: Part A: McClosky and Brill, *Dimensions of Tolerance* (New York, 1983), Table 7.9, 306–9. Totals do not equal 100 per cent because middle categories were excluded from the source table. Part B: Ibid., Table 7.4, 285–9. On these items, we use 'nothing' to designate the response, 'I would do nothing, since I favour the action.' Totals do not equal 100 per cent because we omit the replies of 'I wouldn't get involved, can't help anyway.' Part C: McClosky and Zaller, *The American Ethos* (Cambridge, 1984), Table 7.9, 216–17. The mass public sample excludes respondents who scored in the lower half of a political sophistication index in the original table. Values from the original table do not total 100 per cent, presumably because a middle response was excluded. Part D: Ibid., Table 7.7, 208–10. Again, the public sample is limited to the more politically sophisticated half, and a middle response appears to have been omitted. This table attempts to paraphrase briefly the original questions without altering the meaning. For the precise wording, please see the original sources.

States, between ideology and orientation to civil liberties. But they do not recognize that in establishing the specific impact of ideology they are undermining their overall argument that the politically involved, by virtue of their involvement in politics, are the 'repositories of the public conscience' and the 'carriers of the Creed'. To be sure, they acknowledge that the 'far right' and 'hardcore' conservatives are 'an exception to the greater libertarianism of opinion leaders'.[32] But casting the problem as one of deviation only at the political extremes clearly conflicts with the findings of Table 4. Not only are the 'strong' conservatives—their term—never represented by them as ideological extremists, but also, looking closely at Table 4, one can see that the 'moderate' conservatives—again their term—among the élites are never less likely to favour an anti-civil libertarian alternative than are 'moderate' liberals among the public at large.

How is it possible that we, looking at exactly the same figures as McClosky and Brill, laid out in exactly the same way, should reach diametrically opposed conclusions? The reason is this. McClosky and Brill focus only on the comparison of liberals and conservatives *within* the élite and within the mass samples; they omit to compare and contrast liberals and conservatives across samples. But once comparisons are made across and not just within samples, it is plain that the differences in commitment to civil liberties between competing groups of élites eclipse in size and political significance differences between élites qua élites and the public as a whole; indeed, so much so that conservative élites—notwithstanding their greater involvement in politics—are consistently, and markedly, less committed to basic rights than are ordinary citizens whose political outlook happens to be liberal.

## Conclusions

We believe that there is a tension at the heart of modern empirical democratic theory. The politically active, we are told, constitute a stratum, a class of citizens with a distinctive commitment to democratic norms by virtue of their distinctive involvement in politics. Among other things:

> Members of the political stratum (who live in a much more politicized culture) are more familiar with the 'democratic' norms, more consistent, more ideological, more detailed and explicit in their political attitudes, and more completely in agreement on the norms. They are more in agreement not only on what norms are implied by the abstract democratic creed but also in supporting the norms currently operating.[33]

This we have labelled the consensus claim. But there is also a second claim centrally associated with modern democratic theory. This second claim holds that there is a plurality of élites, and the interests, background, and political outlook of these competing élites can vary from one domain of policy to another and from one point in time to another: hence the fallacy of assuming there is a power élite—a single, unified, homogeneous body presiding over political decisions across-the-board.

Our findings have exposed the tension between the claims of consensus and of pluralism. Figure 1 presents a stylized, but true-to-life illustration of how the fact of élite pluralism undercuts the claim of an élite consensus on civil liberties.

According to the thesis of democratic élitism, the politically aware and influential share a consensus on civil liberties, thanks in large part to their involvement in politics, and that by virtue of this consensus they supply a protective bulwark against mass intolerance and serve as 'repositories of the public conscience'. For simplicity, Figure 1 maps preferences in a two-party system, although exactly equivalent (if more complex) representations can be graphed for multiparty systems. The solid and dotted curves describe the distribution of support for civil liberties among political élites and ordinary citizens respectively; the solid and dotted vertical lines, the average (mean) levels of support for liberties characteristic of each.

Figure 1: A Stylized Comparison of Élite and Mass Means and Modes: Commitment to Civil Liberties

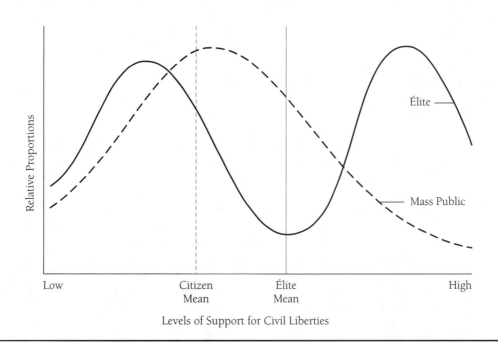

Levels of Support for Civil Liberties

As inspection of the vertical lines makes plain, on average political élites are more committed to civil liberties than are ordinary citizens, the solid (élite) line being significantly to the right of the dotted (citizen) line. But the crucial fact is that the distribution of élite support for civil liberties is bimodal. And the twin-peaked élite distribution means that it is inappropriate to compare the mean level of support for civil liberties among élites with the mean level among ordinary citizens. Quite simply, the mean is a misleading statistic to summarize a multimodal distribution.

The two peaks of the élite distribution graphically illustrate how misleading it is to group together élites as a whole, in order to compare them with the public as a whole. The heart of the thesis of democratic élitism is the élite consensus claim: that political élites tend to consensus on

issues of civil liberties by virtue of being more politically active and aware than the ordinary citizen. The test of consensus, however, is the extent to which the distribution of attitudes on civil liberties among élites is unimodal. All of our results demonstrate the untenability of the consensus claim. As Figure 1 illustrates, partisan groups of élites competing for popular support embody competing points of view on issues of civil liberties. In the United States the electoral choice at state and federal levels is characteristically between the Democratic and the Republican parties—and at the élite level, the two parties markedly and systematically differ in their attitudes towards civil liberties. In a multiparty system like Canada there are comparable differences between political parties, at the élite level, in attitudes towards civil liberties. It would of course be wrong to suggest that élites with a high level of commitment to civil liberties are exclusively assigned to one political party and those with a low level of commitment to civil liberties exclusively assigned to another. The differences between parties, in commitment to civil liberties as in other areas of policy, are a matter of degree. And, as we have seen in the Canadian data, they can vary from one aspect of civil liberties to another. The burden of our empirical results is none the less that differences between competing groups of political élites in support for civil liberties, both in the United States and in Canada, are systematic, deep, and politically significant. The politics of civil liberties can accordingly hinge on which group of élites wins the struggle to constitute the government.

Our claim, we should emphasize, is not that there is an inherent logical necessity requiring political élites to diverge over civil liberties; it is merely that we observe that they systematically and markedly do differ in two contemporary polities. There are strong reasons, however, to expect that partisan élites commonly will differ, both else-where and at other times. Some of those reasons have to do with the dynamics of electoral competition, others with the impact of ideology. And it should be remarked that politics in contemporary democracies—not only the United States and Canada but also Great Britain and Israel, among a great many others—continue to supply fresh examples of how issues of civil liberties can become a central part of the electoral contest.

As Schumpeter argued, ordinary citizens only decide who decides public policy. Of course, there is a risk of mass intolerance. The crucial point, however, is that the danger of mass intolerance is in proportion to contending groups of élites, competing for popular support, themselves differing over issues of civil liberties. The thesis of democratic élitism presupposes that the decisive contrast is between élite and mass, ignoring the differences between political élites. The electoral system, however, operates to choose among, not to average across, competing sets of élites. The fallacy of democratic élitism consists precisely in its indifference to which élites prevail.

## Notes

The research reported here is part of a larger project supported by the Social Sciences and Humanities Research Council (Grant No. 411–85–001). The Centre for Criminology at the University of Toronto has provided a home and indispensable support for the Charter Project, as has the Survey Research Center, University of California, Berkeley. This research was also facilitated by a contribution from the Solicitor General of Canada to the Centre of Criminology, University of Toronto while Gaines received support from the Social Sciences and Humanities Research Council (SSHRC 452–900–1217). We want also to thank Robert M. Boyd for invaluable assistance.

1. See, for example: Samuel Stouffer, *Communism, Conformity, and Civil Liberties* (Garden City, NY: Doubleday, 1955); Bernard Berelson et al., *Voting* (Chicago: University of Chicago Press, 1954); Herbert McClosky, 'Consensus and Ideology in American Politics', *American Political Science Review* 58 (1964): 361–82; Thomas R. Dye and Harmon Zeigler, *The Irony of Democracy*, 7th edn (Monterey, Calif.: Brooks/Cole, 1987); Herbert McClosky and Alida Brill, *Dimensions of Tolerance: What Americans Think About Civil Liberties* (New York: Russell Sage, 1983); David G. Barnum and John L. Sullivan, 'Attitudinal Tolerance and Political Freedom in Britain', *British Journal of Political Science* 18 (1988): 604–14. However, also see James L. Gibson, 'Political Intolerance and Political Repression During the McCarthy Red Scare', *American Political Science Review* 82 (1988): 511–30.

2. Joseph Schumpeter, *Capitalism, Socialism, and Democracy* (New York: Harper and Row, 1962), 269.

3. This article focuses on the research of McClosky, given the centrality of his empirical results to the thesis of democratic élitism. It offers a critique of a

part of the writing, but is in no respect a critique of the writer: on the contrary, McClosky has made a seminal contribution and we would not have been in a position to offer our contribution had he not first made his.

4. McClosky and Brill, *Dimensions of Tolerance*, 434.

5. Stouffer, *Communism, Conformity, and Civil Liberties*; McClosky, 'Consensus and Ideology in American Politics'; McClosky and Brill, *Dimensions of Tolerance*; Herbert McClosky and John Zaller, *The American Ethos: Public Attitudes toward Capitalism and Democracy* (Cambridge, Mass.: Harvard University Press, 1984); Clyde Nunn, Harry Crockett Jr, and J. Allen Williams Jr, *Tolerance of Nonconformity* (San Francisco: Jossey-Bass, 1978); John L. Sullivan, James Piereson, and George E. Marcus, 'An Alternative Conceptualization of Political Tolerance', *American Political Science Review* 73 (1979): 781–94; John L. Sullivan, James Piereson, and George E. Marcus, *Political Tolerance and American Democracy* (Chicago: University of Chicago Press, 1982); Barnum and Sullivan, 'Attitudinal Tolerance and Political Freedom in Britain'.

6. McClosky, 'Consensus and Ideology in American Politics', 374 (emphasis added).

7. Dahl, *Who Governs?* (New Haven: Yale University Press, 1961); V.O. Key Jr, *Public Opinion and American Democracy* (New York: Knopf, 1961).

8. McClosky and Brill, *Dimensions of Tolerance* (e.g., 28–30).

9. Ibid., 32–273.

10. But see Joseph F. Fletcher, 'Participation and Attitudes Toward Civil Liberties: Is There an Educative Effect?', *International Political Science Review* 11 (1990): 439–59.

11. Dahl, *Who Governs?*

12. See, for example, Peter Bachrach, *The Theory of Democratic Elitism* (Boston: Little, Brown, 1967); Dye and Ziegler, *The Irony of Democracy*; Nunn, Crockett, and Williams, *Tolerance for Nonconformity*.

13. The extent to which the thesis of democratic élitism reinforces the arguments for participatory democracy has largely escaped attention. Beyond this, it should be emphasized that merely because a scholar agrees with the consensus and the participation claims as empirical generalizations, it does not follow that he or she personally favours an élite possessing special prerogatives or extra-constitutional powers.

14. Paul M. Sniderman, Joseph F. Fletcher, Peter H. Russell, and Philip E. Tetlock, 'Political Culture and the Problem of Double Standards: Mass and Elite Attitudes Toward Language Rights in the Canadian Charter of Rights and Freedoms', *Canadian Journal of Political Science* 22 (1989): 259–86.

15. Leslie Kish, 'A Procedure for Objective Respondent Selection Within the Household', *Journal of the American Statistical Association* 44 (1949): 380–7.

16. Institute for Social Research, *Attitudes Toward Civil Liberties and the Canadian Charter of Rights—Technical Documentation*, rev. edn (Toronto: York University, 1989).

17. Sullivan et al., 'An Alternative Conceptualization of Political Tolerance'; Sullivan et al., *Political Tolerance and American Democracy*.

18. Sullivan et al., 'An Alternative Conceptualization of Political Tolerance'; Sullivan et al., *Political Tolerance and American Democracy*.

19. The item is taken from McClosky and Brill, *Dimensions of Tolerance*, with permission.

20. Ronald Dworkin, *Taking Rights Seriously* (Cambridge, Mass.: Harvard University Press, 1977).

21. This item is taken, with permission, from McClosky and Brill, *Dimensions of Tolerance*.

22. This item is taken, with permission, from McClosky and Brill, *Dimensions of Tolerance*.

23. Commission of Inquiry Concerning Certain Activities of the Royal Canadian Mounted Police (McDonald Commission), *Second Report: Freedom and Security Under the Law* (Ottawa: Queen's Printer, 1981).

24. A. Allan Borovoy, *When Freedoms Collide* (Toronto: Lester & Orpen Dennys, 1988).

25. To discipline our assessment of issues of wiretapping, the justifications are drawn from the enabling legislation, the Canadian Security Intelligence Service Act, 1984.

26. Joseph F. Fletcher, 'Mass and Elite Attitudes About Wiretapping in Canada: Implications for Democratic Theory and Politics', *Public Opinion Quarterly* 53 (1989): 225–45.

27. The parallels between attitudes now and actual behaviour in the October Crisis are impressive.

28. Schumpeter, *Capitalism, Socialism, and Democracy*.

29. McClosky and Zaller, *The American Ethos: Public Attitudes toward Capitalism and Democracy*, 235; McClosky and Brill, *Dimensions of Tolerance*, 415–38.

30. Herbert McClosky, Paul J. Hoffman, and Rosemary O'Hara, 'Issue Conflict and Consensus Among Party Leaders and Followers', *American Political Science Review* 54 (1960): 406–27; also see Jeanne J. Kirkpatrick, *A New Presidential Elite* (New York: Basic Books, 1976); Warren E. Miller, *Parties in Transition* (New York: Russell Sage, 1986).

31. McClosky and Brill present these results to demonstrate the strength of the connection between liberalism and commitment to civil liberties, among both élite and general population samples.

32. McClosky and Brill, *Dimensions of Tolerance*, 422.

33. Dahl, *Who Governs?*, 320.

# Part IV

# Political Economy

## Introduction

Stephen McBride and Michael Howlett

Political economy is concerned with the interconnection between the economic and the political aspects of human societies. How does economics influence politics? How does politics influence economics? How does the conjunction of economic and political power influence other areas of society such as law, culture, customs, social relations, and values?

To answer such questions, political economists must examine economic and political activity in and across particular societies, consider connections between the economic and political systems and the broader society, understand social divisions and power relations within society, and probe the ideas used to guide and/or rationalize political, social, and economic behaviour. Political economists strive for a multidimensional understanding of power. They recognize that power may be derived from various sources, among which economic position and wealth, social status, and political office-holding are especially important. Indeed, inequalities of political power are often linked to inequalities in other social spheres—including those based on class, gender, and ethnicity.

Generally, the distribution of resources in societies is managed by some mixture of state (political system) and market (prevailing type of economic system). Understanding states and markets, and the relations between them, has therefore been a major focus of political economists. This focus tends to reinforce the operating assumption of most political economists—that the interconnections between the political and economic spheres of social life hold the key to analysis and understanding of central dynamics within the broader society.

At one time the academic study of political and economic issues was united in university departments of political economy. Over time, increased specialization produced political science and economics as separate and often alien academic disciplines. By the 1960s the two subjects were studied in different departments and there was often little connection between the two. Unfortunately, this remains the case today.

Yet it is obvious to even a casual observer that, regardless of how universities choose to organize themselves, politics and economics are intimately linked. As a reaction against the rigid academic division of labour that had come to exist by the 1960s, approaches to the study of the economic and political system as an integrated whole revived in many separate academic disciplines during the 1970s. The reborn 'discipline' of political economy retains its vitality and its interdisciplinary character. Political economists are found in many academic departments, including sociology, anthropology, communications, geography, and economics. In Canada, political science has provided something of a focal point for the new political economy through the inclusion of a Political Economy section at the annual conference of the Canadian Political Science Association. Those who attend the meetings, however, represent many disciplines.

Within political economy there have been various schools of thought, often linked to the ideologies present in society. Thus we find liberal versions of political economy that begin from models of individual self-maximizing behaviour[1] based on a belief in 'rational economic man'. These approaches tend to focus on the advantages of market mechanisms for the production and allocation of wealth and, increasingly, for the delivery of all services as well. Socialist versions of political economy begin from the organization of societies into collectivities, especially classes, and go on to focus on the defects of markets and the need for collective or public intervention to correct them. In addition, in Canada, one school of thought emphasizes the economic development characteristics of societies founded, and still based to an uncomfortably large extent, on the export of 'staples'—natural resources extracted or harvested for export to a metropolitan centre of economic activity. Central to this approach is the contention that a structural inequality of power exists between the resource-dependent economy, often termed the hinterland or periphery, and the more diverse metropolitan economy, which occupies a more central role within the world economy.

## Types of Political Economic Analysis

By the beginning of the twentieth century political economy had produced two very different and contradictory theories of the nature of production. Liberal political economy construes the 'political' far more narrowly than does socialist political economy, basing its analysis on what it considers to be apolitical individual interactions in the marketplace and urging the restriction of any politically derived institutional fetters on market-based activities. Socialist political economy, on the other hand, rejects the liberal, market-liberating understanding of the autonomy of civil society. As such, political economy, as a field of inquiry, provides one the clearest examples of how the definition of the 'political' affects subsequent methodology, the choice of objects of study, the relations of power analysed, and, to a certain extent, the nature of the conclusions reached.

Interestingly, both modern approaches to political economy owe their origins to the same writings in what is usually referred to as 'classical political economy'. As expressed in the writings of Adam Smith (1723–90) and David Ricardo (1772–1823), classical political economists were concerned with identifying the sources of a nation's wealth. They examined the rise and fall of colonial empires, such as Spain and Portugal in the pursuit of pure wealth in the form of gold and silver. From the experiences of these and other countries in what was known as the seventeenth- and eighteenth-century 'mercantilist' system, classical political economists argued that wealth was not a function of the amount of money or booty a nation possessed, but rather was a direct result of the productivity of its workforce.

Given this analysis, many succeeding political economists argued that individuals in society should be allowed to produce what they want and consume what they want, exchanging goods and services in the market without state interference. This system of production and exchange, it was claimed, would generate the greatest returns and fairest distribution of wealth possible.[2] Liberal political economy has argued consistently that market-based forms of production and exchange are superior to state-based forms. Beginning in the works of Smith and Ricardo at the turn of the nineteenth century and moving on to the works of Marshall, Jevons, Walras, and other 'neoclassical' theorists at the turn of the twentieth century, liberal political economy developed a theory of supply and demand whereby free and unregulated markets would produce an optimal level of production and social distribution of goods and services.

The critical assumption in this regard is related to the notion that human beings act to maximize their pleasures while minimizing their pain; they thereby 'maximize their utility'. In this view, individual human beings tend to act in an inherently selfish manner, rationally calculating their advantage prior to undertaking any course of action.[3] This behavioural assumption underlies liberal political economy's theory that supply and demand for goods in unregulated markets will tend to balance each other or 'reach an equilibrium'. In a system of voluntary exchange with individuals attempting to maximize their utility, no one will produce goods that are not wanted or can't be paid for. This principle is then applied to political life as well, and various forms of collective political action—interest groups, electoral behaviour, political parties, and public policy-making—are analysed in terms of the utility-maximizing behaviour of social actors.[4]

Many other political economists, however, drew very different conclusions from the insight that social wealth was ultimately derived from the organization of human labour. Drawing on elements of the classical analysis and especially on its 'labour theory of value', Karl Marx and other nineteenth-century socialist political economists fashioned a critique of classical political economy. Marx and others focused attention on the economic, political, and social relations and mechanisms used by powerful groups to extract labour power and the resulting wealth from other groups. The inequality of social class control over the use of labour power thus prevented an equitable distribution of wealth in society. These analyses centred on the use of private property rights by small groups of property owners to force the non-property-owning majority to sell their labour for wages in order to survive.[5]

In its simplest interpretation, Marxist class analysis suggests a division of capitalist society into two great classes—the capitalist class or bourgeoisie on the one hand, and working class or proletariat on the other. The distinction is based on the ownership or non-ownership of productive property. Inequality of condition between these classes is seen as a fundamental characteristic of capitalist societies. More importantly, because the wealth and position of the bourgeoisie are based on the exploitation of the labour of the working class and appropriation of the social surplus produced by it, an inescapable antagonism exists between the interests of these two classes. Virtually all class analysts agree, however, that the class structure of modern capitalist societies is more complex than this and that, in addition, inequalities based on other factors such as gender and race cannot be explained exclusively in terms of class analysis.

Class-based political economy views individuals not as autonomous self-standing entities but as 'bundles' of social relations. That is, the individual person has various kinds of relations with other individuals—familial, social, cultural, linguistic, religious, workplace. Taken together, these relations define people's characters and circumscribe their needs and wants.[6] This is a complex enough vision of individual psychology when contrasted with the 'self-maximizing' visions of liberal political economy. It is made even more complex in socialist political economy because all of these relations are seen not only to have a spatial dimension, but also a temporal one. That is, it is not enough just to understand these relations at one point in time—they must be analysed historically as well.[7]

## Canadian Political Economic Theory

Political economy was bypassed in the 1960s and 1970s by many political scientists in Canada professing a desire to better understand specifically *political* behaviour. In the great flurry of studies of voting behaviour, political parties, electoral systems, and other aspects of modern political life characteristic of this period, the links between political behaviour and the production and reproduction of social wealth were often ignored or obscured. Recently, however, a renewed desire to reintegrate political and economic phenomena in the study of political life has emerged.

A rich literature now examines the experience of different classes, the relations between them, and the significance, for Canadian development, of class divisions or of the characteristics of particular classes.[8] Some regional conflicts, for example, can be best understood if the class-based dimensions of these conflicts are taken into account. The interwar protest movements of western farmers, for example, can be better appreciated when we see them as independent commodity producers whose disadvantageous relations with bankers, grain trade companies, and farm implement manufacturers meant that their protests were unavoidably directed against central Canadian bankers and industrialists.[9] Other issues seem to involve divisions between different 'fractions' of the same class—during the energy crises of the 1970s and early 1980s, for example, the interests of owners of oil companies, who naturally wanted to maximize prices, were often in conflict with those of manufacturers who wanted to keep the price of their energy inputs down.

Class analyses often overlap with studies that focus on a ruling élite or élites. Many political economists and political sociologists have conducted investigations of the composition and character of Canada's capitalists[10]—in some instances from a class perspective and in others from the standpoint of élite theory. The great wealth of the corporate élite and the density of personal and economic connections among them, for example, through interlocking directorships on corporate boards, make it clear that the distribution of economic power is highly concentrated in relatively few hands.

Discussion of class-based inequalities of condition and power within the economy leads naturally to consideration of possible links between them and inequalities of political power. Since relations of political power tend to find expression in the state, meaning in this case not 'country' but rather the political system that governs a particular country, theorizing the role of the state and investigating who actually wields political power have been important emphases for this school of political economy.

In Canada the most popular variant of political economy has combined the attention to the sources of unequal power relations among classes in the production process with an earlier Canadian tradition that considered the geographic or spatial determinants of social relations in production and trading processes. This variant is usually referred to as 'staples' political economy. It followed the lead of a group of political economists centred at the University of Toronto in the 1930s who studied the consequences of Canada's historical reliance on the export of bulk raw materials—or staples—for its economic wealth.[11] Much fine work in Canadian history has been undertaken by members of the 'staples' school, including well-known classics by Harold Innis on the cod fishery, fur trade, and mineral staples,[12] Arthur Lower on the timber trade,[13] and Vernon Fowke on the wheat economy.[14]

The staples approach of Canadian political economy has been particularly concerned with Canada's location within the international political economy. The essence of the theory is 'that Canada was developed to exploit a series of raw materials for more industrially advanced metropolitan nations. Canada's reliance on resource exports led to a failure to capture the benefits of the "linkages" associated with the inputs into production and processing of the raw materials, thereby locking it into a spiral of dependent relations.'[15] More optimistic versions of staples theory, associated with W.A. Mackintosh, saw dependence on resource extraction and the export of unprocessed natural resources as merely an early stage on the route to full-fledged industrialization. Reaching the mature phase of this development process would involve the Canadian economy increasingly capturing and benefiting from the linkages referred to above—production of the inputs (capital equipment, transportation infrastructure, and so on) necessary to extract the resources, and increased processing of them prior to export. While Canada has experienced some industrialization, much of the political economy literature depicts Canada's industrialization as being truncated or dependent—a result of remaining partly trapped by staples development.[16] This is much as the founder of staples theory, Harold Innis, had anticipated.

## Contemporary Canadian Political Economic Analysis

In the 1990s, Canadian political economy is moving in two directions. In recent years many Canadian political economists have turned to more detailed analysis of social relations, investigating occupational structures, gender relations and other components of the Canadian political economy.[17] They have viewed these transitions as involving a gradual movement from 'Fordism' to 'post-Fordism'.[18] The selection included here by Jane Jenson and Greg Albo is an example of such an analysis. 'Fordism', after auto manufacturer Henry Ford, describes a system of mutually

reinforcing institutions, relationships, and practices—national economic management, a system of mass production and consumption, mild redistribution through the
welfare state, and acceptance of free collective bargaining—that enabled the economy
and society to operate productively and without major social antagonisms for a time.
'Post-Fordism' represents a system in which mass production is replaced by flexible
production, steady jobs by part-time ones, and permanent employment by contract-
ing-out. It has included a redefinition of the goals of economic policy, from full
employment to price stability, together with a reduction in the size and role of the
state, particularly as a provider of such public goods as education and training, and of
social welfare services. Key instruments in achieving this shift include privatization
and deregulation, free trade, and the abolition of the redistributive role of the state.[19]
Changes to the tax system and reduced social services, a reduction in the power of
trade unions, the need for families to have two wage-earners to survive, and other
social and political issues can be traced to this fundamental transition in production
relations. Each of these policy departures has been analysed by political economists.

While this research has progressed, other political economists in Canada have
continued to focus on the implications and results of Canada's recent integration into
a continental trading system under the terms of the Canada-US Free Trade Agreement
(FTA) and the North American Free Trade Agreement (NAFTA).[20]

Staples theorists have always depicted Canada as a disadvantaged actor in an
international economy shaped by others. Our disadvantages sprang from geography,
history, and technology. For some theorists, these disadvantages were compounded by
the tendency of the indigenous business élite to act as local representatives of international capital.[21] Political economists have spelled out the political implications of
recent quasi-constitutional documents such as the FTA and NAFTA, which have altered
many significant components of historical patterns of state-society relations in
Canada. (The article here by Stephen Clarkson is a leading example of this kind of
analysis.) Since international treaties are binding on governments, the trade agreements serve to 'constitutionalize' many of their provisions, as well as the assumptions
behind them. In particular, the ruling assumption is that government interference
with market forces is illegitimate. Corporate property rights are generally enhanced by
the agreements, and the rights of governments, which have at least the potential to act
as expressions of the democratic will of the people, are restricted.[22]

In 'Remapping Canada: The State in the Era of Globalization', Gregory Albo and Jane
Jenson provide a multifaceted, historically grounded account of the changing role of
the Canadian state. Their article focuses on the transition that has occurred between
the postwar period ('Fordism'), characterized by stability and relative prosperity for
most people in Canada, and the post-1975 period, when unemployment and insecurity have again become a reality. Albo and Jenson identify and explain a 'trajectory
towards decline' that incorporates a discussion of the impact of globalization, trade
agreements, and the restructuring, if not dismantling, of the federal state. The changes

carry major implications for citizens whose rights and political and social identities have been undermined.

US President Ronald Reagan once described free trade as an 'economic constitution for North America'. In 'Constitutionalizing the Canadian-American Relationship', Stephen Clarkson applies the concept of a constitution to the relationship between Canada and the US. For much of the postwar period this relationship was governed by conventions—unwritten, informal practices that shaped the relationship while providing for some flexibility in interpretation. With the advent of the trade agreements, neo-liberal principles have become codified and, in this sense, 'constitutionalized'. Further, because of asymmetries of power between the signatories to NAFTA, the provisions of the trade agreements are binding for Canada and Mexico but impose few limits on the United States.

## Notes

1. For an accessible discussion and critique of the model of maximizing behaviour, see C.B. Macpherson, *The Real World of Democracy* (Toronto, 1965).
2. E.K. Hunt, *History of Economic Thought: A Critical Perspective* (Belmont, Calif.: Wadsworth, 1979).
3. See S. Kelman, 'Public Choice and Public Spirit', *The Public Interest* 87 (1987): 80–94; Iain McLean, *Public Choice: An Introduction* (London: Basil Blackwell, 1989).
4. For further insights into the public choice school, see Dennis C. Mueller, *Public Choice II* (Cambridge: Cambridge University Press, 1989); Mark Sproule-Jones, 'Institutions, Constitutions, and Public Policies: A Public-Choice Overview', in M. Atkinson and M. Chandler, eds, *The Politics of Canadian Public Policy* (Toronto: University of Toronto Press, 1983).
5. Maurice Dobb, *Theories of Value and Ideology Since Adam Smith* (Cambridge: Cambridge University Press, 1974).
6. Jean Cohen, *Class and Civil Society* (Boston: Beacon Press, 1982).
7. Branko Horvat, *The Political Economy of Socialism: A Marxist Social Theory* (Armonk, NY: M.E. Sharpe, 1982); Nicos Poulantzas, 'On social classes', *New Left Review* 78 (1973): 27–55.
8. Comprehensive references to this literature can be found in Wallace Clement and John Myles, *Relations of Ruling: Class and Gender in Postindustrial Societies* (Montreal and Kingston: McGill-Queen's University Press, 1994).
9. The classic study using the socialist political economy perspective is C.B. Macpherson, *Democracy in Alberta* (Toronto: University of Toronto Press, 1953).
10. For example, Gustav Myers, *History of Canadian Wealth* (Toronto: J. Lewis & Samuel, 1972, reprint); Libbie and Frank Park, *Anatomy of Big Business* (Toronto: Progress Books, 1962); Wallace Clement, *The Canadian Corporate Elite* (Toronto: McClelland & Stewart, 1975); Peter Newman, *The Canadian Establishment* (Toronto: McClelland & Stewart, 1975); William Carroll, *Corporate Power and Canadian Capitalism* (Vancouver: University of British Columbia Press, 1986); Henry Veltmeyer, *Canadian Corporate Power* (Toronto: Garamond Press, 1987).
11. On the origins of the staples school, see W.T. Easterbrook and M.H. Watkins, *Approaches to Canadian Economic History* (Toronto: McClelland & Stewart, 1967); C.R. Fay, 'The Toronto school of economic history', *Economic History* 3 (1934): 168–71.

12. See Harold Innis, *The Fur Trade in Canada* (Toronto: University of Toronto Press, 1956); Innis, *Settlement and the Mining Frontier* (Toronto: Macmillan, 1938); Innis, *The Cod Fisheries: The History of an International Economy* (New Haven: Yale University Press, 1940).

13. See Arthur Lower, *The North American Assault on the Canadian Forest* (Toronto: Ryerson, 1939); Arthur R.M. Lower, 'Settlement and the forest frontier in Eastern North America', in A.R.M. Lower and H.A. Innis, eds, *Settlement and the frontier in Eastern North America* (Toronto: Ryerson, 1936).

14. Vernon Fowke, *The National Policy and the Wheat Economy* (Toronto: University of Toronto Press, 1957).

15. Wallace Clement and Glen Williams, 'Introduction', in Clement and Williams, *The New Canadian Political Economy* (Montreal and Kingston: McGill-Queen's University Press, 1989), 7.

16. See Mel Watkins, 'The Political Economy of Growth', in Clement and Williams, *The New Canadian Political Economy*.

17. See, for example, the essays in Craig Heron and R. Storey, eds, *On the Job: Confronting the Labour Process in Canada* (Montreal and Kingston: McGill Queen's University Press, 1986); Simon Rosenblum and Peter Findlay, eds, *Debating Canada's Future* (Toronto: James Lorimer, 1991).

18. See Alain Lipietz, 'The Post-Fordist World: Labour Relations, International Hierarchy and Global Ecology', *Review of International Political Economy* 4, 1 (1997): 1–41.

19. That is, redistributive in the direction of greater equality.

20. A good example is Daniel Drache and Meric S. Gertler, eds, *The New Era of Global Competition* (Montreal and Kingston: McGill-Queen's University Press, 1991).

21. G. Laxer, 'The Schizophrenic Character of Canadian Political Economy', *Canadian Review of Sociology and Anthropology* 26, 1 (1989): 180–2. The nature and characteristics of Canada's business class provide a linking issue between the revived schools of Canadian political economy.

22. See Cameron's introduction to D. Cameron, ed., *The Free Trade Papers* (Toronto: Lorimer, 1986).

## Study Questions for the Readings

1. How has the role played by the state differed at different periods in Canadian history?.
2. How can we account for this change from one role to another?
3. Why is it sometimes argued that globalization and continentalism endanger the very existence of the Canadian state?
4. Why was political mobilization against free trade difficult to sustain?
5. Why does Clarkson think that international trade agreements like the FTA and NAFTA have become part of Canada's constitution?
6. What does he mean by 'constitution'?
7. Clarkson believes that in these trade deals Canada gave up much and gained little. Why?

# Remapping Canada:
## The State in the Era of Globalization

Gregory Albo and Jane Jenson

The turbulence of the late twentieth century has wrought major alterations in the structure and policies of the Canadian state. The state's role in economic regulation has changed dramatically. Rather than promoting national markets, the federal government has pursued elimination of borders between the Canadian economy and the rest of the world and made the country's competitive position in global markets the privileged barometer of well-being. Attention to trade is, of course, not new. The Canadian state has long had a development strategy founded on the comparative trade advantage derived from abundant natural resources. It promoted mining, forestry, intensive agriculture, and gas and oil drilling, while also financing the railways, roads, and pipelines that sent the products to market. Now the ecological scars of overexploitation of the Atlantic fishery and Pacific forests are only the most striking signals that the traditional role of the Canadian state in promoting resource-based development is in jeopardy. Indeed, the opposition of a large number of Canadians—and non-Canadians—to resource-driven development means that debate about the state's ecological responsibilities will be as fierce in the future as they have been recently.

The long-sought alternative to reliance on resource exports was the hope of transforming Canada into a major manufacturing economy. Many political economists, including some located throughout the federal and provincial levels of

the state, have advocated a state strategy to foster modern, technologically advanced manufacturing production that would transform Canada into a country of high value-added exports (beyond autos and resources). The establishment of a continental free-trade area and a division of labour in which Canada continues to be most prized as a source of primary resources could well mark the eclipse of that aspiration.

Along with the economic restructuring of the last two decades, there has been divisive political turbulence and change, which have moved Canadian politics far away from the familiar postwar patterns. There are ongoing conflicts over the legitimacy of a unitary 'Canadian' state, with nationalist movements in Quebec and among Aboriginal peoples seeking to redefine the country's boundaries and remake several of its major institutions. But the recent period has also brought redefinition of the proper relationship between state and citizens. There has been fervent struggle over whether the state should even minimally promote social equality or whether everyone must accept 'the discipline of the market', no matter the social costs. Social programs that often served, since the 1940s, to define the essence of Canadian distinctiveness within North America are seeing reduced expenditures and being redesigned to increase market-based incentives. The postwar promise of a 'just society' seems an increasingly distant utopia amid widening social polarization and inequalities. The way in which the 're-engineering' of state policy is being done, as the federal government transfers responsibilities for social programs and other spending to the provinces, means that ties binding Canadians through country-wide institutions are being weakened if not completely severed. In effect, the

From Wallace Clement, ed., *Understanding Canada: Building on the New Canadian Political Economy* (Montreal and Kingston: McGill-Queen's University Press, 1997), 215–39. Reprinted by permission of McGill-Queen's University Press.

Canadian state is dismantling itself, in terms of redistributive policies, while strengthening its capacity to regulate in favour of the priorities of the market.

The Canadian nation-state is not alone, of course, in confronting the strains and questions of its future under the conditions of 'globalization'. If few of the certainties that guided Canada's advance to capitalist modernity through the twentieth century remain intact, the same is true almost everywhere. The years from 1945 to 1974 are sometimes termed those of Fordism and described as a 'golden age' for national production structures and the interstate system of the capitalist world. The combination of mass production for mass consumption that dominated the Western European and North American economies after 1945 produced rapid growth, rising productivity, and higher wages for workers. The reconstruction of the interstate system after 1945 reinforced, albeit only modestly and somewhat contradictorily, the economic autonomy and sovereignty of nation-states. The postwar Keynesian welfare state presumed that national borders were also the primary boundaries for economic exchange and for political community. The autonomous national regimes establishing social and economic rights of citizenship depended on states controlling access of persons to their national territory and to their social programs.

Since the mid-1970s, however, such assumptions have been difficult to sustain as the crisis of Fordism has unfolded. Canadian families seek live-in nannies from the Philippines so that mothers are able to fly to business meetings in Paris. Population flows have multiplied, and countries try to cope with more immigrants and temporary workers in labour markets, which are, paradoxically, both more spatially fluid and stagnant. Economic instability is endemic as the borders of all states become increasingly permeable. The New York bond market's assessment of the Canadian government's deficit has almost as much influence on budgetary policy as does the Toronto Stock Exchange. Economic crisis and the loss of national autonomy in directing the future have marked even the postwar miracle communities of (West) Germany, Japan, and Sweden. Indeed, the Europeans are voluntarily transferring sovereignty to the supranational European Union in the hope that a remapping of economic and political space will ward off the worst effects of globalization.

The current malaise about the role of the Canadian state is still a result, however, of the specific history of Canada's position within the advanced capitalist group of countries and its relationship with the international economy. As other countries moved towards full employment during the postwar 'golden age', Canadian unemployment rates had already begun the climb that produced today's double-digit figures. As European and Japanese growth and productivity rates accelerated, they surpassed Canadian output levels. As recognition of the effects of globalization rose in the 1980s, Canada had the weakest and most foreign-dominated industrial structure among OECD countries, and this had long been the case.[1] The arrival of the 'new world order' seems to offer only further decline. The first task of this chapter is to explain the social and political origins of Canada's trajectory towards decline, via an assessment of the economic development strategies of the Canadian state in earlier economic regimes.

In order to do so, we must assess the capacity of the state to act, both in the past and in this era of globalization. A steady process of trade liberalization, winding down of capital controls, and internationalizing of production has undermined the state's capacity to regulate the entire country as one economic unit. The decision to move towards free trade through the Canada-United States Free Trade Agreement (FTA) of 1989, for example, signalled that the state was willing to move its regulatory powers elsewhere—in this case, to an international treaty that set limits on state actions.

In recent years, too, regional and even local economies have forged new ties beyond national borders and begun to rely more on their local states, either provincial or municipal, to promote their own interests.[2] The restructuring of global economic relations and the transformation of Canada's production structures have only intensified the 'spatial centrifugalism' already provoked by the uneven and disarticulated development of the national economy, which has always characterized Canada and profoundly shaped state institutions.[3]

Nor has this erosion of state autonomy simply evolved. Political actors, taking advantage of the restructuring of production and trade and of the interstate system, have pressed for decentralization, if not dismantling, of Canada's national institutions. This is partly because conflicts embedded in constitutional politics since Confederation provoked demands from Quebec for new state powers. Recognizing Aboriginal peoples' right to self-government also requires a certain devolutionist reordering of state institutions and constitutional power. Demands to alter the division of powers between levels of government continues, then, to be associated with economic restructuring, thereby creating the new spaces in which state action occurs.[4]

These are not the only efforts to shift the way the state regulates the national space, however. Within the federal government promoters of the new right agenda, who seek to reduce the role of the state in the economy and give free play to market forces, have undertaken a significant redistribution of responsibility for social programs and economic development. In tandem with severe program reductions, Ottawa has turned over responsibility to the provinces for providing those that remain. In this way, the federal level has effectively abrogated the responsibility that it assumed at the beginning of the 'golden age' for overseeing country-wide social and labour-market institutions and for setting standards for equitable treatment of all Canadians. An analysis of these

spatial shifts—and the economics, politics, and ideas that underpin them—is also a central task of this chapter.

## Canadian Development and the State

It is commonplace that a unique element of Canadian history is the leading role played by the state in economic development since the nineteenth century. The history of railway building, of Ontario Hydro, and of public health care are frequently evoked to show that Canadians do not 'fear' state intervention and that it has contributed to national well-being. Political economists, from both the staples and the Marxist traditions, share an interest in the formation of the Canadian state, even if they have not agreed on how to understand its relationship to civil society. Nor have such theoretical disputes lost their political urgency today. It is not simply of 'academic' interest whether economic conditions in Canada are interpreted as only a temporary adjustment, as a cumulative process of economic failure specific to Canada, as a mere regional effect of a general crisis of capitalism, or a decline whose institutional origins need to be traced to earlier historical processes. Historical disputes about Canada's early formation shape individuals' positions within the field of political economy and within current political debates about the country's future in an era of globalization.

If there is disagreement about how to characterize the present, there is wider agreement among political economists that its roots reside in history.[5] An understanding of the forces shaping the current trajectory of the Canadian economy and the role of the state must seek their lineage in the legacies of the country's transition to capitalism in the mid-nineteenth century. Canada was both a late follower and a post-colonial state. Britain undertook a transition to capitalism and industrialization first; all other countries were 'followers' of one sort or another, with Canada falling within the group of late followers, whose transition occurred in the second half of the nineteenth century. The Canadian colonies and the post-1867 dominion were, moreover, a 'white-settler' extension of the British Empire, occupying a geographical space in competition with a powerful and expansionist southern neighbour. These political and spatial constraints gave a particular cast to Canada's transition to capitalism. Wedged between a dominant imperial power, which continued to maintain economic ties with its former colonies, and the rising industrial power of the United States, the Canadian colonies confronted an increasingly open and competitive international economy for their exports. The economic task of the late-follower transition to capitalism was either to 'catch up' industrially or to be marginalized as a periphery of a larger, imperial power. Originating as a white-settler colony, Canada never had to break the grip of a feudal aristocracy, as so many European countries did. The political task of the transition was to consolidate the geographical space of Canada politically for European settlement and a national market. Canada's capitalist transition and initial industrialization emerged thus, in a social structure comprised of agrarian small property-holders, large mercantile and financial interests, and an Aboriginal population still occupying much of the territory.

This history has set the parameters of the new Canadian political economy's debates about models of development and state formation. Analyses seek the imprint left on the state from the transition to capitalism, and vice versa. As well, they track the formation of capitalism's classes, particularly the industrial bourgeoisie and proletariat, in relation to other classes and to Aboriginal peoples living on the margins of the capitalist economy. Finally, political economists have tried to assess the effect of the balance between internal development and external dependence that characterizes Canada's insertion into the world economy.

## The Canadian Transition: From One Staple to Another

The staples thesis of Canadian history provides perhaps the most common interpretation of Canada's economic development. Drawing on Adam Smith's *Wealth of Nations* (1776), it describes Canada's transition to capitalism as a successful extension across time and space of exchange relations and state-building.[6] In the work that laid the foundation of Canadian political economy, Mackintosh and Innis present Canadian development as a continuing search for natural resources—that is, staples—to exploit. Fish, fur, timber, and minerals all propelled development forward in time and westward through space. Despite much historical debate and varying emphases in details, all adherents of the staples approach agree that the pace and form of development were determined by geographical possibilities and limitations, technological improvements, the division of labour, and, most crucially, the economic surplus generated by foreign demand for 'resource-extensive exports'.[7]

In Mackintosh's view, for example, industrialization passed through stages. Looking at Canada as an ex-colony of Britain, he said, '[R]apid progress in . . . new countries . . . [is] dependent upon the discovery of cheap supplies of raw materials by the export of which to the markets of the world the new country may purchase the products which it cannot produce economically at this stage of its development.'[8] Innis had a darker vision of the exchange relationship between imperial centre and colonial periphery. He warned repeatedly of the rigidity of overhead costs and the instability of external demand, which could produce 'disturbances incidental to dependence on staples', thereby cumulatively upsetting the development of the periphery.[9] None the less, both authors attributed a successful capitalist transition in mid-nineteenth-century Canada to an export staple that quickly propelled it, as a late industrializer, from the commercial-agriculture to the industrial stage of development.

Despite focusing on economic, technological, and geographical factors, staples theorists did not ignore the state. Indeed they produced two important and varying accounts of the economic and social relations that underpinned Canadian state-building. At the centre of the dispute was the nature of the social projects, especially Confederation and the first National Policy of the 1870s, which generated regional tensions over the unequal terms of exchange of the newly formed national market. Writing from the perspective of central Canada, Creighton identified the commercial élite engaged in the staples trade, and concentrated in the commercial centres of Montreal and Toronto, with the national interest: 'In the commercial group was concentrated a great proportion of economic power—the wealth, the energy and ability of the colony . . . It was a re-enactment . . . of the classic West-European struggle—the struggle between insurgent commercial capitalism and a desperately resisting feudal and absolutist state.'[10] From the vantage point of the West, Fowke documented both that the links provided by its wheat exports were crucial to successful industrialization and that the National Policy exacerbated regional tensions. The unequal exchange relation that fuelled such tensions arose in large part because the Canadian state acted as—indeed was created to be—'an agent within the first national policy . . . [of] its original principals, the commercial, financial, and manufacturing interests of the central provinces.'[11]

When staples theorists analysed state actions they most often described them as direct responses to needs generated by the staples trade.[12] For some theorists, still writing from a Smithian perspective of trade as spur to development, the 'entrepreneurial capacity' of the Canadian state in the National Policy set this country apart from both the British and the American market-led capitalist transitions. Aitken, for example, forcefully argued that the 'defensive expansionism' of the Canadian state was a strategy for territorial integrity. It involved the state in 'facilitating the production and export of staple products . . . to forestall, counteract, or restrain the northward extension of American economic and political influence.'[13] Thus the central responsibility of the state was management of exchange flows between Canada and the world economy.

## An Exceptional Failure

The defensive-expansionism thesis, developed after 1945, was an optimistic reading of the way the Canadian state had managed trade relations and the contribution of resource exports to state-building and economic progress. In later years, some political actors and academics became uneasy about the increasing ties between Canada and the United States. These ties were both economic—as continental trading relationships took precedence over the remnants of the post-colonial link with Britain—and political. In the Cold War interstate system Canada was not only clearly in the Western camp, in which the United States had replaced Britain as the world hegemonic power. Its territorial integrity and sovereignty were also weakened by common North American defence systems and increasing integration of its international actions with those of its southern neighbour.[14] By the early 1960s concerns about economic as well as political sovereignty were emerging.[15]

This was the context in which the nationalist tendency within the new Canadian political economy first began to work. This position can be considered neo-Innisian, as it continued to share the focus of the staples thesis on resources and exchange relations. The traditional staples analysis was supplemented, however, with a dependency approach to the power relations that were formed by unequal exchange between a dominant manufacturing-based centre and a resource-exporting periphery. Where Innis saw constraints resulting from Canada's location on the margins of

Western civilization, the neo-Innisians detected the blockages to development of a periphery.[16] Signs of dependence, which Canada shared with Latin America, were truncated industrial development in manufacturing branch plants that lacked export capacity, reliance on resource exports, and a state that lacked sufficient effective autonomy to direct the country's economy. As Levitt, one of the originators of this approach, summarized, the 'new mercantilism of multinational corporations' prevented formation of a technologically advanced manufacturing sector, and this situation led to the 'silent surrender' of sovereignty through the postwar period.[17]

These political economists sought the economic and social sources, internal as well as external, of Canada's failure to make a successful transition to an autonomous manufacturing economy. One root was clearly external, located in the pattern of trade relations between a resource periphery and manufacturing centre. 'Canada was to be understood as an "effect" of these ongoing and changing relationships with the two great imperial powers of modern capitalism.'[18] The problem, however, was not just international trade patterns. Internal structures forged in a staples-dominated economy had a fundamental effect. The economic surplus earned in the staples trade opened a number of potential alternative paths to development: industrial diversification through import substitution, a switch to a new resource export staple, or a 'staples trap' of continued reliance on a declining resource base. The choice of path depended on entrepreneurial capacity to convert the economic surplus generated by resource exports into economic linkages with other nationally controlled industries. Entrepreneurship, for the neo-Innisians, pivoted around the characteristics of Canada's capitalist class, which controlled the surplus and the staples trade. The new Canadian political economy revealed a Canadian capitalist class comprised of persistently strong mercantile and financial interests, dating back to a commercially based transition to capitalism. Industrial interests, moreover, were stunted, foreign-owned, and technologically backward.[19] It was these interests and class alliances that had kept Canada in a 'staples trap', predisposed to 'development of inefficient non-innovative and backward industrial structures with a penchant for dependence on foreign technology, foreign capital and state assistance.'[20]

In these formulations, mercantile capitalism had been replaced in the nineteenth century not by powerful industrialists but by a 'financial-staples oligarchy', the precursor of the power of today's banks and multinational corporations, which themselves remain dependent on an imperialist centre within the world economy. In these histories the industrial development fostered by the National Policy brought stunted industrialization and loss of economic sovereignty, as American industrialists were induced to jump tariff walls or to buy Canadian firms to create branch plants to serve the Canadian market.

The state had a role to play in this story. It was, however, a different one from that recounted by the early staples theorists. Whereas for the latter the entrepreneurial capacity of the state had helped build the state and forge an autonomous economy, for the nationalist new political economists the Canadian state was foremost a subservient extension of Canada's commercial and financial capitalism.[21] The dominance of financial, commercial, and foreign manufacturing capital in Canadian society translated into a weak state, uninterested in fostering development or sustaining national sovereignty. In this formulation, the root of Canada's development impasse is social: the state was simply an instrument of the powerful élites in a truncated transition to capitalism. It was little wonder, then, that the state had failed to arrest dependence or to respond adequately to the signs of economic weakness and decline becoming visible in the 1970s. As Drache put it, Canada could not 'transcend its commercial status as a supplier of resources and a market for manufactured goods . . . [I]t could not acquire the

capability to revolutionize its own mode of production.'[22] The state was, in the vision of the new
political economy, neither able nor willing to halt
the reconfiguration of economic space in the
direction of continentalism.

## Less Exceptional than Different

For the new Canadian political economy heirs of
Innis, Canada's capitalist transition was one of
exceptional failure. Accordingly, Canada was 'the
world's richest underdeveloped country'[23] and
had an economy that had failed to follow the normal development phases to an industrial society
with an autonomous economy and state. Marxists
and political economists influenced by class
analysis provided a quite different reading of the
same history.[24] Notably, they dismissed the idea
that the country's development was stuck in a
merchant capitalist phase or that Canada's major
characteristic was its 'exceptionalism'.

These political economists argued instead
that Canada had passed through the usual stages
of capitalist development. Pentland, for instance,
traced the transition from pre-capitalist 'personal'
and feudal relations of exploitation to capitalist
social relations at mid-nineteenth century.
Confederation and the National Policy signified a
successful bourgeois revolution, reflecting the
material interests of industrial capitalists facing
monopolistic competition from the United States.
Their state-building and spatial extension yielded
'an undivided protectionist voice'.[25] In Ryerson's
view, the 'unequal union' of Confederation—of
colonial Canada and imperial Britain, Quebec and
Canada, Aboriginals and Europeans—reflected
the growing strength of industrial capitalists, who
required 'a state of their own, under their control,
capable of providing a favourable framework for
the home market.'[26] Labour historians, too, dis-
sented from the picture of an exceptionalism in
Canadian society. They focused on the growing
strength of the working class and its institutions
as industrial capitalism spread.[27]

Despite the similarities between Canada's
history and the emergence of capitalism and state-
building in other countries, there were particularities to the Canadian story that received the
attention they deserve only in later studies. As
Panitch noted, political economists could not
ignore the fact that Canada was 'distinguished
from other advanced capitalist societies in terms of
its dependent industrialism.'[28] Such observations
call for a historicist method capable of exposing
the ways abstract categories take on historical content as the result of the actions of social forces
making their own history and thereby becoming
the specific structures of Canadian capitalism.

The years of state-building at the end of the
nineteenth century and the first National Policy
formed again the terrain worked over in three
studies that sought to depict the origins and
nature of the structural-institutional fusion
between internal conservatism and external
dependence that had perpetuated a model of
development leading to 'technological entropy'. In
Williams's view, the import-substitution strategy
promoted by the National Policy had been a logical choice for state and business élites in a
resource-endowed regional periphery. The
process of 'arrested industrialization' that took
hold was increasingly difficult to overcome,
because makers of state policy were 'loath to disturb the investment climate' that recasting a non-
innovative, branch-plant economy would entail.[29]
It is with a similar sense of the failed 'historical
possibilities' that Laxer located Canada's 'aborted
industrialization'. For him, in Canada, in contrast
to all other late-follower countries, agrarian producers had not penetrated the power bloc and
had never therefore forged the class alliances necessary 'to take a leading role in creating the state
and transforming the economy.'[30] Without a
national-popular movement to deter them, dominant élites maintained a crippling allegiance to the
British (and then American) empire and state policies that sustained 'foreign ownership and a truncated manufacturing sector'.[31] For Mahon, the

hegemony of the staples fraction of Canadian capital meant that 'industrialization remained a secondary objective.'[32] Even though it perceived the threat of deindustrialization, a marginalized nationalist manufacturing fraction and working class lacked enough power within an unequal structure of representation to force elaboration of an industrial policy.[33] In sum, for these authors, with their focus on either business élites or subordinate classes, the specificity of Canada's transition to industrial capitalism was the pattern of class power and the resulting alliances (or failed alliances)—weak national manufacturers (Williams), weak agrarians (Laxer), weak workers (Mahon).[34] The frail manufacturing class, in conjunction with other marginalized groups and classes, could never exercise sufficient political power to provoke normal development of an export manufacturing capacity. The institutional and policy legacies were the growing spectre of deindustrialization in an increasingly open and competitive world economy after 1945.

Building on such class-oriented and institutional studies, without ever ignoring the insight that Canada's dependent capitalism must be explained, it is possible to retell the story of these years of transition and spatial reconfiguration. We now see that the particular character of the Canadian transition lay in the combination of intensive and extensive forms of accumulation, which generated quite impressive productivity advances through the nineteenth century and moved Canada into the upper rank of capitalist countries.[35] Extensive accumulation was made possible by territorial expansion and absorption of new workers.[36] The state's territorial reach extended westward and northward. Territories that had been incorporated into the trading networks of imperialism were directly appropriated. Aboriginal lands were seized, and their pre-capitalist mode of production was liquidated.[37] As well, the labour supply was highly elastic for immigrants from Europe, who brought skills that Canada did not have to pay to develop, at the going wage.[38] Exten-

sive accumulation did not prevent, and indeed encouraged, intensive accumulation by providing the surplus to pay for investment in capital goods (using foreign funds and technology) in both the agricultural and resource sectors. The growth of incomes also provided the inducement for mass-market industries—textiles, shoes, dry goods—to develop. The story told about Canada's economic transition is thus not one of merchant trade preserving pre-capitalist commercial and financial activities. Rather it is the creation of industrialism out of that combination of intensive and extensive accumulation that also implanted capitalist relations of production throughout the territory that became modern Canada.

This model of capitalist development also implied a certain specificity to the Canadian state structure.[39] The country created in 1867 was a liberal democracy, but one whose sovereignty was divided and parcelled. An ex-colony but still a 'dominion' without recognition as a fully independent nation-state, it was also internally divided by competing nationalist claims arising in French and English Canada and the unresolved history of the subjugation of Aboriginal nations. State structures were constructed in response to competing drives. Strong and centralized powers were sought by those whose goal was to create a single socio-economic space and to facilitate development of infrastructure to smooth the transition to industrialism. At the same time there were social forces that would accept only state structures sufficiently decentralized to accommodate the diversity of two nations in a single state and of regionally differentiated, unevenly developed economies. The result was the divided sovereignty of Canadian federalism and a 'place-sensitive societal paradigm'.[40]

These state structures would subsequently be forced to accept the consequences of divided sovereignty as well as the absence of a strong sense of pan-Canadian allegiance. At each moment of economic and political turbulence, the legitimacy of basic state institutions was called into question, so that Canadian history seemed to lurch from 'constitutional crisis' to 'constitutional crisis'. The delicate élite negotiations that generated the new dominion underlined 'the primacy attached to the preservation of property and the prerequisites of the accumulation process'.[41] Popular democratic forces were weak, and the fact that institutions of federalism were privileged as the locale for conflict resolution between political and bureaucratic élites made it even more difficult for them to gain access. The unequal structures of representation of class-divided societies became even murkier in a situation in which the institutional routes to representation were varied and not always open.[42] Such a state did bring in a transition to capitalism based in both extensive and intensive forms of accumulation, but its limited capacity to sustain industrial or labour-market policies hindered Canada's emergence as a major industrial power in its own right.

Throughout this section we have seen that quite different readings of Canada's nineteenth century exist. While everyone agrees that in the last decades of the century Canada set out on a trajectory that shaped the crisis of the late twentieth century, there is much less agreement about the parts played by the state, social actors, and institutions of these years. Some have seen the state as little more than the handmaiden of large historical forces. For others the state was captured by the dominant class forces and did nothing to divert the country from a road of failure, directed towards a 'staples trap' of dependence. For yet others, the pre-capitalist ruling class was displaced in the thoroughgoing capitalist project that was Confederation. This project, led by powerful social forces, created an influential state not simply in their own image but one that reflected and perpetuated the unequal structures of representation and power in Canadian society.

These alternate explanations of Canada's capitalist transition are central to much more than theoretical academic disputes. Many political economists seek to understand the history of their present circumstances as part of the effort to

change them. Their attention turned, therefore, even as they struggled to discern the role of the state in those crucial decades of the nineteenth century, to another matter: how can we comprehend Canada's current economic malaise, and what contribution has the state made to it?

## Postwar Canada and the Long Decline

Just as the forces restructuring Europe and North America in the late nineteenth century provided foreign demand for Canada's primary commodity experts, the post-1945 golden age of Fordism similarly furnished buoyant foreign markets for Canada's primary commodities of hydroelectricity, oil and gas, and metals. The United States had displaced Britain as the undisputed economic centre of the world economy during the war, and as a result Canada's 'permeable Fordism' was profoundly shaped by American technology and manufacturing branch plants.[43]

There were, however, already disconcerting signs of a developing economic malaise during the postwar boom, despite impressive gains in productive capacity. Except in natural resources and a few manufacturing sectors, domestic industry did not fare well when confronted by international competition. A number of trends stood out. The manufacturing sector ranked as one of the West's weakest in output and employment shares of the national economy. Levels of foreign direct investment were at new highs, bringing the expected liabilities for exports and innovation. Exports were concentrated in resources and semi-processed goods, while imports were primarily high-end manufactured goods. Firms undertook only minimal research and development; there were shortages of skilled workers even though substantial unemployment had appeared. All of this combined to produce Canadian productivity and growth rates chronically below the rest of the Western economies, while much of the growth was simply the extensive employment growth of an enlarging market.

The emerging picture was one of relative economic decline. While the roots of this decline might be identified by the various approaches to the new Canadian political economy in the formative processes of the capitalist transition, it was still necessary to trace the history from the nineteenth century to the present. Moreover, the contribution of the postwar state to the patterns of economic development and state-building had to be assessed. Here, again, different approaches emerged.

The Smithian heirs of the original staples theory dominated postwar economic thinking in Canada, within the state and among neoclassical economists. They saw few problems with the patterns of trade and ownership. In their eyes, foreign investment helped address what they saw as capital shortages; resource exports were Canada's natural comparative advantage.[44] None the less, there were some concerns about industrial production. Apprehensions began to mount as early as the Royal Commission on Canada's Prospects (Gordon Commission) in 1957. The Economic Council of Canada's reports of the 1970s picked up this theme, and the Royal Commission on the Economic Union and Canada's Development Prospects (Macdonald Commission) in the mid-1980s sounded an alarm as well. The underlying premise was that the absence of economies of scale prevented full productivity increases and stunted export trade in high value-added goods. This analysis gained the support of both foreign and domestically controlled capital, which also weighed in behind the solution proposed by these reports to the state. This was to foster further continental integration through creation of a common economic space. Indeed, the central recommendation of the Macdonald Report was that Canada seek a free-trade arrangement with the United States. Such an accord would reconfigure economic space by expanding the single market and by harmonizing a broad range of economic policies. The federal government pursued this recommendation, negotiating and then implementing the Canada-United States Free Trade Agreement (FTA) of 1989. In effect, just as political institutions and state power had been crucial after 1867 in the creation of a single economic space from east to west, state institutions in the mid-1980s led the move to redesign this economic space by lifting the barriers that partly separated the two largest North American economies. Extension of the trade pact by inclusion of Mexico within the North American Free Trade Agreement (NAFTA) of 1992 continued this remapping of economic space.

Not surprisingly, the neo-Innisian nationalist tendency within the new Canadian political economy was not enthusiastic about this prescription. Its diagnosis of the economic impasse since the 1970s had focused on political dependence and economic decline.[45] From within the state sector the alarm was sounded by the Science Council of Canada, which warned that Canada's branch-plant model of development was causing technological entropy through 'truncated industries with a low technological capability becoming cumulatively dependent upon foreign industries.'[46] The proposed corrective was a national industrial strategy that could foster 'technological sovereignty' and generate an export-oriented manufacturing sector. This prescription received short shrift, however, as the state definitively moved towards the FTA. Indeed, anything resembling an industrial policy was ruled out of bounds by the prevailing laissez-faire policy, which characterized such activity as an inappropriate intervention by the state in the economy that would cause inefficiencies and as an unacceptable restraint on free trade.

Therefore the run-up to the FTA and the state's increasing enthusiasm for a continentalist strategy forced political economists to seek other strategies for reversing economic decline and to begin to treat the whole of North America as a potential space for political action. The particularities of Canadian economic decline had to be assessed relative to the restructuring occurring across the advanced capitalist countries. Because the inter-nationalization of production was generalized, it was also necessary to reconsider the balance among national, continental, and international strategies as a potential space for political action. Niosi, Resnick, and Carroll, for example, examined the impact of the new conditions for the international economy on the characteristics of Canadian capital, including its ties to foreign capital. They contended that high levels of 'foreign investment' characterized late capitalism as a whole: Canada was not exceptional. Carroll, for example, argued that foreign ownership and its consequences were simply part of a universal 'world-wide process of capitalist internationalization'.[47] Foreign investment in Canada had been declining since the early 1970s, so that the largest portion of assets remained under domestic control.[48] Such patterns belied any notion of a continuous regression to dependence. Canadian businesses were, moreover, investing abroad, while interlocking corporate ties had created a small monopoly of finance capitalists active in both manufacturing and financial sectors. For Resnick, such trends represented a maturing of Canadian capitalism 'over the postwar period, with Canadian banks and corporations increasingly in control of leading sectors of the Canadian economy and better able to project their influence abroad. The Canadian state has played a crucial role in furthering this process.'[49] Bellon and Niosi argued, too, that the 'continental and rentier nationalism' fostered by the state had 'its logical outcome . . . [in] growing integration into the North American market.'[50]

In the view of these authors, 'Canada simply presents the first case of a more *general* phenomenon' that has emerged in this age of globalization.[51] This rejection of Canada as an exceptional, failed late-follower and its reclassification as one of several countries sharing a generalized experience of crisis and globalization elide the unique features of Canada's dependent capitalism. Ob-

servers of a more historicist position have sought not only economic but also political particularities of the 'Canadian case', precisely because it is these specificities that set the constraints for action in the context of free trade and globalization.

In some cases their search led to development of new concepts. Indeed, the major theme of a recent collection is that the central concepts of the first generation of the new Canadian political economy—dependence, class, and state—have been supplanted by three others—production, space, and identity.[52]

Àpropos of the first concept, the implication is that the focus on the dependent status of Canada's production relations has given way to analyses that identify their specific historical forms, as well as their links to social classes. Such studies clarify the ways in which Canada's Fordism continued to depend on extensive accumulation. In postwar Canada, the 'super-profits' that drive capital accumulation came in large part from economic rents from primary commodity production, employment rents generated by forgoing the training costs required for technologically leading production, and absolute growth in the market from immigration.[53] In addition, the pre-1940 politics of post-colonialism and the nascent manufacturing branch plants formed during the National Policy period sent Canada into the Fordist years highly permeable to foreign influences. Previous state policies as well as those promoted in the late 1940s meant that intensive accumulation relied on second-best technology adapted from the US economy, whose capitalists were attracted to the vibrant Canadian economy. The result was a national system of innovation in which minimal research and development occurred, techniques were imported, and education and training structures remained underdeveloped. This industrial structure, with its adaptation of US technology, became increasingly a barrier as the American technological edge in the formation of Fordism declined relative to the later-formed flexible-production techniques of Japan and West Germany.

In other words, earlier state decisions, whether in the late nineteenth century or after 1945, set up the later economic weaknesses. They also shaped the constraints and choices for the 1980s and 1990s. Indeed, it is possible to see the move towards a continent-wide economic space as the most recent effort to build on Canada's strengths in primary products and to 'cut the losses' of earlier hopes to advance a country-wide autonomous industrial economy. Thus NAFTA creates not only a new economic space but a particular division of labour. Canada provides resources, financial input, and some manufacturing, Mexico furnishes cheap labour, and the United States provides technology and representation of the regional bloc in the interstate system.

Second, recognition of the extent to which states as well as other institutions are crucial to the creation of economic and political space is the reason that political economists now pay attention to this concept. The break-up of Fordism has forced us to recognize that the correspondence between nation-states and the capitalist economy can take on new configurations. National states, for instance, are having greater difficulty in regulating their own economies at the same time as they are participating in the redrawing of borders. The free-trade agreements that the federal government signed are potent symbols that nation-states, and the powerful social classes represented in their structures, may choose to limit their own sovereignty.

This lesson is not lost on other social forces and political actors. It was noted above that the political practices of the Fordist period marginalized subordinate classes, particularly the labour movement. This marginalization allowed the state to enter into the free-trade agreements, despite the likely costs to manufacturing and other workers. Indeed, the job losses in the resulting restructuring have driven unemployment and welfare rates to postwar highs. Deregulation of national financial markets, moreover, repeats a historic pattern of capital mobility that is 'dangerously unstable and ultimately economically inefficient'.[54]

Political mobilization against the negative effects of free trade has been difficult to sustain. The political party traditionally associated with the labour movement—the New Democratic Party—structured much of its identity around the processes of national regulation of postwar Keynesianism, and it has not been able to abandon these commitments without consequences. The bourgeois parties have been less encumbered with the legacies of the past. Even the Liberal Party, which constructed Canada's welfare state, has joined the Reform and Progressive Conservative parties in pursuit of the neo-conservative project of globalization. The provincial states controlled by the NDP have had little success in finding a 'progressive competitiveness' option of empowering subordinate groups and protecting them from the adverse winds blowing through the global economy. The crisis has ripped apart the NDP and the labour movement, which now appear to support neither the old economic policies of national regulation nor a new economic project capable of accomplishing egalitarian or redistributive objectives.[55]

Nor have the disputes over regionalism and federalism that had characterized Canada's Fordism been overcome. Constitutional conflict both drove and was exacerbated by economic crisis. The Macdonald Commission itself was established in the early 1980s to inquire into both economic and constitutional restructuring. The existence of the Canadian state itself has been placed in question by the political fragmentation that has been encouraged by economic globalization and continentalism. There has in effect been a 'double shift' away from the national state of the postwar years. The free-trade agreements, as well as the strengthening of the supervisory authority of the International Monetary Fund and the World Trade Organization, cede national sovereignty to opaque international institutions with few democratic credentials. The politics of Québécois and Aboriginal nationalisms seek not only a redefinition of state powers but also a reconfiguration of national political space. The sovereigntist movement in Quebec would redraw the formal borders of Canada, while both Québécois federalist nationalists and Aboriginal nationalists seek to realign the effective borders of political power via a process of devolution.[56]

Third, these movements have made it clear that the identity of Canadians is being altered in these years of crisis and change. The state has a central role to play here because it is the state that recognizes citizens, both those who have the right to call themselves citizens and the rights that citizens obtain. Both these aspects of inclusion are in dispute, and both are linked directly to current politics. Neither Québécois separatists nor Aboriginal nationalists aspire to 'Canadian' citizenship. The former want to realize their own national identities in an independent state, while Aboriginal peoples claim the collective rights of nations within Canada (as do many Québécois nationalists who wish to remain in Canada).

Many more Canadians than these are asking about the content of national identity. Immigrant flows around the globe are one important characteristic of globalization, and they are changing the racial, ethnic, and national composition of the country's population. These changes make any identity as an ex-colony of Britain—or France— very difficult to sustain. The ethnic and racial mix of the population means that Canadians have a multiplicity of links with a wide variety of countries and a political interest in seeing state policies in the realm of human rights, refugee policy, and international military action represent those links. It also means that anti-progressive politics must be combated by, for example, demonstration that an inclusive citizenship policy has been and con-

tinues to be central to the country's well-being, rather than contrary to it.

Citizenship is not simply about the borders between us and others, about the inside and outside. It is also about the rights of citizens within the country.[57] Here the Canadian state has been challenging and changing the postwar social identity of citizenship. The citizenship of Fordism was one that established and extended economic and social rights. There were two dimensions to this notion. First was the idea that the costs and consequences of life's hazards—unemployment, accident, sickness—as well as life's needs—education, and childbearing—should be shared, if not equally, with at least minimal standards of equity. Citizens were not considered to live as isolated individuals facing the risks and costs of everyday life alone. Social solidarity was a 'public good' to be set against the insecurities of the capitalist market. Second, the Keynesian welfare state was organized around the idea that the state would extend and regulate national institutions such as labour markets, health care, and education to provide at least a minimal level of provision regardless of individuals' economic circumstance. Everyone had the right to unemployment insurance, to universal health care, and to access to educational institutions, no matter where she or he lived in the country. In a federal system such as Canada's, 'portability' and 'national standards' were crucial manifestations of the rights of national citizenship.

In the current political situation of post-Fordism, these citizenship rights have been called into question, and with them the political and social identities of Canadians. Citizens are being told that they alone, or with their families, have responsibility for their futures. The market and their own worthiness will determine not only whether they succeed or fail but whether they will live their lives with dignity or in fear of poverty and the other inherent risks of capitalist society. It is not by chance that one of the major fears of opponents of the FTA and NAFTA was that their cit-

izenship right to universal health care would be
threatened by the state's decision to break down
trade borders. Indeed, in recent years we have
been treated to a panoply of arguments emanating
from the state and business élites to explain why
the era of global competition has rendered the old
programs outdated. The question for the future is

whether the Canadian state will be forced, by
democratic mobilization of its citizens, to find new
versions of these programs that retain the same
commitment to solidarity and equity or whether it
will preside over the breaking of the ties that have
bound the country together—and therefore over
the dismantling of the country itself.

## Notes

1. On the economic crisis in Canada, see J. Jenson, R.
Mahon, and M. Bienefeld, eds, *Production, Space,
Identity: Political Economy Faces the 21st Century*
(Toronto: Canadian Scholars' Press, 1993); C.
Gonick, *The Great Economic Debate* (Toronto:
Lorimer, 1987); and S. McBride, *Not Working: State,
Unemployment, and Neo-Conservatism in Canada*
(Toronto: University of Toronto Press, 1992).

2. R. Cox, 'Global Perestroika', in R. Miliband and L.
Panitch, eds, *Socialist Register 1992: New World
Order?* (London: Merlin, 1992), 31; J. Loxley,
'Regional Trading Blocks', in Jenson, Mahon, and
Bienefeld, eds, *Production, Space, Identity*, 305–26.

3. Jane Jenson, 'Mapping, Naming and
Remembering: Globalization at the end of the
twentieth century', *Review of International Political
Economy* 2, 1 (Spring 1995): 96–116.

4. This has been a consistent theme of Canadian
political science. See: J. Brodie, *The Political
Economy of Canadian Regionalism* (Toronto:
Harcourt Brace Jovanovich, 1990); G. Stevenson,
*Unfulfilled Union* (Toronto: Macmillan, 1979); R.
Whitaker, *A Sovereign Idea* (Montreal and
Kingston: McGill-Queen's University Press, 1992);
Jane Jenson, '"Different" but not "Exceptional":
Canada's Permeable Fordism', *Canadian Review of
Sociology and Anthropology* 26, 1 (1989).

5. Neoclassical economists, in contrast, display a
preference for ahistorical and monocausal explanations of the Canadian economic impasse. They
identify either the 'small size' of the national market or 'over-governance' as producing market
rigidities. These analyses do not adequately
address the empirical situation, however. Extending exchange relations through continental free
trade has compounded Canada's economic crisis.
Reducing the public sector—already one of the

most impoverished in the advanced capitalist
zone—has resulted in further disintegration of the
national state.

6. Another way of describing the process is as one of
'nation-building'. We prefer to label it 'state-building' because it was a state and its institutions that
were being built. The question of whether a
'nation' was being forged continues to plague us
today. Our term reminds us of Charles Tilly's
observation that histories of the transition to capitalism and its development trajectories are closely
linked to histories of state-building. See C. Tilly,
*Coercion, Capital and European States* (Oxford: Basil
Blackwell, 1990).

7. M. Watkins, 'A Staple Theory of Economic
Growth', *Canadian Journal of Economics and
Political Science* 29, 2 (1963). For the relationship
between Smith and Innis, see W.T. Easterbrook,
'Innis and Economics', *Canadian Journal of
Economics and Political Science* 19, 3 (1953). For a
thorough neoclassical account of this period that
discounts the role of staples industries, and much
else, see I. Drummond, *Progress without Planning:
Ontario's Economic Development, 1867–1941*
(Toronto: University of Toronto Press, 1987).

8. W.A. Mackintosh, *The Economic Background of
Dominion-Provincial Relations* (Toronto: McClelland
& Stewart, 1964), 13. For essays surveying this
theme, see D. Cameron, ed., *Explorations in
Canadian Economic History* (Ottawa: University of
Ottawa Press, 1985); D. Platt and G. Di Tella, eds,
*Argentina, Australia and Canada Compared: Studies
in Comparative Development, 1870–1965* (New
York: St Martin's Press, 1985).

9. H. Innis, *Essays in Canadian Economic History*
(Toronto: University of Toronto Press, 1956),
381–2. The most important synthesis of this view

of Innis is the insightful paper of D. Drache, 'Harold Innis and Canadian Capitalist Development', *Canadian Journal of Political and Social Theory* 6, 1–2 (1982).

10. D. Creighton, *The Empire of the St. Lawrence* (Toronto: Macmillan, 1956), 40.

11. V.C. Fowke, *The National Policy and the Wheat Economy* (Toronto: University of Toronto Press, 1957), 276. See also K. Buckley, 'The Role of Staple Industries in Canada's Economic Development', *Journal of Economic History* 28 (1958).

12. For a detailed discussion of staples and the state, see G. Albo and J. Jenson, 'The Relative Autonomy of the State', in W. Clement and G. Williams, eds, *The New Canadian Political Economy* (Montreal and Kingston: McGill-Queen's University Press, 1989), 183–7.

13. H. Aitken, 'Defensive Expansionism: The State and Economic Growth in Canada', in W.T. Easterbrook and M. Watkins, eds, *Approaches to Canadian Economic History* (Toronto: McClelland & Stewart, 1967), 220–1. Easterbrook also noted with resignation that in Canada 'centrally directed, "induced" entrepreneurship established a pattern which remains largely intact.' See his 'Long-Period Comparative Study: Some Historical Cases', *Journal of Economic History* 17 (1957): 576.

14. M. Clark-Jones, *A Staple State: Canadian Industrial Resources in Cold War* (Toronto: University of Toronto Press, 1987); E. Regehr, *Arms Canada: The Deadly Business of Military Exports* (Toronto: Lorimer, 1987).

15. See H. Aitken, *American Capital and Canadian Resources* (Cambridge, Mass.: Harvard University Press, 1961); W. Axline et al., eds, *Continental Community? Independence and Integration in North America* (Toronto: McClelland & Stewart, 1974).

16. G. Williams, 'Canada in the International Political Economy,' in W. Clement and G. Williams, eds, *The New Canadian Political Economy* (Montreal and Kingston: McGill-Queen's University Press, 1989), 116–37.

17. K. Levitt, *Silent Surrender* (Toronto: Macmillan, 1970).

18. J. Myles, 'Understanding Canada: Comparative Political Economy Perspectives', *Canadian Review of Sociology and Anthropology* 26, 1 (1989): 1.

19. Levitt, *Silent Surrender*; T. Naylor, 'Dominion of Capital: Canada and International Investment', in A. Kontos, ed., *Domination* (Toronto: University of Toronto Press, 1975); W. Clement, *Continental Corporate Power* (Toronto: McClelland & Stewart, 1977).

20. Naylor, 'Dominion of Capital', 52.

21. For a more detailed presentation of state theory in this approach, see Albo and Jenson, 'Relative Autonomy', 187–93.

22. D. Drache, 'Harold Innis and Canadian Capitalist Development', *Canadian Journal of Political and Social Theory* 6, 1–2 (1982): 42.

23. Levitt, *Silent Surrender*, 24–5.

24. For a detailed consideration of class theorists' view of state power, see Albo and Jenson, 'Relative Autonomy', 193–200.

25. H.C. Pentland, *Labour and Capital in Canada, 1650–1860* (Toronto: James Lorimer, 1981), 173. See also P. Phillips, 'Unequal Exchange, Surplus Production and the Commercial-Industrial Question', in D. Cameron, ed., *Explorations in Canadian Political Economy* (Ottawa: University of Ottawa Press, 1984). Though Pentland was far from an orthodox Marxist, his study was influenced by the transition debate sparked by Dobb's *Development of Capitalism*.

26. S. Ryerson, *Unequal Union: Confederation and the Roots of the Conflict in the Canadas, 1815–1873* (Toronto: Progress Books, 1968), 310.

27. See especially G. Kealey, *Toronto Workers Respond to Industrial Capitalism, 1867–1892* (Toronto: University of Toronto Press, 1980); M. Cohen, *Women's Work: Markets and Economic Development in Nineteenth Century Ontario* (Toronto: University of Toronto Press, 1988).

28. L. Panitch, 'Dependency and Class in Canadian Political Economy', *Studies in Political Economy* 6 (1981): 23. This more historicist Marxist theoretical tendency was associated with the formation of the journal *Studies in Political Economy*, which followed on the heels of L. Panitch, ed., *The Canadian State* (Toronto: University of Toronto Press, 1977).

29. G. Williams, *Not for Export* (Toronto: McClelland & Stewart, 1983), 130.

30. G. Laxer, *Open for Business* (Toronto: Oxford University Press, 1989), 151.

31. Ibid.

32. R. Mahon, *The Politics of Industrial Restructuring* (Toronto: University of Toronto Press, 1984), 14. This is a theme widely shared in Panitch, ed., *The Canadian State*.

33. Mahon, *Industrial Restructuring*, 3. This is a theme Mahon has reiterated: 'The "New" Canadian Political Economy Revisited', in Jenson, Mahon, and Bienefeld, eds, *Production, Space, Identity*, 2–3.

34. On the continuing political blockages to a rearrangement of class power relations, see J. Brodie and J. Jenson, *Crisis, Challenge and Change: Party and Class in Canada* (Toronto: Methuen, 1980).

35. On some of these issues, see M. Abramovitz, 'Catching Up, Forging Ahead, and Falling Behind', *Journal of Economic History* 46, 2 (1986); A. Maddison, *Phases of Capitalist Development* (New York: Oxford University Press, 1982); R. Pomfret, *The Economic Development of Canada* (Toronto: Methuen, 1981), ch. 4.

36. Extensive accumulation can be defined as capital accumulation via an extension of the scale of production, achieved without altering production techniques. This involves drawing on new sectors, workers, land, or a larger portion of the day, or using the same with greater intensity. Intensive accumulation applies science and technology, embodied in skills and machines, so that productivity advances rapidly. No regime of accumulation is exclusively intensive or extensive in specific historical conditions or institutions. It is the mix of forms of accumulation that defines the specificity of a regime.

37. F. Abele and D. Stasiulus, 'Canada as a "White-Settler Colony": What about Natives and Immigrants?', in Clement and Williams, eds, *The New Canadian Political Economy*. The poisonous dynamic of this internal colonialism remains imprinted in the Canadian state structure, just as extensive accumulation via geographical extension of the market remains part of Canada's development model. The westward territorial expansion of North America ran parallel to Europe's classic age of imperialism.

38. These wages were, moreover, relatively high, considering the productivity levels of North America, low living costs, and the possibility of independent commodity production. Panitch, 'Dependency and Class'.

39. For recent, creative efforts to rethink this process of state formation, see G. Bernier and D. Salée, *The Shaping of Quebec Politics: Colonialism, Power and the Transition to Capitalism in the 19th Century* (Washington: Crave Russak, 1992); A. Greer and I. Radforth, eds, *Colonial Leviathan: State Formation in Mid-Nineteenth Century Canada* (Toronto: University of Toronto Press, 1992).

40. J. Jenson, 'Representations in Crisis: The Roots of Canada's Permeable Fordism,' *Canadian Journal of Political Science* 23, 4 (1990): 672.

41. D. Wolfe, 'The Canadian State in Comparative Perspective', *Canadian Review of Sociology and Anthropology* 26, 1 (1989): 107; P. Resnick, *The Masks of Proteus: Canadian Reflections of the State* (Montreal and Kingston: McGill-Queen's University Press, 1990), 43–5.

42. On the unequal structures of representation of class-divided societies, see R. Mahon, 'Canadian Public Policy: The Unequal Structure of Representation', in Panitch, ed., *The Canadian State*, 165–98.

43. Jenson, '"Different"'.

44. This has been most forcefully stressed by Harry Johnson, *The Canadian Quandary* (Toronto: McClelland & Stewart, 1977).

45. See, for example, J. Laxer, 'Canadian Manufacturing and U.S. Trade Policy', in R. Laxer, ed., *Canada, Ltd.: The Political Economy of Dependency* (Toronto: McClelland & Stewart, 1973), 127–52; D. Drache, 'Re-discovering Canadian Political Economy', in W. Clement and D. Drache, eds, *A Practical Guide to Canadian Political Economy* (Toronto: Lorimer, 1978); C. Gonick, *Inflation or Depression* (Toronto: Lorimer, 1975).

46. J. Britton and J. Gilmour, *The Weakest Link* (Ottawa: Supply and Services, 1978), 141.

47. Carroll, *Corporate Power*, 187.

48. J. Niosi, *Canadian Capitalism* (Toronto: James Lorimer, 1981) and *Canadian Multinationals* (Toronto: Garamond Press, 1985); Resnick, *Masks of Proteus*; W. Carroll, *Corporate Power and Canadian Capitalism* (Vancouver: University of British Columbia Press, 1986) and 'Neoliberalism and the Recomposition of Finance Capital in Canada', *Capital and Class* 38 (1989): 81–112.

49. Resnick, *Masks of Proteus*, 187.

50. B. Bellon and J. Niosi, *The Decline of the American Economy* (Montreal: Black Rose, 1988), 153.

51. Carroll, *Corporate Power*, 200, emphasis added.

52. Mahon, 'The "New Canadian Political Economy" Revisited'.

53. This interpretation can be gleaned from the data presented in M. Porter, *Canada at the Crossroads* (Ottawa: Supply and Services, 1991), ch. 2; and Royal Commission on the Economic Union and Development Prospects for Canada, *Report*, Vol. I (Ottawa: Supply and Services, 1985), ch. 2.

54. M. Bienefeld, 'Capitalism and the Nation State in the Dog Days of the Twentieth Century', in R. Miliband and L. Panitch, eds, *Socialist Register 1994: Between Globalism and Nationalism* (London: Merlin, 1994), 112.

55. G. Albo, 'Competitive Austerity and the Impasse of Capitalist Employment Policy', in Miliband and Panitch, eds, *Socialist Register 1994*.

56. Jenson, 'Mapping'.

57. See J. Jenson, 'Citizenship and Equity: Variations across Time and in Space', in J. Hiebert, ed., *Political Ethics: A Canadian Perspective*, Vol. 12 of the Research Studies of the Royal Commission on Electoral Reform and Party Financing (Toronto: Dundurn Press, 1991); G. Albo, D. Langille, and L. Panitch, eds, *A Different Kind of State? Popular Power and Democratic Administration* (Toronto: Oxford University Press, 1993); S. Phillips, ed., *How Ottawa Spends 1993–94: A More Democratic Canada?* (Ottawa: Carleton University Press, 1993).

# Constitutionalizing the Canadian-American Relationship

Stephen Clarkson

## Constitutions and International Change

The world of the 1990s is marked by conflict and confusion: conflict within and between states; confusion about the characteristics that the resulting new political and economic forms are assuming. Great analytical uncertainty accompanies this geopolitical chaos: new realities no longer fit categories such as nation-state that have been used to describe and explain them in the past.

One established concept under strain in the flux of late twentieth-century political economy is that of 'constitution'. Over the past three centuries, when the global system comprised a set of largely autonomous states, the notion of constitution denoted the formal documents and unwritten conventions that determined and reflected the balance of social, ethnic, or regional forces within a political regime. Whether enshrined in written prose or established by legal custom, constitutions demonstrated six basic attributes:

 i) they described common policy-making institutions that had authority over the whole system;
 ii) they defined powers and set limits to what political institutions can do;
 iii) they established rights for citizens of the state;
 iv) they were enforced by mechanisms, whether formal or informal;
 v) they were legitimized by some method of ratification; and

vi) they could be amended only according to specific formulae.

Constitutional analysts confined the scope of their interest to the internal workings of states for the good reason that—with the exception of imperial systems—interstate relations were too anarchic to be comprehended by a paradigm premised on the rule of enforceable law.

One consequence of military, technological, economic, and cultural globalization has been a loss of autonomy by the nation-state, which has taken on increasing obligations to international regimes. The internalization of international constraints can be seen in its most articulated form in the members of the European Community, which accepted new disciplines on their behaviour in exchange for participation in the continent's supranational structures. The treaties and acts that have created the new Europe since World War II can readily be seen to be constitutional because they set up a supranational policy-making apparatus, imposed new limits on the actions of the individual nation-states, defined rights for their members, worked out enforcement and amendment mechanisms, and achieved legitimacy through each participatory government's ratification process.

In sharp contrast with Europe, North America's gradual evolution over the past century as a continental state has been driven until the late 1980s more by forces of economic, social, and cultural integration than by clear political goals articulated by national élites. The recent trade agreements negotiated between Canada, Mexico, and the United States constitute a shift towards the formalization of the previously informal processes of continentalization. They reflect a strategic response by the US to its changing global

From Duncan Cameron and Mel Watkins, eds, *Canada Under Free Trade* (Toronto: James Lorimer & Company, 1993), 3–20.

position and have dramatic implications for the political position of its two neighbours.

In the immediate postwar decades, when the US was enjoying the dominant and benevolent phase of its world hegemony, Congress was loath to abandon any of its sovereign power to a supra-national trade body. Accordingly, the General Agreement on Tariffs and Trade (GATT) was born weak and tied the hands of its smaller members as loosely as it did those of capitalism's superpower. In the overarching context of the Cold War, the United States dealt generously with its allies; it acted as first among equals in the various international bodies that handled the industrialized world's interrelations.

After 1970, when the United States found its economic primacy challenged and entered the second, predatory phase of its hegemonic trajectory,[1] it started to shift its diplomatic energy from ideological Cold War imperatives towards more commercial 'Cold Peace' objectives. Washington came to believe that its competitors in Europe and Asia were using their governments' policies to create unfair advantages for their exporters while protecting their own markets in ways that improperly excluded American products. US trade doctrine assumed that American transnational corporations could still triumph in world markets if only they faced a 'level playing field'. The task of US trade diplomacy was to level the international field.

The Tokyo Round of the GATT's trade liberalization marked a transition by moving beyond simple tariff reductions to the knotty problem of non-tariff barriers, such as countervail and anti-dumping actions against competitors. At the Organization for Economic Co-operation and Development (OECD), a code of investment behaviour was worked out, defining 'national treatment', the principle that policies developed for national firms should be applied to foreign corporations without discrimination.

As a result of the new trade agenda, the economic defences of smaller countries in the OECD and the Third World came under increasing pressure from outside at the very time that the formulae for the Keynesian welfare state and import substitution industrialization were failing to assure prosperity and high employment. Rather than protecting its national society against predators from the outside world, the nation-state was increasingly having to respond to the demands of a globalizing market that required its own political system to reduce its economic defences. The state was becoming 'internationalized' as part of a global decision-making system.[2] The price of membership in the world's trading institutions was to accept increasingly intrusive demands for conformity to internationally defined standards for social, industrial, and even environmental policy.

Although trade negotiators spoke the language of tariffs and non-tariff barriers, the United States kept adding other phrases to the international agenda in its attempt to reach a globally harmonized policy environment: intellectual property (corporations' right to profit from their patents and technology in other countries); free flow of information (the transmission of all kinds of data without political hindrance); services (financial, professional, touristic, and administrative activities that do not involve the exchange of commodities but account for huge financial transactions). In these new areas involving high technology and telecommunications, Washington was convinced that American transnationals enjoyed a significant comparative advantage whose exploitation would do much to restore the US's faltering global standing well into the twenty-first century.

In this period, the United States' attitude became much more demanding towards its trading partners. With the Soviet-bloc countries on their knees, it no longer felt it had to acquiesce to its partners' economic priorities in order to gain their military collaboration. For the United States a properly multilateralized world was one whose policy practices were uniform and modelled on its own. Accordingly, Washington's policy-makers started paying careful attention to the 'unfair' practices of its smaller trading partners, whether rich or poor.

For Canada, the impact of the United States' international economic agenda went one step further, and the political price turned out to be considerably higher.

## Canada and the Continental Economy

Canada's postwar experience in constructing a Keynesian welfare state under a centre-right Liberal Party yielded a high standard of living for three decades, but the experiment was built on weak premises. In the Cold War period Canada's great wealth derived from a series of traditional staple-based, low-value-added, high-volume, export-led industries whose main market was the downstream operations of integrated transnational corporations in the United States. Economic rents from the resource sector were redistributed by a moderately interventionist state to create a considerable degree of social equity for the country's less-developed regions and to support a somewhat inefficient, high-wage, import-substitution 'Fordism' that relied largely on a tariff wall and branch plants that were continental extensions of other US transnationals.[3]

Under these conditions, many sectors of Canada's political economy became continentally integrated. Independent production of complete warplane systems was abandoned in 1958, and the country's military-industrial complex became formally integrated with that of the United States in the Defence Production Sharing Arrangement of 1959, just one year after Canada's air defence was strategically absorbed within the North American Air Defence Command. Automobile production, almost completely controlled by four American companies, was rationalized on the continental level following the signing of the Auto Pact in 1965.

Even beyond such formal agreements, many sectors of Canadian life became completely absorbed by those of the United States. Mass culture industries (entertainment television, movies, advertising, sports) had little national content unless determined by government regulation or produced in the public sector. Canada was being continentalized by stealth. The federal state played an ambivalent role, sometimes as facilitator of Americanization and sometimes as defender of a certain minimal level of Canadian autonomy. One institution, for example, the Canadian Radio-television and Telecommunications Commission, could in the same year both approve the introduction of cable TV, which effectively moved the US's cultural border 300 kilometres to the north, and legislate Canadian content rules that created a reserved programming space for Canadian artistic production on the air waves.

Although the process of Canada's integration in North America was not formalized by an over-arching document or institution, there were clear signs that a continental state was developing with a constitution based on convention.

i) *Common Policy-making Institutions*. Beyond the military sphere created by NORAD, policy-making at a continental level took place mainly within transnational corporations.

ii) *Limits to Government*. Washington accepted limits to the exercise of its superior power over Canada provided that Ottawa supported American anti-Communist foreign policy abroad and refrained from interfering with American capital at home.

iii) *Rights for Citizens*. Individuals had no continental rights. The right of access for American corporate citizens to Canadian resources and the Canadian market was taken as given; Canada was treated to certain fruits of the American system, such as special access to bidding for Pentagon contracts.

iv) *Enforcement*. Enforcement of the rules of this intuitively understood game was assured by the high level of trust and co-operation that had developed among the relevant decision-makers of both political systems.

v) *Ratification*. The conventions of North America's continentalism were periodically legitimized by ritualized statements made by the national leaders, who, in uttering comforting clichés about the 'world's longest undefended border', would confirm the 'special relationship' between Ottawa and Washington with its emphasis on complementarity, not competition, between their economies.

vi) *Amendment*. Significant alterations in the continental system were generally made after extensive consultation. Since changes made by Washington to its macroeconomic policy or its military strategy affected Canada as directly as if it were an American territory, Canadian politicians regularly requested—and just as regularly received—exemptions from particularly damaging measures.

This comfortable continental constitution was disrupted in the early 1970s when, experiencing the inflationary and commercial consequences of its disastrous venture in Asian warfare, the United States realized its global hegemony was being challenged by the emerging economic blocs in west Europe and east Asia. Washington decided it would have to get tough with friend and foe, partner and competitor. In August 1971, the shock of the protectionist measures known as Nixonomics jolted Liberal Ottawa out of its complacency. Overnight, Richard Nixon had changed the continental constitution. Suddenly, Canadian politicians discovered that Washington no longer felt itself limited by a gentlemanly code in what it could do to Canada: instead of communicating through quiet diplomacy, it leaked its demands to the press. Washington wanted to expand the obligations of the Canadian government in responding to US demands and to enlarge the rights of its corporate citizens: domestic international sales corporations (DISCS) were invented to promote the home-country operations of American transnational corporations at the expense of their foreign branch plants. Washington was enforcing these new policies by compulsion not by consensus:

Canada could no longer count on Washington giving it privileged consideration in its policy-making. The American government was amending the conventions of the Canadian-American relationship unilaterally, not by consultation: American leaders stressed competition, not complementarity, in their discourse, thereby delegitimizing the special relationship. Had Nixon not thrown the American presidency into a turmoil that would take a decade to resolve, Canada might have had to bend to Washington's will much sooner.

As it was, Ottawa tried—under Pierre Trudeau's half-hearted leadership—to reduce its vulnerability to American economic nationalism and chart for itself a more national course of development that resembled the social democratic approaches taken in some north European countries. Although it never developed a comprehensive industrial strategy to move the Canadian economy towards a high-value-added, high-technology, nationally directed model, the federal government did take several steps towards making the Canadian economy less vulnerable and more autonomous. It created a national investment company (Canada Development Corporation), an agency to review foreign takeovers and extract greater benefits from the branch operations of transnational corporations (Foreign Investment Review Agency), and a national oil company (Petro-Canada). These efforts by the federal state to develop a more national mode of regulation were largely ineffectual in the face of the deepening continental regime of Canadian capital accumulation patterns.[4]

By the end of the 1970s, Canada's dual-sector model was running into trouble. The terms of trade turned against raw materials in the staples sector, where exploitation was becoming increasingly capital-intensive and uncompetitive as resource supplies dwindled. Foreign ownership was so extensive in the manufacturing and service sectors that they had little of the indigenous innovative capacity in high-technology areas that had been so central to the economic successes of Japan and Sweden. As levels of tariff protection fell, the manufacturing sector lost ground in the home market without being competitive enough to make gains abroad.

In the face of a sullenly unresponsive business community, the Trudeau Liberals took a big gamble. In 1980 they made a bold move to regain national control over the petroleum industry. The National Energy Program (NEP), designed to exploit rising petroleum prices for industrial development, came to symbolize the ambition and the folly of the Liberals' national consolidation strategy. Its ambition was to displace foreign with national ownership of the oil and gas sector; its folly was to attempt this radical action at the very moment that Ronald Reagan came to power in Washington and prices on the world oil market peaked.[5]

## Towards Bilateral Treating

In calling for the establishment of a 'North American accord' during his 1980 election campaign, Reagan showed an extraordinarily intuitive grasp of the continental requirements of American economic strategy. Multilateral and unilateral trade initiatives could only have limited successes; bilateral action in the Western hemisphere promised the best prospects for restoring America to the saddle in the emerging tripolar world.

Washington was bound to continue its active participation in multilateral negotiations for trade liberalization since gains made at the GATT had global effect and so were potentially the most rewarding in the long term. But the United States's clout was no longer great enough automatically to achieve its goal of breaking down its competitors' economic defences. This realization did not prevent American politicians from taking an aggressive stance in the new Uruguay Round of the GATT negotiations; they demanded an abolition of agricultural subsidies, a new regime for intellectual property rights, the inclusion of services in the trade regime, and the declaration of a code defin-

ing what industrial subsidies governments would be allowed to offer their enterprises.

If Washington had least control when working multilaterally at the GATT, it could exert most control unilaterally. Despite the neo-conservatives' rhetorical insistence on trade liberalization, the Reagan years saw a further tightening of Congress's already powerful protectionist legislation. The 1988 Omnibus Trade Act and its infamous 'Super 301' gave the US administration powerful new weapons that could be fired at individual trading partners—whether in the First World or the Third—who were deemed to be unfairly subsidizing their entrepreneurs' exports to the US or using their state policies to constrain the scope for American exporters.

Bilateral action, the third dimension of the Reaganites' approach to trade diplomacy, represented a new twist on an old strategy. Ever since President Monroe had enunciated his doctrine of hemispheric supremacy in 1823, the United States had claimed the Americas as its special sphere of influence. Now its prime geopolitical objective was to stem the US's relative decline in global strength by building a regional base from which to take on its European and Japanese competitors. Enlarging the scope of its transnationals' protected home market and finding them a Third World (maquiladora) labour base within Fortress America would strengthen their competitiveness. Extending tariff and non-tariff barriers against European and Japanese conglomerates would help prevent their competitors from benefiting from the advantages of a single North American market.

The beauty of a bilateral game plan was that it could be executed in parallel with GATT's multilateral negotiations. The successful negotiation of a bilateral trade deal would also signal to the international community that the United States had other arrows in its quiver. Progress made on a bilateral agenda could be applied as precedents at the multilateral level. By signing a bilateral trade treaty with Israel, Washington had already shown that if its global interlocutors were not ready to talk, it had other options for achieving its goals—and they had better be careful lest they find themselves left out in the cold.

By the mid-1980s Canada—the United States's most open and most accommodating partner—was the obvious subject for testing this strategy in the Western hemisphere. Its flirtation with a more autonomous mode of regulation had come to an ignominious end even before Pierre Trudeau resigned as prime minister in 1984. Under his aegis, the Liberal government had shown its interest in expanding the scope of managed trade by tentatively proposing to Washington the negotiation of more free trade sectors on the model of the Auto Pact. Although nothing had come of this probe, it prepared the way for Trudeau's successor, Brian Mulroney, to endorse the notion of continental free trade wholeheartedly.

When Mulroney was first elected prime minister in September 1984, the contradictory label of his party, Progressive Conservative, nicely defined his political position: he claimed to be committed to preserving the social programs of the welfare state as a 'sacred trust', but he was also the spokesman for business interests impatient with the constraints imposed on them by the allegedly interventionist Liberal government. The tensions created by trying to juggle these incompatible positions proved unbearable. Within a year, the prime minister had adopted a mainly neo-conservative agenda, which had been conveniently articulated by a massive public inquiry, the Macdonald Royal Commission. This massive public inquiry, established three years before by the Trudeau government, managed to articulate the Canadian business community's continental interests as theorized by neo-classical economics.[6]

Central to this new agenda for Canada was the achievement of a bilateral free trade agreement with the United States that would, it was argued, gain not just 'secure' but 'enhanced' access for Canadian manufacturers to the huge American market: secure through gaining exemption for Canadian exporters from the application of US protectionist legislation and enhanced from a reduction of US tariffs against Canada's manufactured goods. In effect, free trade was to become Canada's alternative to import substitution as an industrial strategy: it would allow Canadian firms to become globally competitive by exploiting the magic of scale economies. Eagerly promoted by a prime minister who had made 'super relations' with the United States the cornerstone of his foreign policy, bilateral free trade became a matter of life and death for the government. Mulroney promptly asked Washington to begin negotiations. Pleased to be dealing with a government so eager, even desperate, to reach an agreement, Washington played with its northern friend like a game fish, using its considerable bargaining skills and greater strength to toy unashamedly with its interlocutors and land a deal that created many valuable precedents for American trade policy, making breakthroughs in the fields of government disciplines, access to Canadian resources, investment rights, and services trade.

Washington gave up little and gained much when it signed the Canada-United States Free Trade Agreement (FTA).[7] In exchange for eliminating its tariffs along the Canadian border, it secured the elimination of Canadian tariffs that were on the average twice as high. It maintained intact the sovereignty of Congress to pass new trade measures that could supersede the trade agreement. It avoided negotiating a definition of 'subsidy' that might lessen the scope of its countervail actions against Canadian producers or exempt Canadian exporters from the application of its other protectionist laws.

The concessions that Canada made in response to American negotiating demands suggest that what is known as an agreement about 'free trade' can be more properly understood as a constitutional document as important for the future of the northern dominion's political system as the Constitution Act of 1982. The FTA took a hesitant step towards creating common policy-making institutions, set new limits to government, defined new rights, introduced new enforcement mechanisms, was brought into force by acts of the signatory states, and laid out amendment procedures.

i) *Policy-making Institutions.* The Canada-United States Trade Commission (CUSTER) was set up on paper but not in practice. With neither supranational secretariat nor permanent address, it consists merely of periodic meetings of the Canadian trade minister and the United States trade representative plus seconded staff. As an institution CUSTER is a hollow shell.

ii) *Limits to Government.* Those who had read the Macdonald Report had been given the vision of a bilateral agreement that would concentrate on trade barriers and exclude the Auto Pact, agriculture, energy, and culture from its purview. Citizens had heard their prime minister and his negotiators publicly insist that neither the Auto Pact, nor culture, nor energy would be 'on the table'.

In fact, the FTA constrains governmental action in each of these sectors and in many other ways.

- In the energy sector, Canadian governments are prohibited from using the price system to act in the interest of Canadian consumers or Canadian industry over those of American importers.
- In controlling foreign investment, the powers of the federal agency to impose conditions on foreign capital are greatly restricted.
- The Auto Pact has been altered to make future Japanese transplants unable to use Canada as a base for their North American assembly plants.
- In agriculture, the competence of such institutions as the Canadian Wheat Board is severely curtailed.
- In financial services, the Canadian government is prevented from discriminating against American banks, which are given national treatment.
- Cultural policy, while nominally excluded from the scope of the FTA by section 2011/1, is

actually included by the subsequent paragraph, 2011/2, which establishes the United States's right to retaliate by taking 'measures of equivalent effect' in any other economic area to compensate for losses that the American entertainment industry might claim because of future cultural policies enacted by Canadian governments.[8] The practical result of this clause is to prevent Canadian governments from taking any action to protect or extend Canadian cultural industries that impinge in any way on Hollywood's ample bottom line.

The FTA shifts power from the provincial to the federal government. . . . While there has been a stormy debate about the implications of these and many other provisions, defenders and opponents of the FTA alike agree that it will make the undertaking of another National Energy Program impossible. In other words, no future Canadian government would be able to mount an interventionist industrial strategy, whether by leaning on the energy sector to serve the national interest at the expense of supplying the American market or by using other policy tools commonly used by industrialized states.

iii) *Rights for Citizens.* The only 'citizens' whose rights are extended by FTA are corporate entities. In accepting the principle of national treatment, Canada is prevented from providing any help for Canadian firms that it does not also offer American companies. National treatment, the right of establishment, and the right to bid on government procurement contracts effectively grant American corporations access to important new fields, such as services, and represent major extensions of their sphere of operation in Canada.

iv) *Enforcement.* At first glance, the enforcement provisions of FTA are not impressive. No august supranational chamber has been created to act as the supreme court of North America. CUSTER is fraught with so many ambiguities in the FTA document that it is difficult to foresee how various eventualities will be handled.[9] For instance, the federal government is obliged to have the provinces respect the letter and spirit of FTA even though the courts would not necessarily deem Ottawa's jurisdiction adequate to this policing task.

Nevertheless, a second reading makes it clear that the FTA significantly extends Washington's power to monitor and control Canadian political life. Notification is specified as an obligation for each 'party' to give the other 'party' advance warning of any intended local or federal government policy that might affect the other side's interests as defined by the FTA. Implicit is the recognition that the United States has the right to know whatever is going on in the Canadian political system that might have some bearing on its interests. Uncle Sam's desire to know has become Cousin Canuck's duty to inform.

A similar emphasis is put on engaging in bilateral consultations as the means to warding off potential conflicts. The other side's right to know becomes extended to the right to satisfaction through negotiations—even before the democratically elected parliaments of the federal or provincial governments have had a chance to act in what they believe to be their public's interest. This significant extension of political interdependence increases Canada's vulnerability, multiplies the possibilities of linkage between bilateral issues, and introduces new ways for the United States legitimately to intervene in Canadian politics and press its demands.

The dispute-settlement mechanism, over which much ink has been spilled, does not comprise a truly supranational institution.[10] Rather, the panels that the Canada-United States Trade Commission (CUSTER) can establish under the FTA's Chapter 19 for resolving commercial disputes are bodies set up on an ad hoc basis merely to determine whether one government's trade action is consistent with its *own* trade law. The presence of panellists from both jurisdictions represents a minimal concession to the idea of supranationality, but the agreement clearly leaves the implementation of a panel's ruling up to CUSTER, which is a binational body deciding issues by consensus.

Translated into plain American, deciding by consensus means that each country—but, most importantly, the United States—retains a veto power over the actions of the enforcement agency.

As the number of panel settlements grows, a body of precedent is being created. Panel members are not permanent officials, but their experience contributes to a consolidation of American trade-law practice, which directly affects federal and provincial bureaucrats in Canada, who now plan policy so that it will not come up against American contingency protection. In this respect, CUSTER is helping continentalize US trade law, getting it applied at the heart of the Canadian political process.

In the mechanism for settling disputes arising from implementation of FTA that is described in Chapter 18 of the agreement, a party's ultimate sanction is to take retaliatory action against the other. Given the overwhelming disparity in power between the United States and Canada, the FTA's legitimizing of retaliation means that Washington's right to discipline Canadian governments for not performing in a manner satisfactory to it is accepted explicitly.

v) *Ratification*. The passing of the FTA by both the American Congress and the Canadian Parliament, with the ultimate signature of the document by the American president and the Canadian prime minister on 1 January 1989, indicates the weight of legitimacy given by the ratification process.

vi) *Amendment*. If it takes agreement by both Congress and Parliament to alter it, the constitutional quality of the FTA for Canada needs little further substantiation. For Canada, the tablets are chipped from stone on Capitol Hill.

## Constitutional Asymmetry

If the FTA's provisions are so powerful that they can be considered part of Canada's constitutional framework, does it not follow that the FTA is *ipso facto* part of the United States constitution? On the face of it, there are good reasons to think this to be the case. The FTA is a bilateral agreement made between two formally sovereign states that are committed to its application: in most cases, the clauses apply equally to each 'party' to the agreement. Nevertheless, the tenor of the document is not symmetrical, as we can see by estimating the constitutional weight it will bear in the American system.

i) and ii) *Limits to Government*. While the US may be theoretically bound by the same restrictions on its energy policy as is Canada, the effective limitation is negligible because it imports rather than exports petroleum. The provisions affecting the automobile industry are pertinent only for Canada. It is difficult to see in what way it can be maintained that the FTA puts a crimp on future US policy-making. US implementing legislation explicitly asserted Congress's right unilaterally to pass laws that altered the FTA.

iii) *Rights for Citizens*. The Canadian government—which is only too eager to claim every possible benefit on the FTA's behalf—has not suggested that the application of the national treatment principle will force Washington to make the new Clinton administration's industrial strategy incentives and stimuli available to Canadian firms on the same footing as to its own companies. Where the Canadian negotiators had a strong case for reciprocity—getting the same treatment for Canadian banks in the US as Canada was giving US banks in Canada—they were flatly turned down. If the FTA had really given Canadian firms operating in the United States substantially greater rights, there would be no reason for so many to have closed down and moved to the United States to gain access to the US market—but as American corporate citizens.

iv) *Enforcement*. The frail nature of CUSTER's institutional structure underlines how little the FTA has constrained American sovereignty. In establishing a dispute-settlement mechanism, the United States has simply accepted some Canadian personnel participating in a review process with fixed deadlines that is to provide a means for deciding whether determinations made by its quasi-judicial trade bodies correctly apply US law. While dispute-panel decisions are said to be binding, there is nothing beyond political goodwill that makes them so: the United States need not fear Canadian retaliation in cases of its non-compliance with panel decisions.

v) and vi) *Ratification and Amendment*. In a formal sense, the FTA has a constitutional quality for the United States because it can only be ratified and amended with the agreement of the Canadian government. What President Reagan referred to as the continent's economic constitution was ratified by the American president and the Canadian prime minister formally signing the agreement and by the legislature in each country passing legislation to implement the FTA's provisions in domestic law.

While this is true in a legalistic sense, what is far more important is the power Congress has retained for its trade law to take precedence over the FTA. The application of the omnibus trade bill to Canada was not restricted in any way by the FTA. Precedents in the US Supreme Court indicate that provisions of international agreements signed by the US executive do not prevail over subsequent legislation passed by Congress. The FTA accepts in section 1902 that Congress can change its laws affecting trade with Canada so long as such amendments specifically mention Canada. Far from constitutionally tying the hands of Congress, the FTA provides an instrument with which Congress can exert its leverage over Canada by setting up oversight processes that further institutionalize its interest in keeping its competitor to the north under control. In short, the FTA constitutionalizes Canada's continental dependency as a post-national state with barely any limitation on the autonomy of the American hegemon.

## From the FTA to NAFTA

Canadians were astonished when they learned that, having just worked out what was meant to be a historic trade agreement with Canada, the

United States was already in the throes of bilateral trade talks with countries throughout Latin America. Having exploited Mexico's crisis during the 1980s to pressure the Institutional Revolutionary Party (PRI) government into taking a broad range of liberalization measures, Washington wanted, first of all, to institutionalize the Salinas regime's many measures to deregulate, privatize, and downsize the state. However Washington rationalized its initiative with Mexico—to encourage 'democratic values' south of the border; to facilitate employment opportunities there and reduce the pressure of Mexican emigration; to extend the space for American transnationals and secure a cheap labour force for them; to expand the domain of Fortress America and secure it against Japanese competitors—inducting Mexico into a trade agreement would be the next step towards reducing the power of the state throughout Latin America and continuing the World Bank's structural adjustment programs that bring market discipline to government economic policy throughout the Third World.

From the point of view of neo-conservative ideologues in Canada, this was good news, but the Canadian government had barely begun to deal with the consequences of the FTA when it had to face the prospect of the United States signing a separate trade deal with Mexico. Canada feared such a deal could jeopardize what it considered to be its privileged position in Washington if it did not participate in the Washington-Mexico negotiations. It needed to resist the extension of a hub-and-spoke system for the hemisphere, in which Washington was the hub and every other country formed a separate spoke linked only through the emerging continental capital.[11]

While the federal government trumpets American gains in NAFTA as if they were good for Canada—far more invasive provisions for intellectual property rights, higher North American content rules that are already driving Japanese investors from Canada, further extensions of the application of national treatment, broadened definitions of services—two characteristics strike a Canadian eye.

In the first place, NAFTA is as significant a constitutional document for Mexico as the FTA was for Canada. With its wide-ranging prescriptions for what the Mexican government must do and cannot do, with the rights of American corporations spelled out in great detail, with the more elaborate dispute-settlement and enforcement mechanisms, with its three-government ratification, and with its difficult amendment process (agreement by the three signatory states), NAFTA introduces a new dimension to Mexico's constitution.

What is more, the new document is almost as institutionally empty as was the FTA. This suggests that as the constitution for an enlarged continental regime, NAFTA will remain a highly asymmetrical power system. The US will retain the bulk of its sovereignty while its growing band of junior partners are strictly bound by NAFTA and, later WHEFTA (Western hemisphere free trade) into a new post-national dependency in which one of their governments' chief roles will be to enforce US policies on their territories.

## Next Steps

In trying to assess the significance of the FTA and NAFTA for the future of the Canadian political system, it may be helpful to put our crystal ball in a comparative and ideological context. We should first compare the unbalanced, poorly articulated constitutional structure of the emerging North American state with Europe's measured process of continental integration.[12] The European community's more deliberate, more democratic, more balanced, and more gradual process of continentalization has encouraged member states to give up some sovereignty in order to increase their autonomy. The supranational institutions of the European Community (EC) assure its smaller post-national members larger voices in the vital affairs of the continent than they would have as more sovereign nation-states.[13]

We also need to consider the question of ideological conjuncture. Entrenching a radically right-wing agenda in Canada and Mexico through trade agreements at the very moment that America's infatuation with neo-conservatism is coming to an abrupt end presents a conundrum. President Clinton's Washington is committed to playing catch-up with Japan and the European Community by promoting the competitive potential of American enterprise. Yet, with NAFTA, Ottawa and Mexico City have agreed to renounce the very kinds of industrial policy that the 'new Democratic party' in Washington is busily preparing to adopt. In effect, Clinton will be ignoring NAFTA's disciplines while his junior partners blithely tie their second hands behind their own backs and, more important, those of their successors in power.

The passing of the nation-state may well be inevitable, but the kind of continental state in which it is to find a place is not an immutable reality. Constitutions embody ideological values. They express the interests of dominant élites. But an externally enforced constitution like NAFTA, which violates democratic norms (by withdrawing policy power from elected governments), offends popular values (by getting adopted in the face of public opposition), and represents the interests of a generation whose time has come, and almost gone, is unlikely to enjoy a long and happy life.

Political scientists have long affirmed that a constitution can only succeed in directing a state's functioning if it is reasonably attuned to the political and economic forces at play within its boundaries. The new trade agreements that the United States is managing to impose on its neighbours are unlikely to survive in the long term if they awaken the democratic forces they were designed to marginalize.[14] If the new entity created by Washington's trade bilateralism better serves the interests of its corporations than those of its citizens and undermines rather than supports the structures and culture of its member states, it is hard to foresee it living happily ever after. Driven by remorseless global pressure, the Canadian, like the Mexican, state will not be able to avoid engaging in a continuing process of reforming its external constitution. Although it will continue to be difficult to deal with a beleaguered United States, these countries would do well to seek strength in pressing for a recasting of NAFTA by developing concerted demands based on their common position as territories on the United States' immediate periphery. Canada may not agree with many of the Mexican government's views on environmental and labour rights. Nevertheless, the two countries do share a larger interest either in achieving a more articulated set of continental institutions that provide representation of the peripheral countries at the centre or in dismantling the inherently unstable NAFTA. *E pluribus unum* might not be a bad motto for the countries of the Western hemisphere contemplating trade agreements with the USA.

## Notes

1. 'Predatory' compared to 'benevolent' hegemony: Robert Gilpin, *The Political Economy of International Relations* (Princeton, NJ: Princeton University Press, 1987), 90.
2. Internationalization of the state: Robert W. Cox, 'Production and Hegemony: Toward a Political Economy of World Order', in H.K. Jacobson and D. Sidjanski, eds, *The Emerging International Economic Order: Dynamic Processes, Constraints and Opportunities* (Beverly Hills, Calif.: Sage Publications, 1982), 53.
3. Import substitution industrialization: Glen Williams, *Not for Export: Toward a Political Economy of Canada's Arrested Industrialization*, 2nd edn (Toronto: McClelland & Stewart, 1988).
4. National mode of regulation: Stephen Clarkson, 'Disjunctions: Free Trade and the Paradox of Canadian Development', in Daniel Drache and

Meric S. Gertler, eds, *The New Era of Global Competition: State Policy and Market Power* (Montreal and Kingston: McGill-Queen's University Press, 1991), 103–26.

5. Folly and ambition: Stephen Clarkson, *Canada and the Reagan Challenge: Crisis and Adjustment, 1981–85*, 2nd edn (Toronto: Lorimer, 1985), chs 2, 3.

6. Canada, *Report of the Royal Commission on the Economic Union and Development Prospects for Canada, Volume One* (Ottawa: Minister of Supply and Services Canada, 1985).

7. How Washington outnegotiated Ottawa: G. Bruce Doern and Brian W. Tomlin, *Faith & Fear: The Free Trade Story* (Toronto: Stoddart, 1991).

8. See Graham Carr in Duncan Cameron and Mel Watkins, eds, *Canada Under Free Trade* (Toronto: Lorimer, 1993).

9. Stephen Clarkson, 'The Canada-United States Trade Commission', in Duncan Cameron, ed., *The Free Trade Deal* (Toronto: Lorimer, 1988), 26–45.

10. Gary N. Horlick and F. Amanda DeBusk, 'The Functioning of the FTA Dispute Resolution Panels', in Leonard Waverman, ed., *Negotiating and Implementing a North American Free Trade Agreement* (Vancouver: Fraser Institute, 1991), ch. 1.

11. Richard G. Lipsey, 'The Case for Trilateralism', in Steven Globerman, ed., *Continental Accord: North American Economic Integration* (Vancouver: Fraser Institute, 1991).

12. For a masterly comparison of European with North American integration: Bruce W. Wilkinson, 'Regional Trading Blocs: Fortress Europe versus Fortress North America', in Drache and Gertler, eds, *The New Era of Global Competition*, 51–82.

13. On the trade-off between reduced sovereignty and increased autonomy: Albert O. Hirschman, *National Power and the Structure of Foreign Trade* (Berkeley: University of California Press, 1980).

14. For the position of the popular forces in Canada: Maude Barlow and Bruce Campbell, *Take Back the Nation* (Toronto: Key Porter, 1991); Mel Hurtig, *The Betrayal of Canada* (Toronto: Stoddart, 1991).

Part V

# Public Administration

## Introduction

Laurent Dobuzinskis

In the previous edition (1994) of this book, I raised the question: Is public administration in crisis? Today, the answer seems clear. The crisis has been resolved. A new set of values and corresponding practices known as 'public-sector management' are now well entrenched in the public service at the federal, provincial, and municipal levels. These values are in tune with an emerging consensus about the role of the state in society. Governments are now expected to do less on their own, to let the private sector take on some of the responsibilities they used to assume in previous decades, and to pay more attention to the quality of the services they continue to deliver.

Not everyone has rallied to the defence of this new paradigm. Many scholars who study public administration have been critical of some of the implications of the new trends. Public servants themselves are divided. Most senior officials have adopted a more managerial style. Some of them have even become strong advocates of the new style, with its emphasis on innovation and results (as opposed to procedures). However, there is still resistance in the public service taken as a whole, especially in the lower ranks of the bureaucratic hierarchy. Elected officials have raised concerns about the risks associated with loosening parliamentary controls over public-sector managers. These criticisms have slowed down the pace of reform, yet they failed to derail the process of 'reinventing government'.[1] What is true, however, is that the enthusiasm of the pioneers of the new approaches has somewhat cooled off by now. Most people agree that government must become more businesslike. However, even the most ardent reformers now concede that government is not like business in some important respects.

To say that a new 'post-bureaucratic' paradigm has replaced traditional concepts and approaches in public administration is not to say that all issues concerning the future of the public sector have been resolved. In fact, the new paradigm is itself the source of complex dilemmas. Thus, we need to retrace the origins and development of current approaches within government bureaucracies and, secondly, to reflect on their implications and the problems they pose to elected and bureaucratic officials in their dealings with one another and in their relations with the public at large.

Most of these problems concern the inadequacy of traditional accountability structures. As the definition of the tasks and responsibilities of public servants continues to change, the question of how to hold them accountable, to whom, and for what becomes more and more difficult to answer. This renewed concern for account-ability points in the direction of an even more fundamental dilemma. Can government provide the prompt and efficient public services its citizens expect, and at the same time meet a growing demand for more consultation and a more participatory style of democratic politics?

Before these issues can be discussed, however, we should have an overview of the development of modern bureaucracies and of the challenges they have been facing in recent times. Public administration is a field in constant evolution.

## The Origins and Development of the Modern Administrative State

By the end of the nineteenth century, science and technology seemed to fulfil the sec-ular dream of the modern age: to achieve complete mastery over the natural world and to use its resources efficiently in the service of industry and 'progress'. The realization of that project required the development of new organizations capable of mobilizing the energies of large numbers of manual and clerical workers, technicians, and pro-fessionals. Hence the development of some sort of organizational machinery: the assembly plant in industry, the department store in commerce, and the modern bureaucracy in the world of government.[2]

Of course, to describe government agencies as machines is only a metaphor. Like all metaphors, this one has limitations. There have always been talented and innova-tive public servants whose behaviour has been anything but mechanical. Nevertheless, this imagery can serve to highlight certain uniquely important aspects of public administration in its formative years. Some of these attributes still characterize con-temporary public administration, no matter how much the world has changed since the last century and regardless of how hard government officials have worked at reforming the institutions of government.

The political and bureaucratic élites in Western Europe undertook to reform their administrative systems early in the second half of the nineteenth century. Political appointees and those for whom an administrative position was merely a title and a pretext for obtaining privileges were replaced by a new professional class of compe-tent administrators. Standardized procedures were gradually implemented to improve the efficiency of administrative practices. In the 1870s, for example, a politically neu-tral Civil Service Commission in charge of recruiting the members of the professional administrative élite and a rudimentary system of classification were already distin-guishing features of the British civil service. When Max Weber wrote his classical analysis of bureaucracy early in this century, the institutions he was describing could be found in most countries of continental Europe.

Max Weber (1864–1920) was a social theorist of immense stature and his inter-ests were in no way limited to bureaucracy. Thus, to understand his views on this sub-ject, it is important to place them in the broader context of his political sociology. Weber undertook a monumental study of the civilizations and religions of the world in order to analyse the relationship between social institutions and belief systems. He was concerned in particular with the ways in which institutions exercise not just power (which can be defined as the imposition of one's will on someone else, sometimes in the face of considerable resistance) but authority (the ability to issue commands that are obeyed because they are considered legitimate by most members of society). Weber identified three types of legitimate authority, which he described as 'ideal types', meaning that they represent the purest form of a concept. Reality is always a little more messy and only approximates any ideal type.

The first model of authority, the origin of which can be traced back to the very beginning of civilization, rests on the notion of tradition. Thus, traditional monarchs commanded respect and authority because their subjects were convinced that Divine Providence wisely guides royal succession. In such highly personalized political systems, there is little room for the development of impersonal, mechanistic bureaucracies. The second ideal type of authority or leadership finds its justification in the exceptional personality of a leader in whom the people see the mark of divine grace or some other transcendental quality. Historical examples include religious prophets and political leaders such as Joan of Arc, Cromwell, Napoleon, and Hitler.[3] Contemporary leaders whose mastery of the electronic media gives them an edge over their opponents, for example, Pierre Elliott Trudeau in the recent past and Bill Clinton today, have also been described as 'charismatic'; that is not, however, what Weber meant by that term. Charismatic leadership and bureaucracies can sometimes complement each other, but they are just as likely to clash.

The third ideal type proposed by Weber—legal-rational authority—best describes the legitimization process inherent in liberal democracies where the exercise of power is considered to be legitimate if, and only if, it is based in law and serves some rational purpose. By contrast, the arbitrary or capricious use of state resources by government officials is cause for sanctions. The administrative apparatus of the modern state operates in a manner entirely compatible with the notion of legal-rational authority.

Weberian bureaucracy operates very much like a machine that rationally implements policies and programs consistent with legislation enacted by Parliament (or provincial legislatures). The essential characteristics of Weber's ideal-type bureaucracy are:

- a hierarchical organizational structure within which every bureaucrat has an assigned function;
- well-defined jurisdictional boundaries that determine what a government agency can or cannot do;
- specialized training and recruitment based on technical skills (the 'merit principle');
- the use of written documents and files;
- management by detailed but impersonal rules.

In this model, bureaucrats are usually hired at the beginning of their careers to fill positions at the lower end of the hierarchy. They can normally expect tenure for life and promotions at regular intervals if they perform their duties adequately.

That modern government bureaucracies function in accordance with the law is not something that needs to be explained at length. Government departments and other agencies are normally created by statute, and the public servants who staff them are constrained by complex rules and regulations.[4] The idea that there is anything rational about this vast and seemingly absurd administrative machinery requires a little more elaboration. In contrast to the usual clichés about bureaucratic red tape and the ineptness of administrative practices, Weber saw in the bureaucratic mode of organization an efficient means of implementing the impersonal and rational purposes of modern legislation.

In North America, the move towards a professional civil service came a little later than in Europe. Patronage was a firmly entrenched practice; beginning in the 1880s, political pressures began to mount against that practice. As the responsibilities of government changed with the development of industry and the growth of modern cities, the need for professional administrators became fairly obvious. In 1887, Woodrow Wilson—then a university professor, later elected President of the United States—wrote a seminal article in which he drew a clear distinction between administration, i.e., the technical domain of the expert, and the more subjective and chaotic world of politics. However, it took at least two decades for that vision to become, if not a reality, at least an influential model. Two decisive steps towards the development of a more efficient and professional bureaucracy were taken in Canada with the creation of the federal Civil Service Commission in 1908 and, a decade later, with the extension of the jurisdiction of that Commission to the entire federal civil service in 1918.[5]

The distinction between administration and politics endured until after World War II, when it became evident that public servants were actually playing an active role in the development of public policy. Indeed, the establishment and later the consolidation of the welfare state were in large measure the product of active collaboration between politicians and their bureaucratic advisers. If politics in a broad sense means more than partisan politics and also involves participation in making important policy decisions, then one can say that by the 1940s, administration and politics began to overlap. That is not to say, however, that public servants were allowed to immerse themselves in the more partisan aspects of politics.

In the years following the end of World War II, and especially during the 1960s and early 1970s, the state assumed an increasingly larger role in the management of the economy and in the development of a comprehensive social policy system. The metaphor of a mechanically efficient but rigid and unresponsive organization became increasingly irrelevant to the many functions performed by the public service. The public servants' own sense of identity also changed.

The postwar years were a period of rapid growth for government; the federal level took the lead, but the provinces caught up by the mid-1960s.[6] Growth was not only quantitative but also qualitative. Whereas the public servants recruited in the late 1940s and 1950s did not challenge the managerial style of the Ottawa 'mandarins',[7] the better educated and more individualistic university graduates hired in the 1960s and early 1970s pursued personal career objectives and organizational goals that radically transformed the public service.[8]

The increasing complexity of the policy-making process during a period of sustained economic growth, together with the analytical skills brought to the public service by a new generation of public servants, created a favourable climate for the development of new policy initiatives. The structure of incentives began to change. The most successful public officials were those who could provide sophisticated policy advice to their minister and design new policy structures. Consequently, a large number of new government departments, regulatory agencies, and Crown corporations were established in Canada between the mid-1960s and the mid-1970s. Moreover, in Canada as well as in several other Western democracies, new planning techniques were put in place with a view to improve the design and implementation of a wide range of policy initiatives and programs.[9] By contrast, traditional administrative tasks (e.g., personnel management) received relatively less attention; thus a gap was created between the macro-policy concerns of the upper echelons of the public service and the more strictly managerial concerns of middle-ranking officials. This gap was to become more and more pronounced, until it was finally acknowledged in the late 1980s.[10] The same preoccupation with policy issues, as distinguished from the study of public administration, also gripped the academic community in the same period. (For instance, most graduate programs offering a Master's degree in public administration place a greater emphasis on policy analysis than on organizational and managerial problems.)[11]

Other important changes also took place as the size of the public sector increased and the scope of its interventions broadened. But these changes did not make it easier for the new generation of 'technocrats' to pursue their policy-planning goals. On the contrary, they created obstacles that in the space of one or two decades became the dominant preoccupation of government officials.

An essential requirement for the efficient functioning of a modern bureaucracy is the 'merit system'. Its goal is to ensure that only competent and qualified individuals are recruited and promoted, in a manner ostensibly free of partisan political influence. Beginning in the late 1960s, however, it became apparent that the merit system was biased in favour of the dominant socio-economic groups. Thus efforts were undertaken to create new opportunities for members of minority groups to be recruited and/or promoted. In Canada, the target groups include Francophones, women, Aboriginals, and members of the 'visible minorities'.

The public service also confronted new economic, social, and political challenges. On the economic front, new technologies and the effects of the 'globalization' of markets account for a sharp increase in the number of commercial, industrial, and professional interest groups. On the social front, new social movements (environmentalists, feminists, gays and lesbians, animal rights activists, etc.) have become more and more sophisticated in their lobbying activities. These various groups form complex 'policy networks' and 'advocacy coalitions' in which government agencies actively participate, though without always being able to control them.[12] Finally, the fiscal crisis of the last 10–15 years, which involved soaring budget deficits and declining revenues, forced public administrators to shift attention from policy planning and development to more specifically managerial and administrative issues.

## From Public Administration to
## Public-Sector Management

Structural factors (e.g., the scarcity of resources) probably would have brought about a change of style at some point. But the immediate causes of the shift towards a new emphasis on public-sector management, in Canada and in other countries, are linked to the rise to power of neo-conservative governments in the late 1970s and early 1980s. Neo-conservative leaders (Margaret Thatcher in the United Kingdom, Ronald Reagan in the United States, and Brian Mulroney in Canada) were more or less suspicious of entrenched bureaucracies and proclaimed their intention to 'downsize' the welfare state. At the very least, these political events contributed to a redefinition of the incentives and rewards that motivate public officials. Efficiency in the management of scarce resources, together with greater attention to the specific and complex needs of diversified constituencies and 'consumers' of public services, became the new criteria of success. By contrast, advising ministers on how to achieve far-reaching policy goals, implementing new programs, and designing new administrative structures no longer define the foremost tasks of senior and middle-ranking public servants.

The reinvention of government, however, did not result only from such tactical considerations. As Peter Aucoin explains, 'given the hostility of the anti-bureaucrat political environment within which public servants must work'[13] today, reformers within the public service itself turned towards ideas that could give a new and more positive content to the missions of government and new reasons to value the roles played by public servants. So they embarked on the 'reinvention of government' with the purpose of doing away with bureaucratic structures. In their view, these structures produce the bureaucratic style that the public now so strongly despises. Thus they became bureaucracy-bashers to deflect the criticisms coming from bureaucrat-bashers. Aucoin perceptively suggests that this strategy is based on a wrong diagnosis of the situation—structures alone do not make mistakes or determine the behaviour of the people who work within them. However, in an age of rapid change when organizations must become far more dynamic than they have been so far, the realization that there might be something inherently faulty with the very concept of bureaucracy may not be such a bad diagnostic after all!

The phrase 'public-sector management', which is often used to describe the new priorities, has several noteworthy connotations.[14] 'Management' is a term borrowed from the private sector; it is meant to convey a quality of 'businesslike' efficiency. Of course, the world of government and the world of business differ in many ways. For one thing, there are no equivalents to the profit motive or to the proverbial 'bottom line' in the public sector. There is, however, something that brings the private and the public sectors closer to each other. The most important challenge for both has become the management of change, defined not merely as a capacity to respond to change but as the ability to prepare for unforeseen developments.

The latest trends in management theory emphasize a strategic orientation. Strategic management pays attention not only to the efficient use of resources but also to the economic and social environment, and to the changing expectations and values of a wide range of constituencies and stakeholders whose interests coincide or intersect to some extent with those of the organization (e.g., customers, suppliers, the mass media, competitors, interest groups, international agencies, and so on). Successful organizations are adaptive and can renew themselves as circumstances evolve. This involves a process of continuous learning and a willingness on the part of managers to recognize that their role is not to steer the organization towards fixed goals but to steer it away from goals that have outlived their usefulness. Such organizations have learned how to learn new facts and values, and management's function is to see to it that new facts and values are learned and assimilated throughout the organization. (In that sense, the strategic orientation I am describing here differs from 'strategic planning', a popular approach in the 1960s and 1970s that was predicated on the mistaken belief that long-term and comprehensive objectives could be set through methodical analysis of past trends.) This strategic orientation calls for a leadership style that excels at articulating a vision and at motivating employees. Management is not about issuing orders to be executed mechanically by bureaucratic structures but about facilitating the adoption of values and practices to allow an organization to set goals that are appropriate at the level where they are set. This entails empowering the members of the organization by giving them the power to make decisions about how to achieve the goal they have shared in setting. In return for their greater degree of initiative, the newly empowered members of today's ideal organizations are held accountable for their performance. Results, rather than established procedures, serve as the basis of evaluation. Consequently, public servants ought to act more like *entrepreneurs*, taking some risks and innovating in order to deliver better services at a lower cost, than like traditional bureaucrats.

In Canada, many of these ideas found their way into the thinking of the federal bureaucratic élite in the late 1980s. The clearest expression of this changing culture appeared in the reports that came out of Public Service 2000, an initiative launched by Prime Minister Mulroney in December 1989. The guiding principles originated with some of the most influential public servants in Ottawa. Ten task forces were formed, and they reported between 1990 and 1991.

Among all the recommendations made by the various Public Service 2000 task forces, two stand out as best illustrating the new way of thinking: the idea of improved 'service to the public'; and the notion that the old top-down style of management must give way to an environment where 'public servants will be empowered and encouraged to decide themselves how best to use the resources made available to them in order to get the job done in the most efficient manner.'[15] It is not immediately obvious that government is in the business of delivering 'services' to its 'customers'. After all, the traditional functions of government, such as guaranteeing the sovereignty of the state and maintaining law and order, have more to do with coercion and the legitimate use of force than with providing services comparable to those that can be purchased from private suppliers. But, again, the public sector has gone through a profound transformation during the last few decades. More public servants today work in areas that have little or nothing to do with the traditional, coercive functions of government. They are concerned with the delivery of a vast array of services, ranging from social assistance and income maintenance to the provision of technical information and the allocation of grants and scholarships. The inflexible bureaucratic style still characterizing many government agencies is poorly suited to the performance of functions such as these. Hence the new concern for the quality of the service provided by public servants to their 'clients' or 'customers'.[16]

If better services are to be provided to the public, then public servants who deal directly with the public should be given more power to decide what needs to be done. The centralization of power at the top in the name of efficiency and financial accountability served the interests of taxpayers rather well in the past, insofar as it offered certain guarantees against patronage and administrative malpractice, but in today's context it does not serve the interests of the 'clients' of the public sector. Moreover, rigid management may itself cause cost overruns. Empowering front-line public servants should make it easier for them to experiment with new ways of meeting the public's demands and avoiding 'red tape'. It also should improve their morale. Similar trends towards 'delayering' and innovation can be observed in the private sector, as businesses seek ways to adjust to a more competitive climate.

In Canada, movement in that direction began in 1986 with the introduction of the Increased Ministerial Authority and Accountability (IMAA) program. IMAA was intended to relax the control imposed by central agencies like the Treasury Board Secretariat on the departments that implement government policies. But it did not deal directly with the problems faced by managers 'in the field', that is, the public servants who actually deliver services to the public. Public Service 2000 signalled that much more needs to be done in that respect. Not all recommended changes were immediately implemented, however.

A few of the recommendations were put into law: Bill C–26, concerning the management of human resources; and Bill C–52, concerning the organization of 'common services' agencies, that is, government agencies providing services to other government agencies. In part because these bills provoked vigorous debates when opposition MPs expressed fears about the possible effects of the proposed legislative changes on traditional parliamentary controls, no other aspect of the Public Service 2000 exercise was enacted into law. But many recommendations did not require legislative instruments to be implemented.

This was not, however, a completely successful reform. It was perceived by many public servants as a top-down initiative, as indeed it was to a large extent. The architects of Public Service 2000 were caught in a bind: in their haste to signal that the old top-down management style should no longer prevail, they appeared to practise the very thing they argued against! Thus they made only modest progress in their efforts to recast the administrative culture of the federal public service into a more entrepreneurial and innovative mould. They also met with more resistance—from MPs and from some interest groups—than they had anticipated from outside the federal public service, and they did not obtain all the political support they needed from a somewhat embattled Tory government.[17]

And yet the momentum towards the reinvention of government along more managerialist lines did not stop with the partial demise of this federal initiative. In fact, beginning with the paring down of the federal cabinet and the cabinet committee system introduced in June of 1993[18] under Prime Minister Kim Campbell and continuing under the Jean Chrétien government, the pace of reform accelerated in the 1990s. 'Getting Government Right', to quote Marcel Massé,[19] the minister responsible for administrative reform in the first Chrétien cabinet, has meant two things: (1) foremost in the short term, making government more 'affordable' by reducing the size of the public service and eliminating agencies or programs that have outlived their usefulness; and (2) redefining the role of the federal government by entering into partnership agreements with the private sector or provincial governments in those cases where it is determined that a policy goal continues to be desirable but where it would appear that the federal government should not necessarily be responsible for it.

The first goal has by now been successfully reached, through a series of comprehensive 'policy reviews' as well as an exercise known as Program Review whereby government departments and agencies were asked to set financial targets reflecting improved standards of efficiency and effectiveness. At the time of writing, the federal government is expected to produce a budgetary surplus in future years, and the size of the public service has been brought back more or less to where it stood before the growth that occurred during the 1970s and early 1980s. Businesslike management practices are now common in many government departments and regulatory agencies.

Analysts often refer to the second goal as being an application of the principle of 'subsidiarity'. This principle states that responsibilities should be allocated to the level of government or, as the case may be, to non-governmental organizations that are in closest proximity to the individuals or groups who receive needed services. (Another aspect of this principle is that government ought to encourage individuals and groups to become less dependent on its services.) The systematic application of this principle could have consequences that reach far beyond the stated goal of administrative reforms designed to make government more efficient and less bureaucratic. It is still too early to evaluate the results of this new orientation insofar as it is still very much a work in progress. Early accounts of Program Review as an instrument for redefining the role of the state have focused on the haphazard and rather secretive manner in which this goal was pursued.[20] However, it is clear that (1) privatization and deregulation have been pushed by the federal government and most provincial governments, regardless of party affiliations, over the last 10–15 years; and (2) we have already moved towards a less centralized federal system in recent years (for example, devolution to First Nations of responsibilities formerly assumed by the Department of Indian Affairs and Northern Development; devolution to the provinces of responsibilities concerning human resources training and development).

The examples given so far chiefly concern the government of Canada, but similar trends can be noticed at the provincial level. All provincial governments have had to address serious fiscal constraints by cutting costs and eliminating certain programs or winding down agencies. But two provinces, Alberta and Ontario, have gone further than any other jurisdiction in Canada towards the goal of reinventing government not only as a more service-oriented and businesslike institution, but also as an institution that plays a less central and less interventionist role in society. Critics of these measures have argued that the quality of services has actually gone down rather than up in a number of areas (income assistance; arts and culture) where government programs have been severely cut. While the reformist rhetoric of the 1980s was 'doing more with less', public servants in many parts of the country, and in Alberta and Ontario in particular, now have to do 'less with less'.

In the United States, rhetorical attacks against 'big government' were launched with exceptional verve under President Ronald Reagan in the 1980s, but actual results were far less radical, due in large part to the complicated system of 'checks and balances' that characterizes American government. Congress ended up blocking or slowing down many of the measures proposed in piecemeal fashion by Presidents Reagan and George Bush. During President Bill Clinton's first term, a comprehensive reform, spearheaded by Vice-President Al Gore, was initiated. This National Performance Review is worth examining from a Canadian standpoint because its philosophy was remarkably similar to that of Public Service 2000, with a twin emphasis on a service-oriented approach and on the empowerment of 'street-level bureaucrats'. It also resembled Program Review in that it deliberately proclaimed as its priority the reduction of the size of the US civil service. Its implementation, however, was somewhat more successful than was the case with Public Service 2000: there was clear and unambiguous support from the highest levels of the political executive, something that was lacking with the Canadian initiative (although not in the case of Program Review); and more efforts were made to make public servants feel that they 'owned' the goals of the reform, that these goals were their own, as it were.

The trend away from active government involvement in social and economic affairs and an emphasis on result-oriented management are certainly not limited to North America. In fact, policy reviews and government reorganizations have been pursued even more forcefully and with far more radical results in the United Kingdom, New Zealand, and Australia. (Interestingly, the initiative for reforms in these last two countries came from Labour parties rather than from more conservative parties; and in the UK the Labour Party under Tony Blair has indicated that it does not intend to roll back the reforms introduced under Prime Ministers Thatcher and Major.) Similarly, important reforms have been introduced in the Netherlands and Sweden. One could also point to the massive privatization programs undertaken in some countries of the former Eastern Bloc, notably Poland and the Czech Republic. (Countries that did not move as far as fast, such as Ukraine and Slovakia, trail behind in terms of economic growth and development.) Many countries in Western Europe, including Austria, Denmark, Finland, France, Ireland, Italy, and Portugal, also undertook some more modest reforms; so far, however, Germany and Japan have taken relatively few steps towards adopting the new public-sector management style.[21]

## New Challenges

The transition from public administration to public-sector management facilitated the resolution of problems attributable to 'the crisis of the welfare state'. One such problem concerns the impossibility of continuing to finance ineffective programs at a time when fiscal resources are drying up. Fiscal constraints are due in part to a growing resistance to high levels of taxation by citizens who have become less willing to trust government to work in the public interest and in part to the push towards globalization. (The dysfunctional effects on employment and other variables of taxes, which put enterprises at a competitive disadvantage, will be felt almost immediately in open markets.) However, new challenges now confront public-sector managers. Some of these are not so much new as they are being rediscovered; ironically, traditional public administration had become 'bureaucratic' largely in response to such vexing challenges, and they resurface when bureaucratic practices are relaxed. But social and political change has also brought about genuinely new problems that may drive government beyond the limitations of the public-sector management paradigm. A brief discussion of the complexities associated with the notion of accountability, including the question of why these complexities are being revisited today, will take us part of the way towards an understanding of these new challenges. To get a more complete picture, however, we must also tackle the broader issue of democratic governance and the shape it might take in the next century.

In all organizations, tasks must be performed according to certain standards: finished products must be free of defects; services must be delivered to the satisfaction of customers; strategies for dealing with changing circumstances must be planned and implemented. However, the problem of deciding the appropriate standards for monitoring and evaluating the performance of public employees is complicated by two factors. Firstly, the very fact that public-sector organizations are public means that equity, fairness, and openness will count as much as, if not more than, efficiency and quality of service. But it is not easy to reconcile these often conflicting concerns. For example, citizens interested in finding out more about why certain programs exist, and how they are implemented, now have a right to obtain that information from public agencies in jurisdictions where freedom of information legislation has been implemented (i.e., the government of Canada[22] and most provinces). But public-sector managers have not always allocated sufficient resources to meet these objectives; consequently, information about government programs sometimes continues to be difficult to obtain.[23] This does not mean that public-sector managers deliberately act in bad faith. They are under considerable pressure from elected officials and, ultimately, from the public to cut down expenditures and improve the efficiency of their operations, but meeting unexpected requests for information takes time and costs money.

A second complicating factor is that governments must deal with a wide variety of stakeholders. Thus the clients of government agencies often include individuals and groups with little in common or who may be pursuing conflicting interests. The Department of Indian and Northern Affairs, for example, communicates with the representatives of several First Nations organizations, Native band councils, territorial governments, mining companies, and so on.

Public-sector managers work within complex reporting and accountability structures. Deputy ministers, the most senior bureaucrats in government departments, are accountable not only to the minister in charge of the department but also to a host of other political and bureaucratic authorities. These may include one or more secretaries of state assisting the senior minister heading the department; the Prime Minister, who appoints deputy ministers, on advice received from a committee of public servants chaired by the Clerk of the Privy Council, the top-ranking public servant in Ottawa; the Secretary of the Treasury Board with respect to budgetary and human resources management; the head of the Public Service Commission concerning hiring practices; and, in a more indirect manner, several other authorities or committees, such as the Auditor-General or parliamentary committees. Deputy ministers and other senior executives always had to report and consult with most of these authorities, but in the past these relationships were more predictable and routinized. One of the consequences of the trend towards a more entrepreneurial or businesslike approach has been that deputy ministers and other managers, who used to be under the obligation of reporting what they planned to do within a strictly limited range of responsibilities *before* going ahead with their plans, now have obtained much more latitude to take the initiative on their own but must report on the *results* achieved concerning a far broader range of activities. Moreover, they have become increasingly accountable, albeit in a more indirect and informal manner, to attentive stakeholders, to the media, and to other public opinion leaders. Accountability seems to be a concept expanding simultaneously in all directions: up, down, and across government institutions and the political system as a whole.

Now that the goal of transforming traditional bureaucrats into enterprising public-sector managers has been at least partly achieved, the complexity of these reporting and accountability issues is receiving more and more attention. Paradoxically, the reasons why old-style bureaucrats faced more constraints are now being rediscovered. To deflect criticisms about waste and other supposed ills of the public sector, newly empowered managers now find themselves compelled to recover and reinvent the language and practices they wanted to escape from. Hence, there now is a renewed emphasis on professionalism and ethics as means of channelling innovation. Liability after the fact is less often perceived as a solution than as a problem by government officials; it is, however, becoming a growing concern as Canadians, who had been less prone than Americans to sue public authorities for alleged wrongdoings, appear to be catching up.

Political scientists studying public administration can make valuable contributions to these (re-)emerging issues. Indeed, accountability has moved to the top of the research agenda in public administration, as a quick glance through such journals as *Canadian Public Administration* and the American *Public Administration Review* will confirm. Public-sector managers and many elected officials also seem to be paying far more attention to accountability. So far, however, few concrete steps have been taken to implement on a large scale the proposals discussed in various forums organized by think-tanks and public interest groups.

Accountability will always remain a valuable goal. However, citizens of modern democracies now expect more from government than honest and open administration. Increasingly, they demand to be consulted about, or even to play an active part in, policy-making. Elected officials and public servants do not always respond enthusiastically to these demands, but financial constraints have compelled them to find new ways of delivering services by entering into partnerships with non-governmental organizations. (This is usually referred to as 'alternative service delivery' or ASD.) To the extent that these organizations include not only large corporations but also community-based, non-profit associations, citizen expectations and ASD could converge. By entering into partnership agreements in social, cultural, or environmental ventures, citizens could find ways of leading more productive and meaningful civic lives, while government officials could improve efficiency and reduce the stress placed on a shrinking public service.

To make sense of this complex dynamic, we can turn to Albert O. Hirshman's analysis of the options available to us when dealing with organizations in the private and public sectors. Hirshman contends that when confronted with objectionable choices, we can do one of two things: either exercise our right of 'exit', by withdrawing from the market (or resigning from an organization to which we belong), or voice our concerns in order to influence the policies of the organizations we are dissatisfied with.[24] Dissatisfied customers usually have a choice to buy a similar product from a competitor; a manufacturer who is unhappy with the quality of supplies available on the domestic market can look for suppliers in other countries; members of political parties or professional associations can decide not to renew their membership. These examples illustrate how people exit from unsatisfactory situations.

There are many ways of voicing one's concerns but, contrary to the exit solution, they usually require some form of organized action. Consumer advocate groups and other pressure groups, trade unions, and broadly based social movements can have a significant impact on the decisions made by the management of private-sector firms or government agencies. Sometimes, too, groups or individuals seek to influence large corporations indirectly by pressuring government into regulating them; industrial pollution is a case in point. Organizing to protest and taking part in collective action can be costly. This is especially true when protesters meet with opposition from those they are trying to influence. Sometimes, however, exit is not an available option. In situations where, for example, a monopoly exists (e.g., publicly funded hospitals in Canada) or where members of disadvantaged groups are completely dependent on government support, 'voice' is the only feasible option.

Neither one of these two strategies works perfectly at present. In most cases, only an affluent minority can fully take advantage of the 'exit' option. 'Voice', on the other hand, often results in a confrontational style of politics that risks alienating uninterested third parties. It also reinforces a government tendency towards inertia since it presupposes that problems can only be corrected after they have become apparent to a sufficient number of people.

Thus the challenge for government reformers in the future will be twofold. Firstly, the public sector will have to be reorganized to provide more opportunities for 'exit'. This will require that more competition between service providers becomes a practical reality, and that all citizens have equal opportunity to make meaningful choices between such newly available options. Privatization and deregulation go some way towards meeting the first objective, but critics argue that such steps leave fewer options to those who lack the means to take advantage. Clearly, the second target will have to become a priority. A voucher system is often proposed as a solution to that problem, but much research still needs to be done to evaluate the merits of this idea.

Secondly, institutional mechanisms will have to be designed to allow the free expression of dissent by various groups before new policies are implemented, and in such a way that potential conflicts can be resolved in a manner satisfactory to all parties. Public-sector management has to be broadened to include not only the management of financial and human resources internal to the public sector, but also the mediation of a wider range of interests. An important new task for public-sector managers will be the facilitation of communication among the many groups and individuals who together constitute the 'policy communities' within which government agencies operate (e.g., the environmental community, the small business community, the cultural industries community). Of course, not all conflicts can be prevented. Some dissenters will always prefer to voice their objections outside of these new channels. Democracy cannot be limited to consultation and consensus-building. However, there is much room for improvement of the institutions and processes that citizens use to communicate with policy-makers on matters concerning the development and implementation of public policies. Ultimately, these new channels should enable interested citizens to become policy-makers themselves to some extent.

## Conclusion

In spite of the reforms outlined above, many people today have a rather negative view of public administration. The media continue to spread stereotypes about wasteful bureaucrats, and public administration does not attract as many students as other subfields in political science. However, my hope is that the preceding pages will convince some readers that the study of public administration is actually one of the best ways of coming to grips with the fundamental issues of the day about politics and public policy. The reinvention of government and the search for more democratic means of developing and implementing public policies are concerns that affect practically everyone in modern societies.

❧

The first selection is directly relevant to the trend I discussed in the first part of this introduction, namely, the redefinition of public administration as public-sector management. Greg Richards offers a positive assessment of this trend, yet he concedes that some important differences remain between government and the world of business. Because these differences must be taken into account by the proponents of public-sector reforms, some government agencies are more able than others to take advantage of the new public-sector management approaches. But where they can be applied, they should make an appreciable difference in efficiency and in service quality.

The second text underlines the importance—indeed, the urgency—of a rigorous and far-reaching re-examination of all aspects of administrative accountability. The new context created by the new public-sector management makes it necessary but also more complex. Efficiency is obviously something that public-sector managers should strive to achieve. However, as R.L. Gagne suggests, 'politicians and the public cannot have it both ways': at some point, they will have to choose between efficiency and fairness. There are limits beyond which an increase in the former can only be achieved at the detriment of the latter. Public servants must know whether the public wishes to hold them accountable for continuing to move in the direction of greater efficiency gains, or whether the public is ultimately more concerned with due process.

## Notes

1. This by now common phrase was first proposed by David Osborne and Ted Gaebler in their widely read book, *Reinventing Government* (Reading, Mass.: Addison-Wesley, 1992); this text had a decisive impact on administrative reforms in the United States and (to a somewhat lesser extent) in Canada. A recent example that generally champions the achievements of Alberta's Klein government is C.J. Bruce, R.D. Kneebone, and K.J. McKenzie, eds, *A Government Reinvented: A Study of Alberta's Deficit Elimination Program* (Toronto: Oxford University Press, 1997).

2. On the relationship of science, technology, and bureaucracy, see L. Dobuzinskis, 'Science, Technology and Bureaucracy: From the Discourse of Power to the Power of Discourse', *World Future* 28, 1–4 (1990): 183–201.

3. As this admittedly rather eclectic list suggests, charismatic leaders can be more or less benevolent and more or less admirable. The point is, however, that they have in common an exceptional ability to mobilize vast numbers of followers in ways that are difficult to explain on purely rational grounds.

4. The legal framework of the public service forms a more distinctive component of the constitutional and judicial systems of continental European systems than is the case in most English-speaking democracies, and clearly Max Weber had Germany in mind when he formulated the ideal bureaucratic type. But the essential principle of the rule of law (what the Germans call the *Rechtstaat*) remains the same.

5. Today the phrase 'public service' has come to replace 'civil service', at least in Ottawa, and the Civil Service Commission was renamed the Public Service Commission in 1967. (The legislation that brought about this name changed also implemented a series of more substantive changes that redefined the role played by that agency.)

6. Nowhere in the country was this shift more dramatic than in Quebec, where the institutional reforms and policy changes introduced between 1960 and 1966 came to be known as the Quiet Revolution.

7. Highly competent but discreet and rather traditional in their ways, the dozen or so men who held the top positions in the federal public service at that time were colloquially known as 'the mandarins'.

8. See Nicole Morgan, *Implosion: An Analysis of the Growth of the Federal Public Service in Canada (1945–1985)* (Montreal: Institute for Research on Public Policy, 1986).

9. For critical perspectives on these reforms, see George Szablowski, 'The Optimal Policy-Making System: Implications for the Canadian Political Process', and L. Dobuzinskis, 'Rational Policy-Making: Policy, Politics, and Political Science', in T.A. Hockin, ed., *Apex of Power: The Prime Minister and Political Leadership in Canada*, 2nd edn (Toronto: Prentice-Hall, 1977), 197–210, 211–28.

10. See David Zussman and Jack Jabes, *The Vertical Solitude: Managing in the Public Sector* (Halifax: Institute for Research on Public Policy, 1989).

11. See Donald J. Savoie, 'Studying Public Administration', *Canadian Public Administration* 33, 3 (1990): 393.

12. See W.D. Coleman and G. Skogstad, eds, *Policy Communities and Public Policy in Canada: A Structural Approach* (Mississauga, Ont.: Copp Clark Pitman, 1990); Evert A. Lindquist, 'Public Managers and Policy Communities: Learning to Meet New Challenges', *Canadian Public Administration* 35, 2 (1992): 127–59.

13. Peter Aucoin, 'The Design of Public Organizations for the 21st Century: Why Bureaucracy Will Survive in Public Management', *Canadian Public Administration* 40, 2 (1997): 259.

14. See Timothy W. Plumptre, *Beyond the Bottom Line: Management in Government* (Halifax: Institute for Research on Public Policy, 1988); and Barry Bozeman and Jeffrey D. Straussman, *Public Management Strategies: Guidelines for Managerial Effectiveness* (San Francisco: Jossey-Bass, 1990).

15. *Public Service 2000: The Renewal of the Public Service of Canada* (Ottawa: Supply and Services, 1990), 46.

16. See Public Service 2000, *Service to the Public Task Force Report* (Ottawa: Supply and Services, 1990); Brian Marson, 'Government as a Service Enterprise', *Public Sector Management* (Spring 1991): 12–14.

17. See Alasdair Roberts, 'Worrying About Misconduct: The Control Lobby and the PS 2000 Reforms', *Canadian Public Administration* 39, 4 (1996): 489–523.

18. Beginning under Prime Minister Pierre Trudeau and continuing under Prime Minister Brian Mulroney, the number of cabinet ministers had been steadily going up; as a result, the whole cabinet ceased to be a decision-making body and policy decisions were made in cabinet committees dealing with a broad range of issues and linked through a machinery that became more and more complex and cumbersome over the years. This system was radically restructured by Prime Minister Kim Campbell, who cut the number of ministerial positions by almost half.

19. Marcel Massé, 'Getting Government Right', address to the Public Service Alliance of Canada, 12 Sept. 1993.

20. See A. Armit and J. Bourgault, *Hard Choices or No Choices: Assessing Program Review* (Toronto: Institute of Public Administration of Canada, 1995); G. Paquet and R. Shepherd, 'The Program Review Process: A Deconstruction', in G. Swimmer, ed., *How Ottawa Spends, 1996–97* (Ottawa: Carleton University Press, 1996).

21. N. Manning, 'Three Perspectives on Alternative Service Delivery', *Public Sector Management* 7, 4 (1997): 5.

22. The Access to Information Act was passed in 1983.

23. At the federal level, dissatisfied applicants can address a complaint to the Privacy and Information Commissioner, who will investigate the complaint; see the annual reports of the Commissioner for more detail.

24. See A.O. Hirschman, *Exit, Voice, and Loyalty: Responses to Decline in Firms, Organizations, and States* (Cambridge, Mass.: Harvard University Press, 1970).

## Study Questions for the Readings

1.  Many people complain about 'red tape' and what they perceive as unnecessary rules and regulations enforced by municipal, provincial, or federal bureaucrats. Defenders of bureaucracy often respond that such seemingly absurd rules may be needed to ensure accountability and other important principles of good management that, in the end, work to the benefit of all. Is this a convincing argument? Why (or why not)?
2.  Can government operate in a more businesslike manner? And, if so, should government try to achieve that goal?
3.  Should Canadians regard themselves primarily as the clients of government agencies and, as such, expect competent and efficient service, or as citizens to whom government is accountable for the implementation of policies and programs?

# Businesslike Government:
## The Ultimate Oxymoron?

Greg Richards

The basic premise of the new public management is that government operations can and should be more businesslike. The message is that if government managers behave more like private-sector entrepreneurs, they can provide better service at lower cost to the Canadian public. This argument is steeped in history and seductive in its simplicity;[1] but experience suggests that government operations cannot completely emulate private business. The question is, where does one draw the line? This article discusses the concept of businesslike government and uses a case study to make the argument that being businesslike does not mean creating 'Government Inc.'; it does mean making a commitment to operating with the bottom line in mind.

## The New Public Management

The application of businesslike management in government can take many forms, ranging from the introduction of business processes to outright commercialization. But this new public management has its critics. Donald Savoie argues that the concept is fundamentally flawed, that 'private sector management practices very rarely apply to the public sector.'[2] James Gow, writing on the issue of innovation in government, suggests that 'the presence of political and legal restraints makes the analogy to the private corporation inappropriate for the public service.'[3] He concludes that the notion of stewardship—the responsibility for managing the property of others—is a more

appropriate metaphor for government managers than that of the entrepreneur.

Henry Mintzberg, a prominent business professor and management consultant, argues that government should not try to convert public services into business operations. He suggests that the adoption of 'business practices' is a knee-jerk reaction that ignores the fact that government operations have 'different pressures and different stakeholder relationships'.[4] A similar argument is made by Ian Clark, former Secretary of the Treasury Board of Canada, who suggests that the new public management overlooks legitimate constraints of the institutional environment in which public-sector managers work, 'namely, statutory responsibilities and conventions that comprise the body of pertinent public law'.[5] However, he also argues that reform is needed and has been achieved in certain jurisdictions within the constraints of public law.

In Britain, the apparent oxymoron of 'businesslike government' has been tackled through the creation of Executive Agencies (EAs), which operate like businesses but are accountable to the taxpayer. British Prime Minister John Major's Citizen's Charter makes it clear that the ultimate client is the taxpayer. In response, the EAs have adopted specific goals for service to the client. The administrative structure, in return, makes it somewhat easier for them to pursue these goals without some of the political concerns that often hobble government managers.

In Canada, the concept of entrepreneurial government management has taken on the connotation of 'breaking through bureaucracy', suggesting that public-sector managers, constrained by years of bureaucratic controls and procedures, should bash through these barriers by adopting

From *Optimum: The Journal of Public Sector Management* 27, 1 (1996): 21–5. Reproduced with the permission of the Minister of Public Works and Government Services Canada, 1998.

entrepreneurial business practices. This approach is appealing to some because it suggests a maverick role for managers as innovative risk-takers willing to cross the line occasionally to get things done. Anyone who has worked in the public sector knows that sometimes 'creativity' is needed to carry out a specific job successfully, and that there is sometimes an exceptional case where it may be easier to obtain forgiveness than permission. Some authors conclude, however, that if 'bureaucracy bashing' leads to managers contravening public law, then it is an irresponsible approach to public-sector reform, rather like encouraging drivers to ignore traffic lights simply because the lights slow them down.[6]

Obviously both sides have a point. On one hand, public-sector management can benefit from entrepreneurial approaches; on the other, if managers are too entrepreneurial, they run the risk of contravening public law and flouting public administration values such as prudence and probity. Can businesslike practices that challenge outdated operational methods be adopted without encouraging disregard for the controls needed in the public sector?

## Being Businesslike

From a strategic perspective, the government exists to provide services and businesses exist to earn revenue. Revenue generation is driven by the ability to deliver better products or services at lower prices to the marketplace. In the business world, consumers usually look for the best value (roughly defined as the quality of a product compared to its cost); therefore, the actions of competitors force companies to improve the product or service. Most government managers do not face competition as such, but the emphasis on continual service improvement is obviously crucial to businesslike operations. From a service delivery perspective, therefore, both sectors have similar objectives, but to the government, service is the objective, whereas to business, it is a means of earning revenue.

Private companies can be bureaucratic, but they usually do not endure the degree of control evident in government and so have more freedom to operate. In government, where managers are stewards of taxpayers' dollars, there is obviously a need for effective and transparent control over how this money is spent. The argument that control has become an end in itself probably has merit and the debate will occupy the scholars of government operations for some time. But government managers operate in a different arena than do private companies and, within this arena, businesslike management is possible. What this means in a public-sector context is illustrated by the following examples:

- The city of Calgary's utility department managed to increase service and decrease costs through good planning and work-flow redistribution. In a move that is clearly counter to current business practices, the department *hired* staff to save money.[7]
- The city of New York's police department, whose commissioner instituted specific outcome targets, continual measurement, and strict accountability, reduced crime by an average of 28 per cent.[8]

The common element in these cases is the identification of operational and/or strategic activities that would keep the organization profitable if it were a private company. The following case study discusses this issue in more detail.

### A Case Study

An example of a businesslike approach in a large federal department is Transport Canada's Road Safety and Motor Vehicle Regulation Directorate (RSMVR). The Road Safety Directorate is responsible for regulation and compliance related to road safety in Canada. The organizational unit in question, Road Safety Programs (RSP), is responsible for, among other things, collecting information on a wide array of issues, particularly child restraint devices, automobile defects, and importation of vehicles from the United States. The unit includes three main groups: administrative staff (managers), technical staff (who research the technical aspects of road safety equipment), and support staff.

In 1993, the directorate embarked on an ambitious program to improve client service. This program took an approach to service improvement that included understanding and responding to forces for change, analysing user behaviour, and involving staff in decision-making. The goal was better client service at a lower cost to the organization. Although many different projects were involved, this article will examine only one—the development and installation of a Call Centre in RSP.

*Responsiveness*

Businesses that do not respond well to the environment do not survive. Good business leaders can sense the future by understanding their industry as a whole, the products they make, and the markets they serve. In the case of RSP, it was clear that the leaders understood and championed the need for change. In fact, the strategic planning process for the directorate had started in 1988; the Call Centre program became an integral part of this process.

*Forces for Change*

There were three main forces for change: political pressure, equity in client services, and leadership.

- On the political front, a member of Parliament suggested the adoption of an 800 inquiry line to the then Minister of Transport.
- In terms of client service, a major issue at the time was that the blue pages in the annual Ottawa telephone directory listed a telephone number that could be easily accessed by people in Ottawa but not by those in the rest of the country. Thus client service, more specifically

equity in client service, a common concern in government operations, was a key factor.

- Leadership was established by the director-general of RSMVR, who realized that changes were needed. A number of task forces were created, one of which focused on service to the client. At first, there was resistance to the idea of a Call Centre. Some staff believed that the implementation of an 800 line was unnecessary, since RSP already had good networks that included police forces and other accident-reporting groups who knew how to contact the office for information. Instead of forcing the issue, management tested some commonly held assumptions. Using a consulting team to research the problem, they discovered that there was not, in fact, adequate access to information. Therefore, the Call Centre was eventually accepted as a viable response to client service issues.

*Staff Involvement*

Good businesses include their staff in the planning and development of new products and services. Members of the organization who know the client best and who are responsible for ultimately delivering the new service should be involved in its development. This concept is being implemented in many ways in the business world, including through innovations such as self-directed work teams or product development task forces. In RSP, once the decision was made to move ahead, additional research was conducted to find out how staff felt about the project. One finding of the study was that the more employees were involved, the happier they were. Although the consultants could not prove a direct cause-and-effect relationship, it was clear that the employees of the unit valued this involvement. The result was that the employees who would be operating the Call Centre were involved in setting it up, from selecting their own furniture and state-of-the-art equipment to visiting other organizations to find out how other Call Centres operated.

*Client Service*

In a competitive world, businesses that do not serve clients well will lose them. They will take their business elsewhere. Two key elements of successful marketing in the business world are market segmentation (providing the right product to the right person) and understanding buyer behaviour (how customers buy, use, and evaluate the product).

Market segmentation in the business sense is not often applicable to government operations: all taxpayers are usually entitled to the same level of service. But RSP staff clearly applied the concepts of buyer behaviour. From the start, they put themselves into their clients' shoes. They knew that many callers had questions about vehicle child restraints and automobile defects, important issues that could conceivably be a matter of life and death. Using this understanding of its clients, the RSP developed the following guidelines for service delivery:

- *Personal interaction.* Clients want a real person at the end of the phone line. An automated system does not provide enough flexibility. Moreover, people who are calling may have some degree of anxiety about a particular issue and do not want to struggle through a touch-tone jungle to get answers.
- *Relevance.* Information must be up-to-date and accurate. The group installed a number of technological solutions to ensure that all technical information was readily available. It also encouraged regular, open communications between technical officers and Call Centre operators.
- *Consistency.* Clients should be able to get the same information from any operator at any time. Accordingly, all technical briefings are done in groups, and all operators have access to all information on the issues.

Using these basic customer service principles, service standards similar to those in use by EAs in Britain were developed, including:

- *Same-day response.* Calls are responded to on the same day as they are received.
- *One call only.* Clients do not have to call more than one person for a response to their query.

*Results*

The Call Centre was activated in July 1994 and the volume of calls continues to grow steadily as more people become aware of the service. Continual development in software and document management enables Call Centre operators to find information faster than ever. Ongoing training complements the introduction to new technology.

Performance standards can be tracked through the Centre's information system, but according to the Centre's managers, the operators themselves are keenly aware of how well they provide information. They are often the first to understand trends in calling patterns and to make suggestions for dealing with changes.

## The Business of Government

What did government managers in the RSP have in common with their colleagues in Calgary and New York?

- They developed a view of the future that relates to something concrete. Much has been made of vision statements that show that the organization serves a 'higher purpose', which is important, but they must be based on reality. A good vision statement promotes a new way of working that motivates employees. In the case of the Calgary utilities department, for example, the statement that through intelligent routing and scheduling the employees could read twice as many meters for half as much money does not sound like an idealistic, higher-purpose vision. But it does describe the real nuts-and bolts scenario that the organization wanted to achieve. In the case of RSP, ensuring equal access to timely, relevant, and consistent information is a realistic vision for the organization.

• These agencies set measurable, specific, and realistic objectives. The RSP established measurable standards of service, the city of New York set specific targets for reduction in certain types of crime, and the city of Calgary set realistic targets for cost reduction and service improvement. More importantly, each followed up with measurement and accountability that held a particular person responsible for meeting the targets.

• They all focused on client service, which is also a much-talked-about topic under the rubric of new public management. Everyone wants to meet client needs. Understanding what clients want is important, but organizations also need to understand how the client buys, uses, and evaluates the service. With this knowledge, managers can set service targets and standards that provide guideposts for operational priorities.

## Conclusion

Donald Savoie may be right in suggesting that the application of private-sector management techniques to all aspects of government—businesslike management—is unworkable. If businesslike management means breaking through bureaucracy and getting the job done by disregarding public law and the need for prudence and probity, then government managers *can* not and *should* not be businesslike. But there are many examples of government managers operating in a businesslike manner *within* the boundaries of public law and government procedures. Being businesslike simply means determining what has to be done, setting specific objectives, working hard to attain them, measuring performance, then re-evaluating and redefining the objectives.

This cycle takes place within the context of client, stakeholder, and, as far as the government is concerned, political demands. All business managers, private or public, operate within strategic or operational constraints and until these rules are changed, managers must strive to improve performance within the current boundaries while lobbying to do away with these restrictions.

Meeting client needs through producing high-quality products or services can be done in many ways. Some techniques used by the private sector may not be applicable to the public sector, but this does not mean that the public sector cannot be businesslike, as long as we know whose definition we are using.

## Notes

Greg Richards is a consultant with Consulting and Audit Canada. Before joining the federal public service, he spent several years at the municipal level and introduced a number of businesslike practices to the management of not-for-profit agencies. Mr Richards has a Master of Business Administration degree from the University of Ottawa.

1. The idea that government should behave more like the private sector can be traced back to the work of the 1949 Hoover Commission (US government).
2. Donald Savoie, 'What is Wrong with the U.S. New Public Management?', *Canadian Public Administration* 38 (Spring 1995).
3. James Ian Gow, 'Innovation in the Public Service',

Canadian Centre for Management Development, Mar. 1991.
4. 'Mintzberg Takes Aim at Business-Style Government', *Globe and Mail*, 18 Apr. 1996.
5. Ian D. Clarke, 'On Re-Engineering the Public Service of Canada: A Comment on Paul Tellier's Call for Bold Action', *Public Sector Management* 4, 4.
6. Peter Aucoin, 'Canadian Public Management Reform—A Comparative Westminster Perspective', Canadian Centre for Management Development, Nov. 1995.
7. Harvey Schacter, 'Revolution from Within', *Canadian Business* (Nov. 1994).
8. 'A Safer New York City', *Businessweek*, 11 Dec. 1995.

# Accountability and Public Administration

R.L. Gagne

The objective of this paper is to stimulate reflection and informed discussion on accountability in the public service. We will explore, from the perspective of public servants themselves, some of the ramifications of recent changes, primarily at the federal and provincial level, in customary practices dealing with accountability. The accountability of elected officials to the public, although linked, will not be dealt with here.

For the purposes of this paper, the term 'accountability' is defined as the condition of having to answer to someone for one's actions. In addition, the issue will be approached in terms of who is accountable to whom, for what, and under what circumstances. Implicit in this approach is the notion of rewards or penalties attendant upon the result of one's actions.

The foregoing definition of accountability is not, of course, the only one possible. For instance, Caiden says there are three key elements one must consider in any treatment of the topic of accountability: responsibility, accountability, and liability. He defines these as follows:

> To be *responsible* is to have the authority to act, power to control, freedom to decide, the ability to distinguish (as between right and wrong) and to behave rationally and reliably and with consistency and trustworthiness in exercising internal judgment. To be *accountable* is to answer for one's responsibilities, to report, to explain, to give reasons, to respond, to assume obligations, to render

From *Canadian Public Administration/Administration publique du Canada* 39, 2 (Summer 1996): 213–25. Reprinted by permission of the Institute of Public Administration of Canada.

a reckoning and submit to an outside or external judgment. To be *liable* is to assume the duty of making good, to restore, to compensate, to recompense for wrongdoing or poor judgment.[1]

Concerns about the accountability of public servants spring partly from the impact of the pervasiveness of government institutions and agencies on the life of Canadians and partly from a growing perception on the part of the public that government is out of control. The former tends to make the public more aware of the large role government plays in their lives, something with which not everyone is comfortable. The latter predisposes this same public to lose confidence in the ability of the public service to satisfactorily provide them with the services to which they believe they are entitled. Hence the periodic calls for greater control over, and accountability by, public servants. However, as Kernaghan and Siegel have noted,

> [e]nforcing accountability for the exercise of bureaucratic power has become more difficult as our public services have continued to grow in size and as their responsibilities have grown in complexity.[2]

In Canada, the accountability of public servants at the federal and provincial level is grounded in what has been called the Westminster model of responsible government and is inextricably linked to the complementary notions of ministerial responsibility and bureaucratic anonymity. Furthermore, that view is buttressed by the related belief, sometimes called the policy-administration dichotomy, that elected officials decide on policy matters while public servants do no more than administer and implement these policy

## Table 1: Accountability-Streams for Public Servants

| Superiors | Politicians | The Law | Professions | The Public |
|---|---|---|---|---|
| Deputy ministers | Legislature | Acts | Ethics | Individual citizens |
| Asst. deputy ministers | Ministers | Regulations | Codes | Citizen groups |
| Directors | | | Standards | Service quality |
| Managers | | | | |
| Supervisors | | | | |

decisions. This viewpoint is perhaps most clearly expressed in the federal government's Public Service 2000 document:

> When all is said and done . . . in our system ministers are *elected to decide* whereas officials are *appointed to administer and advise.*[3]

Nevertheless, in today's complex governmental environment, it is often extremely difficult to establish where administrative accountability ends, where political responsibility begins, and vice versa. The Al-Mashat affair is a good example of the invidious position in which public servants may find themselves because of this uncertainty.[4]

In practice, questions of who is responsible to whom, for what, and under what circumstances emerge in five contexts: accountability to a superior; accountability to elected officials; accountability under the law; accountability to professional norms and institutions; and accountability to the public at large. Table 1 illustrates the many accountability-streams with which the average public servant in the provincial and federal sphere must take into account on a daily basis.

The accountability of the individual public servant to his or her superior is grounded in the structure of hierarchy sanctioned by tradition and established through administrative procedures authorized by law. The familiar organization chart and its associated formal job descriptions are the most easily recognized representations of the accountability relationships found in government departments and agencies. This relationship is formal and mostly person-to-person. In many instances, it is modified by the provisions of collective bargaining agreements. But in any case, the expectations and rules are usually clear, with rewards and penalties defined. This kind of accountability exists throughout the public-service hierarchy.

Deputy ministers in the federal and provincial systems, their municipal counterparts, city managers, and their equivalents are examples of public servants directly responsible to politicians. It is through these individuals that the whole public administration apparatus is held accountable to elected officials. Other public servants may, from time to time, be required to deal directly with elected officials. But, ultimately, it is generally only the chief executive officer of a department, ministry, or municipal government whose primary accountability exhibits this feature.

Public servants are also accountable (if perhaps indirectly, in most cases) for upholding the laws they administer. For example, the unemployment insurance adjudicator or the social worker administers a law and can, in effect, be held accountable for doing so in accordance with established norms, even though each may well be the junior officer in a long chain of bureaucratic command. However, the public servants who are directly responsible in law are the federal deputy ministers. They are given certain financial responsibilities *directly* under the Financial Administration Act and are delegated authority for personnel matters by the Treasury Board and the Public Service Commission.[5]

Modern governments require the services of all kinds of professionals in order to administer an ever-growing and complex array of programs and services. This leads to a kind of guild accountability, that is, accountability to their profession. Most professions (e.g., medicine in many of its branches, education, accountancy, engineering, law, land surveying, and social work) impose certain standards of competence and behaviour and have, by law, the authority to discipline members who fail to meet these standards. Engineers employed by the Alberta government, for example, are as directly accountable to their professional association for their decisions or recommendations made as public servants, when this involves engineering matters, as their private-sector counterparts are in the discharge of theirs.[6] The point to be made here is that even though a provincial government engineer's judgement may not be challenged by his or her fellow public servants or even by elected officials, it could well be questioned by the Association of Professional Engineers, Geologists and Geophysicists of Alberta (APEGGA). An unfavourable decision by that body could deprive that individual of the right to practise his or her profession. This is the kind of guild accountability over which neither politicians nor the public can have direct day-to-day influence but one which the individual public servant must certainly take into account. Curiously, engineers employed by the federal government and those in the military are not accountable to a professional association, as long as they remain in the federal public service or in the military.

A much more ambiguous and undefined accountability to accommodate in practice is that of accountability to the public. Unlike the cases of accountability to superiors (administrative or political) or in law, accountability by public servants to the public they serve finds no firm footing in either law, administrative structure, or custom. However, the fact that there is no formal mechanism for the expression of accountability to the public by appointed officials does not negate the fact that many public servants firmly believe that they are indeed responsible to the public they serve. Kernaghan and Siegel have called this 'subjective responsibility' and note that it is rooted in the individual's personal beliefs and convictions, rather than in any formal structures, laws, or customs.[7] In other words, individuals see themselves as responsible to those for whom they feel responsible. This reflects an identification with those who are served rather than a notion of accountability in the strictest sense of the word.[8] None the less, this feeling is real and does in many instances govern behaviour.

But, even if public servants were not to believe themselves directly accountable to the public, there is growing evidence that the public itself expects both its elected and appointed officials to be individually accountable for their actions and decisions. In the case of elected officials, the public can indicate its displeasure or loss of confidence through the vote. Appointed officials are immune from that sanction but are not thereby totally protected from the public's ire or mistrust. For instance, the furore that erupted early in 1994 when the killing of policemen by convicted felons on parole led to calls for individual parole board members to be held directly accountable for their decisions reflects a growing demand by individual Canadians that public servants be individually accountable for their actions.

A significant example of this kind of demand is the $6.3 million suit brought against the National Parole Board, the Correctional Service of Canada, and 14 corrections and parole board officials by the orphaned sons of Kittye Schmidt.

She and her new husband were killed by her ex-husband Dean Cyr, who was at large after violating the conditions of his parole. The suit alleges that the murders were the result of negligence of the National Parole Board and the Correctional Service. Commenting on that suit, the president of the Canadian Resource Centre for the Victims of Crime, Scott Newark, connected it directly to the issue of accountability when he said, 'This isn't about money: it's about people who want accountability.'[9] Newark added that this suit is only one of several now being launched against both the Correctional Service and the National Parole Board. The foregoing may well be part of a trend already well established in the United States, where one researcher has estimated that some 17,600 federal public servants at all levels in the hierarchy are being sued over decisions made by them in the discharge of their duties as public servants.[10] Public servants in Canada are not entirely unprotected in such circumstances. For instance, the Alberta government may assist an employee charged with a criminal offence or what is termed a 'quasi-criminal offence' arising from actions taken or decisions made in the performance of duties. Such assistance may involve the province's own legal counsel or paying for outside legal advice. Another example is the provisions made by the city of Edmonton in a policy that requires the city to pay the costs of civil suits brought against members of council and employees for actions taken in the course of their duties.[11] Despite such protections, the public's emerging willingness to challenge administrative decisions in court has the potential of radically changing the nature of accountability in the public service.

Taken individually, the types of accountability described above can have a major impact on how public servants cope with a rapidly changing work environment. But life is never so disconnected; these accountabilities do impinge on one another. Like riding two horses at once, finding an equilibrium between competing accountabilities can become a difficult balancing act.

In practice, however, the issue is more complicated than a simple case of competing accountabilities. According to Savoie, senior officials, deputy ministers, and municipal chief executive officers see themselves as directly and explicitly accountable to their ministers and to the government of the day, but the so-called front-line staff more often see themselves as accountable to the public they serve rather than to the elected officials who are nominally their superiors.[12] The examples cited by Savoie relate to national government public servants in Canada and in Britain, but the same can be said of many front-line provincial public servants.

The Institution of Public Administration of Canada's 'Statement of Principles Regarding the Conduct of Public Employees' states:

> Public Employees are accountable on a day-to-day basis to their superiors for their own actions and the actions of their subordinates. They owe their primary duty, however, to their political superiors. They are indirectly accountable to the legislature or council and to the public through their political superiors. Public servants also have a responsibility to report any violations of the law to the appropriate authorities.[13]

In practice, this statement involves conflicting accountabilities. As Kernaghan and Langford observe, 'Public servants are often accountable in several directions at once and can, therefore, receive conflicting signals as to what is expected of them.'[14]

Politicians in Canada have adopted two basic strategies (the details differ) in their attempts to deal with public demands for greater accountability from appointed officials: downsizing and privatizing to reduce the size and influence of public bureaucracies; and introducing private-sector management systems in order to improve the efficiency of the remaining public service. Downsizing means the government gives up its responsibility for a service without necessarily allocating it elsewhere (this is referred to as 'load-shedding' by Savoie[15]); privatization means shifting the responsibility for providing a good or service to the private sector. Both remove an activity from the public sector and place the issue of accountability for such activities beyond the scope of this paper. This is not to suggest, however, that these measures are not important issues deserving wide public scrutiny—quite the contrary.

The introduction of private-sector management methods into the public service modifies traditional accountability relationships between politicians and public servants and has particular effects on public servants. An examination of the Mulroney government's efforts in this area will illustrate the point. This government's attempt to introduce private-sector management systems was perhaps best exemplified in its Public Service 2000 program. This initiative emphasized 'freedom of action by departments' and a greater discretion for managers to manage for results.[16] It also stressed the concepts of 'service to Canada and Canadians' and 'a more people-oriented public service.'[17] The idea here was to make the public service more flexible and responsive to the needs of Canadians and to do away with some of the centralized controls, which were believed to impede this. This approach has also been called 'an enabling focus', where '[c]onsiderations of uniformity of service are replaced by attention to uniqueness to ensure that key business results are achieved' and where 'public servants will take higher risks to achieve results.'[18]

Donald Savoie argues that Mulroney's attempt to introduce private-sector management systems did not produce the results intended. Savoie claims that these initiatives, which he calls 'managerialism', are, in their application, in conflict with the principle of ministerial responsibility, although they are quite consistent with the policy-administration dichotomy notion. The latter formed the philosophical grounds for the Mulroney government's efforts to regain full control of the policy process for elected officials, as the quotation from

Public Service 2000 cited earlier about the roles of ministers and public servants makes clear.

Savoie also argues that introducing private-sector management systems into the public service not only reinforces the separation of policy-making and administration (something Mulroney and his advisers intended) but also substitutes the private sector's stress on productivity, performance, and service to customers[19] for the traditional public service values of accountability and control. He also makes the point that the equality, fairness, and due process that Canadians want from government come at the cost of the 'bureaucratic dysfunctions' Canadians complain about. Savoie does not explain this term, and every individual who believes that he or she has been badly used by the system would no doubt define it differently. Certainly, delays in response and bureaucratic detachment would rank high among such complaints.

What Savoie seems to be saying is that both the politicians and the public must choose the dominant value they want in their public service—due process or productivity—but that they cannot have both at the same time. One could define due process as the requirement of government to deal fairly and equitably with all its citizens and to consult on issues of significant importance. Productivity means the effective and efficient use of resources to accomplish a given task. One should not assume, however, as some political leaders have done (e.g., Mulroney, Thatcher, and Reagan), that any particular government function can best be accomplished by allocating it to the private sector or by introducing private-sector management methods into the public service. Savoie notes that this may be quite successful in cases where the work is easily understood, where limited decision-making discretion is required, and where the workload can be readily measured.[20] He stresses that management and decision-making in the public and private sectors differ greatly. He also notes that, unlike the fairly clear-cut objectives found in the private sector (i.e., productivity and profitability), public servants operate in (and must be held accountable in) a political environment where goals are often deliberately vague and where political considerations, not efficiency factors, set the priorities.[21] In a slightly modified context, Savoie's argument tends to illustrate the notion advanced by Jane Jacobs that conflict and confusion result when the precepts appropriate to the 'trader' and 'guardian' functions of society are misapplied.[22]

The foregoing suggests that the accountability regime under which many public servants have served in the past has changed. Management principles like decentralization, achieving measurable results, and empowerment (key features of 'managerialism') imply that public-sector managers are to be held accountable for performance results rather than for adhering to due process and to the equitable treatment of individuals. In addition, if the federal experience is any guide, individual public servants may now be held directly accountable for their own actions or for those of their subordinates by parliamentary committees or their surrogates in provincial legislatures or on municipal councils (as the Al-Mashat affair demonstrated), to say nothing of the potential for damages resulting from the increasing tendency for the public to file civil suits against particular public servants. Set against all this is the recent Supreme Court of Canada ruling awarding $1.6 million to a former Crown attorney who sued for libel over remarks made by a defence lawyer about the Crown attorney's conduct in the performance of his duties.[23] The issue here is whether public officials can sue for libel about remarks concerning the performance of their duties, and the Supreme Court has affirmed that indeed they can. It is still too early to tell what effect this may eventually have on the application of accountability in the public service.

Under 'managerialism', public servants are expected to be proactive and entrepreneurial (rather than reactive and control-oriented) and to manage for productivity. If such an initiative is to succeed, honest mistakes must be tolerated by

politicians, as is the case in the private sector. In addition, efficiency considerations must govern public service decision-making. However, as the Al-Mashat affair demonstrates, politicians are seldom willing to tolerate politically embarrassing errors or administrative decisions, no matter how rational they otherwise may be. Savoie comments:

> . . . [I]n business it does not much matter if you get it wrong 10 per cent of the time as long as you turn a profit at the end of the year. In government, it does not much matter if you get it right 90 per cent of the time because the focus will be on the 10 per cent of the time you get it wrong.[24]

The Auditor General of Canada has reported that public-service managers see their rewards coming, not through the most productive use of resources, but rather on whether 'charges of extravagance or inequitable treatment' may embarrass their political masters.[25] On the other hand, as the Kittye Schmidt civil suit illustrates, members of the public are beginning to insist that someone be held accountable for perceived dereliction of duty, incompetence, or errors in judgement that inconvenience them or cause them harm.

But politicians and the public cannot have it both ways. They must choose whether they wish to have public servants become productivity- and efficiency-conscious or to have them remain essentially concerned with due process and fairness in their dealings with the public. If it is to be the former, then public servants must not only be accountable for their actions, they must also be given both the authority and the freedom to make administrative decisions commensurate with the degree of accountability thrust upon them. In like manner, public servants accorded greater authority and freedom to make administrative decisions must accept the risks associated with that authority, and they cannot expect elected officials to shoulder the blame when decisions go awry.

As was indicated earlier, public servants sometimes view accountability as an expression of their personal preferences; they see themselves as primarily accountable to those they directly serve. There is in this view, however, another dimension not often articulated but one which nevertheless colours the manner in which accountability is perceived: the moral aspect of the issue. The linkage here is what Jacobs says is the impossibility of separating the practical matters public servants deal with on a daily basis from what she calls 'moral considerations'. In other words, norms of some kind do indeed inform and guide individuals (public servants included) in their behaviour on the job.[26]

But no matter how it is interpreted or applied, no accountability regime will function effectively if it gets in the way of allowing public servants to do their job. For example, if unemployment insurance payments or welfare cheques stop going out or if air traffic control bogs down because of accountability issues, the public will turn on politicians and administrators alike. Accountability is essentially a relationship that is most likely to succeed when all parties enter into it on the basis of shared goals and expectations and where performance results are explicit and agreed upon by everyone involved. As things stand, the rules governing this relationship are not clear. They not only need to be made clear, but they must also be fair to both elected and appointed officials. And perhaps most important, these rules must be perceived by the public as protecting its interests.

An earlier (and slightly different) draft of this paper distributed to the members of the Edmonton Regional Group of the Institute of Public Administration of Canada posed the following questions: (1) What then is to be done? (2) Would an acknowledgement that the private and public sectors are significantly different, and that this entails the use of differing criteria for holding the managers in each accountable for their actions relieve the situation? (3) Would a reassessment of the principle of ministerial accountability to ascertain if it is still appropriate in today's highly fluid polit-ical, social, and economic environment help? (4) Would a review of the principle of the policy-administration dichotomy in terms of its applicability to current problems satisfy the critics? (5) Would a combination of any or all of the foregoing do the trick? Or, (6) Must we begin the search for a totally new model of governance?

The following is an abstract of the responses to these questions:

1. The notion that there is a moral dimension to the application of any accountability regime implicit in the paper was acknowledged and confirmed.

2. The accountability of public administrators and politicians cannot be separated. Both are involved in the process of governance, and the issue needs to be looked at as a whole.

3. It was argued that ministers cannot be held individually accountable for all administrative decisions taken by their departments, since that would leave them no time to deal with major policy issues.

4. On the other hand, it was also said that the traditional system, where ministers are responsible for what goes on in their departments and where administrators simply implement policy decisions taken by ministers, should be retained.

5. It was asserted that along with the power public servants hold in the modern state should come personal responsibility for their actions.

6. It was also suggested that a totally new model of governance more attuned to the needs of the citizen is required.

7. The public must become an integral part of any new accountability regime.

8. The notion that productivity and due process are mutually exclusive was challenged, and it was argued that, properly managed, public bureaucracies can be as effective at delivering services to the public as private ones.

9. Accountability to individual citizens, as distinguished from the public in general, forms an integral part of an ethical matrix for some public servants.

The complexity of the issue is reflected in the range of responses provided, not all of which were consistent with each other. This suggests that not all public servants see the issue in the same light or agree on what, if anything, needs to be done about it.

In addition, in some cases, the responses themselves appear to raise other important issues. For instance, while there seems to be general agreement that there exists some kind of moral grounding for the notion of accountability, in a pluralistic society such as Canada, whose morality is to predominate? What is moral behaviour for one group may well be anathema to another. Such a clash of values may well be contentious but surely need not be an insurmountable problem for politicians, public servants, and Canadians in general to sort out. Its existence needs to be recognized if it is to be dealt with in a manner acceptable to all involved.

Even if one were to accept as fact the often-voiced contention that public bureaucracies are less efficient than their private-sector counterparts (and this paper does not), the fact would remain that public agencies always operate within a political (not a market) environment where objectives may be kept deliberately vague and where, except in special circumstances, public institutions can-

not select their clientele the way private firms are able to. Again, this is not an insurmountable problem, but public agencies do indeed face circumstances quite different from their private-sector counterparts, and these circumstances require accommodation. This is not to say that efficiency is impossible for public institutions, only that their efficiencies need not be identical to or defined by those of the private sector.

Moreover, there is a need to distinguish more clearly than is normally done between an 'accountability to' and 'advocacy on behalf of' individual citizens in terms of refining the notions of accountability in the public service. This is not to say that there is no place for advocacy within the public service. There is a place for advocacy under certain circumstances, but this should not be confused with accountability.

Today, public agencies of all kinds are under intense scrutiny as politicians, citizens, and the public agencies themselves struggle to redefine the role of the public sector in the face of the centrifugal force of an emerging global economy and the competing thrust of citizen demands for greater local autonomy.[27] It is important to remember that public agencies are different from private firms and operate under significantly dissimilar circumstances that dictate differing accountability regimes. In this maelstrom of change, it is necessary to keep in mind that, ultimately, all elements of government must be accountable to the public for their decisions.

## Notes

The author is chair of the policy committee of the Edmonton Regional Group. He wishes to thank Jean Bara, Iqbal Jamal, Ian Logan, Pauline Peters, Jim Rivait, Tom Smith, and Ian Urquhart for their assistance in the preparation of this paper. He also wishes to thank the anonymous reviewers for their helpful comments.

1. Gerald E. Caiden, 'The Problem of Ensuring the Public Accountability of Public Officials', in Joseph G. Jabbra and O.P. Dwivedi, eds, *Public Service Accountability: A Comparative Perspective* (West Hartford, Conn.: Kumarian Press, 1988), 25 (emphasis added). The foregoing is also a good source of information on differing definitions of accountability as well as on how accountability is implemented in practice in a number of national jurisdictions.

2. Kenneth Kernaghan and David Siegel, *Public Administration in Canada: A Text*, 2nd edn

(Scarborough, Ont.: Nelson Canada, 1991), 323.

3. Public Service 2000, *The Renewal of the Public Service of Canada* (Ottawa: Supply and Services, 1990), 8 (emphasis in original).

4. S.L. Sutherland, 'The Al-Mashat Affair: administrative responsibility in parliamentary institutions', *Canadian Public Administration* 34, 4 (Winter 1991): 573–603.

5. Gordon Osbaldeston, *Keeping Deputy Ministers Accountable* (Toronto: McGraw-Hill Ryerson, 1989), 20.

6. The accountability here is both personal and to the professional body (Alberta Association of Professional Engineers, Geologists and Geophysicists of Alberta) for their engineering decisions. For an example of this, see Licia Corbella, 'Politics and the Paddle River', *Edmonton Sun*, 15 Nov. 1994, 38, regarding the inquiry by that body into the professional conduct of four senior Alberta government engineers involved in the management of the construction of the Paddle River dam. The same kind of accountability process governs registered land surveyors employed by the province.

7. Kernaghan and Siegel, *Public Administration*, 322.

8. This notion comes from Frederich C. Mosher, *Democracy in the Public Service* (New York: Oxford University Press, 1968) and is cited by Kernaghan and Siegel, *Public Administration*, 322.

9. Scott Newark quoted in Bart Johnson, 'More victims fighting back', *Edmonton Sun*, 28 Oct. 1994, 20. See also Kathleen Engman, 'Sons of slain couple file $6.3M suit: Claim cites fatal errors by Corrections, parole board', *Edmonton Journal*, 27 Oct. 1994, A1, A14.

10. Charles R. Wise, 'Suits against Federal Employees for Constitutional Violations: Search for Reasonableness', *American Political Science Review* 45, 6 (Nov./Dec. 1985): 850.

11. Linda Slobodian, 'Deal protects bullies', *Edmonton Sun*, 16 Dec. 1994, 5.

12. Donald J. Savoie, *Thatcher, Reagan, Mulroney: In Search of a New Bureaucracy* (Toronto: University of Toronto Press, 1994), 316–17.

13. 'Statement of Principles Regarding the Conduct of Public Employees: The Institute of Public Administration of Canada', in Kenneth Kernaghan and John Langford, *The Responsible Public Servant* (Montreal: The Institute for Research on Public Policy and the Institute of Public Administration of Canada, 1990), 204.

14. Ibid., 163.

15. Savoie, *Thatcher, Reagan, Mulroney*, 151.

16. Public Service 2000, *Renewal of the Public Service*, 89–90.

17. Ibid., 51–61, 77–87.

18. Carr Douglas Leiren Consulting Ltd, 'The New Accountability', *The Interlocutor* 2, 1 (Spring 1994): 2.

19. Savoie, *Thatcher, Reagan, Mulroney*, 283.

20. Ibid., 321.

21. Ibid., 137.

22. Jane Jacobs, *Systems of Survival: A Dialogue on the Moral Foundations of Commerce and Politics* (New York: Random House, 1992). Jacobs's argument centres around her notion that there are two distinct moral bases for action in society. The first focuses, *inter alia*, on honesty, competition, initiative, efficiency, industriousness, thrift, and optimism. She calls this the 'trader' function. The second emphasizes, *inter alia*, obedience, discipline, tradition, hierarchy, loyalty, fortitude, and honour. She names it the 'guardian' function. She argues that the first is necessary for the economic well-being of society, and that the second is required to protect society from both without and within, including the excesses of the trader function. But her main argument is that one should never confuse the two kinds of functions nor, worse still, apply the elements necessary for the proper functioning of the first (e.g., honesty, competition, initiative, etc.) to the second or vice versa.

23. Stephen Blindman, '$1.6M libel suit award upheld: defamation reform rejected', *Edmonton Journal*, 21 July 1995, A3. See also 'Court upholds libel award to former Crown attorney', *Edmonton Sun*, 21 July 1995, 32.

24. Donald J. Savoie, 'What is wrong with the new public management?', *Canadian Public Administration* 38, 1 (Spring 1995): 115.

25. Office of the Auditor General, *Report of the Auditor General of Canada to the House of Commons: Fiscal Year Ended 31 March, 1983* (Ottawa: Supply and Services Canada, 1983), 58.

26. Jacobs, *Systems of Survival*, 6, 19, 21, 211.

27. For a critical view of this phenomenon, see Benjamin R. Barber, 'Jihad Vs. McWorld: How the planet is both falling apart and coming together—and what this means for democracy', *Atlantic Monthly* 269, 3 (Mar. 1992): 53–63. For more detailed accounts, see Paul Kennedy, *Preparing for the Twenty-First Century* (Toronto: HarperCollins, 1993); Matthew Horsman and Andrew Marshall, *After the Nation State: Citizens, Tribalism and the New World Disorder* (London: HarperCollins, 1994).

# Part VI

# Public Policy

## Introduction

Michael Howlett

Two perennial questions asked of political scientists are: Why do governments do what they do? and Can they do it better? Whether the topic is an old one like social security or a new one like the environment, AIDS, or reproductive technologies, attempting to answer these questions is a complex and challenging task.

Both questions concern public policy-making. Public policies result from the decisions made by governments. These can be decisions to preserve the status quo or to undertake a new course of action. These policies are not necessarily carefully designed and investigated, nor are they always carefully integrated with past and future policies. Most often, however, efforts in these directions are made. Some policies succeed and others fail to meet their objectives, though distinguishing between those that work and those that do not is not the simple task it might seem.

Answering the first question—why do governments do what they do?—raises many issues involved in determining the motivations of government actors. Are governments driven inexorably by long-term social forces such as economic growth, urbanization, and technological development? Or do they have the capacity to act independently of such forces, and to what extent? Are governments engaged in a more or less neutral, technical search for policy-relevant knowledge in the desire to create effective policies and programs? Or do they simply respond to the urgings and needs of powerful groups in society?

Answering the second question—can they do it better?—involves determining the criteria by which policies should be judged. While this is usually thought of as determining whether a government action has addressed the problem it was intended to resolve, such a matching of policy means and ends is not easy. For one thing, a single policy may well serve multiple goals or ends. Thus, welfare payments can provide food to the poor, can be part of a national child-care program, can help to generate social stability, and/or can be part of a crime prevention program. If a policy only addresses one or two of these ends can it be judged a success? And, even if this confusion of ends could be untangled, what constitutes a 'success'? Is it the efficient use of government funds, the elimination of the 'problem' the policy was expected to address, or the satisfaction of those who may have demanded the program, or those who receive its benefits, or those who pay its costs? How likely is it that a 'problem' can ever be entirely eliminated or a social group entirely 'satisfied'?

The study of public policy-making undertaken by political scientists must deal with these and other questions related to the means, motivations, and measures of government. The systematic study of the actions of government, their effects, and their formulation is one of the three key elements of what has been termed the 'second republic' of postwar political science.[1]

Analysis of government actions has, of course, always been a part of traditional political science. In the past, however, such studies were subordinated to examination of founding principles of governments and to studies of institutions such as public administration, law and the constitution, or political parties and legislatures. When contemporary political science moved away from these topics and towards a broader and more empirical orientation to the study of political phenomena during the 'behavioural revolution' of the 1950s and 1960s, the study of public policy as a distinct subfield in political science was born.

At the time, the founder of the 'policy science', Harold Lasswell, argued for the creation of a new kind of political inquiry. He suggested that it should have a distinctive methodology and be very different from traditional political inquiries in both subject matter and orientation. In a famous article setting out his aims for the new subfield, Lasswell argued that the policy sciences, unlike traditional political studies, would be multidisciplinary, relevant, and explicitly normative.[2] By this he meant that policy analysis would cover as many disciplines as required to understand a subject and would not be bound by the legal, historical, or philosophical studies or methods of traditional political science. The policy sciences would also attempt to go beyond understanding political phenomena by seeking to improve policy-making through practical advice to policy-makers. Analysts would explicitly recognize the values contained in their advice and integrate values into their analyses.

Some elements of this original vision have been maintained in the contemporary policy sciences, but some have not. Policy analyses still tend to be multidisciplinary and require analysts to be familiar with a broad range of insights, concepts, concerns, and methodologies in various fields. Although some analysts may have lost sight of the value-laden aspects of their inquiries and investigations, this element of Lasswell's formulations also remains largely intact. The criterion of relevance to policy-makers, however, has been somewhat tarnished. Many initial policies adopted on the basis of early investigation into policy processes and contents proved unsuccessful, and policy analysts and their work tended to become simply another tool in the arsenal of arguments used by political decision-makers to convince their rivals of the superiority of their own position.[3]

Partially as a result of these early difficulties, more attention has been focused over the past two decades on conceptualizing and comprehending the policy-making process than on offering advice to policy-makers. During this period theory development has clearly progressed. Studies have moved from the separate pursuit of analyses of causal factors, policy evaluation, and decision-making to more holistic visions of the entire policy process.[4]

## Early Studies of Policy-Making: Policy Determinants, Policy Evaluations, and Public Policy Decision-Making

From the 1950s through the 1970s, various authors using interpretative, statistical, and comparative methodologies grappled with understanding the factors that led governments to adopt policies. Analysts were concerned, for the most part, with understanding whether or not a finite set of variables could be considered to 'cause' public policies.

Comparative studies in the 1960s challenged earlier assumptions that policies were adopted due to exclusively political factors, such as the nature of the legislative system, the partisan composition of government, and the competence of political leadership. Researchers noted that countries with very different constellations of these factors still adopted similar policies. In Europe, for example, countries with different political institutions, parties, and personalities appeared to be converging on similar policy mixes as they established the basic structures of the welfare state. Policy analysts attributed primary causal status in explaining policy convergence and determining policy content to broad-based socio-economic variables that these countries had in common. These variables included the nature of the economy, the level of technological development, the age and educational attainments of the population, and the wealth of the society.[5]

Soon, however, this approach to explaining policy convergence was challenged by analysts arguing that political parties and institutions did matter.[6] Noting different nuances and arrangements in policies' development and delivery, most analysts by the 1970s had agreed that complex combinations of political, economic, and social factors were responsible for public policies emerging in different countries when they did.[7] They argued that factors such as the nature of political party systems, differences in political ideologies and cultures, and different types of political institutions and social structures affect the types of policies adopted by governments, even if those governments exhibit similar levels of economic development. While this finding reinforced the idea that policies were not simply determined by a single set of causal variables but were consciously constructed and crafted artefacts, it did little to shed light on the nature of the processes by which this construction took place.

In a second general area of investigation in the late 1970s and early 1980s, numerous case studies of particular policies were prepared in an effort to improve government services and program delivery. Many attempts were made to discern criteria for judging policy effectiveness, as well as policy success or failure.[8] Most of these studies found it difficult to establish objective criteria for policy evaluation. Some argued that policies should be assessed according to their cost, others according to their benefits, still others according to distinctive efficiency criteria, and many more according to whether the policy met some normative principle like justice, equity, or fairness.[9]

Like the studies that failed to establish a finite set of policy causes, evaluative studies concluded that policy success and failure were inherently political, conditioned by economic, social, and ideological concerns that varied by locale and policy type. Most analysts contended that policy success or failure, at least in democratic countries, could only be determined by the electoral process in which the public periodically passed judgement on the record of government activities. But while it removed some of the murk surrounding public policy evaluation, this conclusion, again, did little to advance systematic understanding of public policy-making processes.

A third area of concern over the same period was with the process of government decision-making. Studies focused on the information and methods used by decision-makers, and challenged earlier assumptions that decision-making was a 'rational' activity in which maximizing decisions were reached after detailed comparison of multiple policy alternatives. Borrowing heavily from decision-making studies of businesses and other complex organizations, most investigators concluded that the process of public policy decision-making occurred within a context characterized by 'bounded rationality'. That is, investigators considered the constraints placed on decision-makers—limited time, limited information, and an inability to predict the future—and argued that most decisions emerged from a piecemeal, incremental process featuring bargaining among decision-makers. Policy decisions, in other words, seldom resulted from minutely detailed evaluation of policy costs and benefits.[10]

All three of these early types of study depicted public policy-making as an inherently political process. However, the inability of any of these approaches to say much more than this led to new efforts in the 1970s and 1980s to produce accurate and meaningful generalizations concerning the types of processes found in contemporary government, the range of actors involved, and the impact of institutions, ideas, and other factors on policy development and change.

## Visions of the Policy Process: The Policy Cycle

Drawing on some early work of Lasswell,[11] in the mid-1970s and 1980s scholars contended that policy-making is best seen as a series of processes, or a *policy cycle*. In this cycle, the search for knowledge to resolve problems is tempered by the realities of the political processes through which those problems are identified and solutions implemented. In this model, policy-making is usually conceived as an instance of applied problem-solving. Like problem-solving—in which a problem must be recognized, solutions put forward, a decision on action taken, the decision implemented, and the results of the implementation monitored to see if the problem was, in fact, resolved—public policy-making was divided into a series of distinct stages. The policy cycle, it was argued, contained separate subprocesses in which problems emerged on government agendas (agenda-setting), solutions were formulated (policy formulation), a decision taken (decision-making), the decision implemented (policy implementation), and the results monitored or evaluated (policy evaluation).[12]

The policy cycle model was useful. It incorporated the disparate existing literature dealing with policy determinants, decision-making processes, and modes of policy evaluation, which were now seen as parts, or stages, of a larger policy process. In addition, it identified a clear research agenda examining the two stages of the process ignored by earlier studies: policy formulation and policy implementation. Throughout the 1980s and 1990s many investigations sought to fill in these gaps relating to why certain policy options and not others were considered by governments, and why governments tended to use similar sets of tools in implementing policies.

In regard to policy formulation, many studies over the past decade have underlined the role of subgovernments or *policy subsystems* in developing options for consideration when policy decisions are being made. These studies have identified collections of specific governmental and non-governmental actors, groups of individuals tied together by common knowledge of a policy area or by a common, shared interest who are crucial players in affecting the nature of the options considered in the policy-making process.[13]

In the area of policy implementation, a major thrust has been to study the range of techniques—governing tools or *policy instruments*—with which governments implement policy. These studies have noted that governments, regardless of the policy in question, only have certain types of tools at their disposal in implementing their decisions. These instruments rely on the government's ability to collect and disseminate information, to collect and spend money, to pass and enforce laws, and to employ people to perform various activities. A government can use information to attempt to influence non-governmental actors to follow its suggestions, it can spend money with the same end in mind, or it can force a non-governmental actor to follow its wishes through legislation. Finally, it can also employ its own personnel to undertake the task directly. Studies of policy instruments have not only clarified and classified these techniques, but have also investigated the rationales associated with the choice of each type of instrument.[14]

## Reaggregating the Policy Process: Policy Learning, Public Choice, and Discourse Analysis

Taken together, by the 1990s these studies of the different stages of the policy cycle provided a more complete picture of public policy-making than previously existed. But they did so at the expense of providing an integrated, holistic understanding of the entire policy process. That is, the policy process was broken down into a number of substages—agenda-setting, policy formulation, decision-making, policy implementation, and policy evaluation—and the various factors affecting each subprocess were detailed and investigated. How to put the entire cycle back together again is the subject of much current research,[15] and several different 'meta-theories' of how the various stages fit together now compete in the literature.[16]

One approach deals with *policy learning*, or viewing public policy-making as a learning process. The empirical foundations of this approach are typically experiences in previous phases of the policy cycle, or in the experiences of other countries or jurisdictions. This approach contends that governments not only mediate between powerful social actors but also attempt to 'puzzle' their way to successful policy outcomes.[17] Research undertaken from this perspective looks at both domestic and international sources of policy change, and has identified several common methods by which governments draw lessons from their own and others' experiences when considering policy choices.[18]

A second approach—*public choice*—looks at policy-making as a manifestation of the rational calculations of participants at every stage of the cycle.[19] This approach focuses on the nature of the rules and institutions that constrain policy actors and determine their conduct throughout the policy-making process. Research in this area has identified several means by which sets of rules and decision-making opportunities are 'nested' in such a way as to influence heavily the types of decisions policy actors make.[20]

A third approach focuses on the manner in which all stages of the policy process are affected by the nature of the discourses in which policy debate is conducted. This mode of *discourse analysis* investigates the sets of predominant ideas and beliefs that policy actors hold and links these to the specific manner in which agenda-setting, policy formulation, decision-making, policy implementation, and policy evaluation occur.[21]

The selections below help to illustrate the original aims and ambitions of the policy sciences and the types of questions about policy processes and policy actors that investigators have pursued in Canada and elsewhere.

In the first reading, University of Ottawa political scientist Jeanne Laux examines the circumstances surrounding the use of a particular policy instrument—privatization—in Canada. Focusing on the development of this instrument under the federal Mulroney administration of the late 1980s, Laux concludes that ideology was a significant factor leading the government to use this instrument. Significantly, however, she also finds evidence that the government learned from its earlier experiences and from those of other countries in modifying its privatization program during its two terms in office.

In the second reading, Queen's University political studies professor Keith Banting examines the federal Chrétien government's failed attempt to systematically reform Canada's social security system. Banting's analysis highlights the complexity of policy subsystems in a federal state and acknowledges how the social security subsystem has expanded as more knowledgeable and activist citizens demand roles in policy formulation. Coupled with limitations on government's ability to fund new programs, Banting argues, the expansion of policy subsystems can cause major failures in government efforts to change or alter public policy.

## Notes

1. Theodore Lowi, 'The State in Political Science: How We Become What We Study', *American Political Science Review* 86, 1 (1992): 1–7.
2. Harold D. Lasswell, 'The Policy Orientation', in D. Lerner and H.D. Lasswell, eds, *The Policy Sciences* (Stanford, Calif.: Stanford University Press, 1951).

3. Carol Weiss, *Using Social Research in Public Policy Making* (Lexington, Mass.: Heath, 1977).

4. See Peter DeLeon, 'Trends in Policy Science Research: Determinants and Developments', *European Journal of Political Research* 14 (1986): 3–22; Aaron B. Wildavsky, *Speaking Truth to Power: The Art and Craft of Policy Analysis* (Boston: Little, Brown, 1979).

5. Good examples of this first approach are Thomas R. Dye, *Politics, Economics, and the Public: Policy Outcomes in the American States* (Chicago: Rand McNally, 1966); Harold L. Wilensky, *The Welfare State and Equality: Structural and Ideological Roots of Public Expenditures* (Berkeley: University of California Press, 1975).

6. On this point, see Frank Castles and Robert D. McKinlay, 'Does Politics Matter: An Analysis of the Public Welfare Commitment in Advanced Democratic States', *European Journal of Political Research* 7 (1979): 169–86; Douglas A. Hibbs, 'Political Parties and Macro-economic Policy', *American Political Science Review* 71 (Dec. 1977): 1467–87; Anthony King, 'Ideas, Institutions and the Policies of Governments: A Comparative Analysis: Part II', *British Journal of Political Science* 3 (Oct. 1973): 409–23.

7. For overviews of these syntheses see Richard I. Hofferbert, *The Study of Public Policy* (New York: Bobbs Merrill, 1974); Richard Simeon, 'Studying Public Policy', *Canadian Journal of Political Science* 9, 4 (1976): 548–80.

8. See Helen M. Ingram and Dean E. Mann, *Why Policies Succeed or Fail* (Beverly Hills, Calif.: Sage, 1980); Donna H. Kerr, 'The Logic of "Policy" and Successful Policies', *Policy Sciences* 7 (1976): 351–63; James S. Larson, *Why Government Programs Fail* (New York: Praeger, 1980).

9. See Dennis J. Palumbo, *The Politics of Policy Evaluation* (Beverly Hills, Calif.: Sage, 1987).

10. Often cited articles setting out this argument are Charles Lindblom, 'The Science of Muddling Through', *Public Administration Review* 19, 2 (1959): 79–88; Charles Lindblom, 'Still Muddling, Not Yet Through', *Public Administration Review* 39 (1979): 517–29; Herbert Simon, 'A Behavioural Model of Rational Choice', *Quarterly Journal of Economics* (Feb. 1955): 99–118; Herbert Simon, *Administrative Behavior* (New York: Free Press, 1957).

11. Harold D. Lasswell, *The Decision Process: Seven Categories of Functional Analysis* (College Park: University of Maryland Press, 1956).

12. See James E. Anderson, *Public Policy-Making* (New York: Robert E. Krieger, 1978); Charles O. Jones, *An Introduction to the Study of Public Policy*, 3rd edn (Monterey, Calif.: Brooks/Cole, 1984).

13. See, for example, Michael M. Atkinson and William D. Coleman, 'Policy Networks, Policy Communities and the Problems of Governance', *Governance* 5, 2 (1992): 154–80; Franz Van Waarden, 'Dimensions and Types of Policy Networks', *European Journal of Political Research* 21 (1992): 29–52; Maurice Wright, 'Policy Community, Policy Network and Comparative Industrial Policies', *Political Studies* 36 (1988): 593–612.

14. On the tools approach, see G. Bruce Doern and Richard W. Phidd, *Canadian Public Policy: Ideas, Structure, Process* (Toronto: Nelson, 1988); Christopher Hood, *The Tools of Government* (Chatham, NJ.: Chatham House Publishers, 1986); Michael Howlett, 'Policy Instruments, Policy Styles, and Policy Implementation: National Approaches to Theories of Instrument Choice', *Policy Studies Journal* 19, 2 (1991): 1–21; Lester M. Salamon, ed., *Beyond Privatization: The Tools of Government Action* (Washington: Urban Institute, 1989).

15. See Paul A. Sabatier, 'Toward Better Theories of the Policy Process', *PS: Political Science and Politics* (June 1991): 144–56.

16. See Laurent Dobuzinskis, Michael Howlett, and David Laycock, eds, *Policy Studies in Canada: The State of the Art* (Toronto: University of Toronto Press, 1996); William N. Dunn and Rita Mae Kelly, *Advances in Policy Studies Since 1950* (London: Transaction Publishers,

1992).

17. On the learning approach, see Colin Bennett and Michael Howlett, 'The Lessons of Learning: Reconciling Theories of Policy Learning and Policy Change', *Policy Sciences* 25, 3 (1992): 275–94; David Dolowitz and David Marsh, 'Who Learns What From Whom: A Review of the Policy Transfer Literature', *Political Studies* 44 (1996): 343–57.

18. See Peter M. Haas, 'Introduction: Epistemic Communities and International Policy Coordination', *International Organization* 46, 1 (1992): 1–36; Peter A. Hall, 'Policy Paradigms, Experts, and the State: The Case of Macroeconomic Policy-Making in Britain', in S. Brooks and A.-G. Gagnon, eds, *Social Scientists, Policy, and the State* (New York: Praeger, 1990); Richard Rose, 'What is Lesson-Drawing?', *Journal of Public Policy* 11, 1 (1991): 3–30.

19. Good introductions to this approach are Iain McLean, *Public Choice: An Introduction* (London: Basil Blackwell, 1989); Dennis C. Mueller, *Public Choice II* (Cambridge: Cambridge University Press, 1989).

20. See James G. March and Johan P. Olsen, 'The New Institutionalism: Organizational Factors in Political Life', *American Political Science Review* 78, 3 (1984): 734–49; Mark Sproule-Jones, 'Multiple Rules and the "Nesting" of Public Policies', *Journal of Theoretical Politics* 1, 4 (1989): 459–77.

21. See Frank Fischer and John Forester, eds, *The Argumentative Turn in Policy Analysis and Planning* (Durham, NC: Duke University Press, 1993); Marie Danziger, 'Policy Analysis Postmodernized: Some Political and Pedagogical Ramifications', *Policy Studies Journal* 23, 3 (1995): 435–51.

## Study Questions for the Readings

1. What is 'privatization'? What has been the Canadian record of use of this policy instrument since 1980?

2. Did politicians in Canada learn from their own and other countries' experiences with privatization? If so, what lessons did they learn, from whom, and with what effect?

3. In her article Laux suggests that 'when ideology confronts economic and political reality, policy must adapt.' What does she mean by this statement and how does it apply to the Canadian experience with privatization?

4. Banting describes the Chrétien government's 1994 social policy review as 'caught in the tensions existing among three separate agendas: the reform of social policy, the reduction of the federal deficit, and the accommodation of Quebec within Canada.' Discuss how the outcome of the review illustrates the results of these agenda dynamics.

5. Who were the principal actors involved in the social policy review? What positions did they take and why? Which, if any, played a major role in scuttling the federal government proposals?

6. What lessons, if any, can Canadian governments draw from the failure of the review process?

# How Private Is Privatization?

Jeanne Kirk Laux

## Introduction

> The privatization program is a symbol of this government's confidence in the private sector. (Canada, Office of the Minister of State [Privatization], 1987c)

Thus spoke the Minister of State for Privatization as the Conservative government in Canada moved beyond rhetoric to implement its program. By 1991, when the special Office of Privatization and Regulatory Affairs was disbanded, the program had radically redefined the public sector in Canada. Eight wholly owned Crown corporations and other government investments representing book value assets of over $9 billion had been sold, legislation authorizing the sale of others (including oil giant Petro-Canada) passed, and various inactive Crown companies wound up.[1] The positive impact of privatization is now taken for granted in Ottawa and celebrated in the past tense. All of the 'Prosperity Initiative' papers, for example, highlight privatization alongside tax reform, deregulation, and the Free Trade agreement as testimony to the Conservatives' success in creating an environment favourable to growth and global competitiveness (Canada, Industry, Science and Technology, 1991: 9; Canada, Prosperity Initiative, 1991: 4). Harvard business economist Michael Porter (1991: 60) simply repeats the official line in his report commissioned by the Business Council on National Issues and the government of Canada: 'Privatization of a significant number of Crown

From *Canadian Public Policy/Analyse de Politiques* 29, 4 (1993): 398–411. Published by permission of Canadian Public Policy/Analyse de Politiques.

Corporations previously active in commercial markets has also improved the competitive environment for firms in Canada.' No surprise, then, that Prime Minister Mulroney included 'privatizations' in his shortlist of 'tough decisions strengthening Canada's competitive position' cited in his farewell address (24 Feb. 1993).

Looking closely at the implementation, rather than the idealization, of privatization, it becomes clear that when ideology confronts economic and political reality, policy must adapt. In the ideal world as conjured up by neoclassical economics and political rhetoric, the market is a place without barriers to entry or to exit and information is perfect. Of course, no one has illusions that the world conforms to this image, but more important, this paper contends, governments do not in fact want to see that image actualized. After all, in the real world of mixed economy and electoral politics, who produces what and where does matter. Certainly the World Bank, which once unabashedly promoted privatization in the Third World, had to chasten its counsel. The Bank's experience in the 1980s showed that the divestiture process is inescapably political—governments typically engage in tacit collusion with newly privatized firms to offer special benefits or conversely oblige new owners to accept restrictions as a condition of sale.[2] Privatization became 'potentially useful' if regarded as just 'one part of a broader effort to increase market forces' (Shirley, 1988: 35). Likewise in Europe, where a wide range of privatization programs was introduced during the 1980s, the claims of market and state oft-times clashed. Some of these programs were highly ideological (Britain, France), others distinctly pragmatic (Italy, Spain), but in all instances comparative case studies reveal that 'state involvement in the affairs of privatised companies—before, during and after their sale' is habitual (Vickers and Wright, 1988: 27).

This paper will show how Canada's experience with privatization conforms to the broader international experience. The federal Conservative government—first in 1979 and then in 1985—presented privatization as part of a grand ideology which also served an admixture of pragmatic aims such as deficit reduction. Faced with the complexities of the mixed economy in Canada and the evolving concerns of elected politicians, Ottawa would first tolerate and then legislate deviations from the formal norms of a market economy. It would be a mere truism to argue that politicians accomplish less than they claim or that practice and principles diverge. The argument advanced here instead contends that government purposefully adapted policy in order to move its privatization agenda forward. Four types of policy adaptation (which are detailed below) appear to have been necessary in order to make divestiture of Crown corporations a feasible proposition for politicians in Canada. Taken together, these policy adaptations raise the question—just how private is privatization? Not all that private it seems! The federal government, besides maintaining a substantial ownership role and transferring some Crown assets to other levels of government, also facilitated privatization by restricting or protecting the newly privatized.

Section I gives a quick review of the official purposes and actual sales of Crown corporations and other government commercial holdings to remind readers of the scale of privatization and, at the same time, of the continuing role of government as investor. Sections II–V retrace the four principal ways in which the federal government has adapted grand policy to necessity. In the early phase of privatization (1984–7) Ottawa sought out scarce buyers by (1) accepting government purchasers and (2) soliciting bids from market-dominant firms rather than encouraging new competitors. In its next phase of privatization

(1988–92), the Conservative government proved willing (3) to place restrictions on investors to reassure Canadians that foreign takeover was precluded and (4) to impose conditions on managerial freedom to appease concerned stakeholders. Each mode of policy adaptation will be illustrated by reference to specify company cases. These mini-analyses lead to the Conclusion, where it is argued that in remixing the mixed economy through sales of commercial Crown corporations, even a Conservative government has not been so rash as to rely on market discipline alone.

## I Privatization

### The Policy; The Results

From its inception, privatization policy in Canada has been ideologically charged. In 1979 Joe Clark's short-lived Conservative government found time to set up a Privatization Secretariat in order, it was said, to reverse 40 years of excess concentration of power in the hands of the state.[3] Valuations of Crown companies were undertaken and the sale of Petro-Canada proposed. With the defeat of the government in the House this agenda had to be deferred, but was not forgotten. The new party leader, Brian Mulroney, instituted a task force on the future of Crown corporations in 1983. Its report took privatization to be axiomatic and considered the only policy problem to be one of bringing public opinion around.[4] Privatization hit the headlines immediately after the 1984 elections when Sinclair Stevens, the Minister of Industry, announced his intent to sell five companies and proclaimed that 'the discipline and vitality of the marketplace will replace the often suffocating effect of government ownership'.[5] Stevens's somewhat maverick approach to privatizing did not, however, suit the needs of a new government looking to win acceptability from the business community for a wide-gauge policy of economic renewal (Aucoin, 1988; Deblock, 1988).

Only with the 1985 budget speech and the creation of a ministerial task force does privatization become an integral part of Conservative government policy (Canada, Dept. of Finance, 1985). By summer 1986 machinery of government was established to give it an orderly process and the first Minister of State for Privatization (and Regulatory Affairs), Barbara McDougall, publicized the policy objectives which would be maintained by the subsequent two ministers. As set out by the government (Canada, Office of the Minister of State [Privatization], 1987a), the official purposes of privatization are to:

1. Adapt policy instruments to new economic realities—if Crown corporations initially had valid objectives in the Canadian context, today taxation, regulation, etc. may meet these needs.
2. Redirect spending—given fiscal constraints, scarce government funds are needed for other programs while some Crown companies could better finance expansion through private investors.
3. Respond to business objections—unfair competition from subsidized public enterprises contravenes free market rules.
4. Improve company performance—efficiency and service to the customer are better ensured by private ownership.
5. Improve management—rapid, flexible decision-making needed to adapt to changing markets and technologies requires the risk of market failure.

In addition, policy statements after 1988 introduce the notion of popular capitalism, i.e., 'new opportunities for Canadians' to invest, and underscore the need for improved competitiveness in order to meet the challenge of a 'global economy' (Canada, Office of Privatization and Regulatory Affairs, 1989).

And what of the results? Canada's privatization program, as carried out by the Mulroney

government, clearly represents a significant withdrawal of the state from production as a direct producer of goods and services for sale in the marketplace. Comparison of current government holdings with the situation just prior to the election of the Tories in 1984 supports this assertion. According to the official report on public-sector enterprises submitted by the President of the Treasury Board, the federal government then owned 67 parent Crown corporations which in turn had 128 wholly owned subsidiaries. Their combined assets were valued at $50 billion (Canada, President of the Treasury Board, 1985). The truly commercial corporations among them —those which produced goods or services for sale in the market and were intended to be self-financing—played a substantial economic role.[6] Canada's 500 major industrial companies, as listed in the *Financial Post 500* at that time, included 32 wholly owned Crown corporations of which 19 belonged to the federal government (and another 22 companies wherein one or another level of government held at least 10 per cent of the shares). In addition to its direct ownership, the federal government also held a vast portfolio of more than 100 companies and affiliates with a total asset value of $8 billion through its 47 per cent controlling interest in the Canada Development Corporation.

As the Mulroney government's second term drew towards a close, the government's ownership position in commercial enterprises was much reduced. Again according to the President of the Treasury Board, Ottawa now owns outright 58 Crown corporations, with seven of these in the process of being wound up or sold. They represent $80 billion in assets, or closer to $60 billion in constant 1984 dollars. These parent corporations now control 118 wholly owned subsidiaries (Canada, President of the Treasury Board, 1991). The sale of Air Canada and of shares in Petro-Canada in particular dramatically changed the figures. The national petroleum company alone had more than 50 wholly owned subsidiaries, 6,000 employees, and assets worth over $4 billion. By divesting its interest in the Canada Development Corporation (CDC) and privatizing corporations like Canadair, Teleglobe, or Canadian Arsenals the government removed itself as a competitor in sectors ranging from biotechnology, aerospace, and telecommunications to munitions manufacture. Today the *Financial Post 500* (1992) shows 27 companies wholly owned by government, but only eight of them are federal Crown corporations while just three out of the other 16 companies with significant government investment are held at the federal level.

The scale of privatization carried out since 1984 is impressive, but not quite so impressive as government information kits and official speeches would have the public believe. Political rhetoric is by nature inflationary. In his 1991 Budget Speech, the Finance Minister touted the privatization of 'more than 20 Crown corporations'. In truth just eight commercial corporations wholly owned in 1984 had by then been fully divested. Meanwhile a half dozen new Crown corporations were created—for example, when four national museums (e.g., National Gallery of Canada) were each granted Crown corporation status. Three mixed private-public enterprises, wherein the government had the largest shareholding, were also fully divested.

The Finance Minister's higher figure reflects not more sales of parent corporations, but a re-shuffling of corporate holdings. Some Crown corporations had to be invented in order to be privatized. This was the case for two divisions of the Atomic Energy of Canada Ltd (AECL) which were split off to become separate companies (Nordion and Theratonics), held by the Canadian Development Investment Corporation, and then put up for sale. Legal technicalities have made other Crown corporations disappear despite continued majority government ownership. Thus Petro-Canada's 1992 sale of less than 30 per cent of its shares to the public removed the company from the official Public Accounts listing simply because government is no longer the sole shareholder. The government's list of privatized companies also included small Crown corporations which were dissolved, rather than being transferred to private ownership. It also counts the sales of subsidiaries, despite the fact that acquiring or selling subsidiaries is a normal course of business operations for Crown corporations.[7]

Even after political rhetoric is deflated, the results of privatization are considerable. The commercial public sector—defined here as Crown corporations listed on Schedule III of the Financial Administration Act (FAA), their subsidiaries, and mixed enterprises wherein the federal government has a substantial ownership position—appears dramatically circumscribed following nearly a decade of privatization.[8] In this sense, the program must be judged a success. The purpose of our analysis in the coming sections is to consider the means used to attain these sales which, we argue, involve four forms of policy adaptation intended to avoid the full implications of market discipline. Rather than holding to market rules of free entry and exit, or actively looking to maximize competition and managerial discretion, the Canadian government proved ready to tolerate deviations from these norms and indeed to place legal restrictions on private-sector actors. Only such adaptive policy-making could satisfy the government's evolving political imperatives, which included the need to be seen to be privatizing; to remove corporations from the government accounts; and to attract public support for large-scale share offerings.

## II Privatizing to the Public Sector

In the early phase of a privatization program, governments will offload public assets where they may. For centre-right governments like the Conservative government in Canada, which wave the flag of free market principles, there is an urgency to demonstrate to the business and financial community their capacity to reduce public-sector holdings. For governments of every ideological stripe in a period of fiscal restraint, characteristic of the 1980s, there is an anxiety about the financial and bureaucratic burden of overseeing public enterprises. May the seller beware! During the Mulroney government's first term (1984–8) the 'privatization' of several Crown corporations actually increased the corporate holdings of other governments rather than bolstering private ownership. These lateral transfers from government to government took place directly in two cases (Northern Canada Power Commission [NCPC]; Eldorado Nuclear Limited [ENL]), and indirectly in another case (Teleglobe).

*Northern Canada Power Commission*: In the somewhat chaotic days just after the 1984 election, before the Conservatives had put in place machinery of government for privatization, individual ministers tended to speak out and cabinet then scrambled to find a policy cover for their initiatives. Thus David Crombie, Minister of Indian and Northern Affairs, generously offered to devolve the authority for electrical power transmission in the Yukon and Northwest Territories from federal to territorial governments by 'giving' them the Crown corporation (NCPC). Protracted negotiations followed over the next two years concerning, for example, demands by the NWT government that Ottawa convert the corporation's $125 million debt to equity. Finally, in 1987 (Yukon) and 1988 (NWT) the former federal Crown corporation's assets were sold rather than given away to be reborn as twin territorial government-owned corporations![9]

Meanwhile Sinclair Stevens, Minister of Industry, had announced the sale of all commercial Crown corporations held by the Canadian Development Investment Corporation (CDIC) under his tutelage. Cabinet fell into line and agreed to launch the bidding process through the intermediary of the CDIC to expedite sales. Thanks to its Crown corporation status, CDIC had discretionary use of 'off budget' funds to engage lawyers and investment firms to undertake a quick privatization without prior parlia-

mentary approval. New directors brought in from private-sector firms put a special divestiture committee in place. Private bidders were indeed found for de Havilland Aircraft, Canadair, and eventually Teleglobe, but in the case of Eldorado Nuclear Ltd this fast-track privatization process broke down.

*Eldorado Nuclear Limited*, one of Canada's more venerable Crown corporations, created by C.D. Howe to control production and refining of strategic resources in the nuclear era, had become North America's largest uranium producer and one of only five uranium processing companies in the non-Communist world. Yet with uranium prices falling over the 1980s and the worldwide nuclear reactor industry stagnating, the CDIC divestiture committee proved unable to find a private-sector buyer. How then to unburden the new Conservative government of responsibility for a company which was showing losses and had accumulated long-term debt nearly to its statutory ceiling of $600 million? Rather than back away from its promised divestment, the government found a creative solution to taking ENL off the official books as a Crown corporation. CDIC brought in a private-sector chairman, previously employed by mining multinational Falconbridge Ltd, to head ENL and negotiate a deal with the Saskatchewan government, then held by Grant Devine, a dedicated privateer.

When, in 1988, the Conservative government in Ottawa announced ENL's 'privatization', in truth a government-to-government merger had taken place. The provincial Crown corporation, Saskatchewan Mining Development Corporation (SMDC), and ENL combined to form a new supercompany, Cameco, controlling half of Canada's uranium production and all of its refining. Cameco's articles of incorporation allowed for its complete privatization at any time, but four years later the former Crown corporation was still 100 per cent state-owned. The federal government, however, was absolved of its accountability. With a provincial government holding company as the majority owner (61.5 per cent), Cameco became an associate (less than 50 per cent ownership) of Ottawa's holding company CDIC. To encourage private investors, the two governments absorbed the predecessor companies' debts in the form of promissory notes to be repaid from Cameco's eventual bond or share issues. Eventually, an initial share offering to the public was made in 1991, but Cameco today remains a corporation with substantial government ownership.[10]

*Teleglobe Canada* provides an example of Ottawa's willingness to allow indirect government ownership of an ostensibly privatized Crown corporation.[11] In its rush to sell this profitable overseas telecommunications company, the federal government overlooked many complex policy implications of privatizing a monopoly in a regulated industry. The initial guidelines for the bidding process generated such an interdepartmental and business-government tangle that bidding had to start over again in 1986.[12] Finally, after pressure from Finance to finalize a sale before the 1987 budget speech (deficit numbers could be improved by that extra half-million dollars net to the consolidated revenue fund), a surprise bidder was selected. The winner, Memotec Data, a relatively small Montreal data-processing company, had to leverage its buy-out of the Crown corporation. Memotec, as it turned out, was the venture capital vehicle for a consortium of companies, many of which were themselves state-owned: federal Crown corporations Air Canada (now privatized), Canadian National Railways (CN), and Canadian Broadcasting Corporation (CBC); provincial Crown corporations Ontario Hydro, the Caisse de dépôt, and the Société générale de financement (SGF)—all acting through their pension funds.[13]

These examples show one way in which the new Conservative government, committed to reducing the economic role of the state in Canada, adapted policy to necessity—here the need to be seen to privatize—as caveat vendor: it shifted assets from Crown to Crown.[14] In other cases, as

Section III will demonstrate, this sales imperative inspired Ottawa to adapt policy in another way. After seeking and finding interested private-sector buyers, the government selected the dominant market players, ignoring the negative impact on competition within Canada.

## III Concentration not Competition

The privatization of commercial Crown corporations in Canada has typically taken place by way of asset sales. Ottawa ventured into the more complex world of public share offerings only where mixed share ownership existed already (CDC, Fisheries Products International) or where the high public visibility of a Crown company made it politically correct (Air Canada, Petro-Canada). Otherwise, it was deemed easier to unload Crown companies in competitive industries by appealing to established companies which had a strong incentive to invest and the management experience to make privatization work. As in Britain before, this meant that government was willing to adapt its policy favouring market competition to attract an appropriate buyer. Canada's Minister of State for Privatization continued to emphasize that 'privatization promotes market competition and the more efficient allocation of resources' (Canada, Office of the Minister of State [Privatization], 1987b). However, rather than creating new entrants to stimulate competition in a given product market, most sales have constituted privatization-by-merger and served to reinforce the market share of already dominant companies.

The initial sale of de Havilland Aircraft of Canada Ltd provides a striking example of Ottawa's willingness to tolerate market concentration if needed to clinch a sale. Canada's market share for the regional commuter aircraft (then 20 per cent of world sales) was turned over to the world's largest aircraft manufacturer, the Boeing Company (Seattle), as the winning bidder for de Havilland Aircraft of Canada Ltd. Other instances may be cited—such as selling the federal Crown corporation Canadian Arsenals to the SNC Group, already a producer of small calibre arms, and thereby increasing concentration in the munitions industry and bolstering the productive assets of Canada's second largest engineering firm.[15] Our attention will focus on three market-dominant private enterprises in Canada to illustrate how Ottawa permitted their position to be reinforced thanks to the privatization program: Bombardier, Bell Canada Enterprises (BCE), and Canadian Pacific Ltd (CP).

*Bombardier*: Privatization has enabled Bombardier, Canada's 32nd ranking industrial company, to integrate horizontally from mass transit and recreational vehicles (snowmobiles) to aircraft. This Quebec-based transportation equipment manufacturer first bought out the federal aircraft company Canadair in 1986 and then, when Boeing decided to resell former Crown company de Havilland in 1991, Bombardier came in as the new majority owner (having meanwhile purchased Shorts, another regional aircraft competitor, from the British government). Privatization by provincial governments in Canada has further enhanced Bombardier's competitive position as it bought UTDC, the innovative mass transit company, from the Ontario government in 1991 as part of a complex salvage deal after Quebec's engineering firm Lavalin, the original UTDC buyer, collapsed. Bombardier's move up the *Financial Post 500* corporate ranking from 69th position (1984) to 32nd position (1992) is in no small measure attributable to the increased revenues achieved by acquiring government-owned companies rather than by expanding sales of products developed in the private sector.[16]

*Canadian Pacific Ltd* (CP) and *Bell Canada Enterprises* (BCE) have each added to their market power thanks to the government's eagerness to encourage the Crown corporation, Canadian National Railways (CN), to divest itself of several of its subsidiaries. Canadian National's management decided to rationalize its operations by selling off five holdings in trucking, hotels, and telecommunications in order to reduce debt and re-centre operations on the core railway business. The Mulroney government chose to publicize such sales (which require only an *ex post facto* sanction by Order in Council) as indicators of successful privatization policy. The main impact of CN's divestment program has been to confirm the market dominance of two companies now ranked first (BCE) and fifth (CP) by the *Financial Post 500*.

CP seized the opportunity presented by CN's divestment program and paid out $235 million to take over CN's 50 per cent share of their joint venture—CNCP Telecommunications, which had been formed in 1980 to rationalize telex services. CP's subsidiary Canadian Pacific Hotels then bought out its competitor, CN Hotels. When CN divested two regional telecommunications subsidiaries in the Yukon and in Newfoundland, BCE extended its reach as Canada's leading telecommunications company. BCE bought out Northwestel (serving the NWT) from CN for $208 million and indirectly gained control of Terra Nova telecommunications (serving the Maritimes) because it has a 55 per cent controlling share of NewTel Enterprises, the holding company for the direct buyer, Newfoundland Telephone Company Ltd.[17]

The first two sections of our paper make it clear that the Conservative government officially ignored the fact that many purchasers of corporate assets were ill-placed to increase competition either because they were themselves government companies or because they were dominant private-sector players looking to consolidate their market share through further acquisitions. During its first term in office, the government was more concerned with its immediate need to find a buyer than with the impact of the sales on market structures. Why is this? Not connivance, but the political need to appear credible in the pages of the business press appears to have pushed these early sales forward. Regardless of purchaser, any divestment contributed to redefining the traditional policy paradigm which had validated Crown corporations as necessary instruments of policy. More pragmatically, even the transfer of Crown assets to another level of government did remove them from the federal government's accounts.

As privatization moved forward and indeed was moved to the centre of the government's political agenda leading up to the 1988 elections, cabinet ministers confronted new risks especially in the case of public share offerings. Here government may propose, but thereafter the financial market will dispose. To win public acceptance beyond the business community for sales of such flagship companies as Air Canada, the Conservative government adapted policy in another way. Restrictions were imposed to determine who could purchase shares in former Crown corporations and thereby acquire such ownership rights as voting power.

## IV Political Barriers to Entry

A central tenet of economic liberalism—that anyone is free to enter the market—may have awkward political consequences. Rather than remain indifferent to the risks of privatization, Ottawa has systematically imposed its own a priori definition of just which investors constitute 'the private sector'. The main pariah proves to be the foreign investor—somewhat surprising for a Conservative government which in other policies moved from regulating to promoting foreign investment. Part of the explanation may be found in the controversy surrounding the first significant sale of a Crown corporation: de Havilland Aircraft of Canada Ltd. Vociferous opposition greeted the government's 1985 announcement that this Ontario company, acquired by government in 1976 precisely to maintain a Canadian presence in a research- and export-intensive industry, would be sold to a US multinational—Boeing. The sale went through in 1986, but only after many weeks of hearings before a House of Commons committee and unwanted press headlines. Thereafter, the government pre-empted potential opposition by

restricting foreign ownership and control of former Crown corporations.

The federal government has applied its restrictions on foreign ownership of former Crown corporations in various ways. In an asset sale, restrictions are set out in the Letter of Intent co-signed with the buyer and then formalized in the Acquisition Agreement or in a Memorandum of Understanding. For public share issues, the government indicates in the Prospectus all restrictions on shareholding and these are then enshrined in the privatization legislation and/or the Articles of Association under companies law. In this way, while implementing its privatization program, the state in Canada acts as arbiter in financial markets to (i) preordain who may bid for assets or apply to purchase shares, (ii) set a ceiling on overall foreign ownership for all time, (iii) prohibit block voting by foreign interests.

The legislation authorizing the sale of Air Canada offers an example of government-imposed restrictions on corporate ownership. It stipulates that no individual shall hold more than 10 per cent of the common shares while foreign investors are further restricted to a collective 25 per cent interest: 'The articles of continuance of the Corporation shall contain provisions imposing constraints on the issue, transfer and ownership, including joint ownership, of voting shares of the Corporation to prevent non-residents from holding, beneficially owning or controlling, directly or indirectly, otherwise than by way of security only, in the aggregate, voting shares to which are attached more than twenty-five per cent of the votes that may ordinarily be cast to elect directors of the Corporation'.[18] In the mining industry, the federal government imposed stricter conditions. When putting together the deal to merge Eldorado Nuclear Ltd and the Saskatchewan government's Crown corporation with a view to eventual privatization, Ottawa decided to limit non-residents to owning 5 per cent of shares individually (as compared to Canadians, who may hold up to 25 per cent) and 20 per cent in the aggregate. The same 20 per cent ceiling was set for foreign ownership in Teleglobe.[19]

Just who are these non-residents whom the government would exclude from buying shares in otherwise open financial markets? The privatization legislation is always very specific on this matter. When, for example, Ottawa reorganized Atomic Energy of Canada Ltd to permit the sale of two divisions as separate corporations (Nordion and Theratronics), the legislation specified that '"non-resident" means: (a) an individual, other than a Canadian citizen, who is not ordinarily resident in Canada, (b) a corporation incorporated, formed or otherwise organized outside Canada, (c) a foreign government or an agency thereof, (d) a corporation controlled by non-residents as defined in any of paragraphs (a) to (c), (e) a trust (i) established by a non-resident (ii) in which non-residents have more than fifty per cent of the beneficial interest, or (f) a corporation that is controlled by a trust described in paragraph (e).'[20] In an effort to ensure that these barriers to entry by non-residents be respected even after the privatization firms enter the realm of company law, the Mulroney government set out prohibitions. The legislation governing Petro-Canada's privatization is typical in specifying that 'Petro-Canada and its shareholders and directors shall not (a) make any articles or by-laws inconsistent with the Act or the provisions included in its articles of amendment pursuant to subsection [Here reference is made to the section restricting ownership].'[21]

## V Conditional Freedom

Once the Conservative government gained confidence from its initial sales and created a new cabinet committee and Minister of State for Privatization, the sale of Crown corporations began to be celebrated as beneficial to all Canadians. Ottawa imitated the logic of 'popular capitalism' tried in Britain and, with the 1987 sale of Fisheries Products International, initiated a series of divestments through public share issues. In the lead up

to re-election, the government issued a prospectus and financed massive publicity to sell the first tranche of Air Canada shares, allowing the Conservatives to proclaim that: 'privatization encourages individual Canadians to take part in the ownership of companies through equity investments' (Canada, Office of the Minister of State [Privatization], 1987a). In truth, widely held share ownership results in management-run companies. Thus, despite the official claim that 'entrepreneurship is fostered with the withdrawal of political and bureaucratic impediments' (Canada, Office of the Minister of State, 1987a), politicians could not afford to let the market decide. In order to appeal to new investors, all the while ducking the political flak that could come from disgruntled stakeholders of public enterprises, Ottawa placed conditions on management freedom.[22]

The composition of the Board of Directors, or just who among the owners will have the right to make strategic decisions, is one area where the government has interfered with normal shareholders' rights in the private sector. For example, upon selling its majority shareholding in Fisheries Products International, where the Newfoundland government was a co-owner, Ottawa went along with a very narrow definition of who could exercise control. The Articles of Association stipulate that a majority of the 15 members of the Board of Directors must not only be Canadian but must live in the province of Newfoundland.[23] In the case of Teleglobe, which became a publicly traded company after its initial privatization through a bidding process, the federal government retained a broad power to override the board of directors by giving cabinet the right to issue 'a directive to the new corporation with respect to any matter relating to the national security, the foreign policy or the international telecommunications policy of Canada'.[24] Other Western governments have formalized their right to issue directives to former state-owned enterprises. In both France and Britain government holds a special share in some privatized companies (the 'action spécifique' and the 'golden share') to be voted only in specified conditions where the national interest (e.g., defence, energy security, treaty commitments) is affected (Heald, 1985; Bauer, 1988).

Strictures on relocation are another common way by which the Canadian federal government has narrowed managers' decision-making latitude for privatized Crown corporations. While cabinet ministers boasted that the government had decided to allow Air Canada the freedom it needs to grow, the actual legislation governing privatization made that freedom conditional. After placing the company under the Canada Business Corporations Act (CBCA), the government put mandatory provisions in its articles of continuance: '(d) provisions requiring the corporation to maintain operational and overhaul centres in the City of Winnipeg, the Montreal Urban Community and the City of Mississauga; and (e) provisions specifying that the head office of the Corporation is to be situated in the Montreal Urban Community.'[25] Likewise Petro-Canada after privatization would be obliged to keep its head office in Calgary while part of the pay-off to Saskatchewan for the merger with Eldorado Nuclear was privatization legislation maintaining the new company's headquarters in that province.[26] Even in cases where the state-owned enterprise already operated under the CBCA and was sold to a single corporate bidder, government negotiators were able to set similar conditions on corporate freedom. Thus the sale of Canadair involved a Letter of Intent which explained the terms of the Acquisition Agreement wherein the private enterprise buyer, Bombardier, agreed that 'the existing research and development activities will remain in the Province of Quebec.'[27]

## Conclusion

Never a mere necessity, always part of strategy, privatization is celebrated in neo-conservative doctrine for correcting the imbalance between public and private sectors. The Conservative government in Ottawa consistently reiterated the central tenet of its privatization program: 'Our government is committed to building a more competitive and market-oriented economy' (Canada, Office of Privatization, 1989). Politicians, however, cannot afford to be market dependent, in the sense of allowing market forces alone to determine economic outcomes, and thus privatization is nowhere a simple matter of transferring public assets to the private sector. Government, in the process of privatization, purposefully participates in determining who will enter or exit the marketplace and under what conditions. Our analysis of the privatization program implemented by the federal government (1984–92) brings out the principal ways in which policy was adapted to smooth the transition from public to private.

The Conservative government first adapted its broad policy of enhancing market competition to its immediate need to make privatization succeed in the narrow sense of securing buyers for commercial Crown corporations. In this first phase of program initiation, transfers of Crown assets to other governments or to dominant market players were tolerated. The political imperative of being seen by the business and financial community to be privatizing was met. Policymakers' behaviour thus conforms to the public choice notion of credit claiming. There was, however, more at stake. By offloading these companies, some unwanted commitments of future resources were cancelled. The Tories also accelerated the revisions of the prevailing policy paradigm by demonstrating they could dispense with one traditional policy instrument—the Crown corporation.

The dynamics of privatization in Canada altered very quickly following an initial learning process and by 1987 a more calculated adaptation of policy took place. In this second phase of program extension, the federal government set up both barriers to entry and barriers to exit in order to avoid the politically unacceptable consequences of letting the market decide. After being hit by heavy flak from press, opposition, and even business interests when privatizing de Havilland and Teleglobe in particular, the Conservative government showed a new political willingness to place conditions on market freedoms for both investors and managers. Strictures on foreign ownership and prohibitions against relocation are typical and remain in force today. These restrictions reassured the public that privatization could be of benefit to Canadians, thus making it possible to issue shares in the major Crown corporations with perceived national policy roles (Air Canada and Petro-Canada).

The policy adaptations which facilitated implementation of the Conservatives' privatization program have also created an unexpected legacy. As the policy agenda refocuses on trade and competitiveness, and as the idea of a 'new industrial policy' is raised by the Clinton administration in Washington, Canada's privatized companies are not fully free agents, bounded only by general companies law, but remain subject to limits on their management decision-making—limits set by a government concerned to make privatization a politically tolerable proposition.

## References

Aucoin, Peter. 1988. 'The Mulroney Government, 1984–1988: Priorities, Positional Policy and Power', in Andrew Gollner and Daniel Salee, eds, *Canada Under Mulroney*. Montreal: Véhicule: 335–56.

Bauer, Michel. 1988. 'The Politics of State–Directed Privatisation: the case of France, 1986–88', *West European Politics* 11, 4: 49–60.

Canada, Department of Finance. 1985. *Securing Economic Renewal: The Budget Speech*. 23 May.

Canada, House of Commons. 1986. *Minutes of Proceedings and Evidence of the Standing Committee on Regional Development*. Issue no. 37, 29 Jan.

Canada, Industry, Science, and Technology. 1991. *Industrial Competitiveness, a sectoral perspective*. Ottawa: Minister of Supply and Services.

Canada, Office of the Minister of State (Privatization). 1987a. 'Excerpts from Statements made by the Honourable Barbara McDougall on the Reasons for Privatization'.

———. 1987b. 'The Privatization of Crown Corporations', Information kit.

———. 1987c. 'Speaking notes for the Honourable Barbara McDougall to the Ottawa Chapter, Institute of Public Administration of Canada', 23 Mar.

Canada, Office of Privatization and Regulatory Affairs. 1989. Information kit.

Canada, President of the Treasury Board. 1985. *Annual Report to the Parliament on Crown Corporations and Other Corporate Interests of Canada, 1983–84*. Ottawa: Minister of Supply and Services.

———. 1991. *Annual Report to the Parliament on Crown Corporations and Other Corporate Interests of Canada, 1990–91*. Ottawa: Minister of Supply and Services.

Canada, Prosperity Initiative. 1991. *Prosperity through Competitiveness*. Ottawa: Minister of Supply and Services.

Canadian National. 1988. *Annual Report 1988*.

Deblock, Christian. 1988. 'Le programme de renouveau économique: objectifs et priorités', in Christian Deblock and Richard Arteau, eds, *La politique canadienne à l'épreuvre du continentalisme*. Montreal: Éditions ACFAS: 43–56.

*Financial Post 500*. 1992. *Financial Post 500: the ranking of Canada: 500 largest companies*. Toronto: Financial Post.

Heald, David. 1985. 'Will the Privatization of Public Enterprises Solve the Problem of Control?', *Public Administration* 63 (Spring).

Kikeri, Sunita. 1990. *Bank Lending for Divestiture, a review of experience*, Country Economics Department Working Papers [WPS 338]. Washington: The World Bank, May.

Laux, Jeanne Kirk, and Maureen Appel Molot. 1988. *State Capitalism, Public Enterprise in Canada*. Ithaca, NY: Cornell University Press.

Porter, Michael E. 1991. *Canada at the Crossroads, the reality of a new competitive environment*. Ottawa:

Business Council on National Issues and Minister of Supply and Services Canada.

Schultz, Richard. 1988. 'Teleglobe Canada', in Allan Tupper and G. Bruce Doern, eds, *Privatization, Public Policy and Public Corporations in Canada.* Halifax: Institute for Research on Public Policy: 329–62.

Shirley, Mary. 1988. 'The Experience with Privatization', *Finance and Development* (Sept.): 34–5.

Stanbury, William T. 1988. 'Privatization and the Mulroney Government', in Andrew Gollner and Daniel Salee, eds, *Canada Under Mulroney.* Montreal: Véhicule: 119–57.

Vickers, John, and Vincent Wright. 1988. 'The Politics of Industrial Privatisation in Western Europe: an overview', *West European Politics* 11, 4: 1–30 (special issue: 'The Politics of Privatisation in Western Europe').

World Bank. 1992. *Privatization: the lessons of experience.* Washington: The World Bank Country Economics Department.

# Notes

1. The function of overseeing privatization reverted to the Department of Finance, Minister of State (Finance and Privatization). Staff was reduced and the post of Deputy Minister eliminated. These figures on privatization results will be elaborated below in Section I. For background and analysis of the shift away from using Crown corporations as policy instruments towards privatization, see Laux and Molot (1988).

2. See Kikeri (1990). This working paper (which engages the author not the World Bank as such) reports on 70 Bank operations in 35 countries over the 1980s giving myriad examples of the political distortion of divestiture policy. Since then, rejection of state ownership in Central and Eastern Europe has reinvigorated the World Bank's push for privatization. Its latest study refocuses the evidence on Third World success stories and provides a checklist of techniques to remove political impediments. Still, in the Bank's view, privatization remains 'a complement to, and not a replacement for' a range of policies needed to establish a 'market-friendly environment'. See World Bank (1992: ii–xii).

3. This is how Clark's senior policy adviser, Jim Gillies, put it in 'Neoconservatism: some elderly political theories, attractively spruced up', *Globe and Mail*, 27 Aug. 1979, 1.

4. 'Summary of the Task Force's Final Recommendations' (n.d.). For an analysis of the Conservatives' privatization program, see Stanbury (1988).

5. Quoted in the *Toronto Star,* 31 Oct. 1985, 1.

6. Many of Canada's Crown corporations were not (and are not) direct competitors to private-sector enterprises. Some of them are inactive while others provide services which in most countries are carried out by government departments (e.g., Harbours Commission). The bulk of the assets of Crown corporations are controlled by those known as financial intermediaries—conduits for credit extended for, e.g., public housing (Central Mortgage and Housing Corp.), export promotion (Export Development Corp.), or agricultural development (Farm Credit Corp.).

7. Some of the Crown companies which have been dissolved include Loto Canada Inc., the Canadian Sports Pool Corporation, and the Crown Assets Disposal Corporation. Subsidiaries heralded as privatizations belonged to Canadian National Railways.

8. The federal government prefers to restrict the definition of a commercial corporation to those operating in a 'competitive environment' which are listed in Part II of Schedule III of Part III of the FAA. Ottawa remains the sole owner of other corporations not listed in Part III of the FAA, notably the cultural corporations like CBC or Telefilm, subject to a different accountability regime. These, along with the Canadian Wheat Board, employ another 12,000 persons.

9. Canada (1989). NCPC (Northwest Territories) is now owned by the Northwest Territories Power Corporation, a Crown agency regulated by the NWT Public Utilities Board and NCPC (Yukon) is owned by the Yukon Power Corporation, which has contracted out the management to a private company.

10. 'Unresolved policy questions making selling Eldorado tough', *Globe and Mail*, 2 Mar. 1987, B5. Eldorado Nuclear Limited Reorganization and Divestiture Act (1988) Article 8 (1). Following a 1993 share offering Cameco will be 42 per cent government owned with Ottawa's share being 10 per cent.

11. Other tales of indirect transfers from government to government could be told, such as the 1992 sale of Ottawa's 53.7 per cent interest in Telesat, the satellite communications carrier, to Alouette Tele-communications, Inc. Alouette is a new alliance between Spar Aerospace Ltd, Quebec-Telephone, and Telecom Canada (now Stentor) which regroups the telephone companies. Some of them are 100 per cent owned by provincial governments, e.g., Manitoba Telephone System and Sasktel, both of which rank among the top 200 corporations in Canada.

12. For the intricacies of the Teleglobe sale and the competing interests at stake, see Schultz (1988).

13. 'Memotec debourse $488 millions pour Teleglobe', *Le Devoir*, 12 Feb. 1987, 1. The Quebec government's investment company, the Caisse de dépôt, now holds 14 per cent of Teleglobe Inc. (formerly Memotec Data Inc.).

14. Over time some of these companies, notably Teleglobe and ENL, may be expected to become 100 per cent privately owned. Other privatized companies, however, find themselves once again in a government portfolio by virtue of secondary sales. Such is the case for de Havilland Aircraft of Canada (now 49 per cent owned by the Ontario government) and subsidiaries of the Canadian Development Corporation such as Connaught Laboratories (now owned by the French government's Institut Mérieux). Both cases qualify as policy adaptation because they were the subject of cabinet deliberations in Ottawa.

15. An analysis of SNC's purposes in acquiring Arsenals is found in 'Canadian Arsenals', *Ploughshares Monitor* (Dec. 1986): 17. For all key documentation relevant to the de Havilland sale to Boeing, including much that was previously confidential, see Canada, House of Commons (1986).

16. 'Deal Moves Bombardier into Aerospace Elite', *Globe and Mail*, 24 Nov. 1992, B5; 'Bombardier acquires UTDC in Subsidy Deal with Ontario', *Globe*

*and Mail*, 5 Dec. 1991, 1. For a profile of the company's operations and business strategy, see the special series by Jean-Paul Lejeune in *Commerce*, 12 Dec. 1991, 24–37, 46–8.

17. BCE has also worked through the market to become the largest shareholder (27 per cent) in privatized Teleglobe. Ownership positions are traced through the *Financial Post 500*. For CN's strategy and details on these sales, see Canadian National (1988: 5, 11, 34).

18. Air Canada Public Participation Act, Article 6 (1) (b). In the case of Air Canada this restriction conforms to the legal limit on foreign ownership imposed for all airlines by the National Transportation Act. The Mulroney government could have opted to amend the Act, however, but did not so choose, to the irritation of some in the industry like Rhys Eyton, president of Canadian Airlines International Ltd (as reported in 'Clouds in the "Open Skies"', *Maclean's*, 25 Feb. 1991, 32–3).

19. Eldorado Nuclear Limited Reorganization and Divestiture Act (1988), Article 5 (1) (ii) and (iii). The restriction on foreign ownership for Teleglobe is set out in the terms of reference for bidders: 'Conditions and Process of Sale' (see Canada, Office of the Minister of State, 1987b) and enshrined in Article 5 (1) (b) of the Teleglobe Canada Reorganization and Divestiture Act (1987).

20. Nordion and Theratronics Divestiture Authorization Act, Article 6 (7). Foreign ownership ceilings for both companies were set at 25 per cent.

21. Petro-Canada Public Participation Act, Article 10. No apologies for this deviation from free market principles were made—rather, the Minister of State for Privatization proudly announced that 'These restrictions mean that Petro-Canada will remain Canadian-owned and Canadian-controlled' (Office of Privatization and Regulatory Affairs [1990], *News Release*, 1 Oct., 1).

22. Stakeholders include Crown corporation employees, consumers of the goods or services supplied, communities where head office or plants are located, and provincial governments.

23. 'Eager Investors Scoop Up FPI Share Offer', *Globe and Mail*, 25 Mar. 1987, B1. Provincial governments have generally been more vigorous than Ottawa in looking to satisfy stakeholders by

placing conditions on management freedom after privatization. The Conservative government in Saskatchewan, for instance, when offering shares in the Potash Corporation of Saskatchewan (PCS), specified that, in addition to majority Canadian ownership and board membership, at least three directors must reside in the province. See Part III of The Potash Corporation of Saskatchewan Reorganization Act (1989).

24. Directive power for Teleglobe is legislated in Article 18 (1) of the Teleglobe Canada Reorganization and Divestiture Act which makes (2) consultation with and (4) compensation for the corporation optional.

25. Air Canada Public Participation Act, Article 6.1 (d) (e). Deputy Prime Minister Don Mazankowski quoted in Air Canada's *Privatization Bulletin*, 18 Aug. 1988.

26. Petro-Canada Public Participation Act, Article 9 (1) (g) and Eldorado Nuclear Limited Reorganization and Divestiture Act (1988), Article 5 (1) (d).

27. The difference with the other cases is that such negotiated deals do not have the force of law but constitute 'good faith intentions'. Canadair (n.d.), 'Letter of Intent for the purchase of Canadair Ltd. by Bombardier Inc.', 13. Teleglobe is likewise obliged by Article 11 of its divestiture Act to maintain its head office in the Montreal urban community.

# The Social Policy Review:
## Policy-Making in a Semi-Sovereign Society

Keith G. Banting

Setbacks are often as illuminating as success. Certainly in government, the dynamics of the policy process can sometimes be thrown into sharper relief by disappointments than by initiatives that seem to glide through with ease. From this perspective, the social security review launched in October 1994 by the release of the federal discussion paper, *Improving Social Security in Canada*,[1] reveals much about the contradictory pressures shaping contemporary public policy in Canada.

Moreover, the review highlights important tensions surrounding the role of public consultations in an era of tight fiscal constraints, especially when those constraints are reinforced by international economic pressures beyond the reach of domestic politics. On the one hand, public disenchantment with élite-dominated decision processes has created an irresistible and entirely appropriate culture of public consultation surrounding important policy initiatives. On the other hand, the palpable tightening of international economic constraints and Canada's vulnerability to volatile global financial markets have narrowed the range of policy options before government. In the stark words of the Department of Finance, 'we have suffered a tangible loss of economic sovereignty.'[2] The resulting contradiction between a vibrant consultative culture and diminished economic sovereignty is a powerful challenge to contemporary policy-making, a challenge illuminated by the social security review.

From *Canadian Public Administration/Administration publique du Canada* 38, 2 (Summer 1995): 283–90. Reprinted by permission of The Institute of Public Administration of Canada.

## The Social Security Paper and the Budget

From the outset, the social security review was caught in the tensions existing among three separate agendas: the reform of social policy, the reduction of the federal deficit, and the accommodation of Quebec within Canada. The reform agenda is driven by the conviction that the social programs we inherited from the postwar generation are now out of date and need to be restructured. Key priorities include a co-ordinated restructuring of unemployment insurance, social assistance, training, and education in order to equip Canadians for the global economy and to promote adjustment in the economy as a whole. In addition, our transfer programs need to be redesigned to respond more effectively to child poverty and the intense financial stresses being borne by many young families and by workers displaced by changing technology. This broad agenda has been developed through a long series of reports and studies over the last decade and has engaged both federal and provincial policy-makers. Indeed, large demonstration projects are under way on a jointly funded basis in New Brunswick and British Columbia.

The deficit reduction agenda is driven by other imperatives. It reflects the conviction that the level of accumulated federal debt is unsustainable and is eroding the prospects for investment, increased productivity, and job growth in Canada.[3] Moreover, the burden of debt-financing is crippling government. In 1993–4, interest payments on the federal debt were $38 billion, pre-empting one-third of all federal revenues and making budget planning very sensitive to fluctuations in interest rates. The significant growth in taxes in Canada during the 1980s has convinced policy-makers that there is little political room for further tax increases, and attention has therefore focused primarily on the expenditure side. However, as Table 1 makes painfully clear, the deficit, which was $42 billion in 1993–4, is much too large to be tackled through Draconian cuts in discretionary spending alone. In this context, any significant effort to eliminate the deficit puts tremendous pressure on the two biggest categories of program spending: transfers to persons and transfers to other levels of government.

The third agenda, the accommodation of Quebec within Canada, is as old as the country itself. Nationalist forces within Quebec politics have challenged federal leadership in social policy since the days of the Tremblay Commission in the mid-1950s, and since then the politics of social policy in Canada have been fuelled as much by intergovernmental struggles over jurisdiction as by substantive differences over program content. Jurisdictional conflicts came to a head again during the constitutional negotiations of the late 1980s and 1990s. In the aftermath of the defeat of the Meech Lake Accord, support for separatism soared in Quebec, and federalist forces in the province responded with a call for significant decentralization, including the transfer of all federal social programs to the province. The Charlottetown Accord incorporated a more mod-

est package, but did include the transfer of labour-market training to the provinces and tight curbs on the federal government's capacity to launch new shared-cost programs. Although the Charlottetown Accord was defeated in a national referendum, the jurisdictional issues simply flowed into non-constitutional politics. These pressures were powerfully reinforced by the strong showing of the Bloc Québécois in the federal election of 1993 and the election of the Parti Québécois in September 1994, one month before the release of the federal green paper.

Although the Axworthy discussion paper was informed by all of these agendas, the reform agenda was clearly predominant:

[T]he world has changed faster than our programs. In the last decade in particular, the sheer relentless force of technological, economic and social change has reshaped our lives and our livelihoods. Government policies and approaches have been too slow in responding. Social security reform is a matter of making choices together about how best to build a social security system for the 21st century.[4]

By comparison, deficit reduction and constitutional questions constituted secondary themes. One page was dedicated to the 'fiscal context' and proclaimed that 'reform of social security cannot be contemplated in isolation from the fiscal realities facing governments in Canada. Until the fiscal situation improves, there will be no new money

## Table 1: Structure of Federal Public Spending, 1993–1994[5]

| Component | Billions of dollars |
|---|---|
| Interest on debt | 38.0 |
| Transfers to persons | 42.4 |
| Transfers to governments | 27.6 |
| All other spending | 50.0 |
| Total | 158.0 |

for new programs. And existing expenditures must be brought under control and in some instances reduced.'[6] Discussion of the 'federal-provincial partnership' in the green paper was even briefer, calling simply for increased collaboration and 'clarification of roles and responsibilities consistent with the Constitution'.[7] Despite these qualifications, the overwhelming focus of the paper was policy reform and the leadership of the federal government in the process. And certainly, the vast majority of submissions to the parliamentary committee, which held hearings on the paper, emphasized the substance of social policy and the importance of the federal role in the social needs of Canadians.[8]

The social policy component of the federal budget tabled in late February 1995 shifted the balance dramatically towards deficit reduction and decentralization. Officially, the budget simply set in place a framework within which social policy reform is to proceed. In practice, however, the new framework leaves only limited fiscal and political room for the reform agenda. The changes have made explicit very tight fiscal parameters for that process, and they reduced the role of the federal government in the definition of Canada's social future. Established program financing and the Canada Assistance Plan are to be consolidated into one block grant to the provinces—the Canada Health and Social Transfer (CHST)—and the combined cash transfer is to be cut significantly. Although the changes do not alter the principles set out in the Canada Health Act, several of the conditions embedded in the Canada Assistance Plan disappear in the transition to the CHST, leaving provinces with greater flexibility to redefine social assistance and social services. In addition, the budget announced that federal transfer programs such as unemployment insurance and pension programs will be examined during the next year with a view to further reduce expenditure levels.

Officially, the process of social security reform is still alive. According to the budget, the Minister of Human Resources Development is to 'invite all provincial governments to work together on developing, through mutual consent, a set of shared principles and objectives that could underlie the new transfer.'[9] Nevertheless, the prospects for a spontaneous federal-provincial consensus are not great, and the changes to federal transfers to persons are being driven by the fiscal agenda. Although nothing is impossible in politics, the prospects for a co-ordinated modernization of social programs seem dim. Canada is likely to limp into the twenty-first century with a poorer version of a social infrastructure designed for an earlier time. What went wrong?

## The Politics of Social Policy Reform

Comprehensive social policy reform is a complex political operation; it has seldom been achieved in Canada, even in less constrained times. An ambitious reform agenda requires the Minister of Human Resources Development to operate in three separate political arenas: the internal arena of cabinet and caucus, the arena of social policy groups, and the federal-provincial arena. Beyond these arenas of organized politics lies the wider public, whose support is courted by participants in the organized arenas.

The review process foundered most clearly inside the government, in two ways. First, the review was weakened from the outset by the lack of a clear framework and definitive options for debate. Initially the minister promised a clear 'action plan'; but political anxieties within the cabinet, caucus, and the Prime Minister's Office transformed early drafts from the advisory task force into a vague 'discussion paper'. This not only delayed the release of the federal paper, it also produced a document too vague to catalyse a focused national dialogue. An impressive set of supplementary papers dribbled out in subsequent months, but these never attained sufficient profile to define the debate.

For old hands in social policy debates, this process was hauntingly familiar. In the preparations for the social security review in the mid-1970s, Marc Lalonde marched into cabinet with a document containing clear proposals and walked out with a paper full of bland principles but virtually no policy content.[10] History faithfully repeated itself in the summer and fall of 1994. Indeed, by the standards for the mid-1970s, the Axworthy document was relatively pointed. Nevertheless, the open-ended nature of important parts of the discussion paper left the debate without a centre of gravity.

In retrospect, it is also clear that the social policy review was not sufficiently integrated into the fiscal process of the government. There are several reasons for this disjunction. In part, the government's fiscal strategy was not fully resolved when the discussion paper was released, and, in part, the government's fiscal room narrowed after the discussion paper was released as a result of a rise in interest rates late in 1994. Nevertheless, parameters matter. The tightness of fiscal constraint and the implications of the loss of economic sovereignty implicit in Canada's foreign indebtedness did not inform the discussion document from the outset. Indeed, the fiscal parameters were perhaps the vaguest part of the discussion paper.

As a result, the social policy review was launched in a manner that made a bruising confrontation with the fiscal and constitutional agendas inevitable. The real question therefore was whether the social review would mobilize external political support that would strengthen social priorities when that confrontation came. The minister regularly warned that if the social policy community could not agree on a strategy to restructure social policy within contemporary constraints, the job would eventually be done by others less sensitive to the social needs of Canadians. In effect, this is what happened, as the minister received remarkably little support as the review progressed.

The consultative phase of the review process was an open one, and substantial intervenor funding was provided. In this way, the process reflected the new culture of participation in policy-making. It takes considerable effort to remember the major social security review of the mid-1970s was conducted almost exclusively in closed federal-provincial meetings, with public information limited to vague communiqués that only the *cognoscenti* could interpret. Such deference to élite accommodation has largely vanished in Canada; social groups insist on a more open process.

The social policy community in Canada, however, is vigorously pluralistic rather than corporatist, and advocacy groups have little incentive to work within a framework defined by diminishing resources and hard trade-offs. As a result, the prospects that the minister could generate group support beyond the business community were limited from the outset. There was little support even from organizations that might have been thought of as winners in the discussion paper. For example, proposals that unemployment insurance benefits should be reduced but child benefits enriched received scant support from child advocacy organizations. 'You can't rob mom and dad to pay baby', they insisted.[11] Such an approach preserves amity among social groups, but essentially sidelines them from serious politics in an era defined by painful choices.

The reaction of provincial governments was different but hardly more encouraging. Axworthy launched the intergovernmental debate on social policy reform by meeting with his provincial counterparts on Valentine's Day, well before the release of his paper. The romantic implications for the date, however, were lost in the hard world of intergovernmental diplomacy. The traditional mix of jurisdictional rivalry, regional interests, and ideological diversity, which fuels federal-provincial conflict in Canada generally, was in full play. In fact, the mix was made even more volatile than usual by the deep-seated anger in Ontario about the cap on federal transfers to the three richest provinces under the Canada Assistance Plan and by the election of the Parti Québécois in Quebec. The federal approach to the review oscillated between multilateral discussions and a search for bilateral agreements on specific parts of the agenda. Yet, the response was hardly enthusiastic. Only the government of New Brunswick cheered when the discussion paper was released, and little progress on a co-ordinated approach to reform was made in the months that followed.

Given the limited prospects for strong support among groups and other governments, the only strategy available to the minister was to mount a populist campaign to mobilize powerful public support for a reform agenda. On occasion, Axworthy did seem to be appealing over the heads of groups and provinces to the public at large. Such tactics did have potential because a considerable gap existed between the advocacy voices heard by the parliamentary committee and the preferences of the wider public as measured by opinion polls. Survey data available at the time pointed to a hardening of attitudes among Canadians generally towards unemployment insurance and social assistance.[12] However, a populist strategy confronted difficulties. One was the vagueness of the proposals in the federal paper; it is difficult to mobilize public support without a specific direction. In addition, harder public views can imply as much support for simple cuts as for complex restructuring. Finally, the discussion paper's proposals for post-secondary education generated strong opposition among an articulate, middle-class constituency, university and college students.

In the final analysis, the underlying political energy propelling the Axworthy review proved weak and provided limited political protection in the cabinet wars over the budget introduced in late February of 1995. The minister faced powerful pressures from cabinet colleagues more concerned about the fiscal and constitutional agendas, and the resulting compromises left large holes in the original strategy.

## Lessons for the Policy Process

The discussion paper on social security reform launched a modern consultative process designed to engage Canadians in a sophisticated process of policy renewal. The process did engage the energies of many Canadians, and new ideas such as income-contingent loan repayments were injected more firmly into the policy debates of the country. Nevertheless, the problems encountered along the way point to important lessons for such exercises in the future.

First, as long as governments feel politically responsible for every idea and option set out in a discussion document, the traditional distinction between a 'white paper' and a 'green paper' becomes meaningless. The decision to publish a green paper rather than an action plan did not calm the political anxieties or stem the watering down of the document. Clearly, it is time to abandon the distinction between white and green papers, at least in the field of social policy. In this particular case, it would have been much better if the minister had not chaired the task force that advised him and helped him draft the paper. A document from an independent advisory group could have set forth more detailed options and framed a more compelling debate.

Second, in a period of hard fiscal realities, it is important that any consultation process begin with a clear statement of the real parameters of the exercise. This is not to suggest that advocacy groups will happily work within hard fiscal limits; such bliss is not given to modern governments. Indeed, for many the parameters themselves would quickly become the focus of debate. Nevertheless, such a controversy would be more relevant than one in which fiscal constraints are so opaque that the real issues before the country are missed.

This is especially the case in a period when parameters of debate are increasingly influenced by international pressures. The modern state has always stood between the wider global system and its own domestic society, mediating the pressures from these two domains. The scope for domestic autonomy has varied over time, and Canada is clearly in a period when global constraints are tightening in palpable ways. Canadian foreign indebtedness has enfranchised global financial markets and international bond-rating agencies, making them an important component of our fiscal politics.

By contrast, a public consultation process, by its very nature, reflects and amplifies domestic political preferences. In the case of Canadian social policy, the balance of pressures drawn to

such a process tends to an expansive definition of social needs and priorities. Without a clear definition of the parameters at the outset, government ends up striking the balance between domestic aspirations and hard constraints after the public has spoken, almost inevitably in ways that deny public voices. Surely, this is a recipe for frustration. Without transparency from the outset, there is a real danger that elaborate consultation processes will heighten, not reduce, public cynicism about the responsiveness of our political institutions.

## Notes

The author is Stauffer-Dunning Professor of Policy Studies and Director of the School of Policy Studies at Queen's University. He would like to thank Arthur Kroeger for comments on an early draft of this article.

1. Canada, Ministry of Human Resources Development, *Improving Social Security in Canada: A Discussion Paper* (Ottawa: Minister of Supply and Services, 1994).
2. Canada, Ministry of Finance, *A New Framework for Economic Policy* (Ottawa: Department of Finance, 1994), 78.
3. Ibid.
4. Canada, Ministry of Finance, *Creating a Healthy Fiscal Climate* (Ottawa: Department of Finance, 1994), Annex 1, Tables 1 and 2.
5. Ministry of Human Resources Development, *Improving Social Security*, 26–7.
6. Ibid., 7.
7. Ibid., 23.
8. The balance in public submissions to the Standing Committee on Human Resources Development is captured in the title of its report, *Security, Opportunities and Fairness: Canadians renewing their social programs*, and by the summary of those submissions in the report itself.
9. Standing Committee on Human Resources Development, *Security, Opportunities and Fairness: Canadians renewing their social programs* (Ottawa: House of Commons, 1995), 53.
10. Canada, Ministry of National Health and Welfare, *Working Paper on Social Security in Canada* (Ottawa: Information Canada, 1973).
11. 'You can't rob mom and dad to pay baby', *Toronto Star*, 10 Oct. 1994, A3.
12. *Financial Post*, 22–4 Oct. 1994, A1.

# Part VII

# International Relations

## Introduction

Theodore Cohn

Karl Deutsch has defined politics as the 'incomplete control of human behaviour through voluntary habits of *compliance* in combination with threats of probable *enforcement*'.[1] Legislative, executive, and judicial authorities within nation-states seek to ensure that enforcement and compliance occur through the passage and administration of laws and the settling of disputes in accordance with law. In many authoritarian as well as more democratic states, most of the people comply with the laws voluntarily (even if grudgingly) most of the time. In cases where this does not occur, the public authorities may be prepared to use force against those who defy the laws. The international political system, by contrast, is primarily a 'self-help system' in which enforcement and compliance occur in a more decentralized or anarchic fashion. Thus, threats of retaliation by one state against another or one alliance against another carry far more weight than a central body such as the United Nations in ensuring that international enforcement takes place.

The decentralized nature of international politics has inevitably affected how theory in this realm has developed. Thus, a major tenet of *realism* (for many years the dominant school of thought in international relations) is that states are the most important actors in the international system. Realists often refer to the sovereignty principle, which is designed to ensure that nation-states are not subject to the direction of a superior government. The evolution of thinking in international relations can best be illustrated by a series of debates that emerged as the discipline developed. Chronologically, these debates pitted realists against idealists, behaviouralists against traditionalists, and realists against structuralists and interdependence theorists. This section focuses mainly on these debates, but some attention is also given to the literature in Canadian foreign policy and to some of the characteristics of current international relations approaches.

*The History of the Peloponnesian War* by Thucydides (471–400 BC) is often identified as the first important work in international relations, and Thucydides is also credited with being the first writer in the realist tradition.[2] Nevertheless, it was only after World War I that international politics emerged as a distinct academic discipline in universities. The heavy physical and psychological costs of this war made the realist European balance-of-power system seem unacceptable, and attention was directed to reforming the international system so that change could occur peacefully. The *idealist school* of thought therefore became prominent after World War I, and its most important exponent was American President Woodrow Wilson. Wilson called for an end to European power politics, where each state depended on its own or its allies' power for security. Instead, he advocated a collective security system, centred in the new League of Nations, that would assist any member state considered to be a victim of aggression. Another example of idealism in this period was the Kellogg-Briand Treaty of 1928, which was eventually ratified by 65 states. This treaty purported to outlaw war as an instrument of national policy, and relied on nothing more than the inherent rationality and ethical behaviour of policy-makers to bring about such peaceful conditions.

The aggressive actions of Germany, Japan, and Italy in the 1930s, however, clearly demonstrated that idealist thought had little impact on the policies of some major states. The United States had not even joined the League of Nations, and the weak response of the League's most important members—Britain and France—to aggression pointed to the shortcomings of idealism in preventing serious conflict. In *The Twenty Years' Crisis: 1919–1939,* written on the eve of World War II, E.H. Carr strongly criticized the idealist school, stating that 'the inner meaning of the modern international crisis is the collapse of the whole structure of utopianism based on the concept of the harmony of interests.'[3] After World War II the *realist school* of thought dominated the study of international politics. The 'new' realist school in fact adhered to views held by many policy-makers and historians in the old pre-World War I European balance-of-power system. According to the realists, arms and military alliances are far more effective than ethical views and international organizations in preventing war. Realists have been so influential in the discipline that a more detailed description of their ideas is necessary.

Realists view international and domestic politics as being separate and distinct, and they place emphasis on the anarchic, decentralized nature of international relations. They maintain that states are the principal or dominant actors in international politics and that states are 'amoral' (i.e., their foreign policy behaviour is not affected by moral codes). Realists further argue that socio-economic issues are subordinate to strategic-security issues in international relations and that the competition for power is of primary concern to nation-states. Thus, the leading realist writer in the postwar period, Hans Morgenthau, asserted that 'international politics, like all politics, is a struggle for power.'[4] Realists attributed the primary causes of World War II to appeasement with regard to aggressive demands and to the military weakness of the democracies. As the subtitle in Morgenthau's seminal work *Politics Among Nations: The Struggle for Power and Peace* indicates, realists view the balance of power among states and alliances as the best insurance against forceful domination by any single state (or group of states). Nevertheless, realists believe that conflict among states is inevitable, and they therefore argue that each state can best promote its national interest by maximizing its power.

Thinking in Canada has clearly been influenced by realism, but it has also posed a challenge to realist preoccupations with the major powers and the use of force in international relations. The Canadian perspective of 'liberal internationalism' placed more emphasis on developing a peaceful and stable international order than on promoting the national interest. Canadians also opposed the dominance of postwar institutions (such as the UN Security Council) by the great powers alone, and argued that every state should have responsibilities appropriate to its particular capacities. Although the great powers would of course be more influential than others, middle powers (such as Canada, India, and Sweden) should have more influence and responsibilities than lesser powers. These ideas had limited influence outside Canada until recently, however, largely because of the Cold War split among the major and middle powers. The active role of Canada and other middle powers as UN peacekeepers can nevertheless be viewed as examples of this doctrine in practice. Canadian foreign policy literature in general tends to be preoccupied with the country's 'place in the world', and various authors have presented competing arguments that Canada is a middle power, a principal power, or a dependent state.[5] The influence of the realist school on this literature is evident, since so much of the discussion focuses on Canada's power position.

Despite the predominance of realism since World War II, the idealist school continues to have some influence in the study of international politics. As E.H. Carr stated, 'the utopian who dreams that it is possible . . . to base a political system on morality alone is just as wide of the mark as the realist who believes that altruism is an illusion and that all political action is self-seeking.'[6] In recent years, idealist writers have been concerned with a variety of issues, including the ethics of nuclear deterrence, intervention in countries' domestic affairs (to restore human rights, for example), and international distributive justice (the distribution of wealth among as well as within states). Nevertheless, most modern-day 'textbooks in international relations have been conspicuous for the absence of much discussion of normative or value considerations.'[7]

Outside of the realist-idealist debate, a second major debate arose between *behaviouralists* and *traditionalists* in the 1950s. This debate focused on the best method of studying international relations, with the behaviouralists strongly criticizing the traditionalist tendency to rely on history and experience in developing their thought. Instead, the behaviouralists sought to develop a more scientific study of international politics based on the development of quantitative techniques, formal models, and testable hypotheses. The behaviouralist school has contributed to important advances in the study of international relations in such areas as decision-making approaches, game theory, mathematical probability models, and linkage theory.[8] Nevertheless, behaviouralists' expectations that cumulative studies would gradually lead to a general theory of international politics were disappointed, for a variety of reasons. Much of the terminology used in international politics, such as *democracy, dictatorship, aggression*, and *imperialism*, is value-laden; relevant data are often lacking in the field, since international bodies such as NATO and the UN Security Council often hold their most important meetings in secret; and many international relations concepts such as *power* and *sovereignty* are not readily subject to quantification. By the late 1960s, many behaviouralists realized that their insights were not superior to those of the traditionalists and that the two approaches were best viewed as complementary rather than conflicting. Thus, Robert C. North and others entered a 'plea for pluralism in our approaches to international relations . . . and for a higher level of mutual respect and reasoned dialogue between "traditionalists" and "behaviouralists".'[9]

Behaviouralists had often portrayed themselves as providing an alternative to realism, and more specifically to the traditionalism of Hans Morgenthau. Nevertheless, behaviouralists were basically concerned with *methodology*, and they did not question the basic realist assumptions regarding the centrality of states, the importance of power and peace, and the separability of domestic and international politics. The realists clearly dominated the discipline of international relations until the mid-1970s. At this time, several alternative approaches began to pose a serious challenge to some of the realists' most fundamental assumptions. These included both interdependence and structuralist approaches. As Steve Smith has noted, 'for the first time, these accounts actually saw different actors at work and different issues involved, the crucial result of which was to break down the monolithic conception of the state and the very notion of the State as dominant actor.'[10]

*Interdependence theorists* rejected the state-centric approach of the realists and maintained that the proliferation of non-state actors, such as multinational corporations and international organizations, is a significant political development in international relations. While realists tend to portray states as being impermeable units, interdependence theorists view states as 'sieves', which have numerous points of contact with the international system. International interactions are therefore not limited to official contacts at the central governmental level, but also include other types of relations. Robert Keohane and Joseph Nye have produced some of the most important works from an interdependence perspective.[11] New types of relationships identified by these two authors include *transnational relations*, which involve 'interactions across the border in which at least one actor is nongovernmental' (such as a multinational corporation), and *transgovernmental relations*, consisting of 'direct interactions between agencies [governmental subunits] of different governments where those agencies act relatively autonomously from central governmental control' (for example, between environmental officials in two countries).[12]

In view of these numerous points of contact, interdependence theorists reject the realist perception that international and domestic politics are separate and distinct, and they regard many contemporary issues as being *intermestic* in nature; that is, they are 'simultaneously, profoundly and inseparably both domestic and international'.[13] They further believe that socio-economic issues are often more important then strategic-security matters, especially since the end of the Cold War. This contrasts with the postwar realist view that strategic-security matters were *high politics*, at the top of a hierarchy of international relations issues, while socio-economic issues could be relegated to the less important category of *low politics*.

Keohane and Nye have limited their discussion of transgovernmental relations to interactions among bureaucratic subunits of national governments. However, the definition of 'transgovernmental' can be broadened to include cross-border interactions among other types of subunits, such as American states, Canadian provinces, and even municipal governments. This broader meaning is particularly important in a Canadian context, because Quebec has long had political aspirations to act internationally, and some other provinces have also sought to raise their international profiles (though more for economic than political reasons). Thus, Canadian foreign policy analysts have made an important contribution to the interdependence literature by examining the role of subnational governments in international relations.[14]

While Keohane and Nye levelled some potent criticisms at realism, they were not trying to deny that realist preoccupations with interstate relations, power, and national interest were unimportant. Rather, they wanted to expand the realist vision by including important new actors and relationships. Some interdependence critics have gone much further than Keohane and Nye in attempting to replace the entire realist approach with models of a world or global society. These world society theorists argue that interdependence has increased exponentially so that the most important problems today, such as those related to trade, foreign investment, nuclear weapons, and environmental pollution, are global in scope and require global solutions. They envision a global community emerging with interests that are contrary to those of nation-states.[15] Thus, Saul Mendlowitz has stated that 'today we may be in the throes of an . . . epochal change—away from . . . the nation-state system . . . on to a truly global society with a global economy and global culture, and involving global governance.'[16]

A second challenge to the realists came from the *structuralist perspective*. As the name implies, this approach places particular emphasis on the structure of the international system as a factor explaining the behaviour of states. Many structuralists maintain that the most important characteristics of the international system relate to the pervasive domination of capitalism. Like interdependence theorists, structuralists place considerable emphasis on socio-economic factors and on non-state as well as state actors in international relations. Indeed, they believe that multinational corporations and international organizations often serve as means of domination by which some states and classes benefit from the capitalist system at the expense of others. Many structuralists describe the historical development of the rich, northern industrial states as occurring at the expense of the poorer southern states in Africa, Asia, and Latin America: the North is considered to be responsible for the underdevelopment or the dependent development of the South.[17]

Some Canadian foreign policy analysts have relied on structuralist approaches in developing a thesis that Canada is a dependent or satellite state, primarily in relation to the United States.[18] This contrasts with the traditional view of Canada as a middle power and with the more recent claim that Canada is a principal power. Many southern states would understandably maintain that they are in far more peripheral and vulnerable positions than Canada, and Canada's status as a relatively wealthy, industrialized country makes its portrayal as a dependent state highly controversial. The view of Canada as a principal power is also unconvincing, even though it is a member of the Group of Seven most important industrialized nations. While Canada has some characteristics of both a principal power and a dependent state, most analysts continue to accept the traditional view that Canada is a middle power.[19]

The existence of realism, interdependence, and structuralism as competing paradigms indicates that there is no longer either an ideological or a methodological consensus in the contemporary study of international relations. Furthermore, a number of analytical approaches today are 'hybrids' that draw on more than one of these schools of thought. One of the most prominent approaches is referred to as *hegemonic stability theory*. Hegemony is deemed to exist when one state has predominant power in the international system. In its traditional version, hegemonic stability theory asserts that a relatively open and stable international economic system is likely to exist when a hegemonic state is willing and able to provide leadership. When a global hegemon is lacking or a hegemon is declining in power, it is more difficult to maintain economic openness and stability. Most theorists agree that hegemonic conditions have occurred at least twice in modern times—under Britain in the nineteenth century, and under the United States after World War II. Some hegemonic stability theorists argue that American hegemony is declining and that this is contributing to growing economic instability, but all aspects of the theory are the subject of debate within the academic community.[20]

Another prominent approach deals with *international regimes*, which can be defined as 'sets of implicit or explicit principles, norms, rules, and decision-making procedures around which actors' expectations converge in a given area of international relations'.[21] Scholars often focus on the principles and norms governing regimes (such as the trade or monetary regime) and on changes in regimes over time. The global trade regime, for example, is centred in the World Trade Organization or WTO (formerly called the General Agreement on Tariffs and Trade), which helps to uphold such regime principles as non-discrimination, liberalization, and reciprocity in trade. Although trade liberalization has occurred over a number of years, regional trade blocs and new sources of protectionism such as non-tariff barriers pose a threat to the global trade regime.[22]

Some theorists have argued that a hegemonic distribution of power leads to open and stable economic regimes because the hegemon has both the incentive and resources to make such regimes function effectively. Thus, the United States is often credited with helping establish the global monetary, trade, and aid regimes after World War II. Nevertheless, once regimes are established by a hegemonic power, their principles and norms are quite durable, and the regimes may continue to exist even after the hegemonic state declines.[23] The view that principles, norms, rules, and decision-making procedures can provide a degree of order in a trade or monetary regime diverges from the traditional realist perception regarding the anarchic nature of international politics.

It should be noted that the realists have responded to the challenges posed by the behavioural, interdependence, and structuralist approaches. Indeed, a number of neorealist writers have attempted to counteract the deficiencies in traditional realist theory by making it more rigorous and more relevant to contemporary conditions. The term *neorealist* has been closely associated with Kenneth Waltz, who has provided a more elaborate theoretical grounding for realist ideas and a more systematic analysis of such concepts as balance and power.[24] Neorealists such as Robert Gilpin have incorporated the economic dimension as a central feature of their theory and have examined the impact of rising and declining hegemonic states on transformations in international relations. It is interesting that the neorealists' concern with economic issues has similarities with the preoccupations of some pre-World War I realists with trade and other economic matters. It was primarily in the Cold War period after World

War II that a number of realists seemed to forget about economic issues. Thus, Gilpin has stated that he had 'returned to a realist conception of the relationship of economics and politics that had disappeared from postwar American writings, then almost completely devoted to more narrowly conceived security concerns.'[25]

Realism probably continues to be the most influential approach today, and to a large extent this reflects the continued dominance of the discipline by Americans. While American scholars have greatly enriched the study of international relations, the field would certainly benefit from contributions from a wider array of nationalities. In a discipline such as international relations, we face the dual challenge of diversifying the sources and nature of perspectives and at the same time developing a coherent body of theory so that we can build on the theoretical contributions of others.[26]

The readings that follow demonstrate some of the changes in the field of international relations described above. The first selection, from *Environmental Scarcity and Global Security* by Thomas F. Homer-Dixon, discusses the many ways in which environmental scarcity may contribute to violent conflict. Homer-Dixon demonstrates that realists and other international relations theorists concerned with violent conflict today must not only consider traditional strategic-security factors, but also economic, environmental, resource, and demographic issues. While he indicates that most of the violent conflict over environmental issues occurs in the Third World, the advanced industrial states account for most of the world's pollution and have the technological capabilities to provide solutions. Environmental security is very much an interdependence issue today, because it increasingly must be viewed above the nation-state level in regional and global terms.

Historically, there has been a high degree of foreign ownership (especially US ownership) in Canadian industry, and Canadians have long expressed concerns about the effect of foreign ownership on the country's economic prospects. Today as interdependence and globalization have increased, even Americans have become concerned about foreign ownership (which is still well below the level of foreign ownership in Canada). In the US case, attention has been focused on the rapid growth of Japanese investment in the United States.

In his article on the growth of foreign ownership in the United States, Robert Reich argues that large multinational corporations (MNCs) have worldwide interests that differ fundamentally from the interests of their home countries (that is, the countries where they are headquartered). Indeed, a US or Canadian MNC may produce mainly abroad rather than at home if it serves its interests. Thus, Reich argues that the central issue for a state competing in the global economy today is not who owns the manufacturing industries within its territory but whether the state has a skilled, educated workforce. With a skilled workforce, a state will attract the type of investment it requires, whether it is foreign or domestic.

Fred Lazar, in the final selection here, on foreign ownership in Canada, strongly disagrees with Reich's arguments. According to Lazar, those countries with the lead in knowledge-based and high-technology industries are likely to be the most competitive today. Canada's economic prospects are not promising, since it is lagging behind most major industrialized countries in R&D (research and development) investments and capabilities. Lazar attributes Canada's lack of research-intensive industries to the high degree of foreign ownership in the economy. Thus, he notes that Canadian-owned firms generally devote a larger share of their revenues to R&D in Canada than Canadian branch plants of American-owned firms. In sum, Lazar and Reich have sharply differing views regarding 'who is us', and whether 'our' interests as a nation-state depend on having our own multinational corporations. The fact that this debate is going on today demonstrates the degree to which globalization and interdependence are affecting the study of international relations.

## Notes

1. Karl W. Deutsch, *The Analysis of International Relations*, 2nd edn (Englewood Cliffs, NJ: Prentice-Hall, 1978), 19.
2. See, for example, Michael W. Doyle, 'Thucydidean Realism', *Review of International Studies* 16, 3 (1990): 223–37.
3. Edward Hallett Carr, *The Twenty Years' Crisis: 1919–1939* (New York: Harper & Row, 1969), 62 (originally published in 1939).
4. Hans J. Morgenthau (revised by Kenneth W. Thompson), *Politics Among Nations: The Struggle for Power and Peace*, 6th edn (New York: Alfred A. Knopf, 1985), 31 (first published in 1948).
5. The literature on Canada as a middle power is the most extensive, and includes J. King Gordon, ed., *Canada's Role as a Middle Power* (Toronto: McClelland & Stewart, 1966); John Holmes, *Canada: A Middle-Aged Power* (Toronto: McClelland & Stewart, 1976); Andrew F. Cooper, Richard A. Higgott, and Kim Richard Nossal, *Relocating Middle Powers: Australia and Canada in a Changing World Order* (Vancouver: University of British Columbia Press, 1993). Examples of writings on Canada as a principal power and a dependent state, respectively, include David Dewitt and John Kirton, *Canada as a Principal Power* (Toronto: John Wiley & Sons, 1983); Wallace Clement, *Continental Corporate Power: Economic Linkage Between Canada and the United States* (Toronto: McClelland & Stewart, 1977). For critical reviews of the literature, see Michael K. Hawes, *Principal Power, Middle Power, or Satellite? Competing Perspectives in the Study of Canadian Foreign Policy* (Toronto: York University Research Program in Strategic Studies, 1984); Maureen Appel Molot, 'Where Do We, Should We, or Can We Sit? A Review of Canadian Foreign Policy Literature', *International Journal of Canadian Studies* 1, 2 (Spring-Fall 1990): 77–96; David R. Black and Heather A. Smith, 'Notable Exceptions? New and Arrested Directions in Canadian Foreign Policy Literature', *Canadian Journal of Political Science* 26, 4 (Dec. 1993): 745–74.
6. Carr, *The Twenty Years' Crisis, 1919–1939*, 97.
7. Paul R. Viotti and Mark V. Kauppi, *International Relations Theory—Realism, Pluralism, Globalism* (New York: Macmillan, 1987), 519. Some recent works concerned with idealism include Stanley Hoffman, *Duties Beyond Borders: On the Limits and Possibilities of Ethical International Politics* (Syracuse, NY: Syracuse University Press, 1981); J.M. Hare and Carey B. Joynt, *Ethics and International Affairs* (New York: St Martin's Press, 1982); Mervyn Frost, *Towards a Normative Theory of International Relations* (Cambridge: Cambridge University Press, 1986).

8.  Examples of behavioural contributions include Harold Guetzgow et al., *Simulation in International Relations: Developments for Research and Teaching* (Englewood Cliffs, NJ: Prentice-Hall, 1963); Richard C. Snyder, H.W. Bruck, and Burton Sapin, eds, *Foreign Policy Decision-Making* (New York: Free Press, 1963); J. David Singer, *Quantitative International Politics: Insights and Evidence* (New York: Free Press, 1968); Martin Shubik, *Games for Society, Business and War: Towards a Theory of Gaming* (New York: Elsevier, 1975).

9.  Robert C. North, 'Research Pluralism and the International Elephant', in Klaus Knorr and James N. Rosenau, eds, *Contending Approaches to International Politics* (Princeton, NJ: Princeton University Press, 1969), 218.

10. Steve Smith, 'Paradigm Dominance in International Relations: The Development of International Relations as a Social Science', *Millennium: Journal of International Studies* 16 (1987): 201.

11. See Robert O. Keohane and Joseph S. Nye, Jr, eds, *Transnational Relations and World Politics* (Cambridge, Mass.: Harvard University Press, 1972); Keohane and Nye, *Power and Interdependence*, 2nd edn (Glenview, Ill.: Scott, Foresman and Company, 1989). For additional perspectives on interdependence, see R.J. Barry Jones and Peter Willetts, eds, *Interdependence on Trial: Studies in the Theory and Reality of Contemporary Interdependence* (London: Frances Pinter, 1984).

12. Robert O. Keohane and Joseph S. Nye, Jr, 'Introduction: The Complex Politics of Canadian-American Interdependence', in Annette Baker Fox, Alfred O. Hero, Jr, and Joseph S. Nye, Jr, eds, *Canada and the United States: Transnational and Transgovernmental Relations* (New York: Columbia University Press, 1976), 4.

13. Bayless Manning, 'The Congress, the Executive and Intermestic Affairs: Three Proposals', *Foreign Affairs* 55 (June 1977): 309. Manning is credited with introducing the term 'intermestic'.

14. For example, see Douglas M. Brown and Earl H. Fry, eds, *States and Provinces in the International Economy* (Berkeley and Kingston: University of California and Queen's University, 1993); Peter Karl Kresl and Gary Gappert, eds, *North American Cities and the Global Economy: Challenges and Opportunities* (Thousand Oaks, Calif.: Sage, 1995); Theodore H. Cohn and Patrick J. Smith, 'Subnational Governments as International Actors: Constituent Diplomacy in British Columbia and the Pacific Northwest', *BC Studies* 110 (Summer 1996): 25–59.

15. The various theories of global society are discussed in K.J. Holsti, *The Dividing Discipline: Hegemony and Diversity in International Theory* (Boston: Allen & Unwin, 1985), ch. 3.

16. Saul H. Mendelowitz, 'The Program of the Institute of World Order', *Journal of International Affairs* 31 (Fall/Winter 1977): 261. Other works expressing global society views include Richard A. Falk, *This Endangered Planet* (New York: Random House, 1971); John Burton, *World Society* (Cambridge: Cambridge University Press, 1972); James Rosenau, *The Study of Global Interdependence* (London: Frances Pinter, 1980).

17. See Viotti and Kauppi, *International Relations Theory*, 9–10, 399–401. The structuralist literature is vast and diverse in nature. The reader may wish to refer to works such as Peter Evans, *Dependent Development: The Alliance of Multinational, State, and Local Capital in Brazil* (Princeton, NJ: Princeton University Press, 1979); Immanuel Wallerstein, *The Capitalist World-Economy* (Cambridge: Cambridge University Press, 1979); Thomas R. Shannon, *An Introduction to the World-System Perspective*, 2nd edn (Boulder, Colo.: Westview Press, 1996).

18. For example, see Clement, *Continental Corporate Power*; Glen Williams, 'On Determining Canada's Location within the International Political Economy', *Studies in Political Economy*

25 (Spring 1988): 107–40; Daniel Drache, 'The Crisis of Canadian Political Economy: Dependency Theory Versus the New Orthodoxy', *Canadian Journal of Political and Social Theory* (Fall 1983): 25–48.

19. See Kim Richard Nossal, *The Politics of Canadian Foreign Policy*, 2nd edn (Scarborough, Ont.: Prentice-Hall, 1989), ch. 3. The difficulty in reaching a consensus on Canada's power position is a further indication of the problems that behaviouralists have in quantifying variables.

20. As Susan Strange notes, 'today there are variants of hegemonic theory to suit most political tastes.' Susan Strange, 'The Persistent Myth of Lost Hegemony', *International Organization* 41, 4 (Autumn 1987): 557.

21. Stephen D. Krasner, 'Structural Causes and Regime Consequences: Regimes as Intervening Variables', in Krasner, ed., *International Regimes* (Ithaca, NY: Cornell University Press, 1983), 2.

22. For discussions of the trade regime norms, see Jock A. Finlayson and Mark W. Zacher, 'The GATT and the Regulation of Trade Barriers: Regime Dynamics and Functions', in Krasner, ed., *International Regimes*, 273–314; Gilbert R. Winham, *The Evolution of International Trade Agreements* (Toronto: University of Toronto Press, 1992).

23. See Robert O. Keohane, *After Hegemony: Cooperation and Discord in the World Economy* (Princeton, NJ: Princeton University Press, 1984).

24. See Kenneth N. Waltz, *Theory of International Politics* (Reading, Mass.: Addison-Wesley, 1979).

25. Robert Gilpin, *The Political Economy of International Relations* (Princeton, NJ: Princeton University Press, 1987), xii.

26. For a discussion of these challenges see Holsti, *The Dividing Discipline*, and the special issue of *Millenium* 16, 2 (1987), on the development of international relations.

## Study Questions for the Readings

1. Traditionally, security issues were defined in terms of the East-West conflict between the two superpowers, the United States and the Soviet Union. With the decline of the Cold War, should we broaden our definition of 'security' to include environmental and other common threats to humanity? Refer to the Homer-Dixon selection in your discussion.

2. Which of the following two factors has a greater effect on Canada's competitiveness as a nation-state: the amount of foreign ownership in Canadian industry or the skills and education of Canadians? Refer to the selections by Reich and Lazar in your answer.

3. Why does Lazar, a Canadian, have a different view about foreign multinational corporations than Reich, an American? Does the difference in their views relate to the fact that the United States is a major power and Canada is a middle power?

# Violent Conflict, Environmental Scarcity, and Long-term Security Implications

Thomas F. Homer-Dixon

If food production stagnates, if some developing societies slide further into poverty, if large numbers of people leave their homelands, and if institutions and social relations are disrupted, what kinds of conflict are likely to develop?

There is not much information on which to base an answer to this question. This may be partly because environmental and population pressures have not yet passed a critical threshold of severity in many poor countries. Also, environmental problems are very complex, and until recently there was little good research on environment-conflict linkages. But on the basis of the case studies in the project on 'Environmental Change and Acute Conflict', three types of conflict seem most likely.

## Three Perspectives in Conflict

*Scarcity conflicts* are those one intuitively expects when countries calculate their self-interest in a world where the amount of resources is fixed, that is, in a world where the resource pie does not grow. Such conflict will probably arise over three types of resources in particular: river water, fish, and good cropland. These renewable resources are likely to spark conflict because their scarcity is increasing swiftly in some regions, they are often critical to human survival, and they can be physically seized or controlled.

The current controversy over the Euphrates River, discussed at the start of this book, illus-

trates how scarcity conflicts can arise. It is clear, though, that the problem of Euphrates water is tangled up with issues of territorial integrity and relations between government and ethnic minorities in both Syria and Turkey. Although water scarcity is a source of serious tensions between Syria and Turkey, and may produce interstate violence in the future, this dispute is not a pure example of a scarcity conflict. Truly pure examples may be impossible to find.

Experts in international relations who address the security implications of environmental scarcity usually emphasize the potential for scarcity conflicts. Yet research within the project on environmental change shows that these conflicts will not be the most common to arise from environmental stress. Indeed, ethnic disputes and corrosive conflict within countries deserve a greater portion of expert attention.

*Group-identity conflicts* are likely to arise from the large-scale movements of populations caused by environmental scarcity. As different ethnic and cultural groups are pushed together, people in these groups usually see themselves and their neighbours in terms of 'we' and 'they'; in other words, they will use the identity of their own group to judge the worth of other groups. Such attitudes often lead to bitter hostility and even violence. The situation in the Bangladesh-Assam region may be a good example of this process; Assam's ethnic strife over the last decade has apparently been catalysed by immigration from Bangladesh. This case is discussed further below.

Growing population and environmental stresses in poor countries will undoubtedly lead to surging immigration to the industrialized world. Princeton political scientist Richard Ullman writes: 'The image of islands of affluence amidst a

Excerpted from the Foreign Policy Association's Headline Series No. 300, *Environmental Scarcity and Global Security*. Published by the FPA. Reprinted with permission from the FPA, 470 Park Avenue South, NY, NY 10016, USA.

sea of poverty is not inaccurate.' People will seek to move from Latin America to the United States and Canada, from North Africa and the Middle East to Europe, and from South and Southeast Asia to Australia. This migration has already shifted the ethnic balance in many cities and regions of rich countries, and governments are struggling to contain a backlash against 'foreigners'. Such racial or ethnic strife will become much worse.

Although it seems probable that environmental scarcity will cause people to move in large numbers, which will in turn produce conflict, several qualifications are needed. First, refugees tend to have limited means to organize and to make demands on the government of the receiving society. Rather than overt violence, therefore, a common result will be silent misery and death, with little destabilizing effect. Second, government intervention plays a critical role in determining whether population displacement causes conflict; displaced groups often need the backing of a government (either that of the receiving society or of an external one) before they have sufficient power to cause conflict. And finally, it should be noted that migration does not always produce negative results. It can, for instance, ease labour shortages in the receiving society, as has been the case, for instance, in Malaysia. Countries as diverse as Canada, Thailand, and Malawi demonstrate that societies often have a striking capacity to absorb migrants without conflict.

*Deprivation conflicts.* As poor societies produce less wealth because of environmental problems, their citizens will probably become increasingly angered by the widening gap between their actual standard of living and the standard they feel they deserve. The rate of change is key: the faster the economic deterioration, the greater the discontent. Lower-status groups will be more frustrated than others because élites will use their power to maintain, as best they can, the same standard of living despite a shrinking economic pie. At some point, the frustration and anger of certain groups may cross a critical threshold, and

they will act violently against those groups perceived to be the agents of their economic misery or those thought to be benefiting from an unfair distribution of economic rewards in the society.

In general, experts on conflict within societies say that rebellion, revolution, and insurgency are likely when (1) there are clearly defined and organized groups in a society; (2) some of these groups regard their level of economic achievement, and in turn the broader political and economic system, as wholly unfair; and (3) these same groups believe that all peaceful opportunities to achieve change are blocked, yet regard the balance of power within the society as unstable; in other words, they believe there are opportunities for overthrowing authority in the society.

Environmental scarcity helps produce both the second and third of these conditions. A key social effect in poor countries is the disruption of institutions such as the state. Thus, environmental problems may not only increase the frustration and anger within poor societies (through increased deprivation); in addition, by weakening the state and other institutions, environmental problems may open up opportunities for angry groups to overthrow existing authority. These groups will also be more likely to challenge authority in a society if they have good leaders and are well organized. Leaders help the members of their group believe that their situation should and can be changed. All of these factors are evident in the case study of the Philippines, in the next section.

## Case Studies

Three sources of environmental scarcity, identified earlier, are degradation and depletion of renewable resources, population growth, and changes in resource distribution among groups. In this section, the case studies will show how these three sources operate singly or in combination to produce the types of conflict just discussed. The case studies are drawn from the work of the research project on environmental change. They suggest

## Figure 1: Some Sources and Consequences of Environmental Scarcity

Sources of
Environmental Scarcity

Social Effects

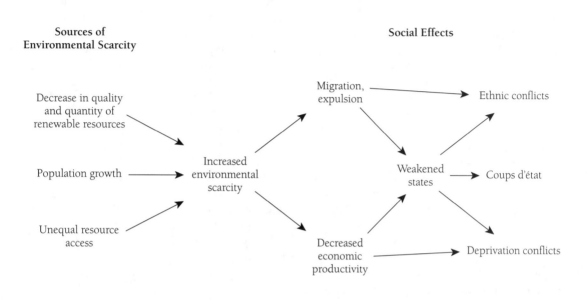

that group-identity and deprivation conflicts will be particularly common outcomes of environmental scarcity (see Figure 1).

### Bangladesh-Assam

Population growth by itself will be a key source of social stress and conflict in some cases. Bangladesh, for instance, does not suffer a critical loss of agricultural land from erosion or nutrient depletion because the normal floods of the Ganges and Brahmaputra rivers lay down a layer of silt every year that helps maintain the fertility of the country's vast plains. But the UN predicts that Bangladesh's current population of 115 million will grow to 235 million by the year 2025. Cropland is already desperately scarce at about 0.08 hectares per capita, but since all of the country's good agricultural land has already been

exploited, population growth will cut this figure in half by 2025. Land scarcity and the brutal poverty and social turmoil it produces have been made worse by repeated severe floods (perhaps aggravated by deforestation in the watersheds of the region's major rivers) and the susceptibility of the country to cyclones.

As noted previously, over the last four decades these stresses have caused millions of people to migrate from Bangladesh, formerly East Pakistan, to neighbouring areas of India. Detailed data are scarce; the Bangladeshi government is reluctant to admit that there has been a significant exodus because the problem has become a major source of friction with India. But one of the researchers on the environmental-change project, Sanjoy Hazarika, an investigative journalist who reports for *The New York Times* from South Asia, has pieced together demographic information and experts' estimates. He concludes that migrants from Bangladesh and their descendants have increased the population of neighbouring areas of India by 15 million people, of which only 1 million or 2 million can be attributed to migration caused by the 1971 war between India and Pakistan that resulted in the creation of Bangladesh. He estimates that the population of the state of Assam has swelled by at least 7 million people, of Tripura by 1 million, and of West Bengal by about 7 million.

This enormous movement of people has produced sweeping changes in the politics and economies of the receiving regions. It has altered land distribution, economic relations, and the balance of political power between religious and ethnic groups, and it has triggered serious intergroup conflict, for example between the Lalung tribe and Bengali Muslim migrants in Assam. In the neighbouring Indian state of Tripura, the original Buddhist and Christian inhabitants now make up only 29 per cent of the state's population, with the rest consisting of Hindu migrants from Bangladesh. This shift in the ethnic balance precipitated a violent insurgency between 1980 and 1988 that was called off only after the government agreed to return land to dispossessed Tripuris and stop the influx. But because the migration has continued, this agreement is in jeopardy.

India offers certain attractions for potential migrants from Bangladesh. The standard of living is often much better; furthermore, Indian politicians have often encouraged Bangladeshis to enter India in order to expand certain segments of the voting population. The region's conflicts must also be seen in the light of history. During the colonial period, for instance, the British used Hindus from Calcutta to administer Assam. The Assamese are therefore particularly sensitive to their growing loss of political and cultural control in the region as more people migrate from Bangladesh. While this historical context is important, it does not obscure the powerful influence of environmental scarcity behind these conflicts.

## The Senegal River Basin

Elsewhere in the world, population growth and damage to renewable resources often encourage large-scale development projects that can shift resource access. This can produce dire conditions for poorer and less powerful groups whose claims to resources are opposed by élites, and this may lead to violence. A good example is the dispute that began in West Africa in 1989 between Mauritania and Senegal over the Senegal River valley which defines their common border.

Senegal has fairly abundant agricultural land, but much of it suffers from high to severe wind and water erosion, loss of nutrients, salinization, and soil compaction caused by agriculture. The country has an overall population density of 38 people per square kilometre and an annual population growth rate of 2.7 per cent, giving a doubling time of about 25 years.

Except for the valley of the Senegal River along its southern border and a few oases, Mauritania is largely arid desert and semiarid grassland. Although its population density is very low, at approximately 2 people per square kilometre, the population growth rate is 2.8 per cent. This combination of factors led the UN's Food and Agriculture Organization (FAO) in a 1982 study to include both Mauritania and Senegal in their list of 'critical' countries whose croplands cannot support their current and projected populations without a large increase in agricultural inputs, like fertilizer and irrigation.

The floodplains fringing the Senegal River are broad and fertile, and have long supported a productive economy—farming, herding, and fishing—based on the river's annual floods. During the 1970s, a serious drought and the prospect of a chronic food shortfall in the region encouraged the region's governments to seek international financing for the high Manantali Dam on the Bafing River tributary in Mali and the Diama salt-intrusion barrage near the mouth of the Senegal River between Senegal and Mauritania. These dams were designed to regulate the river's flow to produce hydropower, expand irrigated agriculture, and provide river transport from the Atlantic Ocean to landlocked Mali. But there were other social and economic consequences that the international experts and regional governments did not foresee.

Senegal's population is mainly black; but prior to 1989 there was a small but vigorous class of white Moor shopkeepers throughout much of the country. Mauritania, in contrast, is dominated by a white Moor élite, and there has been a long history of racism by these Moors toward their non-Arab black compatriots. This racism is deeply resented by black Africans across the border in Senegal.

As anthropologist Michael Horowitz has found, anticipation of the new dams sharply increased land values along the river where irrigation could be installed. The Moor élite in Mauritania suddenly became interested in title to this land and rewrote the legislation governing its ownership. This effectively stripped black Africans of their rights to continue farming and herding along the Mauritanian bank of the Senegal River, as they had done for generations.

In the spring of 1989, tensions in the river basin triggered an explosion of attacks by blacks against Moors in Senegal, which led to attacks by Moors against blacks in Mauritania. Within a few weeks, almost all of the 17,000 shops owned by Moors in Senegal had been pillaged or destroyed, several hundred people had been killed in ethnic violence in both countries, and thousands had been injured. Nearly 200,000 refugees fled in both directions across the border, and the two countries were nearly at war. The Mauritanian regime used this occasion to activate new land legislation, declaring the black population along the Mauritanian portion of the river basin to be Senegalese, stripping them of their citizenship, and seizing their properties and livestock. Many of these blacks were forcibly expelled to Senegal, and some launched cross-border raids to retrieve expropriated cattle.

This case study illustrates the interaction of the three sources of human-induced environmental scarcity identified earlier. Agricultural shortfalls, caused in part by population pressures and degradation of the land resource, encouraged a large development scheme. These factors together raised land values in one of the few areas in either country offering the potential for a rapid move to modern, high-input agriculture. The result was a change in property rights and resource distribution, a sudden increase in resource scarcity for an ethnic minority, expulsion of the minority, and ethnic violence.

### The Jordan River Basin

The water shortage on the occupied West Bank of the Jordan River offers a similar example of how population growth and excessive resource consumption and degradation can promote unequal resource access. While figures vary, one of the project's researchers, Miriam Lowi of Princeton University, estimates that the total amount of renewable fresh water annually available to Israel is about 1,950 million cubic metres (mcm), of which 60 per cent comes from groundwater (i.e., aquifers), and the rest from river flow, floodwater, and waste-water recycling. Current Israeli demand, including the needs of settlements in the occupied territories and Golan Heights, is around 2,200 mcm. The annual deficit of some 200 mcm is covered by overpumping aquifers. As a result, the water table in some parts of Israel and the West Bank is dropping significantly (Israeli experts estimate from 0.2 to 0.4 metres per year), thus causing the salinization of wells and the infiltration of sea water from the Mediterranean. Moreover, Israel's population is expected to increase from the present 4.6 million to 6.5 million in the year 2020, even without major immigration from the countries of the former Soviet Union. Based on this population growth projection, the country's water demand could exceed 2,600 mcm by 2020.

Two of the three main aquifers on which Israel depends lie principally underneath the West Bank, with their waters draining into Israel proper. Consequently, nearly 40 per cent of the groundwater Israel uses originates in occupied territory. In order to protect this important source for Israeli consumption, the Israeli government has strictly limited water use on the West Bank. Of the 650 mcm of all forms of water annually available in that territory, Arabs are allowed to use only 125 mcm. Israel restricts the number of wells Arabs can drill in the territory, the amount of water Arabs are allowed to pump, and the times at which Arabs can draw irrigation water. The differential in water access on the West Bank is marked: on a per capita basis, Jewish settlers consume about four times as much as Arabs.

Arabs are not permitted to drill new wells for agricultural purposes, although the Mekorot (the Israeli water company) has drilled more than 30 wells for settlers' irrigation. Arab agriculture in the region—especially in areas such as Jericho—has suffered because many Arab wells have become dry or saline as a result of deeper Israeli wells drilled in proximity. This, combined with the confiscation of agricultural land for settlers and other Israeli restrictions on Palestinian agriculture, has encouraged many West Bank Arabs to abandon farming. Those who have done so have become either unemployed or day labourers within Israel.

The Middle East as a whole faces increasingly grave and tangled problems of water scarcity, and many experts believe these will affect the region's security. Water was a factor contributing to tensions preceding the 1967 Arab-Israeli war, and the war gave Israel control over most of the Jordan basin's water resources. While 'water wars' in the basin are possible in the future, they seem unlikely given the military predominance of Israel. More probably, in the context of age-old ethnic and political disputes, water shortages will aggravate social tensions and unrest within societies in the Jordan River basin. In recent congressional testimony, political scientist Thomas Naff noted

that 'rather than warfare among riparians [i.e., countries that border or straddle rivers] in the immediate future, what is more likely to ensue from water-related crises in this decade is internal civil disorder, changes in regimes, political radicalization and instability.'

## The Philippines

In many parts of the world, a somewhat different process is under way: unequal resource access combines with population growth to produce environmental damage. This can lead to economic deprivation that spurs insurgency and rebellion.

In the Philippines, Spanish and American colonial policies left behind a grossly unfair distribution of land. Since the 1960s, the government, often in collusion with the country's powerful landowners, has promoted the modernization and further expansion of large-scale agriculture in the country's low-lying coastal plains. This was done to raise the output of grain for domestic consumption and of cash crops such as coconuts, pineapples, bananas, and sugar to help pay the country's massive foreign debt. In general, this has held static or lowered the labour demand per hectare (the 'labour-intensity') of agricultural production. With a population growth rate of 2.3 per cent and with little rural industrialization to absorb excess labour, agricultural wages have fallen, and the number of poor agricultural labourers and landless peasants has swelled. Economically desperate, millions of people have migrated to shantytowns in already overstressed cities, such as the Smoky Mountain squatters camp in Manila, while millions of others have moved to the least productive and often most ecologically vulnerable territories, especially steep hillsides away from the coastal plains (see Figure 2).

In these uplands, settlers use fire to clear forested land or land that has been previously logged by commercial companies closely associated with landowning, government, and military élites. The settlers bring with them little money or

## Figure 2: Some Sources and Consequences of Environmental Scarcity in the Philippines

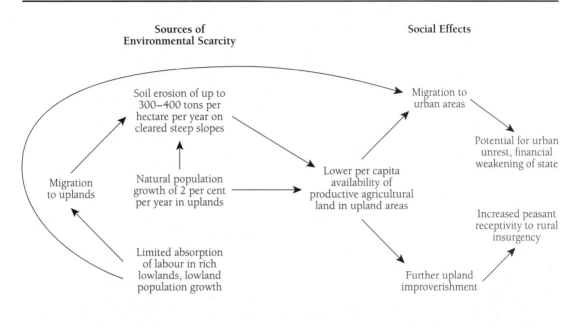

knowledge to protect their fragile ecosystems, and their small-scale logging, production of charcoal for the cities, and slash-and-burn farming often cause horrendous environmental damage, including water erosion, landslides, and changes in the hydrological cycle. This has set in motion a cycle of falling food production, clearing of new plots, and further land degradation. Even marginally fertile land is becoming hard to find in many places, and economic conditions are often hazardous for the peasants.

The country has suffered from serious internal strife for many decades. But two of the project's researchers, Celso Roque, the former undersecretary for the environment of the Philippines, and his colleague, Maria Garcia, have concluded that resource stress appears to be an increasingly powerful force driving the Communist-led

insurgency. Some senior Philippine politicians have reached the same conclusion. Daniel Lacson, the governor of the province of Negros Occidental under President Aquino, identifies two sources of poverty and injustice behind the insurgency: the accumulation of land in the hands of a few who have failed to deal with the problems of the poor; and land degradation that affects small farmers and is not alleviated by government action.

The upland insurgency is motivated by the economic deprivation of the landless agricultural labourers and poor farmers displaced into the hills where they try to eke out a living from failing land; it exploits opportunities for rebellion in the country's peripheral regions, which are largely beyond the effective control of the central government; and it is helped by the creative leadership of the cadres of the New People's Army and the

National Democratic Front. During the 1970s and 1980s, these groups found upland peasants very receptive to revolutionary ideology, especially where the repression of landlords and local governments left them little choice but to rebel or starve. The revolutionaries have built on local understandings and social structures to help the peasants define their situation and focus their discontent.

## Other Similar Cases

Processes similar to those in the Philippines are strikingly common around the planet. Population growth and unequal access to land force huge numbers of people either into cities or onto marginal lands. In the latter case they cause major environmental damage and become chronically poor. Eventually, they may be the source of persistent unrest and insurgency, or they may migrate from these marginal regions yet again, stimulating ethnic conflicts elsewhere or urban unrest. The short but violent 'Soccer War' between El Salvador and Honduras in 1969 involved just such a combination of factors.

As William Durham of Stanford University has shown, changes in agricultural practice and land distribution in El Salvador since the mid-nineteenth century concentrated poor farmers in the country's uplands. Over the years these farmers developed some understanding of land conservation, but inevitably their increasing numbers on very steep hillsides caused serious deforestation and erosion. A natural population growth rate of 3.5 per cent further aggravated land scarcity, and as a result many people migrated to neighbouring Honduras where there was more open land. Tension gradually increased between the newcomers and the local Hondurans, and the eventual expulsion of the migrants from Honduras started the war. Durham notes that the competition for land in El Salvador that led to this conflict was not addressed after the war; it was a powerful factor behind the country's subsequent civil war; and it was a central issue in El Salvador's arduous peace negotiations.

Similarly, in South Africa, the white regime's past apartheid policies concentrated millions of blacks in the 'homelands', created by the South African government in some of the country's least productive and most ecologically sensitive territories, where population densities were made worse by high natural birth rates. In 1980, rural areas of the Ciskei homeland had a population density of 82 persons per square kilometre, while the surrounding predominantly white Cape Province of South Africa had a rural density of two. Homeland residents have little money and few resource-management skills and are the victims of undemocratic, corrupt, and abusive local governments. Sustainable development in such a situation is impossible, and wide areas have been completely stripped of trees for fuelwood, grazed down to bare dirt, and eroded of topsoil. A 1980 report concluded that nearly 50 per cent of Ciskei's land was moderately or severely eroded, and nearly 40 per cent of its pasturage was overgrazed.

This loss of the resource base, combined with a lack of alternative means of employment and social breakdown due to the stresses induced by apartheid, has produced an economic crisis in the homelands. This, in turn, has caused high levels of migration to South African cities, which are still unable to integrate and employ these migrants adequately, due to the social and economic structures remaining from apartheid. The result is the rapid growth of squatter settlements and illegal townships that are rife with violence that threatens the country's move to full democracy.

## Long-term Security Implications

Can poor countries respond effectively to environmental scarcity to prevent the processes described above? If some of them cannot, what will this mean for national and international security over the long term?

## Supply and Demand of Human Ingenuity

Some optimists argue that it is not so much environmental scarcity *per se* that is important as whether or not people are harmed by it. Human suffering might be avoided if political and economic systems provided the incentives and ingenuity that allow people to reduce or eliminate the harmful effects of scarcity. To address this argument, more information is needed about the factors that affect the supply and demand of human ingenuity in response to environmental scarcity.

The combined or 'aggregate' data on world food production might seem to justify optimism. Between 1965 and 1986, many poor regions suffered serious environmental problems, including erosion, salinization, and land loss to urbanization. Yet global production of cereal grains increased 3 per cent a year, meat and milk output grew by 2 per cent annually, while the growth rate for oil crops, vegetables, and legumes was 2.5 per cent. At the regional level, increased food production kept ahead of population growth, except in Africa, and shortfalls were eased by exports from rich countries with huge surpluses. One might therefore conclude that poor countries have sufficient resources and ingenuity, with occasional assistance from grain-exporting countries, to respond to environmental problems.

But such aggregate figures hide large differences in food availability among and within poor countries. Moreover, these statistics are not as promising as they once were: many developing countries have already reaped most of the green revolution's potential benefit, and the rate of increase in global cereal production has declined by over 40 per cent since the 1960s. For three successive years—from 1987 through 1989—global cereal consumption exceeded production. While bumper grain crops were again harvested in 1990, carryover stocks can be rapidly exhausted, and as few as two years of bad harvests in key agricultural regions could produce a global food crisis.

Over the long term, the ability of poor countries to respond well to the effects of environmental scarcity on agriculture will depend on the complex interactions within each society of [a number of] factors. . . . Particularly important factors are the society's dominant land-use practices, land distribution, and market mechanisms within the agricultural sector. The latter is especially important today, since numerous poor countries are giving up state control over their markets, reducing government spending, and allowing more foreign investment.

According to most economists, in a market economy that gives accurate prices to all traded goods and services, environmental scarcity will encourage conservation, technological innovation, and substitution of more abundant resources for scarce ones. Princeton University economist Julian Simon, in particular, has an unwavering faith in the capacity of human ingenuity to overcome scarcity when spurred by self-interest. Many economists point to the success of the green revolution, which they claim was driven in part by market forces, since, among other things, it involved the substitution of relatively cheap petroleum resources (in the form of fertilizer) for increasingly degraded, and therefore more expensive, agricultural land. This powerful argument supports the policies for liberalizing markets in poor countries advocated by international financial and lending institutions, such as the International Monetary Fund and the World Bank. But these policies may not be an effective response to environmental scarcity in the future.

## Cornucopians and Neo-Malthusians

Experts in environmental studies now commonly use the labels 'cornucopian' for optimists like Simon and 'neo-Malthusian' for pessimists like the scientists and authors Paul and Anne Ehrlich. Cornucopians do not worry much about protecting the stock of any single resource because of their faith that market-driven human ingenuity can always be tapped to allow the substitution of more abundant resources to provide the same service. Simon writes: 'There is no physical or economic reason why human resourcefulness and enterprise cannot forever continue to respond to impending shortages and existing problems with new expedients that, after an adjustment period, leave us better off than before the problem arose.'

The neo-Malthusian label comes from the eighteenth-century economist Thomas Malthus, who claimed that severe hardship was unavoidable because human population always grows much faster than food production. Neo-Malthusians are much more cautious than cornucopians in their assessment of human ability to push back resource limits. For renewable resources, they often make the distinction between 'capital' and 'income' discussed above; they contend that human economic activity should leave environmental capital intact and undamaged so that future generations can enjoy a constant stream of income from these resources.

Historically, however, cornucopians have been right to criticize the idea that resource scarcity places fixed limits on human activity. Time and time again, human beings have circumvented scarcities, and neo-Malthusians have often been justly accused of 'crying wolf'. But in assuming the experience of the past pertains to the future, cornucopians overlook seven factors.

## Cornucopian Oversights

First, whereas serious scarcities of critical resources in the past usually appeared singly, now multiple scarcities interact with each other to produce synergistic effects. An agricultural region may, for example, be simultaneously stressed by degraded water and soil, greenhouse-induced changes in rainfall, and increased ultraviolet radiation. The total impact of these interacting problems may be much greater than the sum of their separate impacts. Moreover, thresholds and

extreme events make the future highly uncertain for government decisions. Finally, as numerous resources become scarce at the same time, it is harder to identify substitution possibilities that serve the same purposes at costs that prevailed when scarcity was less severe.

Second, in the past the scarcity of a given resource usually increased slowly, allowing time for social, economic, and technological adjustment. But human populations are much larger and the activities of people consume, on a global average, many more resources than before. This means that critical scarcities often develop much more quickly; whole countries are deforested in a few decades; most of a region's topsoil can disappear in a generation; and critical ozone depletion may occur in as little as 20 years.

Third, today's consumption has far greater momentum than in the past because of the size of the population of consumers and the sheer quantity of material consumed by this population. The countless individuals and groups making up societies are heavily committed to certain patterns of resource use, and the ability of markets to adapt may be sharply limited by these special interests.

These first three factors may soon combine to give a new and particularly severe character to global environmental scarcity: the populace will face multiple resource shortages that are interacting and unpredictable, that quickly grow to crisis proportions, and that will be hard to address because of powerful commitments to certain patterns of consumption.

The fourth reason that cornucopian arguments may not apply in the future is that the free-market price mechanism is a bad gauge of scarcity, especially for resources held commonly by all people, such as a favourable climate and productive seas. In the past, many such resources seemed endlessly abundant; now they are being degraded and depleted, and it is becoming evident that their greater scarcity often has tremendous bearing on a society's well-being. Yet this scarcity is at best reflected only indirectly in market prices. In addition, people often cannot buy or sell in a market in which they have an interest, because they either lack the money or are distant from the market in space or time. For instance, poor coastal communities in the southern Indian state of Kerala see their local fish catches dwindling year-by-year because of overfishing offshore; yet they do not have the money or ability to buy fish in international markets. Similarly, future generations who will suffer from today's overfishing cannot buy fish in today's markets either. In such cases the true scarcity of the resource is not reflected by its price.

The fifth reason is an extension of a point made earlier: market-driven adaptation to resource scarcity is most likely to succeed in wealthy societies. Abundant reserves of money, knowledge, and talent help economic actors invent new technologies, identify possibilities for conservation, and make the transition from old to new patterns of production and consumption. Yet many of the countries facing the most serious environmental problems in the coming decades will be poor; even if they have efficient markets, lack of money and know-how will keep them from responding well to these problems.

Sixth, cornucopians have an outdated faith in human beings' ability to unravel and manage the complex processes of nature. There is no fundamental reason to expect that scientific and technical ingenuity can always overcome all types of scarcity. People may not have the mental capacity to understand adequately the complexities of environmental and social systems. Even with this capacity, it may simply be impossible, given the physical, biological, and social laws governing these systems, to reduce all scarcity or repair all environmental damage. Moreover, scientific and technical knowledge must be built incrementally—layer upon layer—and its diffusion into the broader society often takes decades. Technological solutions to environmental scarcity, if indeed any are to be found, may arrive too late to prevent catastrophe.

Seventh, future environmental problems, rather than inspiring the wave of ingenuity predicted by cornucopians, may actually reduce the supply of ingenuity available to a society. Two kinds of ingenuity are key to dealing with environmental scarcity. 'Technical ingenuity' is needed for the development of, for example, new agricultural and forestry technologies that compensate for environmental degradation. 'Social ingenuity' is needed for the creation of institutions and organizations that buffer people from the effects of degradation and provide the right incentives for people to develop new technologies. The development and distribution of new grains adapted for dry climates and eroded soils, of alternative cooking technologies to compensate for the loss of firewood, and of water conservation technologies depend on an intricate and stable system of markets, laws, financial agencies, and educational and research institutions. Not only are poor countries undersupplied with these social resources, their ability to create and maintain them will be weakened by the very environmental stresses they need to address.

Cornucopians often overlook the role of social ingenuity in producing and maintaining the complex legal and economic climate in which technical ingenuity can flourish. Governments, bureaucrats, and local community leaders must be clever 'social engineers' to design and implement good adaptation strategies and market mechanisms. Unfortunately, though, multiple, interacting, unpredictable, and rapidly changing environmental problems will dramatically increase the complexity and urgency of the setting within which government and community leaders must operate; and they will also generate increased 'social friction' as élites and interest groups struggle to protect their shares of economic and political power. The ability of governments and others to respond to the increased demand for social ingenuity by being good social engineers will likely go down, not up, as these stresses increase.

When it comes to the poorest countries on this planet, therefore, one should not invest too much faith in the potential of human ingenuity to respond to environmental problems once they have become severe. The most important of the seven factors above is the last: growing population, consumption, and environmental stresses will increase decision-making complexity and social friction. These will in turn reduce the ability of leaders in poor countries to intervene as good social engineers in order to chart a sustainable development path and prevent further social disruption. Neo-Malthusians may underestimate human adaptability, but as time passes their analysis will become ever more telling. . . .

# Who Is Us?

Robert B. Reich

Across the United States, you can hear calls for us to revitalize our national competitiveness. But wait—who is 'us'? Is it IBM, Motorola, Whirlpool, and General Motors? Or is it Sony, Thomson, Philips, and Honda?

Consider two successful corporations:

- Corporation A is headquartered north of New York City. Most of its top managers are citizens of the United States. All of its directors are American citizens, and a majority of its shares are held by American investors. But most of Corporation A's employees are non-Americans. Indeed, the company undertakes much of its R&D and product design, and most of its complex manufacturing, outside the borders of the United States in Asia, Latin America, and Europe. Within the American market, an increasing amount of the company's product comes from its laboratories and factories abroad.
- Corporation B is headquartered abroad, in another industrialized nation. Most of its top managers and directors are citizens of that nation, and a majority of its shares are held by citizens of that nation. But most of Corporation B's employees are Americans. Indeed, Corporation B undertakes much of its R&D and new product design in the United States. And it does most of its manufacturing in the US. The company exports an increasing proportion of its American-based production, some of it even back to the nation where Corporation B is headquartered.

Now, who is 'us'? Between these two corporations, which is the American corporation, which the foreign corporation? Which is more important to the economic future of the United States?

As the American economy becomes more globalized, examples of both Corporation A and B are increasing. At the same time, American concern for the competitiveness of the United States is increasing. Typically, the assumed vehicle for improving the competitive performance of the United States is the American corporation—by which most people would mean Corporation A. But today, the competitiveness of American-owned corporations is no longer the same as American competitiveness. Indeed, American ownership of the corporation is profoundly less relevant to America's economic future than the skills, training, and knowledge commanded by American workers—workers who are increasingly employed within the United States by foreign-owned corporations.

So who is us? The answer is, the American workforce, the American people, but not particularly the American corporation. The implications of this new answer are clear: if we hope to revitalize the competitive performance of the United States economy, we must invest in people, not in nationally defined corporations. We must open our borders to investors from around the world rather than favouring companies that may simply fly the US flag. And government policies should promote human capital in this country rather than assuming that American corporations will invest on 'our' behalf. The American corporation is simply no longer 'us'.

## Global Companies

American corporations have been abroad for years, even decades. So in one sense, the multinational identity of American companies is nothing new. What is new is that American-owned multinationals are beginning to employ large numbers of foreigners relative to their American workforces, are beginning to rely on foreign facilities to do many of their most technologically complex activities, and are beginning to export from their foreign facilities—including bringing products back to the United States.

Around the world, the numbers are already large—and still growing. Take IBM—often considered the thoroughbred of competitive American corporations. Forty per cent of IBM's world employees are foreign, and the percentage is increasing. IBM Japan boasts 18,000 Japanese employees and annual sales of more than $6 billion, making it one of Japan's major exporters of computers.

Or consider Whirlpool. After cutting its American workforce by 10 per cent and buying Philips' appliance business, Whirlpool now employs 43,500 people around the world in 45 countries—most of them non-Americans. Another example is Texas Instruments, which now does most of its research, development, design, and manufacturing in East Asia. TI employs over 5,000 people in Japan alone, making advanced semiconductors—almost half of which are exported, many of them back to the United States.

American corporations now employ 11 per cent of the industrial workforce of Northern Ireland, making everything from cigarettes to computer software, much of which comes back to the United States. More than 100,000 Singaporians work for more than 200 US corporations, most of them fabricating and assembling electronic components for export to the United States. Singapore's largest private employer is General Electric, which also accounts for a big share of that nation's growing exports. Taiwan counts AT&T,

RCA, and Texas Instruments among its largest exporters. In fact, more than one-third of Taiwan's notorious trade surplus with the United States comes from US corporations making or buying things there, then selling or using them back in the United States. The same corporate sourcing practice accounts for a substantial share of the US trade imbalance with Singapore, South Korea, and Mexico—raising a question as to whom complaints about trade imbalances should be directed.

The pattern is not confined to America's largest companies. Molex, a suburban Chicago maker of connectors used to link wires in cars and computer boards, with revenues of about $300 million in 1988, has 38 overseas factories, five in Japan. Loctite, a mid-size company with sales in 1988 of $457 million, headquartered in Newington, Connecticut, makes and sells adhesives and sealants all over the world. It has 3,000 employees—only 1,200 of whom are Americans. These companies are just part of a much larger trend: according to a 1987 McKinsey & Company study, America's most profitable midsize companies increased their investments in overseas production at an annual rate of 20 per cent between 1981 and 1986.

Overall, the evidence suggests that US companies have not lost their competitive edge over the last 20 years—they've just moved their base of operations. In 1966, American-based multinationals accounted for about 17 per cent of world exports; since then, their share has remained almost unchanged. But over the same period, the share of exports from the United States in the world's total trade in manufactures fell from 16 per cent to 14 per cent. In other words, while Americans exported less, the overseas affiliates of US-owned corporations exported more than enough to offset the drop.

The old trend of overseas capital investment is accelerating: US companies increased foreign capital spending by 24 per cent in 1988, 13 per cent in 1989. But even more important, US businesses are now putting substantial sums of money into foreign countries to do R&D work. According to National Science Foundation figures, American corporations increased their overseas R&D spending by 33 per cent between 1986 and 1988, compared with a 6 per cent increase in R&D spending in the United States. Since 1987, Eastman Kodak, W.R. Grace, Du Pont, Merck, and Upjohn have all opened new R&D facilities in Japan. At Du Pont's Yokohama laboratory, more than 180 Japanese scientists and technicians are working at developing new materials technologies. IBM's Tokyo Research Lab, tucked away behind the far side of the Imperial Palace in downtown Tokyo, houses a small army of Japanese engineers who are perfecting image-processing technology. Another IBM laboratory, the Kanagawa arm of its Yamato Development Laboratory, houses 1,500 researchers who are developing hardware and software. Nor does IBM confine its pioneering work to Japan: recently, two European researchers at IBM's Zurich laboratory announced major breakthroughs into superconductivity and microscopy—earning them both Nobel Prizes.

An even more dramatic development is the arrival of foreign corporations in the United States at a rapidly increasing pace. As recently as 1977, only about 3.5 per cent of the value added and the employment of American manufacturing originated in companies controlled by foreign parents. By 1987, the number had grown to almost 8 per cent. In just the last two years, with the faster pace of foreign acquisitions and investments, the figure is now almost 11 per cent. Foreign-owned companies now employ 3 million Americans, roughly 10 per cent of our manufacturing workers. In fact, in 1989, affiliates of foreign manufacturers created more jobs in the United States than American-owned manufacturing companies.

And these non-US companies are vigorously exporting from the United States. Sony now exports audio- and videotapes to Europe from its Dothan, Alabama, factory and ships audio recorders from its Fort Lauderdale, Florida, plant. Sharp exports 100,000 microwave ovens a year from its factory in Memphis, Tennessee. Last year, Dutch-owned Philips Consumer Electronics Company exported 1,500 colour televisions from its Greenville, Tennessee, plant to Japan. Its 1990 target is 30,000 televisions; by 1991, it plans to export 50,000 sets. Toshiba America is sending projection televisions from its Wayne, New Jersey, plant to Japan. And by the early 1990s, when Honda annually exports 50,000 cars to Japan from its Ohio production base, it will actually be making more cars in the United States than in Japan.

## The New American Corporation

In an economy of increasing global investment, foreign-owned Corporation B, with its R&D and manufacturing presence in the United States and its reliance on American workers, is far more important to America's economic future than American-owned Corporation A, with its platoons of foreign workers. Corporation A may fly the American flag, but Corporation B invests in Americans. Increasingly, the competitiveness of American workers is a more important definition of 'American competitiveness' than the competitiveness of American companies. Issues of ownership, control, and national origin are less important factors in thinking through the logic of 'who is us' and the implications of the answer for national policy and direction.

*Ownership is less important.* Those who favour American-owned Corporation A (that produces overseas) over foreign-owned Corporation B (that produces here) might argue that American ownership generates a stream of earnings for the nation's citizens. This argument is correct, as far as it goes. American shareholders do, of course, benefit from the global successes of American corporations to the extent that such successes are reflected in higher share prices. And the entire US economy benefits to the extent that the overseas profits of American companies are remitted to the United States.

But American investors also benefit from the successes of non-American companies in which Americans own a minority interest—just as foreign citizens benefit from the successes of American companies in which they own a minority interest, and such cross-ownership is on the increase as national restrictions on foreign ownership fall by the wayside. In 1989 cross-border equity investments by Americans, British, Japanese, and West Germans increased 20 per cent, by value, over 1988.

The point is that in today's global economy, the total return to Americans from their equity investments is not solely a matter of the success of particular companies in which Americans happen to have a controlling interest. The return depends on the total amount of American savings invested in global portfolios comprising both American and foreign-owned companies—and on the care and wisdom with which American investors select such portfolios. Already Americans invest 10 per cent of their portfolios in foreign securities; a recent study by Salomon Brothers predicts that it will be 15 per cent in a few years. US pension managers surveyed said that they predict 25 per cent of their portfolios will be in foreign-owned companies within 10 years.

*Control is less important.* Another argument marshalled in favour of Corporation A might be that because Corporation A is controlled by Americans, it will act in the best interests of the United States. Corporation B, a foreign national, might not do so—indeed, it might act in the best interests of its nation of origin. The argument might go something like this: even if Corporation B is now hiring more Americans and giving them better jobs than Corporation A, we can't be assured that it will continue to do so. It might bias its strategy to reduce American competitiveness; it might even suddenly withdraw its investment from the United States and leave us stranded.

But this argument makes a false assumption about American companies—namely, that they are in a position to put national interests ahead of company or shareholder interests. To the contrary: managers of American-owned companies who sacrificed profits for the sake of national goals would make themselves vulnerable to a takeover or liable for a breach of fiduciary responsibility to their shareholders. American managers are among the loudest in the world to declare that their job is to maximize shareholder returns—not to advance national goals.

Apart from wartime or other national emergencies, American-owned companies are under no special obligation to serve national goals. Nor does our system alert American managers to the existence of such goals, impose on American managers unique requirements to meet them, offer special incentives to achieve them, or create measures to keep American managers accountable for accomplishing them. Were American managers knowingly to sacrifice profits for the sake of presumed national goals, they would be acting without authority, on the basis of their own views of what such goals might be, and without accountability to shareholders or to the public.

Obviously, this does not preclude American-owned companies from displaying their good corporate citizenship or having a sense of social responsibility. Sensible managers recognize that acting 'in the public interest' can boost the company's image; charitable or patriotic acts can be good business if they promote long-term profitability. But in this regard, American companies have no particular edge over foreign-owned companies doing business in the United States. In fact, there is every reason to believe that a foreign-owned company would be even more eager to demonstrate to the American public its good citizenship in America than would the average American company. The American subsidiaries of Hitachi, Matsushita, Siemens, Thomson, and many other foreign-owned companies lose no opportunity to contribute funds to American charities, sponsor community events, and support public libraries, universities, schools, and other institutions. (In 1988, for example, Japanese companies operating in the United States donated an estimated $200 million to American charities; by 1994, it is estimated that their contributions will total $1 billion.)[1]

By the same token, American-owned businesses operating abroad feel a similar compulsion to act as good citizens in their host countries. They cannot afford to be seen as promoting American interests; otherwise they would jeopardize their relationships with foreign workers, consumers, and governments. Some of America's top managers have been quite explicit on this point. 'IBM cannot be a net exporter from every nation in which it does business', said Jack Kuehler, IBM's new president. 'We have to be a good citizen everywhere.' Robert W. Galvin, chairman of Motorola, is even more blunt: should it become necessary for Motorola to close some of its factories, it would not close its Southeast Asian plants before it closed its American ones. 'We need our Far Eastern customers', says Galvin, 'and we cannot alienate the Malaysians. We must treat our employees all over the world equally.' In fact, when it becomes necessary to reduce global capacity, we might expect American-owned businesses to slash more jobs in the United States than in Europe (where labour laws often prohibit precipitous lay-offs) or in Japan (where national norms discourage it).

Just as empty is the concern that a foreign-owned company might leave the United States stranded by suddenly abandoning its US operation. The typical argument suggests that a foreign-owned company might withdraw for either profit or foreign policy motives. But either way, the bricks and mortar would still be here. So would the equipment. So too would be the accumulated learning among American workers. Under such circumstances, capital from another source would fill the void; an American (or other foreign) company would simply purchase the empty facilities. And most important, the American workforce would remain, with the critical skills and capabilities, ready to go back to work.

After all, the American government and the American people maintain jurisdiction—political control—over assets within the United States. Unlike foreign assets held by American-owned companies that are subject to foreign political control and, occasionally, foreign expropriation, foreign-owned assets in the United States are secure against sudden changes in foreign governments' policies. This not only serves as an attraction for foreign capital looking for a secure haven; it also benefits the American workforce.

*Workforce skills are critical.* As every advanced economy becomes global, a nation's most important competitive asset becomes the skills and cumulative learning of its workforce. Consequently, the most important issue with regard to global corporations is whether and to what extent they provide Americans with the training and experience that enable them to add greater value to the world economy. Whether the company happens to be headquartered in the United States or the United Kingdom is fundamentally unimportant. The company is a good 'American' corporation if it equips its American workforce to compete in the global economy.

Globalization, almost by definition, makes this true. Every factor of production other than workforce skills can be duplicated anywhere around the world. Capital now sloshes freely across international boundaries, so much so that the cost of capital in different countries is rapidly converging. State-of-the-art factories can be erected anywhere. The latest technologies flow from computers in one nation, up to satellites parked in space, then back down to computers in another nation—all at the speed of electronic impulses. It is all fungible: capital, technology, raw materials, information—all, except for one thing, the most critical part, the one element that is unique about a nation: its workforce.

In fact, because all of the other factors can move so easily any place on earth, a workforce that is knowledgeable and skilled at doing complex things attracts foreign investment. The relationship forms a virtuous circle: well-trained workers attract global corporations, which invest and give the workers good jobs; the good jobs, in turn, generate additional training and experience. As skills move upward and experience accumulates, a nation's citizens add greater and greater value to the world—and command greater and greater compensation from the world, improving the country's standard of living.

*Foreign-owned corporations help American workers add value.* When foreign-owned companies come to the United States, they frequently bring with them approaches to doing business that improve American productivity and allow American workers to add more value to the world economy. In fact, they come here primarily because they can be more productive in the United States than can other American rivals. It is not solely America's mounting external indebtedness and relatively low dollar that account for the rising level of foreign investment in the United States. Actual growth of foreign investment in the United States dates from the mid-1970s rather than from the onset of the large current account deficit in 1982. Moreover, the two leading foreign investors in the United States are the British and the Dutch—not the Japanese and the West Germans, whose enormous surpluses are the counterparts of our current account deficit.

For example, after Japan's Bridgestone tire company took over Firestone, productivity increased dramatically. The joint venture between Toyota and General Motors at Fremont, California, is a similar story: Toyota's managerial system took many of the same workers from what had been a deeply troubled GM plant and turned it into a model facility, with upgraded productivity and skill levels.

In case after case, foreign companies set up or buy up operations in the United States to utilize their corporate assets with the American workforce. Foreign-owned businesses with better design capabilities, production techniques, or managerial skills are able to displace American companies on American soil precisely because those businesses are more productive. And in the process of supplanting the American company, the foreign-owned operation can transfer the superior know-how to its American workforce—giving American workers the tools they need to be more productive, more skilled, and more competitive. Thus foreign companies create good jobs in the United States. In 1986 (the last date for which such data are available), the average American employee of a foreign-owned manufacturing company earned $32,887, while the average American employee of an American-owned manufacturer earned $28,954.[2]

This process is precisely what happened in Europe in the 1950s and 1960s. Europeans publicly fretted about the invasion of American-owned multinationals and the onset of 'the American challenge'. But the net result of these operations in Europe has been to make Europeans more productive, upgrade European skills, and thus enhance the standard of living of Europeans.

## Now Who Is Us?

American competitiveness can best be defined as the capacity of Americans to add value to the world economy and thereby gain a higher standard of living in the future without going into ever deeper debt. American competitiveness is not the profitability or market share of American-owned corporations. In fact, because the American-owned corporation is coming to have no special relationship with Americans, it makes no sense for Americans to entrust our national competitiveness to it. The interests of American-owned corporations may or may not coincide with those of the American people.

Does this mean that we should simply entrust our national competitiveness to any corporation that employs Americans, regardless of the nationality of corporate ownership? Not entirely. Some foreign-owned corporations are closely tied to their nation's economic development—either through direct public ownership (for example, Airbus Industrie, a joint product of Britain, France, West Germany, and Spain, created to compete in the commercial airline industry) or through financial intermediaries within the nation that, in turn, are tied to central banks and ministries of finance (in particular the model used by many Korean and Japanese corporations). The primary goals of such corporations are to enhance the wealth of their nations, and the standard of living of their nation's citizens, rather than to enrich their shareholders. Thus, even though they might employ American citizens in their worldwide operations, they may employ fewer Americans—or give Americans lower value-added jobs—than they would if these corporations were intent simply on maximizing their own profits.[3]

On the other hand, it seems doubtful that we could ever shift the goals and orientations of American-owned corporations in this same direction—away from profit maximization and toward the development of the American workforce. There is no reason to suppose that American managers and shareholders would accept new regulations and oversight mechanisms that forced them to sacrifice profits for the sake of building human capital in the United States. Nor is it clear that the American system of government would be capable of such detailed oversight.

The only practical answer lies in developing national policies that reward *any* global corporation that invests in the American workforce. In a whole set of public policy areas, involving trade, publicly supported R&D, antitrust, foreign direct investment, and public and private investment, the overriding goal should be to induce global corporations to build human capital in America.

*Trade policy.* We should be less interested in opening foreign markets to America-owned companies (which may in fact be doing much of their production overseas) than in opening those markets to companies that employ Americans—even if they happen to be foreign-owned. But so far, American trade policy experts have focused on

representing the interests of companies that happen to carry the American flag—without regard to where the actual production is being done. For example, the United States recently accused Japan of excluding Motorola from the lucrative Tokyo market for cellular telephones and hinted at retaliation. But Motorola designs and makes many of its cellular telephones in Kuala Lumpur, while most of the Americans who make cellular telephone equipment in the United States for export to Japan happen to work for Japanese-owned companies. Thus we are wasting our scarce political capital pushing foreign governments to reduce barriers to American-owned companies that are seeking to sell or produce in their market.

Once we acknowledge that foreign-owned Corporation B may offer more to American competitiveness than American-owned Corporation A, it is easy to design a preferable trade policy—one that accords more directly with our true national interests. The highest priority for American trade policy should be to discourage other governments from invoking domestic content rules—which have the effect of forcing global corporations, American and foreign-owned alike, to locate production facilities in those countries rather than in the United States.

The objection here to local content rules is not that they may jeopardize the competitiveness of American companies operating abroad. Rather, it is that these requirements, by their very nature, deprive the American workforce of the opportunity to compete for jobs, and with those jobs, for valuable skills, knowledge, and experience. Take, for example, the recently promulgated European Community nonbinding rule on television-program production, which urges European television stations to devote a majority of their air time to programs made in Europe. Or consider the European allegations of Japanese dumping of office machines containing semiconductors, which has forced Japan to put at least 45 per cent European content into machines sold in Europe (and thus fewer American-made semiconductor chips).

Obviously, US-owned companies are already inside the EC producing both semiconductors and television programs. So if we were to adopt American-owned Corporation A as the model for America's competitive self-interest, our trade policy might simply ignore these EC initiatives. But through the lens of a trade policy focused on the American workforce, it is clear how the EC thwarts the abilities of Americans to excel in semiconductor fabrication and film-making—two areas where our workforce already enjoys a substantial competitive advantage.

Lack of access by American-owned corporations to foreign markets is, of course, a problem. But it only becomes a crucial problem for America to the extent that both American and foreign-owned companies must make products within the foreign market—products that they otherwise would have made in the United States. Protection that acts as a domestic content requirement skews investment away from the United States—and away from US workers. Fighting against that should be among the highest priorities of US trade policy.

*Publicly supported R&D.* Increased global competition, the high costs of research, the rapid rate of change in science and technology, the model of Japan with its government-supported commercial technology investments—all of these factors have combined to make this area particularly critical for thoughtful public policy. But there is no reason why preference should be given to American-owned companies. Dominated by our preoccupation with American-owned Corporation A, current public policy in this area limits US government-funded research grants, guaranteed loans, or access to the fruits of US government-funded research to American-owned companies. For example, membership in Sematech, the research consortium started two years ago with $100 billion annual support payments by the Department of Defense to help American corporations fabricate complex memory chips, is limited to American-owned companies. More recently, a government effort to create a consortium of companies to catapult the United States into the HDTV competition has drawn a narrow circle of eligibility, ruling out companies such as Sony, Philips, and Thomson that do R&D and production in the United States but are foreign-owned. More generally, long-standing regulations covering the more than 600 government laboratories and research centres that are spread around the United States ban all but American-owned companies from licensing inventions developed at these sites.

Of course, the problem with this policy approach is that it ignores the reality of global American corporations. Most US-owned companies are quite happy to receive special advantages from the US government—and then spread the technological benefits to their affiliates all over the world. As Sematech gets under way, its members are busily going global: Texas Instruments is building a new $250 million semiconductor fabrication plant in Taiwan; by 1992, the facility will produce four-megabit memory chips and custom-made, application-specific integrated circuits—some of the most advanced chips made anywhere. TI has also joined with Hitachi to design and produce a super chip that will store 16 million bits of data. Motorola, meanwhile, has paired with Toshiba to research and produce a similar generation of futurist chips. Not to be outdone, AT&T has a commitment to build a state-of-the-art chip-making plant in Spain. So who will be making advanced chips in the United States? In June 1989, Japanese-owned NEC announced plans to build a $400 million facility in Rosedale, California, for making four-megabit memory chips and other advanced devices not yet in production anywhere.

The same situation applies to HDTV. Zenith Electronics is the only remaining American-owned television manufacturer, and thus the only one eligible for a government subsidy. Zenith employs 2,500 Americans. But there are over 15,000 Americans employed in the television industry who do not work for Zenith—undertaking R&D,

## Table 1: US TV Set Production, 1988

| Company Name | Plant Type | Location | Employees | Annual Production |
|---|---|---|---|---|
| Bang & Olufsen | Assembly | Compton, Calif. | n.a.† | n.a. |
| Goldstar | Total* | Huntsville, Ala. | 400 | 1,000,000 |
| Harvey Industries | Assembly | Athens, Tex. | 900 | 600,000 |
| Hitachi | Total | Anaheim, Calif. | 900 | 360,000 |
| JVC | Total | Elmwood Park, NJ | 100 | 480,000 |
| Matsushita | Assembly | Franklin Park, Ill. | 800 | 1,000,000 |
| American Kotobuki (Matsushita) | Assembly | Vancouver, Wash. | 200 | n.a. |
| Mitsubishi | Assembly | Santa Ana, Calif. | 550 | 400,000 |
| Mitsubishi | Total | Braselton, Ga. | 300 | 285,000 |
| NEC | Assembly | McDonough, Ga. | 400 | 240,000 |
| Orion | Assembly | Princeton, Ind. | 250 | n.a. |
| Philips | Total | Greenville, Tenn. | 3,200 | 2,000,000+ |
| Samsung | Total | Saddle Brook, NJ | 250 | 1,000,000 |
| Sanyo | Assembly | Forrest City, Ark. | 400 | 1,000,000 |
| Sharp | Assembly | Memphis, Tenn. | 770 | 1,100,000 |
| Sony | Total | San Diego, Calif. | 1,500 | 1,000,000 |
| Tatung | Assembly | Long Beach, Calif. | 130 | 17,500 |
| Thomson | Total | Bloomington, Ind. | 1,766 | 3,000,000+ |
| Thomson | Components | Indianapolis, Ind. | 1,604 | n.a. |
| Toshiba | Assembly | Lebanon, Tenn. | 600 | 900,000 |
| Zenith | Total | Springfield, Mo. | 2,500 | n.a. |

* Total manufacturing involves more than the assembling of knocked-down kits. Plants that manufacture just the television cabinets are not included in this list.

† Not available.

Source: Electronic Industries Association, HDTV Information Center, Washington, DC.

engineering, and high-quality manufacturing. They work in the United States for foreign-owned companies: Sony, Philips, Thomson, and others (see the accompanying table). Of course, none of these companies is presently eligible to participate in the United States's HDTV consortium—nor are their American employees.

Again, if we follow the logic of Corporation B as the more 'American' company, it suggests a straightforward principle for publicly supported R&D: we should be less interested in helping *American-owned companies* become technologically sophisticated than in helping *Americans* become technologically sophisticated. Government-financed help for research and development should be available to any corporation, regardless of the nationality of its owners, as long as the company undertakes the R&D in the United States—using American scientists, engineers, and technicians. To make the link more explicit, there could even be a relationship between the number of Americans involved in the R&D and the amount of government aid forthcoming. It is important to note that this kind of public-private bargain is far different from protectionist domestic content requirements. In this case, the government is participating with direct funding and thus can legitimately exact a quid pro quo from the private sector.

*Antitrust policy.* The Justice Department is now in the process of responding to the inevitability of globalization; it recognizes that North American market share alone means less and less in a global economy. Consequently, the Justice Department is about to relax antitrust policy—for American-owned companies only. American-owned companies that previously kept each other at arm's length for fear of prompting an inquiry into whether they were colluding are now cosying up to one another. Current antitrust policy permits joint production agreements as well, when there may be significant economies of scale and where competition is global—again, among American-owned companies.

But here again, American policy seems myopic. We should be less interested in helping American-owned companies gain economies of scale in research, production, and other key areas, and more interested in helping corporations engaged in research or production within the United States achieve economies of scale—regardless of their nationality. US antitrust policy should allow research or production joint ventures among any companies doing R&D or production within the United States as long as they can meet three tests: they could not gain such scale efficiencies on their own, simply by enlarging their investment in

the United States; such a combination of companies would allow higher levels of productivity within the United States; and the combination would not substantially diminish global competition. National origin should not be a factor.

*Foreign direct investment.* Foreign direct investment has been climbing dramatically in the United States: last year it reached $329 billion, exceeding total American investment abroad for the first time since World War I (but be careful with these figures, since investments are valued at cost and this substantially understates the worth of older investments). How should we respond to this influx of foreign capital?

Clearly, the choice between Corporation A and Corporation B has important implications. If we are most concerned about the viability of American-owned corporations, then we should put obstacles in the way of foreigners seeking to buy controlling shares in American-owned companies, or looking to build American production facilities that would compete with American-owned companies.

Indeed, current policies tilt in this direction. For example, under the so-called Exon-Florio Amendment of the Omnibus Trade and Competitiveness Act of 1988, foreign investors must get formal approval from the high-level Committee on Foreign Investments in the United States, comprising the heads of eight federal agencies and chaired by the secretary of the treasury, before they can purchase an American company. The expressed purpose of the law is to make sure that a careful check is done to keep 'national security' industries from passing into the hands of foreigners. But the law does not define what 'national security' means: thus it invites all sorts of potential delays and challenges. The actual effect is to send a message that we do not look with favour on the purchase of American-owned assets by foreigners. Other would-be pieces of legislation send the same signal. In July 1989, for instance, the House Ways and Means Committee voted to apply a withholding capital gains tax to foreigners who own more than 10 per cent of a company's shares. Another provision of the committee would scrap tax deductibility for interest on loans made by foreign parents to their American subsidiaries. A third measure would limit R&D tax credits for foreign subsidiaries. More recently, Congress is becoming increasingly concerned about foreign takeovers of American airlines. A subcommittee of the House Commerce Committee has voted to give the Transportation Department authority to block foreign acquisitions.

These policies make little sense—in fact, they are counterproductive. Our primary concern should be the training and development of the American workforce, not the protection of the American-owned corporation. Thus we should encourage, not discourage, foreign direct investment. Experience shows that foreign-owned companies usually displace American-owned companies in just those industries where the foreign businesses are simply more productive. No wonder America's governors spend a lot of time and energy promoting their states to foreign investors and offer big subsidies to foreign companies to locate in their states, even if they compete head-on with existing American-owned businesses.

*Public and private investments*. The current obsession with the federal budget deficit obscures a final, crucial aspect of the choice between Corporation A and Corporation B. Conventional wisdom holds that government expenditures 'crowd out' private investment, making it more difficult and costly for American-owned companies to get the capital they need. According to this logic, we may have to cut back on public expenditures in order to provide American-owned companies with the necessary capital to make investments in plant and equipment.

But the reverse may actually be the case—particularly if Corporation B is really more in America's competitive interests than Corporation A. There are a number of reasons why this is true.

First, in the global economy, America's public expenditures don't reduce the amount of money left over for private investment in the United States. Today capital flows freely across national borders—including a disproportionately large inflow to the United States. Not only are foreign savings coming to the United States, but America's private savings are finding their way all over the world. Sometimes the vehicle is the far-flung operations of a global American-owned company, sometimes a company in which foreigners own a majority stake. But the old notion of national boundaries is becoming obsolete. Moreover, as I have stressed, it is a mistake to associate these foreign investments by American-owned companies with any result that improves the competitiveness of the United States. There is simply no necessary connection between the two.

There is, however, a connection between the kinds of investments that the public sector makes and the competitiveness of the American workforce. Remember: a workforce that is knowledgeable and skilled at doing complex things attracts foreign investment in good jobs, which in turn generates additional training and experience. A good infrastructure of transportation and communication makes a skilled workforce even more attractive. The public sector often is in the best position to make these sorts of 'pump priming' investments—in education, training and retraining, research and development, and in all of the infrastructure that moves people and goods and facilitates communication. These are the investments that distinguish one nation from another—they are the relatively nonmobile factors in the global competition. Ironically, we do not ordinarily think of these expenditures as investments; the federal budget fails to distinguish between a capital and an operating budget, and the national income accounts treat all government expenditures as consumption. But without doubt, these are precisely the investments that most directly affect our future capacity to compete.

During the 1980s, we allowed the level of these public investments either to remain stable or, in some cases, to decline. As America enters the 1990s, if we hope to launch a new campaign for American competitiveness, we must substantially increase public funding in the following areas:

- *Government spending on commercial R&D.* Current spending in this critical area has declined 95 per cent from its level two decades ago. Even as late as 1980, it comprised .8 per cent of gross national product; today it comprises only .4 per cent—a much smaller percentage than in any other advanced economy.
- *Government spending to upgrade and expand the nation's infrastructure.* Public investment in critical highways, roads, bridges, ports, airports, and waterways dropped from 2.3 per cent of GNP two decades ago to 1.3 per cent in the 1980s. Thus many of our bridges are unsafe, and our highways are crumbling.
- *Expenditures on public elementary and secondary education.* These have increased, to be sure. But in inflation-adjusted terms, per pupil spending has shown little gain. Between 1959 and 1971, spending per student grew at a brisk 4.7 per cent in real terms—more than a full percentage point above the increase in the GNP—and teachers' salaries increased almost 3 per cent a year. But since then, growth has slowed. Worse, this has happened during an era when the demands on public education have significantly increased, due to the growing incidence of broken homes, unwed mothers, and a rising population of the poor. Teachers' salaries, adjusted for inflation, are only a bit higher than they were in 1971. Despite the rhetoric, the federal government has all but retreated from the field of education. In fact, George Bush's 1990 education budget is actually smaller than Ronald Reagan's in 1989. States and municipalities, already staggering under the weight of social services that have been shifted on to them from the federal government, simply cannot carry this additional load. The result of this policy gap is a national education crisis: one out of five American 18-year-olds is illiterate, and in test after test, American schoolchildren rank at the bottom of international scores. Investing more money here may not be a cure-all—but money is at least necessary.
- *College opportunity for all Americans.* Because of government cutbacks, many young people in the United States with enough talent to go to college cannot afford it. During the 1980s, college tuitions rose 26 per cent; family incomes rose a scant 5 per cent. Instead of filling the gap, the federal government created a vacuum: guaranteed student loans have fallen by 13 per cent in real terms since 1980.
- *Worker training and retraining.* Young people who cannot or do not wish to attend college need training for jobs that are becoming more complex. Older workers need retraining to keep up with the demands of a rapidly changing, technologically advanced workplace. But over the last eight years, federal investments in worker training have dropped by more than 50 per cent.

These are the priorities of an American strategy for national competitiveness—a strategy based more on the value of human capital and less on the value of financial capital. The simple fact of American ownership has lost its relevance to America's economic future. Corporations that invest in the United States, that build the value of the American workforce, are more critical to our future standard of living than are American-owned corporations investing abroad. To attract and keep them, we need public investments that make America a good place for any global corporation seeking talented workers to set up shop.

# Notes

1. Craig Smith, editor of Corporate *Philanthropy Report*, quoted in *Chronicle of Higher Education*, 8 Nov. 1989, A34.

2. Bureau of Economic Analysis, *Foreign Direct Investment in the U.S. Operations of U.S. Affiliates, Preliminary 1986 Estimates* (Washington: US Department of Commerce, 1988) for data on foreign companies; Bureau of the Census, *Annual Survey of Manufactures: Statistics for Industry Groups and Industries, 1986* (Washington, 1987) for US companies.

3. Robert B. Reich and Eric D. Mankin, 'Joint Ventures with Japan Give Away Our Future', *Harvard Business Review* (Mar.-Apr. 1986): 78.

# Corporate Strategies:
## The Costs and Benefits of Going Global

Fred Lazar

## Introduction

Corporations increasingly are becoming global institutions. They are adopting strategies which transcend the influence of the small and medium-sized industrial nations of the world. The largest 500 multinational corporations conduct over one-half of world trade.[1] Trade and, more importantly, investment barriers have been lowered dramatically by the NAFTA and the latest GATT agreement, thus strengthening further the bargaining position of highly mobile capital and the clout of global corporations. It is not surprising, therefore, that in this environment, global companies are becoming the principal actors driving the economic and social agendas of all countries. Canada provides a fascinating case study of the potential problems which many countries may shortly face if they fail to develop their national champions and fail to strengthen and broaden their industrial bases, relegating them to a junior role in relation to the global corporations.

Canada's economic prospects continue to be dependent on resources. For example, resource-based products accounted for 45 of the top 50 Canadian products in terms of world export share at the last economic peak in 1989. But natural resources are no longer the staples of the world economy. Instead, the new staples are ideas.[2] Unfortunately, Canada does not appear to be well endowed with the new 'staples'.

Canada appears to lag behind most major industrialized countries in R&D investments and

capabilities. Part of our poor record in this area stems from the industrial structure of the economy; that is, a disproportionately large share of economic activity accounted for by very low R&D-intensive industries. Part of this results from the high degree of foreign ownership of the industrial sector in Canada. Foreign-owned firms operating in Canada appear to underperform Canadian-owned companies in the high R&D-intensive industries. Canadian-owned companies, on average, allocate a larger proportion of their revenues to R&D expenditures than US companies in the same industries.

It is not surprising, therefore, that McMillan warns that 'huge portions of Canadian industry have fallen by the wayside to international competition, management mediocrity, and technological backwardness.'[3] Canada's heavy dependence on foreign investment has not produced the dynamic, innovative economy needed to be successful in today's global village. As corporations become more global in their strategies and operations, the dearth of Canadian multinationals will place our future very much at risk, despite our appearance today as a wealthy country. Canada continues to rely too heavily on the old staples, and lacks the management skills and autonomy (both in the private and public sectors) to compete successfully in the ever-expanding, global economy. . . .

## Do We Need Canadian Multinationals?

There is little debate regarding the importance of being the home base for international corporations. But do we need Canadian-controlled multinationals to be competitive and to prosper in the evolving and more interdependent global

Abridged from Robert Boyer and Daniel Drache, eds, *States Against Markets: The Limits of Globalization* (London and New York: Routledge, 1996), 270–96. Reprinted by permission of Routledge and the author.

## Table 1: The 500 Largest Industrial Companies in the World: Total Numbers in the G-7 and Selected Other Countries, 1992

|             | 1-50 | 51-100 | 101-250 | 251-500 | Total |
|-------------|------|--------|---------|---------|-------|
| Canada      | 0    | 0      | 3       | 5       | 8     |
| US          | 13   | 19     | 50      | 79      | 161   |
| France      | 5    | 3      | 10      | 12      | 30    |
| Germany     | 7    | 8      | 7       | 10      | 32    |
| Italy       | 3    | 1      | 2       | 0       | 6     |
| UK          | 1    | 4      | 12      | 23      | 40    |
| Japan       | 13   | 7      | 40      | 68      | 128   |
| Australia   | 0    | 0      | 2       | 7       | 9     |
| Switzerland | 2    | 1      | 2       | 4       | 9     |
| Sweden      | 0    | 2      | 3       | 9       | 14    |

Source: *Fortune*, 26 July 1993.

economy? Before we consider this question, let us take a brief look at the track record to date in developing Canadian multinationals which have become major players in their industries.

The Fortune 500 largest industrial companies in the world in 1992 provides a good starting point. There were eight Canadian companies on this list. There were no Canadian companies among the top 100; the largest Canadian company, Northern Telecom, ranked 173 on the list. Only Italy, among the other members of the G-7, had fewer companies among the top 500, but Italy had three companies among the 50 largest. On a per capita basis, Canada had a disproportionately small number of major corporations among the top 500 in comparison to the US, Japan, UK, Germany, and France. It is also interesting to note that Sweden, Australia, and Switzerland had more companies on this list than Canada and that Sweden and Switzerland were both represented among the 100 largest companies (Table 1). The UNCTC [United Nations Centre for Transnational Corporations] has noted that despite 'the comparatively small domestic market, a handful of Swedish transnational corporations have become

global market leaders, and many have done so by well-executed acquisition strategies.'[4]

Even more disappointing is the absence of large Canadian companies in most technology-intensive industries. We have a presence in aerospace, where Bombardier ranks 14 out of 16, and in electronics and electrical equipment, where Northern Telecom ranks 24 out of 46 companies.[5] It is important to note that Bombardier has been strongly supported by both the federal government and the government of Quebec, and that Northern Telecom's early growth was buttressed by its monopoly supply position to Bell Canada. It is conceivable that in the absence of government support and a monopoly position, neither company would be anywhere near the top 500 companies in the world today. As well, Petro-Canada, another Canadian member of the world's largest industrial companies, is entirely a creation of the federal government.

Admittedly, Canada has many more multinationals, but the largest multinationals play a special role because they can serve as the foundations for creating a cluster of domestic companies which can 'benefit from a shared

culture and learning experience, supply capabilities and infrastructure' so that the 'resulting
economies give them a competitive edge in both
domestic and international markets'.[6]

Reich[7] and Porter[8] appear to agree that ownership does not matter in those cases in which a
country becomes the home base for fully integrated operations with decision-making autonomy for
serving a regional market in several product lines
or the global market in a much narrower range of
products. But, as both Porter and Reich point out,
if a country does not attract the fully integrated
complex, it will receive very limited benefits from
foreign direct investment. Porter has indicated that
Canada has tended to attract foreign investment to
gain access to the Canadian market or acquire
resources ('source base factors'). In both cases, the
host country is vulnerable to parent company decisions. According to Porter, '[f]actor sourcing and
market access investment . . . tend to be less permanent; they are prone to being reversed as cheaper inputs are located elsewhere or investment in
the country is no longer needed to gain market
access.'[9] Moreover, these types of foreign investment provide few beneficial spillovers and exter-
nalities to other domestic firms and industries.

The centre(s) for strategic decision-making
within multinationals (the home base) is (are)
critical for Canada since this is where the key
decisions are made. The periphery operations/
subsidiaries serve as a conduit for information to
the centre and for the implementation of the decisions mandated by the centre. The aggressive use
by the US of their panoply of trade laws places
Canada at a competitive disadvantage in attracting
the North American regional headquarters of
non-Canadian multinationals, and structural
shortcomings in technology-intensive activities
diminish our attractiveness as a home base for
many products. Thus, non-Canadian companies
are more likely to select the US as the location for
their North American regional product headquarters and Canada is not likely to rank among the
top locations for a product headquarters within a
non-Canadian, multinational company. In light of
these difficulties and the importance of a home
base, Canadian policy-makers may have no choice
but to concentrate their economic development
strategies on promoting the creation of more
Canadian multinationals with the goal of increasing the Canadian presence among the largest
global, corporate players. . . .

## Notes

1. A.M. Rugman and A. Verbeke, 'Canadian Business
   in a Global Trading Environment', *Ontario Centre
   for International Business, Working Paper Series* No.
   1 ( Sept. 1988), 3.
2. C.J. McMillan, *Building Blocks or Trade Blocs:
   NAFTA, Japan and the New World Order* (Ottawa:
   Canada-Japan Trade Council, 1993), 12.
3. Ibid., 62.
4. United Nations Centre on Transnational Corporations, *The Process of Transnationalization and Transnational Mergers*, UNCTC Current Studies No. 8,
   Series A (New York: UN, 1989), 52.
5. The total number of companies in an industrial
   sector includes only companies on the Fortune
   500 list.
6. J.H. Dunning, 'The Competitive Advantage of
   Countries and the Activities of Transnational
   Corporations: Review Article', *Transnational Corporations* 1, 1 (Feb. 1992): 159.
7. R. Reich, 'Who Is Us?', *Harvard Business Review*
   (Jan.-Feb. 1990).
8. M. Porter, *Canada at the Crossroads: The Reality of a
   New Competitive Environment* (Ottawa, 1991), 73.
9. Ibid., 74.

# Part VIII
# Comparative Politics of the Developed World

## Introduction

Paul Warwick

The term 'comparative politics' immediately raises, or ought to raise, two very fundamental questions: (1) what things are to be compared? and (2) why compare them? Concerning the first question, the assumption most commonly adopted is that the comparison will be a cross-national one, involving some aspect of politics in the researcher's native country and its counterpart in one or more foreign countries. But what if a researcher wishes to compare the Liberal Party in Canada with the Progressive Conservatives, or politics in British Columbia with politics in Ontario or Quebec? Would such investigations not also fall under the rubric of comparative politics? One can go much further still. When indicating to a psychologist some years ago that my main specialty is comparative politics, she responded with what seems now to have been a very sensible question: 'What do you compare—people with animals?'

As it happens, political scientists almost never compare people with animals—although they could, possibly to the benefit of our understanding of politics. And while political scientists do compare political parties or provincial politics in Canada, they do not classify those activities as comparative politics. Instead, the label has come to denote the study of political systems other than one's own. This usage is bizarre because it means that, for an American political scientist, Canadian politics partakes of comparative politics but American politics does not, whereas for a Canadian political scientist the reverse is true.[1] Thus, what is included in the subfield of comparative politics depends on where you live—hardly the best way to define a subfield in a discipline supposedly guided by scientific principles! The usage also implies that the researcher comparing politics in different Canadian provinces is not engaging in the same type of enterprise as a researcher comparing, say, Canadian and US federal politics. What makes them different, however, is not terribly clear.

Another disturbing implication of using the term to refer to studies of politics in foreign countries is that, incredible as it may seem, these studies need not involve any comparisons at all. A book on French or Chinese politics, for example, is typically classified as 'comparative' even when the political system under examination is not explicitly compared with the author's own or any other political system. In this usage, comparative politics becomes a conceptual label that means, well, virtually nothing at all.

The best way to resuscitate the term would be to find some rationale for undertaking comparisons—to address, in other words, the second question. There is, in fact, a powerful rationale for investigating politics in a comparative vein. Consider the case of a political scientist, a Canadian citizen, who is primarily interested in Canadian politics. This researcher would not be considered a 'comparativist' according to the standard usage of the concept. Suppose now that this researcher happens to be interested in the role of special interest groups or 'lobbies', as they are known, in national politics. He or she may believe, as many political observers currently do, that the Charter of Rights and Freedoms adopted in 1982 has enhanced the political leverage of these lobbies and encouraged their proliferation by providing them with a means of challenging government actions and policies in the courts. The researcher therefore poses the following research question: Has the adoption of the Charter led to an increase in the numbers and influence of lobbies in national politics in Canada?

The most obvious way to go about answering this question would be to compare the role of lobbies in Ottawa today with their role before 1982. But how does one determine the influence of lobbies so many years ago? Direct evidence is likely to be scarce or fragmentary and the researcher may find that all he or she has to go by are people's recollections, which are inevitably imperfect. In addition, even if lobbies were less influential before 1982, that fact in itself does not prove that the Charter caused the change. Perhaps the real culprit is the slower rates of economic growth that have induced more groups to turn to government for assistance and obliged governments to cut back on spending—or any of a number of other possible causes.

As long as the researcher focuses exclusively on Canada, it may well be impossible to eliminate the false leads and isolate the true cause or causes. A well-chosen cross-national comparison, however, might help immeasurably in this quest. For example, the researcher might decide to compare the role of lobbies in Canada with their role in Britain. The advantage of this comparison is that Britain, like Canada, has a parliamentary system of government—the basic political structure is thus the same—but it has never entrenched a charter of rights. If the hypothesis is true that the Charter has stimulated lobbying in Canada, one would expect to see a stronger presence for lobbies in Canadian politics than in British politics, other things being equal.

Fortunately, in the case of Britain, some other things are more or less equal: Britain has also experienced economic difficulties in recent years and serious budgetary deficits. If lobbies are less important in British politics than in Canadian politics, presumably it is not due to any differences in these factors. There may, of course, be some other potential causes that are not equal between the two countries, but then it is always possible to bring other political systems into the comparison in order to examine the role of those factors. Indeed, the broader the comparison, the more confident we would be in its conclusions. Thus, to answer a question about politics in Canada, our researcher would be well advised to include as many parliamentary systems as possible.

There is, moreover, no need to stop at this point. A common generalization in political science is that lobbying is less pervasive and less successful in parliamentary systems than in presidential systems such as that of the United States. The reasons go to the root of the differences between the two systems. Most parliamentary systems function on the basis of a fusion of executive and legislative powers: the prime minister and cabinet not only control the enforcement of laws (the executive power) but they also command a disciplined parliamentary majority, which gives them dominance over the legislative process. The separation of powers embedded in the US system means, among other things, that the president and cabinet do not control a majority in Congress; in addition, an absence of effective party discipline in Congress leaves individual senators and representatives free to vote according to their state or district interests (or their own consciences). Unconstrained by the executive branch or by party discipline, therefore, these congressmen and women should be much more open to persuasion by lobbyists, especially those representing important interests back home. If our researcher were to incorporate the US into the comparison, would he or she find that lobbies in Canada are more active and influential than in Britain but considerably less so than in the US? An answer to this question would help put the Canadian situation in a valuable perspective: the influence of lobbies in Canada may seem considerable, even excessive from the viewpoint of democratic ideals, but perhaps it could be a lot worse![2]

The example we have just considered illustrates the important point that a comparative approach can be valuable, even essential, to the understanding of politics in one's own—or any other—country. It also illustrates a second valuable point: comparison need not be confined to similar objects. To assess the importance of lobbies in the Canadian political process, a comparison with other parliamentary systems may be useful, but so may a comparison with non-parliamentary systems like the US presidential system. Indeed, the more diverse the range of political systems investigated, the greater the likelihood that one will be able to assess the full range of the phenomenon under consideration and the full range of influences that may act upon it. We can compare apples with oranges—as long as we remember that they are both fruit.[3]

The ability to assess the full range of possible causes deserves some emphasis because it is one of the most significant strengths of the comparative method. I suggested a comparison of Canada and Britain in the above example because the two systems have similar institutional structures; extension of the comparison to the US is instructive because it allows us to observe what happens under a somewhat different structure. But comparisons can be much more revealing that these remarks suggest. A persistently striking feature of parliamentary democracies, for example, is that, despite their similar structures, they often reveal profoundly different political processes and political outcomes. This phenomenon is no better illustrated than in the comparison of rates of government survival across such systems. While the parliamentary systems of Canada and Britain both typically produce single-party majority governments that are relatively long-lived (four to five years), the norm in Italy is governments formed of between three and five parties and lasting less than one year. The same type of regime, in other words, can experience governmental stability or governmental instability. Thus, a comparative perspective on parliamentary regimes immediately alerts us to the fact that some other influence or influences must be at work.[4]

The rapid development of the subfield of comparative politics in the post-World War II period was stimulated in large part by the realization that non-institutional factors must lie behind the diversity of political processes observable across the globe. The importance of a global perspective was accentuated in the first two postwar decades by the emergence of a large number of new states, the result of the disintegration of European colonial empires. Would these states become successful liberal democracies, like most of their former colonial masters? Or would they fall victim to military takeover or Communist revolution? If the provision of democratic institutions were enough to ensure democracy, there would be little cause for concern because most of these new states initially adopted democratic frameworks, often at the urging of the departing colonial powers. But, clearly, formally democratic institutions cannot guarantee a smoothly functioning democracy—otherwise Italian politics might look more like British politics and German democracy might never have succumbed to a Nazi takeover in 1933. But if democratic institutions are not enough, what is?

🙷

The first article in this section, written in 1956 by the American political scientist Gabriel Almond, is seminal both to this issue and to the development of comparative politics in general because it proposed a profoundly influential answer: political culture. Almond argued that politics in any system is influenced by that system's 'pattern of orientations to political action'. In the Anglo-American political systems, for example, he found a *political culture* that is homogeneous and secular. It is homogeneous in the sense that there is a widespread sharing of political values such as freedom, mass welfare, and security. It is secular in that it emphasizes, not the pursuit of rigid ideologies, but rather a bargaining, pragmatic, experimental political style. These traits, in his view, orient political behaviour in all of the Anglo-American systems (including Canada). In contrast, the continental European political culture is fragmented into pre-industrial, transitional, and industrial subcultures in which 'political affiliation is more an act of faith than of agency'. This fragmentation and the resultant emphasis on ideology that permeates political life in many of these countries have been used by Almond, among many others, to explain why politics in Italy, as in the pre-war German parliamentary regime and certain French regimes, so little resembles politics in Britain or Canada.[5]

Almond's analysis of non-Western political cultures, moreover, provides a handle with which to assess and understand the fate of the newer states, which, as subsequent events have amply demonstrated, have generally not had an easy experience with liberal democracy. For Almond, the political culture of these states is characterized by a conflict between Western and non-Western political cultures, the latter of which may involve more than one distinct subculture. As a result of this conflict over fundamental values and orientations, Almond concludes that instability and violence may, in fact, be 'inescapable'.

The concept of political culture, launched by Almond's article, provided a novel and exciting perspective in the study of politics and stimulated the rapid growth of comparative studies. But it did not go uncriticized. Some feared that it led too easily to a cultural determinism: taken to its extreme, it seemed to imply that neither people nor institutions mattered because culture determined everything. It also appeared value-laden in the eyes of some political scientists: Anglo-American political culture came out as 'good' because it sustained liberal democracy; all other political cultures were 'bad'. Finally, culture is a rather slippery concept, pervasive yet difficult to assess in a rigorous scientific fashion. In the 1970s and 1980s, many political scientists abandoned political culture in favour of a 'rational choice' perspective, which emphasized not how culture affects behaviour but how behaviour flows from the rational pursuit of individual goals.[6]

In the second selection, Ronald Inglehart attempts to revive the concept of political culture by showing that research over the past 30 years has produced a considerable body of systematic evidence supporting the role of political culture as a mainstay of stable democracy.[7] He highlights the importance of interpersonal trust—an individual's belief that most people are basically trustworthy—as an indicator of a homogeneous political culture that is central to the early establishment and successful maintenance of a democratic regime. Also relevant are such cultural traits as an overall satisfaction with life, satisfaction with one's political system, and support for the existing social order. All four traits, in his view, partake of a cultural syndrome that sustains democratic institutions. As for the idea that the political cultures of Anglo-American countries come out best in this type of analysis, Inglehart argues that, while this syndrome can be linked historically to the Protestant Reformation and the rise of modern capitalism in Western Europe, other cultural traditions—most notably the Confucian tradition—also appear well suited to an economic dynamism that ultimately should foster cultural traits supportive of democracy.

This last conclusion, to be sure, is speculative and will undoubtedly be challenged by other scholars. The value of the article for our purposes, however, lies not with Inglehart's demonstration of a linkage between culture and democracy, nor with his speculation about its sources, but rather with its illustration of the larger principle that many of the most important issues in political science can only be tackled adequately if they are approached in a broad comparative perspective. This applies just as much to issues arising from the study of politics in a single country as to issues framed in an explicitly comparative context. Comparative politics may mean, to some, nothing more than the study of foreign political systems, but to take this narrow, atheoretical perspective is, in the final analysis, to miss the whole point.

## Notes

1.  An interesting attempt by American political scientists to view US politics non-parochially is Harold Chase, Robert Holt, and John Turner, *American Government in Comparative Perspective* (New York: New Viewpoints, 1980).

2.  A recent comparative study of the utility of parliamentary and presidential systems for newly emerging democracies is Guiseppe di Palma, *To Craft Democracies* (Berkeley: University of California Press, 1990). See also Juan Linz and Arturo Valenzuela, eds,

*Presidential and Parliamentary Democracy: Does It Make a Difference?* (Baltimore: Johns Hopkins University Press, 1992).

3. This point is developed more fully in Adam Przeworski, 'Methods of Cross-National Research, 1970–1983: An Overview', in Meinoff Dierkes, Hans Weiler, and Ariane Berthoin Antal, eds, *Comparative Policy Research: Learning From Experience* (Brookfield, Vt: Gower, 1987).

4. This type of contrast is the subject of my book, *Government Survival in Parliamentary Regimes* (Cambridge and New York: Cambridge University Press, 1994).

5. Almond and his associate, Sidney Verba, later developed and tested these ideas in *The Civic Culture: Political Attitudes and Democracy in Five Nations* (Boston: Little, Brown, 1965). Their work was critiqued and updated in Gabriel Almond and Sidney Verba, eds, *The Civic Culture Revisited* (Boston: Little, Brown, 1980).

6. A good brief introduction to the rational choice approach is Albert Weale, 'Rational Choice and Political Analysis', in Adrian Leftwich, ed., *New Developments in Political Science* (Aldershot: Edward Elgar, 1990), ch. 12.

7. Inglehart has incorporated this selection into a larger study, *Culture Shift in Advanced Industrial Society* (Princeton, NJ: Princeton University Press, 1990), which focuses on the rise of 'post-material' values in Western countries.

## Study Questions for the Readings

1. On what basis does Almond categorize the countries of the world?
2. Is this a reasonable way to categorize these countries? Explain.
3. What does this categorization leave out that is politically significant?
4. What cultural traits does Inglehart identify as important for liberal democracy?
5. How did these traits arise in the established liberal democracies?
6. Are countries that do not have this 'cultural syndrome' doomed to fail at liberal democracy?

# Comparative Political Systems

Gabriel A. Almond

What I propose to do in this brief paper is to suggest how the application of certain sociological and anthropological concepts may facilitate systematic comparison among the major types of political systems operative in the world today. . . .

The problem to which this paper is a tentative and provisional answer is the following. With the proliferation of courses and special studies of specific 'governments' and groupings of governments on an area or other bases, is it possible to set up and justify a preliminary classification into which most of the political systems which we study today can be assigned? The classifications which we now employ are particularistic (e.g., American Government, British Government, the Soviet Union, and the like); regional (e.g., Government and Politics of the Far East, Latin America, and the like); or political (e.g., the British Commonwealth, Colonial Government, and the like); or functional (e.g., the comprehensive comparative efforts limited to the European-American area, such as Finer and Friedrich, and the specific institutional comparisons such as comparative parties, and comparative administration).

Anyone concerned with this general problem of classification of political systems will find that all of the existing bases of classification leave something to be desired. Dealing with governments particularistically is no classification at all. A regional classification is based not on the properties of the political systems, but on contiguity in space. The existing structural classifications, such as democracy-dictatorship, parliamentary-

presidential systems, two-party and multi-party systems often turn out to miss the point, particularly when they are used in the strikingly different political systems of the pre-industrial areas. There may be a certain use therefore in exploring the possibilities of other ways of classifying political systems. What is proposed here is just one of those ways, and because of the uneven state of our knowledge is necessarily crude and provisional.

In my own efforts to stand far off, so to speak, and make the grossest discriminations between types of empirical political systems operative in the world today, I have found a fourfold classification to be most useful: the Anglo-American (including some members of the Commonwealth), the Continental European (exclusive of the Scandinavian and Low Countries, which combine some of the features of the Continental European and the Anglo-American), the pre-industrial, or partially industrial, political systems outside the European-American area, and the totalitarian political systems. This classification will not include all the political systems in existence today, but it comes close to doing so. It will serve the purpose of our discussion, which is not that of testing the inconclusiveness of this classification but rather the usefulness of sociological concepts in bringing out the essential differences between these political systems.

The terms which I shall use in discriminating the essential properties of these classes have emerged out of the Weber-Parsons tradition in social theory.[1] I shall try to suggest why I find some of these concepts useful. First, a political system is a system of action. What this means is that the student of political systems is concerned with empirically observable behaviour. He is

Abridged from *Journal of Politics* 18, 3 (Aug. 1956): 391–409. Reprinted by permission of the author and the University of Texas Press.

concerned with norms or institutions in so far as they affect behaviour. Emphasizing 'action' merely means that the description of a political system can never be satisfied by a simple description of its legal or ethical norms. In other words, political institutions or persons performing political roles are viewed in terms of what it is that they do, why they do it, and how what they do is related to and affects what others do. The term *system*[2] satisfies the need for an inclusive concept which covers all of the patterned actions relevant to the making of political decisions. . . .

The unit of the political system is the role. The role, according to Parsons and Shils, 'is that organized sector of an actor's orientation which constitutes and defines his participation in an interactive process.'[3] It involves a set of complementary expectations concerning his own actions and those of others with whom he interacts. Thus a political system may be defined as a set of interacting roles, or as a structure of roles, if we understand by *structure* a patterning of interactions. The advantage of the concept of *role* as compared with such terms as *institutions, organizations,* or *groups,* is that it is a more inclusive and more open concept. It can include formal offices, informal offices, families, electorates, mobs, casual as well as persistent groupings, and the like, in so far as they enter into and affect the political system. The use of other concepts such as those indicated above involves ambiguity, forced definitions (such as groups), or residual categories. Like the concept of system it does not prejudice our choice of units but rather enables us to nominate them on the basis of empirical investigation. . . .

My own conception of the distinguishing properties of the political system proceeds from Weber's definition—the legitimate monopoly of physical coercion over a given territory and population.[4] The political systems with which most political scientists concern themselves are all characterized by a specialized apparatus which possesses this legitimate monopoly, and the political system consists of those interacting roles which

affect its employment. There are, of course, simpler societies in which this function of maintenance of order through coercion is diffuse and unspecialized; it is combined with other functions in the family and other groupings. While these systems are also properly the subject matter of political science, there are few political scientists indeed with the specialized equipment necessary to study them.

It may be useful to add a few comments about this definition of politics and the political in order to avoid misunderstanding. To define politics as having this distinguishing property of monopolizing legitimate coercion in a given territory is not the same thing as saying that this is *all* that government does. It is the thing that government does and that other social systems ordinarily may not do legitimately. Other social systems may employ other forms of compulsion than physical coercion. Some indeed may legitimately employ physical coercion on a limited scale. But the employment of *ultimate, comprehensive,* and *legitimate* physical coercion is the monopoly of states, and the political system is uniquely concerned with the scope, the direction, and the conditions affecting the employment of this physical coercion. It is, of course, clear that political systems protect freedoms and provide welfare, as well as impose order backed up by physical compulsion, but even their protection of freedom and their provision of welfare are characteristically backed up by the threat of physical compulsion. Hence it seems appropriate to define the political system as the patterned interaction of roles affecting decisions backed up by the threat of physical compulsion. . . .

Every political system is embedded in a particular pattern of orientations to political action. I have found it useful to refer to this as the *political culture.* There are two points to be made regarding the concept of political culture. First, it does not coincide with a given political system or society. Patterns of orientation to politics may, and usually do, extend beyond the boundaries of political systems. The second point is that the political culture is not the same thing as the general culture, although it is related to it. Because political orientation involves cognition, intellection, and adaptation to external situations, as well as the standards and values of the general culture, it is a differentiated part of the culture and has a certain autonomy. Indeed, it is the failure to give proper weight to the cognitive and evaluative factors, and to the consequent autonomy of political culture, that has been responsible for the exaggerations and oversimplifications of the 'national character' literature of recent years.

The usefulness of the concept of political culture and its meaning may perhaps be conveyed more effectively through illustration. I would argue that the United States, England, and several of the Commonwealth countries have a common political culture, but are separate and different kinds of political systems. And I would argue that the typical countries of continental Western Europe, while constituting individual political systems, include several different political cultures which extend beyond their borders. In other words, they are political systems with fragmented political cultures.

In an effort to overcome understandable resistances to the introduction of a new term, I should like to suggest why I find the concept of political culture more useful than the terms we now employ, such as *ideology* or *political party*. As I understand the term *ideology*, it means the systematic and explicit formulation of a general orientation to politics. We need this term to describe such political phenomena as these and should not reduce its specificity by broadening it to include not only the explicit doctrinal structure characteristically borne by a minority of *militants*, but also the vaguer and more implicit orientations which generally characterize political followings. The term *political party* also cannot serve our purpose, for we are here dealing with a formal organization which may or may not be a manifestation of a political culture. Indeed, we will be gravely misled

if we try to force the concept of party to mean political culture. Thus the commonly used distinctions between one-party, two-party, and multi-party systems simply get nowhere in distinguishing the essential properties of the totalitarian, the Anglo-American, and the Continental European political systems. For the structure we call *party* in the totalitarian system is not a party at all; the two parties of the Anglo-American system are organized manifestations of a homogeneous political culture; and the multi-parties of Continental European political systems in some cases are and in some cases are not the organized manifestations of different political cultures.

But the actual test of the usefulness of this conceptual scheme can only come from a more detailed application of it in developing the special properties of the classes of political systems to which we earlier referred.

## The Anglo-American Political Systems

The Anglo-American political systems are characterized by a *homogeneous, secular* political culture. By a secular political culture I mean a multivalued political culture, a rational-calculating, bargaining, and experimental political culture. It is a homogeneous culture in the sense that there is a sharing of political ends and means. The great majority of the actors in the political system accept as the ultimate goals of the political system some combination of the values of freedom, mass welfare, and security. There are groups which stress one value at the expense of the others; there are times when one value is stressed by all groups; but by and large the tendency is for all these values to be shared, and for no one of them to be completely repressed. To a Continental European this kind of political culture often looks sloppy. It has no logic, no clarity. This is probably correct in an intellectual sense, since this balancing of competing values occurs below the surface among most people and is not explicated in any very elegant way. Actually the logic is complex and is constantly referred to reality in an inductive process. It avoids the kind of logical simplism which characterizes much of the Continental European ideological polemic.

A secularized political system involves an individuation of and a measure of autonomy among the various roles. Each one of the roles sets itself up autonomously in political business, so to speak. There tends to be an arm's-length bargaining relationship among the roles. The political system is saturated with the atmosphere of the market. Groups of electors come to the political market with votes to sell in exchange for policies. Holders of offices in the formal-legal role structure tend to be viewed as agents and instrumentalities, or as brokers occupying points in the bargaining process. The secularized political process has some of the characteristics of a laboratory; that is, policies offered by candidates are viewed as hypotheses, and the consequences of legislation are rapidly communicated within the system and constitute a crude form of testing hypotheses. Finally, because the political culture tends to be homogeneous and pragmatic, it takes on some of the atmosphere of a game. A game is a good game when the outcome is in doubt and when the stakes are not too high. When the stakes are too high, the tone changes from excitement to anxiety. While 'fun' is frequently an aspect of Anglo-American politics, it is rarely a manifestation of Continental European politics; and, unless one stretches the definition, it never occurs at all in totalitarian politics. . . .

## The Pre-Industrial Political Systems

The political systems which fall under this very general category are the least well known of all four of the classes discussed here. But despite our relative ignorance in this area and our inability to elaborate the many subtypes which no doubt exist, a discussion of this kind of political system is analytically useful since it presents such a strik-

ing contrast to the homogeneous, secular political culture, and the complex and relatively stable role structure of the Anglo-American political system.

The pre-industrial—or partially industrialized and Westernized—political systems may be best described as mixed political cultures and mixed political systems. Nowhere does the need for additional vocabulary become clearer than in the analysis of these systems; for here parliaments tend to be something other than parliaments, parties and pressure groups behave in unusual ways, bureaucracies and armies often dominate the political system, and there is an atmosphere of unpredictability and gunpowder surrounding the political system as a whole.

Some clarity is introduced into the understanding of these systems if one recognizes that they are embedded in mixed political cultures. What this means is that as a minimum we have two political cultures, the Western system with its parliament, its electoral system, its bureaucracy and the like, and the pre-Western system or systems. In countries such as India there are many traditional political cultures which intermingle with the Western system. What kind of amalgam emerges from this impingement of different political cultures will depend on at least five factors: (1) the type of traditional cultures which are involved; (2) the auspices under which Westernization has been introduced (e.g., Western colonial powers, or native élites); (3) the functions of the society which have been Westernized; (4) the tempo and tactics of the Westernization process; (5) the type of Western cultural products which have been introduced. As a consequence of this impingement of the Western and traditional political cultures, there is a third type of political culture which frequently emerges in this type of system; what in Max Weber's language may be called a charismatic political culture. It often happens as a consequence of the erosion of a traditional political culture that powerful forces are released—anxieties over the violation of sacred customs and relationships, feelings of rootlessness and directionlessness because of the rejection of habitual routines. The impact of the Western rational system on the traditional system or systems often creates a large potential for violence. One of the typical manifestations of this conflict of political cultures is the charismatic nationalism which occurs so frequently in these areas and which may be in part understood as being a movement toward accepting a new system of political norms, or a movement toward reaffirming the older traditional ones, often both in peculiar combinations. To overcome the resistance of habitual routines backed up by supernatural sanctions, the new form of legitimacy must represent a powerful affirmation capable of breaking up deeply ingrained habits and replacing earlier loyalties. Thus, at the minimum, we must have in these political systems the old or the traditional political culture, or cultures, the new or the Western-rational political culture, and transitional or resultant political phenomena of one kind or another. Needless to say, this typical mixture of political cultures presents the most serious problems of communication and co-ordination. We are dealing with a political system in which large groups have fundamentally different 'cognitive maps' of politics and apply different norms to political action. Instability and unpredictability are not to be viewed as pathologies but as inescapable consequences of this type of mixture of political cultures. . . .

## Totalitarian Political Systems

The totalitarian political culture gives the appearance of being homogeneous, but the homogeneity is synthetic. Since there are no voluntary associations, and political communication is controlled from the centre, it is impossible to judge in any accurate way the extent to which there is a positive acceptance of the totalitarian order. One can only say that in view of the thoroughgoing penetration of the society by a centrally controlled system of organizations and communications, and the special way in which coercion or its threat is

applied, the totalitarian system, in contrast to the others, tends to be non-consensual. This is not to say that it is completely non-consensual. A completely coercive political system is unthinkable. But if one were to place the totalitarian system on a continuum of consensual–non-consensual it would be located rather more at the non-consensual end of the continuum than the others described here. Unlike the other systems where some form of legitimacy—whether traditional, rational-legal, or charismatic—underlies the acquiescence of the individual in the political system, in the totalitarian order the characteristic orientation to authority tends to be some combination of conformity and apathy. This type of political system has become possible only in modern times, since it depends on the modern technology of communication, on modern types of organization, and on the modern technology of violence. Historic tyrannies have no doubt sought this kind of dominion but were limited in the effectiveness of their means. Totalitarianism is tyranny with a rational bureaucracy, a monopoly of the modern technology of communication, and a monopoly of the modern technology of violence. . . .

## The Continental European Political Systems

We refer here primarily to France, Germany, and Italy. The Scandinavian and Low Countries stand somewhere in between the Continental pattern and the Anglo-American. What is most marked about the Continental European systems is the fragmentation of political culture; but this fragmentation is rather different from that of the non-Western systems. For in the non-Western systems we are dealing with mixed political cultures involving the most striking contrasts. The Western political culture arising out of a very different development pattern is introduced bodily, so to speak, from the outside. In the Continental European systems we are dealing with a pattern of political culture characterized by an uneven pattern of development. There are significant survivals, 'outcroppings', of older cultures and their political manifestations. But all of the cultural variations have common roots and share a common heritage.

In view of this developmental pattern it may be appropriate to speak of the Continental European systems as having political subcultures. There is indeed in all the examples of this type of system a surviving pre-industrial subculture (e.g., the Catholic *ancien régime* area in France, Southern Italy, and the Islands, and parts of Bavaria). The historical background of all three of these systems is characterized by a failure on the part of the middle classes in the nineteenth century to carry through a thoroughgoing secularization of the political culture. Thus another political subculture in these political systems constitutes remnants of the older middle classes who are still primarily concerned with the secularization of the political system itself. A third group of political subcultures is associated with the modernized and industrialized parts of these societies. But because they emerged in an only partially secularized political culture, their potentialities for 'political market' behaviour were thwarted. As major political subcultures there are thus these three: (1) the pre-industrial, primarily Catholic components, (2) the older middle-class components, and (3) the industrial components proper. But the political culture is more complex than this. Since in the last century the political issues have involved the very survival of these subcultures, and the basic form of the political system itself, the political actors have not come to politics with specific bargainable differences but rather with conflicting and mutually exclusive designs for the political culture and political system. This has involved a further fragmentation at the level of ideology and political organizations. Thus the pre-industrial, primarily Catholic element has both an adaptive, semi-secular wing and an anti-secular wing. The middle classes are divided into conservative wings in an uneasy alliance with clerical pre-republican elements, and left-wings in uneasy friendship with socialists. Finally, the industrial workers are divided according to the degree of their alienation from the political system as a whole. The organized political manifestations of this fragmented political culture take the form of 'movements' or sects, rather than of political parties. This means that political affiliation is more of an act of faith than of agency.

Perhaps the most pronounced characteristic of the political role structure in these areas is what one might call a general alienation from the political market. The political culture pattern is not adapted to the political system. For while these countries have adopted parliaments and popular elections, they are not appropriately oriented to these institutions. The political actors come to the market not to exchange, compromise, and adapt, but to preach, exhort, convert, and transform the political system into something other than a bargaining agency. What bargaining and exchanging does occur tends to take the form of under-the-counter transactions. Thus demoralization ('*transformism*') is an almost inescapable consequence of this combination of political culture and system. In contrast, the normatively consistent, morally confident actor in this type of political system is the *militant* who remains within the confines of his political subculture, continually reaffirms his special norms, and scolds his parliamentarians.

This suggests another essential characteristic of this type of role structure, which places it in contrast to the Anglo-American. There is not an individuation of the political roles, but rather the roles are embedded in the subcultures and tend to constitute separate subsystems of roles. Thus the Catholic subculture has the Church itself, the Catholic schools, propaganda organizations such as Catholic Action, Catholic trade unions, or worker organizations, a Catholic party or parties, and a Catholic press. The Communist subculture—the subculture of the political 'alienates'—similarly has a complete and separate system of roles. The socialist and 'liberal' subcultures tend in the same direction but are less fully organized and less exclusive. Thus one would have to say that the centre of gravity in these political systems is not in the formal legal role structure but in the political subcultures. Thus 'immobilism' would appear to be a normal property of this kind of political system, and it is not so much an 'immobilism' of formal-legal institutions as a consequence of the condition of the political culture. Needless to say, this portrayal of the Continental European political system has been exaggerated for purposes of contrast and comparison.

Two other general aspects of the role structure of these countries call for comment. First, there is a higher degree of substitutability of roles than in the Anglo-American political systems and a lesser degree than in the non-Western systems.

Thus parties may manipulate pressure groups in the sense of making their decisions for them (the Communist case); interest groups such as the Church and Catholic Action may manipulate parties and trade unions; and interest groups may operate directly in the legislative process, although this last pattern occurs in the Anglo-American system as well. The 'immobilism' of the formally political organs often leads to a predominance of the bureaucracy in policy-making.

A second general characteristic, which is a consequence of the immobilism of the political system as a whole, is the ever-present threat of what is often called the 'Caesaristic' breakthrough. As in the non-Western area, although the situations and causes are different, these systems tend always to be threatened by, and sometimes to be swept away by, movements of charismatic nationalism which break through the boundaries of the political subcultures and overcome immobilism through coercive action and organization. In other words these systems have a totalitarian potentiality in them. The fragmented political culture may be transformed into a synthetically homogeneous one and the stalemated role structure mobilized by the introduction of the coercive pattern already described.

In conclusion perhaps the point might be made that conceptual and terminological growth in the sciences is as inevitable as the growth of language itself. But just as all the slang and neologisms of the moment do not find a permanent place in the language, so also all of the conceptual jargon which the restless minds of scholars invent— sometimes to facilitate communication with their colleagues and sometimes to confound them—will not find its permanent place in the vocabulary of the disciplines. The ultimate criterion of admission or rejection is the facilitation of understanding, and this, fortunately enough, is not in the hands of the restless and inventive scholar, but in the hands of the future scholarly generations who will try them out for 'fit'. If I may be permitted to conclude with a minor note of blasphemy, it may be said of new concepts as it was said of the salvation of souls . . . 'there shall be weeping and gnashing of teeth, for many are called but few are chosen.'

## Notes

1. See in particular Max Weber, *The Theory of Social and Economic Organization*, trans. A.M. Henderson and Talcott Parsons (New York: Oxford University Press, 1947), 87 ff.
2. See David Easton, *The Political System: An Inquiry into the State of Political Science* (New York: Alfred Knopf, 1953), 90 ff.
3. Talcott Parsons and Edward A. Shils, eds, *Towards a General Theory of Action* (Cambridge, Mass.: Harvard University Press, 1951), 23.
4. *From Max Weber: Essays in Sociology*, trans. H.H. Gerth and C. Wright Mills (New York: Oxford University Press, 1946), 78.

# The Renaissance of Political Culture

Ronald Inglehart

It is time to redress the balance in social analysis. Since the late 1960s, rational choice models based on economic variables have become the dominant mode of analysis, while cultural factors have been de-emphasized to an unrealistic degree. This approach has made major contributions to our understanding of how politics works; nevertheless, it underestimates the significance of cultural factors, if only because while economic indicators are readily available for these models, cultural data generally are not.

The incompleteness of models that ignore cultural factors is becoming increasingly evident. In Catholic societies from Latin America to Poland, the Church plays a major role despite the demise often predicted by economic determinists. In the Islamic world, Muslim fundamentalism has become a political factor that neither East nor West can ignore. The Confucian-influenced zone of East Asia manifests an economic dynamism that outstrips any other region of the world. By economic criteria one of the *least*-favoured regions on earth, it is virtually impossible to explain its performance without reference to cultural factors. Even in advanced industrial societies religion not only outweighs social class as an influence on electoral behaviour[1] but actually seems to be widening its lead: while social class voting has declined markedly in recent decades, religious cleavages remain astonishingly durable.

There is no question that economic factors are politically important, but they are only part of

the story. I argue that different societies are characterized to very different degrees by a specific syndrome of political cultural attitudes; that these cultural differences are relatively enduring, but not immutable; and that they have major political consequences, being closely linked to the viability of democratic institutions.

After flourishing in the 1960s, the concept of political culture came under attack. In 1963 the fountainhead of political culture research, Almond and Verba's *The Civic Culture*, represented a tremendous advance. Previous works that attempted to deal with the impact of culture on politics relied on impressionistic evidence. Cultural influences on the distinctive political behaviour of a given people were interpreted in terms of vague but presumably indelible characteristics such as 'national character'. By providing a well-developed theory of political culture based on cross-national empirical data, Almond and Verba moved from the realm of literary impressions to that of testable propositions.

In subsequent years, it was often charged that political culture was a static concept and that Almond and Verba had ethnocentrically asserted the (presumably permanent) superiority of Anglo-Saxon culture over that of other nations. For though their theoretical interests concerned possible changes in political culture, their analysis was based on data from a single time point and was therefore necessarily static. Empirically, the political culture of a given country could only be treated as a constant. The British and US citizens were, as hypothesized, found to rank higher on interpersonal trust, pride in their political institutions, and feelings of political competence than the publics of Germany, Italy, or Mexico. But since these variables were in fact constants for each

Abridged from *American Political Science Review* 82, 4 (Dec. 1988): 1203–29. Reprinted by permission of the author and the American Political Science Association.

country, it was impossible to analyse their relationships with other macrophenomena or to trace changes over time.

The political culture literature argues that the evolution and persistence of mass-based democracy require the emergence of certain supportive habits and attitudes among the general public. One of the most basic of these attitudes is a sense of interpersonal trust. Almond and Verba[2] concluded that interpersonal trust is a prerequisite to the formation of secondary associations, which in turn is essential to effective political participation in any large democracy. A sense of trust is also required for the functioning of the democratic rules of the game: one must view the opposition as a *loyal* opposition, who will not imprison or execute you if you surrender political power but can be relied upon to govern within the laws and to surrender political power reciprocally if your side wins the next election. Almond and Verba found that their German and Italian respondents ranked relatively low on interpersonal trust. With data from only one time point it was impossible to determine whether these findings could be attributed to short-term factors—perhaps the harsh conditions of the postwar era—or whether they reflected more enduring differences. There was some reason to believe that the Italian findings, in particular, might reflect the heritage of long historical experiences.[3]

The relationship between (1) a culture of distrust and (2) the presence or absence of modern social structures has the causal ambiguity of the chicken-versus-egg question: Does southern Europe have low levels of trust because it has not yet developed modern organizational structures? Or (in a variation on Weber's Protestant ethic thesis) did southern Europe industrialize and develop modern organizational structures later than northern Europe because its traditional culture was relatively low on interpersonal trust? We cannot answer this question conclusively with the data now available. Banfield's interpretation implies that low levels of trust are a persisting feature of given

cultures or regional subcultures, which may inhibit economic and political development in those areas. His critics emphasize the impact of economic development on cultural patterns. In our view a reciprocal causal relationship seems likely.

Important though it is, interpersonal trust alone is not sufficient to support stable mass democracy. A long-term commitment to democratic institutions among the public is also required, in order to sustain democracy when conditions are dire. Even when democracy has no reply to the question, What have you done for me lately? it may be sustained by diffuse feelings that it is an inherently good thing. These feelings in turn may reflect economic and other successes that one experienced long ago or learned about second-hand as part of one's early socialization. Evidence presented below indicates that the publics of certain societies have much more positive feeling toward the world they live in than do those of other societies. One of the best indicators of this orientation is satisfaction with one's life as a whole. This is a very diffuse attitude. It is not tied to the current performance of the economy or the authorities currently in office or to any specific aspect of society. Partly because it is so diffuse, intercultural differences in this orientation are remarkably enduring and may help shape attitudes toward more specific objects, such as the political system.

From their 1959 fieldwork, Almond and Verba found that (unlike the British or US citizens) few Germans expressed pride in their political institutions. But one of the few aspects of their society in which they *did* express pride was the way their economic system was working. In the short run, this is an inadequate basis for democratic legitimacy. But in the long run, such feelings may contribute to the evolution of broadly favourable orientations toward the institutions under which one lives. Such feelings may play an important role in sustaining the viability of these institutions even when favourable economic or political outputs are not forthcoming. For cultural patterns, once established, possess considerable autonomy and can influence subsequent political and economic events. To demonstrate this fact, let us now turn to the analysis of data from cross-national surveys carried out during the past 15 years.

## Cross-cultural Differences in Overall Life Satisfaction and Their Political Significance

The study of political culture is based on the implicit assumption that autonomous and reasonably enduring cross-cultural differences exist and that they can have important political consequences. Intuitively, these assumptions seem plausible. But critics of cultural explanations have questioned them, and indeed very little empirical evidence has been presented to support them so far. Since they are crucial assumptions underlying a controversial topic, let us examine a substantial body of evidence in order to see how well these assumptions hold up in longitudinal perspective.

I will start with one of the most basic and central attitudes of all: whether or not one is satisfied with the way things are going in one's life. Figure 1 illustrates the cross-national differences in response to the question, 'Generally speaking, how satisfied are you with your life as a whole? Would you say that you are very satisfied, fairly satisfied, not very satisfied, or not at all satisfied?' This question has been asked repeatedly in the Euro-Barometer surveys carried out from 1973 to the present. Figure 1 sums up the results from the over 200,000 interviews in more than 200 representative national surveys of the publics of nine European Community nations.

I find large and remarkably stable cross-cultural differences. And these differences do not reflect objective economic conditions in any direct or simple fashion. Year after year the Italian public shows the lowest level of satisfaction; from 1973 to 1987 they rank last in every year but one (when they rank second-lowest); at no time during this 14–year period do more than 15 per cent

of the Italian public describe themselves as 'very satisfied'. The French manifest only slightly higher levels of life satisfaction than the Italians, ranking in second-to-last place in all but two years (rising one rank above this level in one year and falling one rank below it in the other year). At no time do more than 17 per cent of the French public describe themselves as 'very satisfied'.

At the opposite extreme, the Danes manifest the highest level of overall life satisfaction in every year but one (when they rank second); at no time do less than 47 per cent of the Danish public describe themselves as 'very satisfied'. On the average, the Danes are six times as likely as the Italians to describe themselves as 'very satisfied'. The Dutch also rank high consistently, throughout the period from 1973 to 1987; at no time do less than 36 per cent describe themselves as 'very satisfied' with their lives as a whole.

The other nationalities maintain their relative positions in remarkably stable fashion, with a sole exception: the Belgians, who consistently ranked among the three most satisfied nationalities throughout the 1970s, show a substantial and protracted decline in the 1980s, falling to sixth place by 1986. In the 1970s, 40–45 per cent of the Belgians consistently described themselves as 'very satisfied'; in 1986, the figure had fallen to 21 per cent. This drop of 15–20 points is not immense when compared with the gap of 50 points that separate the Danes from the Italians, but it does represent a substantial decline in the subjective well-being of the Belgian public and stands in dramatic contrast to the overall stability of the cross-national differences manifested throughout this period. The cultural differences are reasonably stable but not eternal. Short-term fluctuations are present and, as the Belgian case illustrates, significant changes can occur in the relative positions of given nations.

On the whole, the stability shown in Figure 1 is truly remarkable. For one must bear in mind that this was a period of sharp economic upheavals; the crises that occurred in the mid-

## Figure 1: Cross-national Differences in Levels of Satisfaction with Life, 1973-87

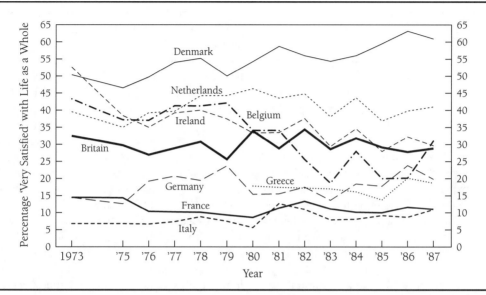

Source: Euro-Barometer surveys.

1970s and the early 1980s constituted the two most severe recessions since the 1930s. Moreover, these crises had a much more severe impact on some societies than others. From 1973 to 1987, life satisfaction declined significantly in both Belgium and Ireland, two of the three countries most severely afflicted by unemployment and inflation during this period. Conversely, life satisfaction showed a modest but perceptible upward trend in Germany, the country with the lowest inflation rates from 1973 to 1987. Thus I find a fairly good fit between short-term fluctuations in life satisfaction and the economic experiences of the respective societies.

But a far more impressive aspect of Figure 1 is the cultural continuity that persisted *in spite of* these short-term fluctuations. Despite dramatic economic upheavals from year to year and despite large differences between the experiences of the different countries, I find remarkable stability in the relative positions of these publics. Through thick and thin, the Italians and French remain near the bottom and the Danes and Dutch near the top. And despite the fact that the German economy ranks high both in absolute terms and in relative performance, the life satisfaction levels of the German public consistently rank relatively low. Conversely, both the Irish and the Dutch have much lower per capita incomes than the Germans, and they experienced considerably higher levels of inflation and unemployment during this era than the Germans did, yet they continued to manifest higher levels of life satisfaction than the Germans. Though cross-cultural differences in life satisfaction respond to economic changes, they do so only with a great deal of inertia.

My conclusion is very simple but very important: there is a durable cultural component underlying these responses. Virtually any survey response is influenced to some extent by the context in which it is asked and this question is no exception: responses reflect both short-term fluctuations (resulting from immediate economic, social, and political events) and a long-term cultural component. Through statistical procedures it is possible to distinguish between the underlying cultural component and the short-term disturbances. In the present case, the long-term cultural differences are so pronounced that one can readily perceive them by mere visual inspection. Enduring cross-cultural differences exist and can be measured.[4]

I suggest that the cultural component of these cross-national differences reflects the distinctive historical experience of the respective nationalities. Long periods of disappointed expectations give rise to dissatisfied attitudes. These orientations may be transmitted from generation to generation through pre-adult socialization. In so far as early learning is relatively persistent, this contributes to the stability of distinctive cultural patterns. The fact that one can to some extent identify the historical causes of given cross-cultural differences does not of course make them disappear. They remain distinctive cultural characteristics with important behavioural consequences.

Is it true that economic security tends to enhance the prevailing sense of life satisfaction in a society, gradually giving rise to a relatively high cultural norm? Empirical evidence supports this supposition. First, as we have seen, there is a tendency for life satisfaction levels to rise or decline gradually in response to short-term economic fluctuations. But one might suspect that the observed cross-cultural differences reflect long-term historical experiences over generations or even centuries, not just the past dozen years or so. We would need survey data covering the past century or two in order to test this hypothesis directly. They are not available, but we can use the cross-sectional pattern to provide a surrogate test: if economic security is conducive to relatively high levels of life satisfaction, we would expect the publics of prosperous nations to show higher

levels of satisfaction than those of poorer ones. The data in Figure 2 test this hypothesis.

The overall correlation between gross national product per capita and life satisfaction in Figure 2 is .67: prosperity *is* linked with relatively high levels of life satisfaction among the 24 nations for which we have data from the 1980s. This point has been a matter of controversy in previous studies. Cantril analysed data gathered in the 1950s from 14 countries and found that the publics of richer nations *did* show relatively high levels of subjective well-being.[5] Easterlin re-analysed the Cantril data and concluded that the correlation was actually rather weak.[6] Emphasizing the fact that some poor nations (such as Egypt) showed higher levels of life satisfaction than some relatively wealthy ones (such as West Germany), he argued that economic development had little impact on subjective well-being. In a more recent study based on a broader range of nations, Gallup found a relatively strong correlation between economic development and life satisfaction.[7] He concluded that the two *are* linked. The present data also show a relatively strong correlation between economic development and life satisfaction. How we interpret this depends on one's theoretical expectations. If one approaches the topic with the expectation that subjective well-being will be found almost entirely a matter of economic factors, as Easterlin apparently did, then the crucial finding is that this is not the case. With the data in Figure 2, a nation's economic level explains less than half of the variance in life satisfaction. In the data Easterlin analysed, economic factors explain an even smaller share of the variance. From Easterlin's perspective, economic determinism was clearly discredited.

However, if one approaches the question with the expectation that a nation's level of economic development is only one of a number of historical factors that influence cross-cultural differences in life satisfaction, then the data clearly do support the hypothesis. Here, as in Easterlin's analysis, one can point to some striking deviant cases. Never-

# Figure 2: Mass Life Satisfaction, by Level of Economic Development

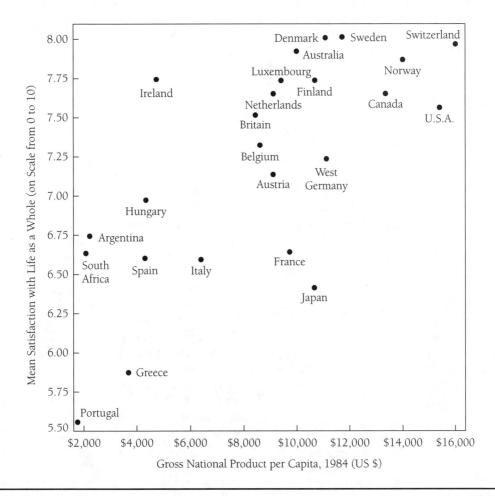

Note: r = .67

theless, the overall pattern is clear: wealthier nations tend to show higher levels of life satisfaction than poorer ones.

The Euro-Barometer surveys also provide regular readings on political satisfaction, which shows much more short-term fluctuation than life satisfaction, for it explicitly refers to the political system and accordingly behaves like an indicator of governmental popularity, fluctuating from one month to the next in response to current economic conditions and political events. When a conservative government is in office, those who identify with the Right show higher levels of political satisfaction; when a government of the Left gains power, those on the Left show higher levels. Political satisfaction fluctuates in response to current economic and political events. But it is clear that a significant cultural component *also* is present underneath these fluctuations: the publics of some countries are consistently more satisfied than others. Moreover, these differences reflect the now-familiar pattern found with life satisfaction and happiness: the publics of France and Italy almost always rank lower on political satisfaction than those of other nations: at the national level, the correlation between life satisfaction and political satisfaction is .41.

Both overall life satisfaction and political satisfaction are correlated with stable democracy. I will examine this relationship below. For the moment let me simply note that political satisfaction levels are only weakly linked with the number of years that democratic institutions have persisted in a given nation ($r$ = .21). But *despite* the direct and obvious political relevance of political satisfaction, life satisfaction is far more strongly linked with stable democracy ($r$ = .85). Democratic institutions seem to depend on enduring cultural traits such as life satisfaction and interpersonal trust, more than on relatively fluctuating variables such as political satisfaction. The latter may well be a better predictor of the popularity of a given government at a given moment. But precisely *because* it fluctuates with short-term conditions, it is less effective in maintaining the long-term stability of democratic institutions.

## Interpersonal Trust, Economic Development, and Democracy

Following Banfield, Almond and Verba, Wylie, and others, I hypothesized that interpersonal trust is part of an enduring cultural syndrome that is conducive to the viability of democracy. The first question one must answer is, Do enduring intercultural differences exist in interpersonal trust? Unless they do, any argument concerning its long-term political impact is on shaky ground.

The evidence indicates that given societies are indeed characterized by distinctive levels of interpersonal trust. This even seems to be true of specific regions *within* given countries. Euro-Barometer surveys in 1976, 1980, and 1986 asked, 'Now I would like to ask about how much you would trust people from various countries. For each country, please say whether, in your opinion, they are generally very trustworthy, fairly trustworthy, not particularly trustworthy, or not at all trustworthy.'

Figure 3 depicts the relative levels of interpersonal trust expressed during this 10-year period toward people of one's *own* nationality. As is immediately evident, trust levels in given countries are extremely stable. In a pattern that is becoming increasingly familiar, the Italian public ranks lowest at every point in time (with four major regions of Italy each retaining their relative positions). The Greeks rank next, followed by the French. The other nationalities are clustered close together, with relative rankings consistently remaining within the band between 85 per cent and 95 per cent. One line in Figure 3, labelled 'G.B. & Neth.', depicts the levels of *both* the British and the Dutch, which are identical at all three points. Remarkably pronounced and durable differences in trust exist among the various regions of Italy. Precisely as Banfield found many years ago, southern Italy seems to be characterized by lower levels of interpersonal trust than northern or central Italy and than any other Western society for which we have data.[8]

These findings of stable regional differences in Italian political culture are consistent with earlier findings by Putnam and his colleagues based on ecological data covering a much longer period of time.[9] In an imaginative and elegant analysis, these authors utilize various indicators of social involvement and political mobilization (such as membership in mutual aid societies, union membership, and electoral turnout) to derive a measure of 'civic culture'. This variable manifests remarkable stability at the regional level: their index of civic culture as measured in the 1970s correlates at $r$ = .91 with the strength of mass parties in 1919–21 and at

## Figure 3: Interpersonal Trust among European Publics, 1976–86

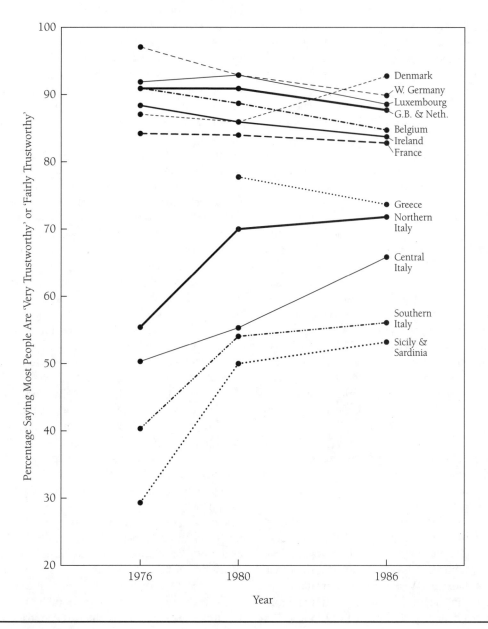

$r$ = .84 with the strength of mutual aid societies from 1873 to 1904. Civic culture in turn proves to be strongly correlated with the relative success of the new regional governments established throughout Italy in 1970. The authors conclude that political success or failure largely reflects the impact of autonomous cultural factors, independent of underlying economic variables:

> Contrary to any simple-minded economic determinism, these regional continuities in political culture are strikingly greater than continuities in economic structure or social well-being. For example, the agricultural share of the regional work force in 1970 correlated $r$ = .02 with the same figure in 1870; the equivalent statistic for infant mortality is $r$ = .01. Those regions with a relatively agricultural economy in 1970 had not been the more agricultural regions a century earlier, and the regions with good public health in 1970 had not been the healthier ones in 1870. But the regions characterized by political activism and social solidarity in the 1970s were essentially the same regions that had been so a century earlier. In short, we can trace with remarkable fidelity over the last hundred years the historical antecedents of just those aspects of regional political culture—mass participation and civic solidarity—that in turn provide such a powerful explanation for contemporary institutional success.[10]

Despite evidence of impressive stability in the propensity to trust others, trust is not a fixed genetic characteristic: it is cultural, shaped by the historical experiences of given peoples and subject to change. Fieldwork carried out for *The Civic Culture* found that the publics of the two, long-established English-speaking democracies had markedly higher levels of interpersonal trust than those of Mexico, West Germany, or Italy. The Italian public, in particular, manifested trust levels that were phenomenally low in 1959. But as our theoretical framework implies, the economic miracles that took place in both West Germany and

Italy during the 1950s and 1960s eventually had an impact on the political culture of those countries. Though the Italian public still remained relatively low on trust in 1981 and 1986, absolute levels of trust had more than tripled by 1981 and almost are reasonably strong grounds for thinking that while it may work both ways, the former of the two processes is mainly responsible for the relationship. First, knowing the relatively modest place that politics has on most people's intellectual horizons, it seems far more plausible that people vote Communist or neo-Fascist because they are dissatisfied and distrustful than that they are dissatisfied and distrustful because they vote Communist (or as a right-wing fantasy might have it, that communism spreads unhappiness and distrust among the public). Secondly, low levels of trust, satisfaction, and happiness are broad cultural characteristics of the French, Greek, and Italian publics, only marginally more prevalent among the electorates of the Communists and extreme Right than elsewhere. If the Communists sow unhappiness, they sow it broadly, not just among their own supporters. The growth of interpersonal trust among the West German public was proportionately smaller, because they started from a higher level. But by 1986 the Germans had actually surpassed the British in interpersonal trust. The other side of the coin is the fact that interpersonal trust had shown a long-term decline in the two English-speaking democracies.

Like life satisfaction and happiness, high interpersonal trust goes with relatively high levels of economic development, as Figure 4 illustrates. The cross-sectional correlation is .53. The available data do not enable one to determine whether this is because interpersonal trust is conducive to economic development or because economic development leads to an enhanced sense of security that is conducive to trust or whether (as we suspect) the two processes are mutually supportive. It is interesting that in the two countries from which I have evidence of a dramatic rise in interpersonal trust (West Germany and Italy), this

## Figure 4: Economic Development and Interpersonal Trust

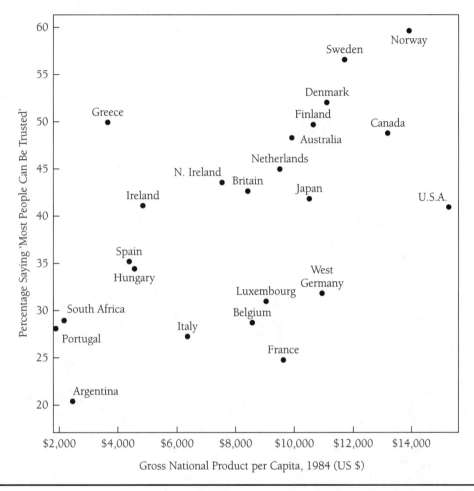

Sources: Data from World Values survey, 1981, and, for Greece, Portugal, and Luxembourg, Euro-Barometer Survey 25 (April 1986).

Note: r = .53

phenomenon took place after a period of dramatic economic recovery. But it is clear that economic factors alone are not decisive; for the publics of both Britain and the United States were wealthier in the 1980s than they were in 1959–60, but both experienced an erosion of interpersonal trust from 1960 to 1981.

As we will see shortly, high levels of interpersonal trust are also linked with stable democracy. But before analysing this relationship, let us consider the implications of a recurrent finding in the data. With remarkable consistency, the publics of France and Italy rank lowest on the syndrome of attitudes that might loosely be called the civic culture. Among those societies for which time series data from 1973 to the present exist, the French and Italian publics nearly always rank lowest on life satisfaction, happiness, political satisfaction, and trust. And these are precisely the countries that have been characterized by the largest antisystem parties: in France since the end of World War I the Communists have normally polled a fifth or more of the total vote in national elections. More recently, a party of the extreme Right, the National Front, won about 10 per cent of the vote in nationwide elections in 1984 and again in 1986, recalling the sudden mushrooming of support for another extreme Right party, the Poujadists, that took place in the 1950s. Similarly, in Italy the Communists have generally won about a third of the vote since 1945, while the neo-Fascist Italian Social Movement has often won as much as 10 per cent of the vote in national elections.

Data from Greece are available only since 1980, but they fit the pattern just described. To be sure, the Greek public has shown relatively high levels of satisfaction with the way democracy is functioning since democratic institutions were restored in the 1970s. But as I have already noted, this variable fluctuates with short-term events. On most of the long-term civic culture indicators such as life satisfaction, happiness, and support for the existing social order, the Greek public ranks relatively low. In keeping with this pattern, support for antisystem parties has been relatively high in Greece. The Communist vote has been higher than in any of the other societies for which time series data exist, apart from France and Italy, and there has also been significant support for parties of the extreme Right.

I believe that relatively low levels of diffuse satisfaction and trust make one more likely to reject the existing political system and support parties of the extreme Right or Left. Again, we have the chicken-versus-egg question: Does a culture of dissatisfaction and distrust give rise to an extremist vote or do extremist parties produce

distrust and dissatisfaction? The available empirical data do not allow me to provide a conclusive answer; but there change *precedes* changes in the vote. Table 1 shows the cross-national pattern of responses to the following question:

> On this card (*show card*) are three basic kinds of attitudes concerning the kind of society we live in. Please choose the one which best describes your own opinion.
> 1. The entire way our society is organized must be radically changed by revolutionary action.
> 2. Our society must be gradually improved by reforms.
> 3. Our present society must be valiantly defended against all subversive forces.

As Table 1 demonstrates, there is wide cross-national variation in response to this question. In the early 1980s, support for the revolutionary option ranged from a low of 1 per cent or 2 per cent in Northern Ireland and Norway to highs of 12–25 per cent in Mexico, Portugal, and South Africa. Conversely, support for the defence of the status quo ranged from highs of 49 per cent and 38 per cent respectively in Norway and West Germany to lows of 10–12 per cent in Mexico, Spain, and Portugal. The revolutionary option was most likely to be endorsed in societies with a relatively low per capita GNP ($r = -.68$) while the conservative option was most likely to be endorsed in societies with a relatively high per capita GNP ($r = .58$). And, as one might expect, support for the revolutionary option is negatively correlated with life satisfaction ($r = -.52$); while support for the conservative option shows a positive correlation with life satisfaction ($r = .31$).

Responses to this question among the nine European Community nations from which we have data from 1976 through 1986 are quite stable, apart from a gradual decline in support for the revolutionary option. In 1976 it was supported by 9 per cent of the public in the European Community as a whole but in 1986 by only 5 per

## Table 1: Support for Radical Change, Gradual Reform, or Defence of Present Society, in 20 Societies, 1981 (%)

| Society | Radical Change[a] | Gradual Reform[b] | Defend Present Society[c] | Number of Cases |
|---|---|---|---|---|
| N. Ireland | 1 | 74 | 25 | 287 |
| Norway | 2 | 50 | 49 | 1,146 |
| W. Germany | 3 | 59 | 38 | 1,149 |
| Denmark | 3 | 69 | 28 | 1,026 |
| Japan | 3 | 71 | 26 | 707 |
| Netherlands | 3 | 70 | 26 | 1,063 |
| Sweden | 4 | 80 | 16 | 797 |
| Ireland | 4 | 76 | 20 | 1,084 |
| Luxembourg | 5 | 69 | 25 | 760 |
| Canada | ˙5 | 74 | 21 | 1,135 |
| Britain | 5 | 73 | 23 | 1,136 |
| USA | 5 | 73 | 22 | 2,101 |
| Belgium | 7 | 73 | 21 | 897 |
| Italy | 8 | 73 | 19 | 1,270 |
| Spain | 8 | 82 | 10 | 2,091 |
| Greece | 9 | 57 | 26 | 2,000 |
| France | 9 | 73 | 19 | 1,123 |
| Mexico | 12 | 77 | 11 | 1,610 |
| Portugal | 14 | 74 | 12 | 813 |
| S. Africa | 25 | 54 | 21 | 1,182 |

Sources: World Values survey, 1981; except the data for Greece and Luxembourg are from Euro-Barometers 15 and 16 (carried out in April and October 1981), and Portuguese data are from Euro-Barometer 24 (carried out in November 1985). These are the earliest such data available from Portugal.

[a] 'The entire way our society is organized must be radically changed by revolutionary action.'

[b] 'Our society must be gradually improved by reforms.'

[c] 'Our present society must be valiantly defended against all subversive forces.'

cent. This decline was gradual, never falling by more than one percentage point per year, and was pervasive, with most nations showing declining support for revolution. But the phenomenon was especially concentrated among the publics of France and Italy, where pro-revolutionaries constituted 14 per cent of the public in both countries in 1976 but only 7 per cent and 8 per cent respectively in 1986. In part, this reflects the deradicalization of the Communist electorates of France and Italy, which *preceded* the electoral decline experienced in the mid-1980s by the

Communist parties of these two countries (and to some extent, throughout Western Europe). Moreover, it may be a harbinger of favourable prospects for the persistence of democratic institutions in these countries, for my data show a correlation of −.73 between support for the revolutionary option, and the number of continuous years that democratic institutions have functioned in a given nation.

## The Consequences of Political Culture: Some Speculations with Data

Let us sum up what we have learned so far. I find a broad syndrome of related attitudes that show substantial and consistent cross-cultural variation, with certain societies being characterized by satisfied and trusting attitudes to a much greater degree than others. The cross-national differences show impressive stability over time. Though they can vary (and the variations are of great substantive interest), they tend to be relatively enduring cultural characteristics. Finally, this syndrome is linked with the persistence of democratic institutions.

Life satisfaction, political satisfaction, interpersonal trust, and support for the existing social order all tend to go together. They constitute a syndrome of positive attitudes toward the world one lives in. And this syndrome goes with enduring democratic institutions. Is the linkage a causal one? Such causal linkages are difficult to demonstrate conclusively. To do so would require political culture data from a large number of nations, some of which became democracies during the course of a long time series, while others did not. My interpretation implies that those societies characterized by high levels of life satisfaction (as well as interpersonal trust, tolerance, etc.) would be likelier to adopt and maintain democratic institutions than those whose publics lacked such attitudes. Conversely, democratic institutions would be more likely to flounder in societies with

low levels of life satisfaction, trust, and so on. Such data are not now available and will be difficult to obtain, both because it will require a long-term data-gathering process in many countries during many decades and because the governments of non-democratic societies usually make it difficult to carry out survey research. In principle, however, it is possible to acquire such data, and this is a goal worth striving for. We may not attain the optimum, but we can certainly improve on what we have now. In the meantime, let us examine the cross-national pattern: do democratic institutions seem to have emerged earlier and persisted longer in societies with high levels of overall life satisfaction, than in those characterized by relatively low levels?

As Figure 5 demonstrates, the answer is yes. There is a remarkably consistent tendency for high levels of life satisfaction to go together with the persistence of democratic institutions over relatively long periods of time. Among the 24 societies depicted in Figure 5, the overall correlation between life satisfaction and the number of continuous years a given society has functioned as a democracy is .85. Needless to say, the causal inference would be on firmer ground if I had survey data on life satisfaction levels from some much earlier point in time, such as 1900, but such data are not available. I use *ex post facto* data from 1981 as an indicator of the relative rankings earlier in history. The evidence indicates that these rankings are pretty stable, but this procedure undoubtedly introduces some error in measurement (which tends to work *against* my hypothesis). Since our focus is on the effects of domestic political culture, I code democracy as having failed to survive only when it collapsed through *internal* causes and not when it did so as a consequence of foreign conquest. By this definition, literally *all* of the 13 societies that have maintained democratic institutions continuously since 1920 or earlier, show relatively high life satisfaction levels (above 7.25 on a scale from 0 to 10). Among the 11 societies in which democratic

## Figure 5: Mass Life Satisfaction and Stable Democracy

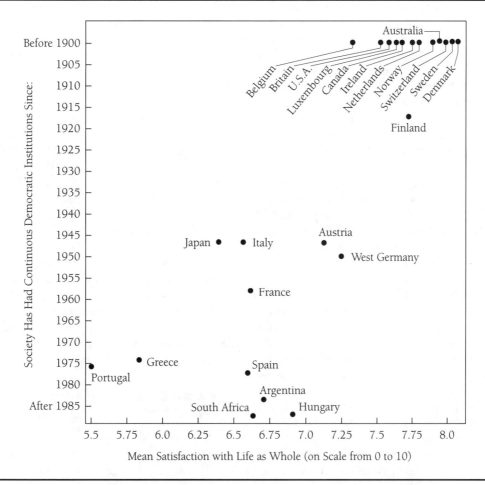

Sources: Data from World Values survey, and Euro-Barometer survey.
Note: r = .85

institutions have emerged only since 1945 or which are not yet fully democratic, all but one show mean life satisfaction levels below 7.25 and in some cases far below it. Some data are also available from Mexico, but because they are not based on a representative national sample, they have been omitted from these quantitative cross-national analyses. For what they are worth, these data show surprisingly high levels of life satisfac-

tion, paralleling earlier findings by Almond and Verba that the Mexican public showed anomalously high levels of satisfaction with their political system despite relatively negative conditions.

The coding of France might seem questionable. It is coded as having continuous democratic institutions only since 1958, since the military uprising that brought the Fourth Republic to an end and brought De Gaulle to power was not of foreign origin but was carried out by the French Army. It is true that the last president of the Fourth Republic invited De Gaulle to form a government. But he did so only under pressure from the French Army. Free elections were held shortly afterward, so the suspension of democracy was very brief; but as the subsequent military uprisings of 1960 and 1962 testify, democracy in France was for a time on shaky ground.

It is conceivable that we have the causal arrow reversed. Perhaps many decades of living under democratic institutions produces greater life satisfaction. We don't rule this factor out. Indeed, we think it *does* contribute to overall life satisfaction somewhat. But theoretical considerations suggest that the process mainly works the other way around. It seems more likely that a global sense of well-being would determine one's overall sense of satisfaction. In keeping with this reasoning, Andrews and Withey[11] find that political satisfaction has only a relatively modest impact on most people's overall life satisfaction; satisfaction with one's job, home, family life, and leisure time all make larger contributions.

Overall life satisfaction is part of a broad syndrome of attitudes reflecting whether one has relatively positive or negative attitudes toward the world in which one lives. Life satisfaction, happiness, interpersonal trust, and whether one supports radical social change or defends one's existing society, all tend to go together in a cultural cluster that is closely related to whether or not democratic institutions have persisted for a long time in a given society. These attitudes seem to be a deep-seated aspect of given cultures, constituting a long-term component underlying absolute levels of satisfaction with governmental performance at any given time. Though political satisfaction shows sharp fluctuations from one month to the next, the publics of some societies consistently manifest higher levels of satisfaction than the publics of others.

This syndrome is also linked with a society's economic level. The more developed societies tend

to rank relatively high on life satisfaction, trust, and the other components of the syndrome. Are both it and liberal democracy simply joint consequences of economic development or does political culture make an autonomous contribution to the viability of democratic institutions, as Almond and Verba have argued? Let me emphasize that we do not yet possess a data base that would enable us to answer such questions conclusively. We have established the presence of an enduring and cross-nationally distinctive syndrome of basic cultural attitudes and demonstrated that this syndrome is much stronger in those societies that have been stable democracies since 1920 than in those that have been nondemocratic or intermittently democratic. But we do not yet have sufficient data to sort out the causal linkages between political culture, economic development, and democracy in any conclusive fashion. To do so would require regular measures of the relevant cultural variables throughout the past century. At present, they are simply not available. Nevertheless, the patterns shown in Figures 2, 4, and 5 are so striking and their implications are so important that they virtually cry out for further explanation. . . .

## Cultural Change and Economic Development

. . . Max Weber argued at the turn of the century that the rise of capitalism and the subsequent rapid economic development of the West were made possible by a set of cultural changes related to the emergence of Calvinist Protestantism.[12] His Protestant ethic thesis gave rise to a controversy that endured for decades. Some of the criticisms seem well founded; and the thesis that economic achievement was linked with Protestantism may seem unconvincing today, when predominantly Catholic countries have higher economic growth rates than Protestant ones. Nevertheless, though I would not defend Weber's thesis in its entirety, I believe that important aspects of it were correct, provided his work is viewed as an analysis of a specific historical phenomenon (as was clearly Weber's intention) and not as asserting an immutable relationship between economic achievement and Protestantism. Particularly crucial is Weber's insight that culture is not simply an epiphenomenon determined by economics but an autonomous set of factors that sometimes shape economic events as well as being shaped by them. . . .

Weber argues that Calvinist Protestantism gradually evolved into a value system that viewed the accumulation of wealth for its own sake (and not as a means to survive or acquire luxuries) as a sign of divine grace and encouraged an ascetic self-control conducive to the accumulation of wealth. This led to an entrepreneurial spirit and an accumulation of capital that facilitated the Industrial Revolution in the eighteenth and nineteenth centuries, which in turn had immense consequences for global economic development in the twentieth century.

I suggest that the Protestant Reformation was only one case of a more general phenomenon: the breakdown of traditional cultural barriers to economic modernization. . . . One feature common to traditional value systems is that they emerge in, and are adapted to, economies characterized by very little technological change and economic growth. In this situation, social mobility is a zero-sum game, heavily laden with conflict and threatening to the social system. In a society undergoing rapid industrialization and expansion, by contrast, social mobility may be widespread. But in traditional agrarian societies, social status is hereditary, except when an individual or group forcibly seizes the lands and social status of another. To preserve social peace, virtually all traditional cultures discourage upward social mobility and the accumulation of wealth. These cultures perform an integrating function by providing a rationale that legitimates the established social order and inculcating norms of sharing, charity, and other obligations that help to mitigate the harshness of a subsistence economy.

By their very nature the traditional value systems of agrarian society are adapted to maintaining a stable balance in unchanging societies. Accordingly, they tend to discourage social change in general and the accumulative entrepreneurial spirit in particular. One of the important functions of the Protestant Reformation was to break the grip of the medieval Christian world view on a significant portion of Europe. It did not accomplish this alone. The emergence of scientific inquiry had already begun to undermine the anthropocentric cosmos of the medieval Christian tradition. But it is difficult to avoid the conclusion that Weber's emphasis on the role of Protestantism captures an important part of reality. For prior to the Protestant Reformation, southern Europe was economically more advanced than northern Europe. During the three centuries after the Reformation, capitalism emerged, mainly among the Protestant regions of Europe and among the Protestant minorities of Catholic countries. Protestant Europe manifested a subsequent economic dynamism that was extraordinary, moving it far ahead of Catholic Europe. Shifting trade patterns, declining food production in southern Europe, and other variables played a role in this shift, but the evidence suggests that cultural factors were also important.

As capitalism led to industrialization and eventually to historically unprecedented levels of prosperity, emulation became more and more attractive, and increasing amounts of cross-cultural diffusion took place. But to a truly remarkable degree, throughout the early stages the Protestant cultural zone was markedly more receptive to industrialization and economic development than any other part of the world. The Industrial Revolution began in England, spreading rapidly to predominantly Protestant Scotland and Wales but leaving Catholic Ireland largely untouched except for the Protestant region around Belfast. Industrialization spread from England to nearby France but lagged there in comparison with its rapid implantation in more distant but more receptive areas such as the United States and Germany, both of which soon became far more industrialized than France. At the start of the twentieth century, the correlation between Protestantism and economic development was still remarkably strong. In Europe, the economically most dynamic nations were Great Britain, Germany, Sweden, Denmark, Norway, the Netherlands, and Switzerland, all of which were predominantly Protestant at that time. The only non-Protestant countries that had attained even roughly comparable levels of economic development were Belgium and France, both of which were geographically near the original core area from which the Industrial Revolution spread and in both of which Protestant minorities played a disproportionately important role in the process of economic development. In the New World, the United States and Canada had also emerged as developed industrial societies, while virtually all of Latin America remained almost totally unaffected by the Industrial Revolution. Even within Canada, the predominantly Catholic region developed much less rapidly than the rest of the country. Economic development seemed wedded to Protestantism.

But culture is not a constant. It is a system through which a society adapts to its environment. Given a changing environment, in the long run culture is likely to change. One major change that took place was the secularization of Catholic (and other non-Protestant) cultures. In much of the world, the role of the merchant and the profit-making entrepreneur became less stigmatized. In some settings the entrepreneur even became the cultural hero, as the captain of industry had been in the United States of the late nineteenth century.

A contrasting process of cultural change began to take place in the more advanced industrial societies during the second half of the twentieth century. . . . Precisely in those regions that had earlier been most strongly influenced by the Protestant ethic, the long-term consequences of

economic development began to be felt, as generations emerged that had been raised in unprecedented prosperity and economic security and were characterized, increasingly, by the presence of postmaterialist values. . . .

This thesis implies that as a result of the historically unprecedented prosperity and the absence of war that has prevailed in Western countries since 1945, younger birth cohorts place less emphasis on economic and physical security than do older groups, who have experienced a much greater degree of economic insecurity. Conversely, the younger birth cohorts tend to give a higher priority to non-material needs, such as a sense of community and the quality of life. Cohort analysis carried out from 1970 through 1987 in six Western countries confirms the presence of substantial differences in the basic societal priorities of younger and older generations.[13] Moreover, it demonstrates that as intergenerational population replacement has occurred, there has been a gradual but pervasive shift in the values of these publics from predominantly materialist priorities toward postmaterialist goals. One consequence of this shift has been a diminishing emphasis on economic growth in these societies together with increasing emphasis on environmental protection and preserving the quality of life—if necessary, even at the expense of economic growth. Postmaterialists place markedly less emphasis on economic growth than do those with materialist or mixed values. And they emphasize a high salary and job security less than working with people they like or doing interesting work.[14] Conversely, postmaterialists place more emphasis on protecting the environment and are far more likely to be active members of environmental organizations than are materialists. Finally, postmaterialists are economic underachievers; that is, *controlling* for the fact that they come from more prosperous families and receive better education, postmaterialists earn significantly lower incomes than those with materialist values.[15] All this suggests that as societies become increasingly influenced by the

## Table 2: Economic Growth Rates in Protestant vs Catholic Countries and Japan, 1870-1984

| Rank | 1870–1913 | 1913–38 | 1949–65 | 1965–84 |
|---|---|---|---|---|
| 1 | USA (P) | Japan (B) | Japan (B) | Japan (B) |
| 2 | Canada (P) | Norway (P) | W. Germany (P) | Norway (P) |
| 3 | Denmark (P) | Netherlands (P) | Italy (C) | France (C) |
| 4 | Sweden (P) | USA (P) | France (C) | Belgium (C) |
| 5 | Germany (P) | Switzerland (P) | Switzerland (P) | Italy (C) |
| 6 | Belgium (C) | Denmark (P) | Netherlands (P) | W. Germany (P) |
| 7 | Switzerland (P) | Sweden (P) | Canada (P) | Canada (P) |
| 8 | Japan (B) | Italy (C) | Denmark (P) | Netherlands (P) |
| 9 | Norway (P) | Canada (P) | Norway (P) | Denmark (P) |
| 10 | Gt Britain (P) | Germany (P) | Sweden (P) | Sweden (P) |
| 11 | Netherlands (P) | Gt Britain (P) | USA (P) | USA (P) |
| 12 | France (C) | France (C) | Belgium (C) | Gt Britain (P) |
| 13 | Italy (C) | Belgium (C) | Gt Britain (P) | Switzerland (P) |
| Mean economic growth rate in Protestant countries[a] | 152 | 120 | 98 | 72 |

Sources: 1870–1965 standings calculated from data in Angus Maddison, *Economic Growth in Japan and the U.S.S.R.* (London: Allen & Unwin, 1969), 148–9; 1965–84 standings from data in *World Development Report, 1986* (Washington: World Bank, 1986).

Note: (P) = countries in which a majority of the population was Protestant in 1900; (C) = countries having a Roman Catholic majority in 1900; (B) = Buddhist majority in 1900.

[a] Percentage of rates in Catholic countries.

growing postmaterialist minority, they will tend to give economic growth a lower priority.

Among those countries for which we have long-term historical data, those that had relatively high growth rates a century ago tend to have relatively low growth rates today. Table 2 illustrates this phenomenon. [During the period] 1870–1913, nearly all Protestant countries had growth rates that were higher than those of almost all Catholic countries. My table actually understates the extent to which this was true, because the few Catholic countries from which we have historical data are precisely the ones that were *most* developed in the nineteenth century. Protestant countries still had more dynamic economies in the interwar years. But in the past few decades, this situation has reversed itself; during 1965–84, the Catholic countries in our sample had higher growth rates than most of the Protestant ones. Within the United States, as recently as 1958, Catholics and Protestants manifested different values concerning various aspects of economic and family life.[16] But these differences have been dwindling.[17]

In part, this reflects the fact that it is easier for a poor country to attain a high growth rate than for a rich one. By importing technology that has already been proven in more developed countries, one can catch up rapidly. But in global perspectives it is clear that this is only part of the story. For plenty of poor societies are *not* showing a rapid economic growth, while others (like those of East Asia) have been growing at an extraordinary pace. Clearly, some societies are more receptive to economic development than others. Conversely, some rich nations (like Japan) continue to develop relatively rapidly—even when they can no longer rely on imported technology but are increasingly developing their own—while others have become relatively stagnant.

High economic growth was once an almost uniquely Protestant phenomenon; today it has become global in scope and is *less* likely to be found in the Protestant societies than elsewhere. This does not mean that the civic culture that emerged in these societies will disappear. On the contrary, these countries are still becoming rich and, on the whole, life satisfaction, political satisfaction, and trust have been gradually rising in recent years. The syndrome that linked Protestantism with wealth and democracy has become less distinctively Protestant because it is permeating other regions of the world.

It is doing so unevenly, however, with its spread being shaped by the cultural traditions of given societies. The Confucian system was virtually unique among traditional cultures in that it institutionalized a socially accepted and even honoured channel for upward social mobility, based on nonviolent individual achievement rather than ascription. By passing a series of difficult academic examinations that were open to any promising young male, one could attain power, status, and wealth as a government official. Consequently, in the sixteenth century a social scientist from Mars might have ranked East Asia, with its Confucian

tradition, as the region of the world that was culturally most conducive to economic development. Though narrowly circumscribed, social mobility through individual achievement was accepted to a degree virtually unknown elsewhere. Education, rather than armed force, was the principal means to rise in society. And a secular orientation was relatively conducive to technology and worldly achievement.

I suspect that the Confucian cultural tradition, its traditional rigidity having been shattered by the impact of the West, is an important element underlying the current economic dynamism of certain portions of Asia. During the period from 1965 to 1984, five of the 10 fastest-growing nations in the world were countries shaped by the Confucian and Buddhist traditions: Singapore, South Korea, Hong Kong, Taiwan, and Japan. China ranked thirteenth. Moreover, three more of the top 20 countries had significant Chinese minorities that in each case played disproportionately important economic roles: Malaysia, Thailand, and Indonesia. Finally, immigrants of East Asian origin have shown disproportionately high rates of economic achievement throughout Southeast Asia and in the United States, Canada, and Western Europe. It is difficult to avoid the conclusion that the Confucian cultural tradition is conducive to economic achievement today. It would be unrealistic to view these traits as indelible, however. My broader thesis suggests that the intense emphasis on economic achievement now found among peoples shaped by the Confucian tradition could emerge only when the static orientation of traditional society was broken and is likely to gradually erode when future generations have been raised in high levels of economic security. For the present, however, it may be a key factor in the world economy.

## Conclusion

Both social analysis and social policy would be much simpler if people from different societies were interchangeable robots. But a large body of evidence indicates that they are not. The peoples of given societies tend to be characterized by reasonably durable cultural attributes that sometimes have major political and economic consequences. If this is true, then effective social policy will be better served by learning about these differences and about how they vary cross-culturally and over time than by pretending that they don't exist.

Rational choice models constitute one of the most promising tools now available for political analysis. As currently applied, they are effective in analysing short-term fluctuations within a given system, taking cultural and institutional factors as constant. But these factors are not constant, either cross-nationally or over time. And current models cannot deal with long-term changes in the basic goals and nature of a system. One of the central debates in the field of political economy seems to reflect this fact. When it was found that political support responded to fluctuations in the economy, it was taken for granted that this reflected the workings of economic self-interest among the electorate. Subsequent research has made this interpretation increasingly doubtful. The linkage between economics and politics seems largely shaped by sociotropic concerns. The classic model of economically determined behaviour has a strong grip on the minds of social analysts, probably because, throughout most of the history of industrial society, it provided a fairly accurate description of human behaviour. In recent decades, the rising role of postmaterialist concerns may have helped make sociotropic concerns increasingly important, particularly among the politically more aware segments of the electorate.

Political economy research has demonstrated convincingly that short-term economic changes have significant political consequences. But the long-term consequences of economic change have barely begun to be analysed in comparable fashion, though they may be at least equally significant. Evidence presented here indicates that the emergence and viability of mass-based democracy is closely related to economic development and that the outcome is contingent on specific cultural changes. Though mass democracy is almost impossible without a certain amount of economic development, economic development by itself does not produce democracy. Unless specific changes occur in culture and social structure, the result may not be democracy but a variety of alternatives ranging from the Libyan to the Soviet. A large body of cross-national survey evidence indicates that enduring cultural differences exist. Though these differences may be related to the economic level of a given nation, they are relatively independent of short-term economic changes. These cultural factors have an important bearing on the durability of democracy, which seems to result from a complex interplay of economic, cultural, and institutional factors. To neglect any of these components may compromise its survival.

Finally it appears that economic development itself is influenced by cultural variables. In my brief analysis of this, I have utilized one indicator of materialist and postmaterialist values that is available from only the past two decades and another indicator—the dominant religious or philosophic tradition of a given society—that is a greatly oversimplified indicator of prevailing world-views at a given time and place but goes back over centuries. Clearly, this analysis cannot be regarded as conclusive. But the available evidence tends to confirm Weber's insight that culture is not just a consequence of economics but can shape the basic nature of economic and political life.

# Notes

1. Arend Lijphart, 'Religious vs. Linguistic vs. Class Voting: The Crucial Experiment of Comparing Belgium, Canada, South Africa, and Switzerland', *American Political Science Review* 73 (1979): 442–61.

2. Gabriel Almond and Sidney Verba, *The Civic Culture* (Princeton, NJ: Princeton University Press, 1963).

3. Edward Banfield, *The Moral Basis of a Backward Society* (Chicago: Free Press, 1958).

4. These findings, incidentally, bear on a question that was recently considered grounds for denying Samuel Huntington membership in the National Academy of Sciences. His opponents charged that it was absurd to argue that relatively high or low levels of satisfaction can be attributed to given nations; but in a very significant sense, it appears that they *can*.

5. Hadley Cantril, *The Pattern of Human Concerns* (New Brunswick, NJ: Rutgers University Press, 1965).

6. Richard A. Easterlin, 'Does Economic Growth Improve the Human Lot? Some Empirical Evidence', in Paul A. David and Melvin W. Reder, eds, *Nations and Households in Economic Growth* (New York: Academic Press, 1974).

7. George Gallup, 'Human Needs and Satisfaction: A Global Survey', *Public Opinion Quarterly* 41 (1976): 459–67.

8. Banfield, *Moral Basis of a Backward Society*.

9. Robert D. Putnam, Robert Leonardi, Raffaella Y. Nanetti, and Franco Pavoncello, 'Explaining Institutional Success: The Case of Italian Regional Government', *American Political Science Review* 77 (1983): 55–74.

10. Ibid., 69–70.

11. Frank Andrews and Stephen Withey, *Social Indicators of Well-Being in America* (New York: Plenum, 1976).

12. Max Weber, *The Protestant Ethic and the Spirit of Capitalism* (New York: Scribners, 1958).

13. Ronald Inglehart, *Culture Shift in Advanced Industrial Society* (Princeton, NJ: Princeton University Press, 1989).

14. Ronald Inglehart, 'Aggregate Stability and Individual-Level Change in Mass Belief Systems: The Level of Analysis Paradox', *American Political Science Review* 79 (1985): 97–117.

15. Inglehart, *Culture Shift*.

16. Gerhard Lenski, *The Religious Factor* (New York: Anchor-Doubleday, 1963).

17. Duane Alwin, 'Religion and Parental Childrearing Orientations: Evidence of a Catholic-Protestant Convergence', *American Journal of Sociology* (1986): 412–40.

# Part IX

# Comparative Politics in the Developing World

## Introduction

James Busumtwi-Sam

The phrase 'comparative politics of the developing world' implies there is something about politics in the 'developing world' that differentiates it from politics in the 'developed world'. However, what makes politics in certain regions of the world distinctive is not so much that the people are different, but the different conditions or circumstances in which people live. The task of understanding these circumstances has informed the subject-matter of the comparative study of politics in Africa, the Middle East, Central and South America and the Caribbean, all of Asia excluding Japan, and the Pacific islands excluding Australia and New Zealand. In all, there are over 120 countries represented here. It is not surprising, therefore, that there have been a number of debates and controversies in the comparative study of politics in these countries and regions.

### Problems of Diversity and Classification

One debate has centred on how best to describe and classify this group of countries. Various terms have been used, including 'the Third World', 'developing nations', 'less developed countries', 'underdeveloped countries', and 'the South'. The main issue of debate here is not simply about terminology, but about whether the terms and concepts are analytically useful. To be able to explain and understand a political phenomenon or event, political scientists must first be able to define and describe in a simplified way the key properties and characteristics of that phenomenon.

Some argue that the concept 'Third World' is no longer a valid descriptive or analytical category in the study of comparative politics.[1] The Third World originally described one of the 'three worlds' that existed during the Cold War—the First World of Western industrialized states; the Second World comprising the Soviet Union and its allies in eastern Europe; and the Third World that included all other countries not aligned with either of the first two groups. Now that the Cold War is over, the argument goes, the classification is no longer applicable. Ideology is less relevant in the contemporary system.

A second reason advanced for the inadequacy of the term 'Third World' is increased diversity. The Third World includes countries like Singapore and South Korea—two of the so-called Newly Industrializing Countries (NICs)—which are among the fastest-growing economies in the world and among the world's leading exporters of manufactured products. By some economic indicators, these countries are similar to, or outperform, many developed states.[2] Also, the Third World includes countries like the United Arab Emirates, which had a per capita national income of US$15,770 in 1988 (compared with Canada at US$16,960 in 1988), and Mozambique, which had a per capita national income of only $100 in 1988.[3]

Some of the other terms, such as 'underdeveloped', 'less developed', and 'developing', are also open to criticism because they do not describe what properties these countries actually possess but rather what they do not possess in comparison to another group of countries. In political science, a central concept such as the 'state', for example, is defined by the properties it actually possesses (i.e., a fixed territory, population, government, and sovereignty) rather than by the properties it does not possess. While the term 'developing countries' minimizes the negative connotations, it still entails a somewhat negative comparison (i.e., they are becoming more like the developed countries, but are still behind these countries).

Given these problems, perhaps the most appropriate concept for describing and classifying this group of countries is 'the South'. The South is mainly a geographic classification that avoids the negative connotations and ideological problems associated with the other concepts and terms. Most of the countries that comprise the 'developing world' are either in the Southern hemisphere or are located south of developed nations, while most of the developed nations are located in the Northern hemisphere. The notable exceptions are Australia and New Zealand, which are developed nations in the Southern hemisphere.

## Common Features of the South

Despite their increased diversity, some analysts point to features shared by countries in the South as a whole that have provided them with a collective identity in the world.[4] One is a shared colonial experience. Colonialism is the ownership and administration of one territory and people by another as if the former were part of the latter. By far the greater part of what is currently the South has historically been subjected to formal colonial rule by European states. Even non-Western societies that retained their independence (e.g., Japan) were forced to come to terms with a world in which European technology and influence were dominant, and had to adapt their own domestic political structures to meet the European prerequisites of statehood.

European colonial expansion began in the mid-fifteenth century and reached its peak in the late nineteenth and early twentieth centuries. During the first phase of colonial expansion, the emphasis was on trade in commodities (gold and textiles) with the New World (the Americas), the Far East, and Africa. This period also saw the development of the slave trade to meet the demands for cheap labour in New World colonies. The second phase of European colonial expansion, which followed the Industrial Revolution in Europe, was characterized by the imposition of formal colonial rule and intense competition among European powers for possession of colonies. The acquisition of territory and raw materials was a key component of this competition.

Thus, almost all present-day countries in the South are the product of a process that began in the mid-fifteenth century in Europe through which scattered peoples throughout the world were brought together into a single society of sovereign states and a single global economy. This colonial experience has left an important legacy— a perception of being objects rather than subjects—that has given countries in the South a degree of cohesion.

While countries like Canada, the United States, Australia, and New Zealand were also once colonies, their experience of colonialism differed in at least two important ways from the majority of countries in Africa, Asia, and Latin America. Firstly, the former were designated colonies of European settlement because, among other things, they had more temperate climates similar to that in Europe. Colonies in the more tropical areas of Africa, Asia, and Latin America were deemed unsuitable for European settlement and were mainly designated for the production of cash crops—sugar, cotton, tobacco, and coffee—for the European market. Secondly, unlike the majority of colonies, in colonies designated for European settlement indigenous populations (such as First Nations peoples in Canada and the US and Aboriginals in Australia) were displaced; and when political independence was achieved, the post-colonial state was controlled largely by peoples of European descent.

Another reason why it is still useful to talk of the South is that despite the successes of countries like Singapore and South Korea, the South as a whole, including the NICs, has a relatively low share of the global economy (trade, finance, investment, and consumption) as compared to the developed countries (the North). For example, the South has 78 per cent of the world's population but accounts for only 17 per cent of global product (1992); the North has 28 per cent of the world's population but accounts for 83 per cent of global product (1992). This gap is also evident in social indicators of development. The average life expectancy in the entire South, for example, is 61 years, while for developed countries it is 76 years. A person living in a typical low-income country in the South consumes only 58 per cent of the required protein nourishment; earns only 8 per cent of what would be earned for a comparable job in Canada; is nine times more likely to be illiterate; and has a life expectancy of only 54 years (76 years for Canada). Children in low-income countries of the South are 7.9 times more likely to die before their fifth birthday.[5] Thus, despite the enormous diversity within this group of countries, which makes generalizing difficult, the harsh reality of poverty is clearly evident for many in the South. According to the World Bank's definition of poverty (an income of less than US$370 a year), over 20 per cent of the world's population—more than one billion people—were living in poverty in 1990.[6]

## Contemporary Issues and Debates

Since 1945, countries in the South have attempted to carve out an identity that reflects their unique historical and contemporary circumstances and differentiates them from countries in the North. Prior to the 1960s, development—political, economic, and social—was not a significant issue on the international agenda. Through the United

Nations system, however, countries in the South were successful in bringing the issue of development on to the international agenda. The most ambitious strategy in this regard was the cluster of reforms known as the New International Economic Order (NIEO) launched in 1974.[7] The NIEO contained three sets of reforms designed to redistribute political power and wealth from the rich countries of the North to the South.

The first were the 'self-reliance' reforms designed to increase the control of countries in the South over their natural resources (e.g., control over multinational corporations). The second set consisted of 'resource-transfer' reforms designed to achieve greater and more regular flows of financial resources from developed countries of the North to the South (e.g., an increase in grants and concessional foreign aid). The third set of reforms emphasized 'international influence'. These reforms were designed to increase the participation of countries in the South in the central institutions that regulated international economic and political interactions, such as the International Monetary Fund (IMF) and the World Bank.

By the beginning of the 1980s, however, the negotiations for the NIEO were overtaken by a series of international crises that effectively removed the NIEO from the international agenda. These crises included the international recession of the early 1980s precipitated by the second round of oil price increases in 1979 and the debt crisis that emerged in 1982. These crises not only undermined the unity of the South vis-à-vis the North and seriously eroded its bargaining position, they were also major catalysts for political changes in much of the South.

By the early 1990s, two significant transformations were occurring in the South. The first was the retreat of the state; the second, closely related to the first, was the transformation of economic policy. With respect to the retreat of the state, the late 1980s and early 1990s witnessed a weakening of authoritarian governments and movement towards democratization in many countries, especially in Latin America but also in Asia and Africa. Thus, democracy and democratization have become important topics in the comparative study of politics in the South.[8] The issue of democratization—the process through which countries move from authoritarian forms of government towards more open, responsive, and accountable forms of government—has generated considerable interest and debate among analysts.

One aspect of this debate has centred on identifying the conditions that allow for 'democratic transitions' and for the consolidation of democratic systems of government.[9] Another aspect has focused on the apparent relationship between democratization, on one hand, and economic development, peace and security, and the advancement of human rights, on the other. The precise nature of this relationship has generated considerable interest among scholars.

For example, is democracy a precondition for economic growth, or is it the other way around? The empirical record presents a mixed picture. While some developing countries with authoritarian-type governments achieved impressive rates of economic growth (the Asian NICs in particular and China more recently), these have been the exception, not the rule. Authoritarianism in most Latin American and African countries turned out to be disastrous economically. With respect to democratic government, the historical record is also mixed. While some democratic nations, such as

Botswana, have been able to manage impressive rates of economic growth, others, such as Bolivia, have not.

Beyond changes in forms of government, at a more fundamental level, the late 1980s and early 1990s witnessed an adjustment in the relationship among state, society, and the economy involving a weakening of the central state machinery and its retreat from society and the economy to varying degrees. In many countries in the South, stronger 'civil societies', determined to carve out more autonomous spheres of political, social, and economic interaction, emerged. Thus, another important topic in the comparative study of the South related to the issue of democratization is the role of civil society (i.e., the non-governmental and non-profit sectors of society, including voluntary associations and other types of formal and informal groupings) in development.[10] Other issues that have become prominent include the gendered division of political, economic, and social activity and, specifically, the role of women in development.[11]

The second major transformation in the South in the late 1980s and early 1990s was the change in economic policy. The most influential model of economic development in much of the South during the 1960s and 1970s emphasized economic nationalism, state intervention, and import-substitution industrialization. During the 1980s, however, there was a dramatic shift in economic policy involving a reduction in the forms and extent of state intervention, the liberalization of trade, and a greater reliance on market forces in the allocation and distribution of resources.[12] Thus, the impact of specific types of economic policies on development has become an important issue of analysis.

The debate here has generally followed two related tracks. The first focuses on the types of policy prescriptions advocated by international agencies such as the IMF and the World Bank as the solution to the development problems faced by countries in the South in the wake of the debt crisis. These policy prescriptions are generally known as 'stabilization' and 'structural adjustment'.[13] The second track focuses on a phenomenon that became more apparent in the wake of the debt crisis: why had the Asian NICs—a relatively small group of countries—performed better economically than the majority of countries in Africa, Latin America, and other parts of Asia? This has led to vigorous debates about the role of the state and the market in economic development, and to debates about whether the success of the NICs could be replicated in other countries.[14]

The problem of violent conflict in the South is also receiving increased attention in comparative politics. Almost all wars since 1945, with the exception of the break-up of Yugoslavia and the USSR in 1991 and 1992, have been in the South. Between 1990 and 1995, there were, on average, 30 ongoing civil wars per annum and most of these were in the South, especially in Africa, Central and South America, and South Asia. What explains this relatively high incidence of political violence and warfare? It is certainly no accident that developing countries experiencing high degrees of violent civil conflict are also those countries whose political, economic, and social institutions are decaying. However, there is considerable disagreement among analysts on how to explain what causes these conflicts.

Some studies, for example, have attempted to show a relationship between socio-economic inequality and resource scarcity, on one hand, and violent conflict, on the other.[15] Others have focused on the ethnic composition of countries in the South and have sought to explain political violence by referring to competition for power among rival ethnic groups. Yet other studies have linked the incidence of violence and warfare to the presence/absence of democratic government.[16]

Another area generating considerable interest and debate is the relationship between the natural environment and development, and population growth and development. This has led to a focus on the concept of 'sustainable development', which meets the needs of the present without compromising the ability to meet future needs.[17] This issue has become particularly important because it is argued that if countries in the South are to develop along the lines of the present-day developed states, there would be severe negative consequences for the natural environment in terms of resource-depletion, deforestation, destruction of ecosystems, atmospheric pollution, and so on. Who should bear the brunt of the costs for protecting the environment—countries in the North or South? What strategies are most effective? Will an emphasis on protecting the environment compromise the ability of southern countries to develop? These are some of the questions currently the focus of debate.[18]

## Theoretical Debates

The study of development is, by definition, a study of change. This fact produced an important debate that centred on the kinds of theories required to understand and explain the present condition of southern countries and, possibly, to predict the future direction of change. What does development entail? What explains why some countries are more developed than others? The answers to these questions have depended on the type of theoretical framework or *paradigm* employed.

The two major paradigms that have dominated the comparative study of politics in the South are the *developmentalist* and the *underdevelopment* paradigms.[19] These two paradigms differ with respect to their views of development, their diagnoses of the problems faced by developing countries, and their prescriptions for change.

The developmentalist paradigm first emerged in the 1950s and 1960s, and included parallel but complementary works in political science and economics.[20] In political science, the most prominent theories were known as *modernization theories* because they saw development as a process of progressive transformation involving national integration and 'nation-building', in which societies evolved from 'traditional' through a series of stages to 'modern' along the lines of the developed Western countries.[21] The model used was the high mass-consumption society typical of Western developed states, which had 'rational' state structures and bureaucracies that governed effectively and efficiently, and political institutions and processes that commanded the loyalty of citizens by allowing them to pursue their material interests. Modernization theories contended that countries in the South could only truly develop if they became more like the developed Western (and northern) countries.

Modernization theories saw underdevelopment as a historical stage or condition through which all states had to pass. The obstacles to development thus lay within the countries of the South—the nature and operation of their political institutions and processes and their economic and social systems prevented the efficient allocation and distribution of resources. These political institutions were still steeped in ancient traditions and cultures and had not yet acquired the rational institutions and processes found in Western developed states. In this regard, modernization theories drew on the work of Max Weber on bureaucracy and public administration, suggesting that southern countries had not yet achieved Weber's third 'ideal type' of authority (the rational-legal authority) found in Western developed countries.[22]

In their prescriptions for change, modernization theories placed emphasis on the development of political institutions and processes that would allow rational public administration and permit economic growth through the operation of a competitive market economy. Another key instrument of change was the diffusion of technology, skills, capital, and other values from richer developed states of the North to the South, through trade and other international transactions.

This developmentalist paradigm had its share of criticisms. Firstly, its modernization theories were accused of being ethnocentric because development required a country to follow the trajectory followed in the eighteenth and nineteenth centuries by Western societies. Development was presented as synonymous with westernization. The view of history in modernization theories was criticized for being unilinear, that is, they assumed there was only one path to development—that followed by present-day developed states.[23] Modernization theories also came under criticism for blaming the poor for their poverty. Their diagnoses of the problems and their prescriptions for change implied that the poor were poor because they were inefficient, or perhaps even irrational. Modernization theories were also criticized for ignoring the international aspects of the problems of development such as the declining commodity prices for exports from the South.

In response to these criticisms, attempts were made to modify modernization theories by rejecting the unilinear view of history and acknowledging the special political and historical circumstances of developing countries.[24] The most serious challenge to the modernization theories, however, came from critics operating in a different paradigm altogether—the underdevelopment paradigm. The concept of underdevelopment emerged in the 1960s and 1970s, and included complementary theoretical developments in political science, economics, and sociology. Within the discipline of political science, there was some degree of overlap between analysts working in the field of comparative politics and those in the field of international relations.[25] In comparative politics, the most prominent theories were those on *neocolonialism*, developed to explain conditions in Africa and Asia, and on *dependency*, developed to explain conditions in Latin America.[26]

The main difference here was historical. African and Asian countries emerged from colonialism and became independent states after 1945, whereas most Latin American countries achieved political independence in the mid- to late nineteenth century. Thus, for the former, the experience of colonialism was more immediate—

hence the term 'neocolonialism'. For Latin America countries, however, dependency theory focused on explaining why they had not developed despite their longer experience as independent states. Despite these differences, theories on dependency and neocolonialism shared similar assumptions, concepts, and methodologies, and over time both sets of theories came to be known generically as dependency theories.

Dependency theories analysed the consequences of international economic specialization on the political, economic, and social development of countries or regions in the South.[27] All theories of dependency recognize a causal relationship between the historical expansion of Western European political and economic influence, beginning with the Industrial Revolution and the expansion of European colonial empires in the nineteenth and early twentieth centuries, and the progressive impoverishment of countries in Africa, Asia, and Latin America.

Modernization theories saw the condition of present-day countries in the South as a 'natural' stage or condition on a process towards development. For theorists of dependency, there was nothing natural about this condition. Countries in the South were not really developing. Instead, their development was distorted or stunted, and thus they were better described as 'underdeveloped'. This condition of underdevelopment was a specific historical creation, a product of unequal political and economic relations between the industrialized North (known as the 'core') and countries in the South (the 'periphery'). As one prominent dependency theorist put it, 'underdevelopment was developed.'[28]

The central concern for dependency theories in their diagnoses of the problems of underdevelopment and prescriptions for change was an analysis of how power was used to allocate and distribute resources in society, especially economic resources. Two broad positions emerged, the Marxist and the structuralist.[29] Marxists focused on the internal class structure within countries on the periphery, while structuralists focused on the international linkages between core and periphery. For the structuralists, the unequal relationships between core and periphery in the contemporary period were described in terms of an 'international division of labour' created by Western states. Within this division of labour, states on the periphery lacked policy-making autonomy because they depended on the core in trade matters and for access to capital and technology. Core states set the development goals for the periphery by virtue of their control over capital, markets, and technology. In effect, in the view of dependency theorists, the poor are poor not because they are inefficient but because of their exploitation by the rich and powerful.

In their prescriptions for change, the differences between the Marxists and structuralists within the underdevelopment paradigm became more pronounced. Marxists tended to share modernization theories' belief that poorer countries could or should develop along the path that developed countries had followed. The Marxists, however, placed emphasis on class conflict as the key mechanism of change. The structuralists, who emphasized the international linkages between core and periphery, argued that development along the lines of the Western countries would never occur as long as relations of dependency were maintained. The prescription thus called for an end to dependency relationships.

Theories of dependency have been criticized for being far better at explaining why countries have not developed than for explaining how specific countries actually did develop.[30] Unlike modernization theories, dependency had no theory of how development occurred, and thus, no vision of the future. If dependency made development impossible, how could the successes of the NICs be explained? In response to these criticisms a 'soft' variant of dependency emerged to account for the apparent successes of the NICs. It argued that 'dependent capitalist development'—a form of development that did not fundamentally alter the unequal relationship—was possible but only when it served the interests of the developed core states.[31] Other analysts in the dependency tradition developed theories of the state suggesting that a strong authoritarian state was required for development.[32]

Dependency theory has had a wide-ranging impact and was embraced by policy-makers in many countries in the South. Here was a major social science paradigm developed largely by scholars from the South. For many in the South, the notion that they had been 'underdeveloped' was appealing because it reflected their sense of (colonial) history and destiny. Indeed, it is more than a little coincidental that the most ambitious strategy by southern countries to transform the international economic order—the NIEO—was launched in the early 1970s when dependency theory was on the ascendancy. Many of the reforms proposed in the NIEO were generally in line with the prescriptions of dependency theories.

By the end of the 1980s there was widespread dissatisfaction with the 'grand theorizing' of both the developmentalist and underdevelopment paradigms. The main criticism was that each sought to reduce the complex realities of the historical and contemporary political, social, and economic conditions of countries in the South to the terms of models or 'ideal types' that distorted a fuller understanding of the actual processes of change in those countries. Critics argued that paradigms produced 'intellectual strictures' that hampered understanding of actual processes of development.[33] Thus, in the 1990s there has been movement away from grand theories applicable to whole groups of countries towards research that focuses on specific countries and specific issues.

Despite the demise of the grand theorizing characteristic of earlier works in the developmentalist and underdevelopment paradigms, modernization and dependency theories continue to exert influence in the comparative study of politics in the South. Indeed, many of the contemporary issues and debates outlined above—studies on democratization and the role of civil society, debates over economic policies and strategies, studies on violent civil conflict, gender, and development, and discussions on sustainable development—employ assumptions, concepts, and other insights grounded in these paradigms.

## Conclusion

The comparative study of politics in the South is a vibrant field with lively debates that address the serious challenges faced by these countries in their quest for development. The field encompasses a wide range of issues and draws on interdisciplinary insights from other subfields in political science, such as international relations and public administration, as well as from other disciplines, including economics and sociology. Given that the study of development is a study of political and social change, the field will continue to be dynamic in order to help us better understand, and possibly anticipate, patterns of change in the South into the twenty-first century.

The first selection was published by the South Commission in 1990. This international commission included scholars and policy-makers from different countries in the South. It analysed the development experience of southern countries and elaborated a vision for the future.[34] The commission's report reflects the concern with specific issues and the rejection of the grand theorizing of the modernization and dependency paradigms. The sections of the report reproduced here show the current emphasis on specific development strategies and economic policies, as well as the current concern for issues such as population and development, gender and development, and the environment and development.

The second article here, by Paul Kennedy, highlights the differences as well as similarities among countries in the South, compares the experiences of different groups of countries, and assesses their prospects for future development in the twenty-first century. Kennedy's analysis draws on insights from both the modernization and dependency perspectives, but to the extent that he emphasizes diversity, he rejects the notion of a general theory applicable to all countries in the South.

## Notes

1. See, for example, Richard E. Bissell, 'Who Killed the Third World?', *Washington Quarterly* 13, 4 (Autumn 1990): 23–32.
2. For example, if we compare the ratio of domestic savings to gross domestic product, Korea at 38 per cent and Singapore at 41 per cent outperform the US, where the ratio was 13 per cent in 1988. Figures from World Bank, *World Development Report, 1990: Poverty* (Washington: World Bank, 1990), Table 9.
3. Ibid., Table 1.
4. See Christopher Clapham, *Third World Politics* (London: Croom Helm, 1985).
5. Figures from John T. Rourke, *International Politics on the World Stage*, 4th edn (Guilford, Conn.: Dushkin Publishing, 1993), 482.
6. World Bank, *World Development Report, 1990*, 1–29.
7. For more on the NIEO, see Jagdish Baghwati and John Ruggie, *Power, Passions and Purpose: Prospects for the North-South Negotiations* (Cambridge: Cambridge University Press, 1984).
8. Larry Diamond et al., eds, *Democracy in Developing Countries* (Boulder, Colo.: Lynne Rienner, 1988); Guillermo O'Donnell and P. Schmitter, *Transitions from Authoritarian Rule: Tentative Conclusions about Uncertain Democracies* (Baltimore: Johns Hopkins University Press, 1986).
9. For an evaluation of studies of democratization, see Doh Chull Shin, 'On the Third Wave of Democratization: A Synthesis of Recent Theory and Research', *World Politics* 47 (Oct. 1994): 135–70.

10. See Alan Fowler, 'The Role of NGOs in Changing State-Society Relations', *Development Policy Review* 9 (1991): 53–84; Michael Bratton, 'Beyond the State: Civil Society and Associational Life in Africa', *World Politics* 11, 3 (1989): 407–30.

11. See, for example, Gita Sen, *Development Crises and Alternative Visions: Third World Women's Perspectives* (New York: Monthly Review Press, 1987); Sue Ellen, Jan Everett, and Kathleen Staudt, eds, *Women, the State and Development* (Albany: State University of New York Press, 1989); Tina Wallace, ed., *Changing Perceptions: Writings on Gender and Development* (Oxford: Oxfam, 1991).

12. See Thomas Biersteker, 'The Triumph of Neoclassical Economics in the Developing World', in James Rosenau and E.O. Czempiel, eds, *Governance without Government* (Cambridge: Cambridge University Press, 1992).

13. See, for example, Valariana Kallab and Richard Fienberg, eds, *Adjustment Crisis in the Third World* (London: Transaction Books, 1984); Joan Nelson, ed., *Economic Crisis and Policy Choice: The Politics of Adjustment in the Third World* (Princeton, NJ: Princeton University Press, 1990).

14. A useful overview of the debate about the success of the NICs is found in Bela Belassa, 'The Lessons of East Asian Development', *Economic Development and Cultural Change* 36, 3 (1988): 273–90; Zeya Onis, 'The Logic of the Development State', *Comparative Politics* (Oct. 1991): 109–26; Frederick Deyo, ed., *The Political Economy of the New Asian Industrialism* (Ithaca, NY: Cornell University Press, 1987).

15. Ted R. Gurr and Mark I. Lichbach, 'Forecasting Internal Conflict: A Comparative Evaluation of Empirical Theories', *Comparative Political Studies* 19 (Apr. 1986): 3–38; Ted R. Gurr, 'On the Political Consequences of Scarcity and Economic Decline', *International Studies Quarterly* 29 (1985): 51–75; Russell Harding, *One For All: The Logic of Group Conflict* (Princeton, NJ: Princeton University Press, 1995).

16. See Crawford Young, ed., *The Rising Tide of Cultural Pluralism: The Nation State at Bay* (Madison: University of Wisconsin Press, 1993); Benedict Anderson, *Imagined Communities: Reflections on the Origins and Spread of Nationalism* (London: Verso, 1983); Paul Brass, ed., *Ethnic Groups and the State* (London: Croom Helm, 1985); Michael Brown, ed., *Ethnic Conflict and International Security* (Princeton, NJ: Princeton University Press, 1993); Ted Gurr, 'Peoples Against States: Ethno-political Conflict and the Changing World System', *International Studies Quarterly* 38 (1994): 347–77.

17. World Commission on the Environment and Development, *Our Common Future* (Oxford: Oxford University Press, 1987).

18. See Alvaro Soto, 'The Natural Environment: A Southern Perspective', *International Journal* 47 (Autumn 1992); Gupta Avijit, *Ecology and Development in the Third World* (London: Routledge, 1987).

19. Charles K. Wilbur and Kenneth P. Jameson, 'Paradigms of Economic Development and Beyond', in Wilbur, ed., *The Political Economy of Development and Underdevelopment*, 4th edn (New York: Random House, 1988), 3–27; Tony Smith, 'Requiem or New Agenda for Third World Studies?', *World Politics* 38, 4 (July 1985): 532–61.

20. In economics, works on economic development within this paradigm were known as diffusionist theories.

21. Among the notable works on modernization in the developmentalist paradigm are: Walt W. Rostow, *The Stages of Growth: A Non-Communist Manifesto* (New York: Cambridge University Press, 1960); Clifford Geertz, *Old Societies, New States: The Quest for Modernity in Asia and Africa* (New York: Free Press, 1963); Gabriel A. Almond and James S. Coleman, *The Politics of Developing Areas* (Princeton, NJ: Princeton University Press, 1960); Edward

Shills, *Political Development in the New States* (The Hague, 1966); David Apter, *The Politics of Modernization* (Chicago: University of Chicago Press, 1965); A.F.K. Organski, *Stages of Political Development* (New York: Knopf, 1965). For a more recent discussion of modernization theory, see Samuel P. Huntington and Myron Weiner, eds, *Understanding Political Development* (Boston: Little, Brown, 1987).

22. For more on Max Weber's ideal types of authority, see the Introduction to Part V in this volume.

23. Smith, 'Requiem or New Agenda for Third World Studies?'

24. See, for example, Samuel P. Huntington, *Political Order in Changing Societies* (New Haven: Yale University Press, 1968).

25. In the field of international relations, the most prominent were the theories of imperialism and the 'world system'. See Immanuel Wallerstein, 'The Rise and Future Demise of the World Capitalist System: Concepts for Comparative Analysis', *Comparative Studies in History and Society* 16 (1974).

26. Prominent works in dependency and neocolonialism include A.G. Frank, *Capitalism and Underdevelopment in Latin America* (New York: Monthly Review Press, 1966); Kwame Nkrumah, *Neocolonialism: The Last Stage of Imperialism* (London: Heineman, 1968); Walter Rodney, *How Europe Underdeveloped Africa* (London and Dar-es-Salaam: Bogle L'overture and Tanzania Publishing House, 1972); Samir Amin, *Accumulation on a World Scale* (New York: Monthly Review Press, 1975); Ronald H. Chilcote, *Theories of Development and Underdevelopment* (Boulder, Colo.: Westview Press, 1984); Clive Thomas, *Dependence and Transformation* (New York: Monthly Review Press, 1976); F. Cardoso and E. Falletto, *Dependency and Development in Latin America* (Berkeley: University of California Press, 1979).

27. In this respect, theories of dependency and neocolonialism can be seen as a subset of the 'world system' theories, which examined the origins and causes of this international specialization. See Anthony Brewer, *Marxist Theories of Imperialism* (London: Routledge & Kegan Paul, 1980). Also see Smith, 'Requiem or New Agenda for Third World Studies?'

28. André Gunder Frank, *Capitalism and Underdevelopment in Latin America* (New York: Monthly Review Press, 1967).

29. See Ronald H. Chilcote, *Dependency and Marxism: Towards a Resolution of the Debate* (Boulder, Colo: Westview Press, 1981); Wilbur and Jameson, 'Paradigms of Economic Development'.

30. Smith, 'Requiem or New Agenda for Third World Studies?'

31. See, for example, F. Cardoso, 'Dependent Capitalist Development in Latin America', *New Left Review* 74 (1972); Peter Evans, *Dependent Development: The Alliance of Multinational, State and Local Capital in Brazil* (Princeton, NJ: Princeton University Press, 1979).

32. See, for example, David Collier, ed., *The New Authoritarianism in Latin America* (Princeton, NJ: Princeton University Press, 1979); P. Evans, D. Reuschemeyer, and T. Skocpol, *Bringing the State Back In* (Cambridge: Cambridge University Press, 1985); Joel S. Migdal, 'Strong States, Weak States, Power and Accommodation', in Myron Weiner and S.P. Huntington, eds, *Understanding Political Development* (Boston: Little, Brown, 1987), 391–436.

33. Albert Hirschman, 'The Search for Paradigms as a Hindrance to Understanding', *World Politics* 22 (1970).

34. The South Commission, *Challenge to the South* (New York: Oxford University Press, 1990), 295.

## Study Questions for the Readings

1. The Report of the South Commission outlines some of the most pressing challenges faced by countries in the South in their quest for development. What are these challenges? What strategies would be most effective in meeting these challenges?

2. Countries in the South have argued there is an obligation on the part of rich industrialized countries of the North to promote development in poorer countries. Do you agree? If yes, what are the nature and the scope of this obligation?

3. Who should bear the brunt of the costs for protecting the environment—rich countries of the North or poorer countries in the South? Which strategies are most effective? Will an emphasis on protecting the environment compromise the ability of the South to develop?

4. Paul Kennedy identifies several factors—political, demographic, and environmental—in his explanation for the differences in the development record of countries in the South. Do you agree with Kennedy's analysis? Why or why not?

5. Kennedy offers a variety of predictions about future prospects for countries in different regions of the South. Which countries are the 'winners' and which countries are the 'losers'? Are his predictions convincing? Why or why not?

6. In Kennedy's view, what role does culture play in development?

# The South and Its Tasks

The South Commission

## A World Divided

Three and a half billion people, three-quarters of all humanity, live in the developing countries. By the year 2000, the proportion will probably have risen to four-fifths. Together the developing countries—accounting for more than two-thirds of the earth's land surface area—are often called the Third World.

We refer to them as the South. Largely by-passed by the benefits of prosperity and progress, they exist on the periphery of the developed countries of the North. While most of the people of the North are affluent, most of the people of the South are poor; while the economies of the North are generally strong and resilient, those of the South are mostly weak and defenceless; while the countries in the North are, by and large, in control of their destinies, those of the South are very vulnerable to external factors and lacking in functional sovereignty.

The countries of the South vary greatly in size, in natural resource endowment, in the structure of their economies, in the level of economic, social, and technological development. They also differ in their cultures, in their political systems, and in the ideologies they profess. Their economic and technological diversity has become more marked in recent years, making the South of today even less homogeneous than the South of yesterday.

Yet in this diversity there is a basic unity. What the countries of the South have in common transcends their differences; it gives them a shared identity and a reason to work together for common objectives. And their economic diversity offers opportunities for co-operation that can benefit them all.

The primary bond that links the countries and peoples of the South is their desire to escape from poverty and underdevelopment and secure a better life for their citizens. This shared aspiration is a foundation for their solidarity, expressed through such organizations as the Group of 77—of which all countries of the South except China are members—and the Non-Aligned Movement, with a large and growing membership from all continents in the South.

The decision-making processes that govern the international flows of trade, capital, and technology are controlled by the major developed countries of the North and by the international institutions they dominate. The countries of the South are unfavourably placed in the world economic system; they are individually powerless to influence these processes and institutions and, hence, the global economic environment which vitally affects their development. For this reason they have made a collective demand for the reform of the international economic system so as to make it more equitable and responsive to the needs of the vast majority of humanity—the people of the South. The struggle for a fairer international system has consolidated their cohesion and strengthened their resolve to pursue united action.

Were all humanity a single nation-state, the present North-South divide would make it an unviable, semi-feudal entity, split by internal conflicts. Its small part is advanced, prosperous, powerful; its much bigger part is underdeveloped,

From The South Commission, *Challenge to the South: The Report of the South Commission* (New York: Oxford University Press, 1990), 1–4, 10–14, 79–82, 99–101, 104–7, 128–41.

poor, powerless. A nation so divided within itself would be recognized as unstable. A world so divided should likewise be recognized as inherently unstable. And the position is worsening, not improving. During the 1970s, there was hope that a New International Economic Order would be generally accepted as an objective and that the North-South gap would narrow. But for most countries of the South that gap has been widening. The world is becoming, not less, but more disparate in the basic conditions of human life. For many in the South, the hope has faded; the prospects have become gloomier than they were perceived to be only a decade ago.

In the three decades after the Second World War, most developing countries made significant economic and social progress. Indeed in the 1960s and 1970s, the developing countries as a group did better than the developed countries in rates of economic growth—and also better than the developed countries in their early stages of development.

The mid-1970s witnessed a shift towards continuing disarray in the world economy. The consequence of this disarray was eventually the world recession of 1980–3. Industrialized countries have since then enjoyed a period of recovery and uninterrupted growth, though at a slower pace than in the previous postwar phases of recovery, but an acute economic crisis continues in many parts of the developing world. In the decade of the 1980s, a large majority of developing countries suffered severe blows to their economic growth and living standards; countries with a heavy burden of external debt suffered most. Retrogression, persistent instability and uncertainty, and recurring financial crises troubled the developing world—although with some important exceptions, notably in Asia—throughout the 1980s.

The impact of these setbacks has been pervasive, and has been reflected in such indicators of public well-being as infant mortality, life expectancy, levels of nutrition, incidence of dis-

ease, and school enrolment. As a result, social discontent and political unrest have been building up, especially among the poorer groups in that population; these, notably women, have borne a disproportionate part of the effect of cuts in social services and employment. Young people, facing reduced opportunities for employment and training, are becoming increasingly disaffected.

The widening disparities between South and North are attributable not merely to differences in economic progress, but also to an enlargement of the North's power vis-à-vis the rest of the world. The leading countries of the North now more readily use that power in pursuit of their objectives. The 'gunboat' diplomacy of the nineteenth century still has its economic and political counterpart in the closing years of the twentieth. The fate of the South is increasingly dictated by the perceptions and policies of governments in the North, of the multilateral institutions which a few of those governments control, and of the network of private institutions that are increasingly prominent. Domination has been reinforced where partnership was needed and hoped for by the South.

Yet, the North too is not homogeneous. There are economic, social, and cultural differences among the developed countries of the West. They also differ in their approach to global issues and, to some extent, in their attitude towards the countries of the South.

The South remains economically linked mainly to the market economy countries of the North—both a legacy of the colonial past sustained by the North's relative economic strength and a consequence of the development strategies sometimes adopted in the South. However, our notion of the North also includes the countries of Eastern Europe, whose attitude towards the South has differed from that of the West. So far, these countries, while strongly supporting the aspirations of the South, have not played a major role in North-South negotiations on economic matters. Links of co-operation between them and the

South have not been fully developed. Conditions in these countries are changing very fast and a new basis for co-operation will need to be evolved as they seek to redefine their position in the global economy. . . .

## Development Defined

The South's vision must also embrace a notion of what development ultimately signifies. In our view, development is a process which enables human beings to realize their potential, build self-confidence, and lead lives of dignity and fulfilment. It is a process which frees people from the fear of want and exploitation. It is a movement away from political, economic, or social oppression. Through development, political independence acquires its true significance. And it is a process of growth, a movement essentially springing from within the society that is developing.

Development therefore implies growing self-reliance, both individual and collective. The base for a nation's development must be its own resources, both human and material, fully used to meet its own needs. External assistance can promote development. But to have this effect, this assistance has to be integrated into the national effort and applied to the purposes of those it is meant to benefit. Development is based on self-reliance and is self-directed; without these characteristics there can be no genuine development.

But a nation is its people. Development has therefore to be an effort of, by, and for the people. True development has to be people-centred. It has to be directed at the fulfilment of human potential and the improvement of the social and economic well-being of the people. And it has to be designed to secure what the people themselves perceive to be their social and economic interests.

People are both individuals and members of society. To articulate their interests—and to influence the course of national development—they have to be free members of their society. They have to be free to learn, to say what they think and

know what others think, to organize in furtherance of their common interests. They have to be able to choose freely those who govern them, and those who govern must be accountable to the people.

Development at the same time takes place in the context of social, economic, and political organization, with the consequence that citizens owe obligations to society. For development means growth of the individual and of the community of which the individual is a part. In the modern world, that community ranges from the family, the village, town, or city to the nation and the world as a whole. At all these levels, and through means appropriate to them, individuals must be able to influence decisions and also join in their implementation and the control of activities which affect them. But their involvement has to conform to a framework of rules set by themselves as part of that larger community and enforced on their behalf by those chosen to govern.

Thus, development necessarily implies political freedom, for individuals as for nations. The interests and desires of the South could not be expressed—or known—until the former colonial territories attained independence. Similarly, the people's interests and desires can only be known when they are free—and have the channels—to express them.

Democratic institutions and popular participation in decision-making are therefore essential to genuine development. Only when there is effective political freedom can the people's interests become paramount within nations. The people must be able to determine the system of government, who forms their government, and in broad terms what the government does in their name and on their behalf. Respect for human rights, the rule of law, and the possibility to change governments through peaceful means are among the basic constituents of a democratic polity.

The form of democracy—its machinery—must be appropriate to the nation's history, size, and cultural diversity. Other nations do not necessarily provide models which can be directly transplanted. Political systems need to be understood by the people they serve and suited to their own value systems. What is vital is that governments should be, through nationally appropriate mechanisms, accountable to the people and responsive to their freely expressed views.

Periodic elections, however free and fair, are insufficient by themselves to secure action tending to achieve genuine development. If a government is to be able to mobilize a country's human and material resources for development and to ensure that the path of development continues to respond to the interests of its people, it needs a system of constant interaction with the people it represents. What the system is, and how it is organized, must again depend on the nature of the society. Nevertheless, continual questioning by citizens, whose freedom of expression should be unencumbered, and by independent observers can stimulate the reforms necessary to maintain the system's democratic effectiveness as the national society develops and changes.

Rapid and sustained economic growth is indispensable for the South's development. Hunger, disease, and ignorance cannot be overcome unless the production of goods and services is greatly increased. Nor can the South's nations be really independent if they have to continue to rely on external aid for such basic needs as food or other vital economic requirements.

It is only a rapidly expanding economy that can create the resources for the improvement of human well-being and of the public services which contribute to it. A fast-growing labour force can also be assured of jobs only if the economy is growing vigorously. Moreover, the social and economic tensions which inevitably arise over the distribution of income and wealth can hardly be resolved unless total output is expanding and productive employment is provided.

Yet it must be emphasized that economic growth as measured by the gross national product (GNP) is not synonymous with development. Not only the growth of the national product but what is produced, how and at what social and environmental cost, by whom and for whom—all this is relevant to people-centred development and should be taken into account in the formulation of policy. A broad assessment of the pace and direction of change and of its impact on the well-being of the people would provide the necessary guidance.

In a development process defined in these broad terms, social questions and social relations are as important as economic matters. Freedom for individuals, or for family and neighbourhood initiative and activities, or for the practice of religious beliefs, are among values for which many people show themselves willing to make large economic sacrifices. Such matters are therefore relevant to our notion of development.

Gross injustices are clearly incompatible with development. Personal insecurity, whether it arises from widespread crime or government action, is incompatible with freedom and therefore with development. So too is the denial of human dignity and equality. Discrimination on the grounds of sex, colour, race, religion, or political belief cannot be justified by economic or social advances which spill over to those who suffer such discrimination. Apartheid would remain the antithesis of development even if black South Africans were able to enjoy a larger share in South Africa's wealth.

To sum up: development is a process of self-reliant growth, achieved through the participation of the people acting in their own interests as they see them, and under their own control. Its first objective must be to end poverty, provide productive employment, and satisfy the basic needs of all the people, any surplus being fairly shared. This implies that basic goods and services such as food and shelter, basic education and health facilities, and clean water must be accessible to all. In addition, development presupposes a democratic structure of government, together with its supporting individual freedoms of speech, organization, and publication, as well as a system of justice which protects all the people from actions inconsistent with just laws that are known and publicly accepted. . . .

## The Need to Reorient Development Strategies

In most regions of the South there is a deep awareness of the limitations of past development strategies and a growing conviction that the way out of the present crisis does not lie in returning to those strategies. At the same time, there is profound disillusionment with the policies that a large number of developing countries are now being obliged to follow under the dictates of the international financial institutions. The need is therefore increasingly felt for finding a path of development that will lead the countries of the South out of the current crisis, into a future of equitable and sustained development.

The South cannot count on a significant improvement in the international economic environment for its development in the 1990s. The development of the South will therefore need to be fuelled by its own resources to a much greater degree than in the past. The countries of the South will have to rely increasingly on their own exertions, both individual and collective, and to reorient their development strategies, which must benefit from the lessons of past experience.

The balance between the different elements of a development strategy must necessarily be country-specific. But a self-reliant and people-centred development path will need to be guided by certain basic principles and objectives.

Priority must be given to meeting the basic needs of the people. Hence there should be a strong emphasis on food security, health, education, and employment, all of which are essential for enhancing human capacities to meet the challenge of sustained development.

The experience since the 1950s has clearly shown that basic needs can be satisfied only with-

in a rapidly expanding economy. It is therefore crucial to revive economic growth, reorient its content, and sustain it at an acceptable pace. The growth strategy should include among its main objectives the broad-based modernization of peasant agriculture and the strengthening of the pace of industrialization while also improving its employment-creating effects, competitiveness, and trade performance.

Concern for social justice has to be an integral part of genuine development. A fairer distribution of income and productive assets like land is essential as a means of speeding up development and making it sustainable. The development of human resources should similarly be an important concern, as it can simultaneously bring equity and efficiency into the economy. In their measures to enrich the capabilities of their people, the countries of the South should seek to achieve, by the year 2000, universal primary health care, literacy, and elementary education; a substantial increase in secondary and higher education and in vocational and technical training; and a slowing-down of population growth.

People-centred strategies of development should be consistent with the evolving culture of the people. While development will necessarily entail changes in cultural norms, values, and beliefs, modernization should not be antithetical to the culture of a people and should contribute to its internal evolution.

A development strategy designed to imitate the lifestyles and consumption patterns of affluent industrial societies is clearly inconsistent with our vision of development for the South. It would accentuate inequalities, for it would be possible to secure such high consumption levels for only a small minority of the population in each country. Because it leads to a high level of imports and energy use, it would also cripple the growth process and intensify economic and environmental strains.

The democratization of political structures and the modernization of the state should also have a high priority. A democratic environment which guarantees fundamental human rights is an essential goal of development centred on the people as well as a crucial means of accelerating development. Not only should democratic institutions be created and strengthened, but there should be encouragement of the formation of non-governmental and voluntary organizations that would be capable of assuming increased responsibility for economic and social advances. By mobilizing local human and financial resources, such grassroots organizations not only help to meet the felt needs of their members, but may in time become important pillars of the democratic system.

For the foreseeable future, most countries of the South will have mixed economies in which the state and market mechanisms will have to complement each other in a creative way if their development potential is to be realized. For this to happen, reforms are required in the machinery of government in addition to the reorientation of policies. The aim should be to modernize the state apparatus, as well as to create a stable and development-oriented macroeconomic framework, encourage entrepreneurship, initiative, and innovation, and make the public sector more efficient.

A people-oriented development strategy will have to take much greater note of the role of women; a nation cannot genuinely develop so long as half its population is marginalized and suffers discrimination. Women, who invariably bear a disproportionate share of poverty, also had to bear the major burden of adjustment to the crisis of the 1980s. Yet, in almost all the countries of the South, they play a vital role in productive activities and in maintaining their families and households. Thus, on the grounds of both equity and growth, development programs must give due prominence to the specific concerns of women and ensure that ample resources are marshalled to satisfy their needs and aspirations.

The creation, mastery, and utilization of modern science and technology are basic achieve-

ments that distinguish the advanced from the backward world, the North from the South. The widening gap in overall development and wealth between the nations of the South and those of the North is to a large extent the science and technology gap. Thus future development policies will need to address with greater vigour the closing of the knowledge gap with the North. Knowledge is vital to the future of the South, for development will depend more and more on the benefits derived from the advances of science and technology. Progress in this field calls for the overhaul of educational systems, in order that more attention may be given to education in science and to training in engineering and technical skills. It will also require science and technology policies which lay down clear sectoral priorities, integrate science and technology in national plans, and provide adequate resources for strengthening scientific and technological capability.

While the nations of the South undoubtedly suffer from the deterioration of the biosphere caused largely by the production and consumption patterns of the North, they are also increasingly facing environmental damage associated with their own development. This includes the degradation of natural resources due to population growth and economic pressures, the contamination of air and water associated with rapid industrialization, and urban pollution due to the unchecked growth of cities. There is therefore a need to take full cognizance of these hazards to ensure that development is indeed sustainable. The utilization of natural resources must be rational and consistent with their preservation, and the use of technologies that are environmentally sound must be promoted in the industries of the South. Developing countries will also have to check rapid and uncontrolled urbanization.

Many of the goals and policies advocated in this chapter can complement each other over time, and our discussion will often stress their mutually reinforcing links. But we recognize that in the design of development policies and the allocation of public investments, many trade-offs, often sharp ones, will arise between the different national objectives—as, for instance, between the creation of social and physical infrastructure, between industrial and agricultural priorities, or between the expansion of exports and domestic demand. Inevitably, difficult choices will have to be made on the range of objectives to be achieved and the balance between them. These choices will necessarily differ from one country to another. . . .

## The Development of Human Resources

Social deprivation remains widespread in the developing world, in spite of substantial improvements during the postwar period in health care, literacy, and education. Almost half of the developing world's children are still not protected by immunization against communicable diseases. In the rural areas of the developing world, nearly two-thirds of families are still without safe drinking water and an even higher proportion is without adequate sanitation. The proportions in urban areas are of the order of one-quarter and two-fifths. With present trends in enrolment and drop-out rates in primary schools, the children—especially girls—of the poorest 15–20 per cent of families in the South are not likely to become literate.

This state of affairs can and should be remedied. The obstacles to remedial action derive from social and cultural as well as economic factors. There are, however, three aspects in the design of policies to which attention needs to be drawn. First, there is the absence of delivery systems to reach the very poorest, particularly in regions that are remote and badly served by roads. In these cases access to health care and education, as well as to water supplies and sanitation, is often sadly deficient. Second, in most developing countries there is a skewed distribution of the benefits of social expenditures. The pyramid of access to social services is such that the people in the upper- and middle-income

groups in the urban areas benefit most from public social spending. Third, in the pursuit of modernization there is a tendency to neglect traditional systems of knowledge and indigenous practices which could be cost-effective in providing some basic social services.

These shortcomings are interconnected and reflect the low social and political weight of the rural poor. Often the establishment of a modern hospital or technical college in an urban centre takes priority over the provision of health and educational services to a remote rural region. Especially in the low-income countries, the scarce resources devoted to social services tend to be concentrated on urban areas. However, if this tendency is unchecked, the result can be a vicious circle. The lack of services in rural areas accelerates the drift to the cities, as the rural poor migrate not only to look for employment but also to secure access to education and health services and a better life for their children. This influx adds to the pressure on schools, clinics, and other social services—and to overcrowding—in the towns. The end result can be seen in many semi-industrial countries in the South: chaos and squalor in the towns while rural areas remain severely deprived of social services.

Breaking this vicious circle requires a committed effort to improve education, health services, water supplies, and sanitation in the rural areas. In middle-income countries, what is called for is a more balanced distribution of public expenditure on social services so that cities are not favoured at the expense of the villages. In low-income countries, with fewer resources, the establishment of efficient delivery systems becomes crucial. Changes in this sphere should, however, be only one element in the redirection of development policies towards the rural poor; their impact would be small if other development policies had a contrary thrust.

Besides their major role as a vehicle of social progress, the development of human resources and the provision of basic public goods invariably broaden an economy's resource base and strengthen its capacity to achieve economic growth. It is true that not all the great advances in the satisfaction of basic needs in the past led to an outstanding pace of economic growth. But there is evidence that the fastest-growing countries in a given period and within a given per capita income group typically had higher than average levels in the development of human resources (especially in education) at the beginning of the period. Large investments on human resources also tended typically to speed up growth performance in comparison with periods preceding such investment. . . .

## Implementing Population Policies

Rapid population growth presents a formidable challenge for most developing countries. The developing countries as a group have the most dynamic demography in the world and, by the end of the century, will have four-fifths of the total world population. However, demographic trends vary greatly in the developing world. In Asia as a whole, population growth has declined to below 2 per cent a year; it is expected to proceed in the 1990s at rates of around 1.2 per cent a year in China, 1.7 per cent in South Asia and the rest of East Asia, and 2.9 per cent in West Asia. In most of Latin America too, rates of population growth are on the decline and are expected to average around 1.9 per cent a year in the 1990s. The trend in most of Africa, in contrast, is still upward, with rates of over 3 per cent a year forecast for the 1990s in sub-Saharan Africa.

Past trends in population will be mirrored in the evolution of the size of the labour force and in the changing structure of the population. The South's labour force is expected to continue growing at the high annual rate of about 2.3 per cent up to the year 2000, subject, however, to great regional diversity. While in China the labour force will grow at about 1.2 per cent a year, it will grow at around 2 per cent in South Asia and the rest of East Asia, 2.4 per cent in Latin America, and at a rate reaching or exceeding 3 per cent in West Asia, North Africa, and sub-Saharan Africa. The age structure of the population by the year 2000 will also show wide differences. The child-dependency ratio (children up to 14 years in relation to the population of working age, i.e., 15–64 years) is expected by then to range from over 70 per cent in sub-Saharan Africa and West Asia, 50 to 60 per cent in Latin America, South Asia, and North Africa, to a low 40 per cent or less in East Asia and the developing countries of Europe. In developed countries, the ratio is expected to drop to nearly 30 per cent. Demographic trends are responses to economic, social, and cultural factors. The vibrant demography of the South is the outcome of its achievements in raising life expectancy and reducing mortality, in particular infant mortality, combined with persistently high fertility. The wide interregional variations in population growth are also in a way consistent with the great differences in population size and density. With its area and natural resources, Africa has the potential to accommodate a much larger population than at present, in contrast, for example, to most of Asia and several Latin American countries. However, in view of the limited availability of financial resources, and of good quality land in several of its countries, action to moderate population growth is a compelling need even in Africa.

A rapidly increasingly population strains the capacity of the economy to provide enough and adequate jobs. For as the number of job-seekers swells, the resources available for creating more jobs shrink. Through its effects on the age distribution within the population, fast demographic growth leads to the situation in which each working person bears a much higher burden of dependency (in terms of demand for food, health care, housing, and schooling) than in countries where the population is growing less fast.

In addition, even though population growth may not be an ultimate cause of poverty, it can drastically impair a country's ability to develop its human capital. Advances in the development of human resources—education, training, health—are of a cumulative nature; past investments create better conditions for later improvements and, vice versa, past neglect compounds the difficulties for the future. Accordingly, where population growth outstrips a country's capacity to develop its human resources, the consequence can be a vicious circle of stagnation and underdevelopment.

The rate of population growth tends to decline as a country becomes more prosperous. But some recent experience in the developing world suggests that a steep decline in fertility can occur in countries at different levels of economic development. The observed decline is attributable to a combination of greatly improved rates of child survival, expanded family planning services, rising educational levels among young girls and, more generally, to advances in the social and economic status of women. Higher rates of child survival improve the predictability of the family's life cycle and encourage parents to adopt family planning practices. Access to family planning services also has a strong effect in the transition to lower fertility rates, as is shown by the high levels of contraceptive use achieved in some poor countries. Educated women and women with their own income and assets tend to delay having children, reducing their child-bearing span. Educated mothers are also better able to care for their children's health and to use contraceptive methods. Changes in male attitudes are, however, also important, and efforts to encourage population planning need to be directed to men as well as women.

The emphasis on checking excessive population growth should be accompanied by attention to the distribution of the population, often concentrated in areas ill-equipped in terms of natural resources or public services. The problem of population pressure in urban areas is acquiring very serious proportions in the South. Ceaseless migration to the cities—the result of both greater economic opportunities in urban areas and poor living conditions in the countryside—has strained the life-supporting capabilities of urban centres. This has happened at a time when public finance to expand public utilities and social services is becoming increasingly limited. Policies offering effective incentives and disincentives to encourage a balanced distribution of population should be vigorously pursued as a matter of priority.

In sum, a strong commitment to slowing down population growth through integrated population and human resource planning can bring large personal and social benefits in most developing countries. High priority for the improvement of child survival rates, expansion of female education, improvement in the economic and social position of women, and the rapid extension of family planning services are the key strategic elements. Their results would be of immediate and direct benefit to couples who, by exercising their preferences, are able to gain greater control over their own lives. But indirect major benefits would also accrue to society as a whole. As population pressure eases, social services, investments in human resources, and employment opportunities can all be increased. . . .

## The Gender Dimensions of Development

Women account for more than half the South's population. They participate in the development process in myriad ways, but their contribution to economic and social change continues to be inadequately recognized and greatly undervalued, because male-dominated cultures have given them an inferior position in society, and custom, taboo, and the sexual division of labour keep them subordinate to men.

Throughout the South, women's labour is vital to the production of goods and services. Now increasingly active in industry, women have throughout been widely involved in agriculture, particularly in the crucial area of food production, providing over half the agricultural labour force in the South. In Africa, for example, most adult women are engaged in agricultural activity, growing and processing the bulk of the food consumed, and marketing the surplus. In Asia and the Pacific, women's labour is important in occupations allied to agriculture and food production, such as fisheries and food processing, as well as in rural household industry. Throughout the developing world, rural women's activities in agro-forestry and soil-conservation schemes not only provide major support to food production, but also add to the environmental balance in ecosystems.

Likewise, in Latin America and the Caribbean, and to a lesser extent in other regions of the South, more and more women are entering the industrial and services sectors, besides becoming prominent in informal economic activities as traders and home-based workers. The majority of women, in both rural and urban areas of the South, combine these economic pursuits with their vital social role as home managers and mothers, bringing up the young and caring for their families.

The majority of women in developing countries carry the double burden of poverty and of discrimination. They are almost invariably paid less than men for the same work, and their entry into better-paid jobs is often blocked. In some countries they do not have the right to own land. They have less access than men to credit, and limited access to such productive resources as irrigation water, fertilizers, and technologies. It is also evident that health services and educational facilities are not equally available to them. For these and other reasons women suffer disproportionately from poverty, illiteracy, and malnutrition. Those who are heads of households are almost always among the poorest 10 per cent of the population.

Economic, social, and cultural factors have combined to produce a situation in which most development efforts have tended to discount the potential social and economic contribution of women, and so fail to mobilize and benefit from this vital human resource. There is a persistent misconception that the value of women's contribution to the economy and to society is adequate-

ly recognized and their needs and interests are satisfied if they are made the beneficiaries of certain welfare programs.

The adjustment programs of the 1980s have made the position of women worse. Many have lost jobs in the formal sector. While some have been able to start certain new activities in the more flexible informal sector, the lack of credit and appropriate training limits the income they can derive from them. Increases in food prices and cuts in educational and health services have meanwhile made it more difficult for women, as home managers, to meet family requirements. In urban areas, increasing economic difficulties have forced women to take to badly paid domestic work and in some cases even to prostitution. In rural areas, non-agricultural activities have become more and more necessary. The result has been to intensify the already severe pressure on women's time, leading in some cases to reduced attention to child care.

The mobilization of women as equal partners in all developmental processes therefore needs the priority attention of policy-makers. The means by which this could be achieved have been outlined in recommendations adopted at United Nations conferences held in 1976, 1980, and 1985 in Mexico City, Copenhagen, and Nairobi, where specific measures were proposed by international consensus, particularly in the Forward-looking Strategy adopted at the Nairobi Conference in 1985, as well as in many national documents. There is now, however, a compelling need to convert this consensus into action.

It needs to be recognized that development policies designed to ensure equity and full participation in society should give priority to raising the social and economic status of women. For example, an agricultural strategy that aims at self-reliance as regards food and nutritional security must give prominence to the role of women as food producers and as providers of health care. An industrial strategy focusing on the cost-efficient provision of consumption goods by using available skills needs to take account of women as major producers and consumers of most essential items of daily life. Women's participation in the fast-growing services sector should be properly reflected as an integral part of national plans to develop this sector.

It is essential, therefore, that the concerns of women should be incorporated within the framework of national development policies in a comprehensive manner. Adequate resources should be made available to meet their needs. The allocation of resources and technological choice in the main sectors, such as agriculture (including irrigation) and industry, need to be examined to determine their likely impact on women's productive activities. Policies to protect and enhance women's income-earning capacity and an upward assessment of their contribution in all economic sectors would lead towards greater equity among all social groups, and promote self-reliance, popular participation, and environmental protection.

The evidence of earlier attempts at integrating women into development planning indicates that it is not enough merely to provide resources or formulate program objectives. There is a need as well for instruments and mechanisms which are responsive to the gender dimension in developmental activity. The design of strategies, training of development agents, and restructuring of legal and administrative systems should reflect the important role of women in the economy and society. What is no less important is that these changes should be accompanied and supported by deliberate endeavours to foster a gender-sensitive culture.

Where necessary, existing legal systems should be modified so as to facilitate the integration of women in the mainstream of the economy. Legal mechanisms may need to be created or strengthened in order to promote women's right to social justice and equity. Concerted efforts must be made to eliminate obstacles women face in such crucial areas as land tenure, to give them equal access to credit, and to grant them legal rights, especially in landownership.

A gender-sensitive approach to development is not just a political imperative, but a basic condition for sustained economic and social progress. It requires changes in all societies, but it calls for radical changes particularly in societies in which traditional perceptions of women as inferior to men continue to prevail and in which the preservation of their culture continues to be invoked to justify the subordination of women. A commitment to people-centred development requires purposeful efforts to weaken the hold of such perceptions and to bring about more enlightened social attitudes to women. Changes will be hastened to the extent that women themselves become actively conscious of their rights, and work to safeguard them. They need to create strong organizations, solidarity networks, and special channels and mechanisms to advance their interests. Aware of their role in the transformation of the nations of the South, they must also mobilize themselves to work in partnership with men to meet the challenges their societies face.

## Culture and Development

We refer here to culture in its widest sense, including:

- The values, attitudes, beliefs, and customs of a society. Paramount among these are religious beliefs and ethnic and national symbols and traditions, but they also include secular views about the human condition and human relations, individual and social priorities, morality, and rights and obligations, all of which may be institutionalized in various degrees.
- The activities in the society which express and enrich, while at the same time transforming, those values, attitudes, beliefs, and customs. The activities range from grassroots endeavours and undertakings (e.g., the production of folk art and handicrafts, the creation and performance of folk music and dance, popular festivities and other forms of collective

entertainment) to specialized cultural forms (literature, music, painting, theatre, dance, film-making, including television, etc.). The products they generate become, in their turn, part of the culture of the society.

Culture must be a central component of development strategies in a double sense: on the one hand, the strategies must be sensitive to the cultural roots of the society, to the basic shared values, attitudes, beliefs, and customs; on the other, they must include as a goal the development of the culture itself, the creative expansion, deepening, and change of the society's cultural stock.

Lack of concern with cultural values in development strategies can produce social reactions, from apathy to hostility, that hinder efforts to implement them. Economistic approaches to development, insensitive to the dominant cultural and social mores of a society, can even evoke fundamentalist and obscurantist responses which are inimical to development and may even set it back.

In order to involve the people as active participants, development must be consistent with their fundamental sociocultural traits; only then can the enthusiasm and creative potential of the people be mobilized. A culture-sensitive process of development will be able to draw on the large reserves of creativity and traditional knowledge and skills that are to be found throughout the developing world. Such enrichment will give development firmer roots in the society and make it easier to sustain development.

But culture is not only an inheritance of the past. In order to survive, a culture needs to renew itself so as to cope with present-day issues. Indeed some traditional cultural traits are inimical to development, and even to human dignity. People in the South should face the challenge of cultural renewal. A good starting-point would be the objective study of their own history. This would help them to reassess traditional values with a view to emphasizing those conducive to renewal and progress.

Further, concern with cultural identity does not imply rejection of outside influences. Rather, it should be a part of efforts to strengthen the capacity for autonomous decision-making, blending indigenous and universal elements in the service of a people-centred policy. Predominant among the latter are the values of democracy and social justice, and the scientific temper.

It is now widely appreciated that the application of technologies has clear social implications. The need for a culturally sensitive approach to the increasingly important function of science and technology in modernization has to be recognized. This will not only further a more harmonious transition to modernization, but could also reinforce the cultural base of the society.

The governments of the South should adopt clear policies and priorities to foster cultural development. In some cases these may take the form of Cultural Development Charters setting out the basic rights of the people in the field of culture, the essential conditions to attain them, and the role of the state in the process. The policies should pay due attention to the following aspects:

- *The right to culture.* This includes both the possibility for the citizen of enjoying the products of culture and of taking part in the creative activities that express and enhance culture. In the modern world, formal education is a principal channel for the transmission and perpetuation of culture. Access to education is therefore a crucial component of the right to culture. At the same time, to serve the goals of development, the education system must be informed by the country's cultural ethos.
- *Cultural diversity.* Because most nations in the South have a mixture of cultures, there should be respect for cultural diversity and concern for the rights of cultural minorities. The decentralization of cultural policy, particularly in the larger developing countries, is an

essential means of ensuring that the interests of all cultural groups are advanced.

- *Cultural role of the state.* The state is responsible for preserving and enriching the cultural heritage of the society, creating the conditions for the flourishing of cultural activities, and guaranteeing access to them for the population as a whole. The state must exercise these functions with due regard to the freedom of cultural and artistic creation, limited only by genuinely superior societal concerns. However, it is crucial that the state should be active in the cultural field. Adequate resources should be devoted to promoting cultural activities at the grassroots level and to encouraging the growth of professional work in the cultural field.

Attention should also be paid to the scope for developing cultural industries—handicrafts, folk arts, book publishing, the music industry, film-making, cultural tourism. This would be a means of blending the preservation and enhancement of the cultural heritage of the countries of the South with productive activities and income generation.

## Development and the Environment

Over the last two decades, concern has deepened about the many adverse environmental consequences of world economic growth. Much apprehension has been expressed about such dangers as global warming and damage to the ozone layer that certain production and consumption patterns have created for the global environment. Increasingly, other types of environmental damage, such as the denudation of important watersheds, desertification, and the destruction of tropical forests—concerns usually specific to a nation or a region—have also received considerable international attention. Calls have been voiced for 'sustainable development' and for estab-lishing environmental standards in industry, and important international and regional protocols have been drawn up to control the emission of certain dangerous gases.

The global and North-South aspects of environmental issues are discussed in Chapter 5. We deal here with the challenges these issues pose for domestic development in the South.

### The Environmental Challenges to the South

The direct environmental hazards faced by the nations of the South are many and varied. They include the continuous degradation of land under cultivation; desertification in the arid and semi-arid zones of the South; degradation of water resources; deforestation in tropical areas; threats to fish resources, both sea and freshwater, from pollution through the dumping of chemical and other waste, or overfishing; the release of noxious gases and the discharge of untreated industrial effluents; and severe pollution and squalor in many of the large cities of South.

The factors behind the increasing environmental stress in many of the countries of the South can be grouped into the following basic categories: increasing pressure on natural resources due to high rates of population growth; systems of property rights and land tenure that accentuate this pressure; the dynamics of agricultural development that result in a bimodal agricultural production system; economic pressure, mainly from the North, leading to overexploitation of natural resources; the imperative of industrialization and economic growth; the adoption of energy-intensive patterns of consumption modelled on those of the North; and unplanned and uncontrolled rural-urban migration.

The South's rapid demographic growth, largely the result of improved nutrition and health services, has put increasing pressure on natural resources, its extent varying according to the availability of cultivable land and the system of land tenure. As land is scarce in many regions of the South, it is cultivated without respite, often resulting in the mining of nutrients and in their depletion. Traditional systems of crop rotation, which usually left some land fallow for regeneration, are increasingly being abandoned owing to the need to grow more food for an expanding population.

A similar phenomenon may also be observed within the system of shifting cultivation found in many parts of tropical Africa and Asia. Here, again, because of population pressure, the fallow periods in which the land regains its nutrients, and which in certain cases used to exceed 20–25 years, are becoming progressively shorter. This leads to increasingly poorer harvests, causing a downward spiral in productivity and leading eventually to the degradation of the land. Population pressure has also resulted in cultivation being extended to unsuitable or marginal lands. Because of the fragility of their soil and also because of exposure to severe water or wind erosion, such areas quickly become unproductive.

Another consequence of population pressure on natural resources is the deforestation taking place in many countries of the South, as farmers seek new lands on which to grow food and raise cattle. Commercial ventures seeking new sources of timber aggravate the problem. FAO [Food and Agriculture Organization] estimates that up to 11 million hectares of tropical forests are cut down each year. This overexploitation has a number of adverse environmental impacts. The soil covered by natural forests is usually fragile, and its use for crop or livestock farming therefore soon degrades it, even making it unsuitable for the replanting of trees. The destruction of the natural plant-cover quickly results in severe erosion and in water run-offs which damage the natural water-regimes. In addition, the clearing of forest on steep water-sheds heightens the risk and volume of floods and landslides. A further damaging consequence is the extinction of plant and animal species unique to tropical forests. These are believed to contain about half of the world's known plant and animal

species; their loss would not only cause ecological imbalances and diminish biological diversity, but also affect the production of valuable industrial and pharmaceutical substances.

Similar to the impact of increasing human pressure on natural resources is that of expanding animal populations on grazing lands in semi-arid and arid zones. Rapid growth in animal herds is partly a result of better veterinary services but is sometimes the result of ill-designed rangeland development schemes. The uncontrolled growth in the animal populations in rangelands has led to overgrazing and the loss of the natural plant-cover. This makes these lands susceptible to wind and water erosion, and to their conversion into deserts. As much as 80 per cent of the rangelands in Africa and the Near East are thought to face a moderate-to-severe risk of desertification.

In addition to these pressures on the land, the economic pressure on countries in the South to earn foreign exchange also accentuates the tendency to overexploit natural resources, particularly forests. Some countries, for example, have allowed private firms (mainly transnational corporations) to carry on an unregulated exploitation of natural forests, often as a way of compensating for falls in export earnings due to a decline in commodity prices.

Further, in many countries, changing systems of land tenure and property have had a negative effect on the way in which natural resources are exploited. In regions where communal property systems used to prevail, as in much of sub-Saharan Africa, external pressure for change has weakened customary rules on the allocation and use of land. While traditional rules limited land access to clan or tribal members and also set conditions on the use of the land, external pressure has made countries open the land to overuse, in disregard of traditional restrictions. Lands under transitory systems of land tenure (i.e., those between customary communal property and freehold) and lands under unstable systems of tenure are perhaps among the most vulnerable to environmental degradation, for in such situations customary protective rules do not apply, nor is there an individual freeholder to take care of his property.

Other forms of tenure that have permitted, or even encouraged, excessive use of land and other natural resources are systems allowing free and unconditional access to all users. Whether these resources are grazing lands, mangrove swamps, or coastal fishing waters, they are invariably overexploited in such circumstances, resulting in their degradation or depletion. For while such areas are generally under the state's nominal ownership or protection, the state is often unable to monitor or regulate their use effectively.

Regimes of property rights and agricultural policies that have allowed dualist or bimodal systems for agricultural production to be applied have also contributed to environmental stress. Where this is the case, while traditional cultivation systems prevail in much of the country, large tracts of land (usually the most productive and irrigable land) are brought under commercial cultivation using modern, capital-intensive technology. This is usually accompanied by the displacement of smallholders or tenant farmers, who are either bought out or evicted, leaving them no option but to encroach on marginal lands. While the pressure on land may not appear to be high when considered nationally, the marginal lands cultivated by the displaced farmers are often under extreme stress and rapidly become degraded.

As in the North, though still to a very much smaller extent, industrialization—which must be a necessary part of economic growth—is responsible for certain environmental dangers. In a number of countries of the South, air pollution by the release of gases and substances from the burning of fossil fuels has begun to be a growing hazard. So has the uncontrolled and unregulated disposal of industrial waste, which contaminates rivers, lakes, and underground water resources.

Severe income inequalities, resulting in particular patterns of demand for industrial goods, also contribute to environmental stress in many countries of the South. Such income maldistribution is invariably accompanied by the adoption by the rich of the consumption patterns of the North, leading to increasing demand for products whose manufacturer or use is highly energy-intensive and has an impact on the levels of atmospheric pollution.

Economic growth and industrialization in the South have encouraged rural-urban migration, which in turn has contributed to the now familiar overcrowding and congestion of urban centres and to the consequential severe environmental damage. Because the growth is unplanned and unregulated, a large proportion of the poor inhabitants of these crowded cities—mainly migrants from the rural areas—usually lacks such basic services and amenities as safe drinking water, waste disposal and drainage, and adequate housing and space. The consequent unsanitary conditions produce serious health hazards, and occasionally the risk of epidemics.

## Domestic Policies for a Better Environment

The countries of the South will need to make a concerted effort to counteract environmental stress, as sustained development will require the preservation and development of natural resources, as well as their rational exploitation. The South has no alternative but to pursue a path of rapid economic growth, and hence to industrialize; it must therefore take action to control the environmental hazards that accompany such growth.

Given the complexity of the environment, it is necessary for countries to adopt an integrated approach. The protection of the environment should not be the sole responsibility of one department or ministry but should be taken into account by all government and non-government bodies concerned, and should be reflected in their plans for new economic activities. Further, all appraisals of new development projects should take their environmental costs into account. The environmental impact of various human activities should also be reflected systematically in the national accounts.

Legal provisions on environmental matters will be required in all countries. Environmental improvement cannot, however, simply be decreed; it requires the concerned involvement of all citizens. It is therefore essential to create a broad awareness of the actual or potential hazards threatening the country's environment and of what the people themselves can do to reduce them. If grassroots institutions are associated with the drawing-up of codes for environmental protection, there is a greater chance that they will be implemented.

Perhaps, in the long term, what could be most crucial in many countries would be policies directed at slowing down population growth and thus reducing the pressure on natural resources. In addition to these broad measures, the countries of the South will need to take specific steps to guard against environmental degradation, while continuing to pursue rapid economic growth.

The reorientation of development strategies to give high priority to smallholder agriculture can assist efforts to prevent the depletion of natural resources. Integrated rural development programs to improve the productivity of land already being cultivated will reduce the pressure on smallholders to bring marginal lands under cultivation. In many cases, land reforms that ensure equitable access to land and water resources will relieve the pressure on marginal and poor lands, which is often intensified by skewed land distribution. Strategies that tend to secure a reasonable balance in the level of regional development can make an important contribution to checking the concentration of population and thus reducing environmental stress in densely populated regions. Governments will, in addition, need to devise systems to regulate open access to natural resources. Such regulation is essential in order to halt the environmental degradation that results from excessive use, and to ensure the economical

exploitation of these resources. Also, the expansion of rural industry will reduce dependence on agriculture for income generation and, correspondingly, the pressure on natural resources.

The expansion of rural industry will, moreover, help to reduce the high rates of rural-urban migration now found in many countries, and to prevent the further deterioration of the environment in their cities. National urban development plans, aimed at reducing the environmental pressures faced by their fast-growing urban centres, must be part of comprehensive action to save the environment.

Another direction in which action should be taken is in encouraging the rational use and management of rangelands that are threatened with desertification. This would involve stabilizing the animal population at levels within the carrying capacities of these lands. In some cases, such action may have to be complemented by measures to protect the livelihoods of nomadic and semi-nomadic herdsmen using these areas.

Environmentally conscious rural development programs must make provision for the sound management of water resources. This will require the protection of river and lake catchment-areas; the more efficient use of water in irrigation schemes; the encouragement of small, community-managed irrigation schemes co-ordinated with larger schemes of irrigation, provided that the latter are efficiently controlled; the protection of surface and underground water from industrial or chemical pollution; and the pricing of water supplies in urban areas to reflect the actual costs of supply and to encourage its more economical use.

The rational exploitation of forests, the encouragement of programs of afforestation, and the search for sources of fuel to replace firewood should also be part of efforts to relieve rural environmental stress. Successful techniques, such as agro-forestry, which allow the use of forest areas for the production of crops and for raising livestock as well as for the rational exploitation of timber and other forest resources, have been evolved in a number of developing countries. These should be applied in countries where there is a risk of forests being destroyed owing to population pressure.

In attempting to build an environmentally sustainable economic and social order, the South should seek to develop and make use of its indigenous systems of agriculture and industry. Such ecologically sound systems have been virtually lost in the North but form the basis of everyday life in large parts of the South. These systems can be usefully adapted and made part of the South's development efforts. Given the substantial contribution they can make, they should not be discarded in the quest for modernization.

In addition to these measures to protect their natural resources, developing countries will need to take action to prevent air and water pollution caused by industrial activities. Regulations to control the emission of gases and the disposal of industrial waste need to be enacted where they do not now exist and existing regulations need to be strictly enforced. The acquisition and develop-ment of technologies that are both energy efficient and environmentally safe are also necessary. All these steps are required to safeguard the global commons shared by the South and the North.

But many of the measures the South can take to curb industrial pollution, particularly the emission of dangerous gases, will depend in large part on co-operation by the North in the transfer of energy-efficient and environmentally safe technologies. Without such co-operation, the South will find it very difficult to reduce industrial pollution, given the necessity to achieve high rates of economic growth. Even with it, however, continued economic growth in the South will in all likelihood necessitate the increased use of fossil fuels. The stabilization or reduction of air pollution throughout the world will thus require the North to reduce its own emissions radically. This is just, as well as necessary, given the enormous disparity in the levels of energy consumption between North and South, and the indisputable right of the South to develop rapidly to improve the well-being of its people.

# Preparing for the 21st Century:
## Winners and Losers

Paul Kennedy

## 1.

Everyone with an interest in international affairs must be aware that broad, global forces for change are bearing down upon humankind in both rich and poor societies alike. New technologies are challenging traditional assumptions about the way we make, trade, and even grow things. Automated workplaces in Japan intimate the end of the 'factory system' that first arose in Britain's Industrial Revolution and spread around the world. Genetically engineered crops, cultivated in biotech laboratories, threaten to replace naturally grown sugar, vanilla, coconut oil, and other staple farm produce, and perhaps undermine field-based agriculture as we know it. An electronically driven, 24-hour-a-day financial trading system has created a global market in, say, yen futures over which nobody really has control. The globalization of industry and services permits multinationals to switch production from one country to another (where it is usually cheaper), benefiting the latter and hurting the former.

In addition to facing these technology-driven forces for change, human society is grappling with the effects of fast-growing demographic imbalances throughout the world. Whereas birth rates in richer societies plunge well below the rates that would replace their populations, poorer countries are experiencing a population explosion that may double or even treble their numbers over the next few decades. As these fast-swelling populations press upon the surrounding forests, grazing lands,

and water supplies, they inflict dreadful damage upon local environments and may also be contributing to that process of global warming first created by the industrialization of the North a century and a half ago. With overpopulation and resource depletion undermining the social order, and with a global telecommunications revolution bringing television programs like *Dallas* and *Brideshead Revisited* to viewers everywhere from Central America to the Balkans, a vast illegal migration is under way as millions of families from the developing world strive to enter Europe and North America.

Although very different in form, these various trends from global warming to 24-hour-a-day trading are *transnational* in character, crossing borders all over our planet, affecting local communities and distant societies at the same time, and reminding us that the earth, for all its divisions, is a single unit. Every country is challenged by these global forces for change, to a greater or lesser extent, and most are beginning to sense the need to prepare themselves for the coming twenty-first century. Whether any society is at present 'well prepared' for the future is an open question;[1] but what is clear is that the regions of the globe most affected by the twin impacts of technology and demography lie in the developing world. Whether they succeed in harnessing the new technologies in an environmentally prudent fashion, and at the same time go through a demographic transition, will probably affect the prospects of global peace in the next century more than any other factor. What, then, are their chances?

Before that question can be answered, the sharp contrasts among the developing countries in the world's different regions need to be noted here.[2] Perhaps nothing better illustrates those

This article appeared in *The New York Review of Books*, 11 Feb. 1993, 32–44. From *Preparing for the Twenty-First Century* by Paul Kennedy. © 1993 by Paul Kennedy. Reprinted by permission of Random House, Inc.

differences than the fact that, in the 1960s, South Korea had a per capita GNP exactly the same as Ghana's (US $230), whereas today it is 10 to 12 times more prosperous.[3] Both possessed a predominantly agrarian economy and had endured a half-century or more of colonial rule. Upon independence, each faced innumerable handicaps in their effort to 'catch up' with the West, and although Korea possessed a greater historical and cultural coherence, its chances may have seemed less promising, since it had few natural resources (apart from tungsten) and suffered heavily during the 1950–53 fighting.

Decades later, however, West African states remain among the most poverty-stricken countries in the world—the per capita gross national products of Niger, Sierra Leone, and Chad today, for example, are less than $500[4]—while Korea is entering the ranks of the high-income economies. Already the world's thirteenth largest trading nation, Korea is planning to become one of the richest countries of all in the twenty-first century,[5] whereas the nations of West Africa face a future, at least in the near term, of chronic poverty, malnutrition, poor health, and underdevelopment. Finally, while Korea's rising prosperity is attended by a decrease in population growth, most African countries still face a demographic explosion that erodes any gains in national output.

This divergence is not new, for there have always been richer and poorer societies; the prosperity gap in the seventeenth century—between, say, Amsterdam and the west coast of Ireland, or between such bustling Indian ports as Surat and Calcutta[6] and the inhabitants of New Guinean hill villages—must have been marked, although it probably did not equal the gulf between rich and poor nations today. The difference is that the twentieth-century global communications revolution has made such disparities widely known. This can breed resentments by poorer peoples against prosperous societies, but it can also provide a desire to emulate (as Korea emulated Japan). The key issue here is: What does it take to

turn a 'have-not' into a 'have' nation? Does it simply require imitating economic techniques, or does it involve such intangibles as culture, social structure, and attitudes toward foreign practices?

This discrepancy in performance between East Asia and sub-Saharan Africa clearly makes the term 'Third World' misleading. However useful the expression might have been in the 1950s, when poor, nonaligned, and recently decolonized states were attempting to remain independent of the two superpower blocs,[7] the rise of super-rich oil-producing countries a decade later already made the term questionable. Now that prosperous East Asian societies—Korea, Taiwan, and Singapore—possess higher per capita GNPs than Russia, Eastern Europe, and even West European states like Portugal, the word seems less suitable than ever. . . .

Relative national growth in the 1980s confirms these differences. Whereas East Asian economies grew on average at an impressive annual rate of 7.4 per cent, those in Africa and Latin America gained only 1.8 and 1.7 per cent respectively[8]—and since their populations grew faster, the net result was that they slipped backward, absolutely and relatively. Differences of economic structure also grew in this decade, with African and other primary commodity-producing countries eager for higher raw-material prices, whereas the export-oriented manufacturing nations of East Asia sought to keep commodity prices low. The most dramatic difference occurred in the shares of world trade in manufactures, a key indicator of economic competitiveness (see chart below). Thus, while some scholars still refer to a dual world economy[9] of rich and poor countries, what is emerging is increasing differentiation. Why is this so?

The developing countries most successfully catching up with the West are the trading states of the Pacific and East Asia. Except for Communist regimes there, the Pacific rim countries (including the western provinces of Canada and the United States, and in part Australia) have enjoyed a lengthy

## Figure 1: Shares of World Trade in Manufactures[10]

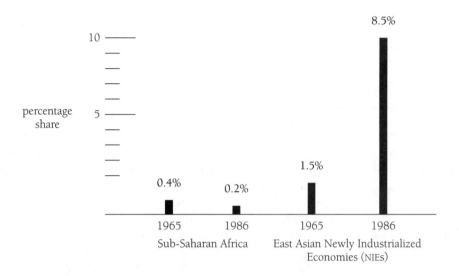

boom in manufacturing, trade, and investment; but the centre of that boom is on the *Asian* side of the Pacific, chiefly fuelled by Japan's own spectacular growth and the stimulus given to neighbouring economies and trans-Pacific trade. . . .

East Asia's present boom is not, of course, uniform, and scholars distinguish between the different stages of economic and technological development in this vast region. Roughly speaking, the divisions would be as follows:

(a) Japan, now the world's largest or second largest financial centre and, increasingly, the most innovative high-tech nation in the nonmilitary field;

(b) the four East Asian 'tigers' or 'dragons', the Newly Industrialized Economies (NIEs) of Singapore, Hong Kong, Taiwan, and South Korea, of which the latter two possess bigger populations and territories than the two port-city states, but all of which have enjoyed export-led growth in recent decades;

(c) the larger Southeast Asian states of Thailand, Malaysia, and Indonesia which, stimulated by foreign (chiefly Japanese) investment, are becoming involved in manufacturing, assembly, and export—it is doubtful whether the Philippines should be included in this group;

(d) finally, the stunted and impoverished Communist societies of Vietnam, Cambodia, and North Korea, as well as isolationist Myanmar pursuing its 'Burmese Way to Socialism'. . . .

Of those states, it is the East Asian NIEs that have provided the clearest example of successful transformation. Although distant observers may regard them as similar, there are notable differences in size, population,[11] history, and political system. Even the economic structures are distinct; for example, Korea, which began its expansion at least a decade later than Taiwan (and democratized itself even more slowly), is heavily dependent upon a few enormous industrial conglomerates, or *chaebol*, of whom the top four

## Table 1: Comparative Savings Ratios, 1987[12]

| | |
|---|---|
| Taiwan | 38.8% |
| Malaysia | 37.8% |
| Korea | 37.0% |
| Japan | 32.3% |
| Indonesia | 29.1% |
| US | 12.7% |

alone (Samsung, Hyundai, Lucky-Goldstar, and Daewoo) have sales equal to half Korea's GNP. By contrast, Taiwan possesses many small companies, specializing in one or two kinds of products. While Taiwanese are concerned that their firms may lose out to foreign giants, Koreans worry that the *chaebol* will find it increasingly difficult to compete in large-scale industries like petrochemicals and semiconductors and shipbuilding at the same time.[13]

Despite such structural differences, these societies each contain certain basic characteristics, which, *taken together*, help to explain their decade-upon-decade growth. The first, and perhaps the most important, is the emphasis upon education. This derives from Confucian traditions of competitive examinations and respect for learning, reinforced daily by the mother of the family who complements what is taught at school. . . .

Perhaps nothing better illustrates this stress upon learning than the fact that Korea (43 million population) has around 1.4 million students in higher education, compared with 145,000 in Iran (54 million), 15,000 in Ethiopia (46 million), and 159,000 in Vietnam (64 million); or the further fact that already by 1980 'as many engineering students were graduating from Korean institutions as in the United Kingdom, West Germany and Sweden combined.'[14]

The second common characteristic of these countries is their high level of national savings. By employing fiscal measures, taxes, and import con-trols to encourage personal savings, large amounts of low-interest capital were made available for investment in manufacture and commerce. During the first few decades of growth, personal consumption was constrained and living standards controlled—by restrictions upon moving capital abroad, or importing foreign luxury goods—in order to funnel resources into industrial growth. While average prosperity rose, most of the fruits of economic success were plowed back into further expansion. Only when economic 'take-off' was well under way has the system begun to alter; increased consumption, foreign purchases, capital investment in new homes, all allow internal demand to play a larger role in the country's growth. In such circumstances, one would expect to see overall savings ratios decline. Even in the late 1980s, however, the East Asian NIEs still had high national savings rates (Table 1).

The third feature has been a strong political system within which economic growth is fostered. While entrepreneurship and private property are encouraged, the 'tigers' never followed a *laissez-faire* model. Industries targeted for growth were given a variety of supports—export subsidies, training grants, tariff protection from foreign competitors. As noted above, the fiscal system was arranged to produce high savings ratios. Taxes assisted the business sector, as did energy policy. Trade unions operated under restrictions. Democracy was constrained by the governor of Hong Kong, *dirigiste* administrations in Singapore, and the military regimes in Taiwan and Korea. Only lately have free elections and party politics been permitted. Defenders of this system argued that it was necessary to restrain libertarian impulses while concentrating on economic growth, and that democratic reforms are a 'reward' for the people's patience. The point is that domestic politics were unlike those in the West yet did not hurt commercial expansion.

The fourth feature was the commitment to exports, in contrast to the policies of India, which emphasize locally produced substitutes for imports, and the consumer-driven policies of the United States. This was traditional for a small, bustling trading state like Hong Kong, but it involved substantial restructuring in Taiwan and Korea, where managers and workers had to be trained to produce what foreign customers wanted. In all cases, the value of the currency was kept low, to increase exports and decrease imports. Moreover, the newly industrialized economies of East Asia took advantage of favourable global circumstances: labour costs were much lower than in North America and Europe, and they benefited from an open international trading order, created and protected by the United States, while shielding their own industries from foreign competition.

Eventually, this led to large trade surpluses and threats of retaliation from European and American governments, reminding us of the NIES' heavy dependence upon the current international economic system. The important thing, however, is that they targeted export-led growth in manufacturers, whereas other developing nations continued to rely upon commodity exports and made little effort to cater to foreign consumers' tastes.[15] Given this emphasis on trade, it is not surprising to learn that Asia now contains seven of the world's 12 largest ports.

Finally, the East Asian NIES possess a local model, namely Japan, which Yemen, Guatemala, and Burkina Faso simply do not have. For four decades East Asian peoples have observed the dramatic success of a non-Western neighbour, based upon its educational and technical skills, high savings ratios, long-term, state-guided targeting of industries and markets, and determination to compete on world markets, though this admiration of Japan is nowadays mixed with a certain alarm at becoming members of a yen block dominated by Tokyo. While the Japanese domestic market is extremely important for the East Asian NIES, and they benefit from Japanese investments, assembly plants, engineers, and expertise, they have little enthusiasm for a new Greater East Asia co-prosperity sphere.[16]. . .

Will this progress last into the twenty-first century? Politically, Hong Kong's future is

## Table 2: Comparative Living Standards[17]

| | Life Expectancy at Birth (years), 1987 | Adult Literacy Rate (%), 1985 | GNP per capita, 1988 US$ |
|---|---|---|---|
| Niger | 45 | 14 | 300 |
| Togo | 54 | 41 | 310 |
| India | 59 | 43 | 340 |
| Singapore | 73 | 86 | 9,070 |
| South Korea | 70 | 95 | 5,000 |
| Spain | 77 | 95 | 7,740 |
| New Zealand | 75 | 99 | 10,000 |

completely uncertain, and many companies are relocating their headquarters elsewhere; Taiwan remains a diplomatic pariah-state because of Beijing's traditional claims; and South Korea still worries about the unpredictable, militarized regime in the north. The future of China—and of Siberia—is uncertain, and causes concern. . . .

On the other hand, these may simply be growing pains. Savings ratios are still extremely high. Large numbers of new engineers and technicians pour out of college each year. The workers' enhanced purchasing power has created a booming domestic market, and governments are investing more in housing, infrastructure, and public facilities. The labour force will not grow as swiftly as before because of the demographic slowdown, but it will be better educated and spend more.[18] A surge in overseas investments is assisting the long-term balance of payments. As the populous markets of Indonesia, Thailand, and Malaysia grow at double-digit rates, there is plenty of work for the trading states. . . . Barring a war in East Asia, or a widespread global slump, the signs are that the four 'tigers' are better structured than most to grow in wealth and health.

## 2.

For confirmation of that remark, one need only consider the present difficult condition of Latin America, which lost ground in the 1980s just as East Asia was gaining it. Here again, distinctions have to be made between various countries within the continent, with its more than 400 million people in an area almost 7 million square miles stretching from the Rio Grande to Antarctica, and with a range of political cultures and socio-economic structures. Argentina, which around 1900 had a standard of living suggesting that it was a 'developed' economy, is very different from Honduras and Guyana. Similarly, population change in Latin America occurs in three distinct forms: such nations as Bolivia, the Dominican Republic, and Haiti have high fertility rates and lower life expectancies; a middle group—Brazil, Colombia, Mexico, Venezuela, Costa Rica, and Panama—is beginning to experience declines in fertility and longer life expectancy; and the temperate-zone countries of Argentina, Chile, and Uruguay have the demographic characteristics of developed countries.[19]

Despite this diversity, there are reasons for considering Latin America's prospects as a whole: the economic challenges confronting the region are similar, as are its domestic politics—in particular, the fragility of its recently emerged democracies; and each is affected by its relationship with the developed world, especially the United States.

Several decades ago, Latin America's future appeared encouraging. Sharing in the post-1950 global boom, benefiting from demand for its coffee, timber, beef, oil, and minerals, and enjoying foreign investments in its agriculture, industry, and infrastructure, the region was moving upward. In the 30 years after 1945, its production of steel multiplied 20 times, and its output of electric energy, metals, and machinery grew more than tenfold.[20] Real gross domestic product (GDP) per person rose at an annual average of 2.8 per cent during the 1960s and spurted to an annual average increase of 3.4 per cent in the 1970s. Unfortunately, the growth then reversed itself, and between 1980 and 1988 Latin America's real GDP per person steadily fell by an annual average of 0.9 per cent.[21] In some states, such as Peru and Argentina, real income dropped by as much as one-quarter during the 1980s. With very few exceptions (Chile, Colombia, the Dominican Republic, Barbados, the Bahamas), most Latin American countries now have per capita GDPs lower than they were a decade earlier, or even two decades earlier.

The reasons for this reversal offer a striking contrast to the East Asian NIES. Instead of encouraging industrialists to target foreign markets and stimulate the economy through export-led growth, many Latin American governments pursued a policy of import substitution, creating their own steel, cement, paper, automobiles, and electronic-goods industries, which were given protective tariffs, government subsidies, and tax breaks to insulate them from international competition. As a result, their products became less attractive abroad.[22] Moreover, while it was relatively easy to create a basic iron and steel industry, it proved harder to establish high-tech industries like computers, aerospace, machine-tools, and pharmaceuticals—most of these states therefore still depend on imported manufactured goods, whereas exports chiefly consist of raw materials like oil, coffee, and soybeans.[23]

Secondly, economic growth was accompanied by lax financial policies and an increasing reliance upon foreign borrowings. Governments poured money not only into infrastructure and schools but also into state-owned enterprises, large bureaucracies, and oversized armed forces, paying for them by printing money and raising loans from Western (chiefly US) banks and international agencies. The result was that public spending's share of GDP soared, price inflation accelerated, and was further increased by index-linked rises in salaries and wages. Inflation became so large that it was difficult to comprehend, let alone combat. According to the 1990 *World Resources* report, 'in 1989, for example, annual inflation in Nicaragua was more than 3,400 per cent; in Argentina inflation reached 3,700 per cent, in Brazil almost 1,500 per cent, and in Peru nearly 3,000 per cent. Ecuador, with only 60 per cent inflation, did comparatively well.'[24] In such circumstances the currency becomes worthless, as does the idea of seeking to raise national savings rates for long-term capital investment.

Another result is that some Latin American countries find themselves among the most indebted in the world. Total Latin American indebtedness now equals about $1,000 for every man, woman, and child. But instead of being directed into productive investment, that money has been wasted domestically or disappeared as 'capital flight' to private accounts in United States and European banks. This has left most countries incapable of repaying even the interest on their loans. Defaults on loans (or suspension of interest payments) then produced a drying up of capital from indignant Western banks and a net capital outflow from Latin America just when it needed capital to aid economic growth.[25] Starved of foreign funds and with currencies made worthless by hyperinflation, many countries are in a far worse position than could have been imagined 25 years ago.[26] For a while, it was even feared that the region's financial problems might undermine parts of the international banking system. It now appears that the chief damage will be in the continent itself, where 180 million people (40 per cent) are living in poverty—a rise of 50 million alone in the 1980s.

Given such profligacy, and the conservative, 'anti-big government' incumbents in the White House during the 1980s, it was predictable that Latin America would come under pressure—from the World Bank, the IMF, private bankers, Washington itself—to slash public spending, control inflation, and repay debts. Such demands were easier said than done in the existing circumstances. Islands of democracy (e.g., Costa Rica) did exist, but many states were ruled by right-wing military dictatorships or social revolutionaries: internal guerrilla wars, military *coups d'état*, labour unrest were common. Even as democracy began to reassert itself in the 1980s, the new leaders found themselves in a near-impossible situation: inheritors of the high external debts contracted by the outgoing regimes, legatees in many cases of inflationary index-linked wage systems, targets of landowner resentment and/or of guerrilla attacks, frustrated by elaborate and often corrupt bureaucracies, and deficient in trained personnel. While grappling with these weaknesses, they discovered that the Western world, which applauded the return to democracy, was unsympathetic to fresh lending, increasingly inclined to protectionism, and demanding unilateral measures (e.g., in the Amazon rain forests) to stop global warming.

Two other weaknesses have also slowed any hoped-for recovery. One is the unimpressive accomplishments of the educational systems. This is not due to an absence of schools and universities, as in parts of Africa. Many Latin American countries have extensive public education, dozens of universities, and high adult literacy rates; Brazil, for example, has 68 universities, Argentina, 41.[27] The real problem is neglect and under-investment. . . .

Presumably, if resources were available, those decaying educational and health-care structures could be resuscitated, helping national recovery; but where the capital can be raised in present circumstances is difficult to see. Moreover, in the strife-torn countries of Central America there is little education to begin with; in Guatemala, the latest census estimated that 63 per cent of those 10 years of age and older were illiterate, while in Honduras the illiteracy rate was 40 per cent.[28] Unfortunately, it is in the educationally most deprived Latin American countries that resources are being eroded by swift population increases.

Despite these disadvantages, recent reports on Latin America have suggested that the 'lost decade' of the 1980s will be followed by a period of recovery. The coming of democratic regimes, the compromises emerging from protracted debt-recycling talks, the stiff economic reforms (cutting public spending, abandoning indexation) to reduce inflation rates, the replacement of 'state protectionism with import liberalization and privatization',[29] the conversion of budget deficits into surpluses—all this has caused the Inter-American Development Bank to argue that 'a decisive and genuine takeoff' is at hand, provided the new policies are sustained.[30] Growth has resumed in Argentina, Mexico, and Venezuela. Even investment bankers are reported to be returning to the continent.

Whether these changes are going to be enough remains uncertain, especially since the newly elected governments face widespread resentment at the proposed reforms. As one commentator put it, 'Much of Latin America is entering the 1990s in a race between economic deterioration and political

progress.'[31] Whereas Spain, Portugal, and Greece moved to democracy while enjoying reasonable prosperity, Latin America (like Eastern Europe) has to make that change as its economies flounder—which places immense responsibilities upon the political leadership.

Although it can be argued that the region's future is in its own hands, it will also be heavily influenced by the United States. In many ways, the US-Latin America leadership is similar to that between Japan and the East Asian NIES, which are heavily dependent upon Japan as their major market and source of capital.[32] Yet there is more to this relationship than Latin America's economic difficulties, and they would benefit greatly from a resumption of growth. . . .

Thus, while the region's own politicians and citizens have to bear the major responsibility for recovery, richer nations—especially the United States—may find it in their own best interest to lend a hand.

## 3.

If these remarks disappoint readers in Brazil or Peru, they may care to glance, in grim consolation, at the world of Islam. It is one thing to face population pressures, shortage of resources, educational/technological deficiencies, and regional conflicts, which would challenge the wisest governments. But it is another when regimes themselves stand in angry resentment of global forces for change instead of (as in East Asia) selectively responding to such trends. Far from preparing for the twenty-first century, much of the Arab and Muslim world appears to have difficulty in coming to terms with the nineteenth century, with its composite legacy of secularization, democracy, *laissez-faire* economics, industrial and commercial linkages among different nations, social change, and intellectual questioning. If one needed an example of the importance of cultural attitudes in explaining a society's response to change, contemporary Islam provides it.

Before analysing the distinctive role of Islamic culture, one should first note the danger of generalizing about a region that contains such variety. After all, it is not even clear what name should be used to describe this part of the earth. To term it the 'Middle East'[33] is, apart from its Atlantic-centred bias, to leave out such North African states as Libya, Tunisia, Algeria, and Morocco. To term it the 'Arab World'[34] is to exclude Iran (and, of course, Israel), the Kurds, and the non-Muslim tribes of southern Sudan and Mauritania. Even the nomenclature Islam, or the Muslim world, disguises the fact that millions of Catholics, Copts, and Jews live in these lands, and that Islamic societies extend from West Africa to Indonesia.[35]

In addition, the uneven location of oil in the Middle East has created a division between super-rich and dreadfully poor societies that has no equivalent in Central America or sub-Saharan Africa.[36] Countries like Kuwait (2 million), the United Arab Emirates (1.3 million), and Saudi Arabia (11.5 million) enjoy some of the world's highest incomes, but exist alongside populous neighbours one-third as rich (Jordan, Iran, Iraq) or even one-tenth as rich (Egypt, Yemen). The gap is accentuated by different political systems: conservative, anti-democratic, traditionalist in the Gulf sheikdoms; demagogic, populist, militarized in countries such as Libya, Syria, Iraq, and Iran.

The 1990 Iraqi attack upon Kuwait, and the different responses of the Saudi élites on the one hand and the street masses in Amman or Rabat on the other, illustrated this divide between 'haves' and 'have-nots' in the Muslim world. The presence of millions of Egyptian, Yemeni, Jordanian, and Palestinian *Gastarbeiter* in the oil-rich states simply increased the mutual resentments, while the Saudi and Emirate habit of giving extensive aid to Iraq during its war against Iran, or to Egypt to assist its economic needs, reinforces the impression of wealthy but precarious regimes seeking to achieve security by bribing their larger, jealous neighbours.[37] Is it any wonder that the unemployed, badly housed urban masses, despairing of

their own secular advancement, are attracted to religious leaders or 'strongmen' appealing to Islamic pride, a sense of identity, and resistance to foreign powers and their local lackeys?

More than in any other developing region, then, the future of the Middle East and North Africa is affected by issues of war and conflict. The region probably contains more soldiers, aircraft, missiles, and other weapons than anywhere else in the world, with billions of dollars of armaments having been supplied by Western, Soviet, and Chinese producers during the past few decades. In view of the range and destructiveness of these weapons, another Arab-Israeli war would be a nightmare, yet many Muslim states still regard Israel with acute hostility. Even if the Arab-Israeli antagonism did not exist, the region is full of other rivalries, between Syria and Iraq, Libya and Egypt, Iran and Iraq, and so on. Vicious one-man dictatorships glare threateningly at arch-conservative, anti-democratic, feudal sheikdoms. Fundamentalist regimes exist from Iran to the Sudan. Terrorist groups in exile threaten to eliminate their foes. Unrest among the masses puts a question mark over the future of Egypt, Algeria, Morocco, Jordan.[38] The recent fate of Lebanon, instead of serving as a warning against sectarian fanaticism, is more often viewed as a lesson in power politics, that the strong will devour the weak.

To the Western observer brought up in Enlightenment traditions—or, for that matter, to economic rationalists preaching the virtues of the borderless world—the answer to the Muslim nations' problems would appear to be a vast program of *education*, not simply in the technical, skills-acquiring sense but also to advance parliamentary discourse, pluralism, and a secular civic culture. Is that not the reason, after all, for the political stability and economic success of Scandinavia or Japan today?

If that argument is correct, then such an observer would find few of those features in contemporary Islam. In countries where fundamentalism is strong, there is (obviously) little prospect of education or advancement for the female half of the population.[39] Where engineers and technicians exist, their expertise has all too often been mobilized for war purposes, as in Iraq. Tragically, Egypt possesses a large and bustling university system but a totally inadequate number of jobs for graduates and skilled workers, so that millions of both are underemployed. In Yemen, to take an extreme example, the state of education is dismal. By contrast, the oil-rich states have poured huge resources into schools, technical institutes, and universities, but these alone are insufficient to create an 'enterprise culture' that would produced export-led manufacturing along East Asian lines. Ironically, possession of vast oil reserves could be a disadvantage, since it reduces the incentive to rely upon the skills and quality of the people, as occurs in countries (Japan, Switzerland) with few natural resources. Such discouraging circumstances may also explain why many educated and entrepreneurial Arabs, who passionately wanted their societies to borrow from the West, have emigrated.

It is difficult to know whether the reason for the Muslim world's troubled condition is cultural or historical. Western critics pointing to the region's religious intolerance, technological backwardness, and feudal cast of mind often forget that, centuries before the Reformation, Islam led the world in mathematics, cartography, medicine, and many other aspects of science and industry; and contained libraries, universities, and observatories, when Japan and America possessed none and Europe only a few. These assets were later sacrificed to a revival of traditionalist thought and the sectarian split between Shi'ite and Sunni Muslims, but Islam's retreat into itself—its being 'out of step with History', as one author termed it[40]—was probably also a response to the rise of a successful, expansionist Europe. . . .

## 4.

The condition of sub-Saharan Africa—'the Third World's third world', as it has been described—is even more desperate.[41] When one considers recent developments such as *perestroika* in the former Soviet Union, the coming integration of Europe, and the economic miracle of Japan and the East Asian NIES, remarked a former president of Nigeria, General Olusegun Obasanjo, and 'contrasting all this with what is taking place in Africa, it is difficult to believe that we inhabit the same historical time.'[42] . . . In the view of the World Bank, virtually everywhere else in the world is likely to experience a decline in poverty by the year 2000 *except* Africa, where things will only get worse.[43] 'Sub-Saharan Africa', concludes one economist, 'suffers from a combination of economic, social, political, institutional and environmental handicaps which have so far largely defied development efforts by the African countries and their donors.'[44] How, an empathetic study asks, can Africa survive?[45]

The unanimity of views is remarkable, given the enormous variety among the 45 states that comprise sub-Saharan Africa.[46] Nine of them have fewer than one million people each, whereas Nigeria contains about 110 million. Some lie in the desert, some in tropical rain forests. Many are rich in mineral deposits, others have only scrubland. While a number (Botswana, Cameroun, Congo, Gabon, Kenya) have seen significant increases in living standards since independence, they are the exception—suggesting that the obstacles to growth on East Asian lines are so deep-rooted and resistant to the 'development strategies' of foreign experts and/or their own leaders that it may require profound changes in attitude to achieve recovery.

This was not the mood 30 years ago, when the peoples of Africa were gaining their independence. True, there was economic backwardness, but this was assumed to have been caused by decades of foreign rule, leading to dependency upon a single metropolitan market, monoculture, lack of access to capital, and so on. Now that Africans had control of their destinies, they could build industries, develop cities, airports, and infrastructure, and attract foreign investment and aid from either Western powers or the USSR and its partners. The boom in world trade during the 1950s and 1960s, and demand for commodities, strengthened this optimism. Although some regions were in need, Africa as a whole was self-sufficient in food and, in fact, a net food exporter. Externally, African states were of increasing importance at the United Nations and other world bodies.

What went wrong? The unhappy answer is 'lots of things'. The first, and perhaps most serious, was that over the following three decades the population mushroomed as imported medical techniques and a reduction in malaria-borne mosquitoes drastically curtailed infant mortality. Africa's population was already increasing at an average annual rate of 2.6 per cent in the 1960s, jumped to 2.9 per cent during the 1970s, and increased to over 3 per cent by the late 1980s, implying a doubling in size every 22 years; this was, therefore, the highest rate for any region in the world.[47]

In certain countries, the increases were staggering. Between 1960 and 1990, Kenya's population quadrupled, from 6.3 million to 25.1 million, and Côte d'Ivoire's jumped from 3.8 million to 12.6 million. Altogether Africa's population—including the North African states—leapt from 281 to 647 million in three decades.[48] Moreover, while the majority of Africans inhabit rural settlements, the continent has been becoming urban at a dizzying speed. Vast shanty-cities have already emerged on the edges of national capitals (such as Accra in Ghana, Monrovia in Liberia, and Lilongwe in Malawi). By 2025, urban dwellers are predicted to make up 55 per cent of Africa's total population.

The worst news is that the increase is unlikely to diminish in the near future. Although most African countries spend less than 1 per cent of GNP on health care and consequently have the highest infant mortality rates in the world—in Mali, for example, there are 169 infant deaths for every 1,000 live births—those rates are substantially less than they were a quarter-century ago and will

tumble further in the future, which is why demographers forecast that Africa's population in 2025 will be nearly three times that of today.[49]

There remains one random and tragic factor which may significantly affect all these (late 1980s) population projections—the AIDS epidemic, which is especially prevalent in Africa. Each new general study has raised the global total of people who are already HIV positive. For example, in June 1991, the World Health Organization abandoned its earlier estimate that 25–30 million people throughout the world would be infected by the year 2000, and suggested instead that the total could be closer to 40 million, and even that may be a gross underestimate.[50] . . .

The basic reason why the present demographic boom will not otherwise be halted swiftly is traditional African belief-systems concerning fecundity, children, ancestors, and the role of women. Acutely aware of the invisible but pervasive presence of their ancestors, determined to expand their lineage, regarding childlessness or small families as the work of evil spirits, most Africans seek to have as many children as possible; a woman's virtue and usefulness are measured by the number of offspring she can bear. 'Desired family size', according to polls of African women, ranges from five to nine children. The social attitudes that lead women in North America, Europe, and Japan to delay childbearing—education, career ambitions, desire for independence—scarcely exist in African societies; where such emerge, they are swiftly suppressed by familial pressures.[51]

This population growth has not been accompanied by equal or larger increases in Africa's productivity, which would of course transform the picture. During the 1960s, farm output was rising by around 3 per cent each year, keeping pace with the population, but since 1970 agricultural production has grown at only half that rate. Part of this decline was caused by the drought, hitting countries south of the Sahara. Furthermore, existing agricultural resources have been badly eroded by overgrazing—caused by the sharp rise in the number of cattle and goats—as well as by deforestation in order to provide fuel and shelter for the growing population. When rain falls, the water runs off the denuded fields, taking the topsoil with it.

None of this was helped by changes in agricultural production, with farmers encouraged to grow tea, coffee, cocoa, palm oil, and rubber for export rather than food for domestic consumption. After benefiting from high commodity prices in the early stages, producers suffered a number of blows. Heavy taxation on cash crops, plus mandatory governmental marketing, reduced the incentives to increase output; competition grew from Asian and Latin American producers; many African currencies were overvalued, which hurt exports; and in the mid-1970s, world commodity prices tumbled. Yet the cost of imported manufactures and foodstuffs remained high, and sub-Saharan Africa was badly hurt by the quadrupling of oil prices.[52]

These blows increased Africa's indebtedness in ways that were qualitatively new. Early, post-colonial borrowings were driven by the desire for modernization, as money was poured into cement works, steel plants, airports, harbours, national airlines, electrification schemes, and telephone networks. Much of it, encouraged from afar by international bodies like the World Bank, suffered from bureaucratic interference, a lack of skilled personnel, unrealistic planning, and inadequate basic facilities, and now lies half-finished or (where completed) suffers from lack of upkeep. But borrowing to pay for imported oil, or to feed half the nation's population, means that indebtedness rises without any possible return on the borrowed funds. In consequence, Africa's total debt expanded from $14 billion in 1973 to $125 billion in 1987, when its capacity to repay was dropping fast; by the mid-1980s, payments on loans consumed about half of Africa's export earnings, a proportion even greater than for Latin American debtor nations. Following repeated debt reschedulings, Western bankers—never enthusiastic to begin with—virtually abandoned private loans to Africa.[53]

As a result, Africa's economy is in a far worse condition now than at independence, apart from a few countries like Botswana and Mauritius. Perhaps the most startling illustration of its plight is the fact that 'excluding South Africa, the nations of sub-Saharan Africa with their 450 million people have a total GDP less than that of Belgium's 11 million people'; in fact, the entire continent generates roughly 1 per cent of the world GDP.[54] Africa's share of world markets has shrivelled just as East Asia's share has risen fast. Plans for modernization lie unrealized. Manufacturing still represents only 11 per cent of Africa's economic activity—scarcely up from the 9 per cent share in 1965; and only 12 per cent of the continent's exports is composed of manufactures (compared with Korea's 90 per cent). . . .

Two further characteristics worsen Africa's condition. The first is the prevalence of wars, *coups d'état*, and political instability. This is partly the legacy of the European 'carve-up' of Africa, when colonial boundaries were drawn without regard for the differing tribes and ethnic groups,[55] or even of earlier conquests by successful tribes of neighbouring lands and peoples; Ethiopia, for example, is said to contain 76 ethnic groups and 286 languages.[56] While it is generally accepted that those boundaries cannot be unscrambled, most of them are clearly artificial. In extreme cases like Somalia, the 'state' has ceased to exist. And in most other African countries, governments do not attract the loyalty of citizens (except perhaps kinsmen of the group in power), and ethnic tensions have produced innumerable civil wars—from Biafra's attempt to secede from Nigeria, to the conflict between Arab north and African south in the Sudan, to Eritrean struggles to escape from Ethiopia, to the Tutsi-Hutu struggle in Burundi, to clashes and suppressions and guerrilla campaigns from Uganda to the Western Sahara, from Angola to Mozambique.[57]

These antagonisms have often been worsened by struggles over ideology and government authority. The rulers of many new African states rapidly switched either to a personal dictatorship, or single-party rule. They also embraced a Soviet or Maoist political economy, instituting price controls, production targets, forced industrialization, the takeover of private enterprises, and other features of 'scientific socialism' that—unknown to them—were destroying the Soviet economy. Agriculture was neglected, while bureaucracy flourished. The result was the disappearance of agricultural surpluses, inattention to manufacturing for the world market, and the expansion of party and government bureaucracies, exacerbating the region's problems.

The second weakness was the wholly inadequate investment in human resources and in developing a culture of entrepreneurship, scientific inquiry, and technical prowess. According to one survey, Africa has been spending less than $1 each year on research and development per head of population, whereas the United States was spending $200 per head. Consequently, Africa's scientific population has always trailed the rest of the world (Table 3).

Despite these relative weaknesses, some observers claim to have detected signs of a turnaround. With the exception of intransigent African socialists,[58] many leaders are not attempting to institute reforms. In return for 'structural adjustments', that is, measures to encourage free enterprise, certain African societies have secured additional loans from Western nations and the World Bank. The latter organization has identified past errors (many of them urged on African governments and funded by itself), and encouraged economic reforms. Mozambique, Ghana, and Zambia have all claimed recent successes in reversing negative growth, albeit at considerable social cost.

Democratic principles are also returning to the continent: the dismantling of apartheid in South Africa, the cease-fire in Angola, the independence of Namibia, the success of Botswana's record of democracy and prosperity, the cries for reforms in Gabon, Kenya, and Zaire, the rising awareness among African intellectuals of the transformations in East Asia, may all help—so the argument goes—to change attitudes, which is the prerequisite for recovery.[59] Moreover, there are local examples of economic self-improvement, cooperative ventures to halt erosion and improve yields, and village-based schemes of improvement.[60] This is, after all, a continent of enormous agricultural and mineral resources, provided they can be sensibly exploited.

Despite such signs of promise, conditions are likely to stay poor. Population increases countered only by the growing toll of AIDS victims, the diminution of grazing lands and food supplies, the burdens of indebtedness, the decay of infra-

## Table 3: Numbers of Scientists and Engineers per Million of Population[61]

| | |
|---|---:|
| Japan | 3,548 |
| US | 2,685 |
| Europe | 1,632 |
| Latin America | 209 |
| Arab States | 202 |
| Asia (minus Japan) | 99 |
| Africa | 53 |

structures and reduced spending on health care and education, the residual strength of animist religions and traditional belief-systems, the powerful hold of corrupt bureaucracies and ethnic loyalties . . . all those tilt against the relatively few African political leaders, educators, scientists, and economists who perceive the need for changes.

What does this mean for Africa's future? As the Somalian disaster unfolds, some observers suggest that parts of the continent may be taken over and administered from the outside, rather like the post-1919 League of Nations mandates. By contrast, other experts argue that disengagement by developed countries might have the positive effect of compelling Africans to begin a *self-driven* recovery, as well as ending the misuse of aid monies.[62] Still others feel that Africa cannot live without the West, although its leaders and people will have to abandon existing habits, and development aid must be more intelligently applied.[63] Whichever view is correct, the coming decade will be critical for Africa. Even a partial recovery would give grounds for hope; on the other hand, a second decade of decline, together with a further surge in population, would result in catastrophe. . . .

## 7.

Is there any way of turning these trends around? Obviously, a society strongly influenced by fundamentalist mullahs with a dislike of 'modernization' is unlikely to join the international economy; and it does not *have* to enter the borderless world if its people believe that it would be healthier, spiritually if not economically, to remain outside. Nor ought we to expect that countries dominated by selfish, authoritarian élites bent upon enhancing their military power—developing world countries spent almost $150 billion on weapons and armies in 1988 alone—will rush to imitate Japan and Singapore.

But what about those societies that wish to improve themselves yet find that they are ham-

pered by circumstances? There are, after all, many developing countries, the vast majority of which depend upon exporting food and raw materials. With dozens of poor countries seeking desperately to sell their cane sugar or bananas or timber or coffee in the global market, prices fall and they are made more desperate.[64] Moreover, although much international aid goes to the developing world, in fact, far more money flows out of impoverished countries of Africa, Asia, and Latin America and into the richer economies of Europe, North America, and Japan—to the tune of at least $43 billion each year.[65] This outward flow of interest repayments, repatriated profits, capital flight, royalties, fees for patents and information services, makes it difficult for poorer countries to get to their feet; and even if they were able to increase their industrial output, the result might be a large rise in 'the costs of technological dependence'.[66] Like their increasing reliance upon northern suppliers for food and medical aid, this has created another dependency relationship for poorer nations.

In sum, as we move into the next century the developed economies appear to have all the trump cards in their hand—capital, technology, control of communications, surplus foodstuffs, powerful multinational companies[67]—and, if anything, their advantages are growing because technology is eroding the value of labour and materials, the chief assets of developing countries. Although nominally independent since decolonization, these countries are probably more dependent upon Europe and the United States than they were a century ago.

Ironically, three or four decades of efforts by developing countries to gain control of their own destinies—nationalizing Western companies, setting up commodity-exporting cartels, subsidizing indigenous manufacturing to achieve import substitution, campaigning for a new world order based upon redistribution of the existing imbalances of wealth—have all failed. The 'market', backed by governments of the developed economies, has proved too strong, and the struggle against it has weakened developing economies still further—except those (like Korea and Taiwan) which decided to join.

While the gap between rich and poor in today's world is disturbing, those who have argued that this gap is unjust have all too often supported heavy-handed state interventionism and a retreat from open competition, which preserved indigenous production in the short term but rendered it less efficient against those stimulated by market forces. 'Scientific socialism for Africa' may still appeal to some intellectuals,[68] but by encouraging societies to look inward it made them less well equipped to move to newer technologies in order to make goods of greater sophistication and value. And a new 'world communications order', as proposed a few years ago by UNESCO to balance the West's dominance, sounds superficially attractive but would in all likelihood become the pawn of bureaucratic and ideological interests rather than function as an objective source of news reporting.

On the other hand the advocates of free market forces often ignore the vast political difficulties which governments in developing countries would encounter in abolishing price controls, selling off national industries, and reducing food subsidies. They also forget that the spectacular commercial expansion of Japan and the East Asian NIEs was carried out by strong states which eschewed *laissez-faire*. Instead of copying either socialist or free market systems, therefore, the developing countries might imitate East Asia's 'mixed strategies' which combine official controls and private enterprise.[69]

Although the idea of a mixed strategy is intriguing, how can West or Central African countries imitate East Asia without a 'strong state' apparatus, and while having a weak tradition of co-operation between government and firms, far lower educational achievements, and a different set of cultural attitudes toward family size or international economics? With the global scene less welcoming to industrializing newcomers, how likely are they to achieve the same degree of success as the East Asian NIEs did, when they 'took off' a quarter-century ago?[70] Even if, by an economic miracle, the world's poorest 50 nations *did* adopt the Korean style of export-led growth in manufactures, would they not create the same crisis of overproduction as exists in the commodity markets today?

How many developing nations will be able to follow East Asia's growth is impossible to tell. The latest *World Development Report* optimistically forecast significant progress across the globe, provided that poorer nations adopted 'market friendly' policies and richer nations eschewed protectionism.[71] Were Taiwan and Korea to be followed by the larger states of Southeast Asia such as Malaysia and Thailand, then by South Asia and a number of Latin American countries, that would blur the North-South divide and make international economic alignments altogether more variegated. Moreover, sustained manufacturing success among developing countries *outside* East Asia might stimulate imitation elsewhere.

At the moment, however, the usual cluster of factors influencing relative economic performance—cultural attitudes, education, political stability, capacity to carry out long-term plans—suggests that while a small but growing number of countries is moving from a 'have-not' to a 'have' status, many more remain behind. The story of winners and losers in history will continue, therefore, only this time modern communications will remind us all of the growing disparity among the world's nations and regions.

# Notes

1. Discussed further in my new book, *Preparing For the Twenty-First Century* (New York: Random House, 1993).

2. For reasons of size and organization, China and India (containing around 37 per cent of the world's population) are not treated here: for coverage, see ch. 9, 'India and China', of *Preparing For the Twenty-First Century*.

3. *World Tables 1991* (Washington: World Bank, 1991), 268–9, 352–3.

4. Ibid.

5. See the World Bank publication *Trends in Developing Economies*, 1990, 299–303, for Korea.

6. For descriptions, see F. Braudel, *Civilization and Capitalism: Vol. 3, The Perspective of the World* (New York: Harper and Row, 1986), 506–11.

7. See P. Lyon, 'Emergence of the Third World', in H. Bull and A. Watson, eds, *The Expansion of International Society* (Oxford: Oxford University Press, 1983), 229 ff.; G. Barrclough, An *Introduction to Contemporary History* (New York: Penguin, 1967), ch. 6, 'The Revolt Against the West'.

8. J. Ravenhill, 'The North-South Balance of Power', *International Affairs* 66, 4 (1990): 732.

9. W.L.M. Adriaansen and J.G. Waardensburg, eds, *A Dual World Economy* (Groningen: Wolters-Noordhoff, 1989).

10. S. Fardoust and A. Dhareshwan, *Long-Term Outlook for the World Economy: Issues and Projections for the 1990s*, a World Bank report (Feb. 1990), 9, Table 3.

11. While Korea has a population of around 43 million and Taiwan about 20 million, Hong Kong possesses 5.7 million and Singapore only 2.7 million.

12. Lest this 1987 figure appear too distant, note that Korea's sixth Five-Year Plan calls for a national savings rate of 33.5 per cent in the early 1990s: see *Trends in Developing Economies*, 300. This table is taken from p. 31 (Table 10) of T. Fukuchi and M. Kagami, eds, *Perspectives on the Pacific Basin Economy: A Comparison of Asia and Latin America* (Tokyo: Asian Club Foundation, Institute of Developing Economics, 1990).

13. See especially, 'Taiwan and Korea: Two Paths to Prosperity', *The Economist*, 14 July 1990, 19–21;

also 'South Korea' (survey), *The Economist*, 18 Aug. 1990. There is a useful comparative survey in L.A. Veit, 'Time of the New Asian Tigers', *Challenge* (July-Aug. 1987): 49–55.

14. Figures taken, respectively, from J. Paxton, ed., *The Statesman's Yearbook 1990–1991* (New York: St Martin's Press, 1990); and from R.N. Gwynne, *New Horizons? Third World Industrialization in an International Framework* (New York/London: Wiley, 1990), 199.

15. The table on p. 4 (Table 1) of Fukuchi and Kagami shows the different rates of growth, and of export's share of total GDP, of the Asian Pacific nations compared with those of Latin America. See also H. Hughes, 'Catching Up: The Asian Newly Industrializing Economies in the 1990s', *Asian Development Review* 7, 2 (1989): 132 (and Table 3).

16. 'The Yen Block' (Survey), *The Economist*, 15 July 1989; 'Japan Builds A New Power Base', *Business Week*, 20 Mar. 1989, 18–25.

17. 'Development Brief', *The Economist*, 16 May 1990, 81, for the first two columns; the GNP per capita comes from *World Development Report, 1990*, 178–9.

18. See the detailed forecasts in 'Asia 2010: The Power of People', *Far Eastern Economist Review*, 17 May 1990, 27–58. On industrial retooling, see pp. 8–9 of 'South Korea' (Survey), *The Economist*, 18 Aug. 1990.

19. N. Sadik, ed., *Population: The UNFPA Experience* (New York: New York University Press, 1984), ch. 4, 'Latin America and the Caribbean', 51–2.

20. A.F. Lowenthal, 'Rediscovering Latin America', *Foreign Affairs* 69, 4 (Fall 1990): 34.

21. Figure from 'Latin America's Hope', *The Economist*, 9 Dec. 1989, 14.

22. As mentioned earlier, Japan and its East Asian emulators also sought to protect fledgling domestic industries, but that was in order to create a strong base from which to mount an export offensive—not to establish an economic bastion within which their industries would be content to remain.

23. For details, see the various national entries in *The Statesman's Yearbook 1990–91*; and *The Economist World Atlas and Almanac* (Englewood Cliffs, NJ:

Prentice-Hall, 1989), 131–57. R.N. Gwynne's *New Horizons?* has useful comments on Latin America's 'inward-oriented industrialization' (ch. 11), which he then contrasts with East Asia's 'outward orientation' (ch. 12).

24. World Resources Institute, *World Resources 1990–91* (Oxford: Oxford University Press, 1990), 39.

25. In 1989, the net transfer of capital leaving Latin America was around $25 billion.

26. For the above, see pp. 33–48 of *World Resources 1990–91*: 'Latin America At a Crossroads'; B.J. McCormick, *The World Economy: Patterns of Growth and Change* (Oxford: Oxford University Press, 1988), ch. 13; 'Latin American debt: The banks' great escape', *The Economist*, 11 Feb. 1989, 73–4.

27. For educational details, see *The Statesman's Yearbook 1990–91*, 95, 236; for literacy rates, see especially those of Uruguay, Costa Rica, Argentina, and Venezuela in the table 'Development Brief', *The Economist*, 26 May 1990, 81.

28. *The Statesman's Yearbook, 1990–91*, 584, 605.

29. T. Kamm, 'Latin America Edges Toward Free Trade', *Wall Street Journal*, 30 Nov. 1990, A10.

30. C. Farnsworth, 'Latin American Economies Given Brighter Assessments', *New York Times*, 30 Oct. 1990; 'Latin America's New Start', *The Economist*, 9 June 1990, 11; N.C. Nash, 'A Breath of Fresh Economic Air Brings Change to Latin America', *New York Times*, 13 Nov. 1991, A1, D5.

31. 'Latin America's Hope', *The Economist*, 9 Dec. 1989, 15; Nash, 'A Breath of Fresh Economic Air'.

32. J. Brooke, 'Debt and Democracy', *New York Times*, 5 Dec. 1990, A16; P. Truell, 'As the U.S. Slumps, Latin America Suffers', *Wall Street Journal*, 19 Nov. 1990, 1.

33. This is the subdivision preferred by *The Economist World Atlas and Almanac*, 256–71, which discusses the North African states (except Egypt) in a later section, under 'Africa'.

34. 'The Arab World' (survey), *The Economist*, 12 May 1990.

35. See 'Religions', p. 21 of the *Hammond Comparative World Atlas* (New York: Hammond, 1993).

36. The few oil-producing countries in Africa, such as Gabon and Nigeria, still have relatively low per capita GNPs compared with the Arab Gulf states.

37. G. Brooks and T. Horwitz, 'Shaken Sheiks', *Wall Street Journal*, 28 Dec. 1990, A1, A4.

38. 'The Arab World', *The Economist*, 12.

39. In 1985, adult female literacy in the Yemen Arab Republic was a mere 3 per cent, in Saudi Arabia 12 per cent, in Iran 39 per cent. On the other hand, many women from the middle and upper-middle classes in Muslim countries are educated, which suggests that poverty, as much as culture, plays a role.

40. M.A. Heller, 'The Middle East: Out of Step with History', *Foreign Affairs* 69, 1 (1989–1990): 153–71.

41. D.E. Duncan, 'Africa: The Long Good-bye', *Atlantic Monthly* (July 1990): 20.

42. J.A. Marcum, 'Africa: A Continent Adrift', *Foreign Affairs* 68, 1 (1988–1989): 177. See also the penetrating article by K.R. Richburg, 'Why Is Black Africa Overwhelmed While East Asia Overcomes?', *International Herald Tribune*, 14 July 1992, 1, 6.

43. C.H. Farnsworth, 'Report by World Bank Sees Poverty Lessening by 2000 Except in Africa', *New York Times*, 16 July 1990, A3; Marcum, 'Africa: A Continent Adrift'; Duncan, 'Africa: The Long Good-bye'; and 'The bleak continent', *The Economist*, 9 Dec. 1989, 80–1.

44. B. Fischer, 'Developing Countries in the Process of Economic Globalisation', *Intereconomics* (Mar./Apr. 1990): 55.

45. J.S. Whitaker, *How Can Africa Survive?* (Washington: Council on Foreign Relations Press, 1988).

46. As will be clear from the text, this discussion excludes the Republic of South Africa.

47. T.J. Goliber, 'Africa's Expanding Population: Old Problems, New Policies', *Population Bulletin* 44, 3 (Nov. 1989): 4–49, an outstandingly good article.

48. *World Resources 1990–91*, 254.

49. Ibid., 254 (overall population growth to 2025), and 258 (infant mortality). L.K. Altman, 'W.H.O. Says 40 Million Will Be Infected With AIDS by 2000', *New York Times*, 18 June 1991, C3 (for percentage of GNP devoted to health care).

50. Altman, 'W.H.O. Says 40 Million Will Be Infected With AIDS by 2000'; and for further figures, see Kennedy, *Preparing For the Twenty-First Century*, ch. 3.

51. See Whitaker, *How Can Africa Survive?*, esp. ch. 4, 'The Blessings of Children', for a fuller analysis; and J.C. Caldwell and P. Caldwell, 'High Fertility in Sub-Saharan Africa', *Scientific American* (May 1990): 118–25.

52. 'The bleak continent', *The Economist*; Whitaker, *How Can Africa Survive?*, chs 1 and 2; Goliber, 'Africa's Expanding Population', 12–13.

53. Whitaker, *How Can Africa Survive?*; Duncan, 'Africa: The Long Good-bye'.

54. 'Fruits of Containment' (op-ed), *Wall Street Journal*, 18 Dec. 1990, A14, for the Africa-Belgium comparison; H. McRae, 'Visions of tomorrow's world', *The Independent* (London), 26 Nov. 1991, for Africa's share of world GDP.

55. In this regard, East Asian nations like Taiwan and Korea, possessing coherent indigenous populations, are once again more favourably situated.

56. *The Economist World Atlas and Almanac* (Englewood Cliffs, NJ: Prentice-Hall, 1989), 293.

57. Apart from the country by country comments in *The Economist World Atlas and Almanac*, see also K. Ingham, *Politics in Modern Africa: The Uneven Tribal Dimension* (London: Routledge, 1990); 'Africa's Internal Wars of the 1980s—Contours and Prospects', United States Institute of Peace, *In Brief* 18 (May 1990).

58. P. Lewis, 'Nyere and Tanzania: No Regrets at Socialism', *New York Times*, 24 Oct. 1990.

59. 'Wind of change, but a different one', *The Economist*, 14 July 1990, 44. See also the encouraging noises made—on a country by country basis—in the World Bank's own *Trends in Developing Economies*, 1990, as well as in its 1989 publication *Sub-Saharan Africa: From Crisis to Sustainable Growth* (summarized in 'The bleak continent', *The Economist*, 80–1).

60. See especially P. Pradervand, *Listening to Africa: Developing Africa from the Grassroots* (New York: Greenwood, 1989); B. Schneider, *The Barefoot Revolution* (London: I.T. Publications, 1988); K. McAfee, 'Why The Third World Goes Hungry', *Commonweal*, 15 June 1990, 384–5.

61. T.R. Odhiambo, 'Human resources development: problems and prospects in developing countries', *Impact of Science on Society* 155 (1989): 214.

62. See Edward Sheehan's article 'In the Heart of Somalia', *The New York Review*, 14 Jan. 1993. See also Duncan, 'Africa: The Long Good-bye', 24; G. Hancock, *Lords of Poverty: The Power, Prestige, and Corruption of the International Aid* (Boston: Atlantic Monthly Press, 1989); G.B.N. Ayittey, 'No More Aid for Africa', *Wall Street Journal*, 18 Oct. 1991 (op-ed), A14.

63. Whitaker, *How Can Africa Survive?*, 231.

64. D. Pirages, *Global Technopolitics: The International Politics of Technology and Resources* (New York: Brooks-Cole, 1989), 152.

65. McAfee, 'Why the Third World goes Hungry', 380.

66. See P.K. Ghosh, ed., *Technology Policy and Development: A Third World Perspective* (New York: Greenwood, 1984), 109.

67. C.J. Dixon et al., eds, *Multinational Corporations and the Third World* (London: Croom Helm, 1986).

68. For a good example, B. Onimode, *A Political Economy of the African Crisis* (Atlantic Highlands, NJ: Humanities Press International, 1988), esp. 310 ff.

69. M. Clash, 'Development Policy: Technology Assessment and the New Technologies', *Futures* (Nov. 1990): 916.

70. L. Cuyvers and D. Van den Buicke, 'Some Reflections on the "Outward-oriented" Development Strategy of the Far Eastern Newly Industrialising Countries', esp. 196–7, in Adriaansen and Waardensburg, eds, *A Dual World Economy*.

71. *World Development Report 1991: The Challenge of Development*, a World Bank report (New York: Oxford University Press, 1991). See also the World Bank's *Global Economic Prospects and the Developing Countries* (1991).

# Part X

# Canadian Politics

## Introduction

Andrew Heard

It is ironic that while Canada was ranked number one in the world in 1997 for human development and freedom by a United Nations agency, it should also be a country that has faced the threat of disintegration for almost two decades.[1] Canada's success as a nation has been based on a combination of economic prosperity and political stability, but that outward appearance of stability belies enormous political strains that have been at work for decades. While there have always been deep divisions in Canadian society, with fierce competition for political power, these strains have been overcome by political leaders who practised brokerage politics and found a middle ground between the contending interests. In recent decades, however, there has been an erosion in the faith that Canadians have in their politicians and political institutions to resolve, or at least defuse, these conflicts. As a consequence, there are pressures to reform Canada's political institutions and process. One can be optimistic and hope that these pressures will lead to lasting changes that leave Canadians better equipped to face the problems of the next century. However, there are many potential risks as well. It is vital, therefore, that we appreciate some of the main divisions and strains facing the Canadian political system.

### Contemporary Canadian Political Conflicts

Politics may be defined as the competition over who gets what, when, and how.[2] Whenever there are specific goods or benefits that can be shared, there is likely to be some rivalry over their distribution; when those goods or benefits are in short supply, the contest for them will become fiercer. The type and nature of political contests vary tremendously. Some are the stuff of normal political disputes, but others can threaten the very existence of the state. Sometimes the struggle occurs between very specific private interests, such as the battles between Air Canada and Canadian Airlines over the future of the airline industry, or it may involve more volatile public issues, such as gun control or euthanasia. While these sorts of political feuds may flare into sharp battles, they are in a sense everyday politics because all involved accept that the disputes will be settled according to the normal political processes. What matters most in the end is the degree to which people agree on the rules and processes through which their disagreements are to be settled. The greatest danger arises when the basic 'rules of the game' are themselves challenged or rejected.

Significant problems emerge when the conflicts pit large blocks of the population against each other, such as the English against the French or Ontario against the prairie provinces. At other times, one sees larger groups in a local conflict, such as the dispute between Aboriginal and non-Native fishermen in British Columbia over who will be allowed to catch how many salmon. The dangers mount when a long-lasting conflict over fundamental issues goes unresolved. It does not particularly matter, for example, if western lawyers complain that the federal government awards the lion's share of Queen's Counsel titles to Ontario lawyers. However, it very much matters if a majority of Québécois or westerners complain bitterly that Canadian economic policy has for decades favoured industry in Ontario at a substantial cost to businesses and consumers in their regions. But even these larger political conflicts can be resolved, or at least contained, if there is general agreement on the institutions and process through which these arguments should be settled.

Much greater dangers, however, lie in the range of contemporary challenges to the basic institutions and rules of the Canadian political system. At the same time that we argue over the usual political issues of who gets what, Canadians have also been engaged in a deeply divisive debate for decades over, to use Lasswell's terms, 'who' is to decide 'about what', 'for whom', and 'how'. Although the defeat of the 1992 referendum on the Charlottetown Accord temporarily ended formal constitutional wrangling, it also exposed just how split Canadians are about the division of powers between the provinces and the national government, the character of the Canadian constitution, and the degree to which equality or uniformity among citizens' rights and provincial powers should be maintained. The difficulty of reaching a consensus on new constitutional rules was evident in the turbulent debates that surrounded the Meech Lake Accord of 1987, its related negotiations that lasted until 1990, and finally the negotiation and referendum on the Charlottetown Accord.[3]

Perhaps the biggest challenge to the orderly resolution of political disputes in Canada lies in deeply opposed views as to how, or even if, Quebec could become an independent country. On the one side, the Parti Québécois believes that a majority vote in a referendum would be sufficient for Quebec to declare itself a sovereign state and enter the world stage. However, many Canadians believe that a simple majority would not be sufficient for such a momentous decision. They argue that the Quebec government and legislature lack any legal authority to declare independence unilaterally, whether backed by a popular referendum or not. The federal government has referred these questions to the Supreme Court of Canada, but the current Quebec provincial government refuses to accept that this court can legitimately set the rules for the people of Quebec. More troubling still is a debate over whether the territory of the province of Quebec could be partitioned in the event of a declaration of independence, so that those areas of the province where a majority wishes to stay within Canada would be carved out of a sovereign Quebec. This scenario raises the alarming prospect of a possible armed confrontation in order to give effect to any partition. Should a future referendum in Quebec be carried in favour of separation, there is the potential for serious political upheaval, and even violence, because the participants do not agree on what rules or processes should be followed to resolve this issue.

## Canadian Political Development

Several profound reforms have shaped Canada since Confederation. The most important has been Canada's acquisition of independence from Great Britain. Contrary to popular belief, Canada did not actually gain independence in 1867; only a new, larger, self-governing colony was created within the British Empire. Independence was only gained slowly, and often informally, through developments in the twentieth century. In 1923 Canada negotiated its first international treaty without British involvement. Only with the passage by the British Parliament of the Statute of Westminster in 1931, Canadian legislatures received the legal power to pass laws that conflicted with British legislation.[4] Canadian governments secured the right to choose the Canadian Governor-General in 1930, but it was only in 1952 that we started choosing Canadians instead of Britons for this position. The British Parliament still retained the final legal control over amendments to the Canadian constitution until 1982, when the governments of all provinces except Quebec agreed with the federal government on an amending formula. The growth of Canada's independence has profoundly, and irrevocably, changed both the substance and the process of Canadian politics.[5]

Canada may see some aspects of its independence compromised through commitments made to other countries, such as the important treaties promoting free trade signed with the United States in 1988, and again with the United States and Mexico in 1992. A number of Canadians are concerned that these agreements not only hurt Canadian industry, but also result in a loss of independence in the ability to set our own economic and social policies. Only time will reveal the full effects of these free trade agreements. In the meantime, considerable debate continues among politicians, union leaders, and various business groups over the desirability, and inevitability, of pursuing closer economic integration with other countries, especially the United States.

A crucial and lasting change to Canada's political system took place with the Charter of Rights and Freedoms that came into force in 1982.[6] Prior to the Charter, the courts were limited to interpreting the meaning of legal rules and to acting as constitutional referees who declared which level of government had jurisdiction over particular issues. The Charter, however, granted the courts the power to decide on the acceptability of laws passed by the legislatures or actions by government officials. Judges now are able to decide whether particular government policies violate the range of rights enshrined in the Charter, such as the freedom of expression or the right to liberty. Judges first have to define what a right means and then decide whether a violation falls within acceptable limits on that right. A tremendous range of criminal, social, and other policies now frequently come under judicial scrutiny because of the Charter. Judges have had to decide whether the Charter protects Canadians from such policies as mandatory retirement, restricted access to abortions, limitations on the right to strike, Sunday closing laws, and censorship. The judiciary has become a very important political actor, vetoing legislation or setting guidelines for the implementation of fundamental political and social policies.

The increasingly powerful role the courts play in developing social policies has arisen in large measure because of the dissatisfaction that many Canadians have felt

towards their politicians and political institutions. This unease is due to several perceived weaknesses. As a group, politicians have lost the trust of many people because
of conflicts of interest and political patronage in awarding jobs and contracts, which
have sometimes degenerated into blatant corruption. This loss of trust is seen in opinion polls that reveal the low esteem in which Canadians hold their politicians; for
example, one poll found that about 60 per cent of Canadians would prefer judges,
rather than politicians, to define their rights. As a consequence, there is a preference
for judges to make important political decisions.[7]

The Charter of Rights has also had a more diffuse, but still important, impact on
the Canadian political system by structuring many debates into the language of
rights. Disputes in which groups assert that they are *entitled* to their desired policy
benefits offer fewer prospects of resolution in the normal political process than those
in which the groups begin their campaign on the basis that they need to convince
others of the wisdom and desirability of their demands; disputes between competing
claims to entitlement may not readily lend themselves to compromise and negotiation. As a result, many disputes are taken to the courts rather than left to the elected
politicians, which can make some problems more difficult to resolve. The positive
benefits of this may be seen in groups that felt marginalized and powerless in dealing
with the political process, but now have an opportunity to put their claims to the
judiciary for authoritative resolution.[8] In one of the selections included here, Jeffrey
Simpson provides some general reflections on the effects of this 'rights talk' on
Canadian politics.

## Reforming Canada's Political Institutions

Much of the impetus to require a referendum to ratify the Charlottetown Accord in
1992 came from this widespread belief that the politicians could not be trusted to
reflect the real interests of their electorate. The 1992 referendum marked the first time
a national vote has been held on constitutional revisions negotiated by the first ministers. With this precedent, it will be difficult for another comprehensive constitutional package to be achieved without a referendum. Indeed, British Columbia and
Alberta have legislation requiring that proposed constitutional amendments be
approved by the electorate before their legislatures can sanction them.[9]

There is also increasing concern that representatives in Parliament and provincial
legislatures are not truly representative of the Canadian population, since the overwhelming majority of elected politicians are white males and the population is not.[10]
Only 21 per cent of the members elected to the House of Commons in 1997 were
women, even though there are slightly more women than men in Canada.[11] While this
underrepresentation has long been thought of as undesirable, only recently have parties taken active steps to redress the problem. Parties have primarily relied on searching out and encouraging suitable female candidates, although some parties have set
an 'ideal' quota for the number of women; for example, the Liberal Party of Canada
tries to ensure that 25 per cent of its candidates are women, while the NDP has a goal
of an equal number of male and female candidates. Another solution to the problem

of representation was offered by the Royal Commission on Electoral Reform, which recommended that the underrepresentation of Aboriginals be dealt with by assigning additional, specific seats for Aboriginal MPs in provinces with large Native populations.[12] The Nunavut Transition Commission even proposed a formal requirement that half the seats be reserved for women in the legislature that will be created for the new territory. However, this measure was voted down in a referendum in 1997. Furthermore, a proposal for the reform of the Northwest Territories' constitution went so far as to argue for a separate Aboriginal Peoples' Assembly as part of the legislature.[13] While there is general agreement that better participation of all groups in Canadian society should be promoted, there is considerable debate over resorting to quotas or reserved seats. Some believe that such measures undermine the notion that legislators, regardless of gender or ethnic origin, can and should act on behalf of all their constituents rather than on behalf of one social group.[14]

There is increasing concern that rigid party discipline over MPs also stifles their fundamental role of speaking and acting on behalf of their constituents' interests. Party discipline has the benefit of ensuring efficiency in the legislatures and providing Canadians with clear choices at election time.[15] But a 1992 poll revealed that only 9 per cent of Canadians have quite a lot or a great deal of faith in political parties.[16]

## Reforming Canadian Federalism

Important political problems facing Canada arise from its federal structure.[17] Since Confederation, there have been continuous struggles between the national and provincial governments over which level of government should have the power to do what. This is a dispute over how *centralized* the country should be. When Canada was created in 1867, the constitution provided for a powerful central government and created provinces with limited powers related to local matters. The provinces were in many ways subordinated to Ottawa, as well, through the powers of reservation and disallowance. A lieutenant-governor could reserve any bill passed by a provincial legislature in order for the national government to decide whether it should be approved; 70 bills have been reserved since 1867 and only 14 of those have been approved. In addition, the national government could simply 'disallow' (declare void) provincial legislation; 112 provincial laws have been disallowed by the government in Ottawa. However, the powers of both reservation and disallowance have been effectively eliminated through informal constitutional rules called conventions.[18] In addition, certain judicial decisions have given very generous interpretations of the powers listed as provincial jurisdictions, especially the provincial power to legislate on 'property and civil rights'. By the same token, the courts have narrowed the scope of such powers listed for the federal government as the jurisdiction over 'trade and commerce', which has been limited to apply only to interprovincial and international trade. As a result, the powers and status of the provinces have increased over time. Nevertheless, some provincial leaders continue to demand even more powers.

The difficulty with federalism is that it creates some problems in the very way it solves others. A country is divided into provinces or states because there are important differences among the regions of a country. A federal system ensures that some policies can vary across the country and reflect the different values of the regions. However, the formal partitioning of the country also permanently divides a nation into segments, and those divisions become a source of friction and conflict as one or more provinces feel they are losing out in particular issues to other provinces.[19]

Thus, the federal nature of Canada provides continuing political controversies as the provinces dispute with each other and the federal government. These conflicts become quite destabilizing when they centre on the basic division of powers between the two levels of government. When time, energy, and goodwill are consumed in arguments over who should have jurisdiction over a particular policy, there is much less likelihood that those issues will be dealt with substantively or successfully.

The federal system in Canada has also created problems because some parts of the country are much poorer than others. A system of equalization payments and other transfer payments allows the federal government to spread the tax money raised in the more prosperous provinces to the others.[20] In some provinces, this money is essential to the government's ability to provide essential services to its population; in Prince Edward Island, for example, federal money can account for up to half of the provincial budget.

The system of transfer payments leads to difficulties in times of economic recession, as there is less money to go around. In the early 1990s the federal government tried to deal with its own deficit problems by unilaterally cutting back the amount of money transferred to the provinces. This reduction led to severe financial difficulties in some provinces and an unsuccessful court challenge to the federal government's action.[21] In many ways the success of Canadian federalism depends on the goodwill of the federal government and of the richer provinces to give money to the less fortunate provinces, but this will is eroded by prolonged economic recession.

## The Quebec and Aboriginal Challenges

The potential for damaging conflict found in the federal system is most clearly seen with the calls in Quebec for greater powers, or even separation from the rest of Canada. Since the 1960s, a growing wave of popular sentiment among the Francophone majority in Quebec has called for more complete control over their own affairs.[22] At first this nationalism centred on cultural issues, to preserve the French culture that was felt to be under threat of eventual extinction. But the nationalist movement in Quebec has broadened its scope and the claims now extend to exclusive provincial control over many aspects of the economy.[23]

One must bear in mind, however, that the nationalist movement in Quebec takes many forms. There are those, in the Quebec Liberal Party, who support more provincial powers within the existing federal system. Others have argued for sovereignty-association, which would give Quebec control over most matters while retaining formal links with the rest of Canada in a new form of association that would replace federalism. Finally, a growing number of Québécois want complete independence from Canada.

The nationalist demands have come to a head three times in votes on the future of Quebec. In 1980 a referendum in Quebec defeated the Parti Québécois government's proposal for sovereignty-association. Then, in 1992, another referendum in Quebec coincided with the national referendum on the Charlottetown Accord, a whole constitutional package that would have seen a number of new powers being given to the provinces within the existing federal framework. This proposal was voted down in Quebec, as it was in most other provinces. In 1995, the people of Quebec very narrowly rejected the Parti Québécois government's referendum proposal to lead Quebec to independence.

The defeat of these initiatives has not ended the challenges that Quebec nationalism poses to Canadian federalism. The Parti Québécois remains strong in Quebec provincial politics and the Bloc Québécois, another separatist party, has become a substantial force in Quebec's participation in national politics. The Parti Québécois is committed to holding referenda until the goal of independence is achieved. In short, there is still the very real possibility that Quebec will become independent and the rest of Canada will be split into two distant sections.

A similar political energy is surfacing in the Aboriginal population. Most First Nations leaders favour a new level of government in which the Native communities have the power to govern their own affairs, much like the provinces. As with Quebec, however, a small but growing force of separatism exists among Aboriginal politicians. Many Aboriginals simply do not recognize the legitimacy of the Canadian state and argue that their people have never willingly been a part of Canada. To them, self-government means the recognition of their status as sovereign nations. The explosive potential of these beliefs is not widely appreciated but is very present. The debate over Quebec separation has raised much annoyance among Aboriginal leaders, who argue firmly that the right to self-determination of the Québécois does not mean that the Aboriginals who live in Quebec must leave Canada if a majority of the general population votes for independence. Mary Ellen Turpel examines these issues in one of the readings here, arguing that the Aboriginal peoples have just as legitimate a right to self-determination as the Québécois, and that they must decide their future for themselves.

The treatment of Canada's Aboriginal peoples only gained substantial public attention in the 1980s. Native political groups had been banned for many decades and the pursuit of self-government was actively suppressed. However, many Canadians in the larger society have become far more conscious of the abysmal conditions of many First Nations communities, and there is now widespread support for some form of self-government.[24] The quest for self-government almost bore fruit with the inclusion of a commitment to Aboriginal self-government in the Charlottetown Accord constitutional package. This reform would have created a brand new order of government in the constitution. While the package was voted down, polls have shown that about 60 per cent of the Canadian public supported the self-government provisions.[25] Although this initiative has stalled for the moment, Aboriginal leaders continue to strive for self-government, and its attainment could radically alter the structure of Canadian government.

## Conclusion

Politics in Canada are played out at many levels. The more usual stuff of politics is seen in the countless disputes that arise over relatively narrow issues and benefits. Other more important political debates continue because Canadians disagree profoundly over the basic structures and institutions that should be used as forums to resolve normal political issues. Too many Canadians believe that their politicians and institutions are not properly serving their communities. There are increasingly serious conflicts over the rules of the game, as more groups and individuals voice their feelings that the political system as a whole has failed to provide them with their perceived needs. As students of political science, we must be aware of the danger to a country when the consensus needed to keep it together begins to erode.

❦

Mary Ellen Turpel, in 'Does the Road to Quebec Sovereignty Run through Aboriginal Territory?', argues that separatist aspiration in Quebec cannot be adequately resolved without coming to terms with Aboriginal self-determination. She points out that any claims to sovereignty by the Québécois are just as effectively put by the First Nations peoples in Quebec. Quebec separatists have an opportunity, in Turpel's opinion, to negotiate with the province's Aboriginal population and form common alliances based on their shared interest in the self-determination of their own groups.

Jeffrey Simpson's article, 'Rights Talk', explores the effect that the Charter of Rights has had on political debates and process in Canada. Several ideas are proposed, some of which relate to the erosion of the public's trust in the political élite to respond effectively to their demands. One of the main consequences of the Charter has been, in Simpson's view, the elevation of what had been matters of discussion and compromise to issues of rights to which one is 'entitled'. This change can lead to a greater difficulty in resolving sensitive political conflicts.

## Notes

1. United Nations Development Program, 'Human Development Report, 1997', http://www.undp.org/undp/hdro/97.htm, 20 Nov. 1997.
2. See Harold Lasswell, *Politics: Who Gets What, When and How?* (New York: McGraw-Hill, 1936.
3. For an account of this period, see Patrick J. Monahan, *Meech Lake: The Inside Story* (Toronto: University of Toronto Press, 1991).
4. For a review of the development of Canadian independence, see Peter W. Hogg, *Constitutional Law of Canada*, 3rd edn (Toronto: Carswell, 1992), ch. 3.
5. See R.I. Cheffins and P.A. Johnson, *The Revised Constitution of Canada* (Toronto: McGraw-Hill Ryerson, 1986).
6. See Ian Greene, *The Charter of Rights* (Toronto: Lorimer, 1989); Rainer Knopff and F.L. Morton, *Charter Politics* (Scarborough, Ont.: Nelson, 1992); Michael Mandel, *The Charter*

*of Rights and the Legalization of Politics in Canada*, 2nd edn (Toronto: Wall and Thompson, 1993); F.L. Morton, 'The Political Impact of the Charter of Rights and Freedoms', *Canadian Journal of Political Science* 20 (1987): 31–55.

7.  Peter H. Russell, 'Canada's Charter of Rights and Freedoms: A Political Report', *Public Law* (1988): 398.

8.  Alan C. Cairns, *Reconfigurations: Canadian Citizenship and Constitutional Change*, ed. Douglas E. Williams (Toronto: McClelland & Stewart, 1995).

9.  Quebec had specific legislation that required a referendum on constitutional issues in 1992.

10. A classic study of the nature of representation is Anthony Birch, *Representation* (New York: Praeger, 1972). For two collections on underrepresentation in Canada, see Kathy Megyery, ed., *Ethno-Cultural Groups and Visible Minorities in Canadian Politics: The Question of Access* (Toronto: Dundurn, 1991); Jane Arscott and Linda Trimble, eds, *In the Presence of Women: Representation in Canadian Governments* (Toronto: Harcourt Brace, 1997).

11. *Globe and Mail*, 26 Jan. 1993, A11.

12. Royal Commission on Electoral Reform and Party Financing, *Reforming Electoral Democracy: Final Report*, vol. 2 (Ottawa: Supply and Services, 1991), 139–50.

13. The Constitutional Working Group, 'Partners in a New Beginning', http://www.ssimicro.com/~xpsognwt/Net/two.html, 20 Nov. 1997.

14. See Birch, *Representation*, 106–23. For a contemporary discussion that proposes some new insights, see Jill Vickers, 'Towards a Feminist Understanding of Representation', in Arscott and Trimble, eds, *In the Presence of Women*, 20–46.

15. See C.E.S. Franks, *The Parliament of Canada* (Toronto: University of Toronto Press, 1987), ch. 3; Peter Aucoin, ed., *Party Government and Regional Representation in Canada* (Toronto: University of Toronto Press, 1985).

16. *Halifax Chronicle Herald*, 17 Mar. 1992, A12.

17. For general discussions of various issues relating to federalism in Canada, see David V.J. Bell, *The Roots of Disunity* (Toronto: Oxford University Press, 1992); François Rocher and Miriam Smith, eds, *New Trends in Canadian Federalism* (Peterborough, Ont.: Broadview Press, 1995); P. Shugarman and Reg Whitaker, eds, *Federalism and Political Community: Essays in Honour of Donald Smiley* (Peterborough, Ont.: Broadview Press, 1989); D.V. Smiley, *The Federal Condition in Canada* (Toronto: McGraw-Hill Ryerson, 1987); Martin Westmacott and Hugh Mellon, eds, *Challenges to Canadian Federalism* (Scarborough, Ont.: Prentice-Hall, 1998).

18. See Andrew D. Heard, *Constitutional Conventions: The Marriage of Law and Politics* (Toronto: Oxford University Press, 1991), 102–5.

19. For some classic pieces on the nature of federalism and prerequisites for its success, see William S. Livingstone, *Federalism and Constitutional Change* (Oxford: Oxford University Press, 1956); K.C. Wheare, *Federal Government*, 4th edn (Oxford: Oxford University Press, 1963).

20. The web of financial relations between the federal and provincial levels of government is described as 'fiscal federalism'. For a discussion of this topic, see Gérald Bernier and David Irwin, 'Fiscal Federalism: The Politics of Intergovernmental Transfers', in Rocher and Smith, eds, *New Trends in Canadian Federalism*, 270–87.

21. *Re Canada Assistance Plan*, [1991] 2 S.C.R. 525.

22. See William D. Coleman, *The Independence Movement in Quebec* (Toronto: University of Toronto Press, 1984); Kenneth McRoberts, *Quebec: Social Change and Political Crisis* (Toronto: McClelland & Stewart, 1988).

23. See Pierre Fournier, *A Meech Lake Post-Mortem: Is Quebec Sovereignty Inevitable?* (Montreal and Kingston: McGill-Queen's University Press, 1991).

24. For various views on Aboriginal self-government, see Michael Asch, *Home and Native Land: Aboriginal Rights and the Canadian Constitution* (Toronto: Methuen, 1984); Leroy Little Bear, Menno Boldt, J. Anthony Long, eds, *Pathways to Self-Determination* (Toronto: University of Toronto Press, 1984); Frank Cassidy, ed., *Aboriginal Self-Determination* (Montreal: Institute for Research on Public Policy, 1991); Royal Commission on Aboriginal Peoples, *Aboriginal Self-Government: Legal and Constitutional Issues* (Ottawa: Supply and Services Canada, 1995).

25. *Globe and Mail*, 1 Dec. 1992, A7.

## Study Questions for the Readings

1. What does Mary Ellen Turpel mean when she says that Aboriginal peoples and the Québécois have the right to self-determination? Can a majority of one group decide to leave or stay in Canada and make all the others of that group do the same? How would you resolve the potential for conflict between the right to self-determination of the First Nations in Quebec and that of the general population in that province?

2. Who should be able to decide whether Quebec can become an independent country, and how much of the existing province's territory and population must leave?

3. As Jeffrey Simpson points out, many Canadians turn to the courts to press their claims. What can they find in the judicial enforcement of the Charter of Rights that they believe elected politicians are unable to provide? What is not working in the legislatures so that people feel a need to turn to the courts?

4. What are the long-term consequences for a political system where competing claims are phrased as 'rights' to which people are 'entitled'? Are some types of disputes suited to rights claims, while others are not?

# Does the Road to Quebec Sovereignty Run through Aboriginal Territory?

Mary Ellen Turpel

The problem here is a denial of the past, or a narrowness of vision that sees the arrival and then spread of immigrants as the very purpose of history.
—Hugh Brody[1]

Québec's resources are permanent; we do not owe them to a political system, or to specific circumstances. They are a gift of nature, which has favoured us more than others in this respect by allowing us to play a more important economic role, thanks to our resources . . .
—Government of Quebec[2]

It is important to respect the aspirations of Québécois to self-determination, if they act in accordance with international law.

At the same time, it is difficult to address in a totally dispassionate way the spectre of 'Quebec secession'. Every time I begin to write about the international legal and Canadian constitutional dimensions of Quebec separation or accession to full sovereignty from the perspective of Aboriginal peoples'[3] status, one area of my so-called professional and personal 'expertise' as an Aboriginal woman and law professor, I am confronted with my concern for the status and rights of those most marginalized in this discussion—the Aboriginal peoples in Quebec.

The claim by Québécois for full sovereignty, as it has been conceived by many secessionists,[4] appears to rest on the erasure of the political status of Aboriginal peoples and the denial of their most fundamental rights to self-determination. These are two most critical points, seemingly resisted by the main political parties in Quebec, and not taken seriously enough outside Quebec by Canadian politicians, intellectuals, or the academic community. I am cautious with terminology here because just writing the expression 'Quebec secession' poses a problem—it conjures up an image of a single territory and a homogeneous people setting up a new state. The point of this essay is to demonstrate that it is not this simple.

How can it be presumed that there can be an accession to sovereign status for Quebec without considering the pivotal matter of the status and rights of the Aboriginal peoples in this scenario? What does it mean to 'consider' the status and rights of Aboriginal peoples in a secessionist scenario? It is not a perfunctory matter, or an administrative decision considering how best to transfer a head of jurisdiction (Indians and lands reserved for the Indians)[5] from the federal authority to a newly independent Quebec state. It is more complex than this, in both a legal and political sense.[6] The political success of the secessionist movement will ultimately be judged on its democratic process, its respect for fundamental human rights and, in the end, its political legitimacy in the eyes of the international community. I believe that the relations with Aboriginal peoples could prove to be the key to assessing that legitimacy and could well influence the international recognition and acceptance of any new Quebec state.

Who are the Aboriginal peoples in Quebec? Most people know something about the Crees in northern Quebec because of their current opposition to the Great Whale hydroelectric project in the James Bay territory, or perhaps because of the James Bay Northern Quebec Agreement.[7] However, it is not only the Crees whose homeland is

From Daniel Drache and Roberto Perin, eds, *Negotiating with a Sovereign Québec* (Toronto: James Lorimer & Company, 1992), 93–106.

captured in some sense by the provincial boundaries of Quebec. There are also Inuit, Naskapi, Mikmaq, Maliseet, Mohawk, Montagnais, Abenaki, Algonquin, Atikawekw, and Huron whose homelands are at least partially within the geographical boundaries of the province of Quebec. I say 'partially' because, using the Mikmaq as a case in point, the Mikmaq of Gaspé comprise one of the seven districts of the Mikmaq nation, Mikmakik, which extends into Nova Scotia, New Brunswick, Newfoundland, and Prince Edward Island. A District Chief from this region sits on the Mikmaq Grand Council, the traditional governing body of the Mikmaq people situated in Cape Breton, Nova Scotia. The administrative boundary of the province of Quebec for Mikmaqs in Gaspé is an arbitrary boundary unrelated to their identity, both territorially and spiritually.

To note this is nothing new for Aboriginal peoples given that all provincial boundaries are somewhat arbitrary from an Aboriginal historical perspective. These provincial boundaries, internal to Canada, do not demarcate Aboriginal homelands. Indeed, even certain international boundaries suffer likewise from a similar arbitrariness. I will use the Mohawks at Akwesasne as another case in point. Their community extends over two provincial boundaries (Ontario and Quebec) and an international boundary with New York state. Their sense of division is compounded by the existence of three boundaries which in no way correspond to their own territorial, spiritual, or political identity as Mohawks or members of the Iroquois Confederacy. What about 'Quebec secession' for these First Nations? While some Aboriginal peoples in Quebec do speak French, their cultural and linguistic identities are first and foremost shaped by their own First Nations culture, history, and language.[8]

While the province of Quebec is undoubtedly no worse than any other province in terms of its history of a strained relationship with Aboriginal peoples (although I would argue this is not an appropriate threshold for assessment), the recent confrontation with Mohawks at Oka in 1991 and the ongoing battle with the Crees over further hydroelectric development in the James Bay territory seem to have particularly embittered relationships between Aboriginal peoples and the provincial government. Not surprisingly, when a future is laid out by the secessionists which envisages a fully sovereign state, claiming to exercise complete jurisdiction over peoples and resources within the current provincial boundaries, Aboriginal peoples express concern. Given the recent political history of Quebec, the impact of the change in political status of the province on Aboriginal peoples' historic relationship with the Crown presents a chilling potential for a complete breakdown in the political relationship between Aboriginal peoples and Quebec.

Open discussion, dialogue, and consideration of Aboriginal peoples' status and rights need to begin immediately in Quebec, but they also require an *informed basis*, founded on principles of equality of peoples, mutual respect, and self-determination. There are basic human rights principles at issue in this debate and the legitimacy of the sovereignist movement may well stand or fall on how these principles are reconciled. The sovereignist movement cannot continue as a virtual steamroller ignoring or denying Aboriginal peoples' status and rights and still hope to be successful. Thus far, the secessionists have not presented a framework for dialogue which embraces basic principles of respect for Aboriginal peoples and their status and rights. Instead, Aboriginal peoples have been offered vague assurances that they will be treated well by a new Quebec state. When Aboriginal peoples have articulated their concerns and set out some basic principles upon which to begin a dialogue with Québécois, they have been unjustifiably attacked and diminished. It seems that, on the part of the Quebec sovereignists, there is no genuine commitment to understanding the Aboriginal perspective on full sovereignty for Quebec.

## Self-determination: The Competing Claims

The explosive political atmosphere encircling the debate over full sovereignty and Aboriginal peoples was revealed when the National Chief of the Assembly of First Nations, Ovide Mercredi, appeared in 1992 before the Quebec National Assembly's Committee to Examine Matters Relating to the Accession of Quebec to Sovereignty.[9] The National Chief, appearing with the Chiefs and Elders from a number of First Nations in Quebec, told the Committee:

> There can be no legitimate secession by any people in Quebec if the rights to self-determination of First Nations are denied, suppressed or ignored in order to achieve independence. Our rights do not take a back seat to yours. . . . Only through openness, of the mind and of the heart, can questions of such vital importance to your people and ours be reconciled. The alternative, which we do not favour, is confrontation. . . .

The response to this, and other submissions, both by the Quebec media and some members of the Committee, was one of outrage. It was as if the sovereignists were wilfully blinded to the principles articulated by Aboriginal peoples in support of their rights. This is particularly frustrating given that, at many levels, the principles that Aboriginal peoples advance for the basis of a political relationship with Canada or a sovereign Quebec are not very different from Quebec's position (self-determination, territory, identity). At least in some cases, I believe the Aboriginal position could prove stronger legally and politically. Since the Lesage era in the 1960s, French Canadians have argued that they want to be masters of their own house (*maîtres chez nous*). Aboriginal peoples have asserted an equally powerful concept—self-determination or self-government.

Sovereignists seem to see threats only when Aboriginal peoples articulate their own perspec-tives. The worrisome point in this fury over the National Chief's appearance before the Committee on Sovereignty is that he is a committed moderate. There were no threats of violence, only pleas for dialogue and for measures to prevent a confrontation over the competing positions. As Chief Mercredi stated: 'I, as National Chief, welcome constructive dialogue between First Nations and Quebecers on constitutional issues. We should build partnerships in support of our respective rights and not construct hierarchies of your rights over ours.' Nevertheless, there seems to be a powerful drive towards castigating Aboriginal peoples for advocating Aboriginal and treaty rights. For example, the National Chief was chastised by Claude Masson of *La Presse* for speaking 'exaggerated, insulting and outrageous words' and said that the Aboriginal leadership 'must behave like reasonable and responsible human beings and not like warriors or criminals with a right of life and death over everybody else.'[10] This utter misrepresentation of the basic principles advanced by the National Chief, a leader who has worked hard to build alliances and open dialogue with Quebec, demonstrates how wide the gulf is growing between sovereignists and Aboriginal peoples. The era of disciplining Aboriginal peoples for being different is over. Political support for the aspirations of Québécois will not be won in Canada or around the world with this type of denigration.

There has been an obvious strategic decision in the Quebec independence movement to view Aboriginal issues as business for a later date—after the accession to full sovereignty. The executive of the Parti Québécois has recently adopted a resolution to this effect. There seems to be little priority placed on dealing with Aboriginal peoples' status and rights before accession.[11] In response to Aboriginal suggestions that the situation is critical in Quebec, there is a 'why only pick on us' sentiment in the secessionist movement's response to Aboriginal peoples, which is ill-informed. Aboriginal peoples have been vigorously advancing their right to self-determination, territory, and cultural rights at all levels in Canada and internationally. The *Delgamuukw* action in British Columbia is a case in point. This case, which is now before the British Columbia Court of Appeal, is an assertion of Gitksan and Wet'suwet'en political and territorial sovereignty against the federal and provincial Crown.

The movement for adequate recognition of Aboriginal and treaty rights is not confined to Quebec. With or without the prospect of Quebec's secession, the rights will be advanced in that province, too. But in light of the sovereignist agenda, it is seen as critical here because the movement for full sovereignty calls into question Aboriginal peoples' status and rights in a most immediate and far-reaching way—there will be a decision made about the future of all peoples in Quebec, in a referendum to be held by October 26, 1992. Issues relating to that referendum—self-determination, territory, and identity—are brought directly to the fore by the sovereignist agenda which, once engaged through Bill 150, is a veritable juggernaut. Aboriginal peoples cannot be expected to ignore what is coming at them full force.

Moreover, these issues deserve more than just passing consideration in the context of the discussions in this text of negotiating with a sovereign Quebec. From a human rights perspective, could there legitimately be a fully sovereign Quebec without according equal consideration to the aspirations and choices of Aboriginal peoples? To simply begin the discussion by sketching the contours of negotiations with a sovereign Quebec may be putting the cart before the horse. For Aboriginal peoples, Québécois, and Canadians there is a great deal at stake. Either one legitimizes a priori the reduction of First Nations peoples to the status of ethnic minorities with no right of self-determination, or one recognizes that there would be several other potential sovereign entities with which a Quebec state would have to negotiate.

Negotiating with a sovereign Quebec could only mean, for Aboriginal peoples, a political

relationship based on negotiating international treaties between emerging independent peoples. Existing treaties involving Canada, Aboriginal peoples, and Quebec, such as the James Bay Northern Quebec Agreement, would not have continuing validity, and Quebec would not be able to claim the benefits of such treaties. If full sovereignty is declared by Quebec, this would amount to a unilateral breach of that agreement. The James Bay Northern Quebec Agreement was not only explicitly negotiated and ratified in a federal context, but also contained perpetual federal and provincial obligations that cannot be altered without the Aboriginal parties' consent. A unilateral declaration of independence would be a clear breach of that agreement and Quebec could not claim the benefits of the agreement while not respecting its negotiated terms.

Aboriginal peoples are not simply a head of jurisdiction, as seems to have been presumed by many Québécois and others outside the province. The first peoples in Canada are political entities—'peoples' in the international legal sense. This means that as peoples (with distinct languages, cultures, territories, populations, and governments), Aboriginal peoples have full rights of self-determination. For the purposes of discussions over sovereignty, Aboriginal peoples must be seen to enjoy the status of peoples with a right to self-determination. This position is supported by both Canadian and international law. The International Bill of Rights (an instrument which I presume a fully sovereign Quebec would want to respect in order to gain entry into the international community) recognizes the right of all peoples to self-determination. By this it is meant that peoples should freely determine their political status and that this should not be determined for them by a state, or an external actor.

Aboriginal peoples are independent political entities with distinct languages, cultures, histories, territories, spiritualities, and governments. As such, they can choose or determine their future relationship with Canada or a sovereign Quebec. This should not be determined for them by other peoples or governments. At present, the position of many sovereignists does not embrace self-determination for Aboriginal peoples. It presumes that Aboriginal peoples are not peoples or are too insignificant and dispersed to be independent political actors.[12] As academics and intellectuals, we should not promote recognition for a fully sovereign Quebec if it means that Aboriginal peoples' competing rights of self-determination will be compromised.

We need to recognize that when the political discourse shifts to Quebec's secession, it moves from the familiar realm of federalist considerations of distinct society and the recognition and protection of distinct identities to the less certain context of political and territorial sovereignty. With this shift, there is a different grid structuring the debate, one with far broader implications. Once basic concepts of control over territory and peoples are put so squarely on the agenda by people in Quebec, the struggles in which Aboriginal peoples are engaged across Canada come sharply into focus. The basic presumption which operates in the minds of many sovereignists is that they either have, or will automatically acquire, sovereignty over Aboriginal peoples in Quebec. Flowing from this sovereignty, some Québécois believe that the French-Canadian majority in Quebec can decide what it wants to do with Aboriginal peoples. But what is the source of their sovereignty over Aboriginal peoples and territories? Is it the right of the French-Canadian nation in Quebec to self-determination?

It would seem clear that the French-Canadian people are faced with the competing rights to self-determination of Aboriginal peoples. Moreover, the right to self-determination is not a right of the province of Quebec.[13] In international law, provinces do not enjoy a right of self-determination, peoples do. Consequently, other peoples who may have competing claims, especially to territory, cannot be ignored. Sovereignists in Quebec have, in effect, constructed their claim on the basis of the province of Quebec as the entity which will exercise the right of self-determination. However, this would unjustly efface the competing and legitimate rights of Aboriginal peoples.

As this short discussion illustrates, the competing self-determination claims by French Canadians and Aboriginal peoples need to be carefully examined before we can deal with referenda or territory in an equitable and mutually respectful manner. Indeed, these three issues—self-determination, referendum, and territorial claims—are critically interwoven in the current Canadian context. No single issue can stand alone without the others being considered. An independent Quebec state would not meet with international recognition if Aboriginal peoples were not treated as peoples, with full enjoyment of human rights, including the right of self-determination. Self-determination for Aboriginal peoples may well require that they be involved as full, equal, and independent participants in the decision about the accession of Quebec to full sovereignty. I emphasize 'independent' because Aboriginal peoples must be dealt with as 'peoples', not 'minorities' subject to the political will of the province. As distinct political entities, Aboriginal peoples must participate in that process through their leadership and not be presumed to be 'represented' by members of the Quebec National Assembly or the federal parliament.

The federal government also has obligations to recognize Aboriginal peoples' rights to self-determination. If there are to be negotiations with Quebec on secession, then Aboriginal peoples cannot be treated as a head of jurisdiction along with monetary issues or other items. Aboriginal peoples must each decide their relationship with a new Quebec state. As United States President Woodrow Wilson stated in 1917, '. . . no right exists anywhere to hand peoples about from sovereignty to sovereignty as if they were property.'[14] Aboriginal peoples cannot be handed from one sovereign (the federal Crown) to another (an independent Quebec state) as if they were property. Yet this seems to be the presumption operating in Bill 150, the Allaire report, and the Bélanger-Campeau Commission report, where Aboriginal peoples are viewed as minorities, authority over which can be simply transferred to a sovereign Quebec.

The persistence of this mindset of viewing Aboriginal peoples as minorities or of an inferior status to French or English newcomers goes to the very problem Hugh Brody identifies in the quotation set out at the beginning of this essay: there is a narrowness of vision here which sees the arrival and spread of immigrants (whether they be French, English, or otherwise) as the very purpose of history, including Canadian history. It is this vision which selects immigrant political objectives as superior to and more compelling than those of Aboriginal peoples. Aboriginal perspectives and political aspirations are treated as secondary within the immigrant vision. Yet the immigrant vision has been vigorously challenged. Even some voices in Quebec have challenged it, although they seem to fall on deaf ears. For example, Professor Daniel Turp (Université de Montréal), a leading sovereignist academic frequently cited by the Parti Québécois, acknowledged, when he appeared before the Committee on Accession, that 'in my opinion [Aboriginal peoples] constitute peoples who are self-identified as peoples . . . this would confer on them a right to self-determination at the same level as Quebec . . . the same rules apply to Aboriginal peoples as to Québécois.'[15] This aspect of his opinion has been largely ignored by sovereignists who instead emphasize the right of the French in Quebec to self-determination.

We know that the Canadian constitution is premised on a privileged reading of history, or the immigrant vision of (only) two founding nations, and that it has marginalized or excluded Aboriginal visions. Aboriginal peoples, Québécois, and other Canadians should strive to establish a more honourable and collaborative

process. This entails fundamental changes to existing political processes and constitutional structures. Moreover, in the context of secession, it requires a full airing of opinions on Aboriginal peoples' status and rights.

## Territory

In 1992, David Cliche, the Parti Québécois 'Native policy' adviser and a member of the executive of the Parti Québécois, argued that, upon secession, Quebec will naturally take the territory within the current provincial boundaries. This position was endorsed by the leader of the Parti Québécois, Jacques Parizeau. What it ignores is that Aboriginal peoples have no say in the matter. The decisions over the control of Aboriginal territories should be made by Aboriginal peoples, not Quebec or the federal government. Cliche opposes this view and suggests that the sovereignists would offer the Aboriginal people the best deal they could ever get. But this promise misses the point, because self-determination for Aboriginal peoples is not about the prospects of a good deal some time in the future. It is about peoples deciding freely their political and territorial status now and not being forced into political arrangements without that independent collective decision.

The gulf in our respective understandings of the situation is a broad one. I believe that from an international legal perspective, and in terms of the political legitimacy of the sovereignist movement, only Aboriginal peoples can decide their future status. This cannot be usurped by the sovereignists, just as French Canadians want to decide their future without this being unilaterally usurped by the federal government.

Much of the sovereignist argument on territorial claims has rested on a doctrine of international law called *uti possidetis juris*, which is offered to support the claim that they will enter independence with the territory they had before. In this case, the secessionists say the territory they had before is Quebec within the current provincial boundaries. They sometimes call this the principle of 'territorial integrity'. This doctrine is said to displace the ordinary principle of occupation as a basis for territorial sovereignty. The international law on whether *uti possidetis* is compelling is dubious at best, with the leading scholars in the field wondering whether the doctrine is even a norm of international law.[16] Even the International Court of Justice has cautioned that this doctrine is problematic as it conflicts with a significant principle in international law—self-determination.[17] The sovereignist claim to take the territory within the current provincial boundaries is weak, internationally, especially given that much land in the province is subject to Aboriginal claims which have yet to be resolved, and which are tied in to Aboriginal self-determination. The secessionists will have to present other arguments that can satisfy international legal standards if they hope to be recognized as a legitimate state with the existing provincial boundaries as their territorial base.

Control over Aboriginal peoples' territories has been essential for the prosperity of Quebec. This certainly has been the experience following the boundary extensions of 1898 and 1912. It is clear that the secessionist position is rooted in a realization that these territories are of continued significance. Issues of control over territory are fundamental to the secessionists because mass development projects like James Bay II (Great Whale) are part of their economic plan. Aboriginal peoples have legitimate concerns about the territorial consequences of full sovereignty. Would this mean that a new Quebec state can unilaterally make development decisions? James Bay may be but a glimpse of what Aboriginal peoples could face with Quebec secession and full claims to jurisdiction over their territories. It has been an enormous struggle, albeit increasingly successful, for the Crees to gain support for their opposition to further James Bay hydroelectric development. As Grand Chief Coon-Come reflects:

Bourassa's dream [of hydroelectric development] has become our nightmare. It has contaminated our fish with mercury. It has destroyed the spawning grounds. It has destroyed the nesting grounds of the waterfowl. It has displaced and dislocated our people and broken the fabric of our society. And we have decided, knowing the behaviour of the animals, that we will not be like the fox who, when he sees danger, crawls back to his hole. We have come out to stop the destruction of our land.[18]

In this quotation the Grand Chief says 'our' when he refers to the land and to the fish. This contradicts the view of the government of Quebec (excerpted at the outset of this essay) that the land and resources of the province are a gift of nature to the people of Quebec, in which regard they are more favoured than others.

The territorial claims of the secessionists to the current provincial boundaries are legally and politically insecure. The territory was not given to Québécois as a gift of nature. It was a gift of the federal government in 1898 and 1912—a gift made without the consent of the owners, Aboriginal peoples. French Canadians will have to support their territorial claim to the lands within the existing provincial boundaries with something other than erroneous theories about gifts of nature or *uti possidetis*.[19] No one can presume these are theirs to take when the original occupants of the land, Aboriginal peoples, assert their rights. Voting in a referendum in support of this position is not enough either, legally or politically.

## Referendum: The Who/Whom

In 1902, Lenin posited the critical question in politics as 'who/whom': who rules whom, who decides for whom? Bill 150 provides for a referendum sometime between October 12 and 26, 1992. The who/whom question is pivotal. Bill 150 states that if the results of the referendum are in favour of secession, they will 'constitute a proposal' that Quebec acquire the status of a sovereign state one year to the day from the holding of the referendum. What question will be put to voters, who will vote, and the weighing of the results are all unclear at this point. For Aboriginal peoples in Quebec, the ambiguity of the referendum is threatening because if a vote is registered in favour of sovereignty, it could legitimize the appropriation of Aboriginal territories and the assumption of authority over them. They would be the 'whom' ruled by the 'who' in a simple majority referendum.

Is a simple 50-plus-1 majority enough in these circumstances? If it was, this could mean that Aboriginal peoples' self-determination rights would be overridden, as Aboriginal peoples may simply be outvoted by larger populations in non-Aboriginal regions of Quebec. This kind of a referendum could not be held up internationally as supporting accession to sovereignty because of its implications for Aboriginal peoples. Referendums are numbers games and Aboriginal peoples would be set up for exclusion unless double majorities or separate referendums are employed. Aboriginal peoples will have to insist on double majorities, or independent (traditional) means for expressing their views on accession to full sovereignty. They cannot be lumped into a general referendum if the result is to be accepted for any purposes as a legitimate mandate for statehood.

While concerns about the status and rights of Aboriginal peoples are grave, it is nevertheless important to stress that this is a great opportunity for the sovereignists to lead the way on self-determination. There is a natural alliance which could be struck between Aboriginal peoples and the secessionists whereby Aboriginal self-determination could be respected as a priority. This requires an immediate dialogue with Aboriginal peoples within a framework of respect for the equally compelling right of Aboriginal peoples to self-determination. This dialogue cannot be informed by the 'trust us, we'll give you a good deal later' attitude which seems so popular among sovereignists.

Such an alliance would be a historic event and could lead to interesting and innovative political arrangements with Canada and a new Quebec state. However, the basic principles for such an alliance, such as Aboriginal self-determination, must be discussed and openly embraced by the sovereignist movement. This requires a reconsideration of elements of its vision of a new Quebec state. Particularly, the territorial integrity position would have to be revised to embrace at least the principle of shared and co-managed resources. Currently, there is no indication that this is happening and the responsibility is really on the sovereignist side to demonstrate a willingness to respect the right of Aboriginal self-determination.

As the title of this essay would suggest, the road to full sovereignty for Quebec runs through Aboriginal territory. There is no detour, no other path. There is only one road, and it must be a course of justice and respect for Aboriginal peoples. The secessionists will be well advised to look carefully at the map of this road now that they have chosen the path of statehood. Should Québécois fail to deal with Aboriginal self-determination, their movement stands to lose a great deal of legitimacy and support both in Canada and the international community.

## Notes

*Meegwetch* to Paul Joffe for our discussions about the issues discussed in this paper and for what he symbolizes for me in this struggle: a non-Aboriginal Quebecer deeply committed to justice for Aboriginal peoples. *Meegwetch* also to Paul for inspiring the title of this paper. Responsibility for the views expressed in this paper are strictly my own.

1. H. Brody, *Maps and Dreams* (Vancouver: Douglas & McIntyre, 1988), xiii.
2. Government of Quebec, *Quebec-Canada: A New Deal* (Éditeur Officiel, 1979), 89. This is the official Parti Québécois publication circulated prior to the referendum on sovereignty-association in 1980.

3. Although my preferred expression is 'First Nations', I use the phrase 'Aboriginal peoples' throughout this paper because I want it to be clear that I am referring to both the First Nations (sometimes called 'Indians') and Inuit. In the province of Quebec there are First Nations and Inuit people, each with distinctive perspectives, status, and rights.

4. Here I am particularly mindful of the comments of the members of the Committee on the Accession of Quebec to Full Sovereignty, established pursuant to Bill 150 (An Act Respecting the Process for Determining the Political and Constitutional Future of Quebec). It has been before this committee that the sovereignist position has become most clearly articulated in the past months, in terms of the comments of members of the committee, background studies, and the submissions of witnesses.

5. Now section 91(24) of the Constitution Act, 1867.

6. Of course, law and politics are hardly distinct. Legal arguments are interconnected with politics at every level in this context. I have deliberately made this essay less technical and 'legal' than it could have been. Some of the detail for the legal argument, at least on the issue of territory, can be found in Kent McNeil, 'Aboriginal Nations and Québec's Boundaries: Canada Couldn't Give What It Didn't Have', in Daniel Drache and Roberto Perin, eds, *Negotiating with a Sovereign Québec* (Toronto: James Lorimer, 1992). For a detailed and superb legal analysis of Aboriginal peoples' concerns *vis-à-vis* full sovereignty for Quebec, see Grand Council of the Crees of Quebec, *Status and Rights of the James Bay Crees in the Context of Quebec's Secession from Canada*, Submission to the United Nations Commission on Human Rights, 48th Session, 21 Feb. 1992.

7. This is a land claim agreement or modern treaty entered into in 1975 by Cree, Inuit, and the federal and provincial governments.

8. As Zebeedee Nungak, spokesperson for the Inuit Tapirisat of Canada and the Inuit in northern Quebec, rather graphically illustrated at the federally sponsored constitutional constituency assembly, 'Identity, Values and Rights', he identifies as an Inuk first, a Canadian second, and a Québécois third (7 Feb. 1992, Royal York Hotel, Toronto). I say 'graphically' because he held up a map of Quebec which divided the province into the north and south, arguing that (to paraphrase) 'the distinct society of the south cannot override the distinct society of the north'.

9. The National Chief of the Assembly of First Nations, Ovide Mercredi, appeared on 11 Feb. 1992. A copy of his text is on file with the author.

10. From the translation, reprinted in *Globe and Mail*, 18 Feb. 1992, 19.

11. The sovereignists often refer to a 20 Mar. 1985 National Assembly resolution as a starting point for engaging with Aboriginal peoples on issues relating to full sovereignty. However, it is important to note that this resolution was unilaterally imposed on the First Nations in Quebec. The Aboriginal leadership in the province wrote a letter to Premier Lévesque on 25 June 1985, reminding the Premier of the First Nations' objections to the tabling of the resolution and the unilateral way in which the government behaved. This letter expressed concern about the substance of the resolution. As a unilaterally imposed document, it is not a basis for a relationship which respects self-determination for Aboriginal peoples.

The Crees suggest, in their brief to the United Nations, that 'it is unacceptable for the National Assembly or government of Quebec to unilaterally impose policies on First Nations. The contents of an acceptable Resolution were in the process of being negotiated. Also, a prior commitment had been expressly made by the Premier of Quebec that he would not table any resolution on this matter in the National Assembly without aboriginal consent.' Submission of the Grand Council of the Crees of Quebec, 166.

12. The secessionist position has been articulated in detail by Professor J. Brossard in his text, *L'accession à la souveraineté et le cas du Québec* (Montréal: Les Presses de l'Université de Montréal, 1977). This text has been referred to by the Committee on the Accession of Quebec to Sovereignty as an accurate statement of the rights of French Canadians to self-determination.

13. Brossard acknowledges that the basis of the claim to accession is the rights of French Canadians to self-determination. He goes further to suggest that in theory it is only the French-Canadian nation that could participate in the decision on full

sovereignty, thus excluding the Anglophones. *L'accession à la souveraineté*, 183–5. He admits that politically such an alternative is impracticable.

14. This is quoted in the Submission of the Grand Council of the Crees of Quebec to the United Nations Commission on Human Rights.

15. He appeared before the Committee on Accession on 9 Oct. 1991.

16. See, for example, I. Brownlie, *Principles of International Law*, 4th edn (Oxford: Clarendon Press, 1989), 135, who suggests that 'the principle [of *uti possidetis*] is by no means mandatory and the states concerned are free to adopt other principles as the basis of settlement.'

17. *Frontier Dispute (Burkina Faso/Mali)*, 80 ILR 440 at 554 (separate opinion of Judge Luchaire).

18. Quoted in H. Thurston, 'Power in a Land of Remembrance', *Audubon* 52 (Nov.-Dec. 1991): 58–9.

19. As the National Chief of the Assembly of First Nations stated in his presentation to the Committee on Accession, 'The Quebec government's proposed principle concerning the territorial integrity of Quebec is an affront to First Nations. It is obvious that territorial integrity serves to consolidate your legal position to the extreme prejudice of the First Nations.'

# Rights Talk:
## The Effect of the Charter on Canadian Political Discourse

Jeffrey Simpson

A journalist may be forgiven for beginning with a reference to today's news. This morning, we read of the federal government's plans for a referendum bill. Two reactions immediately ensued, both illustrative of contemporary political discourse, one traditional, the other rather new. First, the opposition parties, as is typical, healthy, and traditional in a parliamentary democracy, immediately raised questions about this or that aspect of the proposed legislation. Second, third-party actors—so-called interest groups—threatened to bring a Charter challenge against the legislation, alleging that its provisions infringed, among other possibilities, on the rights of free speech and free association. That interest groups should condemn all or part of government legislation is a traditional part of parliamentary democracy; that they should threaten a Charter challenge is a decade-old twist.

One day's news on the referendum front illustrates the Charter's impact on Canadian affairs in two ways. The government indicated that it could not allow spending limits and umbrella groups because its lawyers had indicated such a bill would not be 'Charter-proof'—that is, it would not withstand a court challenge on Charter grounds. That illustrates what all close observers of government now realize: that almost every move any government makes these days, especially in the field of legislation, is reviewed and reviewed again for its Charter implications. Departments of Justice in Ottawa and the provinces have become like treasury boards: new central agencies. Whether this has made for better

From Philip Bryden, Steven Davis, and John Russell, eds, *Protecting Rights and Freedoms* (Toronto: University of Toronto Press, 1994), 52–9. Reprinted by permission of University of Toronto Press Incorporated.

legislation is a moot point; that it has added another complication to governing is not. Similarly, the immediate threat of a Charter challenge took what I would argue is a profoundly political question—the holding and organizing of a referendum on the country's future constitutional arrangements—and partly deformed it into a legal one. The terms of the debate—what was important, and which side stood where—were transformed from consideration of the essence of the bill into narrow matters concerning the details of the referendum's organization. Such is the almost inevitable impact of the legislation of political debate, a legacy of the Charter.

The Charter, in the space of a decade, has become the country's most important symbol. Polls have their limitations, so I offer these results with due modesty. But consider the results of a November 1991 Focus Canada survey by Environics Research of Toronto. Eighty-nine per cent of respondents were aware of the Charter, a very high number given the appalling ignorance of so many Canadians about the basic institutions of their country. Seven in ten respondents—six of ten in Quebec—considered it a 'very important' part of the Canadian identity, higher than for any other symbol.

Just how important the Charter has become as a national symbol can be seen from these Environics results. Outside Quebec, 75 per cent of respondents considered the Charter a 'very important' symbol, compared to 71 per cent for the flag, 69 per cent for the anthem, 38 per cent for multiculturalism, 31 per cent for the CBC, 25 per cent for the monarchy, and 22 per cent for bilingualism. Inside Quebec, the Charter still topped the list of national symbols: 64 per cent for the Charter, followed by bilingualism (52 per cent), anthem (39 per cent), flag (38 per cent), Radio-Canada (31 per cent), multiculturalism (29 per cent), monarchy (5 per cent). The same poll pointed to another intriguing impact of the Charter: the degree to which it is seen as advancing the cause of minorities. Twenty-eight per cent believed their personal rights had improved under the Charter, 18 per cent believed they had deteriorated, and 53 per cent had seen no change. Thirty-nine per cent believed the 'rights of the average citizen' had improved, 16 per cent thought they had deteriorated, and 38 per cent thought that there had been no change. But when respondents were asked whether minorities' rights had improved, 56 per cent said yes, 9 per cent said no, and 26 per cent believed there had been no effect.

No one can be definitive in interpreting these numbers. It may be that Canadians are proud of their country's treatment of minorities, or pleased that the Charter is protecting minorities, there being so many of them in Canada, and therefore the Charter will grow in popularity and legitimacy if it continues to be perceived as principally a shield and sword for minorities. It may also be, however, that a Charter whose principal beneficiaries are minorities will begin to lose appeal among the majority, or at least among those on whom the Charter has had little direct effect, and that eventually a backlash against either the Charter or its interpretation by activist judges may set in. It is obviously too soon to draw any conclusions.

The Charter is part of a worldwide concern for human rights, a concern that was once used in the moral battle against Communism, but that even without the Communist 'threat' still evokes an emotional appeal beyond the liberal democracies. Next year, for example, the United Nations will be sponsoring a large international conference—like the Rio conference on the environment—dedicated to human rights. Countries from Czechoslovakia to Australia are giving themselves written charters, or thinking about such a move. To be for human rights is apparently to be

for written charters which can be used against state infringement of rights or to promote more respect by states of those rights. Even Great Britain, which has managed to struggle along without a Charter yet still be considered among the world's democracies, has found itself bound by certain European rights codes to which it had to subscribe upon joining the European Community. Canada is therefore part of a worldwide trend, a point repeatedly made by Charter proponents in the debates of 1980–1.

The Charter reflects and encourages the broader trend towards the 'Americanization' of politics in Canada. In particular, the Charter is inspired by the suspicions of state power which find their logical expression in the US balance-of-power, or checks-and-balances, system of government, which allocates to the courts a wide latitude for checking or reversing government decisions that found no echo in Canadian courts. Such is the distaste for what government has wrought in recent years in Canada that a series of proposals—some constitutional, others political—have been advanced, which have as their common thread the curtailment of the power of the prime minister and cabinet through the control of a parliamentary majority. An elected Senate, the devolution of powers to provinces, the creation of Aboriginal self-government, referenda, direct recall of members, free votes in the Commons and, of course, the Charter are all part of this trend. In the same Environics poll quoted above, Canadians were asked in 1986 and 1991 which institutions they considered superior to those in the United States. Of 14 categories, in only one—system of government—had respect for Canadian institutions sharply fallen. In 1986, 52 per cent of Canadians believed Canada had the better system of government; by 1991, only 32 per cent of Canadians so believed.

Third, but related to the 'Americanization' of Canadian politics, has been the breakdown of the old élite accommodation model of governing Canada. The Charter has played an important role here, in abetting the creation and strengthening of interest groups, in judicializing many political decisions, in increasing the amount of 'rights talk' in political discourse, and in making compromises more difficult.

Why has there been more 'rights talk' in recent years? In part, this increase reflects the worldwide trends noted above. But there are far more profound domestic reasons. The old élite accommodation model disintegrated because it could not reflect adequately the desire to be represented by a plethora of new groups, which themselves reflected social, economic, and demographic trends. The changes to Canada's immigration policies in 1976–7, for example, opened the doors to many more immigrants from Third World countries, thereby increasing the number of 'visible minorities' who found themselves severely underrepresented among the 'élites' who made the country's political decisions. The huge entry of women into the workforce both changed the nature of the family, and propelled many of them against the glass barriers that existed in all walks of Canadian life. Women, too, found themselves underrepresented in the 'élite groups', and therefore some of them rejected the model whereby élites made the decisions, then 'sold' them to the public. Aboriginals, of course, continued to reject all models of assimilation. They were not going to be 'sold' anything by élites other than their own. The Charter, with its clauses specifically directed to each of these groups, became an instrument for their affirmation as distinct entities in the Canadian body politic.

Government scrambled to keep up with these social, economic, and demographic changes, but the political system was unable to produce policy outputs or become sufficiently representative to satisfy these groups. This failure sent groups searching outside government for redress and help, and the Charter provided one such avenue through court challenges to government sins of omission or commission. The Charter, too, was given life by lawyers, who are always dispropor-

tionately represented in politics. They were, to use Professor Peter Russell's term, represented heavily among the early 'hopers' and 'believers' in the Charter. And, of course, there were some historical grievances involving linguistic minorities, Japanese Canadians and the like, which it was argued would not have occurred had a Charter been in place. Finally, a yearning for something durable and pan-Canadian emerged from the constitutional impasses of the 1960s and 1970s. A desire grew from the interminable federal-provincial bickering, and from the apparent lack of cohesion in Canada, for something unifying, ennobling, and enduring, a desire perfectly met by the Charter, which spoke to rights, values, and principles. That the Charter has not produced the unity so fervently desired, at least in English-speaking Canada, and may even have contributed to widening the existing gaps, is just one of the document's many ironies.

The governance of a heterogeneous society such as Canada has always been a supreme challenge, and that challenge is now more difficult than ever with the multiplication of groups clamouring for attention. It is also a time when respect for government and elected officials has never been lower. The political culture of Canada these days, within which public policy must be conceived and executed, reflects the increasingly self-evident facts that judges are considered more trustworthy, capable, and desirous of advancing the public interest than politicians; courts more appropriate institutions for the rectification of wrongs and the elaboration of solutions than parliaments; the Charter a surer guide to respect for and expansion of human liberties than parliaments; legal cases a better vehicle for confrontations from which will flow ringing affirmations of rights than messy compromises required by parliamentary debates, party politics, and national elections.

At a minimum, the Charter has influenced a generation of Canadians who look upon it as a supplement to parliamentary and political institutions. As the Canadian Advisory Council on the Status of Women said in its report *One Step Forward; Two Steps Back?*, 'The full support of both government and the courts is needed for women to take their rightful place in Canadian society. Women must press for changes in both arenas.' At worst, the Charter is seen as a surrogate for these institutions. Courts are now immersing themselves in, or being asked to concern themselves with, issues that I would argue are largely if not exclusively political. I say 'political' in the non-partisan sense of questions in which all members of civil society in their capacity as citizens might be interested and affected. These would include Sunday shopping, street soliciting, mandatory retirement, tobacco advertising, tax law, spousal benefits, unemployment insurance, and abortion, among others.

Any innocent observer of public discourse in contemporary Canada must be aware, if not amazed, at the escalation of 'rights talk', a phrase used by Harvard Professor Mary Ann Glendon in her book of the same name. 'In its simple American form, the language of rights is the language of no compromise', she writes. 'By indulging in excessively simple forms of rights talk in our pluralistic society, we needlessly multiply occasions for civil discord. We make it difficult for persons and groups with conflicting interests and views to build coalitions and achieve compromise, or even to acquire that minimal degree of mutual forbearance and understanding that promotes peaceful coexistence and keeps the door open to further communication.' What Professor Glendon observes about her own excessively litigious society is creeping into Canadian discourse and infecting the political culture.

Let me offer a few contemporary Canadian examples of Professor Glendon's observation about the elevation of issues to ones of rights. When the government cut Via Rail services, those opposed to the cuts insisted that Canadians had a 'right' to a national rail service. When Air Canada, even before the Crown corporation was priva-

tized, stopped flying to certain Canadian cities, mayors and others opposed to the decision said their cities had a 'right' to air service. When the government announced changes to the unemployment insurance program, taking $800 million from the fund and using it for training, opponents said recipients had a 'right' to UI payments. On the east coast it was argued that Canadian fishermen had a 'right' to stocks. The fish themselves became bearers of rights. In the *Singh* case, non-citizens, non-landed immigrants, were given 'rights' as outlined in the Charter even though they had not been accepted as legitimate entrants into Canada. And the *Singh* case precedent is now being used in lower court appeals to argue that anyone who appears at a Canadian mission abroad has a 'right' to the full protection of the Charter, including a face-to-face meeting. Smokers lobby their case in terms of their 'right' to smoke; those who oppose them insist upon their 'right' to enjoy a smoke-free environment. I could go on.

A distinguishing characteristic of this 'rights talk' is the degree to which discretionary decisions of government and the normal and sometimes healthy tensions in a pluralistic, democratic society are elevated to those of apparently fundamental human rights. Of course, when issues are so elevated, compromise and accommodation become more difficult because rights are involved. These rights, by virtue of being rights, cannot easily be compromised. They can only be defended to the maximum. These rights also seldom have obligations or responsibilities attached to them. They 'exist,' therefore they 'are': political statements whose underpinnings are apparently immune from examination because the use of the language of rights has raised the moral stakes. This 'rights talk' can gravely deform the nature of political discourse, and, as such, can be considered the particular contribution of lawyers to our politics. Like economists, social workers, sociologists, political scientists, or other intellectual species, lawyers frame issues in terms most familiar to them. Certainly, no self-respecting interest group, labour union, or business association would make a move these days without first vetting everything with a lawyer. 'Rights talk', like the fascination with the constitution itself, pleases lawyers and puts public debate within a framework where lawyers can shine. Whether this produces an appropriate framework for resolving disputes, determining priorities, and conveying a realistic sense of what can be expected from public policy is quite another matter.

What the Supreme Court and other courts cannot do effectively is consider the costs of decisions and whether the extension of benefits or the elaboration of new rights are the most urgent matters requiring governmental and societal attention in an age of straitened fiscal circumstances and inevitably jostling priorities. Judges deal with the case at court; cabinets must balance dozens of simultaneous claims. Judges try to find the balance within a case; politicians look for balances among many dossiers. Judges may have the interests of two, three, or four parties to a case to consider; politicians often must take account of the interests of a multiplicity of groups. The weakness of the judiciary in balancing competing claims, especially on the public purse, is perhaps of little consequence in an age of munificence. It can become increasingly burdensome in an age of distinctly limited government resources.

The battle over the Charter was fought a decade ago, and won by the proponents. The Charter has changed, for better and worse, the political culture of Canada. It is the single most Americanizing influence on our country's political life; yet, in a curious way, it is the hardening glue defining English Canada's sense of community.

Of all the changes wrought by the tempestuous 1980s in Canada, the Charter has been the most consequential. I am sceptical, however, that in contributing to smashing the old political order, the Charter and the 'rights talk' it has spawned produced anything cohesive with which to replace the old order, which, whatever its sins and deficiencies, was based on a recognition of compromise and accommodation and balance—albeit often imperfectly—of competing claims and regional interests inherent in a geographically immense, linguistically divided, and culturally heterogeneous country. On my more optimistic days, I believe we are groping towards something, including new institutions, that can accommodate the new pressures in our society, including the impact of the Charter. On my pessimistic days, I wonder if we have not imposed upon ourselves Procrustean institutions that cannot fit the kind of country we are, and that only by shrinking Canada's size can the country be made to fit the institutions we are giving to it.

# Part XI

# Provincial Politics

## Introduction

Michael Howlett

Protecting the environment, running universities, administering hospital insurance, caring for the poor and elderly, and many other activities fall under provincial jurisdiction in Canada. From highways and electrical generation to transit, municipal government, and human rights, provincial governments provide an entire range of goods and services to their citizens. In fact, if a modern welfare state is one in which governments have programs devoted to health, social security, and universal education, then in Canada we have not so much a single welfare state but rather 10 provincial welfare states, since all of these activities are in provincial hands. The provincial governments together with their urban, hospital, and educational counterparts, spend more money and employ more people than the federal government, and, until recently, collectively approached federal levels of deficits and indebtedness.

The study of political life in Canada, then, is not complete without a look at the provinces. This is also true of many other countries. The states in the United States and in Mexico and Brazil, the *lander* in Germany, and the provinces of many African and Asian countries are all examples of subnational governments, which play an important role in national political life. Like national governments, these subnational units are the subjects of hypotheses, investigation, and theory testing in political science.

Many people in Canada, however, are still not aware of the significant powers and responsibilities of Canada's provincial governments. This general level of ignorance is itself an interesting phenomenon. It reflects on the varied nature of Canadian federalism and the very different opinions expressed over the course of Canada's history on the proper role and responsibilities of subnational government in the federation, as well as on the manner in which these debates have been treated by students of Canadian government.

## The Provinces and Confederation

Most of the provinces have colonial histories that predate the creation of the federal political system in 1867. Only three of Canada's 10 provinces—Manitoba, Saskatchewan, and Alberta—have non-Native histories shorter than that of the federal government, having been created in 1870 and 1905 out of land purchased from the Hudson's Bay Company in 1869, and initially settled by European immigrants through federal immigration policy. The other provinces have much longer histories, extending back to the first days of French, British, Russian, and Spanish exploration of North America in the sixteenth and seventeenth centuries.

Throughout that time, the provinces existed as separate colonies of France and Britain. Following the British conquests of New France and Acadia, these colonies began a long struggle designed to achieve some measure of local control over local activities. By the mid-nineteenth century most had obtained self-governing status under British rule. Colonial legislative bodies and administrations controlled their lands and resources, trained and financed their own militias, built and operated public works, administered justice, and carried out most of the functions of contemporary states with the exception of trade, defence, and external relations. Confederation was negotiated by representatives of three of the most advanced provinces—Nova Scotia, New Brunswick, and the United Province of Canada—with the aim of creating a common market throughout the northern half of North America. From the inception of unity talks in 1864, debates over the provincial and federal government roles in the new country have been a prominent aspect of Canadian politics.

Just prior to Confederation in 1867, the United States had been embroiled in a civil war led by secessionist states. Reflecting on this, Sir John A. Macdonald, who would become Canada's first Prime Minister, argued that provincial governments should be no more than glorified municipal governments, with a minor and declining role in the governance of the new nation. Provincial leaders did not share this view, however, and all parts of the country were soon engaged in struggles over provincial rights and provincial powers with the federal government.

Following crises in New Brunswick and Nova Scotia over the terms of Confederation, the bitterest struggles were waged between Ontario and the federal government over the Manitoba boundary question, and between British Columbia and the federal government over the question of 'Oriental immigration'. Other major struggles involved the Manitoba and federal governments over north-south railway construction and the Nova Scotia and federal governments over freight rates and railway tariffs.[1] These struggles were waged largely in the court system, and in the 1880s and 1890s the provinces won a series of crucial cases before the highest court of appeal in the British Empire, the Judicial Committee of the Privy Council (JCPC), which upheld and expanded upon provincial powers.[2] During this time provincial governments also strategically curtailed the ability of the federal government to veto provincial laws through the use of the federal powers of reservation and disallowance of provincial legislation.[3] Provincial governments continued to pass and repass the same legislation until the federal government eventually abandoned its efforts to prevent its passage by fiat, turning instead to negotiation with the provinces as the preferred means of resolving federal-provincial disputes.

By the turn of the century the federal government was forced to recognize the large areas of social, political, and economic life affected by the continuing powers and responsibilities of the provinces. Federal and provincial leaders ushered in a new era of federal-provincial diplomacy in which the two orders of government attempted to resolve their differences. By 1896, in Canada's first major attempt at constitutional reconciliation, Prime Minister Sir Wilfrid Laurier took many leading provincial premiers and politicians into his federal cabinet in an attempt to end federal-provincial feuding. Such efforts only temporarily halted federal-provincial wrangling, however, which soon began again in earnest over the question of the division of tax revenues in the country.[4]

The establishment of provincial rights and the creation of a new system of federal-provincial relations resulted in much more attention being paid to the provinces in analysis of Canada's political system. Thus, in 1914, when two of Canada's first political scientists, Adam Shortt and Arthur G. Doughty, set out to explain the country to the outside world they named their multi-volume work *Canada and Its Provinces*. Their work was organized around the politics, economy, cultures, and societies of the country's then nine provinces and two territories.[5]

The status of the provinces in Canada's pendulum-like system of federal-provincial relations waned during World War I. Under emergency legislation, the federal government assumed many provincial powers to prosecute the war effort. These powers were returned to the provinces in the 1920s after the expiry of the War Measures Act, but the provinces were able to do little with these powers for some time. During the Great Depression of the 1930s large demands were placed on the provinces for welfare and unemployment relief at a time of drastically reduced provincial finances.[6] None the less, despite these problems, the provinces continued to block attempts by the federal government to expand its formal areas of jurisdiction. During World War II the federal government again took over direction of the economy and usurped many significant provincial powers over natural resources, labour, and taxation under the terms of its emergency powers.[7] By the end of the war, the federal government completely dominated the provinces.

Throughout this lengthy period academic efforts tended to follow political practice: the provinces were virtually ignored in studies of Canadian politics. The major political studies texts of the era failed to mention the provinces or their role in Confederation. Major works by Dawson and Corry, for example, both concentrated exclusively on the 'colony-to-nation' theme of Canada slowly earning its own place in the international system.[8]

Academic attention swung once again to provincial politics in the 1950s and 1960s, however, as the provincial governments slowly began once again to reassert their constitutional rights and responsibilities, and questioned the continuing federal dominance of national affairs in the postwar atmosphere. Intrigued by the election of the first socialist government in North America in Saskatchewan in 1944, American foundations funded studies of several western provincial governments in the 1950s[9] and then in several other provinces in the early 1960s.[10] The development of an independence movement in Quebec spurred studies of that province,[11] while the continual problems plaguing Newfoundland's economy since its entry into Confederation in 1949 led to many studies of that province.[12] Development issues emerging in the two territories resulted in the first studies of the Canadian North at around the same time.[13]

Provincial governments continued to expand in size and scope throughout the 1960s and 1970s, asserting their jurisdiction in areas such as pensions, resources, and transportation and developing a broad array of regulatory agencies and Crown corporations to pursue their ends.[14] By the 1970s the modern era of studies of provincial governments and provincial societies had begun. Most Canadian scholars now acknowledged that understanding the general dynamics of Canadian government required that serious attention be paid to provincial government and politics.

## Modern Studies of Provincial Politics

Studies since the early 1970s have been both idiosyncratic and comparative in nature. Emphasis has been placed on chronicling the development of specific provinces; comparing developments in one jurisdiction to those in others; and developing theoretical models to explain the differences and similarities among provinces.

In the 1970s several case studies helped fill gaps in coverage of the provinces occasioned by previous piecemeal approaches taken to their study.[15] The first serious effort at comparative treatment of the provinces was also produced,[16] as was the first theoretical treatment of provincial life—Elkins and Simeon's 'political culture' approach.[17]

Elkins and Simeon used a framework developed in American studies of comparative politics that emphasized the impact of national differences in values, attitudes, traditions, and beliefs on the nature and type of national political institutions. Different regime types were identified as correlating with characteristic 'political cultures' in different countries. Simeon and Elkins applied these same techniques to the analysis of subnational governments and societies. Analysing survey data, they found that different provincial populations had distinct attitudes towards both government and modes of political participation. However, they questioned the usefulness of such findings, given the similarities of provincial political regimes and histories. They often had difficulty explaining the origins of the differences they had found. Other critics noted that, despite these differences, it was apparent that most provincial governments adopted similar policies and engaged in similar activities, therefore calling into question the utility of the entire approach.

An alternate theoretical perspective emerged from the interest in Canadian political economy occasioned by concerns in the early 1970s about American penetration of the Canadian economy. In the course of re-examining Canada's role in the continental and international economies, a number of scholars viewed the economic, social, and cultural history of the provinces in the context of a resource-hinterland perspective.[18] This analysis argued that the provinces and provincial governments were significant players in a system of continental resource exploitation in which Canadian wheat, timber, minerals, and energy were exported to the US in exchange for manufactured goods.

This system, it was argued, resulted in the systematic political and economic underdevelopment of the eastern and western regions of the country, as these regions remained resource hinterlands to wealthier metropolitan areas in the US and central Canada.[19] However, as critics of this approach noted, many areas of Quebec and Ontario were as dependent on resource exploitation as any in the eastern or western provinces. More significantly, critics also noted that in some cases trade in resources—especially energy resources like oil, gas, and hydroelectricity—resulted in large amounts of money remaining in the producing provinces. Like the political culture approach that preceded it, this political economy approach was eventually abandoned in the face of such criticism.

In the 1980s the insights of the political culture and political economy perspectives were synthesized into a third general approach to Canadian provincial politics. This focused not only on the nature of provincial societies and provincial economies, but also on the capacity of provincial states to alter and affect the pattern of provincial development. Building on early work that had noted the key role played by provincial political institutions in the life of the nation,[20] this approach proposed a fundamental reinterpretation of the dominant perspective on Canadian federalism by focusing not only on the federal government's role in 'nation-building', but also on the provincial governments' roles in a concurrent process of 'province-building' over the course of Canadian history. This province-building approach stimulated examination of the effect of political institutions on social and economic development, reversing a theoretical perspective focusing on societal actors and events that had been characteristic of both earlier perspectives on provincial government and politics.[21]

Although criticized in the mid-1980s for its exaggerated claims and lack of precision,[22] the impact of the province-building perspective should not be underestimated. It has greatly influenced contemporary studies of provincial politics, which now generally fall into two types. Firstly, many new case studies of individual provinces have been made. These studies tend to focus on a common set of political, economic, social, and cultural characteristics. They are concerned with the development of provincial societies and provincial states, and with the results of modernization efforts. Some focus on social services, some on public-sector growth, some on economic development, and some on the alterations to provincial social structures and political systems resulting from these changes.[23] Rather than simply describing the historical development of provincial states and societies like earlier case studies, these more recent studies examine the nature of provincial and territorial states and societies, and the interactions and interrelationships existing among them.

The second thrust of current studies is more explicitly comparative. It includes systematic efforts to evaluate provinces' experiences while identifying causes and consequences of provincial state action. Such studies have examined causes of public expenditure growth, determinants of provincial party systems, methods of provincial budgetary control, and ways in which provinces consciously copy or emulate each others' policy initiatives.[24]

Studies of provincial politics have come a long way since 1970. The major problem encountered with the fluctuating status of the provinces in Canadian affairs has been largely overcome. Provinces have been accorded their due status as important state institutions in their own right. Different theoretical approaches have been tried and the political significance of distinctive provincial societies and provincial economic structures underlined, while the need to carefully evaluate state-society linkages at the provincial level has also been made apparent. Case studies continue to examine specific aspects of these state-society relationships, while provincial comparisons reveal which aspects are common and which are not. Such scholarly work may be setting the stage for comparisons of Canadian subnational politics with those of other countries, or perhaps an integration of the findings of these studies with general theories of national politics and political life. At any rate, the wide range of case and comparative studies now being undertaken in Canada should help ensure that the dynamics of provincial politics, and their impact on national political affairs, come to hold a more prominent place in the study of Canadian politics.

The readings presented below help to illustrate the evolution of studies of provincial politics in Canada. In the first reading, Stephen Tomblin of Memorial University re-examines the 20-year period in office of the Social Credit government of W.A.C. Bennett of British Columbia from 1952 to 1972. Applying the notion of 'province-building' to his analysis of the period, Tomblin finds evidence that the Bennett government was not simply an unorganized, reactive administration but, rather, was engaged in an entire series of infrastructure and other development projects consciously designed to build the province and its institutions. This article brings into focus the merits and difficulties of the 'province-building' approach to the study of Canadian provincial politics.

The second selection appeared in *Publius*, a leading journal of federal studies. Gordon R. Brown examines the continuing controversy over the extent and nature of federal and provincial powers in Canada and the claim that these powers overlap to such an extent as to wastefully duplicate government services and activities. Brown notes that three major studies of the question have found areas of overlap but have failed to establish that such overlap causes governments in Canada to be inefficient or wasteful. As he concludes, the current concerns with efficiency in government merely reflect the latest round in the ongoing struggle between the federal and provincial governments to define, and protect, their powers.

## Notes

1. On the history of these disputes, see E.R. Forbes, *The Maritime Rights Movement 1919–1927* (Montreal and Kingston: McGill-Queen's University Press, 1985); J.C. Morrison, *Oliver Mowat and the Development of Provincial Rights in Ontario: A Study in Dominion-Provincial Relations* (Toronto: Department of Public Records and Archives, 1961).
2. R.A. Olmsted, *Decisions of the Judicial Committee of the Privy Council relating to the British North America Act 1867 and the Canadian Constitution 1867–1954* (Ottawa: Department of Justice, 1954).
3. G.V. LaForest, *Disallowance and Reservation of Provincial Legislation* (Ottawa: Department of Justice, 1955).
4. J.A. Maxwell, *Federal Subsidies to the Provincial Governments in Canada* (Cambridge, Mass.: Harvard University Press, 1937).

5. Adam Shortt and Arthur G. Doughty, *Canada and Its Provinces: A History of the Canadian People and Their Institutions, by One Hundred Associates*, 23 vols (Toronto: Glasgow, Brook, 1914–17).

6. William Archibald Mackintosh, *The Economic Background of Dominion-Provincial Relations: A Study Prepared for the Royal Commission on Dominion-Provincial Relations* (Ottawa: King's Printer, 1939).

7. P.A. Crepeau and C.B. Macpherson, eds, *The Future of Canadian Federalism* (Toronto: University of Toronto Press, 1965).

8. J.A. Corry, *Democratic Government and Politics* (Toronto: University of Toronto Press, 1951); Robert MacGregor Dawson, *The Government of Canada* (Toronto: University of Toronto Press, 1947).

9. See S.M. Lipset, *Agrarian Socialism* (Berkeley: University of California Press, 1950); C.B. Macpherson, *Democracy in Alberta* (Toronto: University of Toronto Press, 1962).

10. Included in this series were Murray S. Donnelly, *The Government of Manitoba* (Toronto: University of Toronto Press, 1963); Frank MacKinnon, *The Government of Prince Edward Island* (Toronto: University of Toronto Press, 1951); F.F. Schindeler, *Responsible Government in Ontario* (Toronto: University of Toronto Press, 1969); Hugh Thorburn, *Politics in New Brunswick* (Toronto: University of Toronto Press, 1961).

11. See, for example, K. McRoberts and D. Postgate, *Quebec: Social Change and Political Crisis* (Toronto: McClelland & Stewart, 1980); Herbert Quinn, *The Union Nationale: Quebec Nationalism from Duplessis to Quebec's Quiet Revolution* (Toronto: University of Toronto Press, 1979).

12. For example, S.J.R. Noel, *Politics in Newfoundland* (Toronto: University of Toronto Press, 1971).

13. K.J. Rea, *The Political Economy of the Canadian North* (Toronto: University of Toronto Press, 1968).

14. See M. Chandler and W. Chandler, *Public Policy and Provincial Politics* (Toronto: McGraw-Hill, 1979); M. Chandler and W. Chandler, 'Public Administration in the Provinces', *Canadian Public Administration* 25, 4 (1982): 580–602; Margot Priest and Aron Wohl, 'The Growth of Federal and Provincial Regulation of Economic Activity 1867–1978', in W.T. Stanbury, ed., *Government Regulation: Scope, Growth, Process* (Montreal: Institute for Research on Public Policy, 1980); A.R. Vining and R. Botterell, 'An Overview of the Origins, Growth, Size, and Functions of Provincial Crown Corporations', in J.R.S. Pritchard, ed., *Crown Corporations: The Calculus of Instrument Choice* (Toronto: Butterworths, 1983).

15. Martin Robin, ed., *Canadian Provincial Politics: The Party Systems of the Ten Provinces* (Scarborough, Ont.: Prentice-Hall, 1972); Martin Robin, ed., *Canadian Provincial Politics* (Scarborough, Ont.: Prentice-Hall, 1978).

16. See David J. Bellamy, Jon H. Pammett, and Donald C. Rowat, eds, *Provincial Political Systems: Comparative Essays* (Toronto: Methuen, 1976).

17. See David Elkins and Richard Simeon, eds, *Small Worlds: Provinces and Parties in Canadian Political Life* (Toronto: Methuen, 1980).

18. See T.W. Acheson, 'The National Policy and the Industrialization of the Maritimes, 1880–1910', *Acadiensis* 1 (1972): 3–28; David Alexander, *Atlantic Canada and Confederation* (Toronto: University of Toronto Press, 1983); H.V. Nelles, *The Politics of Development* (Toronto: Macmillan, 1974); J. Richards and L. Pratt, *Prairie Capitalism: Power and Influence in the New West* (Toronto: McClelland & Stewart, 1977).

19. See, for example, R.J. Brym and R.J. Sacouman, eds, *Underdevelopment and Social Movements in Atlantic Canada* (Toronto: New Hogtown Press, 1979); Michael Clow, 'Politics

and Uneven Capitalist Development: The Maritime Challenge to the Study of Canadian Political Economy', *Studies in Political Economy* 14 (1984); Larry Pratt and Garth Stevenson, eds, *Western Separatism: The Myth, Realities and Dangers* (Edmonton: Hurtig, 1981).

20. E.R. Black and A.C. Cairns, 'A Different Perspective on Canadian Federalism', *Canadian Public Administration* 9, 1 (1966): 27–44.

21. See Harold Chorney and Phillip Hansen, 'Neo-Conservatism, Social Democracy, and "Province-Building": The Experience of Manitoba', *Canadian Review of Sociology and Anthropology* 22, 1 (1985): 1–29; Larry Pratt, 'The State and Province-Building: Alberta's Development Strategy', in Leo Panitch, ed., *The Canadian State: Political Economy and Political Power* (Toronto: University of Toronto Press, 1977). Also see the essay by Stephen G. Tomblin included here.

22. R.A. Young, Phillipe Faucher, and Andre Blais, 'The Concept of Province Building: A Critique', *Canadian Journal of Political Science* 17 (1984): 783–818.

23. See, for example, James Bickerton, *Nova Scotia, Ottawa, and the Politics of Regional Development* (Toronto: University of Toronto Press, 1990); Keith Brownsey and Michael Howlett, eds, *The Provincial State: Politics in Canada's Provinces and Territories* (Toronto: Copp Clark Pitman, 1992); Jacqueline S. Ismael and Yves Vaillancourt, eds, *Privatization and Provincial Social Services in Canada: Policy, Administration, and Service Delivery* (Edmonton: University of Alberta Press, 1988); Melville McMillan, ed., *Provincial Public Finances*, vol. 1, *Provincial Surveys* (Toronto: Canadian Tax Foundation, 1991).

24. For example, L.R. Jones and Jerry L. McCaffery, *Government Response to Financial Constraints: Budgetary Control in Canada* (New York: Greenwood Press, 1989); James M. Lutz, 'Emulation and Policy Adoptions in the Canadian Provinces', *Canadian Journal of Political Science* 22, 1 (1989): 147–54; J.A. McAllister, 'Fiscal Capacity and Tax Effort: Explaining Public Expenditures in the 10 Canadian Provinces', paper presented to the annual meeting of the Canadian Political Science Association, 1984, Guelph, Ont.; P. McCormick, 'Provincial Political Party Systems 1945–1986', in A. Gagnon and A.B. Tanguay, eds, *Canadian Parties in Transition* (Toronto: Nelson, 1989). See also Christopher Dunn, *Provinces* (Peterborough, Ont.: Broadview Press, 1996).

## Study Questions for the Readings

1. Describe the principal elements of the Bennett government's activities in BC between 1952 and 1972. Why would these be considered to be efforts at 'province-building'?

2. What role did the federal government play in British Columbia's development over the period 1952–72? Are 'province-building' and 'nation-building' contradictory or consistent processes?

3. Is Canada's federal system of government 'wasteful'? How can this be measured?

4. Why has concern with federal-provincial 'overlap' increased since 1980?

5. What is the link, if any, between overlap and efficiency? Is the duplication of federal and provincial services necessarily negative?

# W.A.C. Bennett and Province-Building in British Columbia

Stephen G. Tomblin

One of the great myths in the study of British Columbia politics is the dominant view that the rise of the W.A.C. Bennett administration in 1952 introduced an era of incompetent and short-sighted political leadership. Richard Simeon, in his study of federal-provincial relations, singled out Bennett's 'personalized style' as being important in explaining the province's poor record in defending provincial interests during intergovernmental negotiations.[1] Walter Young and Terence Morley depict the Bennett administration as being an 'amateur government'.[2] Donald Smiley reports that the Social Credit leadership had 'no vision, no plan, no real urge, to remake society. In spite of its constant appeals to morality, Social Credit is at heart the pursuit of power divorced from purpose.'[3] And Martin Robin, Bennett's greatest critic, suggests:

> Past Liberal critics of the government party, confused and dazzled by Social Credit's sometimes idiosyncratic style prefer to define Social Credit not as a political and legislative coalition which represents different groups and balances one interest against the other, but as an unpredictable bond of latter-day Poujadists and political nihilists who have no purpose in mind except to retain power and do so by cynically waging war on all established elites whether of the left or right. The Socialist critique abjures both views and defines Social Credit in a more traditional way as primarily a spokesman and representative of the established economic elites, both within and without the province.[4]

First published in *BC Studies*, 85 (Spring 1990): 45–61. Reprinted by permission of BC Studies.

In contrast to these criticisms, much evidence—and particularly that presented at the Royal Commission on the BC Railway in 1977—suggests that the Bennett government did understand, and very clearly, what it was trying to do. Its 'vision', manifest in its grasp of the importance of provincial control over transportation and communication policy in signifying possession, and in stimulating new opportunities in the interior and north, was in fact very obvious.[5] The premier made plain his belief that the provincial leadership must have its own development scheme as a defence against Ottawa and Alberta. He and his colleagues therefore designed a development plan that would, in their view, defend BC's territorial interests and allow it to grow as they believed it should.[6] Indeed, the premier maintained that he was pursuing the same types of objectives as those undertaken by the Fathers of Confederation—though his concern with the north-south axis led him to challenge the development and expansion of the national transportation system because he believed it reinforced interprovincial communication and transportation instead of an intraprovincial network.[7]

## Defensive Expansionism

Utilizing infrastructure development to consolidate a territory under the control of an entrepreneurial leadership is not a new approach in the politics of state intervention in Canada. As discussed by Aitken, the national policy of 1867 featured a defensive expansionist strategy that aimed at defending the territory of Canada against American expansionism.[8] Primary emphasis was placed on building the infrastructure necessary to launch a new experiment in nation-building while defending territory from outside political competition.

Implicit in a defensive expansionist approach is the assumption that it is political élites who dominate the public agenda with the objective of preserving or increasing their territorial-jurisdictional control over a particular region.[9] The defensive model asserts that political élites are the key actors who assert their independence through controlling patterns of spatial interaction within the economy and society through the construction of infrastructure in a new frontier. Such an approach proposes that the primary purpose of such a strategy is to promote development, but within the spatial and temporal constraints governing the actions, and defining the interests, of the political élites who design and implement the policy.

## Dependency and the Battle for Territorial Integrity

When W.A.C. Bennett became premier in 1952, he set out to develop the hinterlands of the province and to reverse the problem of underdevelopment in the interior and north by building a new intraprovincial transportation system. He contended that Vancouver-based economic and political élites had not done enough to defend the province's territorial integrity against Ottawa and Alberta. He felt that it made good sense to exploit infrastructural development as a means of reversing the problems created by a long history of external political and economic dependence.[10] While the premier's ideas about restructuring the BC economy were not based upon challenging the province's reliance on outside markets and capital, he believed that he could resolve the problem of underdevelopment on the periphery if he could gain more control over the timing and location of economic development within the province. Thanks to the premier's popularity and his domination of the policy process, his ideas had a major impact on shaping the government's infrastructural development program between the years 1952 and 1972. As the available case studies show,

province-building does not necessarily require a large or effective bureaucratic structure. Certainly it did not during the Bennett years in BC.

Early in his political career, Bennett concluded that a mix of factors was responsible for the province's transportation problems. One of the premier's major targets was the system of power-sharing in the province. In early 1952, Bennett determined that weak political leadership was primarily responsible for the low level of rural BC's socio-economic and political development.[11] He believed that the political and economic élites of British Columbia were either unable or unwilling to defend the interests of the frontier against outsiders. The 'city slickers' that dominated both the socialist party and the coalition government were singled out for being weak defenders of the general provincial interest. Consequently, the premier concluded that the political infighting and open debates during the coalition era had focused too much attention on cost-effectiveness rather than on the needs of the interior and north. His administration adopted a different approach.

The British Columbia of 1952 was characterized by rugged frontier, recent immigration, weak provincial loyalties, a resource-dependent economy, and sporadic and isolated settlement.[12] If the province were ever to become a more integrated economic and political entity, it seemed essential to establish new transportation and communication links as quickly as possible. Bennett firmly believed that the stagnation and underdevelopment of the frontier would be reversed only if the provincial government took a more active role in building a substantial infrastructure. He conjectured that the externally controlled and spatially fragmented economy required stronger provincial control if the people of the frontier were ever to gain the benefits of a more integrated economy and society.

The federal government was Bennett's second obstacle. In an interview conducted by Roger Keene and David Humphreys, Bennett clearly stated that he first became involved in politics because he was convinced that national transportation policy and local élites were undermining economic and social development in the hinterland.[13] He openly condemned the BC government for walking away from negotiations and not challenging the Rowell-Sirois report's conclusions that the prospects for economic development in the interior and north were poor because of high transportation costs.[14] His solution was to gain power and develop the infrastructure required to open up the territory to the rest of the province. He thus moved—the items on the list are well known—to complete and extend the Pacific Great Eastern Railway, link the Lower Mainland with the interior and north, stimulate northern development by implementing the two-river policy, construct an oil and gas pipeline, service coastal communities by creating a new ferry system, build a superport at Roberts Bank, and upgrade and expand the provincial highways network.[15]

Central to Bennett's vision of a better-integrated and autonomous society was the building of a new communication and transportation network. Consequently, the Social Credit leadership became embroiled in several conflicts with the federal government, other provincial governments, and business interests in defending its priorities for development. The key to winning support was the ability to quickly implement the government's development plans. Once each piece of infrastructure was built, and as more and more communities came to depend upon the new services, the criticism subsided. By restricting public debate and by refusing to build a complex bureaucracy, Bennett was able to implement his priorities for development rapidly. Under these circumstances even the federal government was ultimately forced to accept Bennett's development scheme.

Premier Bennett consistently went out of his way to exploit transportation policy to defend the needs of the periphery against outside governmental and entrepreneurial interests. In relation to national rail policy, he thought,

the pattern was clear, British Columbia had to pioneer on its own. The national railway, content with the conventional operation and cash flow of the Edmonton to Prince Rupert corridor, ignoring both north and south, shied away from virgin and pioneer territory. Only when the risks were taken by this province and the hard work completed, did the CNR and Ottawa express interest in the open frontier.[16]

Despite the high costs, Bennett built an integrated railway system to make the interior and north accessible to the rest of the province.

He adopted a similar position in the case of the oil pipeline. The construction of an oil transportation facility in the Peace River region was intended to help the provincial government to increase its power to direct development, and Bennett stuck to his plan to do it despite much criticism. When he insisted that the oil industry build an integrated oil pipeline connecting northern and southern regions of the province, the industry argued that the abundance of relatively cheap oil reserves in Alberta, and presence of oil transportation facilities there, made the policy economically unfeasible. In a determined effort to defend his northern policy, 'Bennett forced the oil industry to build an all British Columbia oil pipeline south from the Peace River though the corporate economic judgement insisted it would be better routed through Alberta.'[17] The premier even threatened to transport oil through the rail network and then to legislate that the refinery companies accept the much more expensive product this would create. While the rail-building program was a financial nightmare and the costs of installing the pipeline were very high, the government thus succeeded in opening up the frontier to the rest of the province through its highway, ferry, railway, hydro, and oil and gas policies.[18] It was, however, in the contest for control of the frontier between the province and Ottawa that Bennett's enthusiasm for his grand design emerged most clearly.

The Social Credit leadership believed that the province had entered a critical period and that only through governmental action could British Columbia hope to defend its territorial ambitions. Matters were complicated by the fact that there was a kind of Alberta-Ottawa alliance. Thanks to it, the Bennett government adopted the position that unless the province quickly implemented its own development scheme, the goal of 'displacing Alberta's growing influence on the activities covering almost one quarter of this province's land mass, would be lost',[19] perhaps forever. Indeed, even more was at stake, for Alberta, with the support of Ottawa, stood to become a major gateway between California and the north.[20] Tying the north to the rest of the province was essential to counteract this possibility.[21]

By the time Bennett was selected as premier in 1952, the Alberta government, with help from Ottawa, had already built some of the infrastructure necessary to ensure that Alberta became the gateway and main supplier for the north.[22] This process continued. As one submission to the Royal Commission on the BC Railway would put it, 'Alberta has made considerable progress to date in advancing and upgrading its transportation links with the Northwest Territories, knowing that trading and transportation patterns, once established, would be difficult to change. Similar efforts are long overdue by British Columbia to create a trading corridor from the Arctic to the Pacific, opening up the Yukon and Northwest Territories.'[23] This was the kind of view Bennett had tried to take.

The Social Credit government's commitment to building a more integrated system of transportation in BC was based upon the belief that only if this were done would the province have the power necessary to play a more productive role in developing the province's resources, and to defend the needs of the frontier against outside governments. Indeed, as Ray Williston, a member of Bennett's cabinet, once noted, more than transportation was involved: the Social Credit government had a long-term development plan which

intentionally exploited rail transportation, oil and gas resources, and the Peace River power project in order to defend its development plans and territorial ambitions.[24]

## Peace River Hydro Development

The 'two rivers' controversy flared up during the late 1950s and early 1960s as the federal and British Columbia governments fought to gain control over hydro development in the province.[25] The controversy's emergence provided Bennett with an opportunity to focus on the development needs of the province and thereby challenge the shortcomings of the national development policy. The premier insisted that the Peace River project would proceed, arguing that it was the only site fully under the control and jurisdiction of his administration.[26]

The proposal by the Peace River Power Development Company to open up the north was a major one and led to the two-rivers policy. But Bennett's interest in the matter ensured that the commitment to northern expansion was not solely the creation of private commercial interests. The original decision to support the Peace River Power Corporation's large-scale investment scheme appears, indeed, to have been based more on a government concern to promote new cost-effective links in the province than on a desire to protect the interests of any single power broker. The fact that the company lost millions of dollars in financing the project certainly suggests that the government did not grant big business any special favours.

The decision to push for public involvement was based on at least two political considerations. The lack of initiative shown by Swedish industrialist Wenner Gren was a major factor.[27] He had failed to provide the funding and leadership required to open up the north. Since the power industry was unwilling to gamble, the government decided it should proceed alone. Northern development and the provincialization policy were too important to be sacrificed.

Second, William Mainwaring, past vice-president of BC Electric and president of Peace River Development Company between 1958 and 1961, was unable to carry out Bennett's development scheme without a contract with BC Electric to purchase Peace River power.[28] But BC Electric, reversing its position of 1959, had refused to commit itself to purchasing Peace River power in 1960. The corporate giant adopted the position that other sources of energy, including Hat Creek thermal and Columbia hydro power, were more cost-effective.

In view of these considerations, the premier asked the BC Energy Board to compare and contrast the advantages and disadvantages of Peace vs Columbia development. The board played a major role in helping to rationalize the takeover of Wenner Gren's Peace River Power Development and BC Electric on 1 August 1961. It is no coincidence that the premier introduced the Energy Board's commissioned study on the same day that the assets of BC Electric and Peace River Power Development Company were seized by government.[29] As noted by Neil Swainson, 'the Energy Board's comparison of the cost of power from the two river systems paved the way for the Peace River Company's takeover. The substance of its findings was that under similar conditions and public ownership, there would be little to choose between the power costs averaged over the period to 1985.'[30]

There was little inclination among business leaders or the general public to support the takeover of BC Electric.[31] At the time the decision was made, major commercial interests had their own sources of energy. Cominco's mining operations and Alcan's Kitimat-Kemano mega-projects were already well established.

The federal government was also critical of Bennett's plan. After 1957, Ottawa held serious reservations about the cost-effectiveness of the northern development scheme. Its view was supported by federal government and private industry studies on Peace River hydro potential. Much of the criticism focused on the problem of securing adequate funding for both hydro development projects, and the high cost of building an integrated power system spanning the province. The federal government also felt that the simultaneous development of both rivers would create a surplus of energy. Its preferred scheme for development of the Columbia River basin included delaying the Peace River power project, introducing the downstream power benefits generated in the US directly into the BC power grid, and building a major upper Kootenay storage facility in Canada for a major diversion.[32] Such a development scheme would, it thought, create new industrial opportunities in western Canada, rather than in the US.

The provincial takeover of the power industry increased the opportunity to regulate development in BC. A major benefit of the step was that it helped to preserve the revenue lost to the federal government through corporate income tax paid by BC Electric. The Bennett government had been a major critic of the federal tax system, and the takeover of the power industry provided a vehicle for registering its dissent.[33] The premier felt that the federal tax system was responsible for removing essential provincial resources that could be spent rectifying underdevelopment in the interior and the north. The takeover meant that revenues which had gone to Ottawa would now stay in the province.

A second benefit of the takeover was the increased likelihood that the Americans would accept Bennett's demand for compensation for downstream benefits.[34] As noted by Ronald Worley, 'before the Premier's announcement, the U.S. had felt in a good bargaining position regarding the Columbia. The Americans were confident the province would have to develop the Columbia anyway, even if they refused to give back any power from downstream benefits, now the shoe was on the other foot.'[35] The policy forced the Americans to accept the premier's demands for downstream compensation.[36] The Columbia River Treaty signed between the US and Canada formally recognized Canada's right to downstream flood control benefits.[37]

Notwithstanding these gains, several groups mobilized to oppose the actions of the provincial government. The Vancouver Board of Trade, the British Columbia Chamber of Commerce, and the Canadian Chamber of Commerce led various business interests in rallying opposition to the expropriation of BC Electric.[38] In addition, a survey conducted for the *Province* confirmed that the general public preferred Ottawa's scheme for power development.[39]

The provincial government none the less proceeded with the policy, and found that implementation of it did in fact increase its power to control development, and to mobilize and create support for its position. When Canada signed the 1961 treaty before a federal-provincial agreement was completed, Bennett was therefore in a position to threaten to veto the agreement until his demand for downstream power sales was allowed.

With the support of Gordon Shrum and the other members of the Energy Board, the premier entered the most bitter confrontation in the history of his administration. The Energy Board raised serious doubts about the accuracy of past comparisons on Peace vs Columbia power costs.[40] Specifically, the Energy Board report suggested that the two-river policy was both feasible and desirable. To be sure, as noted by Swainson, 'the board had loaded its figures to a degree.'[41] Its report none the less served a useful political function.[42] Rather than capitulating to the demands of intellectuals and business interests, the premier exploited the talents of experts to legitimize his policy in the public's eyes.

In the end, all parties accepted hydro development on the premier's terms. The federal government reversed its opposition to long-term power exports to US markets. The Americans acknowledged Canada's right to compensation for downstream flood benefits, and also agreed to accept the sale of Canadian entitlement to Columbia power. The final agreement was ratified on 22 January 1964.

# Roberts Bank

In the late 1960s the provincial economy continued to expand. David Mitchell commented that

> one of the most important features of this period was British Columbia's developing Pacific presence; Canada was only beginning to realize that it was a Pacific as well as an Atlantic nation. Bennett promoted his province throughout the Pacific Rim and made special overtures to the resource-hungry Japanese who often showed a keener understanding of B.C.'s development potential than did Central Canadians. Always the publicist, Bennett declared: 'There are great mountains separating British Columbia from Ottawa, but between us and Japan there is only the peaceful sea.'[43]

The series of events leading to the construction of a major coal port facility at Roberts Bank clearly illustrates that federal-provincial disputes over development priorities do not always promote zero-sum conflicts where there is only one winner. As noted by Ian Urquhart, country-building and province-building are often 'complementary community-building activities'.[44] So they turned out to be in this case.

In the early stages, of course, the federal and BC governments did square off to debate whether the construction of a new facility at Roberts Bank was necessary. However, because of the initiatives of the Bennett government, an intergovernmental compact was eventually formed to serve the interests of both governments.

The precipitating event which spurred the Bennett administration into action was the decision taken in May 1966 by Crowsnest Industries of Fernie Ltd to export coal to Japan. The coal would be transported through Montana to a US port via the Great Northern Railway. The coal company's goal was the most efficient and cost-effective means of transporting its product to Japan by way of a deep-water port. The Bennett government, on the other hand, wanted to see the project completed, but only if it served the territorial and jurisdictional interests of the province.

On 3 September 1966, Energy Board secretary J. Southworth made public a special report which recommended that the province construct an alternative facility at Roberts Bank which would protect all BC's general commodity exports.[45] In November, after closely studying the proposal, the Bennett government adopted the policy as its own.

Once the decision was made, Bennett announced plans to construct a major industrial complex near the port site. Attorney General Robert Bonner, minister responsible for the deep-sea superport, unveiled the cabinet's ambitions for an innovative scheme calling for oil-tank facilities and containerized cargo and lumber assembly wharves at the site.[46]

This announcement sparked a major controversy. Led by the federal government, many of the most powerful economic interests in the province strongly opposed the scheme for port development.[47] Because the Saskatchewan Wheat Pool, Transmountain Oil Pipeline Company, Canadian National Railway, Pacific Coast Bulk Terminals, Vancouver Wharves Ltd, Neptune Terminals Ltd, and the National Harbours Board had collectively spent $100 million to upgrade the port of Vancouver, they did not take kindly to a scheme that would create a rival to it at public expense.[48]

The premier's commitment to the project was, in part, a response to the fact that the Port of Vancouver was unable to accommodate 100,000-ton tankers. Equally, however, he wanted an alternative facility to one in Washington state. Bennett was not prepared to be simply a spokesman for the coal barons who originally proposed an American route.

In September 1966, Transport Minister Bonner recommended that cabinet should approve the establishment of a BC Harbours Board to oversee port construction and maintenance at Roberts Bank.[49] The new initiative was not well received by major commercial interests. The consensus among members of the shipping community and the National Harbours Board was that the proposed Roberts Bank port alternative was not economically feasible.

In November 1966, Ottawa responded by announcing its intention to defend its jurisdiction over the waterfront area. The federal government was not against port development *per se*. Its major criticism was that the Bennett scheme threatened the existing facilities in the Port of Vancouver.[50] But there was, in its view, room for compromise. As stated by then federal Transport Minister Pickersgill, 'there is no reason why such a facility could not be provided by the provincial government or by private interests as long as they fit into the overall scheme.'[51]

Ottawa's move triggered a major confrontation between the two levels of government. Suspicious of what he saw as Ottawa's lack of concern for the development needs of British Columbia, the premier reacted by claiming provincial control over the project on the ground that the province had jurisdiction over the area 'between low tide and the shore'.[52]

By March 1967, the Social Credit government was moving forward with its plan to build a superport at Roberts Bank 'with or without federal government participation'.[53] Since the port was to be constructed and operated by the province, Transport Minister Bonner introduced a bill to create a provincial harbours board with the authority to borrow up to $25 million.[54] It would have a staff of between three and seven members with the premier as fiscal agent. The proposed legislation allowed the provincial harbours board to enter co-operative agreements with Ottawa, but on the province's terms.

Preparations for a major assault on shipping interests in the Port of Vancouver as well as on the federal government were well under way with the creation of the provincial harbours board. Certainly, as press reports show, the creation of the BC Harbours Board in March 1967 significantly altered the focus of debate.[55]

The federal government responded by sending a number of different signals.[56] At first, Prime Minister Pearson joined Jack Davis, MP for Coast-Capilano, in denouncing the Roberts Bank scheme. But the criticism quickly subsided.[57] The federal government was clearly reassessing its options in light of the jurisdictional challenges put forward by the Bennett government.

Having attracted Ottawa's attention, Bennett took the opportunity to focus attention on rail transportation's relation to the scheme. In April 1967, the premier raised serious questions about the ability of the two national railways to service the proposed port facility.[58] An alternative connection, he thought, should be established with the Great Northern Railway to the south, in case the national rail lines failed to deliver on time. The premier also proposed that a provincial line be constructed connecting the superport with the Canadian and American railways.[59] This would ensure British Columbia's full control over rail operations.

The Bennett government faced major opposition in its drive for new rail and port facilities in the province. Pacific Coast Bulk Terminals Ltd, a subsidiary of Cominco, joined the Canadian Pacific Railway in criticizing the decision to build a superport at Roberts Bank. The president of Pacific Coast Bulk Terminals, the largest bulk facility in BC, thought that Roberts Bank was 'at least eight years premature'.[60] If Bennett had been solely concerned with servicing the needs of the local business community, he would most likely have avoided locking horns with Cominco and the CPR. These were powerful economic interests in the Pacific province. Yet the premier continued to press on.

By October 1967, Ottawa was shifting its position concerning Roberts Bank. In November, federal Transport Minister Paul Hellyer indicated that the National Harbours Board was considering contributing $50 million for the superport,[61] pro-

viding it was built as part of an integrated scheme involving Vancouver harbour. The federal transport minister clearly hoped to build a coal facility at Roberts Bank which would complement rather than compete with existing infrastructure.

While the provincial government was prepared to welcome federal funding, provincial Attorney General Robert Bonner stated publicly that the provincial leadership would continue to operate on the premise that Roberts Bank was a provincial project.[62] Hellyer's plan for upgrading harbour facilities over a 30-year construction period was, he claimed, unrealistic. It was, indeed, pretty clear that the province's leadership viewed the federal offer as a delaying tactic. BC therefore went ahead with plans to build the superport by itself. Bennett was simply not convinced that Ottawa shared his development priorities.

Many observers of the political struggle for control were upset by the extraordinary dedication to preserving provincial autonomy exhibited by the premier, especially when taking such a stance might place the project in additional jeopardy. Various commercial interests were concerned that the confrontational approach might threaten the project, and Alberta and Saskatchewan expressed a fear that Bennett planned to invoke a tariff on out-of-province cargo.[63] One journalist, noting all this, warned that 'Mr. Bennett is mistaken if he thinks the people of this province are willing to pay such a price for his empire-building and self glorification.'[64] While the British Columbia government blamed Ottawa for promoting confrontation, a public relations spokesman for Kaiser Steel Corporation expressed the view that the Bennett government, and not Ottawa, was 'dangerously close to pushing the derail button'.[65]

Bennett and his colleagues were undismayed. In an effort to increase the competitive advantage of the provincial government in the fight for jurisdictional authority over the superport, the chairman of the newly created BC Harbours board, Robert Bonner, spearheaded a new campaign. Bennett himself set the scene by declaring that his government was more capable than its federal counterpart of ensuring that the superport was built on time and in accordance with the development needs of British Columbia.[66] He dismissed the constitutional argument as being a federal ploy to defer further action.[67] And he showed little respect for Ottawa's constitutional position, using an Order in Council in March 1968 to expropriate the land surrounding the designated site.[68] The province was clearly set to go it alone, despite Ottawa's reassurances and efforts to promote a compromise.

The response from Ottawa was swift. The federal government threatened to challenge the legality of the provincial initiative, to expropriate the provincial land, and to build the facility by itself. While the prospect of a long drawn-out court battle threatened the $650 million coal contract, each government continued to defend its own interests.

In the end, Premier Bennett backed away from the issue of provincial participation in all areas of port development, but he managed to influence port construction. The provincial government got significant input into the timing and planning of the mega-project.[69] Moreover, in an effort to control the major decisions concerning rail transportation, it ensured that BC Hydro and BC Rail would provide the only rail link to the facility.[70]

## Conclusion

In light of the foregoing, it seems clear that there is a need to reconsider the significance of the role played by W.A.C. Bennett's leadership in shaping the growth of the BC economy and society. Whether it was hydro development policy, rail policy, pipeline policy, or Roberts Bank, the Bennett government actively built alliances, forestalled external challenges, and intervened to promote and implement a self-designed infrastructural development program. Aiming at once to increase political and economic autonomy and to reverse the problem of underdevelopment and dependency in BC through the building of physical infrastructure, Bennett and his government devised, and successfully implemented, a strategy of major importance.

While, then, the Bennett government has been characterized as concerned mainly with votes, with defending business interests, or with being short-sighted in its planning, the history of infrastructural development provides evidence that the premier was more than a simple broker of conflicting societal interests. When we consider the extent to which the provincial government went out of its way to defend its own political ambitions and territorial goals against the private sector and Ottawa, it is hard not to conclude that the political leadership had its own set of objectives which were not simply a product of interest group pressure.

While the policy was often criticized by the federal government, academics, business interests, and others who questioned the costs of the various development schemes, the building of new transportation and communication links in BC was central to the territorial interests and goals of the entrepreneurial leadership. The so-called unprepared 'amateur government' was able to battle with its critics, and in the end, the Bennett administration won more battles than it lost in exploiting physical infrastructural development to defend its territorial ambitions.

Reforms in the field of transportation were given top priority in the Social Credit's plan of action. Emphasis was placed upon exploiting infrastructural development to ensure that economic development assumed a different spatial pattern than it would have otherwise—a pattern more consistent with the government's plans for territorial integration. It is time for scholars to recognize that the propensity to pursue provincial initiatives, with the intention of shaping economic and political interests along provincial lines, was a strong determining force under W.A.C. Bennett. It was a period of government-sponsored province-building.

## Notes

Much of the detail provided in this paper was drawn from my Ph.D. thesis. I wish to thank Alan Cairns, Donald Blake, Keith Banting, Paul Tennant, David Close, Gail Tomblin-Murphy, Dianne O'Brien, Jimmy Tindigarukayo, and the readers of *BC Studies* for their comments, encouragement, and suggestions.

1. See Richard Simeon, *Federal-Provincial Diplomacy: The Making of Recent Policy in Canada* (Toronto: University of Toronto Press, 1972), 217.
2. Walter Young and Terence Morley, 'The Premier in the Cabinet', in Terence Morley et al., eds, *The Reins of Power* (Vancouver: Douglas & McIntyre, 1983), 64.
3. Donald Smiley, 'Canada's Poujadists: A New Look at Social Credit', *Canadian Forum* 42 (Sept. 1962): 121.
4. Martin Robin, 'British Columbia: The Politics of Class Conflict', in Robin, ed., *Canadian Provincial Politics* (Scarborough, Ont.: Prentice-Hall, 1972), 53.
5. See University of British Columbia, Main Library, Special Collections Division, *Presentations to Royal Commission on British Columbia Railway*, Exhibits: 172, 173A, 186, 256, 285.
6. See 'Presentation to Royal Commission on the B.C. Railway from W.A.C. Bennett', and 'Presentation to Royal Commission on B.C. Rail from Ray Williston', Sept. 1977, Exhibits 173A and 186 respectively.
7. See *B.C. Government News,* Jan. 1954, 4, 6.
8. H.G.J. Aitken, 'Defensive Expansionism: The State and Economic Growth in Canada', in W.T. Easterbrook and M.H. Watkins, eds, *Approaches to Canadian Economic History* (Ottawa: Gage Publishing, 1980), 181–221.
9. Ibid., 209–10.
10. For further discussion on dependency, élite alliances, and underdevelopment, see Andre Gunder Frank, *Capitalism and Underdevelopment in Latin America* (New York: Monthly Review Press, 1967).
11. Resnick and Marchak have concluded the same thing. For details, see P. Resnick, 'B.C. Capitalism and the Empire and the Pacific', paper presented at the Western Sociology and Anthropology Association meetings, 4–6 Mar. 1981; Patricia Marchak, 'A Contribution to the Class and Regional Debate', *Canadian Issues* (1983): 81–8.
12. For further information, see Edwin Black, 'British Columbia: The Politics of Exploitation', in Dickson Falconer, ed., *British Columbia: Patterns of Economic, Political and Cultural Development* (Victoria: Camosun College, 1982), 250–66.
13. Roger Keene and David Humphreys, *Conversations with W.A.C. Bennett* (Toronto: Methuen, 1980), 30.
14. Ibid.
15. For further details on the history of infrastructural development in BC, see S.G. Tomblin, 'In Defense of Territory: Province-Building Under W.A.C. Bennett', Ph.D. thesis (University of British Columbia, 1985).
16. 'Presentation to Royal Commission on the B.C. Railway from W.A.C. Bennett', 6 Sept. 1977.
17. Paddy Sherman, *Bennett* (Toronto: McClelland & Stewart, 1966), x.
18. For details on the costs of these various projects, see Alfred Carlsen, 'Public Debt Operations in B.C. Since 1952', *Canadian Journal of Economic and Political Science* 27, 1 (Feb. 1961): 74–81; Martin Crilly, 'Analysis of British Columbia Ferries and Its Commercial Vehicle Policy', MBA thesis (University of British Columbia, 1973); H.L. Purdy, *Transport Competition and Public Policy in Canada* (Vancouver: University of British Columbia Press, 1972); Patrick McGeer, *Politics in Paradise* (Toronto: Peter Martin, 1972); John Munro, 'Highways in British Columbia: Economics and Politics', *Canadian Journal of Economics* 8, 2 (May 1975): 192–202; K. Rupenthal and T. Keast, *The British Columbia Railway—A Railway Derailed* (Centre for Transportation Studies, University of British Columbia, 1979); A.D. Scott, 'The Columbia River Treaty', *Canadian Journal of Economics* 2, 4 (1969): 619–26; Kenneth Strand, 'The B.C. Hydro Project', in Paul Weiler et al., eds, *Megaprojects* (Canadian Construction Association, 1981); Neil Swainson, *Conflict Over the Columbia* (Montreal and Kingston: McGill-Queen's University Press, 1979); P. Sykes, *Sellout: The Giveaway of Canada's Energy Resources* (Edmonton: Hurtig, 1973); G.W. Taylor, *Builders of British Columbia: An Industrial History* (Victoria: Morriss Publishing, 1982).
19. 'Presentation to Royal Commission on the B.C. Railway from Ray Williston'.

20. 'Presentation to Royal Commission on the B.C. Railway from W.A.C. Bennett', 6 Sept. 1977.

21. For further details, see Rosemary Neering, W.A.C. Bennett (Vancouver: Fitzhenry & Whiteside, 1981), 47.

22. See Geoffrey Willis, 'Development of Transportation in the Peace River Region of Alberta and British Columbia', MA thesis (University of Alberta, 1966).

23. Royal Commission on the B.C. Railway 35 (1978): 4911.

24. See University of British Columbia, Main Library, Special Collections Division, 'Presentation to Royal Commission from Ray Williston', Sept. 1977, Exhibit 186, 2.

25. The two-rivers policy refers to the commitment made by Bennett to develop the hydro potential of both the Peace and Columbia rivers.

26. For further discussion, see Sherman, Bennett, 221–7, 239–42.

27. For details, see Swainson, Conflict Over the Columbia, 82; and Roger Keene's Collections, Provincial Archives, 'An Interview by Jack Webster with W.A.C. Bennett, CJOR, 22 Oct. 1976'.

28. Ronald Worley, The Wonderful World of W.A.C. Bennett (Toronto: McGraw-Hill Ryerson, 1971), 232.

29. Swainson, Conflict Over the Columbia, 201.

30. Ibid., 202.

31. For evidence of poll conducted by Hugh S. Hardy and Associates, see Vancouver Sun, 24 Aug. 1957, 9.

32. For an account on the House of Commons' view of hydro development, see Government of Canada, House of Commons Second Session—Twenty-Sixth Parliament Standing Committee on External Affairs, 'Columbia River Treaty Protocol', Minutes of Proceedings and Evidence (Ottawa: Queen's Printer, 1964).

33. For examples of this criticism, see B.C. Government News, Dec. 1955, 4–8; Feb. 1956, 3–4; Mar. 1957, 2, 6; Feb. 1960, 3; Feb. 1962, 2.

34. For further details, see Martin Robin, Pillars of Profit (Toronto: McClelland & Stewart, 1973), 208–17.

35. Worley, The Wonderful World of W.A.C. Bennett, 226.

36. Victoria Daily Times, 28 Feb. 1958.

37. See Swainson, Conflict Over the Columbia, 1.

38. See Vancouver Province, 13 Sept. 1961; Vancouver Province, 20 Sept. 1962; Vancouver Sun, 4 Oct. 1961.

39. Vancouver Province, 2 Oct. 1961.

40. See Victoria Daily Colonist, 2 Aug. 1961; Vancouver Sun, 29 Aug. 1961; Province of British Columbia, British Columbia Energy Board Annual Report, 'Interim Report on the Columbia and Peace Power Projects', Victoria, BC, 1 Mar. 1961.

41. Swainson, Conflict Over the Columbia, 203.

42. For further information on Strachan's criticism of the two-river policy, see letter from R.M. Strachan, Leader of Opposition, to T.C. Douglas, National Leader of the NDP, 7 Sept. 1961; Press Release from Robert Strachan, 4 May 1964, Province of British Columbia Archives.

43. David Mitchell, W.A.C. Bennett and the Rise of British Columbia (Vancouver: Douglas & McIntyre, 1983), 385.

44. Ian Urquhart, 'Country-building and Province-building', MA thesis (Queen's University, 1980).

45. See Vancouver Province, 3 Sept. 1966, 1; British Columbia Research Council, Vancouver Harbour Traffic Trends and Facility Analysis (Vancouver, 1967).

46. See Vancouver Province, 9 Nov. 1966.

47. For further discussion on the merits and demerits of the Robert Banks proposal, see Richard Hankin, 'An Investigation of the Utility of Benefit-Cost Analysis in Waterfront Allocation', MA thesis (University of British Columbia, 1968), 61–117; Environment Canada, A Statement of Deficiencies in the Environmental Assessment of Roberts Bank Port Expansion (issued to the National Harbours Board by Environmental Assessment Panel, Feb. 1978); Beak Hinton Consultants Ltd, Response to 'A Statement of Deficiencies in the Environmental Impact Assessment for Roberts Bank Port Expansion' (National Harbours Board, June 1978).

48. Vancouver Province, 9 Nov. 1966.

49. Ibid., 3 Sept. 1966.

50. See the Government of British Columbia, Department of Industrial Development, Trade and Commerce, British Columbia Business 1972 (Victoria: Queen's Printer, 1972).

51. Vancouver Sun, 10 Nov. 1966.

52. See Vancouver Province, 14 Mar. 1967.

53. Ibid.

54. The Act provided that 'the Board is established for the purposes of developing or encouraging the development of harbour facilities, and to assist and promote the industrial development of the

Province in conjunction with harbour development.' See province of British Columbia, 'An Act to Establish the B.C. Harbours Board', *Statutes of British Columbia* (1967), 9.

55. See *Vancouver Province*, 14 Mar. 1967.

56. A former member of the Bennett cabinet indicated in an interview with the author that the federal government supported the Roberts Bank scheme primarily because of the proposals for development put forward by the Bennett government. It was felt that Ottawa's major concern was preserving its jurisdictional integrity over port development rather than servicing the needs of the province.

57. *Victoria Daily Times*, 20 Mar. 1967; *Vancouver Province*, 1 Apr. 1967.

58. *Vancouver Province*, 25 Mar., 5 Apr. 1967.

59. For an overview of the federal government's position on the question of rail access, see Letter from Don Jamieson, Minister of Transport, to Premier Bennett, 2 Apr. 1970.

60. *Victoria Daily Times*, 10 Aug. 1967.

61. *Vancouver Sun*, 20 Oct. 1967.

62. See *Victoria Daily Times*, 1 Nov. 1967; Province of British Columbia, Department of Trade and Industry, *B.C. Government News* (Victoria: Queen's Printer, Aug. 1968), 16.

63. See *Vancouver Province*, 2 Mar. 1968; *Vancouver Sun*, 5 Mar. 1968; *Vancouver Province*, 14 Mar. 1969.

64. *Vancouver Sun*, 5 Mar. 1968.

65. *Victoria Daily Times*, 9 Nov. 1967.

66. Ibid., 7 Mar. 1968.

67. Ibid.

68. Ibid., 15, 23 Mar. 1968.

69. For further details on the role played by the province in developing Roberts Bank, see *B.C. Government News*, July-Aug. 1969, 16.

70. For further information, see *Vancouver Sun*, 7 June 1968.

# Canadian Federal-Provincial Overlap and Presumed Government Inefficiency

Gordon R. Brown

The claim that overlapping government activity in Canada's federal system causes significant government inefficiency has gained considerable currency. The popularity of such a claim is not surprising, because it links the perennial Canadian debate over the division of federal and provincial powers to growing concern about government finances. One recent analysis arguing for greater provincial powers makes this link especially clear:

> While public finances are in a state of crisis, many sectors (economic development, agriculture, immigration, health, education, manpower training, etc.) are still plagued by sterile and unproductive duplication of government programs. This overlapping dilutes resources and blurs the focus of government action as a whole. There is no concerted action and public funds are not put to optimal use.[1]

Over the past 15 years, there have been three Canadian studies devoted entirely to the question of overlap: the studies by Germain Julien and Marcel Proulx,[2] the Alberta government,[3] and the federal Treasury Board.[4] Have these studies demonstrated that, indeed, overlap causes considerable government inefficiency? That is the question addressed here. A positive finding would be significant. Governments in federal political systems would have an opportunity to spread their limited tax dollars further and, presumably, an incentive to resolve ongoing disputes over jurisdiction.

However, Canadian studies have not demonstrated that overlap causes significant government inefficiency. The studies have only demonstrated the existence of extensive overlap between federal and provincial government activity. The studies resort to qualitative arguments and anecdotal evidence when assessing the link between overlap and efficiency. This explains the studies' differing conclusions on the effect of overlap on efficiency. Julien and Proulx and the Alberta study take the traditional provincial position that overlap causes significant government inefficiency. The federal Treasury Board argues that overlap is managed fairly well. Thus, the debate about overlap remains essentially a debate about federal and provincial power, not about efficiency. This is apparently unavoidable, due to the difficulty of measuring the effect of overlap on efficiency.

The terms 'overlap', 'entanglement', 'duplication', and 'redundancy' describe similar phenomena. Overlap is given a wide range of meanings in the literature. It can entail more than one government providing similar or identical goods and services to similar or identical clients; it can also entail more than one government acting in a given policy area. The latter meaning is also applied to entanglement, although the word 'entanglement' carries a more pejorative connotation. Duplication and redundancy are more restricted terms, indicating that two governments are providing the same goods or services to the same clients. In the case of duplication, both governments provide some benefit. In the case of redundancy, the second government provides absolutely no additional benefit.[5] In this article, the terms 'overlap' and 'overlapping' are used to cover all these meanings. When a precise meaning is intended, it is indicated. The French terms

From *Publius: The Journal of Federalism* 24, 1 (Winter 1994): 21–37.

*chevauchement* and *dédoublement*, found in the Canadian literature, can be translated as overlap and duplication, respectively.

The term 'efficiency' also requires consideration. Should one use the accountant's conception of efficiency or the economist's? The accountant's conception of efficiency, sometimes referred to as productive or technical efficiency, focuses on the production process.[6] Productive efficiency involves the relation of outputs to inputs, and can be expressed as the amount of output obtained from a given input. An efficient program yields more output for a given input than an inefficient program. For the economist, efficiency involves maximizing welfare. Does the distribution of resources maximize the welfare of the populace?

This article discusses both productive efficiency and economic efficiency, because studies of overlap have dealt with both conceptions. Supporters of the provincial position, critical of the current level of overlap, generally use arguments related to productive efficiency. They argue that it would be cheaper for one government to handle a given policy area than for two governments to do so. In the Canadian context, this argument can be used to favour the provinces because they have constitutional jurisdiction in most areas of social policy. Defenders of the status quo, under which the federal and provincial governments coexist in most policy areas, respond in two ways. They either minimize the impact of overlap on productive efficiency, as the federal Treasury Board study does, or they turn to the concept of economic efficiency, arguing that two governments are more responsive to the public's demands than one government would be. This latter argument, focusing on the greater variety of choices overlapping programs offer the public, is associated with public choice theory.[7]

The focus of this article is on government efficiency. It would also be possible to address efficiency at the user level. Users may waste their own resources because they have to sort out which government provides which services, or because they have to deal with overlapping regulations. The issue of overregulation has an extensive literature of its own. To keep the subject manageable, this discussion relates to overlapping government programs rather than overlapping regulations. After a historical review of the debate about overlap, the findings of the three major Canadian studies of overlap are reviewed and the arguments concerning productive and economic theory are assessed.

## Overlap as a Recurring Theme in Canadian Federalism

The claim that overlap causes government inefficiency is not new. Furthermore, the provinces have usually been on the offensive, opposing the federal presence in most areas of provincial jurisdiction.

In the late 1930s, the federal government's Royal Commission on Dominion-Provincial Relations, better known as the Rowell-Sirois Commission, included an assessment of overlap's effect on government efficiency. Officials from the federal government and all provincial governments were invited to identify problems of overlap and duplication. All provinces except Quebec and Alberta agreed to send officials to appear before the commission. In addition, two commission staff members conducted a special survey of federal and provincial services.[8] The Rowell-Sirois Commission identified three areas of significant overlap: transportation, tax collection, and police service duplication between the Royal Canadian Mounted Police and three provincial forces.[9] Overall, however, the commission found that provincial criticism of overlap was overstated. The authors concluded:

> the Commission's inquiries failed to disclose the measure of overlapping and duplication between governments which has been charged from time to time. This conclusion is supported by the testimony of witnesses whose close contact with administrative conditions should have placed them in a

position to detect any substantial degree of such wastes. Every provincial government, as well as the Dominion government, was asked to permit officials to appear and give evidence about overlapping. During the Ontario hearings, questions were addressed to the Government of Ontario seeking precise evidence regarding allegations of overlapping made in the Ontario brief. Further information was promised but was not received. Similar requests to provide us with concrete evidence were made of business organizations, which had deplored the amount of duplication in government, but again with negative results.[10]

Overlap has also been an important issue more recently. In the early 1970s, Ontario budget papers identified the need for better co-ordination of economic policies.[11] At premiers' conferences, the Ontario premier drew public attention to his claim that duplicate federal and provincial services wasted money.[12] In 1975, overlap was addressed as one chapter of a special report aimed at controlling Ontario's expenditures. The study did not investigate problem areas in detail, recommending that be done in the future, but it did name areas 'identified by the provincial ministries as being significantly related to existing federal programs, if not directly overlapping with or duplicating such programs.'[13] Julien and Proulx, two academic researchers whose work was partly funded by the Quebec government, quantified the extent of overlap in their 1978 study of overlap between the federal and Quebec governments.[14] Also in the late 1970s, the western provinces documented 'the extent of federal intrusions' in areas of provincial jurisdiction.[15] Together, the provinces called on the federal government to reduce overlap.[16]

In 1978, the federal government offered to work with the provinces to harmonize programs. A recent federal assessment of this exercise concluded that it led to significant improvements, through better co-ordination and through federal withdrawal from some areas, including urban affairs. However, the same assessment noted that

'Few specific instances of purely wasteful duplication were identified.'[17]

In the mid-1980s, the federal government's Task Force on Program Review, better known as the Nielsen Task Force, gave some consideration to overlap. The new Conservative government charged the task force with investigating 'concern about waste, duplication, and red tape in federal departments and agencies'.[18] Although the focus was on federal programs, an assessment of federal waste and duplication required consideration of similar provincial programs. The task force noted overlap in regulations, services, and subsidies to business, and in services to veterans.[19] It also noted opportunities for smoother or rethought relationships with provincial governments in housing, health, justice, and Indian and Native affairs.[20] While this criticism of overlap was unusual for the federal government, it may be partly explained by the newness of the government and the Conservative Party's traditional support of provincial power. At about the same time, the Royal Commission on the Economic Union and Development Prospects for Canada, better known as the Macdonald Commission, sponsored research having some bearing on overlap. The research included studies dealing with the division of powers[21] and the harmonization of law in Canada.[22] Overlap received some theoretical discussion,[23] but no detailed analysis.

There has been renewed concern about overlap in the late 1980s and early 1990s, a period marked by recession and two failed attempts to amend the Constitution. Criticism of overlap is especially widespread in Quebec. The Chambre de commerce du Québec has identified the losses from overlap at 'many billions of dollars'.[24] The president of the Mouvement Desjardins, Quebec's leading financial institution, has claimed that overlapping jurisdictions and duplication have forced Ottawa to impose a heavy tax load on Canadians.[25] The president of the Banque Nationale has called for Ottawa to withdraw from some areas of activity, claiming that overlapping jurisdictions, waste, and ineffectiveness have become intolerable.[26] Quebec's two major political parties (the Liberal Party and the Parti Québécois) have also pointed to overlap as a source of government inefficiency.[27] That view was reflected by the Quebec government's Bélanger-Campeau Commission, established in 1990 to assess Quebec's constitutional status.[28]

Concern about overlap extends beyond Quebec. In 1990 and 1991, the western finance ministers argued for 'disentanglement' of federal and provincial spending responsibilities.[29] Soon after, Alberta conducted its overlap study. In 1991, the Canadian Chamber of Commerce surveyed its members about overlap. Thirty per cent of respondents reported they had personally encountered overlap or duplication in government expenditures.[30] In 1993, New Brunswick Premier Frank McKenna wrote to other first ministers, urging them to work together to reduce overlap. New Brunswick itself was studying more than a dozen areas of overlap.[31]

In 1991, the federal government responded to the widespread criticism of overlap with a study by its own Treasury Board, conducted during the height of the constitutional debate that followed the failure of the Meech Lake Accord. The study was part of a broader exercise to formulate federal constitutional proposals leading up to the Charlottetown Accord with the provinces, and the results were provided to the parliamentary committee studying renewed federalism.[32] The study was met with some scepticism, with even the prime minister's chief of staff noting that it would be unlikely for people responsible for programs to recommend their abolition.[33] Since then, the Liberal government elected in 1993 has promised to reduce overlap.

## The Extent of Overlap

How extensive is the overlap found in the studies conducted by Julien and Proulx of the École nationale d'administration publique (ÉNAP), the federal Treasury Board, and the Alberta government? The studies found significant overlap in government activity, with half to two-thirds of government activity occurring in areas of both federal and provincial involvement. Before detailing these findings, a word on the studies' methodologies is in order.

## Methodologies of the Studies

The 1978 ÉNAP study assessed overlap between federal and Quebec programs. The 1991 federal Treasury Board study assessed overlap between federal programs and the programs of all provincial governments. The 1992 Alberta study assessed overlap between federal and Alberta programs. Overlap was measured in terms of government programs. Other alternatives would have been to assess the number of areas that overlap in the Constitution, or the number of organizations that overlap (i.e., the number of federal and provincial departments or agencies dealing with similar concerns). The analysis of programs has the advantages of assessing actual overlap (versus constitutional overlap) and of allowing more precise measurement than the analysis of organizations (since programs are generally smaller units than organizations).

The studies differed in their source of information. The Treasury Board and Alberta studies used information from government managers with day-to-day involvement in their program areas. The ÉNAP study was based on an assessment of publicly available information in budgets and annual reports.

The studies also differed in what was counted. The ÉNAP study counted the number of non-administrative federal *and* Quebec programs involving some element of overlap. The extent of overlap was calculated by dividing the *number* of overlapping programs by the number of all programs. The Treasury Board study totalled expenditures for federal programs having some or all clients and services in common with provincial

## Table 1: Federal-Provincial Program Overlap Categories, 1991–1992 (Percentage of Total Federal Program Expenditure)

| Type of services | Type of clients | | |
| --- | --- | --- | --- |
| | Same | Partially same | Different |
| Same | Category 1<br>1.7%<br>Direct program overlap | Category 2<br>0.9%<br>Direct program overlap | Category 3<br>5.6%<br>Parallel programs overlap |
| Partially same | Category 4<br>26.8%<br>Direct program overlap | Category 5<br>12.7%<br>Direct program overlap | Category 6<br>1.0%<br>Parallel programs overlap |
| Different | Category 7<br>15.3%<br>Transfer programs | Category 8<br>1.3%<br>(No name given by Treasury Board) | Category 9<br>34.8%<br>No overlap |

Note: Table adds to 100.1% in the original document.

Source: Treasury Board Secretariat, *Federal-Provincial Overlap and Duplication: A Federal Program Perspective* (Ottawa: TBS, 1991), 16.

programs. The extent of overlap was calculated by dividing federal *expenditures* on overlapping programs by total federal program expenditures. The Alberta study totalled federal program expenditures in Alberta for activities in which Alberta also had expenditures. The extent of overlap was calculated by dividing the federal *expenditures* on overlapping programs by total federal expenditures apportionable to Alberta.

### The Findings on Overlap

Julien and Proulx found that 60 per cent of non-administrative programs had some element of overlap, whether considering federal programs (58 per cent) or Quebec programs (61 per cent).[34] This 60 per cent comprised programs with some element of direct overlap (roughly 50 per cent of all programs) and programs with some element of indirect overlap, in which one government merely provides financial or technical assistance to another government (roughly 10 per cent of all programs).

The Treasury Board study found that 65 per cent of federal program expenditures involved programs with some form of overlap.[35] The study presented nine categories. Those categories were based on a matrix of services and clients, with both services and clients ranging from being completely the same to partially the same to completely different. The percentage of program expenditures falling into each category is shown in Table 1.

Category 9 clearly indicated no overlap. The remaining 65 per cent of expenditures were classified into three types of 'apparent overlap'.[36]

Category 7 programs were classified as transfer programs. The study noted that transfer programs constitute a complementary activity and require few additional resources to administer. For instance, federal administration for the $5.8 billion in health insurance cash transfers only requires 21 staff.[37] Categories 3 and 6 were classified as parallel programs, which offer the same services to different clients. The study stated that these programs 'do not appear to cause problems of a program overlap nature', because roles and responsibilities are different.[38] For example, federal correctional institutions house offenders with sentences over two years, while provincial institutions house offenders with sentences under two years. However, co-operation is important, and can lead to such arrangements as renting space in another government's correctional institutions.[39]

Only categories 1, 2, 4, and 5 were classified as areas of direct program overlap. Even in category 1, the study found no cases of complete 'duplication' (i.e., redundancy). For example, both orders of government contribute to the Program for Older Worker Adjustment, and they oversee the program through joint federal-provincial/private-sector committees.[40]

The Alberta study found that 55 per cent of the $7.8 billion in federal program expenditures apportionable to Alberta involved areas in which the province also had expenditures.[41] This 55 per cent was broken down as 29 per cent in direct entanglement, providing the same or similar programs to the same or similar clients, and 26 per cent in indirect entanglement.

The studies found overlap across a broad range of activities. Julien and Proulx reported that only two of their 36 sectors—postal service and defence/veterans—had absolutely no overlap.[42] Likewise, the broad range of overlapping activities was noted by the Alberta study,[43] and it is evident in the Treasury Board's listing of programs.[44] However, the Alberta study found that most expenditures on activities with direct or indirect entanglement were in the social sphere

(92 per cent) and had individuals as beneficiaries (91 per cent).[45]

What do the studies' findings of extensive overlap mean? Do they mean that over half of everything the federal government does is also being done by the provincial governments? The answer is no. The studies' overlap percentages of roughly 50 to 65 per cent must be qualified. Each study was performed at the program level. Within any program, there may be some aspects which overlap with another government's activities, and there may be some element of overlap. If there was any aspect of overlap, the entire program or its expenditures were included in the total for overlapping programs. Therefore, it would be wrong to conclude that over half of government activity overlaps. Indeed, the studies did not report a single case of complete redundancy, and most expenditures were for social programs benefiting individuals.

## The Link between Overlap and Efficiency

In spite of their similar findings on the extent of overlap, the studies differed on whether overlap causes significant inefficiency. Julien and Proulx stated that overlap is not consistent with good public management and that there was an urgent need to find solutions.[46] Julien and Proulx published an assessment of the ramifications of their study in a separate volume.[47] They repeated the arguments and conclusions of that assessment in a more recent article reviewing the 1991 federal Treasury Board study.[48] Likewise, the Alberta study took the traditional provincial view that overlap, much of it resulting from federal spending in areas of provincial jurisdiction, causes significant inefficiency.[49] Meanwhile, the federal Treasury Board argued that overlap is fairly well managed.[50]

The difference of opinion can be explained by the lack of quantitative analysis linking overlap to efficiency; none of the studies assessed the cost of lost efficiency resulting from overlap. In the absence of cost estimates, the authors used qualitative arguments and anecdotal evidence to support their positions. The arguments dealt primarily with productive rather than economic efficiency (as well as with other considerations such as accountability). The arguments regarding both technical and economic efficiency are discussed here in turn.

## Overlap and Productive Efficiency

Four arguments link overlap to productive efficiency. First, overlapping programs may be completely redundant. Second, overlapping programs may conflict, and thus cancel out any benefits. Third, overlapping programs may require additional co-ordinating costs. Fourth, overlapping programs may prevent either order of government from realizing economies of scale.

*Redundancy.* The work of two orders of government could sometimes be redundant. According to this argument, the federal system is inefficient to the extent that the involvement of a second government adds nothing to a given outcome. Such involvement wastes inputs.

Redundancy does not just require that both governments provide the same service to the same client. It also requires that all the service from the second government be of absolutely no value to the client.[51] This can be explained with an example. Suppose the federal government funds a municipal swimming pool and the provincial government funds a second municipal swimming pool. The second pool benefits the municipality's citizens through less crowding, alternative schedules or activities, and, for some citizens, a closer location. This is not a case of redundancy because there is benefit from the second pool.

Admittedly, administrative costs might be lower if only one government was involved in the review and awarding of pool funding, but this is a separate argument against government overlap. It is discussed later as lost economies of scale. In addition, the municipality may receive decreasing benefit from governments providing two pools. Perhaps there was a great demand for the first pool, but a more limited demand for the second pool. This is also a separate argument against government overlap, and is discussed later as oversupply of government activity.

The three Canadian studies of overlap reported no cases of redundancy. A report prepared for the Quebec commission responsible for investigating sovereignty after the Bélanger-Campeau Commission also failed to find redundancy.[52]

*Conflicting Objectives.* The work of the two orders of government may conflict. According to this argument, the federal system is inefficient to the extent that the outcomes achieved by both orders of government cancel each other out. Both governments waste inputs. The argument can also be expressed in terms of economic efficiency, because the wasted resources could have been used elsewhere. However, Julien and Proulx and the Alberta and Treasury Board studies treat conflicting objectives as an issue of productive efficiency, focusing on the possibility that the actions of two governments are counterproductive.[53]

Julien and Proulx and the Alberta study cite many areas where the federal and provincial governments have had conflicting objectives. Julien and Proulx illustrate the issue of conflicting objectives by referring to federal involvement in municipal affairs in the 1980s.[54] The federal government was making direct grants to municipalities at the same time as the Quebec government was trying to encourage municipalities to rationalize their finances. Julien and Proulx also note there was federal-provincial conflict in regional development strategy during the same period. Similarly, the Alberta study notes the existence of conflicting objectives in petrochemical development, transportation policy, assistance to the forest industry, labour market training, energy development, and environmental protection.[55]

In contrast, the federal Treasury Board emphasizes areas of co-operation, including park programs, animal health testing, health promotion, justice, and agricultural price stabilization.[56] In park programs, for example, the federal government operates large parks which are primarily aimed at preservation. The provinces operate parks which are generally smaller and are primarily aimed at recreation. The Treasury Board acknowledges there is room for improved co-operation in regulatory programs and inspection programs, but those examples involve overregulation rather than conflicting objectives.[57]

None of this literature suggests how the significance of conflict and co-operation could be assessed. There is an important methodological problem. The program evaluation and value-for-money auditing communities have been attempting to assess efficient and effective performance for years, with limited success.[58] The same difficulty would face an attempt to assess inefficiency due to overlap. It would be even harder to single out the cost of one element of inefficiency: inefficiency due to conflicting objectives. Even the concept of conflict is problematic because it involves a judgement, as shown by the studies of overlap. Where the Alberta government sees general conflict, the federal Treasury Board sees general co-operation. Thus, it is doubtful the cost of conflicting objectives could be quantified; the methodological and conceptual problems are too great. As a result, anecdotal evidence can be used to support any position.

*Co-ordinating Costs.* Special mechanisms may be necessary for the two orders of government to co-ordinate their activities. According to this argument, the federal system is inefficient to the extent that it requires otherwise unnecessary co-ordinating mechanisms. Such mechanisms waste inputs.

The overlap studies did not estimate the costs of co-ordination or refer to any estimates in the literature. All that is quantified in the literature are estimates of the number of intergovernmental meetings and committees. Kenneth Kernaghan has estimated that there are 1,000 federal-provincial committees,[59] and Julien and Proulx

state that close to 1,000 federal-provincial meetings are held each year to co-ordinate government activities.[60] Julien and Proulx note that the exact cost of this activity is impossible to determine without analysing every case of overlap in detail.[61]

*Lost Economies of Scale.* Economies of scale may be lost due to overlap. According to this argument, the federal system is inefficient to the extent that delivering services through two orders of government does not let either order of government take advantage of economies of scale. A single organization is in a better position than several smaller organizations to increase productivity through greater specialization of labour, or to spread administration and fixed costs for such things as equipment or computerized systems over more output.[62] Lost economies of scale result in lower output for a given input.

There is no agreement in the literature on the extent to which economies of scale exist in the public sector.[63] Indeed, there may even be diseconomies of scale, with larger governments operating less efficiently than smaller governments.[64] Given the uncertainty about the existence of economies of scale, it would be impossible to estimate potential cost savings.

Julien and Proulx cite lost economies of scale as a negative consequence of the involvement of two orders of government in a single policy area.[65] However, they acknowledge the point is debatable, given that large government organizations can become more bureaucratic and less efficient. Julien and Proulx also note that there is overlap in internal government services. For instance, computer systems, accounting systems, and payroll systems are required by both orders of government. Julien and Proulx raise this point in discussing redundancy and duplication, insofar as internal federal and provincial government services could be considered to be redundant or duplicate programs.[66] The argument can also be framed in terms of economies of scale; one government could spread the cost of these services over more output. Taken to its extreme, this is an argument for a unitary state, because many of these services would be required even if the two orders of government operated in completely separate fields.

Albert Breton notes that the economies-of-scale argument is normally an argument for greater centralization, something Canadian critics of overlap do not generally favour. Breton criticizes Julien and Proulx for only being concerned with 'vertical overlap' between the federal and provincial governments. He argues that Julien and Proulx ignore the 'horizontal overlap' that exists when an activity is decentralized.[67] Decentralization requires each province to establish its own organization and policies. This may be more wasteful than if the federal government handled some aspects of the activity centrally. Thus, the economies-of-scale argument can be used to support greater centralization. This may partly explain why Julien and Proulx downplay the importance of the argument and why the Alberta study does not mention it. The Treasury Board mentions the economies-of-scale argument as justification for federal involvement, but the Treasury Board does so fairly cautiously by only including the argument in introductory, theoretical remarks.[68]

*Cost Estimates.* Some sources have attempted to estimate the cost of lost productive efficiency resulting from overlap. However, the estimates are either based on extremely broad assumptions or there is not enough public information to judge their credibility.

In its submission to the Bélanger-Campeau Commission, the Chambre de Commerce du Québec identified the losses from overlap at 'many billions of dollars'.[69] In order to determine the original source for this claim, the Chambre de Commerce du Québec was contacted. In turn, the Chambre referred to the data of Professor Pierre Fortin. In 1990, Fortin provided a working paper to Quebec's Bélanger-Campeau Commission in which he assessed the effects of overlap as follows:

> Since Ottawa and the provinces spend together more than $225 billion per year (not including the

service of the debt) and since overlaps affect directly or indirectly up to 60% of the expenditure programs, I would not hesitate to characterize as conservative an estimate of $5 billion, or 2% of the total, to quantify, at the national level, the waste of public funds. One must not forget the historical importance of the role played by shared federal-provincial programs in health, education and, still today, social assistance in the establishment of a system in which the provinces could spend dollars which only cost them 50 cents. Canadian federalism has not often been noted for promoting the economic use of funds, and today we are political prisoners of the acquired rights which the system has created.[70]

This assumption, that 2 per cent of all non-debt-service government expenses are wasted due to overlap, is the basis for Fortin's claim that $5 billion is 'wasted'. It also seems to be the source for the claim by other concerned parties, such as the Chambre de Commerce du Québec, that billions are wasted.

Several other figures have been cited for the cost of overlap in individual sectors. Julien and Proulx refer to a press account of a Quebec government figure of $250 million for workforce training.[71] However, newspapers are far from ideal sources for financial analysis. Julien and Proulx note that other figures reported at the Bélanger-Campeau Commission were $233 million in transport and communication charges and $289 million in duty and tax collection.[72] Julien and Proulx do not indicate the exact nature (or page number in the extensive Bélanger-Campeau documentation) of these savings.

## Overlap and Economic Efficiency

Two major arguments link overlap to economic efficiency. Critics of overlap claim that it results in an oversupply of government activity. Defenders of overlap counter that overlap increases government responsiveness.

*Oversupply of Government Activity.* Overlap could result in an oversupply of government activity. According to this argument, total government involvement increases merely because two governments, and their bureaucracies, are competing in the same area. Economic efficiency suffers because society receives less benefit from the resources directed toward government activity than it would receive if some of those resources went elsewhere.

Oversupply was not treated directly by Julien and Proulx nor by the Alberta and Treasury Board studies, although it is suggested by the former two sources' discussion of the waste caused by conflicting objectives. The argument is dealt with directly elsewhere in the literature. According to Fortin, federal-provincial competition leads to each order of government outbidding the other, creating an oversupply of government services.[73] This dynamic has also concerned Richard Simeon.[74] He has argued that interest groups and bureaucrats press both orders of government to address new issues and problems whether or not they have jurisdiction. Alan Cairns has outlined a similar process of expansion through public and bureaucratic pressure on two competing orders of government.[75] He has characterized the result as a crisis, in which Canadians are faced with 'powerful, dirigiste government at both levels'.[76]

While federal-provincial competition may contribute to government growth, the presence of two orders of government does not necessarily result in more government. William Robson has reported that, for the Organization for Economic Co-operation and Development (OECD) countries, the government sector accounted for 47.1 per cent of 1989 gross domestic product (GDP) in unitary states versus 40.7 per cent of GDP in federations.[77] The figure was 42 per cent in Canada. In addition, government growth was more than one-third faster in unitary states over the prior two decades. Keith Banting notes that such findings have been reported in the literature for some time.[78] He also notes that the oversupply thesis is a fairly recent criticism of federalism, with federalism traditionally being associated with weak, divided government.[79] Banting argues that a new, expansionary dynamic has been imported in Canada's case because of the 'territorial imperative', the desire of the federal government and the provinces to establish their claim to jurisdiction. This expansionary dynamic is reinforced by the competition between Ottawa and Quebec for the allegiance of Quebecers. Nevertheless, Banting argues that the conservative dynamic of federalism outweighs the expansionary dynamic in Canada.[80]

*Government Responsiveness.* The major defence made for overlap is that it results in greater government responsiveness.[81] If individuals or businesses do not find their interests well served by one order of government, they can turn to the other order of government. According to this public-choice argument, the public should be the judge between competing federal and provincial programs;[82] competition should not be prevented by arbitrary rules about which government may respond in what manner. One can even argue that overlap does not exist at all, because governments are fulfilling different objectives and catering to different preferences. Economic efficiency is increased because governments direct resources to the areas of greatest public demand.

The responsiveness argument is essentially the flip side of the argument that overlap leads to an oversupply of government. Under either argument, there may be more government, but whether the additional intervention is warranted depends on whether one believes such intervention is an indication of responsiveness or of government meddling. It should also be noted that increased responsiveness does not necessarily require more government; it could involve smarter government. Governments could develop a 'competitive advantage' with existing resources by better tailoring programs to public demand.

The responsiveness argument described here involves federal-provincial competition, so it is important to distinguish between federal-provincial and interprovincial competition. The distinction can be understood by considering what it is governments compete for. Governments do not compete with each other for votes. Voters do not choose between the federal government and various provincial governments on a ballot.

What, then, do governments compete for? In the case of interprovincial competition, governments compete for people and companies. If people or companies are not satisfied with government services, or with costs, they can move to another province. Federal-provincial competition does not involve geography; it involves the relative power of two governments. The two orders of government compete for favour or, as Banting suggests, allegiance.[83] In the event of a federal-provincial conflict, each government wants public support. Canadians can play the federal and provincial governments against each other to increase government services, but Canadians cannot leave if the resulting cost becomes too high (unless they emigrate). Stated another way, the federal and provincial orders of government compete on services but not on costs, because people have no exit option. Thus, federal-provincial competition may increase government responsiveness, but it also fuels government growth. Both the responsiveness and oversupply arguments have some merit, but the net result on efficiency is not known.

The Treasury Board study does not discuss federal-provincial competition, but it does state that the involvement of two governments can result in better service and more responsive governments.[84] Julien and Proulx critique the view that federal-provincial competition increases responsiveness.[85] Their argument takes three parts. First, citizens do not pay directly for government services. Second, there is little point moving between provinces because provincial programs do not differ markedly. Third, the tendency of the federal government to compete with provinces standardizes services across the country,

so that local preferences are not recognized. These arguments, however, do not convincingly refute the notion that federal-provincial competition increases responsiveness. The first argument recognizes the drawback of federal-provincial competition, the cost of more government services, but it ignores the benefits resulting from those services. The second argument concerns interprovincial competition, not federal-provincial competition. The third argument is an argument against centralization, not against competition.

## Conclusion

The three Canadian studies of overlap conducted over the past 15 years found significant overlap in government activity, with half to two-thirds of government activity occurring in areas of both federal and provincial involvement. However, due to the difficulty of measuring the effect of this overlap on government efficiency, the studies have not demonstrated that overlap causes significant government inefficiency. The inability to conclusively link overlap to government inefficiency has also been noted by the Economic Council of Canada.[86] Referring to the United States, Alice Rivlin notes there has been little investigation of the effects of overlap.[87]

These comments do not imply that overlap has no effect on government efficiency. However, the effects of overlap on government efficiency have proven elusive to measure. No studies have found complete redundancy. The costs of conflicting objectives, additional co-ordination, and lost economies of scale are unknown. Indeed, the overlap literature makes no suggestion on how the cost of conflicting objectives might be assessed, and such an assessment would pose serious methodological and conceptual problems. The Canadian literature on intergovernmental relations has only estimated the number of intergovernmental meetings and committees, not the cost of co-ordination. Public finance literature is divided on whether economies of scale even generally exist in the public sector. These measure-ment problems relate to productive efficiency. Economic efficiency is even more elusive, involv-ing the assessment of welfare. Thus, it would be unrealistic to expect cost estimates of the effect of overlap on government efficiency. Simeon was apparently right to state in the mid-1970s that 'It is impossible to measure the extent of these costs.'[88]

Given the difficulty of measuring the effect of overlap on efficiency, the apparently technical issue of overlap becomes part of the discourse on power. While the Canadian studies on overlap present similar findings on the extent of overlap, they draw different conclusions on the signifi-cance of overlap for government efficiency. Those differing conclusions represent the traditional provincial and federal positions on overlap, reflecting the interests of each side. Thus, the debate about overlap and its effect on government efficiency may generate more heat than light but, as part of the wider Canadian debate on constitu-tional powers, it is unlikely to go away.

## Notes

Author's note: I wish to thank Professor J. Garfield Allen of the University of New Brunswick and the jour-nal's anonymous reviewers for their useful comments on this research.

1. Québec Liberal Party, *A Québec Free to Choose: Report of the Constitutional Committee of the Québec Liberal Party* (QLP, 1991), 20.
2. Germain Julien and Marcel Proulx, *Les chevauche-ments des programmes fédéraux et québécois* [Overlaps between Federal and Québec Programs] (Québec: École nationale d'administration publique, 1978).
3. Alberta, *Improving Efficiency and Accountability: Rebalancing Federal-Provincial Spending Responsibi-lities* (Edmonton: Government of Alberta, 1992).
4. Treasury Board Secretariat, *Federal-Provincial Overlap and Duplication: A Federal Program Perspective* (Ottawa: TBS, 1991).
5. Economic Council of Canada, *A Joint Venture: The Economics of Constitutional Options*, 28th edn (Ottawa: ECC, 1991), 73.
6. M.J. Farrell, 'The Measurement of Productive Efficiency', *Journal of the Royal Statistical Society* 120 (Part III 1957): 253–81; Robin Boadway, *The Constitutional Division of Powers: An Economic Per-spective* (Ottawa: Economic Council of Canada, 1992), 23.
7. Kenneth Norrie, Richard Simeon, and Mark Krasnick, *Federalism and Economic Union in Canada* (Toronto: University of Toronto Press, 1986), 12.
8. Royal Commission on Dominion-Provincial Rela-tions, *Report of the Royal Commission on Dominion-Provincial Relations, Book II* (Ottawa: King's Printer, 1940), 172–3.

9. Ibid., 177, 179, 183.
10. Ibid., 183.
11. See, for example, Ontario, *1970 Budget* (Toronto: Ontario Department of Treasury and Economics, 1970), 52–3.
12. Norman Webster and William Johnson, 'Govern-ments Duplicate Services, Waste Money, Davis Says', *Globe and Mail*, 24 May 1973, 41.
13. Ontario, *The Report of the Special Program Review*, chairman W. Darcy McKeough (Toronto: Govern-ment of Ontario, 1975), 81.
14. Julien and Proulx, *Les chevauchements des pro-grammes fédéraux et québécois*, 63.
15. Alberta, *Improving Efficiency and Accountability*, 5.
16. See, for example, Annual Premiers' Conference, *Press Release No. 1* (Waskesiu, Sask., 1978); Annual Premiers' Conference, *Press Release No. 4* (Pointe-au-Pic, Québec, 1979).
17. Treasury Board, *Federal-Provincial Overlap and Duplication*, 28–9.
18. Task Force on Program Review, *An Introduction to the Process of Program Review* (Ottawa: Supply and Services Canada, 1986), 1.
19. Ibid., 28, 31, 37.
20. Ibid., 33–6.
21. Richard Simeon, ed., *Division of Powers and Public Policy* (Toronto: University of Toronto Press, 1985); Norrie, Simeon, and Krasnick, *Federalism and Economic Union in Canada*; Thomas J. Courchene, *Economic Management and the Division of Powers* (Toronto: University of Toronto Press, 1986); Mark Krasnick, ed., *Fiscal Federalism* (Toronto: University of Toronto Press, 1986);

Richard Simeon, ed., *Intergovernmental Relations* (Toronto: University of Toronto Press, 1985).

22. Ronald C.C. Cuming, ed., *Perspectives on the Harmonization of Law in Canada* (Toronto: University of Toronto Press, 1985); Ronald C.C. Cuming, ed., *Harmonization of Business Law in Canada* (Toronto: University of Toronto Press, 1986).

23. Norrie, Simeon, and Krasnick, *Federalism and Economic Union in Canada*, 7–15; Garth Stevenson, 'The Division of Powers', in Simeon, ed., *Division of Powers and Public Policy*, 110, 115.

24. Québec Liberal Party, *A Québec Free to Choose*, 20 (author's translation).

25. Laurier Cloutier, 'Claude Béland ébranle les dirigeants de l'Association des manufacturiers' [Claude Béland Shocks the Leaders of the Manufacturers' Association], *La Presse*, 27 Mar. 1991, B1.

26. 'Bérard plaide en faveur de changements constitutionnels' [Bérard Speaks in Favour of Constitutional Changes], *La Presse*, 30 Mar. 1991, F2.

27. Québec Liberal Party, *A Québec Free to Choose*, 20; Pierre April, 'Coupes budgétaires: Daniel Johnson se sent appuyé par le public' [Budget Cuts: Daniel Johnson Feels Supported by the Public], *La Presse*, 20 Feb. 1993, F1.

28. Québec, *Report of the Commission on the Political and Constitutional Future of Québec* (Québec: Secretariat de la Commission, 1991), 41.

29. Western Finance Ministers, *1991 Report of the Western Finance Ministers* (Nipawin, Sask., Western Premier's Conference, 1991), 5.

30. Gallup Canada, *Canadian Chamber of Commerce 1991 Members' Survey: Analytical Report* (Toronto: Gallup Canada, 1991), 28.

31. 'Premier Seeks End to Duplication', *Daily Gleaner*, 3 Apr. 1993, 1.

32. Canada, *Minutes of Proceedings and Evidence of the Special Joint Committee of the Senate and of the House of Commons on a Renewed Canada, Issue No. 9* (Ottawa: Queen's Printer, 1991), 38.

33. Chantal Hébert, 'Le dédoublement des pouvoirs avec le Québec n'est pas évident à Ottawa' [The Duplication of Powers with Québec Is Not Obvious to Ottawa], *Le Devoir*, 27 Mar. 1991, A1.

34. Julien and Proulx, *Les chevauchements des programmes fédéraux et québécois*, 33, 42.

35. Treasury Board, *Federal-Provincial Overlap and Duplication*, 16.

36. Ibid., 17–19.

37. Ibid., 18.

38. Ibid.

39. Ibid.

40. Ibid., 17.

41. Alberta, *Improving Efficiency and Accountability*, 14–16.

42. Julien and Proulx, *Les chevauchements des programmes fédéraux et québécois*, 35.

43. Alberta, *Improving Efficiency and Accountability*, 16.

44. Treasury Board, *Federal-Provincial Overlap and Duplication*, 43–79.

45. Alberta, *Improving Efficiency and Accountability*, 16.

46. Julien and Proulx, *Les chevauchements des programmes fédéraux et québécois*, 63–4.

47. Germain Julien and Marcel Proulx, *Analyse des conséquences du chevauchement des programmes fédéraux et québécois* [Analysis of the Consequences of Overlap between Federal and Québec Programs] (Québec: École nationale d'administration publique, 1978).

48. Germain Julien and Marcel Proulx, 'Le chevauchement des programmes fédéraux et provinciaux: un bilan' [Overlap between Federal and Provincial Programs: An Appraisal], *Canadian Public Administration/Administration publique du Canada* 35 (Autumn 1992): 402–20.

49. Alberta, *Improving Efficiency and Accountability*, 7.

50. Treasury Board, *Federal-Provincial Overlap and Duplication*, 19.

51. Economic Council of Canada, *A Joint Venture*, 73.

52. Consortium Lamonde Mallette, 'Gestion de la prise en charge des services fédéraux' [Management of the Takeover of Federal Services], *Les implications de la mise en oeuvre de la souveraineté: Les aspects juridiques, les services gouvernementaux* [Implications of the Implementation of Sovereignty: Legal Aspects, Government Services], Presentations and Studies, vol. 2 (Québec City: Commission d'étude des questions afférentes à l'accession du Québec à la souveraineté, 1992), 76.

53. Julien and Proulx, 'Le chevauchement des programmes fédéraux et provinciaux: un bilan', 414; Alberta, *Improving Efficiency and Accountability*, 7; Treasury Board, *Federal-Provincial Overlap and Duplication*, 7.

54. Julien and Proulx, 'Le chevauchement des programmes fédéraux et provinciaux: un bilan', 414.

55. Alberta, *Improving Efficiency and Accountability*, 7.
56. Treasury Board, *Federal-Provincial Overlap and Duplication*, 20–2.
57. Ibid., 22–3.
58. S.L. Sutherland, 'The Evolution of Program Budget Ideas in Canada: Does Parliament Benefit from Estimates Reform?', *Canadian Public Administration/Administration publique du Canada* 33 (Summer 1990): 133–64.
59. Kenneth Kernaghan, 'Intergovernmental Administrative Relations in Canada', Kernaghan, ed., *Public Administration in Canada: Selected Readings*, 5th edn (Toronto: Methuen, 1985), 154.
60. Julien and Proulx, 'Le chevauchement des programmes fédéraux et provinciaux: un bilan', 413.
61. Ibid., 414.
62. Ibid., 413.
63. William B.P. Robson, *Dynamic Tensions: Markets, Federalism, and Canada's Economic Future* (Toronto: C.D. Howe Institute, 1992), 25; Steven C. Deller and Edward Rudnicki, 'Managers' Efficiency in Local Government Implication on Jurisdictional Consolidation', *Public Choice* 24 (Sept. 1992): 221, 229; Dick Netzer, 'State-Local Finance and Intergovernmental Fiscal Relations', in Alan S. Blinder, Robert M. Solow, George F. Break, Peter O. Steiner, and Dick Netzer, eds, *The Economics of Public Finance* (Washington: Brookings, 1974), 381–3.
64. Graham White, 'Big Is Different from Little: On Taking Size Seriously in the Analysis of Canada's Governmental Institutions', *Canadian Public Administration/Administration publique du Canada* 33 (Winter 1990): 548; John Richards, 'Suggestions on Getting the Constitutional Division of Powers Right', in Jean-Michel Cousineau, Claude E. Forget, and John Richards, *Delivering the Goods: the Federal-Provincial Division of Spending Powers* (Toronto: C.D. Howe Institute, 1992), 18.
65. Julien and Proulx, 'Le chevauchement des programmes fédéraux et provinciaux: un bilan', 413.
66. Ibid., 412.
67. Albert Breton cited in Louis-Philippe Rochon, 'Cité Libre rencontre Albert Breton: Le fédéralisme de concurrence' [*Cité Libre* Meets Albert Breton: Competitive Federalism], *Cité Libre* (Dec. 1991–Jan. 1992): 17.
68. Treasury Board, *Federal-Provincial Overlap and Duplication*, 4.
69. Québec Liberal Party, *A Québec Free to Choose*, 20
70. Pierre Fortin, 'Le choix forcé du Québec: Aspects économiques et stratégiques' [Québec's Unavoidable Choice: Economic and Strategic Aspects], *Les avis des spécialistes invités à répondre au huit questions posées par la Commission* [The Opinions of Specialists Invited to Respond to Eight Questions Posed by the Commission], Working Document, no. 4 (Québec: Commission sur l'avenir politique et constitutionnel du Québec, 1991), 353–4 (author's translation).
71. Julien and Proulx, 'Le chevauchement des programmes fédéraux et provinciaux: un bilan', 411.
72. Ibid.
73. Fortin, 'Le choix forcé du Québec', 353.
74. Richard Simeon, 'The Federal-Provincial Decision Making Process,' *Intergovernmental Relations* (Toronto: Ontario Economic Council, 1977), 26.
75. Alan C. Cairns, 'The Other Crisis of Canadian Federalism', *Canadian Public Administration/Administration publique du Canada* 22 (Summer 1979): 182–3.
76. Ibid., 178.
77. Robson, *Dynamic Tensions*, 26.
78. Keith G. Banting, *The Welfare State and Canadian Federalism*, 2nd edn (Montreal and Kingston: McGill-Queen's University Press, 1987), 41.
79. Ibid., 41, 73.
80. Ibid., 73–6.
81. Norrie, Simeon, and Krasnick, *Federalism and Economic Union in Canada*, 12–15; Gérard Bellenger, 'The Division of Powers in a Federal System', in Simeon, ed., *Division of Powers and Public Policy*, 16.
82. Breton cited in Rochon, 'Cité Libre rencontre Albert Breton', 17.
83. Banting, *The Welfare State and Canadian Federalism*, 74–5.
84. Treasury Board, *Federal-Provincial Overlap and Duplication*, 8.
85. Julien and Proulx, 'Le chevauchement des programmes fédéraux et provinciaux: un bilan', 416–19.
86. Economic Council, *A Joint Venture*, 73.
87. Alice M. Rivlin, 'A New Vision of American Federalism', *Public Administration Review* 52 (July/Aug. 1992): 319.
88. Simeon, 'The Federal-Provincial Decision Making Process', 28.

Part XII

# Local Government

## Introduction

Patrick J. Smith

'Local governance' has been defined as many things. Central to these definitions are notions of local democracy: these range from ideas about neighbourhood influence or control over decisions affecting community to broader conceptions about Aboriginal self-government. As such, they go well beyond simple ideas about local-municipal government with which most of us are familiar. Local government, particularly its conceptual underpinnings, remains rather vague for many people.

'Local government' itself has been defined as the 'first order of government'; as the 'cornerstone—and training ground—of democracy'; as the 'most responsive and accountable form of government'; and as the 'most efficient provider of local services'. Local governments have alternatively been described as 'tenants at will' or 'creatures' of senior constitutional authorities; as a base 'for imposing unwanted responsibilities (and taxes) upon local communities'; as the 'third level' of government and 'largely administrative arms for senior jurisdictions'; and, simply, as 'puppets on a shoestring'.

The contradictions inherent in these—upside vs downside—attempts to demarcate the most salient feature of local government go some way to explaining the sometimes ambivalent position this local order of governing has held in our framework of governance. As each of these definitional points has a grain, or more, of truth, a brief review of the basis for each provides a useful introduction to the study of local governance.

### Upside Images

The 'first order of government' interpretation finds contemporary expression as the theme of the Federation of Canadian Municipalities' 1993 conference and in subsequent FCM positioning; it also relates to the historical—representative—roots of local government in our development of governing institutions.[1] In Canada, apart from the not insignificant constitutional governance orders in existence in such pre-contact Aboriginal settings as the Iroquois Confederacy, the *syndic d'habitations* under the French regime provided the first European representative institutions (in Montreal, Quebec, and Trois-Rivières), through an elected mayor, councillors, and *syndic d'habitations*, for local input to the central authority in New France. First established in 1647 (though abolished in 1663 by the central government in France as 'a dangerous innovation'), this early representative role of local government re-emerged in Canada with the influx of Loyalists fleeing to British North America from the American Revolution. As a result, in 1793, the Upper Canada legislature passed the Parish and Town Officers Act, the first legislation providing for aspects of local governance. With the incorporation of a Board of Police in Brockville and the establishment of the City of York (Toronto) between 1832 and 1834, the Rebellions of 1837–8 for responsible government and Lord Durham's subsequent Report, and the passage in 1849 of the Baldwin Act, the general framework for the development of representative municipal institutions throughout Canada was largely put in place.[2]

The view of local government as the 'cornerstone and training ground for democracy' related not only to its place in the development of representative institutions, but also came from the significance of the local governmental experience in developing ideas of responsible government. In his famous 1840 Report following the Rebellions of 1837–8, Lord Durham argued that local self-government was 'the foundation of Anglo-Saxon freedom and civilization'.[3] In proposing responsible government as the solution to governance in British North America, Durham noted that 'the people should have been entrusted with the complete control over their own local affairs, and been trained for taking their part in the concerns of the Province, by their experience in the management of that local business which was most interesting and most easily intelligible to them.'[4] In the context of contemporary politics, Robert Bish has noted that 'many political scientists and political philosophers have emphasized the role of local government as a training ground for democracy, enabling local citizens to participate in collective endeavours and thus to learn how to temper individual ambitions with concern for others.'[5]

The idea that local government is the most responsive and accountable type of government has been expressed in debates about such key terms of local democracy as 'representation', 'accountability', 'participation', and 'access'. As explained by Plunkett and Betts,

> at the local government level . . . the basic concepts of representative democracy may appear obvious—the universal franchise, one person one vote, representation by population, qualifications to vote and run for office, equal size of electoral districts, direct rather than indirect election, appointment or co-option, elections to office held on a regular and frequent basis . . . —yet they are deceiving in their simplicity. In practice, many of these apparently straightforward concepts . . . have proved difficult to achieve or have contained within their seeming simplicity contradictions which present difficulties for today's larger urbanized municipalities.[6]

Ongoing debates about wards vs at-large elections and the implications for local democracy[7] and enlarged metropolitan government restructuring (e.g., in Megacity Toronto, Metro Halifax, Unicity Winnipeg, the Montreal Urban Community, and Greater Vancouver) suggest we are not necessarily closer to resolution of such basic questions.[8]

In terms of accountability, local governments are closest to their citizens, yet accountability can apply to traditional methods, such as through the ballot box, or it can mean 'the ability of municipal government to respond to the changing needs and desires of its citizens in a more flexible way',[9] such as through more ongoing account-ability to various citizens' groups. As well, a definition of 'accountability' might be expressed in the debate over the desirability of having local political parties. Those who would speak for such partisan politics argue in terms of accountability for spe-cific programs and policies; those against party politics at the local level claim that local government should be 'non-partisan'.[10] This issue hinges on questions about the compatibility of accountability and efficiency in local government. Peter Self has con-cluded that these values are opposite (zero-sum);[11] others, such as the 1979 Lambert Royal Commission on Financial Management and Accountability, found efficiency and accountability to be positively related in democratic governance.[12]

Participation, equally, means many things, including 'taking part in the formula-tion of and setting of objectives, in the elaboration of alternatives, in the actual deci-sion, in implementing the decision and in evaluating the results.'[13] Sherry Arnstein's 'Ladder of Public Participation' itemizes vastly different definitions and their implica-tions for those involved in local government.[14] As part of the debate about governance and public decision-making since the 1960s, pressure for meaningful participation meant 'a major change in the practice of local government. Citizen participation is more than a desirable adjunct; it is an essential basis. If citizen participation does not work, the system will collapse.'[15] Public response to Canadian constitutional reform efforts since the late 1980s related as much to process as to substance and suggests the applicability of this 'public participative' requirement to other policy areas and to questions of governance more generally. As Dilys Hill concluded, participation 'has become a widely used term and . . . in some contexts it is almost the same as the definition of democracy itself.'[16]

Finally, on local government being accessible, David Siegel has defined 'access' as 'responsiveness . . . one of the basic values of public administration'.[17] It is also one of 'the two major values which local government alone can provide'.[18] According to the 1967 Ontario Committee on Taxation, access involves 'the most widespread partici-pation possible . . . [by] virtually all individual citizens' and the maximum 'capacity to influence public policy decisions and to enforce responsive and responsible adminis-tration'.[19] The proximity of local government to the people, combined with its rela-tively small size, makes this order of government the 'most responsive to citizens' desires'.[20] For Kenneth Crawford, this responsiveness relates to the fact that 'local authorities have a more intimate knowledge of the local conditions and can provide greater flexibility in the application of policies than is possible for a central authority.'[21]

The conception of local government as the 'most efficient provider of local ser-vices' has been described as the second major value that 'local government alone can provide'. Here 'service' is defined as 'not only the economical discharge of public func-tions, but the achievement of technical adequacy in due alignment with public needs and desires.'[22] For Siegel, 'service . . . becomes analogous to the values of efficiency and effectiveness.'[23] The idea of efficiency found clearest expression in the era of met-ropolitan reform. The premise, generally, was that 'bigger was better'—at least in terms of the efficient delivery of local services. Examples include the creation of two-tiered local/regional governance with Metropolitan Toronto in the 1950s, the development

of regional districts in British Columbia, of metropolitan councils such as Greater
London in England and Unigov in Indianapolis in the 1960s, and the establishment
of Unicity in Winnipeg in the 1970s. Initially hailed as examples of local governmen-
tal efficiency, by the 1980s the 'bigger/better' answer was less certain. Margaret
Thatcher abolished the Greater London Council and six other Metropolitan County
Councils in England; and in British Columbia, regional districts such as Greater
Vancouver had their planning authority taken away by the provincial government.
Both moves came as a result of policy friction between the major regional authorities
and their senior governmental 'creators'.[24]

In the Toronto region, the province and local/regional authorities have wrestled, so
far unsuccessfully, with a new 'Greater Toronto Area' (GTA), as urban sprawl stretched
beyond the existing borders of Metro. Here, 'the structural tangle of local government
[is] worse' than anywhere in Canada, despite the fact 'that this area has experienced
more municipal reorganization and upheaval than any other in Canada.'[25] Abandoning
GTA reform, the radical Conservative provincial government of Premier Mike Harris
imposed a Megacity solution, abolishing the six cities of the former Metropolitan
Toronto and creating one single city. Other senior jurisdictions, such as in Europe, have
also concluded that abolition is the answer, as in Barcelona and Copenhagen.

In his review of this early era of metropolitan reform, Andrew Sancton concluded that it had generally failed: 'the establishment of metropolitan and regional
government in various Canadian provinces was once seen as an indication of the
importance of urbanization. Paradoxically, the general failure of such governments to
live up to their initial expectations can be explained by that same process of pervasive and extensive urbanization.'[26] For Sancton, the efficiencies promised did not
materialize: 'the simple truth is that urban areas in Canada, and elsewhere, have
become too big to be governed by the . . . regional authorities of the type introduced
. . . from the 1950s to the 1970s. Their time is past.'[27] Others, including Sancton,
have been more optimistic about continuing possibilities for other 'less formal' forms
of metropolitan governance.[28]

## Downside Definitions

On the downside, local governments have been described as 'creatures' or 'tenants at
will' of senior jurisdictions. In the United States, Judge Dillon's 'rule' of 1868 has largely defined the state-local relationship: 'municipal corporations owe their origin to and
derive their powers and rights wholly from the [state] legislature. . . . As it creates, so
may it destroy. If it may destroy, it may abridge and control. . . . [T]he legislature might
. . . sweep from existence all of the municipal corporations of the state. . . . We know
of no limitation on this right . . . so far as [municipal] corporations are concerned.
They are, so to phrase it, the mere tenants at will of the legislature.'[29]

In Canada, most local government texts start simply with the definition of local
governments as 'creatures of the province'.[30] The Constitution Act of 1867, S. 92(8),
is clear and explicit: 'exclusive powers of provincial legislatures' include 'municipal
institutions in the province'. As described by Plunkett and Betts,

the boundaries, functions and institutional forms of municipal government are all derived from, and sanctioned by, the over-riding authority of provincial legislatures. Local authorities can be no more and no less than what is expressly laid down in provincial statutes. Thus any powers that municipalities have . . . are clearly within the realms of provincial responsibility. . . . In addition, the provinces have unrestrained power to create, alter and abolish municipalities, and to exercise whatever degree of control over municipalities and their actions, as the provincial governments think fit.[31]

Others, such as Magnusson, have argued that local governments developed in Canada and elsewhere simply 'for imposing unwanted responsibilities (and taxes) upon local communities'.[32] As Magnusson notes, historically, in places like Halifax and St John's, local government did not develop because of a struggle for local representative democracy as much as it derived from central governments seeking to get local authorities established. Many of the local élites feared more representative and responsible local governmental institutions because these might make 'spendthrift' local decisions 'to the detriment of the more materially privileged minority'.[33]

Bish identified senior governmental offloading of responsibilities for financial reasons on Canada's Pacific coast over a century ago in the colony of British Columbia. 'As the colony had a shortage of funds, it incorporated the City of New Westminster in 1860, so that the clearing of streets and the creation of a city could be proceeded with.'[34] In contemporary terms, the 1991 Municipal Bill of Rights proposed to the Federation of Canadian Municipalities called for 'no downloading of responsibilities from senior governments to municipalities without compensatory revenue-raising capacity'.[35]

The view that local governments are merely 'administrative arms for senior jurisdictions' (a 'third level' of government) represents one end of a continuum. Higgins distinguished between local government and local self-government in terms of the assignment of municipal responsibilities or functions.[36] At the imposed/administrative end of this continuum, the French system stands out:

based on Napoleon's framework of 1799 . . . the French system of local government . . . is characterized by close linkages between the central government and the units of local government. From top to bottom, the hierarchy includes the central government, regions, departements, arrondissements, cantons and communes . . . . Although mayors of communes are locally elected, for some purposes they function as agents of the central government and are therefore subject to prefectural/central direction. . . . With regard to functions, central supervision of local affairs extends beyond the service functions that communes must perform . . . to include whatever things that communes do under their general grant of power.[37]

At the other end of the spectrum is local self-government, 'not characterized by direction and control from above but by relative independence. . . . Local policies are formulated internally; there is a high degree of discretion in implementing policy.'[38]

In Higgins's assessment, 'central-local relations in France come closest to "local government" in the sense of deconcentrated public administration, exemplified by the word *tutelage*, which means that organs of local government are under the guardianship of the central government.'[39] Bish has argued that for those interested in 'structuring government according to economies of scale, some go so far as to see no significant distinction between decentralized central administration and local self government.'[40] Higgins concludes that neither end-point model of local government is the norm:

> the fact that one must search for examples that come at all close to illustrating these two models of central-local relations is indicative that neither model is presently operative in a pure form. Municipalities everywhere are subject to a greater or lesser degree of control by central government, and at the same time municipalities everywhere have a greater or lesser degree of initiative and discretion that distinguishes them from central governments.[41]

Neil Swainson has described this local-senior governmental relationship slightly differently: for Swainson, one 'characteristic of the provincial-local government relationship stems from a growing recognition by both province and municipality that each has the capacity to frustrate the other and yet, in the long run, is likely to derive little advantage from this type of behaviour.'[42] A more apt response to this 'frustration thesis' might be Victor Jones's suggestion of the need to distinguish between the senior governmental 'legal *authority* to act' and its '*power*, or the ability of the authority to act in full or in part, to exercise unfettered choice, to act at any time, any place, or to any extent it chooses.'[43] In the American context, Jones has noted the 'multiple cracks' in the political system that allow 'local governments . . . to make a systemic difference'. He also notes that 'state and national governments . . . are able to exert their authority often enough that local governments can still be called "tenants at will".'[44] Jones says that the central questions for local governments are 'when, how and where will the state [i.e., senior] governments exercise their will against their recalcitrant or innovative children.'[45]

P.J. Smith's 'local intergovernmental/power corollary' is that 'the incidence and extent of "when, how and where" senior authority will be exercised against local governments is substantially correlated with the extent of local frustration of senior governmental policy intentions.'[46] Margaret Thatcher's abolition of the seven major metropolitan authorities in Britain in the late 1980s is the best example of the 'nuclear option' here; BC's dismissal of three school boards (Vancouver and Cowichan in the 1980s and North Vancouver in the 1990s), its abolition of regional district planning authority, and its temporary removal of authority for the regional watershed from the Greater Vancouver Regional District also stand out as good reminders over the past decade that 'institutional/ constitutional relationships do affect local-senior governmental relations' in Canada.[47] Tony Blair's 'New Labour' review of 're-metropolitanization' of urban governance in the UK, Mike Harris's Megacity Toronto option, and similar governance changes in other urban settings such as Halifax and Winnipeg[48] all attest to the continuing agenda of placing local governance issues in larger policy settings.

One of the ways that senior jurisdictions affect the behaviour of local governments is through controls on the revenue-raising capacity of municipal units. In

Canada, local governments have defined themselves as 'puppets on a shoestring'.[49] This image of local governments highlights the essential nature of municipal finance in Canada; and while extravagant in language, the theme of local financial exigency is repeated in many political systems. The early 1970s 'bankruptcy' of New York City, the incapacity of many cities to rebuild urban infrastructure, and cutbacks to traditional municipal services all attest to a pattern of continuing local dependence on inadequate fiscal capacity—whether it is the property tax as in Canada, or local sales taxes as in some American jurisdictions. Senior governmental financial assistance is part of the norm. Much of this senior aid is in the form of 'conditional' grants that limit local self-government decision-making.

Ongoing senior downloading of responsibilities onto local governing authorities suggests this remains a problematic area. Municipal appeals for more recognition and capacity demonstrate the continuing nature of local fiscal need, as do continuing—and largely unsuccessful—efforts to fund the rebuilding of basic urban infrastructure in Canada and around the world.[50]

## Conclusions

Finding a generally accepted balance between these competing upside and downside views of local governance is not easy. In some instances, senior provincial authorities simply opt for one side of the equation, often over the objections of many who live in the cities affected. The creation of 'Megacity' Toronto by Ontario's Harris government is one case in point;[51] so is much of the experience in creating the Halifax Regional Municipality.[52] In Manitoba, proposals for change to Winnipeg city governance appear to be based more on a city-provincial consensus.[53] And in British Columbia, the passage of a provincial Growth Strategies Act and the development of a Greater Vancouver Livable Region Strategic Plan also emerged from a more consensus style of decision-making.[54]

British Columbia's 1997–8 review of and revisions to its Municipal Act sought to base changes on a series of principles that emerged out of widely based discussions among provincial and local interests. Out of this, nine principles, which might equally apply to all governance in current political contexts, emerged. Many of these sought to untangle the conflicting rationales posed historically for local governance. The principles proposed that local government legislation should:

- balance the interests of citizens, local government, and the provincial government.
- be clearly written and understandable.
- replace specific, narrow local government authority with greater local government authority to do business in new, innovative, and more effective ways.
- enable local governments to respond practically to specific local needs and circumstances, including obtaining additional or customized powers where/when needed.
- ensure that provincial government involvement in local government should be justifiable and limited to instances where the provincial government has a clear purpose, responsibility, or interest.

- ensure that local governments are answerable to citizens, and include a variety of ways to determine citizen interest and enable citizen input on issues of concern to them. It should also ensure that the local government decision-making process is fair and open.
- enable local governments to obtain the financial resources they need to meet their responsibilities and provide the level of service expected of them.
- require provincial consultation with local government on matters which directly impact local government decisions and activities.
- establish the means for consultation, collaboration and closure on issues, to guide inter-local government relationships.[55]

So where do these principles and this discussion leave a student of political science trying to place the study of local governance within a discipline? As noted at the outset, each of the images of local government discussed here refers to an important dimension of its existence. The local governance experience in this country and elsewhere has contributed to democratic development. Local governments remain relatively responsive and accountable and have been generally efficient providers of local services. They have also been 'tenants at will' of senior authority and have provided a base for downloading of unwanted responsibilities or as an administrative arm for senior jurisdictions. Local governments have certainly been dependent—sometimes overly so—on financial assistance from senior governments often prepared to play the piper calling the tune.

Yet for all that, local governments have proved more than resilient: they have remained significant cultural repositories and centres of our democratic traditions,[56] they are important bases in sustaining national economies,[57] they have become significant global actors despite lack of formal authority in international affairs,[58] and they have established themselves as major players in ensuring liveability and sustainability both locally and globally.[59]

Some of the key elements in these debates about differing conceptions of local government find expression in the first selection presented here, in which James Lightbody considers why we should study city politics, government, and local democracy. Caroline Andrew, in the second selection, challenges us to rethink just how we conceive our urban spaces and governance. Attempts to base resolution of differences on principles also affect potential outcomes.

Both readings demonstrate that questions about local government deal with central issues in political science. Whether focused on the nature of democracy, the capacity of institutions to be responsive, or the potential for self-governance, the study of local government is part of the challenge to find answers not only about how we conceive our politics and government but also about how we actually govern ourselves. In a democracy, local or otherwise, there is no better challenge.

# Notes

1. See, for example, C.R. and S.N. Tindal, *Local Government in Canada*, 3rd edn (Toronto: McGraw-Hill Ryerson, 1990), 13–42.

2. The four basic principles of the Baldwin Act were: municipalities were creatures of the province and subject to provincial authority; the powers of a municipality should vary according to its size and character; local councils should be elected by and from local property holders; and municipalities were to be assigned the functions of property management. See Warren Magnusson, 'The Development of Canadian Urban Government', in Michael Howlett and David Laycock, eds, *The Puzzles of Power: An Introduction to Political Science* (Toronto: Copp Clark Longman, 1994), 510–11.

3. Gerald Craig, ed., *Lord Durham's Report* (Toronto: McClelland & Stewart, 1963), 60, 67. Durham argued that 'the utter want of municipal institutions giving the people any control over their local affairs, may indeed be considered as one of the main causes of the failure of representative government, and of bad administration in the country.'

4. Ibid.

5. Robert Bish, *Local Government in British Columbia*, 2nd edn (Richmond, BC: Union of BC Municipalities, 1990), 1.

6. Thomas J. Plunkett and George M. Betts, *The Management of Canadian Urban Government* (Kingston: Institute of Local Government, Queen's University, 1978), 131.

7. On this, see Kennedy Stewart, 'Measuring Local Democracy: The Case of Vancouver', *Canadian Journal of Urban Research* 6, 2 (Dec. 1997): 160–82.

8. On some of these examples, see 'Making Cities Work' issue of *Policy Options* 17, 7 (Sept. 1996).

9. Ibid., 129.

10. For an early discussion, see, for example, Jack Masson and James Anderson, eds, *Emerging Party Politics in Urban Canada* (Toronto: McClelland & Stewart, 1972).

11. Peter Self, *Administrative Theories and Politics* (London: Allen & Unwin, 1977), ch. 8.

12. For a discussion of this, see P. Smith and P. Nicoll, 'Municipal Planning Administration in England and Canada', *London Review of Public Administration* 12 (Nov. 1979): 29–64.

13. Plunkett and Betts, *Management of Canadian Government*, 129–30.

14. Sherry Arnstein, 'Ladder of Citizen Participation in the USA', *Journal of the Town Planning Institute* 54, 4 (Apr. 1971).

15. Barry Cullingworth, *Town and Country Planning in England and Wales*, 3rd edn (London: Allen & Unwin, 1970), 320.

16. Dilys Hill, *The Planning and Management of Human Settlements with Special Emphasis on Participation* (The Hague: International Union of Local Authorities, Habitat Report, UN Conference on Human Settlements, 1975), 12.

17. In Kenneth Kernaghan and David Siegel, 'Structures and Politics of Local Government Administration', in Kernaghan and Siegel, eds, *Public Administration in Canada* (Toronto: Methuen, 1987), 587.

18. Ibid.

19. Ontario Committee on Taxation, *Report*, vol. 2 (Toronto: Queen's Printer, 1967), 503.

20. Kernaghan and Siegel, 'Structures and Politics', 588.

21. K.G. Crawford, *Canadian Municipal Government* (Toronto: University of Toronto Press, 1954), 9.

22. Ontario Committee on Taxation, *Report*, vol. 2, 503.

23. Kernaghan and Siegel, 'Structures and Politics'.

24. On this BC experience, see P. Smith, 'Regional Government in British Columbia', *Planning and Administration* 13, 2 (Autumn 1986): 7–20.

25. Andrew Sancton, 'Canada as a Highly Urbanized Nation: New Implications for Government', *Canadian Public Administration* 35, 3 (Autumn 1992): 290.

26. Ibid., 288.

27. Ibid., 292.

28. See, for example, H. Peter Oberlander and P.J. Smith, 'Governing Metropolitan Vancouver: Regional Intergovernmental Relations in British Columbia', in D. Rothblatt and A. Sancton, eds, *Metropolitan Governance: American/Canadian Intergovernmental Perspectives* (Berkeley: Institute of Governmental Studies, University of California Press, 1993), 329–73. Here the argument is made for recognition of metropolitan 'governance' versus the more formal metropolitan 'government'. That appears to be the case in metropolitan Vancouver. See also Patrick J. Smith and H. Peter Oberlander, 'Restructuring Metropolitan Governance: Greater Vancouver-British Columbia Reforms', in Donald N. Rothblatt and Andrew Sancton, eds, *Metropolitan Governance: American/Canadian Intergovernmental Perspectives*, 2nd edn (Berkeley: Institute of Governmental Studies Press, 1998).

29. *City of Clinton v. Cedar Rapids and Missouri River R.R. Co.* (1868), 24 Iowa 455, 475.

30. Magnusson makes this point in his discussion of the Baldwin Act (1849) and its implications. See Magnusson, 'Development of Canadian Urban Government', 509–38.

31. Plunkett and Betts, *Management of Canadian Urban Governments*, 66. This general municipal power is reinforced by exclusive provincial lawmaking powers in 92(10): 'local works and undertakings' and 92(16): 'all matters of a merely local . . . matter'.

32. Magnusson, 'Development of Canadian Urban Government'.

33. Ibid.

34. Bish, *Local Government in British Columbia*, 15.

35. The 'Local Government Bill of Rights' was approved by Vancouver City Council and taken by then Vancouver Mayor Gordon Campbell to the Union of BC Municipalities and to the Federation of Canadian Municipalities' think-tank session on 'Municipalities and the Constitution', Saint John, New Brunswick, 4 Sept. 1991. It was a theme returned to in 1997, for example in the 'consultation' principle included in the BC Discussion Paper on Principles for revisions to the Municipal Act.

36. Donald Higgins, *Urban Canada: Its Government and Politics* (Toronto: Macmillan, 1977), 46.

37. Ibid., 47.

38. Ibid., 48.

39. Ibid., 47–8.

40. Bish, *Local Government in British Columbia*, 1.

41. Higgins, *Urban Canada*, 49.

42. Neil Swainson, 'The Provincial-Municipal Relationship', in J.T. Morley, N. Ruff, N. Swainson, J. Wilson, and W. Young, eds, *The Reins of Power: Governing British Columbia* (Vancouver: Douglas & McIntyre, 1983), 263.

43. Victor Jones, 'Beavers and Cats: Federal-Local Government Relations in the United States and Canada', in H. Peter Oberlander and Hilda Symonds, eds, *Meech Lake: From Centre to Periphery—The Impact of the 1987 Constitutional Accord on Canadian Settlements* (Vancouver: University of British Columbia, Institute For Human Settlements, 1988), 89–126

44. Ibid.

45. Ibid.

46. P.J. Smith, 'Local-Federal Government Relations: Canadian Perspectives, American Comparisons', in Oberlander and Symonds, eds, *Meech Lake*, 127–40.

47. Ibid.

48. For a discussion of recent city-region changes in Canada, see *Policy Options* 17, 7 (Sept. 1996).

49. Canadian Federation of Mayors and Municipalities, *Puppets on a Shoestring: The Effects on Municipal Government of Canada's System of Public Finance* (Ottawa: CFMM, 1976). This was the CFMM's response to the *Report of the Tri-Level Task Force on Public Finance in Canada* (Ottawa, 1976). *Puppets on a Shoestring* predicted 'the decline and fall of municipal government . . . in Canada within five years.'

50. See, for example, the FCM brief to the (Macdonald) Royal Commission on the Economic Union and Development Prospects for Canada (Nov. 1983).

51. On this, see Frances Frisken, 'The Greater Toronto Area in Transition: The Search for New Planning and Servicing Strategies in a Period of Economic Change and Government Restraint', in Donald Rothblatt and Andrew Sancton, eds, *Metropolitan Governance: American-Canadian Comparisons*, 2nd edn (Berkeley: Institute of Governmental Studies, University of California Press, 1998).

52. See Allan O'Brien, 'Municipal Reform in Halifax', *Policy Options* 17, 7 (1996): 20–3.

53. See, for example, the Cuff Report on Winnipeg reforms: George B. Cuff and Associates Ltd, *Organizational Review and Performance Assessment* (Winnipeg, Mar. 1997).

54. See Patrick Smith, 'Metropolitan Governance: Vancouver and BC Reforms', *Policy Options* 17, 7 (1996): 7–11.

55. From *Getting Our (Municipal) Act Together: A Discussion Paper on Principles* (Victoria: Ministry of Municipal Affairs and Housing, Province of British Columbia, 1997).

56. See P. Smith, 'Toward Canadian Local Democracy', in J. Lightbody, ed., *Canadian Metropolitics: Governing Our Cities* (Toronto: Copp Clark, 1994).

57. Jane Jacobs contends that national economies have become dependent on the economies of their major city regions. See Jane Jacobs, *Cities and the Wealth of Nations: Principles of Economic Life* (New York: Random House, 1984).

58. See, for example, T. Cohn, D. Merrifield, and P. Smith, 'North American Cities in an Interdependent World: Vancouver and Seattle as International Cities', in E. Fry et al., eds, *The New International Cities Era: The Global Activities of North American Municipal Governments* (Provo, Utah: Brigham Young University Press, 1989), 73–117; P.J. Smith, 'The Making of a Global City: The Case of Vancouver 1943–1992', *Canadian Journal of Urban Research* 1, 1 (June 1992): 90–112.

59. See, for example, T. Cohn and P. Smith, 'Developing Global Cities in the Pacific Northwest: The Cases of Vancouver and Seattle', in Peter Kresl and Gary Gappert, eds, *North American Cities and the Global Economy: Challenges and Opportunities* (Thousand Oaks, Calif.: Sage, 1995), 251–85.

## Study Questions for the Readings

1. Why do city politics matter?
2. What makes local politics different from politics at the provincial or federal levels?
3. What are the major challenges facing local government today?
4. What are the essential features of a 'feminist city'?
5. How would you overcome impediments to the creation of a more gender-sensitive 'feminist city'? What role(s) might civil society or the state play?
6. How would a feminist agenda impact on an emerging municipal agenda? Why might this feminist agenda potentially have more impact at the level of local governance?

# Why Study City Politics?

James Lightbody

. . . Although Canadians often like to think of themselves in sylvan terms, there is no denying that Canada is an urban community. The federal government's statistical definition of urbanism is a population centre of 1,000 or more people in an area with a population density of 400 per square kilometre. In the 1991 census, 76.6 per cent of Canadians were counted as urban. For statistical purposes, a census metropolitan area [CMA] is defined as 'a main labour market of a continuous built-up area having a population of 100,000 or more' and, by 1991, 61 per cent of the national population lived in such areas. All 25 Canadian CMAs increased their population from 1986 to 1992 and substantially over half of us live in the Quebec City through Windsor urban corridor.

What constitutes a 'city' is quite another matter. Demographers, and other social scientists, have many fascinating differences among themselves as to the definition of a distinct city (especially within intensively built urban corridors), often using commuter-sheds to the main place of work as a key variable. Fine, but most citizens hold to their own personal sense of identity and location, depending on the situation. For example, there may be important psychological villages without government form even within the boundaries of our largest cities, places such as the Beaches in Toronto, Gastown in Vancouver, and Old Strathcona in Edmonton. At the same time, however, few persons vacationing at Disney World, for instance, would go to the bother of volunteering that they are from 'Etobicoke' rather than simply saying 'Toronto'.

From *Canadian Metropolitics: Governing Our Cities* by James Lightbody. Copyright © 1995 Addison Wesley Longman. Reprinted by permission of Addison Wesley Longman.

Yet, once a year, when property taxes are due, people come to the poignant recollection that they reside in Dartmouth, say, and not Halifax. Cities in Canada are institutions, legally incorporated under provincial statutes, and their boundaries are seldom the same as their metropolitan environments. For particular reasons, Calgary and Winnipeg are the main exemptions to this rule. Most metropolitan areas in Canada are governed by a number of local municipalities. For example, the largest city within the Victoria metropolitan area is Saanich. There are over 5,000 incorporated units of local government among the provinces; Canada has about 120 cities as such. And the defining characteristic of Canadian metropolitics is that, even where an area-wide second tier of government exists, the local town or city commands a powerful allegiance based on the political orientations of citizens.

The practical consequence of this is that any attempt to reduce the large number of local-level municipalities through some form of consolidation is virtually predestined to fail. The strength of this community attachment to local cities, often underestimated by metropolitan reform advocates, is hard to understate: in 1980, to take one example, the school children of St Albert (a small suburb of Edmonton then under threat of amalgamation) were all urged to send Valentine's cards to Premier Peter Lougheed deploring the initiative, with the wording, 'We love our city, let us keep it.' Prior to this, in a publicity-stunt variation on a medieval ceremony, their parents had physically beaten the length of the community's borders with birch fronds to ward off evil spirits (presumably residing in the core city to which most of them commuted to work). For whatever reasons, St Albert exists today as an autonomous municipality.

One theme that has lingered over practical discussions of Canadian city politics is the persistent sense of nostalgia for our roots in some fictitious, but glorious, rural past. This belief partly derives from a strong cultural heritage in which the city itself was thought to be evil; a decision to move into such a place was somehow inherently immoral and a desertion of civilized values. Why else indeed would otherwise sensible citizens cast rodents as city mascots? Even today, as a nation, a large chunk of our shared cultural mythology is defined by the romance of the farm, the frontier, and the wilderness. How little of our currency, for instance, bears other than rustic symbols! To move from the sublime to the ridiculous, what images do big city telephone books present of their communities? In 1986 Quebec City's book portrayed a shed in a maple sugar bush, while Montreal's showed pink foxtails in the Laurentian mountains; Calgary produced a montage of elk, a kodiak bear, a person in a kayak; Victoria unveiled a farmer's field at the steps of a mountain, and, as John Sewell has noted, Halifax's book had a drawing on the front cover of lush foliage viewed from a cabin window while the back cover boasted 'a stretched out dead chipmunk and other collector's specimens'.[1] Only Edmonton and Vancouver, among the major cities, had urban vistas.

The more serious side of this honest misrepresentation is reflected in patterns of political representation. All of Canada's provincial legislatures through the present have endured a rural imbalance in representation greater than that permitted federally. For instance, in Alberta, for the provincial election in 1993, 15 of the province's 83 ridings were 25 per cent larger (urban) or smaller (rural) than the size of the average provincial constituency. Edmonton's constituencies were 11.3 per cent, and Calgary's 15.4, larger in population than the provincial average. At the extreme, Calgary-Egmont's 27,858 voters had the same legislative power as Cardston's 8,675. What this means in practical terms is that the urban Calgary elector had about one-third the value to a government seeking re-election as a rural Cardstonite. The recent stance of the Supreme Court of Canada has not given much support to appeals under the Charter of Rights and Freedoms for representational parity between urban and rural voters.[2]

This legislative imbalance has clear consequences for the types of policy questions raised in cabinet, caucus, and Commons. In Alberta, no municipal affairs minister represented an urban riding for the entire span of Social Credit (1935–71), and no such Manitoba minister represented a Winnipeg area riding until 1969 despite the fact that by shortly after the Second World War more than half of the province's population lived there and 19 of the 24 major municipal governments in the province lay within the metropolitan zone. Departments of municipal affairs, symbolically and practically, became service agencies for rural and small-town Canada.

So cities have had to fend for themselves, and often they have done this quite well as the skill of the respective political leadership has permitted. In the province of Quebec, the mayor of Montreal ran roughshod over the provincial department of municipal affairs to impose his form of metropolitan government on Montreal island in the aftermath of the 1969 police strike. For a further example, to obtain a better share of revenues locally generated, the city-owned telephone system in Edmonton reprogrammed its computers on Valentine's Day, 1984, to prevent the provincial telephone company from recording the origins of long distance calls.

More fundamentally, in law and in character, our general local government framework still displays its nineteenth-century origins. . . . [D]espite numerous reform initiatives the heart and soul of Canadian city form and structure, its ideas and applications, has remained Ontario's Municipal Corporations (Baldwin) Act of 1849. This fact has placed serious restrictions upon what even the most intelligent and progressive city councillor may accomplish when in office. Seven generations later,

## Table 1: Public-Sector Employment, 1992

|  | Employees (000s) | % change from 1991 | % of total paid workers |
|---|---|---|---|
| *Public sector* | 2,685 | 0.0% | 23.0% |
| Federal | 562 | –1.5 | 3.8 |
| Provincial/terr. | 1,111 | –0.5 | 10.0 |
| Local | 1,012 | +1.4 | 9.2 |
| *Government (excludes business enterprises)* | 2,335 | +0.3 | 19.9 |
| Federal | 413 | –1.3 | 2.5 |
| Provincial/terr. | 964 | –0.2 | 8.7 |
| Local | 959 | +1.5 | 8.7 |

Source: Statistics Canada data as reported in the *Globe and Mail*, 2 Nov. 1993.

the style of governance promoted by the Baldwin Act—a style that took root and flourished at a time when government as a whole was intended to accomplish very little and popular democracy as we understand the concept today was still widely mistrusted—continues to cramp severely the interventionist ambitions of city governments.

## City Politics Matter

Canadian cities make important policy choices that have a direct impact upon our personal lives. In its varied forms, the policy that emanates from city hall codifies important social values, regulates personal privacy, and generates and restricts economic activity over and above the protective, social, and recreational services we most directly notice. Cities such as Edmonton [and] Calgary . . . are each four times the size of the province of Prince Edward Island. As corporations, they are themselves very big businesses. Measured by its purchases of goods and services from small business, for instance, Edmonton is annually among the 20 largest Canadian corporations. Metropolitan Toronto and Montreal would be, by population

alone, the third and fourth largest Canadian provinces. Cities own telephone companies, railway lines, airports, parking garages, and billion-dollar utilities such as Edmonton Power and its Genessee power plant. Cities also license businesses, bicycles, massage parlours, taxis, and dogs.

Taken together, Canadian municipalities are major actors in the national economy. If we were to look at total government expenditures as a percentage of gross domestic product (GDP) in 1989, the federal government accounted for 18.62, the 10 provinces for 14.68, and the combined local authorities for 8.02 per cent. Further, the data in Table 1 demonstrate rather vividly the scale of combined municipal operations in the area of government employment. It is twice that of the national government and equivalent to that of the provinces. Of course, significant questions of accountability arise when the self-professed amateur politicians in cities raise and spend such large sums in a non-partisan system with neither governmental nor any comprehensive extra-governmental opposition.

All that said, the fiscal position of local governments in the intergovernmental arrangement,

## Table 2: Expenditures/Revenues in the National System before Transfers (in $ millions), Calendar Year 1990

|  | Federal | Provincial | Local |
|---|---|---|---|
| Revenues | $126,313 | 114,541 | 28,762 |
| Expenditures | 125,081 | 98,575 | 53,886 |
| Surplus/Deficit | +1,232 | +15,966 | –25,124 |

Source: Statistics Canada data as presented by the Canadian Tax Foundation, *Provincial and Municipal Finances*, 1991 (Toronto, 1992), 3:2.

as shown in Table 2, is difficult at best, and it must be remembered as well that most local authorities, by law, are not allowed to enter into debt on current (or operating ) budgets. When one looks at the pattern of revenues and expenditures overall, we see that for the calendar year 1990 Canadian municipalities stood deeply in debt. But this is *before* transfer payments from other levels of government. The subordinate financial position of even our greatest cities stems from unchanged and by now outdated revenue sources: local government direct revenues, as a percentage of GDP (4.28 per cent), are almost exactly as they were in 1926. Even the most casual observer of the system would recognize that demands for city expenditures have changed significantly in number and nature from that earlier time. The disparity between the cities' limited funding sources and their ever-growing responsibilities accounts for much of the rancour underpinning intergovernmental relations in Canada. Nor is this all. If, as is currently suggested, the 1990s will be the decade of the deficit for all levels of authority, then the broader levels of government can be expected to try to restrict their expenditures. In the past it has often been possible, after the usual alternatives of privatizing, user-pay, and slashbacks have been explored, to 'off-load' programs onto Canada's cities. Whether the resource of the property tax base has become exhausted for this purpose will increasingly become the object of intense debate.

Still, there is a perception that cities do not deal with the grand issues of 'high politics' and so their politics usually possess a low level of salience for most citizens. Issues of war and peace, economic and fiscal policy, employment and health standards, and the never-ending constitutional debates (which hold direct relevance for very few Canadians) are debated and occasionally resolved at the national level. Provincial governments in the 1990s play major roles in devising standards for the implementation of important federal programs (social assistance, medicare, hospitalization, post-secondary education) and directly involve themselves in the exploitation of natural resources, the development of transportation arteries, and the provision of schooling.

Set against these concerns, how can the local issues of planning, potholes, and police protection compete? None of this is often the arena of media hype; few civic policies hold the attention of the community cosmopolitans for long, and those which do suggest that the agendas of city élites, and their very focused lobbies, are not the same as those of local electors. To put this another way, whereas the urban political leadership cadre seems to be drawn from those who are concerned with such concepts as 'progress' and 'modern government', neighbourhood electors tend to be concrete, parochial, and short-term in their demands of councils. For the former, environmental issues are 'writ large' (ozone depletion, global warming); for most of the rest of us, what our neighbours do to, and in, their backyards holds more immediate, sustained environmental consequence.

If cities are theoretically at the heart of generating wealth in our civilization because of their accumulation of a critical mass of abilities, they have turned this phenomenon into a somewhat tawdry affair in the twentieth century. The infatuation with unrestrained growth, often expressed in brazenly sophomoric terms, has become synonymous with the Canadian metropolis. It is a coveted form of recognition for Canadian cities to be singled out in a survey by a major national publication as one of 'Canada's best cities for business'. Winnipeg, Moncton, Vancouver, Edmonton, and Montreal were so chosen in 1993 by the *Globe's Report on Business* as the finest coddlers of business in the country! A US businessman is cited: 'We looked at Provo, Utah, and Omaha, Nebraska—but those cities' "special treatment" and TLC are perfunctory and institutionalized at this point. We were looking for a city that would develop an infrastructure for us as a partner. And in Winnipeg, Manitoba, you're admitted like an adopted son.'[3]

Now, for most people, to be chosen ahead of some small town in Utah or Nebraska, even for the better surfing, would be no big deal. But Canadian cities have given away the keys consistently. In this, Winnipeg has had a solidly typical track record; to attract the CPR main line in the 1870s, that city's council not only provided land grants, a $200,000 bonus, and a $300,000 bridge over the Red River but also exempted railway lands 'from city taxation forever'. These days it seems more fashionable for city promoters to lobby for major league sports franchises but business boons still abound. Even social-democratic municipal partisans have been swept up in unabashed hucksterism as their labour supporters (especially among the building trades) have clamoured for the jobs that come with large-scale developments. This is one reason for the persistently observed shift to the right by leftist city councillors over their time in office.

Boosterism has had direct consequences for the general direction of city politics, in both senses of that word; that is, who should be in charge and what they should be charging towards. In his insightful analysis of Winnipeg's formative period, Alan Artibise wrote of the city's business élite and its role in civic government: 'There was never any doubt as to who would control the government . . . a centralized form of government assured Winnipeg's businessmen that their conception of desirable public policy would prevail.'[4] The same comment could apply to virtually any other Canadian city. The business concept of public policy meant, very simply, that the expansion of economic enterprise should be the primary focus for local government: all of its energies and concerns ought to be directed towards sustained commercial growth even if such an approach were to mean the neglect of all other objectives. This has been the single most dominant theme in twentieth-century Canadian urban development.

## The Apolitical World of City Politics

One of the most strongly held myths about Canadian metropolitics is that city elections are non-partisan. Few communities have actually gone so far as Vancouver, where the dominant electoral coalition since the depression of the 1930s has actually been called the Civic Non-Partisan Association. But little seems as frowned upon, outside unbridled evidence of graft, as the mere thought that some party-like entity is organizing to take control of the municipal agenda. And, where the local branches of national parties have actually tried to enter the municipal fray (as with the Liberals in Toronto in 1969, and the NDP in Winnipeg in 1971), traditional organizational support was lacking and the voters were markedly unamused.

While there may be many reasons for this outlook, the fundamental salience of Canadian civic non-partisanship can be directly traced back a century to the municipal reform movement in the United States. This movement arose in reaction to the spoils system, which in turn was a product of the boss rule and machine politics of major American cities. The reformers devised a package of institutions intended to de-politicize city government and to model it instead upon the apolitical form of the business corporation. Central to their approach was an abhorrence of party organization, which was seen to lead inexorably to patronage, graft, and all the other splendid kinds of ward-heeling. Canadian municipal reformers took to these bright ideas as readily then as our winter snowbirds now enjoy the seasonal culture of Palm Springs and Miami.

There are probably very few town halls across Canada where the insiders cannot identify accurately the federal or provincial party associations for most sitting councillors. Political attachments are a part of an active social life. Those who may be active at one level of politics are those most likely to be interested in any electoral race, at any level of politics. Although the small scale of the operations in most Canadian cities renders these partisan affiliations of little practical importance in policy-making, party-like activity has been a constant in our municipal life. The great success stories, as judged by electoral victories and longevity, have been cadre organizations (small in number, focused on elections, comprised of local notables with access to wealth) such as the Civic Non-Partisan Association (NPA) in Vancouver, the Independent Citizens' Election Committee (ICEC) in Winnipeg, and, possibly, Jean Drapeau's Civic Party in Montreal. Usually formed to confront a rising challenge from labour, these shadowy coalitions of local Liberals and Conservatives produced little ideological coherence in the form of platform policy except a solid dose of boosterism, civic-government efficiency, and 'common sense' (that being theirs, as it turned out). A unifying theme was always that the partisanship evident at senior levels was somehow irrelevant to the municipal scene.

It now seems somewhat ironic, then, that the more obvious the past federal and provincial partisan ties (and experience) of major candidates in Canadian metropolitics, the more their municipal campaigns have emphasized leadership style and personality at the expense of substantial ideological divergence over more serious policy matters. In fact, it may not be going too far to say that past partisanship has now become a most positive advantage in cities, an almost critical element in the success of 'non-partisan' mayoralty campaigns in the Canadian metropolis. Party ties mean strategists and workers, donors of funds, name recognition, and, often, credibility with the local press gallery. In this way, a past party life is a valuable political resource not available to the innocent newcomer. Even though partisan ties at the federal or provincial level are hardly ever advertised, the gladiators lurk behind the scenes of all municipal election contests, their political affiliations submerged under a flood of rhetoric about 'business-like' government and the pursuit of some amorphous common good.

Because of the often issue-specific and hands-on nature of many local government decisions, the question of political ideology is seldom baldly debated at city hall. The corollary is that the ideological underpinnings of most decisions are not immediately recognized. Ideologies have been often muted at the municipal level, especially as policy coalitions emerge, dissolve, and reform, both inside council and out, according to the particular decision at hand. Canadian cities present the true politics of immediacy. For instance, the urban reformers of the 1970s were widely perceived as radicals because of the comprehensiveness of their challenge to local authority; however, the reality may have been that they were genuine conservatives committed to preserving an existing neighbourhood against freeway or developer intrusion.

Finally, it has become somewhat of a standing cliché in Canadian local government texts that it is the provinces which directly dictate what cities may do, may not do, and must do anyway. Specifically, permissive and mandatory powers are outlined for them by provincial government statute. The former are normally established by a general municipal government Act, while the mandatory functions are set by specific legislation such as the Public Health Act. Importantly, no city can do anything not expressly permitted by some provincial statute or regulation.

Having said this, within the framework set by the respective province, types of city policy decisions will vary. Policies that require taxation and expenditure may be said to be either allocative or redistributive in nature. Allocative policies produce public goods such as fire protection which apply equally to all citizens. Redistributive schemes such as social services attempt to apply or redirect accumulated wealth selectively to those in need. The policy choices of council ultimately take the form of by-laws either requiring certain actions or prohibiting them (zoning by-laws or parking restrictions, for instance). A city council may also delegate its authority to make decisions in a particular policy arena either to its permanent bureaucracy or to a specialized agency such as a development appeal board, transit authority, or police commission. Other decisions might be purely symbolic, as when folkloric heroes or civic pioneers are honoured by the naming of streets, parks, or bridges. Seldom are living politicians so recognized.

Curiously, policy might also be considered to have been made when city councillors choose not to decide. In such an instance they may not be certain as to whether or not there is sufficient support behind a demand for change, or they may not have a clear understanding of the interests of specifically affected groups. So the decision is made not to decide (usually pending further study) and the matter may be referred 'back to committee'. To the casual eye it may even seem as though councillors are sitting about like Greyfriars' Bobby, waiting for something to pop up. But the important point is that a decision has been made not to decide and this choice usually reinforces the status quo. This would certainly characterize the approach taken by most traditional town councils.

But the newer style of urban councillor is more interventionist, asserting an action agenda which, as it comes into conflict with provincially imposed limitations (statutory and fiscal), establishes the flashpoints for intergovernmental conflict regardless of partisan loyalties. Ontario's NDP government of the 1990s, for example, has not held an easy working relationship with the many city councillors associated with that party, just as jurisdictionally inspired conflict ruffled federal-provincial feathers during the few months in 1979 when Conservative Prime Minister Joe Clark dealt with Alberta's Conservative Premier Lougheed. The lesson here is that cities have become more important, more independent, governmental actors. They have become more partisan as they have become more interventionist. While partisan ties may ease some intergovernmental relations (and cause friction in others), they do not cause basic jurisdictional differences to disappear.

No matter how partisan it has become, the governmentally splintered metropolis produces multiple public goods from a number of jurisdictions. At the heart of the public-choice school of political science is the thought that the sum total of these goods would be smaller if each metropolitan area was subject to unitary government. That is, each of many municipalities might find it desirable to maintain a community swimming complex, resulting in a dozen or more for a metropolitan centre, whereas if the region were governmentally unified it could get by with far fewer. Given the numerous problems that otherwise beset the governmentally polycentric metropolitan region, it is certainly a judgement call, ultimately from the user's perspective, as to which form makes the more effective use of public funds. . . .

## Participation in City Politics

. . . There are many limitations upon the creative capacities of councils to facilitate involvement. The most imposing and persistent is the burden of sheer size. As Canadian cities emerged from the reforms of the 1970s, simple largeness became a huge psychological barrier to direct citizen action. There is no longer any physical town hall big enough to accommodate the traditional face-to-face town meeting. Even reforms of upper-tier governments in Ontario over the last few years have neglected to reconcile size with democracy. For example, in 1989 Sarnia, with 58 per cent of the voters in Lambton County, received but 15 of 37 positions on regional council; and, in another case, Mississauga, with 63 per cent of the voters in Peel Region, 10 of 21 councillors.[5] May this be an indication of provincial dismissal of the importance of local representative democracy? Should the serious pattern of electoral misrepresentation not soon be subject to judicial review under the Charter? Ultimately, ought urban voters to accept the legitimacy of such political systems when responsible authorities themselves do not?

A further perennial problem stemming from as far back as the turn of the century is the role of boards and agencies in the city's policy affairs. When these bodies were created, it was felt that specific areas (such as education, policing, and public health) were too specialized and sensitive to be left to the dimwit generalists on councils and ought properly to be handled by panels of 'blue ribbon' citizens. While the existence of such agencies does increase the potential for direct citizen participation in policy-making, it also seriously detracts from the general authority of the elected representatives since many of their major responsibilities are spun off to quasi-subordinates. The delicate question of patronage also arises whenever these 'objective experts' are to be appointed by council, and campaign workers are often asserted by the councillors to be very good citizens indeed. . . .

Some citizens have neither the time nor tastes for the largely electoral politics we have been considering but are still intensely interested in municipal policy-making. They may, therefore, choose to participate in pressure-group activities intended to influence the choices or strategies of city councillors. These activities are essentially of only

two kinds; groups are institutionalized into the process or not. Institutional groups are bodies such as the local Chamber of Commerce, certain professional associations (architects, engineers), government-clientele associations (social service groups, cultural organizations), and many well-established neighbourhoods (usually upper class). They employ their political resources of social standing, professional knowledge, and corporate wealth in an ongoing policy dialogue with city hall. Normally they deal with the senior administrators, and, should they lose on a particular fight, maintaining this long-term relationship is far more important than the immediate decision.

Newer types of groups over the past generation have directly challenged this established way of doing business. They have been based in certain neighbourhoods (threatened by redevelopment), on single issues (freeway expansion plans), and around specific functional areas of government (social services). The behaviour of these groups has been generically described as noisy, negative, and reactionary. This is often the kindest description they will hear. They are noisy because the whole point is to exploit the media to gain attention to counteract institutionalized power and resources. They are negative by definition because they exist to oppose what they view as offensive initiatives on the part of the city. And they are reactionary because by their nature they have not been built into the consultative process. In the 1990s, the NIMBY (Not in My Backyard) phenomenon is a less creative offshoot of the single-issue group, a spontaneous explosion of dissent over a project or plan (such as a dump location). While NIMBY protest is not at all irrational behaviour in politics, it tends to consider no alternative but the termination of the offensive initiative. The groups that rally under this banner claim, very rightly, that the suggestion of other alternatives is not their responsibility.

Recourse to the basic tools of direct democracy in the form of the initiative (a technique by which, through petition, laws crafted by citizens are put directly to a referendum), the referendum (a decision by all electors defined as 'a binding verdict of the people'), and the recall (a process by which an elected official's position is legally declared vacant) has become the legitimate child of 1990s cynicism. Widespread calls for the use of these devices are a symptom that both governing élites and the broader public, each concerned with the manipulations, motives, and apparent fickleness of the other, have become jaded with the established order. The pressures are growing in intensity as the 500-channel super-universe unfolds and politics becomes more immediate, direct, interactive, and accessible for the many outside the old circles. As with any time of serious political change, there will be concomitant stress. What seems most probable is that it will be the city political arena which first tests whether established procedures can be adapted to this new era or not.

In all of this, it is important to understand that what we 'know' about metropolitics comes primarily from two sources. There is the first-hand contact we acquire in our daily lives through such obvious and specific things as parking meters, potholes, and police. Our more general knowledge of city affairs derives from the various news media, which provides the descriptive basis on which we evaluate events. In theoretical terms, the role of these media is not only to report the details but also to place events into the context of civic culture. Importantly, they might be considered filters sifting what is important from what is less so. In reality, however, in towns and most

cities the city hall press gallery is 'in the loop', a part of the system upon which they are reporting. The better reporters trade on insider information, treating favoured councillors and the more accomplished administrators with kid gloves, often floating policy trial balloons for them. There is an acknowledged tendency among the media to view outsiders such as new groups and non-establishment candidates in the same light as incumbents do, as a threat to the established order of business. As to the critical capacities of local electronic newsreaders, most communities are fortunate if their television and radio stations can reproduce the lead paragraphs from the morning tabloids accurately: in short, these media usually follow the lead of the newspapers on most stories.

It is necessary also to remember that newspapers are businesses. To read the commercial pages and the principal local business affairs columnist is to view tub-thumpers for the local board of trade who are just as ingenuous as the sports writers who boost the city's major league franchises. Finally, in an age when the significant municipal politics of other major cities tend not to be covered locally at all, this vigorous 'villaging' of the mass media means that few citizens can fashion independently objective standards against which to measure the local political agenda and the performance of their city's indigenous political classes. For this, city electors are abandoned to the leadership of the already dominant cosmopolitan city élites, who develop interpretations and make assessments based on their personal and professional sources and travels outside the community.

## Notes

1. *Globe and Mail*, 10 Apr. 1986.
2. Andrew Sancton, 'Canada as a Highly Urbanized Nation: New Implications for Government', *Canadian Public Administration* 35, 3 (Autumn 1992): 287.
3. Ann Walmsley, 'City Lights: Best Cities for Business', *Globe and Mail Report on Business* (Aug. 1993): 49.
4. Alan F.J. Artibise, *Winnipeg: A Social History of Urban Growth, 1874–1914* (Montreal and Kingston: McGill-Queen's University Press, 1975), 58.
5. Sancton, 'Canada as a Highly Urbanized Nation', 287.

# The Feminist City

Caroline Andrew

A feminist city. What would it look like? What would define it as feminist? Let's think of the concrete things that would have to be part of our feminist city.[1]

It would have a well-developed network of services dealing with the issue of violence against women and children.[2] These services would be designed with the goal of eliminating violence; they would provide services consistent with an understanding of the structural causes of violence against women and children. Each of the services would operate independently, but they would also be linked as a network. This network of services would co-ordinate the legal, social, educational, psychological and cultural services that presently exist and that need to be created, thus making sure that the entire system of services is accountable to the women who are victims of violence.

A wide variety of services would make genuine choices available to women. Specifically designed services would be put in place for doubly disadvantaged groups of women with disabilities. Participation in these services and influence over their direction would be real and would be encouraged.

A feminist city would be also concerned with the elimination of public violence against women.[3] To this end it would have an agency, financed by the city but independent of it. This agency would function as part of the network of services described above but particularly on issues of public violence against women.[4] It would have a broad mandate to make the city not only violence-free for women but also a comfortable place for women to live. In so doing, it would also ensure a city that is friendly to children and to the elderly. Without suggesting a simplistic physical determinism, urban planning would be carried out in such a way as to create public spaces that encourage widespread public use of the city. Seeking to combine Jane Jacobs's 'mixed use' friendly neighbourhoods and the civic architecture of Italian city centres, which are packed with pedestrians and free of automobiles, the city would welcome suggestions as how to design usable, and used, public space. Streets and squares filled with people are safer spaces for women than deserted streets and empty parks.

A feminist city would have a first-class public transportation system. As women use public transportation more than men, the quality of public transportation is a feminist issue.[5] The system would provide transportation that is not only safe but also cheap and efficient. By providing for women, the system would again service the elderly and the young, providing a transportation system adapted to their needs for mobility and for autonomy.

Our feminist city would also have an active social housing policy. Housing is a feminist issue for a number of reasons.[6] Since women earn less than men, their housing costs represent a greater percentage of their revenue.

Women who lead households and elderly women have a particularly difficult housing situation. Studies show that obtaining secure housing is fundamental to women trying to gain control over their lives.[7]

Therefore the social housing policy would include a range of options, including second-stage housing for women leaving transition homes,

From Henri Lustiger-Thaler, ed., *Political Arrangements: Power and the City* (Montreal: Black Rose Books, 1992), 109–20. Reprinted by permission of Black Rose Books.

co-operative housing, special housing for women with disabilities, and a variety of forms of housing for women living in economic difficulties. Again, this housing policy would be sensitive to issues of class, race, and sexual orientation as well as gender.

Good day care is another essential feature of the feminist city.[8] Day care would be available to all who want to use it. Since once again the question of choice is fundamental, a wide variety of services would be available: full-day or flexible hours or drop-in services, at workplaces or residential neighbourhoods or transportation nodes,[9] with programming sensitive to language and cultural questions.

Our feminist city would actively promote community-based economic development, emphasizing the creation of meaningful and socially productive jobs for women. Training and employment programs would be combined and would be well co-ordinated with day-care programs.

## Urban Planning

Finally, the urban planning component for our feminist city[10] would be sensitive to the impact of physical form on patterns of urban living. Therefore it would strive to create environments that are supportive of women.[11] In general, the single-use zoning found in most late twentieth-century North American cities does not encourage this kind of supportive environment. Suburbs with few or no services, separated from commercial and office zones that afford few or no facilities for family living, do not nurture the intricate patterns of interrelationship between the worlds of production and consumption so typical of women's lives.[12] Urban planning should therefore encourage physical forms that allow a close relationship between services, residences, and workplaces.

However, urban planning should not take for granted that women will always be more concerned than men with the planning and management of the sphere of consumption and thus more sensitive to the interface between production and consumption. Although feminist urban planning would have as its goal the creation of an environment entirely free of sexism, this planning must at the same time take into account the present reality that women are disproportionately responsible for the double and triple schedules needed to combine work, family, and social responsibilities. It should therefore have as its first priority the encouragement of mixed urban land use and the freeing up of urban planning from the overly rigid single-use zoning that has characterized the post-war period.

In style, too, urban planning for the feminist city would be markedly different from the present insistence on the expertise of the planner and the elaboration of a master plan for the whole population. Feminist planning would be attuned to working with the population rather than about the population; it would be sensitive to the multiplicity of groups and interests that comprise the public. Planners would have to devise imaginative strategies to encourage groups and individuals to articulate their needs. The needs of doubly disadvantaged women in particular would be taken into account.

## Public Art

One small element, but one of symbolic importance, that would help define the feminist city is public art.[13] Statues and monuments would be representative of women and of women-centred activities. A few examples suggest the almost endless list of possibilities—Madeleine Parent,[14] Maria Campbell,[15] Nicolletta and Virginia.[16] And not to forget those who have already been more recognized—Marie de l'Incarnation,[17] Lucy Maud Montgomery,[18] Gabrielle Roy,[19] Kenojuak.[20] Of course, as soon as global feminism is considered, the list becomes endless.

In summary, these are just some of the elements that would be part of the feminist city: a network of services designed to reduce and eliminate violence against women, good public transportation, adequate social housing, sufficient day care, and imaginative urban planning.

## Practical and Political Space for Feminists

But how would these be created? How do these ideas become reality? We have shown that there are feminist concerns particular to the city and that a feminist city should have policies directed to these issues. But what does this mean in terms of political processes? How can these policies become implemented in the cities we now know in Canada?

In order to answer these questions, we need to look at feminist political practice and feminist methods of political organizing.

What are the organizing processes of feminist groups and how do these relate to constructing the kind of city we have been describing? Although the Canadian literature on feminist organization is growing rapidly,[21] it is still relatively sparse. This literature does suggest, however, a number of traits of feminist organizing that are consistent with and even conducive to the kind of city we have been describing.[22]

These characteristics include the use of networks and networking, the integration of service provision and other organizational objectives, a strategy of parallel activity within civil society and within the state, a concern for organizational democracy and innovation and, finally, the creation of collective identities and meanings through inter-organizational links and activities.

The importance of networking to the organizational behaviour of feminist groups has been underlined by most of the analysts of the women's movement. Susan Phillips describes social movements in general as 'differentiated but interconnected networks of organizations',[23] and Anadon et al. emphasize the growth of networks among women's groups: '. . . depuis quelques années, le développement des réseaux constitue un élément important de la dynamique des groupes de femmes du Québec.'[24] Michaud, in discussing

different networking strategies, also underlines the importance of this form of organizing.

One also finds diversity in approaches to networks and coalitions, ranging both from the networks of regional and national organizations around specific women's issues (Vickers, 1989) to women's political struggles for the building of solidarity coalitions within the movement itself around general issues (Adamson, Briskin, and McPhail, 1988); and from small networks built regionally and/or nationally to participation in large solidarity coalitions around issues shared with other social movements.[25]

The interrelation between the provision of services and other goals within women's organizations has been much debated. 'The evolution of feminist organizations from pressure groups to service groups'[26] has been variously condemned as an illustration of state co-optation and/or a decline in militancy and applauded as focusing on concrete assistance to women and/or as providing innovative models for services.

Whatever its interpretation, there has been a clear trend towards emphasis on service delivery. In our view this is an indication of the multidimensionality of the work undertaken by feminist organizations—service deliverers they are, but concerned with the transformation of society as well, including the education of their members and the general public, and with questions of internal democracy.

The strategy of parallel activity within civil society and the state is one of the recurrent themes in the Canadian literature on relations between the women's movement and the state. As Vickers observes, 'This tradition of a public but sub-state focus, far from being displaced in recent decades, continues to run parallel to a tradition of increasing support for state-level intervention.'[27] The linking of autonomous activity on the terrain of civil society to activity within the state by bureaucrats and politicians is viewed as being one of the characteristics of organized feminism in Canada.[28]

Concern for internal democracy and organizational innovation has marked women's organizations. Susan Wismer stresses this point in discussing the contribution of the women's movement to the debate on sustainable development; her argument is that its major contribution has been less one of content than one based on the experience of organizational innovation. For Wismer, sustainable development will emerge in societies in which grassroots energy and initiative are organizationally transmitted to the policy process.[29] The women's movement has been in the forefront of creating these kinds of organizations. Using the vantage point of a feminist analysis of power, Yolande Cohen suggests the same possibilities for voluntary associations in general.

> C'est à ce niveau que les groupes volontaires doivent jouer leur rôle de contre-pouvoir: pour ouvrir des perspectives politiques à celles et ceux qui en font la demande. Ils doivent devenir des courroies de transmission des solutions qui au niveau local sont considérées comme adéquates. Lieux d'innovation et d'expertise, les associations ne sont pas uniquement des organes de défense d'intérêts corporatistes. Elles peuvent devenir des outils puissants dans les mains de leurs membres, si tant est que la démocratie y règne, et qu'elles n'hésitent pas à manifester sur la place publique les solutions qu'elles préconisent.[30]

The work of Anadon et al. on women's groups and regional development in the Saguenay-Lac-St-Jean area also views the internal organization and modes of decision-making of feminist groups as one of their major contributions. They have been innovative not only in their chosen target areas, in the kinds of solutions proposed, but also in the way they go about making decisions. This last feature recalls Susan Phillips's insight when she states that social movements are 'sponsors of meaning'.[31] The networks of groups and individuals involved in providing public education, advocacy, and services to women share common understandings. These networks then offer channels for the creation and reinforcement of shared symbolic meanings.

Our work on women's groups in the Outaouais[32] has illustrated the importance accorded by groups to maintaining their identification with the women's movement at the same time that they uphold their commitments to specific areas of public policy. Networking fills this role through strengthening the sense of identity with, and participation in, the women's movement. Adamson, Briskin, and McPhail's *Feminist Organizing for Change* (1988) also examines the kind of shared meanings that are created within and carried along by organizational networks. Their analysis of 'the personal is political' and 'sisterhood is powerful' as central themes in the women's movement demonstrates the impact of these shared understandings.

## Inventing the Feminist City

Having outlined the major characteristics of feminist organizations, it remains to link them to the creation of the concrete programs and activities that we have already described as essential to our feminist city. How do these kinds of political processes relate to the governance of cities?

Our argument is that these characteristics are particularly well adapted to urban political systems. Networking as a political process, and the kind of networks formed by feminists, are compatible with the governance of a spatially limited area such as a city. Through connected groups, associations, and agencies, the networking process can encompass the whole of the city while at the same time allowing for direct face-to-face politics. Politics can be inclusive and at the same time functional on a small enough scale to encourage participation by large numbers for people operating in areas of comfortable size. Italian city-states, for instance, suggest a kind of politics that allows participation in a variety of arenas, forming a basis for the governance of the city.

The importance assigned to services, together with the desire to link them to public education, organizational questions, and political advocacy, is arguably a mode of functioning positively associated with the task of governing cities. Just as service delivery is essential for city governance, the ability to understand service delivery in its ideological and political context is essential to a reinvented city politics. Municipal politics has always included the provision of concrete services and the necessity to work out in detail the relationships between different services directed to the same population. This ability to link the practical and effective delivery of services to larger political questions is one of the hallmarks of feminist organizations and is also one of the necessary characteristics of a reinvented city politics.

The same thing can be said for the 'outside and inside' political strategy; that of simultaneously working in civil society—voluntary associations—and within the state. Municipal government in Canada has had a rather narrow set of responsibilities and forms only a small part of what could be defined as the local state.[33] Local reform therefore relates not only to changes in municipal government, including the widening of the concerns of municipalities, but also to changes in a wide variety of other local bodies. Civil society and the state must be simultaneously reformed. A political practice that works in both areas is clearly preferable to one that is either state-centred or working only in civil society.

## The Role of Feminist Practice

The feminist preoccupation with organizational innovation and internal democracy is also compatible with a reformed city politics. The scale of city government means that face-to-face encounters play a much larger role than at other levels of politics.

This degree of intimacy means that the democratic experiences of feminist organizations are of practical applicability and of great importance.

The collective identity and shared meanings that have been developed and nurtured through networks linking groups, individuals, associations, agencies, and services are of considerable political significance to a reformed city politics.

One of the obstacles to more progressive political activity at the municipal level is the widespread view that municipal government is simply a matter of technical administration rather than of political choices. The kind of transformatory vision that is part of the collective identity of the women's movement may be able to supply the political vision for change that is a precondition to a reformed city politics. Unless there is a sense that this is an arena where significant political choices can be made, it will be difficult to mobilize for political action.

This brings us to the major paradox of our argument: despite the fact that all the elements of the feminist city are both attainable and clearly feminist, and despite the compatibility between feminist organizational practices and the functioning of city politics, feminist politics has been, up until now, very little concerned with municipal governance. The construction of the feminist city has not been high on the feminist agenda.

There are two main reasons for this. The development of the welfare state in Canada left most areas seen as crucial to feminism in the hands of provincial or federal governments. Feminist demands on the state were therefore focused on these levels of government. In addition, municipal government was defined in such a way that to feminists it was uninteresting or worse. Most social issues at the local level came under the purview of special purpose bodies and not municipal governments. School boards are the clearest example, but this has often been true for health and social services and for certain cultural activities.

The responsibilities of municipal government were seen to focus on the servicing of private property and on debates about the provision of infrastructures to permit and support the profitable expansion of the city. This vision of municipal government supported, and was supported by, municipal political personnel who came predominantly from the property sector[34] and who were almost exclusively male.

The disjuncture between feminist organizing and municipal politics can therefore be explained by the role of provincial and federal governments in issues of primary concern to feminists. Further, municipal government appeared not only not to be involved in these issues but also not interested in being involved.[35]

## Feminism and the New Municipal Agenda

There are some indications that this is beginning to change and that feminist issues are emerging on the municipal agenda. Certain municipal concerns, such as housing and public transportation, are increasingly being recognized as feminist issues. New concerns, such as safety, are being thrust on the municipal agenda and articulated in a way clearly relevant to feminists. Indeed, initiatives are emerging across the country that link women's safety and municipal responsibility— METRAC and the Safe City Committee in Toronto,[36] the Women's Safety Bureau in Ottawa-Carleton, the Task Force on Violence against Women in Dartmouth, the 'Femmes et villes' Committee in Montreal, and the Urban Safety for Women and Children Project in Winnipeg, to mention only a few examples.

This transformation is due to a variety of factors, one of which is a mutual reinforcement of recent trends. Changes in political personnel first help produce and accelerate changes in activity; this new activity helps stimulate further changes in political personnel. The increased number of women in municipal government is one of the factors underlying the growing link between the feminist agenda and municipal politics.[37]

This transformation relates also to the crisis of the welfare state and the pressures for decentraliza-

tion and privatization as federal and provincial governments try to cut their fiscal deficits. From these pressures come new questions about the allocation of responsibilities for municipal governments. The questions raised are obviously difficult ones for the women's movement. Federal and provincial governments often use decentralization as a rhetorical tool while reducing services. In addition, municipal governments have not historically been sympathetic to feminist arguments. Therefore the tendency has been for the women's movement to oppose moves towards decentralization and to see these moves as part of the neo-conservative agenda for dismantling the welfare state.

## The Feminist Potential in Decentralization

On the other hand, it is also argued that decentralization has a progressive potential for feminists. This potential does not lie in decentralizing existing local governments but rather in efforts that try to transform them.

Decentralization should give local governments greater policy capacity, a greater interest in redistributive policies, and an agenda less skewed towards the provision of profit-enhancing infrastructure. This implies major shifts in the distribution of power among all levels of government. Indeed, recognition of cities as important actors would change the nature of present-day federalism in Canada.

Despite the neo-conservative drive behind many of the current moves towards decentralization, does decentralization not have a potential for achieving the kind of vision described in our feminist city? We would argue that the very strengths of the feminist model of organizing can be realized in the context of city politics—spatially limited, intricately inserted in its community, directly accessible, and highly concrete. It is possible to observe even now changes that are consistent with this optimistic vision that an enhanced and more socially progressive local state could emerge through decentralization. Taking the area of housing, for example, one can point to increased municipal initiatives for the provision of low-cost units[38] together with the increased understanding of low-cost housing as a feminist issue.[39]

Our argument is therefore that enlarging the scope of municipal government is an important element in the construction of the feminist city. In this regard, as in others, the constitution is a feminist concern. Feminists should see the municipal agenda as crucial to those issues which are central to them. This will be a double process: first, through the better understanding of municipal issues as feminist and second, through the increased activity by local government in areas that have been central to the women's movement.

## The Struggle for the Social Terrain

Such a transformation of local politics would make it of great interest to feminist political agendas. Local politics has become more clearly an arena for political struggles, and particularly struggles of specification, of connection, and of imagination central to feminists. With this transforming decentralization, local politics could provide an example of what Nancy Fraser calls the 'terrain of the social', to be used by feminists in the 'coming welfare wars'.[40] The importance attached by Fraser to people's capacity 'to articulate alternative, politicized interpretations of their needs as they engage in processes of dialogue and collective struggle' argues for a political arena intimately related to daily life and therefore able to encourage the widest participation possible in struggles about the interpretation of needs.[41]

Certainly, in modern times, local government has had narrow and formal conceptions of the needs of those it would see as its 'clients'. The ad-ministrative and highly hierarchical relationships between provincial and local governments reinforce the technical nature of need identification at the local level, as does the ideological vision of the majority of the local political personnel. However, as we have argued here, this is changing.

It is changing because of decentralizing thrusts from provincial and federal governments and because of protests and mobilizations from social movements. And, even more generally, it is changing because of globalization. The nature of globalization creates opportunities for urban political systems to become more important political actors. This increasing importance does not, of course, ensure a more feminist local politics but it does not preclude it.

## Feminism as Local-Global Politics

Feminist political practices are particularly compatible with local politics in the global context of transformation. The 'local-global' character of feminism is clear, visible both worldwide and locally, and it is comfortable moving between the two. Urban feminist projects started in London are shared by local groups in Montreal, Toronto, and across the world.

However, this by no means implies that we can take for granted the construction of the feminist city. It will be the outcome of political struggles, struggles that will involve the rearticulation of local politics, global politics, and feminist politics alike.

So, if we cannot take for granted the construction of the feminist city, we can at least urge this as an important and feasible goal. And perhaps we should prepare ourselves for the next question, no doubt soon to be asked—what is the sex of sewers?

# Notes

1. Two general bibliographies to this area can be found in Caroline Andrew and Beth Moore Milroy, eds, *Life Spaces* (Vancouver: UBC Press, 1988), and by Celine Cloutier and Dominique Masson in *Recherches féministes* 2, 1 (1989).

2. 'Violence against Women', *Canadian Woman Studies* 11, 4 (1991); Jacinthe Michaud, 'The Welfare State and the Problem of Counter Hegemonic Responses within the Women's Movement', in William K. Carroll, ed., *Organizing Dissent* (Toronto: Garamond Press, 1984); Linda MacLeod, *Freedom from Fear: A Women's Right, A Community Concern, A National Priority* (Ottawa: Secretary of State Canada, 1991). My description of this area has been much influenced by my observation of the Regional Co-ordinating Committee to End Violence Against Women of Ottawa-Carleton. The committee, established in 1985, regroups some 150 organizations and individuals working with issues of violence against women and children. The monthly meetings bring together about 50 people on a regular basis.

3. Rachel Pain, 'Spaces, Sexual Violence and Social Control: Integrating Geographical and Feminist Analyses of Women's Fear of Crime', *Progress in Human Geography* 15, 4 (1991): 415–32; *Women and Environments*, 'Urban Safety', 1989–90.

4. My description of this area has been much influenced by my participation in the creation of the Women's Safety Bureau of Ottawa-Carleton and by the information published by METRAC in Toronto. See 'Women and Urban Safety Committee of Ottawa-Carleton', *Women and Urban Safety: A Recommendation for Action* (Ottawa, 1991); Urban Safety for Women and Children Project, *A Safer Winnipeg for Women and Children* (Winnipeg, 1991); Metro Action Committee on Public Violence against Women and Children (METRAC), *The W.I.S.E. (Women in Safe Environments) Report* (Toronto, 1987).

5. Gerda Wekerle, 'Framing Transportation Planning as a Women's Issue and Getting It on the Public Agenda', conference presentation, 1988.

6. See Françoise Mondor, 'Le logement: point d'ancrage pour un nouveau départ', *Canadian Woman Studies* 11, 2 (1990): 46–7; Femmes et logement,

'Un dossier à ouvrir', Actes du colloque, Montréal, 1987; Janet McClain and Cassie Doyle, *Women and Housing* (Ottawa: Canadian Council on Social Development, 1984); 'Women and Housing', *Canadian Woman Studies* 11, 2 (1990); Willem Van Vliet, ed., *Women, Housing and Community* (Aldershot: Avebury, 1988).

7. Françoise Mondor argues this point based on her studies in downtown Montreal. 'Si elles réussissent à rencontrer un minimum de conditions décentes leur permettant d'exercer un certain contrôle de leur espace premier (le logement) dans un milieu social réceptif, elles peuvent alors amorcer une réflexion position sur le présent et sur l'avenir. La stabilité résidentielle apparaît comme une des conditions nécessaires à une amélioration socio-économique on à tout le moins à une possibilité de s'en sortir, et d'émerger d'une situation de pauvreté, d'insécurité et d'isolement.' Mondor, 'Le logement, point d'ancrage pour un nouveau départ', *Canadian Woman Studies* 11, 2 (1990) 46–7.

8. Damaris Rose, '"Collective Consumption" Revised: Analysing Modes of Provision and Access to Childcare Services in Montreal, Quebec', *Political Geography Quarterly* 9, 4 (1990). Rose and Nathalie Chicoine, 'Access to School Daycare Services: Class, Family, Ethnicity and Space in Montreal's Old and New Inner City', *Geoforum* 22, 2 (1991).

9. Denise Roy, 'La garderie de trajet: un lieu de garde entre la résidence et le travail', Colloque Les Bâtisseuses de la Cité, ACFAS, conference presentation, May 1992.

10. It is important to acknowledge the contribution that the review, *Women and Environments*, published since 1978 from Toronto, has made to reflection on issues relating to women and planning. In addition, mention should be made of the work of Women Plan Toronto who, since 1985, have been active in this area. Another particularly interesting document is the one produced by the collective Femmes et ville, *Pour une ville où il fera bon vivre au féminin* (Montréal, 1988).

11. Andrew and Milroy, eds, *Life Spaces*; Dolores Hayden, *The Grand Domestic Revolution* (Cambridge, Mass.: MIT Press, 1988); Beth Moore

Milroy, 'Taking Stock of Planning, Space and Gender', *Journal of Planning Literature* 6, 1 (1992): 3–15; Denise Piché, 'Des villes au féminin: projets d'ici et d'ailleurs', *Recherches féministes* 2, 1 (1989): 115–24; Lise Drewes Nielsen, 'Flexibility, Gender and Local Labour Markets: Some Examples from Denmark', *International Journal of Urban and Regional Research* 15, 1 (1991): 42–54.

12. Nielsen makes this point eloquently. 'Suburban areas are the ghettos of reproduction. It is the women who have the responsibility for solving the division of everyday life which the obsolete town structure forces on families.' Nielsen, 'Flexibility, Gender and Local Labour Markets'. See also Suzanne MacKenzie, 'Building Women, Building Cities: Toward Gender Sensitive Theory in the Environmental Disciplines', in Andrew and Moore Milroy, eds, *Life Spaces*.

13. I am grateful to the organizers (*l'Autre Montréal*) of the *Montréal au féminin* bus tour that took place during the meetings of ACFAS (Association canadienne-française pour l'avancement des sciences) in May 1992, for making me aware of this question. The analysis of the existing public monuments in Montreal shows that they are overwhelmingly male. And Queen Victoria counts for a high percentage of those statues recognizing women.

14. Labour organizer since the 1940s, Madeleine Parent played an important role in the struggles in Quebec during the Duplessis era to improve working conditions. She has continued to play an active role in labour organizing through her involvement in the Confederation of Canadian Unions, and in the women's movement through her involvement in NAC (the National Action Committee for the Status of Women).

15. Writer, notably of the autobiography, *Halfbreed*. Maria Campbell was also involved in founding the Women's Halfway House and Women's Emergency Shelter in Edmonton.

16. These are names of two of the southern Italian immigrant working women described by Franca Iacovetta in her article 'From Contadina to Worker: Southern Italian Immigrant Working Women in Toronto, 1947–1962', in Veronica Strong-Boag and Anita Clair Fellman, eds, *Rethinking Canada: The Promise of Women's History* (Toronto: Copp Clark Pitman, 1991).

17. Founder of the Ursuline order in Canada, Marie de l'Incarnation is remembered for her educational work.

18. Author of *Anne of Green Gables* and a number of sequels, Lucy Maud Montgomery is now one of the pillars of the tourist industry in Prince Edward Island.

19. *Bonheur d'occasion* is perhaps the best book in urban sociology written in Canada. So our feminist city would be recognizing not only the author but the urban analyst.

20. Inuit artist and creator of perhaps the best known Inuit print, 'The Enchanted Owl'.

21. See Nancy Adamson, Linda Briskin, and Margaret McPhail, *Feminist Organizing for Change* (Toronto: Oxford University Press, 1988); Marta Anadon, Dominique Masson, Marielle Tremblay, and Pierre-André Tremblay, *De l'organisation aux pratiques d'auto développement* (Chicoutimi: Université du Québec à Chicoutimi, 1992); see also by the same authors, 'Les collectives des femmes: une démocratie sociale', *Nouvelles pratiques sociales (1991) and Vers un développement rose* (Chicoutimi: GRIR [Groupe de recherche et d'intervention régionales], 1990); Yolande Cohen, 'Le rôle des associations dans la démocratie', *Questionnements et pratiques de recherches féministes* (Montréal: UQAM, Centre de recherche féministe, 1990); Susan D. Phillips, 'Meaning and Structure in Social Movements: Mapping the Network of National Canadian Women's Organizations', *Canadian Journal of Political Science* 24, 4 (1991): 755–82; Jill Vickers, 'Feminist Approaches to Women in Politics', in Linda Kealey and Joan Sangster, *Beyond the Vote: Canadian Women and Politics* (Toronto: University of Toronto Press, 1989).

22. In drawing up this list of traits, I have been particularly influenced by the analyses done by Marta Anadon, Dominique Masson, Marielle Tremblay, and Pierre-André Tremblay of their research on women and regional development in the Saguenay-Lac-St-Jean region, by that of Susan Phillips on national women's associations in Canada, and by the papers presented at the November 1990 conference on 'Women and the Canadian State'. The proceedings of the conference, edited by Caroline Andrew and Sandra Rogers, are forthcoming from McGill-Queen's University Press.

23. Phillips, 'Meaning and Structure in Social Movements'.
24. Anadon et al., *De l'organisation aux pratiques d'auto développement*.
25. Michaud, 'The Welfare State'.
26. Ibid.
27. Vickers, 'Feminist Approaches to Women in Politics'.
28. This comes out particularly clearly in a number of the presentations made at the 'Women and the Canadian State' conference. See also Adamson, Briskin, and McPhail, *Feminist Organizing for Change*; Kealey and Sangster, *Beyond the Vote*.
29. Susan Wismer, 'Creating Sustainable Communities in Canada: The Role and Importance of the Women's Movement', paper presented to the Canadian Urban and Housing Studies Conference, Winnipeg, 1988.
30. Cohen, 'Le rôle des associations dans la démocratie'.
31. Phillips, 'Meaning and Structure in Social Movements', 756.
32. Caroline Andrew, Hélène Dion, and Brigitte Jacques, 'Les groupes de femmes de l'Outaouais et l'identité régionale: étude explorative', *Cahiers de géographie du Québec* 33, 89 (1989): 253–62.
33. Warren Magnusson, 'The Local State in Canada: Theoretical Perspectives', *Canadian Public Administration* 28, 4 (1985): 575–99.
34. James Lorimer, *The Developers* (Toronto: James Lorimer, 1978).
35. Caroline Andrew, 'Le pouvoir local: stratégie de pouvoir ou nouvelle impasse pour les femmes?' in Conseil du Statut de la femme du Québec, *L'égalité: les moyens pour y arriver* (Québec: les publications du Québec, 1991), 63–75.
36. Wekerle, 'Framing Transportation Planning'.
37. Chantal Maillé, *Les femmes et la politique: à quand la véritable égalité?* (Ottawa: Canadian Advisory Council on the Status of Women, 1987).
38. J.D. Hulchanski, M. Eberle, M. Lytton, and K. Olds, *The Municipal Role in the Supply and Maintenance of Low Cost Housing: A Review of Canadian Initiatives* (Vancouver: UBC Centre for Human Settlements, 1990).
39. 'Violence Against Women', *Canadian Woman Studies*; Van Vliet, ed., *Women, Housing and Community*.
40. Nancy Fraser, 'Women, Welfare and the Politics of Need Interpretation', in Peter Lessman, ed., *Politics and Social Theory* (London: Routledge, 1989), 104–22.
41. Ibid.